# A Sociological
Phenomenology of
# Christian
# Redemption

Paul Gilfillan

The right of Paul Gilfillan to be identified as the author of this
work has been asserted by him in accordance with Section 78
of the Copyright, Designs and Patents Act 1988

The book cover picture is copyright to Paul Gilfillan

This book is published by
Grosvenor House Publishing Ltd
28-30 High Street, Guildford, Surrey, GU1 3EL.
www.grosvenorhousepublishing.co.uk

A CIP record for this book
is available from the British Library

ISBN 978-1-78148-737-2

dedicated to

Fr. Eamonn O'Brien

friend & mentor

&

in memory of my father

David Gilfillan (1939–2013)

# Table of Contents

# (ii) Special Ontology

# Part 2

# The Supernatural

# Introduction

In light of the fact that for a long time I never dreamt of writing a phenomenology of redemption, a word of explanation about the title and the range of content of this book is in order. In explaining how an ethnography of Scottish nationalism ended up also becoming a sociological phenomenology of Christian redemption, I can only say that if it is the final end-point of a journey that reveals the final meaning to the road travelled, then this goes some way to explaining the unexpected trajectory that is described here. The book emerges from two periods of research in my natal Fife village of Cardenden in the east of Scotland. Firstly, from doctoral fieldwork conducted between 1998 until 2003 and, secondly, from fieldwork conducted throughout 2013 into locals' views on the upcoming Independence Referendum on 18 September 2014. At the time of my initial doctoral studies I felt fortunate to be researching working-class politics at a time of unprecedented questioning and contestation of Scottish identity, and I was certain that my informants who were living through the restoration of the Scots parliament in 1999 would be likely to voice their sense of 'the nation' and its *politicisation*. However, if my doctoral research was fortuitous in terms of timing, the preparation of this book for publication was done living through an even more significant turning point in Scotland's history i.e. the run-up to Scotland's 'date with destiny' in the Independence Referendum of 2014 as a result of the Scottish National Party's victory in 2011.

For a long time I imagined the book that I might write from my doctoral fieldwork would be a straightforward ethnography of nationalism that fortuitously captured the moment of its historic triumph, and at no stage did I imagine I would end up writing on the range of experiences covered here or the question of transcendence as my original aim was to present a 'fundamental ontology' of the Scottish working class and proceed to an understanding of the working-class nationalism that is emergent in Scotland today. However, in trying to understand contemporary

Scotland's "present as history" (Jameson 1984; Hobsbawm 1997) the historic events of 1999 which saw the triumph of the desire to re-organise political life in Scotland upon exclusively national grounds and which turned several generations of yesterday's wisdom into today's foolishness, meant that it was not only appropriate but fundamentally necessary to ask at this precise point in Scotland's history the question: if the elite who defended a depoliticised relation between nation and state for so long are destined to be remembered as having defended an obsolete imagining of Scotland, what other false wisdoms must be suspected and dismantled at this time? What other false wisdoms are we still labouring under and what other relationships require liberating from their current form? If Scottish nationalists, who throughout the modern industrial period were confidently dismissed insofar as they were held to advocate an impossible return to a hopelessly out-of-date 'medieval' programme of resurrecting the Scottish State *in fact articulated a superior wisdom in their de-differentiated conception of the relation between nation and state*, what other tasks of de-differentiation are necessary today?

Insofar as these questions emerged onto my horizon I began to lose control of what I needed to address and more or less lost sight of the end point to which I might arrive. Where I have arrived to is arguing for the need to rethink (Scottish) human being outwith the established mirrors of modernism, industrialism and secularism and that such is one of the tasks awaiting post-industrial generations recently liberated by literacy and affluence (Galbraith 1969). It is my view that beneath the rise of nationalism and the imminent prospect of the restoration of Scotland's historic independence, something more fundamental is happening and identifying what this 'something' is has taken me some years to see with any kind of clarity. I argue that nationalism is only a fraction of what is emerging and that the retrieval of the repressed 'medieval' nation is only a fraction of what must be retrieved if we are to become equal to the task of understanding "the present as history" (Jameson 1984, p. 65) or "comprehending our era in thought" (Hegel 1991, p. 21).

I argue in what follows that in taking up the task of representing a social class recently empowered by literacy and affluence and provoked by political events from 1979 onwards, the task that devolves to the social researcher is the challenge of re-thinking human being *within* the 'mirror of production' (Baudrillard 1975) but outwith a debilitating *modernist* consciousness[1] and taking up this task has led to the range of concerns tackled here. A focus upon contemporary nationalism has meant a process of coming to understand that to properly contextualise my data I had to situate it within a broader European context and within the question of modernity. In what follows I locate the beginning of the modern era in the gradual shift to living in 'society' begun in the twelfth century, which saw the shift from an agrarian-based organic community to the cash nexus and the urbanisation of human living (Haskins 1927; Pirenne 1936; Hollister 1969; Trinkaus and Oberman 1974; Gimpel 1977; Constable 1996; Chenu 1997; Bisson 2008) and the growth in individual freedom (Morris 1987) and the gradual disappearance of serfdom from this time onwards (Lyon, cited in Warren-Holister 1969, pp. 59-67). In locating the advent of modernity in the twelfth-century I have simply learned from a range of scholars better informed than myself, such as Castoriadis (1987, p. 48):

> What we see in the twelfth–to nineteenth–century Europe is not a great number of different types of society appearing, and then all dying away except for one because they are incapable of surviving. We see one phenomenon, the birth... of the bourgeoisie.

---

[1] The terms *modernist* and *modernism* are used interchangeably with the latter term not being used in the sense of the 'literary modernism' of, for example, Hugh McDiarmid or James Joyce where it denotes the literary depiction of the mundane at the expense of the heroic and the Greco-Roman classical tradition. The aesthetic modernism which turned to the mundane and everyday in a conscious rejection of classical aesthetics is not my understanding of modernism. Rather, I use the term to denote the myth that modern societies either have or must effect a break or caesura with their past in order to either become or remain modern.

I define the condition of 'being modern' as the advent of living a particular and defining tension: the tension involved in living a 'perennial' or pre-modern set of beliefs in a modern stratified market society characterised by a complex division of labour. In giving an account of 'the present as history,' recognising the importance of the twelfth century has become a feature of my thinking which is at odds with *modernists* within the sociological tradition such as Kilminster (1998). I use the term *modernist* to describe, as a first approximation, those who share the "belief in the once-for-all distinction between the present age (called 'Modern') and the past" (Ardener, cited in Overing 1985, p. 47) and who generally imagine the advent of the modern and the advent of 'society' to be a far later development in European history than historical scholarship advocates. My emphasis upon the twelfth century as the beginning of the modern era, then, comes from reading historians such as Bisson (2009) who has argued that the crisis of the twelfth century saw the shift, after 1150, from the experience of power as the exercise of 'personal lordship' to the experience of power as impersonal Government, so that it is from the twelfth century there emerged from the experience of locality and lordship the beginning of the European experience of Government, Society and the State. In contrast to this periodisation of modernity, the modernist sociologist Kilminster (1998, p. 11) writes:

> Of the seventeenth and eighteenth centuries one could say that people did not experience their social interconnectedness as 'society,' but rather the experience of society resulted from the actions of leading people such as kings and ministers.

If the project or tension of 'being modern' was originally specific to European Christians (Morris 1949, pp. 9-24), subsequent to this original twelfth-century advent of modernity saw the emergence of non-Christian or purely naturalistic forms of living this tension. The tension of 'being modern' then is no longer exclusive to Christians (nor Europeans) insofar as it includes non-religious beliefs such as Marxism, for example, so that the struggle to reconcile the current market order with beliefs and values surrounding conceptions of 'the good society' establishes a tension and dialectic of 'being modern' within non-religious biographies, so that the tension lived by the contemporary Christian fated to struggle with Royce's (2001, p. 62) question, "Can the modern man be a Christian?" has become a universal tension.

What unites the varied range of concerns I will address in due course is the basic proposition that today's post-industrial working-class generations face the question of 'being modern' in a unique and fresh manner as they are living through the death of various wisdoms that imagined they had solved the question of 'being modern.' If some tried and tested imaginings of Scotland have been revealed as 'foolish' and are on the brink of obsolescence, the challenge to those producing representations of Scotland today is to articulate fully contextual imaginings of 'being modern' and fully contextual accounts of individuation based upon empirical research in particular localities and communities. I argue that successfully prosecuting this task means nothing less than effecting a re-orientation of the Scottish imagination and psyche and in this task it is necessary to return to the original twelfth-century source of the modern era to take our bearings. On the eve of the Independence Referendum, taking this long durée perspective is appropriate and must be integrated into our understanding of Scotland's "present as history" (Jameson 1984, p. 65) as it allows onto our horizon an emergent working-class project of systematic integralism that has been prepared for by literacy and affluence and political events and the retrieval of the nation by a younger working-class generation liberated by these same forces.

If, so far, the response of a younger working-class generation to the question of being modern has come in the still-emerging shape of constituting a politics without England, this is only a fraction of an emergent integralist vision insofar as what is 'at hand' is a new imagining of cultural and psychological and social and spiritual and intellectual development beyond the established sources and imaginings of modernism. My answer to the challenge of thinking the present as history is a vision of modern class-informed individuation and sociation beyond the twin errors of supernaturalism and secularism as a direct result of "the free appropriation of one's whole Dasein" (Heidegger 1998, p. 53) which only now is a real possibility thanks to the advent of affluence and literacy in the nineteen-eighties. In light of the recent reversal of modernist understandings at a political level, my view is that working-class producers of culture will proceed to widen their horizon to the whole modernist mythology as they construct their own social imaginary and produce a post-supernaturalist and post-secular literature, music and theatre, for example, free of industrialism and modernism.

The phrase *being modern* then is used in two ways. Firstly, drawing upon the work of historians, 'being modern' denotes a series of macro or large-scale social, economic, demographic, political and intellectual changes that occurred from the twelfth century. Secondly, the term is used to denote an existential condition that I propose only arrives to the Scottish central-belt working class after the end of the "dictatorship of scarcity" (Beck 1992, p. 20) in the nineteen-seventies. I distinguish 'being modern' in two senses then: in the sense of the first arrival of 'society' as opposed to 'community' and the advent of government as opposed to 'personal lordship' (Bisson 2009), the advent of new technology and urbanisation and a range of macro processes resulting in society being volatilised to the extent that we can say the twelfth century saw the end of a non-dynamic or static view of human society, and that from this time onwards social change disrupting settled convention became normal. This macro view of modernity, then, is related to but also should be distinguished from the use of the phrase 'being modern' to describe a condition of the lifeworld of the individual. In this latter sense 'being modern' describes the condition of exercising *real freedom* concerning one's social fate. A person can be modern, then, in the sense of living in a modern society characterised by change and innovation in knowledge and technology while in their own life and consciousness they may remain largely immune to the second sense of 'being modern.' Societies and periods of time then may be modern while many living through those times may not be modern in their consciousness or behaviour.

From the evidence of historians, twelfth-century European Christians were alive to the new tension of being modern in the sense of living the predicament of reconciling their new social conditions free of agrarian conventions and fixed political and social arrangements laid down by custom since 'time immemorial.' The advent of the volatilisation of social and economic and political conditions in the twelfth century has remained, as has specifically intellectual problematics and an existential condition mediated by a shared Christian consciousness that was never the preoccupation of an elite but of much of the general population, and that may be expressed as having to bear the weight of the historicisation of Christian redemption in changing social conditions. Today, this condition in its non-religious guise is known as the 'crisis of the West' which as a result of affluence and deep literacy is becoming a democratic existential predicament insofar as it is increasingly difficult not to have one's lifeworld impacted by the drama of reflexive modernisation and the drama of being post-conventional.

Being modern then volatilises the realm of culture and belief because of the objective pressures to exercise reflexivity in order to *practice a predicament*, and one of those predicaments par excellence is the burden of exercising *sovereignty*. Only a clear sighting of the 'present as history' frees one to assume the responsibilities of being modern and make one's way as an individual or a locality or a class or a nation under one's own steam or upon the basis of one's specific 'secondary nature' – whether the 'condition of reduction' for the worker-inquirer (see Chapter 2) or the geographical or territorial 'second nature' of the nation (Chapter 5). I will argue that the contemporary significance of the twelfth century is its being a historical period when the 'present as history' was imagined in a way that was free of modernist despoliation, so that this era models how we today might retain a holistic or integral vision of ourselves and correctly depart towards our future upon the basis of the deepest historical continuity with the past that our fully-contextualised *dasein* in conscious and free possession of itself is capable of. Because new generations are living through the demise of old answers to the tension and conundrum of being modern, the original twelfth-century advent of modernity provides useful ballast as it knew nothing of the 'separation of powers' but thanks to the great Investiture Controversy knows the defining tension between the sacred and the secular, and is a significant resource for a contemporary working-class integralism which will form the basis for a genuine pluralism within the public realm, instead of the current toxic cleansing of political and public life which is too rarefied to support working-class life. To the question whether a working-class generation has been liberated by literacy and affluence simply to reproduce the same materialist and modernist 'evacuation of Scottish being' practiced by their modernist masters throughout the "dictatorship of scarcity" (Beck 1992, p. 20) period there can be only one answer, and an important part of that answer is likely to come in the 2014 Independence Referendum.

While there is a consensus of opinion that there has been a shift to a nationality-based politics of identity in Scotland away from traditional all-British materialist conceptions of class politics among the working class (Brown et al. 1996; Paterson 1996), this 'new' class politics remains a politics of identity, and if a central thesis in what follows is that the politics of nationality in Scotland today is being driven by class realities, within the term 'class realities' is an entire social ontology that is in-formed by national identity which I propose to think through. Part of the significance of the 2014 Independence Referendum lies in this retrieval of the original European non-modernist advent of the modern era to overcome nihilism and meet the epidemic of post-foundationalist scepticism which characterises much of European intellectual culture. In what follows I will outline the contours of a post-affluent and post-liberal working-class generation's systematic integralism based upon their own 'integral contingency,' and give an account of integral liberation upon the rock of socio-historic *contingency*, a decentred and class-specific ontology opposed to any pretence of being a universal ontology.

As what follows is a phenomenology of working-class being, the influence of Husserl and Heidegger is never far away and along with Heidegger (1962, p. 155) I conceive *dasein* as *mitsein* because "Being-in-the-world, the world is always the one I share with Others. The world of Dasein is a *with-world* [*Mitwelt*]. Being-in is *Being-with* Others."[2] My use of the Heideggerian terms *dasein* ('being there') and *mitsein* ('being with') then is largely interchangeable given that "for Heidegger *Dasein* is *Mitsein*; what it means to be a person is indistinguishable from my being with others" (Critchley 2007, p. 59). My view is that the project of understanding Scottish nationalism via thinking working-class *dasein* is necessary because I categorically reject the idea that one can rise to the challenge of grasping the 'present as history' without a fundamental ontology of the class that constitutes much of the social reality of the force that is dominating political life i.e. nationalism. Also, working-class nationalism rather usefully frames its desire to have the Nation and State congruent without recourse to prefabricated metaphors of 'blood and soil' or stranded appeals to 'civic nationalism' or 'civil society' (Yack 1996; Hearn 2000).

Why there are Scots while 'North Britons' are long extinct is a problem for modernist theorists of nationalism who maintain the nation can be imagined *ex nihilo* or 'out of nothing' (Gellner 1997, pp. 90-101). Chapters 4 and 5 attempt to understand why a 'medieval patrimony' has not only survived but is driving current events in Scotland, and I explain this state of affairs by arguing an important consequence of maintaining *the local mediates the national* is to abandon the illusion of 'civil society' as either constituting the nation or having been responsible for nursing the nation through its exile from statehood. Hence, "re-framing Scottish nationalism" via the prism of "social contract theory"

---

[2] The term *phenomenology* is used in the widely accepted sense of an approach that is concerned with the way things appear to the human person as opposed to how they may appear to a detached observer or a God-like point of view. As a description of methodology, I use the word phenomenology in the Heideggerian sense of that process of conducting research that highlights "the process of letting things manifest themselves" (Heidegger, cited in Relph 1989, p. 15) thanks to an iterative process whereby the researcher's perception is increasingly freed from the clichéd and hackneyed understandings of human affairs that are conveniently 'at hand.'

(Hearn 1998, 2000) or "liberal nationalism" (Tamir 1993; MacCormick 1996) not only offers little purchase upon working-class reality but are examples of the cleansing of nationalism of its social density and class reality. The general argument I will pursue is also a direct challenge to those nationalists who, having abandoned political modernism in the shape of the failed geo-political experiment of the United Kingdom, wish to cling onto cultural and philosophical forms of modernism. These more fundamental forms of modernism which will remain intact after independence is achieved, means many nationalists fail to catch sight of what is at stake and what is possible in Scotland today at this historic turning of the tide. Among the SNP membership and leadership are those who prefer their 'medieval particularism' (Lenin) to be *lite*, their territorialisation of identity and freedom to be 'civic' and their return to a 'medieval' patrimony to be as brief as possible. While these *civic* nationalists celebrated the return of a Scottish parliament in 1999 and hope for the return of a Scottish state after 2014, they propose a highly selective and short-lived 'return of the repressed' insofar as what horrifies the *modernist* imagination in a globalising twenty-first century Scotland is the prospect of an 'integral particularism' which enthusiastically takes to the reconstruction of the many tasks that three centuries of modernism among social and cultural elites, as well as 'scarcity thinking' among the dominated, have left unsuspected, untouched and unimaginable.

If the official State-opening of the Holyrood parliament that took place on 1 July 1999 represents the partial 'putting right' of the failure of modernity and the long trek 'back to the future,' the restoration of Scotland's political structures to its 'ancient' standards signals the failure of modernism as a politics but is only the beginning of a longer struggle against *metaphysical* forms of modernism such as modernism as an anthropology and a philosophy of history. Chapters 4 and 5 argue the modernist legacy in Scotland must be replaced by the intellectual and cultural triumph of a species of particularism and the return of a repressed twelfth-century integralism that may be described as a *perennial* template in view of the fact that the historico-symbolic complex that first imagined and achieved national sovereignty has been resurrected and mobilised at the ballot box to return a genuine political dialectic to Scotland and rescue affluent and literate Scotland from the modernist no man's land of the past three centuries. I argue that what we are witnessing in Scotland today is the retrieval of a more fundamental medieval-come-modern project that, long abandoned, has been mobilised in response to the 'long event' of 1979-1997; a politicisation of national identity and a disposition to de-differentiate what liberal modernity sought to differentiate, so that what is 'at hand' is a disposition to reject traditional accommodations to modernist understandings of history and the bourgeois anthropology which views modern man as a variant of *homo economicus* and, thanks to the deployment of a long inert historico-symbolic complex, seeks to put in its place not an era that comes after modernity but a more balanced project of modernity and in the process break from inherited geo-political, intergenerational, political and cultural relations and self-understandings.

I will develop the argument that Scotland has once again begun to address the question of what it means to be modern upon the basis of freedom from political union with England, and fundamental to the sociology of Scottish nationalism is the fact that by destroying all-British strongholds among the Scottish working class such as all-British industries and all-British trade unions, the 'post-national' neoliberal globalisation of the economy pursued in the nineteen-eighties and nineteen-nineties was integral to deconstructing the geo-political relationships which have characterised Scotland's modernity insofar as it destroyed the mundane bases for the symbolic reproduction of Britain among the post-industrial working class. If an older generation of Scots who traditionally did not question union with England are becoming rare, opting for political unionism at the ballot box among a younger working-class generation is becoming ever-rarer in light of modern forces such as affluence and higher literacy (Seawright and Curtice 1995) as well as political and historic events coming into alignment with the nationalist project and releasing long suppressed cultural and historical exigencies to such an extent that, sociologically speaking, young people voting for union with England makes as much sociological sense as voting for communism or marginal socialist parties. I argue, then, that the signature weakness of unionism as it fights for its very life in Scotland today is that it is not alive to the task of 'being modern' or the task of thinking the present as history and for many signifies the tired turning to a prefabricated solution that has been tried for three centuries and has been found wanting.

If there has emerged a re-articulation of the political field among younger generations in the shape of a politics without England, a deeper question is what uses will a post-affluent working-class generation put its recently-acquired access to higher education to? In answering this question I recognise counter-evidence to my thesis concerning an emergent re-imagining of working-class *dasein* free from modernist mythology as even in the 'renaissance' of working-class writing that occurred in Scotland during the nineteen-eighties and nineteen-nineties, those authors who now enjoy iconic status as working-class writers still struggle to shed the modernist or 'mono-chromatic' anthropology they have internalised and struggle to model how to re-think working-class human being free from the corruptions of modernism, materialism and secularism. In the likes of Irvine Welsh and James Kelman, then, we still see depictions of working-class *dasein* with some of the primary colours of human being removed as a matter of realist principle, which I take as evidence of how recent and fragile is an emergent working-class literature free from "the yoke of scarcity" (Sartre 1963, p. 34) and the truncated materialist vision of working-class *dasein* which inspires this use of literacy. In this regard the words of Dolan (1999, p. 49) are apposite: "It's hard to write purely in the abstract when you're surrounded by poverty and blighted lives. But it's also a grave misunderstanding to think that realism itself hasn't moved on."

Against Nairn's characterisation of nationalism as the bourgeoisie inviting "the masses into history" (1981, p. 340) I take the mainstream sociological position that Scottish nationalism is more accurately described as the working class inviting a traditionally unionist middle class into playing its part in the creation of Scottish history and an independent State in light of sociologists' findings (Brown et al. 1996, p. 153) that "support for a Scottish parliament has been higher in working-class than in middle-class groups in every survey that has ever asked the question." The working-class integralism that has already (partially) achieved a nation-state of its own thanks to the re-convening of the Scottish parliament is just one element of a much larger and more fundamental 'politics of being' that is at hand, so that in contrast to characterisations of the present era as an incredulity towards foundationalist projects (Lyotard 1984), the late-modern condition of Scotland offers an empirical opportunity to research a systematic integralism that is emerging (Kravitz 1997, pp. xi-xxxvi).

Having spent the last fifteen years taking advantage of this historic opportunity, what follows is essentially an ethnographic account that is based upon a prolonged period of "being there" (Geertz 1988) and the longitudinal data that this long-term project has brought into view. For example, in August 1998 when beginning doctoral fieldwork my tenancy agreement with Fife Council stipulated a monthly rent of £137.28 and still in Cardenden some fifteen years later in 2013 my monthly mortgage is £789.66. In 1998 the Jamphlars garage in Cardenden advertised MOTs at £17.50 and in 2013 an MOT now costs £45; in 1998 a litre of unleaded petrol at the Robertson's garage in Cardenden (which has since closed) cost 74.9 pence and in 2013 a litre of unleaded petrol costs 136.9 pence at the nearest garage in Kirkcaldy. In 1998 a pint of lager at the Railway Tavern cost £1.60 while in September 2013 the same pint costs £2.90. In 1998 my weekly wage when working with East of Scotland Water authority was £186.06 and in 2013 my weekly wage was £929.31. Longitudinal ethnography, then, allows such data to emerge and conducting fieldwork meant I was able to appropriate the benefits of participant observation:

> As a technique of research, participant observation distinguishes itself by breaking down the barriers between observer and participant, between those who study and those who are studied. It shatters the glass box from which

sociologists observe the world and puts them temporarily at the mercy of their subjects...the ethnographer confronts participants in their corporeal reality, in their concrete existence, in their time and space.

(Burawoy et al. 1991, p. 291).

However, I am sure that I would never have dared to cover the range of topics that follow were it not for the additional confidence that comes from conducting "anthropology at home" (Jackson 1987) and drawing upon my insider status as a result of having been brought up in the village I studied. This study also emerges from conducting anthropology at home as an undergraduate in 1987, as well as Master's degree research in 1997 on the miners' strike of 1984-1985 and then doctoral level study. Because in what follows I am 'writing' my natal village I am engaged with the "writing culture" debate (Marcus & Fischer 1986) and the general post-positivist emphasis upon reflexivity which accepts that an ethnographer's embeddedness in his or her home culture plays an integral part in the production of anthropological knowledge. I share the same class and national identity of my informants and in this respect hope to emulate anthropologists such as Obeyesekere (1979, 1981) and Tambiah (1986) who have exploited their shared background with the nationalists they write about. As a local among other locals, then, I apply Emmett's comment to myself: "The fact that I have been living in rather than studying Blaenau, have been my own informant as much as an ethnographer, I count as an advantage (cited in Cohen 1982, p. 165).

Conducting ethnography at home was an advantage as it enabled me to comply with the specifically ethnographic approach to nationalism whereby in the words of my doctoral supervisor: "Local experience mediates national identity and, therefore, an anthropological understanding of the latter cannot proceed without knowledge of the former" (Cohen 1982, p. 13). This requirement to understand the local social and cultural context out of which nationalism emerges has enabled me to evidence the consubstantial link that exists between different 'realms of belonging:' from the intimate and domestic everyday realm to the national political realm. Likewise, in light of Eriksen's contention that: "[National identity's] great emotional power, and its unabashed linking up with the intimate sphere" (in Olwig & Hastrup 1997, p. 109) is of a piece with Herzfeld's (1997) urging anthropologists of nationalism to attend to how ordinary people experience 'being national' and aligns with current thinking among anthropologists (Handler 1984 & 1985; Smith 1986; Segal & Handler 1992; Brubaker 1996) which stresses that it is necessary to understand traditional forms of community and belonging in order to achieve ethnographic accounts of nationalism. In a small Fife village such as Cardenden, then, belonging is experienced and expressed largely through the idiom of kinship so that a person belongs because, like his or her mother and father before, he or she was "born and brought up" in Cardenden. Kinship and residence, then, are the traditional means through which belonging is articulated in everyday life so that longevity of residence and kinship-based metaphors of belonging are an integral aspect of the larger construction of national identity and belonging and confirm Herzfeld's argument in *Cultural Intimacy: Social Poetics in the Nation State* (1997) regarding the special relevance of anthropology's ability to achieve theoretical purchase upon the popular appeal of nationalist discourse insofar as it is able to explain why "marginal communities...are often the source of the national-character models" (1997, p. 7). In what follows, then, I argue that Cardenden affords an ethnographic site for investigating the iconicity between local and national identity, an idiom of 'sameness' to mark boundaries of identity and belonging.

In terms of the geographic location of my research I make my own Macdonald's (1997, p. 9) description of her study of the Hebridean island of Skye: "The geographically defined 'community'...constitutes not the boundaries and limits of my investigation but the position from which to begin, and through which to focus, the discussion." While the clear geographic focus of what follows is the post-industrial village of Cardenden, I view this study as directly relevant not only to the former coalfield areas and former pit villages of Fife but to the many post-industrial lives and localities throughout central Scotland. If the local mediates the national there is the need to articulate working-class culture before focusing upon national identity and its politicisation. However, in terms of the available scholarly representations of 'working-class Scotland,' it seems working-class Scotland doesn't much exist in the minds of working-class Scots in light of the fact that from the outset of fieldwork I was struck by informants' matter-of-fact insistence that "there's nothing here," so that my informants set me the challenge of constructing 'something from nothing' insofar as they refused to claim the presence of a local substantive culture, and so a research question became: if not from substantive cultural traditions, then from what 'stuff' is Scottish working-class nationalism being drawn from?

If conducting anthropology at home has several advantages, one obvious difference between this and traditional anthropological fieldwork carried out in far-flung fields is that instead of being faced with a surplus of data in the shape of a strange language or unfamiliar practices and beliefs that stand out for the ethnographer's attention, researching at home meant *the question of what to research* was far from straightforward due to the absence of any strange language, beliefs, customs or practices. From the outset I was faced with Foley's (1989) question whether the working class has a culture in the anthropological sense and in this regard Nade-Klein (1997) has argued that ethnographers of Scotland have reproduced the Highland/Lowland distinction because they have failed to engage in anthropology at home due to their persistent preference to conduct research in remote rural areas which are unrepresentative of the lives of the vast majority of Scots. This study, then, is very much an ethnography of the Scottish working class and is offered in the belief that it speaks to the post-industrial central belt of Scotland where the majority of Scots live.

Constituting the *what* to represent, then, has been a defining and ongoing issue for me and has been a question posed within the context of many theorists having struggled with the realisation that working-class *dasein* and *mitsein* are defined by their separation from any form of substantive culture or 'tradition.'

As opposed to the production and inheritance of a literature, a language, an architecture or some other defining quality to rescue the researcher from the problem of constituting 'the what' to represent, I argue that what there is to study are defining *relations* and it is these relations that in large measure constitute the reality of being working class. In what follows I begin my answer to the question of what there is to represent by an immersion into the world of manual labour and gradually rise to a viewpoint which stresses a subjectivity and an intersubjectivity and a range of communicative practices and a politics specific to the working class, before finally arguing this 'something' is a class-specific departure point for an insertion into and appropriation of the wider European cultural tradition. Grappling with the problem of how to produce 'something from nothing' was how I began my journey to a structuralist perspective and to understanding that *the real is structural or relational.* The move to a *relational* definition of reality and a structuralist theory of meaning echoes Caws's (1997, p. 249) conclusion that the "most general insight of structuralism...is that the elements of the human world are constituted out of the relations into which they enter," and is something I have found particularly relevant for capturing the decentred nature of working-class experience.

I argue that *relations generate 'stuff' or reality; not only the what of that which is present to the subject in his experience but the means to experience his experience* so that working-class nationalism, for example, is the politicisation of a highly structured social ontology characterised by a radical openness to incarnating time, history, locality, society and work etcetera. Fully-contextual Man, then, is more or less fated to make himself through the relations he is made to enter or through the relations he is not able to enter so that, as a rule, ontology is at the mercy of relations which are at the mercy of social and historical forces. A structuralist theory of human being, then, points to the conclusion that the working class is the social group most incapable of escaping their relations to being, time, society, history etcetera due to their lacking the means to resource any thought, far less practice, of removing themselves from their material conditions or instantiating a 'forgetfulness' of their objective being and time and their structuring consequences. Insofar as human reality is fundamentally structural/relational, I systematically develop the conclusion that the working class are the social group most conformed to their relations and the world *in their being* and that to grasp this is to grasp all there is to grasp about working-class *dasein*. Because the working class are the social class who more than any other have been reduced to the exigencies of the wage-capital relation, they are the social group most incapable of substantivist illusions regarding themselves and their localities, so that if we turn our attention to nationalism, for example, it is rare to hear nationalism articulated as *discourse*, and this lack of nationalist discourse was the clue that set me on the road to understanding the 'ontological work' which relations must perform and the 'ontological density' which relations are capable of constituting and carrying. This structuralist understanding when turned to the realm of meaning was the key to realising locals' nationalism borrows its 'substance' from the various relations they inhabit as opposed to being sourced in a discourse of values such as civic society or civic nationalism.

The ethnographer who wishes to think about working-class experience but is wary of hackneyed and clichéd language has an obvious affinity with Husserl's phenomenological project of a "return to the things themselves" (Husserl 1975, p. 252). I also believe this concern to avoid cliché is shared by locals themselves insofar as they refuse to claim the existence of a living working-class tradition in contemporary conditions of deindustrialization. For my informants, the existence and reality of a 'working-class culture' is easier to discern when looking back to the era of coal and the years of economic and political struggle and the heyday of locality, and as an ethnographer of this post-industrialised locality I often felt faced with an obvious yet intangible 'nothingness,' with fieldwork often feeling like being on a treadmill chasing a passed 'something.' It seems to me that the ethnographer of any working class is faced with the problem characterised by Marcus when discussing Willis's ethnography of the English working class and the ethnographer "having to invest richness of meaning in "thin" cultural forms purely generated by responses to capitalism" (Marcus and Fischer 1986, p. 178), and as someone who "strains to invest positive meaning and richness in a cultural form that seems entirely oppositional" (Marcus and Fischer 1986, pp. 178-9). This concern directly relates to Hoggart's question in *The Uses of Literacy: Aspects of Working Class Life* (1957) as to the uses made of literacy by the first Scottish working-class generation socialised in conditions of post-scarcity, and I argue that to answer this question is to fashion not only a new relationship to language in light of the relationship to empirical material conditions having been considerably 'loosened,' but to fashion a new sociology that is capable of reflecting an image of contemporary Scotland and working-class *dasein* free from materialism, secularism and modernism. If affluence fundamentally sets working-class *dasein* free in unpredictable ways, it also frees a new kind of sociology to come into being which presupposes the successful dismantling of the mirrors in which working-class *dasein* has misrecognised itself, and an accompanying consciousness that belongs to the "dictatorship of scarcity" era which has come to an end.

In everything that follows the reality of 'social class' is fundamental and my departure point is that: "In the industrial West, class culture *is* the only culture that defines the form of life of many people" (Marcus, cited in Clifford & Marcus 1986, p. 178), along with Willis's (1977, p. 147) insistence that labour "is the main mode of *active* connection with the world: the way *par excellence* of articulating the innermost self with external reality." However, I am mindful of the 'ontological difference' between reality and its representation and that the 'work experience' cannot be represented directly, and theorising the effects of work are highly problematic for sociology and ethnography as they are among the least 'showable' aspects of *dasein's* structuration in light of the fact that there is a physical aspect to disappearing the effects of labour from the consciousness of the worker as noted by Connerton (1989, p. 102):

[I]ncorporating practices...provide a particularly effective system of mnemonics. However, *sui generis*, this suggestion is very difficult to back up with direct evidence since incorporating practices...are largely traceless and that, as such, they are incapable of providing a means by which any evidence of a will to be remembered can be left behind.

This absence of literary traces has meant a sensitivity to the *embodied* nature of much of working-class experience was fundamental to my fieldwork, and meant participating in practices such as production-line work to enable me to observe locals and share their daily practices. Taking jobs as an agricultural labourer at *Kettle Produce* and as a manual operative with *East of Scotland Water* was integral to 'fleshing-out' the fundamental interpretive idea of *embodied discourse* and as methods to position me to gain the necessary data to write an ethnography that would deliver the level of understanding I sought, as well as being able to comply with my supervisor's view that, "if one's ambition is for the intimate knowledge which is afforded by genuinely participant observation...One has to acquire the idiom of the locality, and then learn within it. The acquisition of the idiom is the starting point for investigation" (Cohen 1978, p. 6). My view is that so long as accounts of manual labour, for example, are couched in hackneyed terms such as *exploitation* and *oppression* there is little prospect of the lived reality of manual work 'appearing,' and having read my fair share of texts purporting to deal with working-class experience only to conclude that misplaced goodwill effectively colonises an aspect of working-class being for the observing gaze so that working-class *dasein* remains a *terra incognita* insofar as much of the issues involved stand pre-judged, I was of the view that an original effort was required to conceptualise working-class ontology and so I have pursued the task of naming and bringing the world of workers' embodiment and intentionality to the level of the concept, thereby producing an appropriate vocabulary of this particular *dasein*.

Based upon working as a day-labourer for local farmers and a production line agricultural worker at *Kettle Produce* (Fife) as part of fieldwork, I introduce the notion of a physical reduction as a result of manual labour and in Chapter 6 introduce the terms *reductio ad sensum* and *reductio ad humanum* as a conceptualisation of the 'worked self' in order to establish the autonomy of working class being at a conceptual level. In this effort my guiding departure point has been Castoriadis (1987, p. 168) who has noted the culprit of the piece is the absence of *an ontology of doing*: "There has not been the slightest concern with knowing what *doing* means, what the being of doing is and what it is that doing brings into being." In my treatment of this area of working-class experience I begin from my own practice and recognise that in terms of achieving an embodied point of view immanence changes everything (Tanner et al. 1992), and the issue of realistic representation is further complicated by the fact that articulating the 'worked self' requires a sensitivity to a way of being-in-the-world which cannot be caught by the metaphysics of 'thinghood,' so that another 'culprit' in the long misrepresentation of work has been the Marxist tradition in which subjectivity and immanence have been marginalised by the traditional representation of the worker as 'alienated' from himself and his fellow workers and the products he or she produces, so that what has been lost sight of is that one 'product' the worker is never alienated from is his or her *worked self*.

My focus upon the body as a source of data follows upon many qualitative researchers who similarly recognise embodiment as an important source of non-discursive data and who draw upon their own body as a source of field data (Ellingson 2006). However, if going beyond the philosophy of consciousness tradition in favour of developing an embodied standpoint as a means of accessing the necessary data and producing knowledge through this sensitivity to embodiment is increasingly commonplace, how to properly conceive this drawing upon embodiment has also led me to include in what follows *my own cognitional acts* which were sourced in conceptualising an embodied condition. Significantly, this inclusion of natives' reflexive acts (Myerhoff & Ruby, in Ruby 1982, p. 17) as a source of data meant I felt more or less obliged to include not only an account of my own intellectual self-appropriation but my supernatural experience so that, beginning from an unremarkable inclusion of embodiment, I found myself on a slippery slope that more or less directly led from the inclusion of cognitional acts to the inclusion of the acts of *my soul as a source of field data.*

Trying to find a way to avoid this and then finally surrendering to this methodological slippery slope or 'turn to the subject' has meant I have had to learn to embrace an integral sociology and learn the view expressed many years ago by Marcel Mauss who appealed for social scientists to study the 'total man.' "In reality, in our science, in sociology, rarely or even hardly ever...do we find man divided into faculties. We are always dealing with his body and his mentality as wholes, given simultaneously and all at once. Fundamentally body, soul and society are all mixed together" (Mauss 1979, pp. 24-5). Mauss described the working class as particularly good examples of this fusion of 'body, soul and society' due to its peculiar structuration or the particular relatedness to environment that makes the lived reality of structuration intensely personal, embodied, emotionally charged and determining. As Mauss wrote (1979, p. 28):

[T]he more we regress toward the less evolved forms of social life... the more we are dealing with instinctive men, or, if you will permit the expression, let me rather say total men. Similarly, it is these 'total' men that we meet in the broadest strata of our own populations and above all in the most backward strata. Hence it is they who form the majority of the statistical data available to us...

The average man of our days – and this is true above all of women -...is a 'total' man...The study of this 'totality' is crucial.

The ground covered in the proceeding chapters reflects my journey from a residual positivism to interpretivism and the shift to auto-ethnography until the final position which I describe as integral sociology, in light of the initial starting point that both the range and the meaning of experience "is not susceptible to objective description, but only to interpretation" (Cohen 1985, p. 98). In exploiting my native status I have had to deal with a residual suspicion that the entire project was tainted as a result of my own personal experiences directly impacting "the conditions of production of ethnographic knowledge" (Bell et al. 1993, p. 19). As Chapter 3 will detail, a confrontation with my residual positivism was more or less forced upon me as a result of living with antisocial neighbours and my wish to ignore much of the field because of my fears that writing an ethnography that emerged from my experience of the field meant producing an unrepresentative account of Cardenden. It was grappling with the unsustainable position of ignoring the field and its data to produce an ethnography that in classic positivist fashion could be reproduced and verified by another researcher which forced the issue and made me reject the scientistic 'ideal of knowledge' in favour of a reflexive sociology. This more or less coerced choosing between positivism and interpretivism set me on the path towards auto-ethnography and delving not only into the 'lived experience' (Dilthey) of locals but my own inner experience as a source of knowledge.

If initially I was happy to set myself the task of piecing together the phenomenology of how locals experienced particular housing conditions because I was still writing about realities within the range of ordinary experience, this sense of security was short-lived because, having made the initial break into interpretivism and drawing upon my own lived experience of the field, it was only a matter of time before moving from auto-ethnography as a legitimate methodology to including my own cognitional acts as legitimate sources of data and, upon this basis, making a second break from ordinary experience and a second break from locals themselves insofar as I wished to theorise their experience beyond their own representations of it and beyond what they themselves were familiar with. At this point, if my fieldwork experience became the basis for a sociologically-informed project of self–appropriation (Lonergan 1957; Bourdieu and Wacquant 1992), the successful achievement of this project and the acts of knowledge and love and the experience of the supernatural that arose from prosecuting this ethnographically-informed project of self appropriation compelled my break with a purely naturalistic understanding of working-class *dasein* as incomplete and unable to contain or recognise or represent the full range of working-class experience. This, then, is the basis for the section on Special Ontology.

The decision to include an account of 'higher experiences' or the reflexive acts that working-class *dasein* is capable of fundamentally changed the scope of the book I have written and perhaps even the kind of reader it will attract. In making this decision I draw a parallel between the fact that just as authors of fiction have depicted working-class *dasein* using an impoverished epistemological basis that was more or less adequate to representing the "dictatorship of scarcity" (Beck 1992, p. 20) era these authors were writing within, so among the representations produced by social theorists there has been a similar 'scarcity' epistemology that was felt adequate to describing the 'realm of meaning' as lived by most people in pre-affluent societies. We are the heirs to generations of social theorists and literary authors who have resisted using the full range of colours to depict human reality because to do so was not felt to be empirically justified and so it would have been unrepresentative to do so. I argue, however, that painting with this 'scarcity palette' is at an end and must be replaced by integralism as a more up-to-date and adequate epistemology for accessing the 'world of meaning' not simply as it currently empirically exists but in order to anticipate the dynamism and potentialities being liberated within working-class *dasein* today thanks to affluence and higher education.

The methodological debates that occurred in the nineteen-seventies within the social sciences concerning a post-positivist sociology have been swept away by a comprehensive victory of qualitative and interpretive approaches, and what has also been swept aside is any prospect of a unified standpoint for doing sociology in the wake of the proliferation of different standpoints for doing sociology such as gender, class, sexuality, ethnic identity and geo-political location. However, one standpoint yet to be legitimated is that of religious belief, so that in 2000 when the European Association of Social Anthropologists addressed the question of "how those anthropologists who embrace religion in their personal lives situate themselves within the secular ethos of professional anthropology (Stewart 2001, p. 323), Kapferer identified a 'blinding prejudice' and 'secularist zeal' in much professional anthropology as it struggles to leave behind its methodological atheism in favour of genuine openness to the field, an openness which "offends most of all that secular rationalism, that virtually religious secularism...[so that]... the commitment to secularism in the form of belief (rational secularism as such) militates against openness" (Kapferer 2001, p. 344).

If openness to transcendence horrifies members of an older generation it also signals the coming to an end of a long-held understanding of sociology, and in this regard Kilminster's *The Sociological Revolution* (1998) reminds us that sociology originally believed itself capable of 'liquidating' philosophy and theology insofar as sociology solved the questions that philosophers and theologians had traditionally raised. Kilminster narrates how following the likes of Comte and Marx philosophy and theology were earmarked for obsolescence within the early sociological imagination because questions such as the good life and the good society and human happiness were largely determined by social conditions and therefore were the proper domain of sociology rather than philosophy or theology. However, this early promise of the 'sociological revolution' has failed insofar as sociology has not only failed to tell us what the good society or social order consists in or how we might arrive there, but no longer even understands such tasks as the concern of sociology, far less its special provenance. If the original promise of an engaged or *public sociology* was to take over erstwhile philosophical questions such as the nature of human freedom and agency because social conditions were fundamental to how real human beings exercise agency and freedom, then sociology has failed. While previously sociology promised to dissolve the pretentions of 'pure reason' found in philosophy and theology, the same socialisation and historicisation of reason that dissolved the ambitions of philosophy and theology have been turned upon sociology itself and so it has become mired in the 'sociology of knowledge' (Mannheim 1936) debate for half a century and shows no prospect of escaping.

If the sociological revolution is at an end, then, it is because sociologists no longer believe they are capable of answering such philosophical or theological questions and do not proclaim upon the nature of wisdom, happiness and the good society nor imagine their use of reason can escape the forces of contextualisation. However, in answering in the affirmative that a public sociology can serve society and is able to contribute to the liberation of the individual and the nation in a way that surpasses the contributions of theology and philosophy, I will argue that a properly sociological reading of the self is able to answer traditional philosophical and theological questions such as, what is Man's natural end or perfection, or in what proportionate end does our happiness lie? The section Special Ontology, then, provides a description of an act of understanding which I describe as the natural apotheosis or *ne plus ultra* of working-class *dasein* and that the silence of philosophers, theologians *and sociologists* on the question of what is Man's proportionate natural beatitude is the result of this question having had to await the current post-Enlightenment ethos to arrive and allow a hearing for the proposition that only a post-secular or integral sociology can satisfactorily answer this question.

In what follows the distinction between nature and 'secondary natures' is vital as it has been for much of the history of social theory (Bauman 1976). As a working definition, "what is second nature to the individual is accumulated and sedimented history" (Jacoby 1997, p. 31) so that an integral sociology develops the argument that there has to be a moment of 'pure nature' – in opposition to every kind of supernaturalism – as natural or purely social and cultural human being has to be understood on its own terms before its relation to any kind of transcendent or supernatural destiny can be discussed. More generally, retrieving this dialectic is an important part of re-founding the Scottish imagination at this pre-Referendum point in time because Scotland by the sixteenth and seventeenth centuries saw the development of the theory of the 'divine right' of kings to rule (Wolter 2001, p. 13n) and by the eighteenth and nineteenth centuries' advent of industrialism an original twelfth century advent of the modern era had degenerated into a one-dimensional modernism as a result of the failure to maintain a dialectical tension between immanence and transcendence. Our 'present as history' is characterised by post-industrial working-class generations being more or less coerced into posing the question of what it means to 'be national' and 'be in history' and 'be modern' in a new manner, so that what is needed today is the retrieval of the original twelfth and thirteenth century discovery of the *sui generic* causality of 'secondary natures' free of metaphysical errors such as modernism, secularism, naturalism and materialism that stand in the way of achieving a non-reductionist or integral reading of Scottish *dasein* and an integral reading of the 'present as history.' Having previously described how I began to suspect that beneath the rise of nationalism and the imminent restoration of Scottish independence something more fundamental was involved, this something more is the original European project of modernity so that the Scottish project of independence in Europe needs to be aligned with thinking that is freed from the baleful influence of supernaturalism (Tyrrell 1909) and the 'scarcity thinking' of secularism and materialism.

While it has long been recognised that the 18th century Scottish Enlightenment holds a special place within the history of sociology, historians now identify the twelfth century as the point when across Europe after 1150 there emerged into documentation and awareness a new era characterised by social and economic change where 'public things' or *rei publica* became the object of inquiry and reflection among incipient State officials (Bisson 2009). At this time there occurred the shift towards recognising 'society' in theory and practice as a sui generic category of reality in light of "the appearance after about the year 1000 of new social groupings, including urban guilds and a consolidated family structure, and, on the other hand, the emergence of the anonymous poor and the urban crowd, with the accompanying sense of alienation and *anomie* and the polarization of society and threats of disorder" (Constable 1996, p. 301). In this new periodization, then, the modern era 'begins' with the likes of Duns Scotus (1266-1308) articulating a "complete statement of the theory of sovereignty and the social contract, not unlike that enunciated later by Hobbes, Locke, and Rousseau" (Harris 1927, p. 347) and a theory of human society which "was to revolutionize not only the thought but the practice of the Western world, and it is to him that we can trace in a very real sense the beginning of modern political science" (Harris 1927, p. 357). According to Wolter (2001, pp. 16-17) "[Scotus] does not derive the power of princes directly from God...but rather from the consent of the community given in the voluntary compact of the social contract" and so there is a clear link between Scotus's modern theory of the communitarian basis of political sovereignty and the *Declaration of Arbroath* of 1320 where we find the same modern doctrine stated.

When we remember that Scotus was twenty years old when Alexander III died in 1286 when riding his horse only a few miles from present-day Cardenden, and that this event saw the English king Edward I initiate the Wars of Independence between Scotland and England, and that Scotus upon his arrival in Paris soon thereafter became embroiled in the great topic of the day which was the long-standing feud between Philip the Fair and Boniface VIII over whether Philip owed his political authority to the pope as the Vicar of Christ or through his own authority, we see how useful and timely is Scotus's communitarian theory of political sovereignty in resisting not only ecclesial rulers over-reaching themselves into secular affairs, but useful and timely in peoples having the right to resist secular rulers such as Edward I overreaching themselves into other kingdoms. More philosophically stated, then, modernity begins with Scotus's critique of fideism or supernaturalism and papal theocracy in order to allow humanity to embrace its proper freedom and autonomy. Hardt and Negri (2000), then, locate the origin of European modernity in Scotus's turning to the realm of immanence and the mundane at this time and the Anglo-Catholic theologian John Milbank (2006, p. xxvn) sees Scotus as *the* turning point of the European mind to the extent that Scotus exemplified the signature innovation of modern thought which was to understand created finite reality on its own terms i.e. as a secondary nature exercising its own 'secondary causality' independently of its divine origin:

> The new insistence that Scotus is perhaps the central figure (amongst many others including Avicenna, Gilbert Porreta, Abelard, Roger Bacon, Henry of Ghent, etc.) in *the* crucial shift within Western thought *within which* Kant is still located is not original to RO [Radical Orthodoxy], but has been elaborated by L. Honnefelder, J.-F. Courtine, O. Boulnois, J.-L. Marion and J. Schmutz, amongst many others, ultimately in the wake of Etienne Gilson.

According to Hardt and Negri (2000, p. 74), however, this revolutionary innovation of Scotus provoked a counterrevolution or "second mode of modernity" in the shape of the Renaissance's ambition to "oppose the reappropriation of power on the part of the multitude" (2000, p. 74) so that since the twelfth century European history has been "the uninterrupted conflict between the immanent...and the transcendent" (2000, p. 76) and the development of a fully modern contextual sociology and theology has been prevented because of counterrevolutionary forces for whom "it was paramount to avoid the multitude's being understood...in a direct, immediate relation with divinity and nature" (2000, p. 78) and because what was to be resisted was "every movement of self-constitution of the multitude" (2000, p. 79). The relevance of these long durée concerns to our present-day ethnographic study is that while the existential discovery of both the purely natural apotheosis of fully contextualised Scottish working-class *dasein* and the supernatural realm *is not dependent upon* any kind of knowledge or awareness of developments within eleventh, twelfth or thirteenth century Europe, and while it is clear that a holistic or integral conception of a Scottish and European modernity and the development of an integral sociology do not depend for their arrival upon the conclusions of historians, the fact is that acknowledging the 'return' to the twelfth century is far more than scholarly etiquette or acknowledging one's historical debts as this long durée historicity is the necessary ballast that is required to ensure the 'tasks of freedom' released by affluence do not descend into nihilism and the 'crisis of the West' and to ensure that 'Scotland' authors a new alliance or covenant with the Christian legacy upon a new synthesis and avoids pagan forms of holism that would otherwise threaten Scotland's historical continuity with the European imagination.

Before such grand vistas are opened up to view, however, there is the mundane task of describing and articulating what working-class *dasein* is capable of as this is the central concern of an integral sociology. In what follows the shift beyond a purely naturalistic sociology is founded upon a purely natural achievement so that a moment of 'pure nature' (Long 2010) is the keystone of an integral sociology. In what follows I adopt a 'two-storey' anthropology where human beings or fully-contextualised Scottish working-class *dasein* has two distinct and separate ends: a natural or proportionate end vis-à-vis their human nature and a supernatural end or perfection that is disproportionate to their human nature. This two-storey model is fundamental to ensuring an integral sociology is kept separate from what Milbank (1990) has termed 'the integral revolution' in Catholic theology which seeks to collapse the two orders of the natural and the supernatural into each other. In Chapter 8 I will argue this is a temptation that must be consciously resisted as it is a residual form of supernaturalism which I identify in Milbank, de Lubac, Luigi Sturzo, Karl Rahner and other advocates of Christian sociology and Latin American liberation theology.

In resisting 'theologism' and maintaining a two-storey model a price to be paid is to be accused by supernaturalists of advocating the separation of the natural and the supernatural or the separation of faith from reason. I not only distinguish between these two orders but argue that events in the natural order are the precondition for the advent into the natural order of the supernatural. According socialised human nature its due ontological density is non-negotiable for an integral sociology and talk of a Scotist position leading to the 'secularisation of social theory' is facile and needs to be replaced with the recognition of a perennial tension which can only be resolved by a living synthesis between the two orders.

Strictly maintaining the two-storey model of the human being distances an integral sociology from all theologies and all forms of supernaturalism which have no use for purely natural and social realities, nor how such realities are capable of opening the human being up to his or her supernatural destiny.

Predictably, 'integralists' do not engage in ethnographic or sociological research in order to construct their account of redemption so that, in contrast, an integral sociology is built upon a foundation of 'integral contingency' or a moment of 'pure nature' and a performative account of the natural desire for beatitude or perfection at work upon the basis of a determinate socio-economic context; something which safeguards integral sociology from being an adjunct or ancillary discipline to theology. Importantly, only a two-storey model of human being safeguards against the twin errors of supernaturalism and secularism. Finally, insofar as the twelfth-century view was "that it was harder and more worthy to achieve salvation in the world than in solitude" (Constable 1996, p. 311), then this view is of special relevance to a social class freshly configured by the advent of affluence and deep literacy. I argue then that defending a secularist social theory reproduces the original counter-modernity of the Renaissance and against this I argue that an integral sociology using purely 'profane' material gives an ethnographic 'demonstration' of grace or redemption thanks to the operationalisation of situated being as a result of a sociologically-come-ethnographically constituted act of self-understanding (Chapter 6).

If this achievement is an 'original moment' in the history of spirit it signals the need to succeed in the twenty-first century where the twelfth century failed insofar as if the great success of the European intellect in the twelfth century was the discovery of 'secondary natures' and 'secondary causality' and the invention of the secular and the political and social realms, which thereby opened the way for the natural and social sciences, its great failure was not developing a fully-contextual account of how a universal objective truth is historicised and particularised in different times, places and social contexts so that Long (2010, p. 1) has observed that: "Many contemporary Roman Catholic theologians – to the degree that they engage this question – incline to accept an account of the relation of nature and grace that dissolves the entire structure of human nature and its proportionate end." Both Feingold (2010) and Long (2010) have characterised the Christian mind as being mired in a non-Christian *supernaturalism* which I define as the view that 'secondary natures' and 'secondary causality' are not integral to Christian redemption. This diagnosis is the result of the failure to articulate a fully contextual or fully socialised phenomenology of redemption and is the failure that explains why "theologians barely know how to think about the proportionate nature of the human *ens creatum* any longer" (Long 2010, p. 2). An integral public sociology, then, intervenes into this long durée failure to free Christianity from supernaturalism as well as free sociology from secularism and I will demonstrate how to accomplish these tasks by not only giving a credible account of Man's purely natural beatitude or happiness but an account of how Man brings into view and prepares for his disproportionate or super-natural beatitude by demonstrating the sociological constitution of Man's natural end and his supernatural sanctification, thereby fulfilling the original twelfth century discovery of secondary causality and the original project of modernity.

In light of Long's (2010, p. 2) observation that, "precisely insofar as human nature has an ontological density and proportionate end, just so far is the knowledge of these *essential* to the work of the theologian," the question is how is the philosopher or theologian to come to know Man's proportionate end or which discipline will pronounce upon Man's proportionate end? Will the philosopher or theologian pronounce upon the realm of secondary natures or the social structures in which Man is immersed from the point of his conception until his last breath? How can a theologian or philosopher acknowledge what Scholastics term the 'obediential potency' of Scottish working-class *dasein*, for example, unless a sociologist or ethnographer articulates it for him? How can a theologian or philosopher give an account of an individual's natural beatitude, happiness and perfection unless a sociologist or ethnographer articulates for him the ontological density of working-class human being and a phenomenology of how the working-class person achieves his proportionate end? In the absence of breaking free of philosophy and theology it is difficult to see how Long's claims can be known by the philosopher or theologian except as a matter of abstract formalism, so that the question is how is it possible for the non-sociologist to recover a rigorous *theonomic concept of secondary natures and secondary causality* unless they engage in non-philosophical and non-theological research that *genuinely discovers* these contingent secondary natures to be theonomic and of soteriological value?

It seems to me that this kind of research is a fundamental prerequisite and the philosopher or theologian who fails to venture outside of philosophy and theology in his attempt to recuperate the ontological density of secondary natures must be fated to fail as a Christian theologian, and this is why the school of liberation theology that emerged in Latin American distinguished itself from previous ways of doing theology by acknowledging the findings of sociologists as fundamental material for the work of the theologian. For the individual sociologist, achieving this task is to achieve a sociology which delivers upon the promise of sociology if not to 'dissolve' theology and philosophy (Kilminster 1998) then to safeguard the theonomic potency of social reality. Hence, while St. Thomas taught the doctrine of a specifically proportionate natural end for the human being (Feingold 2010), we require more than abstract philosophic reasoning, and while the natural desire for knowledge of God via his essence is a natural *elicited* desire that must be awakened as a result of knowledge and cognitional development on the side of the knower (Feingold 2010), it is an integral sociology that effectively elicits such a desire and does so *not* upon the basis of divine revelation or a priori belief but upon the basis of an act of self-appropriation achieved upon the basis of integral contingency; and this is a more efficacious departure point for the supernatural than merely philosophical or metaphysical knowledge as in any number of Scholastic texts one can find the truism that *nature is preamble to grace* and in an a priori manner speculate about the relationship between socio-historical conditions and the supernatural. Metaphysical propositions, however, no matter how true can never replace the need to actually instantiate metaphysical truths and can not move anyone one inch closer to their real accomplishment. While the medieval distinction between nature and grace (Viladesau 2006, p. 145) involves the discovery and affirmation of nature as a *sui generic* realm of its own, the existential verification of the claim that *nature is preamble to grace* is something that must be performed if it is to be existentially known to be true, so that, if not the subject of a performative verification then the project of an integral sociology must fail.

It is because the human being has a twofold end– a natural end proportionate to nature as well as a supernatural end that is disproportionate to his or her nature – that means a sociology that is adequate to theorising human being must integrate these two elements and cannot be satisfied with the binary thinking of the twin errors of supernaturalism and secularism. An integral sociology will be Thomistic and Scotist insofar as it articulates the proportionate end of Man and, thereafter, approaches the question of his final supernatural or disproportionate end. However, it is necessary for the doctrine of a specifically natural or proportionate human beatitude to break free from the grip of philosophy and theology and only a sociology can provide an example of socialised human nature achieving its proportionate end and thereby being opened up to the supernatural upon that basis. That the contingent socio-historical realm has theonomic significance is fundamental for an integral sociology given the fact that, were it otherwise, men and women would have to resort to supernaturalism to have any experience or intimation of the divine. By overcoming supernaturalism, then, an integral sociology safeguards the ongoing historical and social nature of Christian redemption.

The theologian not weighed down by the painstaking investigation of 'secondary natures' pays the heavy price of not knowing whether nature or integral contingency are able to bear up the natural man to receive the free gift of his supernatural life. Indeed, any such role or function of socialised *dasein* must be lost sight of for such a theologian. The cognitional life informed by purely natural acts of understanding and loving are 'secondary causes' or *causis secundis* and contingent means that are revealed *a posteriori* as providentially related to the eternal offer of salvation. If secondary natures were not so ordered, both the contingent social order and the structure of cognition and Man's intellectual life could not be described as theonomic or within the ambit of divine providence. In contrast to supernaturalism, then, our purely natural cognitional life and our purely natural acts of love and understanding are not accidental extras to the main event but are essential elements of divine providence over the purely natural, the modern era and the realm of man-made secondary natures. *The alternative to the position that integral contingency is providentially designed to bear the full weight of mediating the supernatural is the twin errors of naturalism and supernaturalism.* Hence, instead of 'hot-wiring' nature to the supernatural and dispensing with the purely natural end of Man by integrating it with his supernatural life via 'the integral revolution' as in Sturzo or de Lubac or Milbank or via the 'supernatural existential' of Karl Rahner, an integral sociology anchors the supernatural in ordinary socialised contingent *dasein* that it may bear that socialised and historicised human being to its supernatural destiny.

An integral sociology by definition rejects any effort to prematurely 'integrate' *the social means* by which the supernatural is 'made real' as the only adequate foundation to ensure escape from supernaturalism is to take social-historical human nature as the starting point as no other basis can hope to avoid the charge of fostering either supernaturalism or its frustrated offspring of naturalism and secularism. If proportionate integral contingency cannot bear the full weight of achieving man's proportionate end as well as provide "the very act which bears us up" (Maritain 1954, p. 110) to the supra-natural level, it does not deserve the name of a sociology because it does not genuinely achieve this elevation through a purely social mediation. An integral sociology, then, is constituted by what socialised *dasein* is capable of achieving as well as what it is capable of *receiving* thanks to bringing to perfection its natural active powers; so that a purely naturalistic sociology is driven to transcend itself as a result of its own inner dynamism into becoming an integral sociology. It is because working-class human being is revealed as theonomic and has soteriological potency as a result of exercising its ownmost nature and powers that means sociology must allow the reality of the supernatural onto its horizon, just as the individual who triggers the advent of the supernatural into his life upon the basis of exercising his purely natural powers would act contrary to reason if he were to deny or refuse this development of himself in his capacity as a social researcher and social theorist.

If the intellectual agency of successfully reducing contingent *dasein* to a pure (proportionate) act of self-understanding is possible, then an understanding of redemption in which a man's being working class is accidental and irrelevant to how he co-operates in his redemption would reveal the soteriological and sociological orders as fundamentally discordant and that nature is not in fact preamble to grace. The notion of secondary natures and secondary causality having significance for redemption and how the two orders of 'the social' and 'the supernatural' are brought into alignment (or to use theological language a covenantal relationship) is what I propose to show in due course. From the standpoint of an integral sociology, for a person to become redeemed is to undergo the odyssey of bringing one's natural or contingent socialised self to a purely natural 'moment of truth' or a point of luminosity that orders and readies the self for the advent of the supernatural so that we may speak of a sociology of the living God. This 'taking aim' at a radical act of self-appropriation is integral to the phenomenological account of Christian redemption that follows because sociological knowledge is necessary for (working-class) human being to achieve its natural or proportionate end. An integral sociology then should be judged according to whether it is able to take the full weight of individuals' immersion in secondary natures and be prepared to be judged as to whether it provides an illuminating and empowering self-knowledge or not, and this should be the test as to whether or not sociology is delivering upon its promise to end philosophy (Kilminster 1998).

An integral sociology rejects the idea of an *innate* efficacious natural desire for God as this would make any contribution sociology might make redundant. If human beings enjoyed a constant innate desire for God regardless of class or gender or culture or education, then all contingent secondary natures would have no role to play in the drama of redemption and would have nothing to add to the story of such a desire; a desire which could happily remain the preserve of philosophers and theologians. However, because the desire for both our natural and supernatural good is not innate but must be elicited, its fate in the life of any individual is dependent upon social conditions and it is these which determine whether such a natural desire is elicited and comes to dominate the life and efforts of an individual, so that the sociologist has something to say about how men and women achieve their supernatural destiny insofar as they are able to explain how the person prepares for grace thanks to reducing himself to act via the understanding of his socialised *dasein* and *mitsein* and upon this basis orders himself to his supernatural beatitude. An integral sociology, then, is indispensable in overcoming 'pure reason' to the extent that it understands how *free* and contingent elicited desires for natural and supernatural happiness can be sufficiently efficacious because of their anchorage in the real, and as a result of this anchorage can bear the weight of a purely natural liberation and subsequent opening onto the supernatural.

As I will argue in Chapter 8, neither liberation theology nor previous attempts at a Christian sociology can be the departure point for an integral sociology because both presume to know precisely that which must be evidenced: the existence of the supernatural. No theology or philosophy can articulate Man's natural or proportionate end in a concrete existential sense and so it is sociology's task to do this and thereby assume the responsibility of 're-founding' the Christian doctrine of nature as preamble to grace upon the basis of integral contingency. The current situation where the Christian does not inherit a model of how to integrate the mundane and the divine remains the defining aporia of Christianity in the modern era in the West because the inability to locate the supernatural at work in the post-*gemeinschaft* industrial order exerts a pressure for de-Christianisation insofar as it puts the very existence of the supernatural into doubt among individuals living with this failure and everyone alive to "this singular and crucial loss of the Catholic intellectual life" (Long 2010, p. 2).

In what follows I give an ethnographic account of the integration of the two distinct realms of the social and the supernatural from a particular class and national standpoint at a particular point in time; an account of supernatural experience upon the basis of socialised 'second nature' which alone can justify the contention that if social theory is to address the reflexive acts of human beings then it must also address the experiences and realities these reflexive acts make Scottish working-class *dasein* capable of receiving. The term 'integral sociology' then adverts to giving a complete picture of the range of human experience, and in this regard openness to the supernatural is just one defining characteristic as the task of articulating the properly natural end or beatitude of the human being is equally foundational as an integral sociology is not merely about the inoffensive task of integrating the social order with the supernatural or refusing to settle for the unsatisfactory choice between supernaturalism or secularism, but pressing the claim that *the class structure mediates the structure of salvation.*

This is what I mean by the idea of putting the full weight of people's destiny upon secondary structures and secondary causality, and until this position is achieved I see no prospect for the desire for a post-secular social theory being fulfilled (Archer et al. 2004; Habermas et al. 2010) nor any reason to dissent from Turner's (1991, p. 61) view that Christianity "does not provide a genuinely satisfactory solution to the problem of class and class conflict in industrial society." Indeed, from this perspective, non-ethnographically grounded and non-sociologically constituted theologies are partly responsible for the privatisation of religion in contemporary Western societies as unless a theology (by which I mean a level of discourse beyond fundamental catechesis) is sociologically constituted it must be ranked as another species of pre-sociological 'pure reason' that will have little conceptual purchase upon real men and women and remain unable to address the challenge of articulating the soteriological value of integral contingency. Those advanced Western societies that have become most de-Christianised are likely to remain so and theology will remain in its pre-modern and pre-sociological state until it comes-of-age not simply by rejecting the immaculate and 'infantile' universalism of much theology but produces a theology constituted by *the class-inflected nature of the constitution of redemption*.

The departure point followed here will be an empirical and ethnographic engagement with real mundane conditions of post-industrial locality and work and housing and a step-by-step inquiry and construction of conditions, consciousness and comportment which rejects any appeal to theological principle or religious belief. Instead, appeal will only be made to ethnographic data and particular acts of understanding which create new realities and which justifies the move beyond naturalistic or secular sociology, and upon this basis is also achieved a decisive break with supernaturalistic accounts of the relation between the natural or the social and the supernatural. The 'pursuit of being' made possible by the sociological imagination fulfils this traditional concern of Western culture thanks to thinking industrialised human being, and in light of which comes the recognition that thinking human being with the non-industrialised tools of pure reason, whether it be philosophy or theology, is unable to generate sufficient purchase on the reality we ourselves are. From the standpoint of integral sociology, the super-natural is mediated through each human being's contingent 'secondary nature' and in post-*gemeinschaft* industrialised societies, without the necessary social and cultural mediation of 'causality' a person cannot exercise the secondary causality he must exercise if he is to order himself towards the supernatural. If the actual advent of the gratuitous gift of sanctifying grace requires a 'triggering' event on the part of the individual and if we accept Kerr's argument that "it is by one's own activity that one is drawn into God" (2002, p. 173), then the advent of the supernatural is dependent upon the occurring of a purely natural event within the person, and insofar as the individual by achieving his or her purely natural or proportionate perfection "gives the created agent a special participation of the pure act of being" (2002, p. 163) we have the solution to a problematic first sighted in the twelfth century and whose lack of a solution condemned attempts at an integral sociology throughout the twentieth century to failure: evidencing the supernatural upon the basis of 'integral contingency' and thereby achieving a way out of the 'modernisation as secularisation' paradigm of much European sociology.

The book is divided into two parts: Part 1 gives a set of initial descriptions and a series of conceptualisations of different aspects of working-class *dasein*, followed by an account of understanding and a series of liberations that follow upon this act of self-understanding. If the first five chapters constitute a more or less standard ethnography, Chapters 6, 7 and 8 are far from standard as they deal with Special Ontology and have as their basis a performative verification of the project of self-appropriation outlined in Lonergan's *Insight* (1957). In this project, the defining tension within the manual labourer is that between two very different worlds and two very different aspects of the self. On the one hand, the self to be appropriated is the situated labouring self that may care nothing for intellectual inquiry, and to complicate matters further there is the question of which self is to be appropriated? Lonergan's (1990, p. 193) answer is that the self to be appropriated is "the rational, intelligent, experiencing man" and so from the existential standpoint of a particular individual labourer this means he must embark upon the intellectual pursuit of himself and in doing so will need to break with an established 'immediate' relationship to himself and make the shift from being a worker to a *worker-inquirer*. The final three chapters are devoted to articulating this journey and the issues involved in successfully accomplishing this shift. In these chapters I trace the development of an initial set of data and give an account of self-appropriation in which the manual *worker* of Chapters 1 to 5 becomes a *worker-inquirer* and proceeds to the further development of himself as a *worker-inquirer-knower*, and in giving my account of these developments I take my doctoral supervisor's words that,

"The self is *the* essential element of anthropological fieldwork" (Cohen 1987, p. 207) as far as I am able.

While an integral sociology is built upon the fact that "there does exist a proportionate natural end distinct from the supernatural end" (Long 2010, p. 3), the pressing need is for an ethnographer-come-sociologist to give an account of that natural end and this is what I provide in Chapter 6 because the *dasein* it unfolds is not readily available either to working-class people themselves or to the social researchers who reflect upon working-class lives. This 'special ontology' is working-class *dasein* considered from the point of view of being in reflexive possession of the truth of itself; of being 'structured in the truth' insofar as a particular 'operationalisation of being' via an act of self-understanding is achieved. The section entitled Special Ontology is written in the wake of secularist humanists having failed to articulate the working-class human being's natural or proportionate beatitude but also in light of Christian theologians' failure which has been noted by Long who has observed that "the natural end that de Lubac and Balthasar find so mysteriously impossible to locate in man as he is" (2010, p. 90) is a failure that is widespread among theologians.

My view is this inability to locate any natural end and the cognition that achieves it is also endemic within the social sciences and humanities, so that an integral sociology must succeed where a number of disciplines have failed to deliver the original twelfth century project of modernity which included the need to effect "the refraction of the gospel's truths throughout a determinate social structure" (Chenu 1997, p. 38). This signature task of 'being modern' also comes to the aid of Lukacs's *History and Class Consciousness* ([1923] 1971) where the task of articulating a phenomenology of how the proletarian subject achieves the Hegelian condition of being 'identical-with-itself' is outlined. I argue that Lukacs's classic text simultaneously contains the great promise and the great failure of Marxism and the left-Enlightenment tradition to give an account of the proletarian subject's purely natural beatitude. Similarly, while the fundamental anthropology of existentialist texts such as Sartre's *Being and Nothingness* (1966) is compatible with the dynamism of Christian anthropology, existentialists likewise evidence the failure to articulate an account of the natural and proportionate perfection available to Man, to say nothing of the happiness that is 'above nature.'

I contend that not only Christian but major post-Christian intellectuals have failed to provide a credible account of (working-class) Man's purely natural beatitude, so that providing such an account will be the ground upon which this text will dialogue with others. To this end the first five chapters consist of empirically-based descriptions and follow a standard ethnographic strategy of establishing some of the fundamental elements involved in a description of a working-class population, beginning with a consideration of the relationship to community/locality (Chapter 1). This emphasis upon locality draws upon the insights of Herzfeld (1997) and Cohen (1996, 1997) who are exemplary in their appreciation of the role of locality for the practice of imagining the nation. Chapter 1 also introduces the idea of the 1945 and 1979 generations which I develop as a heuristic device to organise my data and begins by focussing upon the local perception of the decline in local public space as a result of deindustrialization and cultural change.

Chapter 1 is followed by a description of the social practice of manual labour and the first steps in conceptualising manual labour as a fundamental 'category of being' of working-class *dasein* based upon working as an agricultural labourer and drainage operative with *East of Scotland Water* as well as other pre-doctoral periods of working as a day-labourer in the fields of Fife. Being employed meant being able to conduct participant observation in a crucial social context and was fundamental to my research strategy and methodology since being a worker gives access to conversations and groups and gives an identity that others readily understand and accept and access to rich 'webs of signification' which form the substance of belonging. Doing a manual working-class job, then, guaranteed me access to areas of practice and discourse where working-class structuration occurs, and if the problem of method and data-gathering largely involves the search for locations that afford access to learning what points of 'structuration' there are in the field,

Chapter 2 comes to grips with 'worked subjectivity' as a preliminary step to being able to understand the subsequent politicisation of this worked subjectivity. This emphasis upon manual labour has fallen out of favour among social theorists and researchers for many reasons, such as the shift from blue to white-collar work in late-capitalist economies and changes in the international division of labour so that "the labouring body has been displaced from current consciousness and is not merely separated from the consuming body, which exists in its own right, but does not even stand next to it as an alternative conceptualisation" (Lyon and Barbalet, cited in Csordas 1994, p. 52). There is a palpable representational deficit insofar as the labouring body is conceptually non-existent in much social science literature and I argue in this regard that just as the local without a job is more or less in a state of crisis, so the ethnographer without a grasp of the structuring relevance of manual labour and its consequences for *dasein* is likewise more or less in a perpetual crisis of understanding vis-à-vis working-class reality whether aware of it or not.

More broadly, insofar as the social sciences have failed to achieve an "anthropology from the body" (Csordas 1994) and have failed to adequately conceptualise labour from the labourer's point of view, it is guilty of the same fatal weakness of (Hegelian) Marxism which, while it philosophically intuits the significance of labour, is unable to render labour as a sui generic category of being and so is unable to convert labour into a category and *conditione sine qua non* of 'cognitional agency.' It is in the work experience then that I locate a fundamental element of working-class structuration and the keystone to working-class *dasein* upon which I build my conception of working-class subjectivity and structuration and its purely natural beatitude.

Chapter 3 is based upon my time spent as a Fife Council tenant at 51 Cardenden Road and describes how the nineteen months of fieldwork conducted while living there was dominated by the experience of contesting antisocial neighbours. This chapter seeks to appreciate and understand temporality as a structuring force and seeks to articulate the 'temporal horizon' of working-class being by drawing upon the prolonged process of having an upstairs neighbour evicted, and drawing upon this fieldwork experience as "a limited area of transparency on the otherwise opaque surface of regular uneventful social life (Turner 1957, p. 93). Only via the attempt at constituting neighbourliness were the hegemonies which constitute particular lives made visible; only by being drawn into this antisocial space did I gain insight into the existential ground of neighbours' experiences and begin to suspect the reach of working-class structuration and, in particular, begin to understand *the agency of time* upon *dasein*. Chapter 3 also details the beginnings of my break with positivism insofar as the data that forced itself upon my attention was evermore personal and specific to my fieldwork situation so that I faced a choice of either ignoring the data to keep alive the positivist 'ideal of knowledge' or embrace the 'slippery slope' of the interpretive turn.

Chapter 4 emerges from data gathered while attending weekly meetings of the local history group for over two years. In this chapter national identity is conceived diachronically or in relation to 'being in history' and in relation to the rejection of or the appropriation of a long durée symbolic patrimony. To understand working-class nationalism is to advert to *historicity* as more or less integral to *dasein* and to firstly study the relationship between social class and the 'realm of meaning' and resist the temptation to reduce nationality and/or historicity to ciphers for social forces. After this attempt at incorporating an understanding of historicity as an integral element of Scottish working-class *dasein*, the section General Ontology concludes with a description and analysis of the relations between social class and politics and the ongoing movement towards political independence that was already evident in the nineteen-nineties and, at the time of writing some sixty-four days before the 2014 Referendum, may well be upon us.

While working-class nationalism involves an imagining of the national community, explaining Scottish nationalism using the idea of the nation as 'imagined' is somewhat hazardous as 'Scotland' has survived despite a long campaign of 'forgetting' and 'non-imagining.' Chapter 5 is based upon the material gathered from conducting door-to-door interviews with residents from selected streets from each area of the village in the aftermath of the first elections to the new Scots parliament in May 1999. Of particular importance in my account of nationalism is the notion of embodiment and the link to *practice* (Bourdieu 1977; Brubaker 1996) in an effort to overcome the "pervasive substantialist, realist cast of mind that attributes real, enduring existence to nations" (Brubaker 1996, p. 15n) and the move to define nationalism as "a category of practice, not (in the first instance) a category of analysis" (Brubaker 1996, p. 7) and I further mediate this emphasis upon practice by attending to the practice of manual labour. What emerges is a post-substantivist emphasis upon action as a source of being which points to the conclusion that what observers of nationalism are immune from grasping insofar as there is a crucial link between an ontology informed by labour and nationalism as a subsequent politicisation of that ontology is what Bourdieu (1977, pp. 1-71) has named "the objective limits of objectivism." The victim of his own habitus, defined by Bourdieu (1990, p. 56) as "embodied history, internalised as a second nature," the scholar's detachment and privileged positionality which he believes empowers him to observe nationalism 'fairly and impartially' in fact traps him into the philosophy of consciousness tradition and what Bourdieu names the "synoptic illusion" (1977, p. 101).

Chapter 5 also addresses the task of explaining why Scottish nationalism is such a recent phenomenon and the answer given is that, thanks to the continuing absence of a middle-class national-ism, it is only within the last forty years (1967-2007) that the relation of union has became a working-class issue so that uncovering "the social bases of nationalism" (Gellner 1983, p. 113) requires an investigation of how the working class have mobilised a symbolic patrimony for class ends. In explaining why this has occurred only recently I argue a new post-affluent working-class generation mobilises via nationalism because unlike previous generations during the long durée of the "dictatorship of scarcity" (Beck 1992, p. 20) a new generation is entering a new relationship to the realm of meaning in stark contrast to previous generations immersed in 'scarcity thinking' who entertained a very limited and very dominated relationship to the realm of meaning. Across what I call the 1945 generation and the 1979 generations, one relationship is over and another is at hand.

If Chapters 1 to 5 are standard ethnographic descriptions the final three chapters take the data of the first five chapters to a higher level beyond the words and experiences of informants and beyond standard academic texts that have a focus upon working-class experience such as Charlesworth's *Phenomenology of Working Class Experience* (1999) which is not only resolutely naturalistic in its horizon but does not articulate the purely natural perfection working-class *dasein* is capable of. Charlesworth's text not only leaves working class being in a pre-supernatural state but fails to alert the reader to the purely natural cognitional agency and performance working class being is capable of, and so this work fails to articulate an adequate understanding and account of empowerment from the standpoint of labouring humanity as a result of failing to give an account of the 'integral operationalisation' of situated humanity.

In constructing a standpoint which relies upon a psychological and intellectual development within the worker-inquirer-knower, Chapter 6 privileges the specifically intellectual nature of liberation and argues that a turning to cognitional theory is necessary in light of texts purporting to deal with liberation but which suffer from more or less completely undeveloped theories of cognition and which as a direct result fail to give an account of intellectual liberation that is in any way rigorous or convincing. Chapter 6 is written in the shadow of Marx's view that "liberation is an historical and not a mental act" (Marx and Engels 1974, p. 61) and makes the counter-argument that 'liberation' for human beings is above all a mental act. I argue that how this act of understanding is achieved is important not simply because of the metaphysical truism that "before a man can contemplate his own nature in precise but highly difficult concepts, he has to bring the virtualities of that nature into the light of day" (Lonergan 1957, p. 535), but because of the paradox that a nest of cultural and social conditions stand in the way of the working-class individual achieving this self-understanding and yet are the conditions for making this radical act of understanding (and act of love) possible. Chapter 6 develops the Thomist-Scotist realism or 'moderate nominalism' by drawing upon the developmentalism that lies at the heart of Thomas's account of human beatitude which according to Kerr (2002) emphasises the insight that sanctification occurs at the end of a journey of the human being operationalising his situated or socialised 'secondary nature.'

While traditional Thomism affirms the need for an operationalising of our intellectual nature, contemporary Thomism emphasises the need for an ethnographic turn to achieve this operationalising of that intellectual nature. Because it has been my experience that "it is precisely in relation to the end proportionate to human nature that the supernatural end comes properly into view" (Long 2010, p. 29), the need to give an account of the purely natural end or perfection of working-class human being was necessary before proceeding to give an account of the disproportionate or supernatural capacities of working-class *dasein*. Chapter 6 was written, then, because it seemed wilful not to proceed by way of auto-ethnography to give an account of this act of understanding which is the key stone in my own intellectual itinerary and in light of the fact that: "Up to that decisive achievement, all leads. From it, all follows" (Lonergan 1957, p. xviii).

The significance of Chapter 6 derives from the fact that the notion of a natural proportionate end and beatitude available to Man is a doctrine which even non-religious humanists routinely deny or certainly do not trouble themselves to give an account of, while as for the subject of supernatural or religious experience, this for many Western intellectuals trapped in metaphysical modernism is nowhere to be found among their concerns. Chapters 6, 7 and 8, therefore, pose a direct challenge to those whose imagination and representations are immersed in what I term 'scarcity thinking' and these final three chapters argue that a realistic account of fully-contextualised Scottish working-class *dasein* is the anthropological basis that makes a subsequent experience of supernatural grace possible and intelligible. To this end, I give an account of how the worker-inquirer-knower prepares for the utterly gratuitous gift of supernatural grace by acts of understanding and loving and argue that the moment of sanctifying grace occurs in the aftermath of the worker-inquirer-knower achieving his natural proportionate end and when most reduced to intelligibility, love and understanding, when the worker-inquirer-knower is "actually, actively and repletely knowing and loving" (Kerr 2002, p. 190).

If some writers such as Charlesworth (1999) fail to overcome naturalism in their representations of working-class experience, others who are open to the supernatural fail to overcome supernatural*ism*. Hence, if Chapter 6 was written to articulate the purely natural achievements working-class *dasein* is capable of and bring to perfection the naturalism found in Charlesworth's *Phenomenology of Working Class Experience* (1999), Chapter 8 identifies what I see as the residual supernaturalism of a text such as Milbank's *Theology and Social Theory: Beyond Secular Reason* (1990) which raises the question of the relationship between theology and the social sciences but fails to give a satisfactory answer. Milbank's important intervention is another text of 'pure reason' which maps a particular history of ideas in an objectivist manner and fails to model a living synthesis of the social and the supernatural from any particular social or ethnographic context. In contrast, my final three chapters are built around a performative emphasis that models how working-class *dasein* is actually liberated through its own agency or by its own hand in a purely natural manner because it is an account of integral liberation based upon a cognitional performance grounded in the very social ontology it constructs, conceives, understands, liberates and sanctifies.

As already stated, going beyond the bounds of ordinary or General Ontology in order to complete or perfect the ethnographic data and the exigencies outlined in the first five descriptive chapters meant writing the section on Special Ontology and once this decision was made the logical thing to do next was to add the final chapter on transcendence upon the basis of the preceding act of self-understanding. Chapter 8 then details the supernatural element of working-class *dasein* and is the final stage in the journey begun with a series of descriptions of the *worker*, who in Chapter 6 becomes the *worker-inquirer* and finally the *worker-inquirer-knower*. Chapter 8 details the *worker-inquirer-knower-Christian* in light of the advent of the supernatural as a result of the worker-inquirer-knower reaching the apotheosis of his natural powers and these four stages comprise the journey that is outlined. The final three chapters, then, make common cause with those social theorists who call for a holistic sociology (van Steenbergen 1990; Game and Metcalfe 1996; Bhaskar 2012) and who wish to renew sociology and see the long overdue reconciliation of the social sciences and the question of transcendence and seeks to make common cause with the view that the time has come for social theory to transcend its residual secularist self-understanding as belonging to a 'scarcity era' that has passed and needs to be transcended in a post-secular turn in light of the "emergent anthropological orthodoxy on secularization is that it hasn't happened" (Stewart 2001, p. 323).

Having completed my study of nationalism only to realise nationalism was a fraction of what is emerging in contemporary Scotland, I felt obliged to give my version of what this 'more' is in the shape of the question of what Habermas has termed the unfinished project of European modernity. Chapter 5 and subsequent chapters pursue this 'deeper element' by adding to the description of contextual *dasein* the further element of its reaching the apotheosis of its natural powers. In terms of explaining my decision to include far more of myself than I had bargained for, I cite Gouldner's (1971, p. 493) observation that: "The knower's knowing of himself...and of others and their social worlds...are two sides of a single process [and]...the search for knowledge about social worlds is also contingent upon the knower's *self-awareness*. To know others he cannot simply study *them*, but must also listen to and confront *himself*." I take, then, my lead from Gouldner (1971, p. 481) who has written:

> I have come to the end of my work here, and I am aware that...there remains the uneasy feeling that something more

needs saying...that something has been omitted or glossed and that if I fail to clarify it the preceding work will be not only incomplete but dishonest.

The final three chapters, then, were written not only upon the basis of field data but as a result of developments within myself that went back to undergraduate research and intellectual and spiritual breakthroughs which influenced doctoral fieldwork to the extent that to pass over these developments in silence would have been dishonest. Thanks to these developments I share with Bhaskar (2012, pp. 117-164) a deep interest in the relationship between "social science and self-realisation" and understand sociology as having an indispensable role in articulating the purely natural beatitude or self-realisation of the fully-contextual human being. More generally, in light of the recognition among Scottish intellectuals such as MacIntyre, Muir, MacColla and McDiarmid that "the failure of Scottish culture to *be* whole" (Craig 1999, p. 22) is the central problematic, the final three chapters give the existential grounding of an integral or whole *dasein*, the reconciliation between Christian tradition and the Scottish 'present as history' and an answer to 'the death of God' in modern Europe proclaimed by Nietzsche. In describing how Nietzsche characterised his own 'present as history' Fried (2000, p. 258) has put it as follows:

> In his fundamental outlook towards beings, Nietzsche took as his starting point the knowledge that historical Dasein is not possible without God and without the gods. But God is God only if he comes [*kommt*], and indeed, if he must come; and his coming is possible only if the creative preparedness and the daring wager based on the ultimate limits are held up to him.

The final chapters contextualise Nietzsche's challenge to retrieve a tension that has been lost in the European mind, the tension between Christianity and modernity and seek to articulate a credible response. If Scottish culture and the Scottish imagination has suffered from 'tension-less' anthropologies as a result of the 'Knoxian deformation and destruction' (McRoberts 1959) and the loss of parliament and independence, then other national contexts across the North Atlantic share in this condition. In light of the long and tortuous path that the Scots have taken to politicise their national identity I am more aware than most of how easy it would be to conclude that the 'tasks of freedom' I begin to refer to in passing in Chapters 4 and 5 would be regarded as fanciful or perhaps well-meaning projections of pure reason unless some description or account of them was given. To meet this not unreasonable scepticism the final three chapters are dedicated to giving an account of the free development of the intellectual and psychological aspects of working-class *dasein* that open it towards transcendence in order to 'flesh out' claims made concerning the emergence of a free Scottish modernity.

The final chapters deal with 'special data' as they concern aspects of contextual *dasein* that my informants were not able to help me with by supplying the data as the data is simply too rare and intimate for it to have been handed to me as an ethnographer. To explicate the data further, then, anthropology 'at home' had to become auto-ethnography and this meant drawing upon the example of other ethnographers who have found it necessary to do likewise. In this regard Engelke (2002, p. 4) has argued that Evans-Pritchard and Victor Turner both 'de-privatised' their research methodology as "each tried to fold their 'inner lives' into the work of their anthropology. For Evans-Pritchard and Turner belief became an element of method." Similarly, when Coleman (cited in Pina-Cabral 2008, p. 43) asks "should one study…Christianity by letting the faith 'get inside' oneself," my response has been to dissolve the Chinese walls between the personal and professional as a result of the fieldwork process. In Chapter 2 my method was to access the reality of the labouring body myself by becoming a labourer and then to bring this to the page via writing, and in Chapter 3 my method was to study housing conditions by recognising how these housing conditions entered and determined myself and again to bring this to the page via writing. However, thanks to the experiences

I describe in Chapters 6 and 8 my problem became more radical as from that point onwards I was more or less coerced into seeing as integral to the question of an honest reflexivity the question of transcendence and how to account for the advent of the supernatural as an existential fact *as a result of achieving a sociologically-constituted act of self-understanding.* In light of these developments it seemed that to *not* develop an integral sociology that described these two 'perfections' would be to misrepresent what the purely natural was capable of making itself capable of achieving and receiving i.e. its own apotheosis and the free advent of the supernatural. Finally, mindful of the example of others such as Blondel (1984) and Heidegger (1962) but primarily as a result of having achieved these developments within myself (as well as being mindful of the great MacDiarmid who called upon the poet to assume the burden of his people and to dare to break their living tomb), it seemed daft to contemplate not giving an account of that performative cognitional act "whereby [working class] Dasein is liberated *for* its uttermost possibility of existence" (Heidegger 1962, p. 350).

Having embarked, then, upon the 'slippery slope' of reflexivity or what Levi-Strauss (1908-2009) memorably termed 'the swamps of experience,' the ethnography that follows may be described as an ethnography of *becoming fully modern* insofar as it is a sociological mediation of that 'daring to know' (*aude sapere*) upon the basis of contemporary and contingent social conditions that Foucault identified as defining of modernity; the concern with "the ephemeral, the fleeting, the contingent" (cited in Rabinow and Sullivan 1987, p. 164) and, echoing Chenu (1997), defining the modern condition as the necessity of "recapturing something eternal that is not beyond the present instant, nor behind it, but within it" (Foucault, cited in Rabinow and Sullivan 1987, p. 164). This capture of the eternal upon the basis of the contingent is why modernity begins in the twelfth century and the Franciscan secular turn and the mendicant reform of Christianity. The view that giving 'secondary natures' their due means entrusting the full weight of the supernatural to the shoulders of integral contingency is the true ancestor of the various 'politics of identity' movements we see in post-affluent societies as more social groups attempt to make a stand upon their preferred 'integral contingency' – whether it be gender, sexuality, ethnicity, class identity - as the foundation for the democratic up-take of the twelfth-century project of seeing how far 'secondary natures' can go in bearing the full weight of identity, liberation and salvation.

In attempting an integral sociology I have had to reveal much more of myself than I ever imagined when first entering the field and I am reassured by Ortner (1995, pp. 173-4) who has eloquently written that ethnographic research "has always meant the attempt to understand another life world using the self – *as much of it as possible* – as the instrument of knowing…Classically, this kind of understanding has been closely linked with fieldwork, in which the whole of the self physically and in every other way enters the space of the world the researcher seeks to understand." Because what follows is an ethnography 'at home' I am, of course, involved in the trajectory which I describe the 1979 generation(s) as instantiating and am caught up in the present moment as a Scot among fellow Scots upon the cusp of an unprecedented act of national self-determination on 18 September 2014. Having spent much of my adult life arriving to this point, then, and viewing the effort as a whole I identify with the following point made by Spencer (cited in Ingold 1990, p. 21):

> Many years ago, at a seminar at the University of Edinburgh, I remember Jimmy [Littlejohn] commenting that in order to attempt the task of anthropological comparison we should aspire to 'become coeval with our own history.'

What follows, then, is my attempt and my journey towards becoming coeval with my times and my class and my nation and my people as a native ethnographer who believes that "if anthropology cannot enlighten the complexities of its own national contexts, then it is impotent and trivial" (Cohen 1987, p. 17). I have managed to secure the privilege of attempting and completing a rather long journey that has convinced me that a public sociology and sociological theory and anthropological inquiry are far from impotent and trivial but are rather unique and indispensable sources of liberation. Whether what follows succeeds in making a convincing case for such claims is of course for each reader to decide.

# Part 1
## (i) General Ontology

# 1

# Cardenden: Post-Industrial Village

This is Cardenden. This is Scotland.

Anne-Marie Hankin (age 6)
Good Friday, 1999

## 1.1 Ethnography from Nothing

If identifying a particular day on which fieldwork began is quite artificial as I was researching my natal village, my doctoral fieldwork began in July 1998 after returning from getting married in Spain, and when some twenty months later I began the process of writing up my research, I found myself sitting in front of a blank computer screen on 15 March 2000 facing the problem of where to begin. Which story, event or observation about Cardenden should I start with? Ordinarily, it would have made sense to begin by communicating my 'first impressions' of Cardenden or the moment of my first arrival but in light of conducting ethnography in the village I grew up in, there was no first impression or 'arrival narrative' to solve the problem of how to begin. Instead, I settled upon the strategy of beginning by communicating a sense of local history and the predicament Cardenden shares with many former industrial-era villages in Fife and many locations throughout central Scotland that have recently been made to enter the post-industrial era. Struggling to find a way to capture this reality, however, I stood up from my computer and began pacing around

1

the cramped converted attic that served as my study to relieve the tension of sitting in front of a computer screen that I fancied was patiently waiting for me to begin. I then thought to begin writing up my years of research by describing how I had moved to a new address in Station Road that overlooked *Cardenden Mining Archives* and how I had been able to confirm my suspicion that the Archives had closed before the death of its seventy-seven year old curator. As I paced back and forward I thought that perhaps the view from my study might be a fitting way to begin describing how those locals who remember the industrial era of the village were themselves passing away, and how 'the human means' of curating the memory and identity of the industrial era were coming to an end. I sat down again at my computer, only to immediately stand up to look outside for another look at the Archives, perhaps hoping for some inspiration to begin writing an account of the contrast between the industrial past and the post-industrial present. To my surprise, however, the always-drawn shutter of the Archives was drawn up and upon seeing this novel sight I assumed a new curator had been appointed and the Archives were reopening, and having only been inside on one occasion where the premises had to be specially opened for me after I had arranged an appointment, I was only too glad to escape the problem of how to begin writing and see the collection of mining memorabilia one more time as an obvious way to begin writing about a sense of locality and history in a former pit village like Cardenden.

Stepping inside the Archives, a sudden and palpable sense of disappointment hit me as I scanned empty walls and empty floor space and saw that, far from reopening, the premises were being cleared with all of the mining memorabilia already having been removed, leaving only dark and empty display cabinets ready for dismantling. As I stood taking in this scene Wullie Braid emerged from an open door at the back of the room. Wullie was a former miner who had been responsible for establishing and financing the Archives "tae the tune e eighty thousand pounds" as he presently informed me. I introduced myself and explained I had been hoping for a last look at the Archives but could see that I was too late.

Wullie asked me my name, if I was "connected to the Gilfillans in the village." As we chatted I told Wullie I was in my last year of doing research in the village, at which he told me his daughter was doing her honours year in psychology at Stirling university. While cursing myself for not having previously taken advantage of an ethnographic site that was literally on my doorstep I tamely enquired what was to happen to the collection. Wullie told me he would have "given the lot to Fife Council" if the Council guaranteed the collection would be displayed but, as the Council did not promise this, he had declined the option of having the collection put in storage by the Council and the collection was to be split up between a local mining historian Dan Imrie († 2010), the *Scotspeak* project at the Greig Institute in Leven (Fife) with the rest going "down to Wales." Standing among the empty shelves and cabinets we talked briefly with no enthusiasm of the demise of the Archives. Wullie identified a lack of interest, and at this I remembered when interviewing the late curator he had told me that the problem the Archives faced was not being located "on the Queen's highway" as he had put it, and that this accounted for the failure to attract interest from tourists and casual visitors. With nothing left to say and not wanting to interrupt his work any further I asked Wullie about the Visitors' Book as for a long time I had wanted to see the entry made by Dom Helder Camara and record any comments the eminent Brazilian churchman made when he had visited the Archives. Wullie advised me to come back the next day when his wife would pick out the book for me.[3]

I returned home to face my blank computer screen again but instead of writing I tried to come to terms with what I had just learned. I was saddened the more it sunk in that a local attempt at 'remembrance' and curating the identity and history of the village had come and gone. As myself and Wullie had talked,

---

[3] I had previously been in the Archives on Sunday 23 March 1997 interviewing the curator (Bien Bernard) who had mentioned the visit of Helder Camara. I never saw the Archives open again and never did see the Visitors' Book. Sometime later the space occupied by the Archives was taken over by the offices of Ore Valley Housing Association.

neither of us mentioned the fact that anyone under twenty years of age in the village could have any direct or even indirect experience of the coal mining era, and that the real problem facing the Archives was overcoming locals' fragile connection to their own industrial past; that the circle to be squared was how to establish any kind of 'living relationship' to an era that had passed into history. For the years 1991-2000 the village had been fortunate to possess a well-designed and well-maintained venue dedicated to its industrial past but after two years of fieldwork, even the unexpected occurrence of the Archives closing quickly felt like a familiar tale: a lack of interest, the inability to generate an audience or clientele and thereby revenue to keep the premises financially viable, made all the more poignant as the Archives as a space for memory and local identity was unique and there was no other comparable effort at memory and representation of locality. In the historical shift to a post-industrial economy and society it seemed that even well-resourced efforts at remembering in small localities were fated to offer little resistance to new forces whose "historic role is to destroy history, to sever every link with the past" (Berger 1979, p. 213). As the curator himself had told me:

> You're researchin' because it's a race against time. What wis this a' aboot? An' it's a fascinatin' story, there's no' a story like it. Bit a lot e the community disnae even want tae listen tae that. They're jist no interested. They're no interested... Ma ain brither says as faur as Ah'm concerned, the history e the miners firget it. Ah'm oot the bloody pit; Ah've got ma redundancy money and that's it!

To explain why the end of the Archives felt like 'a familiar tale' it was necessary to start at the beginning of fieldwork and so as I sat in my study at the end of the doctoral-phase of fieldwork I recalled the beginning of fieldwork which had started ten months after the referendum of September 1997 to establish a mandate for the new Scots parliament, and what stood out were the numerous instances when locals expressed puzzlement as to why someone would want to research Cardenden. For example, on a Saturday morning in

July 1999 when buying bread from Bayne's bakery opposite my flat in Cardenden Road, as it was early and business was slow, I spent some time chatting with the woman who had served me behind the counter and informed her I was a student researching Cardenden. At this, she told me her son had graduated the week before from Heriot-Watt University in physics and that he was "waiting for clearance before going down south" to join the Ministry of Defence. "Well..." she concluded, "there's nothing up here, is there?"

Similar views were expressed by retired miner Hugh Young (2 May 2000) when he told me that: "The only thing Cardenden is handy fir is Glenrothes an Kirkcaldy," and I found among local residents who enquired what it was I was studying that I stood a good chance of eliciting recognition of the value of my research if I replied "working-class nationalism" as locals intuitively regarded this as a real and more or less important 'something.' Alternatively, I invited bemused incredulity if I simply replied: "I'm studying Cardenden," as if that answer was intuitively regarded as insufficient and in need of further elaboration and justification. I implicitly presumed the non-plussed reaction to asserting 'I'm studying Cardenden' was based upon locals' view that "there's nothing here" as they so often said, so that in interpreting Hugh's remark cited above the obvious interpretation is that the ethnographer who wishes to capture something important or meaningful should go to Glenrothes or Kirkcaldy as nothing much can come from studying Cardenden, and that by studying Cardenden I was setting myself the challenge of how to make something from nothing.

Nearly three years into fieldwork on a sunny afternoon in April 2001 I took a walk with my then three-year-old daughter in her buggy to the local park. As it was a working day the park was empty except for a local taking his dog a walk and a local unemployed history graduate practicing his golf swing on one of the football pitches created from land that had been reclaimed from the mining industry in the nineteen-nineties. My walk took me through the landscaped area that had been planted with large patches of trees interspersed with small paths to allow locals to walk through and 'enjoy' these new 'post-industrial' spaces;

5

spaces that throughout my childhood had been off-limits as the entire area until the nineteen-nineties was a huge smouldering bing. As usual, I had not particularly enjoyed the walk as I was coerced as usual to think about how the poor quality of soil used to reclaim the land resulted in Nature having little to work on so that its task of reclaiming space from the ravages of the industrial period or making 'something from nothing' would be a depressingly long-term generational affair. Walking through what I fancied was not Nature but the endless monotony of what seemed to be the same tree repeated again and again thanks to the same one species of tree having been used everywhere, I noted the absence of wildlife and birdsong so that the silence and the landscape through which I was walking and trying to spot something interesting to point out for my daughter to look at eventually became a depressing sign of the advent of 'industrialised nature' and a lost opportunity to properly post-industrialise local space.

On this particular day, however, I had heard an unfamiliar sound coming from somewhere in the village that I couldn't identify. Thinking no more about it, I continued my walk before turning back to head home to 113 Main Street. As I turned into my street the town clock which I hadn't even suspected was capable of sounding the hours suddenly started to chime, and at that instant I realised that the strange noise that I had been hearing whilst out walking had been the town clock: a town clock that only at that moment did I realise had been silent all my life; a town clock that only then did I realise had been designed to chime the hours. Only upon hearing the clock sound, then, did I realise it had been *broken* all these years. After more than sixty years of silence the *Number 1 Goth* town clock which had been installed in 1920 but which I was informed had never chimed since the Second World War of 1939-1945, began chiming the hours again. Such was my surprise and delight that throughout that evening as each hour approached I stopped what I was doing and made my way to a part of the house where I'd be sure to hear the hour being sounded; as if still not believing it was true until I heard the clock strike. My taking delight in the sounding of the clock was shared by other locals. As community activist Wullie Duncan informed me later: "Ah wanted tae greet when Ah heard the toon clock chimin. That's how Ah felt." If the task of the ethnographer is to study others in "their space and time" (Burawoy 2000, pp. 3-4) then it seemed the sounding of the passing hours was so pleasing because it called to mind or 'called to presence' the long history of silence residents had endured; as if the 'lived experience' or meaning of the sounding clock within every local inhabitants' hearing was its *liberating* the accumulated years of silence.

The chiming of the hours was architecturally significant as the town clock forms the top part of the Goth building which is the most recognised landmark within the village, and thinking upon my own and Wullie's response, the significance of the clock chiming seemed to be because it felt as if for more than sixty years local 'public time' had stood still, and so for at least one sunny April afternoon and evening a 'spell' that had been cast and then been long forgotten had suddenly been broken and locality had awakened, and local time had returned and been re-united with local space and in our hearing the clock, sixty years of space-time "distanciation" (Giddens 1981, pp. 90-108) had come to an end. Perhaps also, this public marking of time gave inhabitants a new medium through which they could experience their *mitsein* or 'being alongside' each other in their local space and this temporality was a new mediation of sociality and so residents were decanted and delivered from a long unnoticed *mitsein* characterised by a kind of sonic privatism. Throughout that first evening it felt as if *publicness* had returned in a new and unsuspected manner; as if this new temporal-come-aural mediation of locality or sonic structuring of *mitsein* revealed something primitive about the nature of sociality that had been lost, as if the town clock made present once again the original 'publicity-making' function of time-keeping. Insofar as time was made public thanks to the town clock chiming, it made public the prior privatisation of time so that it suddenly felt as if locality itself began again or came freshly into being because time literally *took place* that evening and Cardenden was returned to an era when "time and space were inseparable, congealed in locale, that is in 'place'" (Burawoy 2000, p.3), so that a clock striking reunited

7

everyone within earshot into an aural community of listeners by making a physical connection 'out of thin air.'

If the town clock resuming striking meant the history of silence was made present, something else that was made present was the question as to who was responsible for this long silence, and local history group members informed me that the Community Council's achievement in renovating the clock came after the Goth closed as a pub and after previous offers by the Goth management to pay for the clock's restoration were refused. When inquiring why it had taken more than half a century to fix a clock I received no clear answer, although one community council member informed me the reason was a long-time Community Council member who lived opposite the clock objected that it would disturb his sleep and this was why the clock stopped chiming after 10 p.m. and before 9 a.m.

If the resumption of the town clock sounding the hours had intimations of a post-industrial return to a slower bucolic pre-industrial era, the industrial era of locality as 'pit village' (1895-1965) had its own way of marking time as revealed by one of the members of the local history group (Adam Ingram) who recounted his memories of locality and in particular the colliery whistle sounding throughout the day:

> The first blast of the day was at five twenty-five a.m. and lasted for five minutes. Shorter blasts were then emitted at six a.m., nine-thirty a.m., nine-fifty a.m., one-thirty p.m., two p.m., five-thirty p.m., five-fifty p.m., nine-thirty p.m. and finally at ten p.m. There was, too, the sound of silence. I can recall five: learning the deaf and dumb alphabet at the Cubs; watching the funeral procession of Johnny Thomson, the Celtic goalkeeper, in September 1931 and eight weeks later, the funerals of nine of the ten men killed in the Bowhill Colliery disaster; looking at the first pictures of Belsen Concentration Camp in the Pathé news at the Goth;[4] and

---

[4] There was once a Goth picture house adjacent to the No. 1 Goth pub which has long since been demolished and recently made into a small car park where I would park my *East of Scotland Water* van each night when living in Station

finally the two-minutes silence at eleven a.m. on November 11th every year in remembrance of those who died in the service of their country in two World Wars.

This evocation of the pit horn sounding to mark the progress of the working day is a poignant representation of village and provincial life in light of the practice of all the collieries throughout Fife sounding their horns in unison every year at midnight on Hogmanay to greet the New Year. What is also clear is that time was not simply marked by industry but time itself was industrialised as time did not stop or come to rest or follow any natural or seasonal rhythm but was subject to 'total mobilisation' as every hour of every day was dedicated to economic activity. Also within this context of industrialism, there is a clear evocation in the above testimony of a sense of a shared experiencing of day-to-day time and the passing of the years and sharing in the major events of world history. This era, however, has passed thanks to the process termed 'deindustrialization' which must dominate any attempt at rendering 'the present as history' in light of the fact that the original *raison d' être* of industrial locality has passed, raising questions as to the meaning of place and highlighting the problem as to which generation's view of locality will prevail and which generation will assume responsibility for naming and interpreting the post-industrial present.

## 1.2 The Advent of the Post-Industrial Era

The shaft for Bowhill Colliery was sunk in 1895 and seventy years later in 1965 the colliery closed. In 1931 the village population peaked at over 10,000 while the current population estimate for Cardenden stands at 5,270.[5] Among the material gathered by the local history group I attended during fieldwork were many

---

Road. The only remains of the cinema's existence is a rusted rectangular metal frame still attached to a wall of the pub where the cinema bill was displayed.

[5] General Register for Scotland. www.gro-scotland.gov.uk/statistics. [Accessed 8 December 2010]

newspaper clippings and photographs depicting the social history of the village, and what I found striking about many of the photographs were the ubiquitous crowd scenes such as gala evenings, summer balls and the many annual dances of the many local clubs, civil and church associations and various branches of national organisations. Photographs, for example, of the formal opening of new local amenities such as the cinema or the local park with its meticulously cared-for gardens, which are a record of a confident industrial era. Another striking feature of the photographs is the formality and visible ranking of the subjects posing for the camera: prominent members of the local middle and even upper class such as mine owners, local landowners, managers or business proprietors in their top hats accompanied by wives wearing expensive gowns in the forefront, clearly illustrating social standing and their ongoing patronage of locality and local events and financial investment in locality, all surrounded by the 'rank and file' and illustrating an era where attending such local events was a spectacle and source of distinction. Adding to the formality and significance of such photographs is the fact that they were taken long before cameras were affordable to most people so that this technology remained largely monopolized by professionals, with the result that older locals tend to have little or no photographic record of their early lives with the local history group having very few photographs of miners in informal settings or depictions of mundane domestic life.[6] The preponderance of colliery managers, businessmen and their wives in the photographic record of locality is also reflected in the present-day architecture of the village where, as a rule, simply walking through the village and noting large detached stone-built houses is to identify the former residence of pit managers, doctors and other local professionals of the industrial era before this professional class more or less vacated Cardenden

---

[6] On New Year's Day 2012 one elderly informant told me of a woman in Cardenden who was married to one of her husband's brothers, and not only did she not possess a photograph of her dead husband but did not possess a single photograph of her wedding day.

as a result of post-industrialisation. What is also clear from the photographic record is that the industrial era of the village was also the heyday of class distinction and unambiguous social ranking. As one older informant (Bien Bernard) told me:

See when ye were a boy, if ye saw the minister comin' ye crossed the street, if ye seen the docter comin' ye crossed the street. If ye saw the police comin' ye crossed the street. See that wis the elite, the literati, ye didnae...ye jist never mixed. Never. Never the twain shall meet, right? The minister wis a pal e the coal owners, he wis in the manager's pocket. They were a' in the manager's pockets; a' the business men. Oh no, ye never mixed wi naeb'dy, never mixed wi naeb'dy.

While most of the practices and visible significations of class difference and social status are now long gone, such class-based practices were endemic throughout the first half of the twentieth century when Cardenden was economically profitable and attracted primary and secondary businesses and private investment as well as workers, which meant Cardenden had its own local bourgeoisie and saw the cultivation of an intense localism and the minute organisation of locality in great detail. If the obviousness of the class system has sharply retreated there has also occurred a parallel decline in the practice of local politics from being something assiduously cultivated and competed for among local professionals as part of a commitment to civic life, to the present day Community Council of little power comprised of pensioners backed up by popular apathy.

In addition to a certain retreat of the class system, a description of the advent of the post-industrial era must also include the physical transformation that began in the nineteen-eighties and the many land reclamation schemes[7] to treat the widespread physical and environmental scarring caused to the Fife landscape

---

[7] On the outskirts of Cardenden is the Purvis land reclamation site where rubble from the building trade is recycled and resold. The site is shared with the RWE npower renewables depot which supplies timber-based fuel for the new biomass

by the industrial coalmining which have returned Cardenden to something of its pre-industrial rural appearance.[8] Growing up in Cardenden in the late nineteen-sixties and early nineteen-seventies I remember playing on the long-abandoned bing and buildings of the old Cardenden pit that even then had been long abandoned with no effort having been made to make the land fit for commercial activity or agriculture; as well as playing on the vastly larger bing beside the much larger Bowhill colliery complex which dominated the local landscape until the late nineteen-eighties and which, because it remained too hot to touch just below its encrusted and smoldering surface, was always a tempting playground for local young boys looking to 'get chased.'[9]

If we look to the literature on post-industrialisation the following definition or description from Castoriadis (1997, pp. 32-3) is a useful starting point:

Something in reality corresponds to the term postindustrial. Briefly speaking, in the rich countries at least (but not only), production (whatever that may mean) is moving away from old dirty factories and blast furnaces toward increasingly automated complexes and various 'services'... Automation and data processing were supposed to transform

---

power plant supplying power to the Tullis Russel papermaking plant in nearby Markinch.

[8] An excellent photographic illustration of this return to a pre-industrial appearance is the aerial photograph of Cardenden in Alastair Campbell's *Fife From Above* (2011, p. 76).

[9] The history group members have so far been unable to locate the dates of Cardenden pit which closed circa 1920. Bowhill Colliery (Lady Josephine) officially closed in 1966 (although locals advise the year 1965 because this was when coal production ceased) with a peak employment figure of 1,544 in 1962. The Minto pit closed in 1967 with a peak employment figure of 757 in 1957. The Lady Helen pit closed in 1960 with a peak employment figure of 474. The Number 1 Dundonald pit closed in 1961 with a peak employment figure of 260 in 1952. Bowhill (Cardenden) Power Station had a peak employment figure of 36 in 1974. Further afield, Seafield Colliery (Kirkcaldy) closed in July 1987 with a peak employment figure of 2,472 in 1974 and The Michael, the largest pit in the Fife coalfield, closed in 1988 and had a peak employment figure of 3,296.

the repetitive, alienated industrial toil of old...In actuality, none of all this has materialised...For the bulk of the remaining employees, in industry or in services, the nature of work has not fundamentally changed...'redundant' [industrial] workers, and youth, have mostly found employment in second-rate, poorly paid, 'service' industries.

With this definition in mind the following interview transcript from a former miner and his wife gives us a precise point in time for the end of the industrial era in Cardenden.

**Me:** The miners went back in nineteen-eighty-five. Was that when a' the redundancies were?
**Eileen:** At the end e the year. They hid a tae come oot. The last day e nineteen-eighty-five.
**John:** The last day e nineteen-eighty-five Ah worked.
**Eileen:** Right up tae the thirty-first e December cause if they didnae come oot then, they widnae a got dole the next year. Because they hid nae stamp fir nineteen eighty-four. That wis the year they were on strike. Ye hid tae leave in eighty-five.
**John:** Ye hid tae leave the pit in eighty-five. Ah cannae mind e the reason fir it. It hid somethin tae dae wi the benevolent system.
**Eileen:** They'd nae stamp on their caird 'cause they hid never worked that year so they hid nae stamp fir nineteen-eighty four. Eighty-five he [John] come oot. Eighty-six we got the dole. Fae then we've lived like that.
**Me:** So basically the last day e nineteen-eighty-five?
**Eileen:** He worked the last shift.
**Me:** So basically fir maist Cardenden miners that wis there last day?
**John:** Aye. The pit broke aff fir new year holidays. An that wis yer last day e work. A lot e boys came aff days afore it, a week afore it. Ah says no. Ah went right up tae the very last day, the last minute. Ah didnae even come up the pit early. Ah came up wi the rest e the men, come up richt on ma time. They were even sayin 'What the hell e you daen

oot tae yer work?' They says, 'Yer packin up next week.' They says, 'That's you finished!' Ah says 'Ah'm needin a' the money Ah can git, even though it's jist a days wage, Ah've a lot e debt. Ah cannae afford tae take time aff.' Ah'll tell ye, if they hid asked me tae come back an worked on as casual labour Ah'd a come back. If Ah could get ma dole. See when we first moved up here [from Cluny Park to Whitehall Avenue] this wis a' miners. No everybody bit the majority, the majority were miners. Danny Laferty and Wullie Blair an Balfour an Howie an Cockie, auld Martin, Eck Kenny, Kennedy, Ned Campbell across there.

**Eileen:** They were a' miners wane time.

**John:** A' miners. The majority.

**Eileen:** An they hid a meetin in the [Bowhill War Memorial] Club[10] mind an they were bringin folk in fae ootside.

**Me:** What dae ye mean they brought folk fae ootside?

**John:** They were bringin boys in fae the West e Fife. They hid tae bring in folk tae agitate. Whenever somebody got up tae speak 'Away ya shower e gutless...' An' a' this.

**Me:** Is that right?

**John:** Oh aye! A' the agitators brought in. Agitators. Strangers. They didnae live in the village.

**Eileen:** Ah mean they never hid a vote or anythin.

**John:** That's when Arthur Jack got up an Ah'll gie that boy his due. The hall wis packed an ye could see he wis shakin. He says: 'There's a feelin in the village among a lot e the men, they want the strike tae finish. They want tae go back tae work an Ah think we should have a vote.' An Ah'll tell ye, see when he done that, a' the agitators comin an shoutin ya shower e gutless so an so's an a' the rest e it.

**Eileen:** An it's no only that, when they did go back tae work a bing e men fae the East coast hid a' been workin! Eh? Up the coast. They'd a' went tae their work.

---

[10] Locals recall that into the 1990s the Club was the centre of weekend nightlife and anyone wanting a seat had to be in by 6 p.m. On Sunday 2 June 2013 The Club closed as a result of unpaid utility bills.

**John:** See places like Glenrothes, Kirkcaldy, an' even Leven, they're big toons, folk could hide bit ye cannae hide here.
**Eileen:** 'Cause a' body kent ye.
**John:** Ye cannae hide in a minin village...Kinglessie, Ballingry, Lohore, Bowhill. There nae wiy ye could hide, ye couldnae hide here. An they boys that stayed in Kirkcaldy, Glenrothes...a bing e thum were workin. Ken, you're in a big city, an wane neebor works in a factry an wan neebor works in a thing. He's no bothered whether you're scabbin or no! He couldnae care less! Bit doon here it's different. Anyway, as Ah wis sayin, whenever there's a wee bit e trouble between workers an employers there boys is in. Young socialists, an' Marxists, an' a' the Communist party. They were right in. An they were telln boys how tae organise their strike an' everythin. How tae hiv maximum effect an everything. Create the maist damage.

If the last day of 1985 was the end of life as a miner, it was not until 1990 that Cardenden became 'post-coal' as this was the year when many informants advised me they had gas central heating installed in their former Council houses and when they began living without coal in their lives. It was the summer of nineteen-ninety, then, that coal as a 'way of life' came to an end and became a memory so that today, apart from the chimneys atop every house that was built after the War in the late nineteen-forties and fifties, the only other physical evidence of the coalmining era are the original coal bunkers that remain in the back gardens of elderly widows.

When the older generation and former miners in particular attempt to articulate 'the present as history,' the strike of 1984-1985 is their usual departure point for discourse upon a wide variety of topics: the experience of becoming 'postindustrial,' the meaning of their lives, working-class history and the problematic question of what remains of local identity and community. When locals talk of the strike they remember a period of crisis but also that they did not suspect the advent of a new order, so that the strike today symbolises the advent of post-industrialisation and a sense of 'loss' that many informants openly expressed to me. *Only in the aftermath* of the strike has it taken on a powerful symbolising function for the ending of a way of life, so that closely related to talk of the miners' strike were queries about the cause of the present-day 'collapse' of shared values. For some of my informants there is no doubt that a certain symbolic order, as revealed in the self-assured semiotics of workers' struggle reproduced in trade union banners for example, has fallen apart and a way of life has been made redundant by events. As a National Union of Mineworkers (NUM) official at the time of the strike (Alex Howie) told me:

> It wis a Monday durin' the strike; Ah cannae even tell ye the month an' the front page e *The Sunday Mail*: 'Ravenscraig To Shut.' The front cover an' we were there hudin it up at the gate; an' ken the shift jist walkin' in. Ken they widnae even jist stop tae talk tae ye. Ah could aye mind that. Ye wonder if it'd a' been any different ken if the steel worker boys had helped us. Fae what Ah've seen Ah'm still convinced she [Margaret Thatcher] wis wantin' tae defeat the lot e us.[11] She jist wanted tae f***in' destroy us an' she succeeded tae the extent that Ah think she f***ed the country. An Ah'll tell ye this: any joab Ah've had since Ah left the minin' industry it's dae this, dae that. Dae it or yer oot the door. Ye'll never ever hae a workin' class union noo. Never. Ye'll never ever have a workin' class union. In any joab noo ye'll never have a workin' class union. Cause ye cannae even trust yer neebor. They'll play wane against wane. They'd rather shop wane anither thin stick thegither. Management's actually got everybody tae obey the rules or yer oot the f***in door. When Thatcher beat the miners she beat every industry. They're no' like the management that

---

[11] In the aftermath of the death of the former Prime Minister Margaret Thatcher on 8 April 2013 it emerged that Alex was right to have his suspicions as it emerged in television footage that the British government delayed the closure of the Ravenscraig steel mill as a reward for the Scottish steelworkers' refusal to help the miners during the 1984-1985 strike.

wis in the pit. Once upon a time in the pit ye could talk tae management how you seen it. Ye could f***in argue hammer an' tong, bit ye still hid a union. Noo ye cannae.

In a similar vein, former miner Bien Bernard told me:

In Cardenden here, ye hid little or no choice, there were two thousand miners here, ye hid little or no choice. Ye were lucky if ye were a joiner or an electrician. Bit there werenae they type e jobs tae be had. An' they wernae sae ready gi'en miner's sons better type joabs. So yer more or less bogged down tae the pit...yer faither worked in the pit an' yir grandfaither worked in the pit, an' that wis it. Ye jist followed in his fitsteps ye ken. As a matter e fact ye went doon the pit at fourteen, the smells in a pit, the water smells, the earth smells, the coal smells, the stones smell. A' different smells, an' ye ken ye remember them a' yer lifetime. Ah stull git thum yit. Bit naeb'dy wanted Communists but ye see in this village, the hale lot e us, the minute ye rebelled yir a Communist, disnae maitter if ye *ir* a Communist ye were branded a Communist...yir jist dirt...ye were a coal Jock... yir dad wis a miner ye were nuhin...we were a' branded Communist. See the minute ye rebelled yir a Communist. The first Communist upon this earth wis Christ. The first one tae rebel. He was a Communist! An yet what did we ever want? We wanted a pint at the weekend, a guid drink at the weekend, an' their bauchy an' their bet at the horses. Ye see that wis the life. An' ye couldnae change that. That wis the environment ye ken. That wis their way e life. An' you couldnae change that. They didnae want tae own a hoose; they wid a felt oot e place' if they hud owned a hoose. 'Oh no Ah'm stayin' the same as the rest. Ah'm no changing.' Ye ken what Ah mean? That wis oor environment ye ken. An' Ah'll tell ye somehin, classes will never mix. Ah mean until the end e time. Burns said, 'Man tae man the world o'er shall brothers be fir a' that.' It'll be fine if it did bit that's the perfect utopia, bit that'll never happen. There's

17

no' a lot e people look back wi' pride onywiy on that strike, as when they did wi' 1926. See we were broucht up wi stories fae the old men. When we were young, used tae sit an' men tell'n us a' the stories e what they did durin' the strike an' everythin' ye ken? Auld Cocky Wotherspoon ken? They were a' young boys durin the strike ye see. What they used tae dae durin' the strike. Bit when the strike finished a' they boys thought they would be like their uncles, their faithers and the grandfaithers. They wid dae the same thing ye ken. Bit the spirit wisnae there, the heart wisnae there. It wis different. We hid a lot mair money in oor pocket. We were a lot mair sophisticated noo. At that time the miner hid nuhin onywiy. Even when they were workin they hid nuthin.

Reflecting upon my interviews and conversations with local miners and members of the local Strike Committee and their wives, and some of the women involved in running the soup kitchen set up during the nineteen-eighty-four strike, I am struck by the idea that within the mind of many informants a fundamental thesis underpinning much of their recounting of the strike is that at this time a normally drawn veil was lifted, and that the longer the strike wore on the further the veil was lifted and the more informants glimpsed the true nature of the society they lived in, and they were remembering what it historically had meant to be working class, so that the longer the strike wore on the more they were becoming 'class-conscious.' As one former-miner informant told me when remembering the strike:

Go against the establishment and see how f***in free ye are! There's boys that have tried it. An' boys that have went against the establishment an' jist aboot hid the revolution. In 1926 when Wullie Gallacher an' a' that wis oan the go. A school maister tae! An' they pit him up in Peterhead [prison] an' poisoned um. Cause he wis gonnae lead it, an' it wis on. The revolution in Scotland wis on then. That wis 1926. An' we're that f***in naive we'll never learn. They sat aroond the table in 1974 and said the workin' class will never do this tae us again. They brought oot a' the golden carrots. Sell their hoose, gie them that. There'll be nae mair wane third deposit fir a car. Gie thum the money. Got oor hooses, car. That wis us beat! Gie them a taste, make wee capitalists oot e us. There's only two people boucht their hoose in this street, an' they've changed. Utterly changed. Attitudes changed. An' that's hoo they done it. Ah think the community's changed. Some e the attitude in the community has changed. Ken, at wane time we were a close knit community, we a' helped eachither oot. Noo that disnae happen. Ah dinnae think so, no' tae the same extent it used tae. Ken we've no' got the same neighbourly love, friendship, that we used tae have. Ye ken, it wid a been a guid thing if somebody hid kept a diary. Ah got tellt, after the strike they tellt me tae get rid e a' the minutes e the meetins. They a' went up the lum. Ah got tellt fae the hierarchy in Dysart... instructed us tae burn a' the meetins. It's a pity somebody didnae keep a diary. See ye wernae wantin tae leave nuhin thit could be fund at a later date. A' they boys were watchin' their ain position, watchin' their ain back cause ye actually didnae ken what ye were gaun back tae. See ye've got tae cast yer mind back. Well afore the strike ye hid a' yer local pits gaun. Dundonald, Bowhill, they were a' village pits. An' then when Ah went tae Seafield [Kirkcaldy] ken it wis cosmopolitan. Miners always identified theirsels wi' the pit they came fae. Ken, they were always Michael men, Bowhill men or ken whatever. There wis a sort e a thing wi' the pit they come fae. At that time minin' wis local, everybody lived in each ithers pockets. Ye kent sort e everybody's business ye ken. It wis a close knit community at that time. That's no here noo. It's a different thing a' thegither. It's a different ball game. There's somethin' missin in the community, the companionship, the camaraderie. The pits is a' shut, there's somethin' missin'. Pit it this way. You're gaun doon workin' in a stinkin' black hole, ye depend on folk. Noo your sort e lookin' oot fir him an' he's lookin oot fir you. He's there tae protect you an' you're there tae protect him. Ye dinnae get that noo. That's a' gaun noo. It wis clannish. The East coast boys wis bad. Seafield wis mainly West Fife men.

Similarly, from the following testimony from Davy Murdoch and Shay Kenny when interviewed in Bowhill Bowling Club, we can glimpse how abstractions such as 'class solidarity' and 'internationalism' and notions of the nineteen-eighties involving a formative experience of the 'crisis of the State' emerge from a real and ongoing set of concrete circumstances and experiences:

The strike meant a lot of aggro. Special boys in wi nae numbers on. Six foot police men. The local boys [police] didn't go o'er the score. Trainloads and busloads e cops. And some e thum werenae even cops. Word got oot aboot a mass picket in The Frances [pit]. Boys (police) comin fae as far as Paisley. Pig wagons. Monkey cages. Ah mind eh the Inverness caper. Wane weekend every month we'd go up picketing, monitorin. See there wiz nae coal gaun doon the Caledonian canal. Invergordon and Ardesier was where the coal was bein delivered. A' the wee oot the way harbours. The coal wis lorried doon tae power stations. Anyway, Dysart [strike committee] would organise lots e pickets to Invergordon... The railway workers were brilliant. They refused to touch it [the coal]. That's why it was lorried tae wherever. At the coal depots there was plenty picketing there. The coal deposit here at Bowhill was still supplying schools and hospitals. Drivers had a dispensation slip signed and dated fae Dysart [strike committee]. The bugbear wis Ravenscraig when they started takin coal in there. Yuill and Dodds was the firm that lifted coal to Ravenscraig. A Kirkcaldy firm! Hunterston to Ravenscraig. They were shippin coal in fae Australia. They were also bringing Polish coal intae Perth... See Maggie [Thatcher] wis determined she wis gonnae break the union. We hid a rally in London. Davey wi a stick, a walkin stick, got done fir carryin an offensive weapon...Freddy Karate [proprietor of local fish and chip shop] used tae fry the chips fir us. He'd be supplied wi the tatties. Dundee was a good supply e food, sendin butcher meat an everythin. Dundee has always had an affiliation, a history wi the Fife miners. Expectant mothers were gien a liette fir the bairn. We got grub fae Germany, a boat load of it come intae Dysart [harbour]. Cardenden delivered food fae Dysart tae Kinglassie too. They got landed wi a' the tomato soup cause naeb'dy here liked it. They sent soap. Smelly soap. Cases e jars e pickled cellery. Tony Pavers wis a Latvian, a displaced person durin the war. He got the full case e it. Anyway, Ah'm no sure if it wis because Germany wis a communist country fightin capitalism or what. The French miners sent toys at Christmas. They were stored at the [Miners'] Institute. Ah've still got a set e bools in the hoose. Bit as fir support here, Ah wid say Dundee really wis brilliant. The boys fae Mossmoran [local ethylene production plant] - at that time it wis under construction - took us through tae Glesgae tae the big warehoose. Toys fir the kids' Christmas. Solely fir the bairns roond aboot here. They also set up a fund. The dockyard in Rosyth helped oot wi the grub. They had a fund too. Kelty Club. A' the local shops were good. Bowhill pipe band marched. Andy Donaldson wis the pipe leader. There's three world championship pipe majors stay here in this village. 'There's nae way Ah'm gaun up here oot e tune,' he says! We hid the Gala doon in the park. Summer e 84. Like the Bowhill treat. Tossin the welly etcetera. An then when ye were back at work at Seafield they were spying in the tower at a' the pickets. Ah wis sent tae work wi three scabs. They boys got a privilege o'er the tap e us. In an argument the scab wis always right. They boys used tae get up a tow their sel. They got a tow, and up and through the bath afore us. Right efter the strike they were never on the same shift as us. It wid a been great tae keep a record. Bit the minutes e meetins were all pit up the lumn. The hierarchy in Dysart instructed us tae burn a' the meetings. They never ordered me, bit they made it known.

Macintyre's study *Little Moscows* (1980) argues that 'being local' is an important aspect of working-class *dasein* insofar as more or less throughout the twentieth century in small mining villages in Scotland the experience of locality and work were contiguous, resulting in an intense identification with work and locality that was impossible to reproduce in larger urban contexts. It is not simply then that miners belong to Cardenden but Cardenden belongs to them, their localities are 'theirs' in an uncontested fashion in the sense that, with the end of the local mining industry in the late nineteen-sixties and nineteen-seventies and the local bourgeoisie having vacated locality, there is an uncontested appropriation of and identification with locality: locality is *theirs* and belongs to them in the sense that there is no 'them and us' in this identification with locality, so that what might appear as a remarkable level of *class unity* during the miners' strike of 1984-1985 is indistinguishable from a defence of and identification with their locality.

The historic significance or even 'trauma' of the miners' strike of 1984-1985 stems from the fact that it was the last great strike of the industrial era. The defeat of the miners was not just another instance of defeat comparable with other defeats but was unique because it marks in time the end of a way of life and so has come to symbolise the end of an era and the beginning of an uncertain post-industrial present. When the *Mining Archives* opened in June 1991, then, this was the point in time when a way of life was transformed into a heritage. The village's will to remember its history was similarly evidenced when locals gathered in September 2011 for the annual Johnny Thompson tournament to commemorate the 80th anniversary of the death in September 1931 of the young Celtic and Scotland goalkeeper, and soon thereafter on 30 October 2011 when locals gathered to mark the 80th anniversary of the Bowhill Pit disaster where ten miners died after an explosion on 31 October 1931.

The one hundred and seventy-four people who processed through the village to lay wreaths in Bowhill cemetery on this day were demonstrating their will to retain their connection to their past, and while the era of heavy industry has passed the basic 'laws of motion' governing a free-market economy and society continue into the post-industrial era, so that something else which continues across the industrial and post-industrial eras and continues to connect the generations is the enduring structural weakness of working-class agency. During the 1984-1985 strike, then, something informants that I interviewed told me they were increasingly aware of the longer the strike continued was that *in defending their jobs and their way of life, the miners were putting their jobs and that same way of life in jeopardy*. The dependency upon economic relations and the resultant dependency on the persistence of these relations for survival in the free-market economy and society is a truism of their lives that enjoys ample empirical verification, so that a 'first principle' of being working class is that it is a class that is not the master of its fate, is condemned to be dependent upon an ever-changing 'capitalist industrialisation' so that any local working-class population is condemned to be either playing 'catch up' to the new economy or being 'finished off' by the latest phase of capitalism, so that forms of working-class consciousness are likewise condemned to be either 'polished nostalgia' in an older generation or incoherent and unformed consciousness in the next upcoming generation.

When researching the strike of 1984-1985, then, I was struck by the relevance of Gorz's (1997, p. 75) observation that: "Both the strength and the weakness of the post-industrial proletariat lie in the fact that it does not have an overall vision of future society." In terms of their daily *practice* both generations across the industrial and post-industrial eras agree that there is no escape from the need to internalise the 'mirror of production' (Baudrillard 1975), so that the strike for each miner and his family was a defining event because people defined themselves and their behaviour in relation to it, and it was a character test they had to pass in their own eyes and in the eyes of their neighbours. When interviewing former miners and noting their ease and fluency when remembering the strike, when I asked about the shape of the future there was a marked silence as their narratives came to an end and informants lost their surefooted conviction and fluidity. Whereas the past has a definite shape, then, representations of the future have yet to take shape in their minds, and an awareness of a traditional habitus giving way to new conditions explains the paucity of representations of the future, so that while the strike grounds the older individual in history and gives him biographical and personal security (Berger and Luckmann 1987), this very embeddedness makes the future obscure for this generation.

## The 1945 and 1979 Generation(s)

Prior to beginning interviewing I selected a number of streets from each area of the village where I would conduct door-to-door interviews, and in preparation I obtained a copy of the electoral register for Cardenden and copied the details of each household of each selected street onto an A5 size card. A few days prior to the first elections to the new Scots parliament on 6 May 1999, then, I was walking through the village finalizing the streets where I would conduct interviews and found myself in Cluny Park standing in the middle of the road with clipboard and electoral register in hand. As I stood there, a young girl approached on her bike and stopped to have a look at me, perhaps trying to figure out who I was and what I was doing in her street. "Hiya" I said, to acknowledge her presence. I then tried to anticipate the girl wondering what I was doing by telling her: "It's okay. I'm not lost." After a few seconds, she got back on her bike and cycled off and as she did so she turned her head and shouted in my direction: "This is Cardenden. This is Scotland."

Immediately after the elections to the new parliament as I began interviewing locals about their views on politics and a whole range of issues and began transcribing my interviews, I began to organise my data according to two Weberian 'ideal types' and began classifying interviewees into what I call the *1945 generation* and the *1979 generation*. As a generalization, members of the 1945 generation include those born before nineteen-fifty, while those born from nineteen-sixty onwards I classify as belonging to the 1979 generation. While this leaves those born in the nineteen-fifties in something of a classificatory no-man's land, I intend this simple distinction as a shorthand device to indicate whether a particular interviewee tended to identify with the industrial past or the post-industrial present of the village. As fieldwork and interviewing progressed, however, these two categories also came to indicate a range of related opinions so that I began to use this distinction as a heuristic device to frame social change via the lived experience of these two generations and as a way of *generationalising* the major ruptures and continuities in the experiences of locality, society, culture and politics across the industrial and post-industrial divide.

Each generation or 'ideal type,' then, has its own 'signature sociology' as a result of having its own characteristic socialisation or acculturation. Again as a generalization, I characterise the primary socialisation of the 1945 generation as dominated by the era of the 'dictatorship of scarcity' (Beck) and a comparatively stable cultural and social sphere along with a stable, though far from uneventful, experience of locality. Also, among the 45 generation, their being-for-others or *mitsein* is characterised by the experience of 'thick' locality and thick intersubjectivity along with the 'heavy' presence of society and a non-privatised experience of society, morality, belief and conventions. In contrast, the younger '79 generation's primary socialisation is dominated by the advent of affluence and post-industrialisation that occurred during the nineteen-eighties, and the massive production and importation of commodified culture, along with the decline in the ability to remember, far less reproduce, a substantive local public realm in comparison to the '45 generation which is able to look back with nostalgia at 'something lost,' while the 1979 generation(s) is hard-pressed to identify their experience of locality as 'something' at all.

With the closure of Bowhill Colliery in 1965 and the closure of the local coal washer in 1974 and the closure of Seafield pit in nearby Kirkcaldy in 1986, the relationship among the '45 and '79 generations to locality is different. However, this generational gap is not confined to the shift from an economy of heavy industry to a service sector economy and the consumer society as, in addition to the historical and economic differences that separate the two generations, there are just as significant technological and *cultural* differences that separate them as a result of social change since the nineteen-seventies, radical changes in family formation, the revolution in sexuality from the nineteen-seventies and the integration of working-class mothers into the occupational landscape and the normalization of dual-earner families. Finally, the ideal types of the 1945 and 1979 generations usefully maps the sharp differences in the *political socialisation* of each generation and draws attention to watershed events such as the election of Margaret Thatcher in 1979, the miners' strike of 1984-5, the end of the Cold War in 1989 and the 1979-1997 years of 'democratic deficit' which, when taken together, constitute a sea-change in political, social and economic conditions that more or less separate and define the formative experiences of the two generations.

Deploying these two categories, then, allows for the handling of large amounts of otherwise disparate data and brings into view the fundamental positions behind empirical data and particular details, so that much of this ethnography is about arguing the point that the 1979 generation(s) faces a new and a defining social and economic and cultural and political situation and that the 'nothing' which 1945 generation locals describe is an opportunity for a new 'public emergence of working-class reality' and a new practice and conception of a Scottish modernity (Chapters 4 and 5). Finally, if these new conditions give rise to an unprecedented recognition of the continuing reality of class, they simultaneously give rise to an unprecedented disappearance or 'forgetting' of class reality among the '79 generation(s), so that holding onto the truth contained in both positions is necessary for an accurate understanding and representation of the new way in which each generation experiences personal, public and national space.

Fundamental to mapping the many issues involved in this fundamental change-over between the two generations is the advent of affluence and the 'post-materialist' politics and the new possibilities for human being and human sociality that it makes possible among the affluent '79 generation.[12] Where members of

---

[12] 1945 generation housewives say it was only in the 1970s that beggars knocking on a back door in search of something spare to eat disappeared from their experience.

the '45 generation remember: "In 1953 there were three tellys in Cardenden. One in Mrs. Spence's hoose watchin the Stanley Matthews cup final. We aa thought this wis oot e this world;" and another can advise that: "Everybody's no the same noo. Aa tryin tae keep up wi the Joneses. So that's the Tory part e ye" (Roberta Catherine, Orebank Road), such declarations which may be interpreted as 'primitive' attempts at post-materialist or post-scarcity thinking and which advert to the caesura of affluence and the shift from behaviour shackled to material necessity to the collective entrance into the realm of symbolic goods and the new kinds of individuation it brings, are very strange to members of the '79 generation. The 1945 generation, then, is the last generation that will be able to remember the first time they got into a car, saw the change from gas lamps to electric street lighting, remember the first time they watched a television programme or ran barefoot during the summer months in the Back Raw, or recall their parents hiding the newspaper if the front page reported a murder. This older generation remembers society and locality as an occupational community and its female members remember their first job being "in service" as a maid to an upper middle-class household. This generation remembers the experience of sociality before the post-war penetration of everyday life by technology and the rise of the consumer society, and instantiates a resilient Britishness which has survived eighteen years of democratic deficit and Tory minority rule from 1979-1997 and again from 2010-2015, the miners' strike of 1984-1985 as well as deindustrialization thanks to a 'background' British identity that is the product of a primary socialisation where from early childhood this generation was literally schooled into an identification with Britain and its Empire at the expense of all other identities. As the local history group tutor (Anne Mead) recalled in an article in one of the local history group booklets:

Auchterderran was my primary school in the thirties...The school had no wireless. I especially remember that. On the day of the launching of the Queen Mary, a pupil was dispatched to the lodging of Miss Mackay in Woodend

Road, near the school to await the naming of the liner. Her landlady listened to the launching on the wireless, then the pupil was sent back to school with the name written down and sealed in an envelope. The message went round the classrooms and the pupils were able to pass the news on to their families at home, for few people had wirelesses at home either.

Local History Group, vol. 2 (np)

## 1.3 The Lived Experience of 'Being in Cardenden'

The idea that we live in society is taken for granted but the notion of 'society' is an abstraction. Where we actually live is in particular places such as Cardenden, Dunfermline, Kirkcaldy or St Andrews and even this level of particularity such as 'Cardenden' is an abstraction that misses the further nuance that the village is nucleated into the areas of Auchterderran, Bowhill, Cardenden and Dundonald with each area having its own shops and pub and identity. Also, writing about a post-industrial locality over time involves engaging with the relationship between 'place' and economic forces; the doctrines of neoliberalism and the free-market economy and the many consequences for those localities 'suffering' macro-social and economic processes; questions about whether the free economy is better than the planned or command economy in terms of creating village life *ex nihilo* and bringing that life to an end; questions about whether locales can be 'humane' enclaves relatively free from market forces, or should be thrown open to free-market forces to decide whether they thrive or barely survive, and whether locals would be best-advised to leave rather than remain faithful to a sense of belonging whose time has come to an end. Imagining an answer to the question whether a village or locality is economically viable impacts upon an individual's decision to stay or leave his natal village; impacts upon how his remaining local is deemed rational or baffling, a sign of talent or a sign of a lack of ambition, of embracing a new post-industrial modernity or a hiding from the challenges of 'being modern.'

28

While Cardenden is physically present to its inhabitants as they live there and leave it in the morning and return to it after a day's work, a question for the ethnographer who would attempt to grasp locals in their own space and time (Burawoy 2000, pp. 3-4) and how residents think and feel about their village is what is Cardenden's *psychological reality* or *psychological presence* within its inhabitants. If residents by definition physically live in Cardenden, do they also psychologically or imaginatively live there or perhaps elsewhere?

Early on in fieldwork (10 December 1998) when leaving the flat to do some shopping I passed a newspaper board outside Kooner's corner shop (opposite the police station) which had the words *Scotland's Children of the Damned* indicating the day's top story, while next door to the newsagent was a hairdresser's shop not yet open and on its wooden shutters I noticed fresh graffiti: *Mellon Wiz Ere* and *Rikki M. Sucks C\*\*\* for 10p*. While waiting to be served in the newsagents I listened to two women talking about a woman who had been sacked for stealing petty cash in one of the local shops. I headed next to the local Costcutter mini-supermarket[13] which is the main shop in the area, and while waiting to be served I noticed a number of Milk Tokens pinned to the perspex barrier separating customers and staff, and each token had a name written on it and what looked like an ongoing record of the amount of credit remaining. When it was my turn to be served I asked the assistant about the tokens and she advised they were part of a Department of Social Security welfare food scheme for those on state benefits with young children, adding that it wasn't unknown for people to ask if they could use the cash value of the tokens to buy cigarettes instead of milk.

---

[13] Locals still refer to this building as 'the Store' in reference to the Co-Operative Store that was based in the building for many years and which they grew up with since before the Second World war. Sometime in the mid-to-late nineteen-eighties the Co-Op closed but locals kept the building open as "The Community Store." Initially this venture proved successful and was publicised in the local press as an example to be followed, but after a few years this effort ended due to a lack of profit and today it is run and managed by the *Costcutter* chain of stores.

In terms of official statistics, then, Cardenden is an area that suffers relative deprivation. The Scottish Index of Multiple Deprivation (SIMD) database, for example, which divides Scotland into 6,505 areas ranked according to their level of deprivation (which is calculated by measuring seven variables: income, employment, health, education, geographic access, housing and crime). According to SIMD, then, the area with the ranking of number 1 is the most deprived area in Scotland and the area ranking number 6,505 is the least deprived area in Scotland. In the SIMD database Cardenden is divided into seven data zones and they are currently ranked 1047th, 1100th, 1196th, 1341st, 1475th, 2476th and 3585th. When ranked solely according to income, Cardenden's seven data zones are ranked 661st, 1196th, 1269th, 1368th, 1410th, 2216th and 3990th, so that three of Cardenden's data zones are within the bottom 15-20% of this scale of poverty or at least 80% of Scotland is more affluent than these three areas. [14]

While there is an objectively measurable and well documented material poverty, locals also point to the reality of *cultural decline*; a topic that was never far from many elderly residents' conversation when I talked to them. At one local history group meeting (18 May 1999) I noted the following exchange:

**Tam:** Ye're feared ta gane doon Bowhill noo.
**Jock:** Once being auld wis yet guarantee e safety. Noo yer a target.
**Anne:** Would you walk through Lochgelly at night? Folk being put up in the Hotel. Some fae Alloa. Scumbags! Paedophiles! Dae ye ken there's seven paedophiles in Cardenden? An they complain aboot the food. It's all DHSS[15] folk in Piates and in the Central. [16]

---

[14] See http://www.scotland.gov.uk/Topics/Statistics/SIMD. Accessed 10 January 2013.
[15] Department of Health and Social Security, a UK government department from 1968-1988.
[16] The names of local pubs which also offer accommodation.

**Jim:** Johnny Hamilton fae Carden Avenue. He's banned fae the [Corrie] Centre. The Youth club. He's always in trouble. His dad's got a new girl friend, so Ah'm told. So watch that name, ye'll hear it again.

**Ronnie:** That young arsehole Johnny Hamilton's mum, she wis at college, an on the till at Poundstretchers [shop in Kirkcaldy]. Nae faither on the scene of course.

**Bill:** Wee Hughie fae Bowhill, he's away tae Kirkcaldy noo. We were well gled tae get rid e him.

**Ann:** There was a boy wi an ear ring the day asking for a meter to pay his electricity. He'd been cut off. Standin there in the office. They'll no remember comin hame tired. Or struggling tae pay their rent.

**Jim:** Young folk the day'll no walk the length e theirsel.

As an ethnographer of a deindustrialised space such as Cardenden, there is a sense that an integral part of my job is to research what might be termed the flotsam and jetsam of deindustrialization, and to capture this sense of decline which for some has reached dystopian levels, as for example in the comments of Ena Herd (Orebank Road, 14 November 1999):

Imagine getting tae ma age an everythin's worse! Ken, everywhere ye look aboot ye. At ma age, every value, everythin Ah ever thought aboot the way tae go aboot things, every idea Ah ever hud, every value that Ah ever had, every way e daen things, everythin Ah've got in ma heid, jist turn that aboot, totally roonaboot, totally completely reverse everythin Ah've ever believed in an Ah might jist get it right fir 1999.

In the above testimony it is clear that there is a deep sense of locality having lost its way, and mapping the specifically cultural changes that animates and exercises older inhabitants it is clear that underlying their many anecdotes of change for the worse was the insistence that, having moved from a 'society of scarcity' they now found themselves living in conditions that may be described as 'scarcely any society.' Alongside their repeated lament regarding

31

the 'end' of locality and the family was a parallel lament for the 'thinning' of and decline of sociation and interpersonal association now that 'everything' has been liberated from tradition and convention, so that the crisis in reproducing village life or family life is only a fraction of the crisis faced by younger generations. In trying to capture something of the concrete empirical content that is the basis for these firmly-held views concerning a precipitous decline in the quality of social life, my living in 51 Cardenden Road meant I was able to observe the daily comings and goings within the shopping area in this part of the village, and when I later moved to the main street of the village (Station Road) I was again able to witness a range of behaviours to substantiate locals' concerns.

For example, then, when putting my daughter Candela to bed one summer evening when living in Station Road and well before it was dark outside, I heard the screech of car tyres breaking and looked out to the street and saw two young men in a car that was reversing in order to confront two older men coming out of the *Caspian* take-away and who, judging by their dress and physical appearance, were from the Indian sub-continent. With his car stopped in the middle of the road and the engine still running, the driver got out and walked towards the two men. Although I could not hear what was said, I could clearly see the young man said something to the two 'foreigners.' Faced with what I assume was a calculated insult or provocation, the two older men exchanged words between themselves rather than reply directly to the young 'native.' At this, the youth stood his ground and seemed to repeat his verbal challenge or insult and, again, stood waiting for an answer. As this confrontation was unfolding, I looked and saw the other youth in the passenger seat of the car laughing and making what seemed like an exaggerated show of enjoying his companion's brinkmanship and the predicament of the two 'foreigners.' By this stage, cars were being held up in the street while this confrontation was unfolding and pedestrians in the street were now alerted to what was going on so that this scene was now commanding general attention. After a few more seconds of waiting, the youth returned to his car and drove off with tyres screeching, while the two older men exchanged a few words to each other before walking the few yards to their parked car and driving off.

At the time of this incident Cardenden did not have a non-white resident population to speak of as it was comprised solely of three or four Pakistani families who owned or worked in local shops or a retired professional and his family who had worked in the village for years. Despite this nominal presence, however, shop shutters in the main shopping area of Bowhill during fieldwork were daubed with graffiti such as *NF* [National Front] and *Blacks Out*, while the local health centre had *NF, BLACKS OUT* and *PAKI B******S* spray-painted on the metal security shutters and this was visible for all to see when the shutters were drawn each night. However, to judge by its faded appearance it seems likely that this graffiti was done in the wake of the first arrival of Asian shopkeepers to the village in the nineteen-eighties so that, while it is evidence of 'racial' prejudice, I would not confine its meaning as evidence simply of 'racism' as the real source of such prejudice is a more general 'personality structure' which I would characterize by a general intolerance or an indiscriminate 'disposition to discriminate' that over its lifetime will have many targets in addition to non-white ethnic minorities. For example, then, objectionable graffiti such as the word 'wankers' scored into the front doors of the local and exclusively white Church of Scotland building I would judge as sourced in a youthful disposition of *ressentiment* characteristic of a minority of local youth, so that any building whatsoever or any minority social group whatsoever are likely to be targeted as such a disposition can always find a symbolic 'other' to target as somehow inferior in a hierarchy of status, such as a member of the underclass, a long-termed unemployed individual or any other low-status identity.

As a result of the legacy of the British Empire among the post-Protestant working class, the disaffected Scottish proletarian youth has available to himself a colonial or imperial 'British' relation to the rest of humanity. What is clear is that consubstantial with visible signs such as dress, appearance and language and related differences of religion and culture, these signifiers of 'difference' provoke acts of discrimination and forms of violence, whether purely imaginary or behavioural, from a fraction of young white working-class boys and men who, armed to the teeth with such dispositions as the inheritors of a toxic cultural legacy, are more or less fated to come across occasions to be provoked – such as the eve of the 80th anniversary of the death of Scotland and Celtic footballer Johnny Thomson which provoked supporters of an anti-Catholic football club in Glasgow to pour blue paint over Thompson's grave in the local cemetery in an effort to spoil the wreath-laying ceremony at Thomson's grave which forms part of the annual football tournament held in Cardenden in his memory.

### Language as cipher for fully-contextualised Dasein

Language and labour are outer expressions in which the individual no longer retains possession of himself *per se*, but lets the inner get right outside him.

Hegel 1967, p. 340.

More juvenile forms of this toxic element within Scottish working-class culture include a range of resentments that are expressed in a variety of antisocial expressions such as a bus shelter advertisement for an American brand of rice being made to read '*Uncle Ben is a Child Molester*,' while the graffiti on the lamp-post opposite this advert on the main street reading:

> Nessie is a f***ed up hore
> who has AIDS and
> recks of pish and fish
> and crabs and HIV plus scabies.

When interviewing a resident of Orebank Road quoted earlier she recalled an incident that had taken place while she had been walking in the local park and had been confronted and verbally abused by two young boys.

> Ah wondered where the hatred fae they two laddies...
> imagine bein born intae a world when only bein fourteen an

34

havin a' that hatred inside ye. And nae respect fir a woman oan her ain. Ian ma husband he said tae me 'You mind you keep yer mooth shut! You just let them dae whatever they're gonnae dae. You just let them dae it because you could end up, they could batter ye,' ye ken. Well the young ones dinnae ken ony different. Ah mean that fourteen year auld an sixteen year auld on that motorbike they didnae ken how tae be any ither wiy, right? And we were a million miles apart an Ah wis standin there an there is basic hatred starin inches fae yer face and ye've come tae that in Cardenden park.

The use of language by local boys who may be described as 'armed to the teeth' with *ressentiment* ('re-feeling' and re-living something over and over again) indicates that nothing much has changed since Muir (1935, pp. 118-119) wrote of working-class youth and commented upon: "The terror and corrupt knowledge of these children can be heard in their voices... This terror breaks out in early youth, that is as soon as these boys are strong enough to fight for themselves, in revengeful violence and cruelty." This use of language is valuable data insofar as how people speak and use language is a cipher for their social and cultural and political condition, so that language and the social practice of speaking is socially determined insofar as it passes through the gauntlet of a particular social and cultural context, so that the textual violence referred to above is isomorphic with the linguistic violence of teenage boys and girls in public. When a young teenage boy and his girlfriend, for example, are greeted by a teenage boy beside the busy children's play area in the public park shouting: "Are ye shagging her yet? Eh? Have ye hid a blow job yet?," such use of language by young people involves the "open publication of their degradation" (Muir 1935, p. 122) *and a coming to terms with their objective social position.* Following the quote from Hegel, this use of language reveals a profound intergenerational failure of autonomy insofar as it is firstly through the medium of language that young people take their first steps as individuals, so that data gathered on language-use among young working-class individuals-in-groups is more or less fated to reveal that:

"Individual consciousness is not the architect of the ideological superstructure, but only a tenant lodging in the social edifice of ideological signs" (Volosinov 1986, p. 13).

This heavy social determination of language and thought has been seen and described before by the local writer Joe Corrie in *Black Earth* (1939) where he asked of his fellow Cardenden residents: "Was there ever such a set of people who actually knew so little? They lived in a mean little narrow world of their own, each with the same views, the same thoughts" (1939 p. 70). Likewise, from the vantage point of the 'society of affluence,' historian T. C. Smout describes novelists such as Corrie depicting the depression years of the nineteen-thirties as confronted by lives as "miserable as the 'insect life' lived by Sir James Barrie's characters" (Smout, cited in Muir 1985, p. xxiv), so that when Corrie (1939, p. 239) wrote: "Mrs. Gow never minced her words and if there was a vulgar alternative for a decent word she used it, it gave her more satisfaction," he is describing how discourse is *inter alia* a cipher for a structured and socialised libidinal 'economy of expression' characterised by *ressentiment* that is constantly satisfying itself via language because language is a source of satisfaction insofar as it expresses this condition of resentment.

Because pre-eighteen year olds are not allowed into pubs, a feature of local street life in the village at weekends was pre-teens and teenagers congregating in the local park and its environs such as bus stops and fast-food outlets, which meant the issue of unsupervised teenagers gathering and binge drinking was a well-worn theme among locals and letters to local newspapers. I recall on one occasion when driving along Station Road at five o'clock on a summer evening stopping with a friend to help a young girl who was laying face-down on the pavement and unconscious as a result of having drunk too much. After trying to persuade other young people in the street to come forward and tell us who she was or where she lived, it seems she had been abandoned where she had collapsed because anyone drawn into answering questions from the police or having to accompany her home or to hospital was inviting problems for themself. As a result of the regular occurrence of young people from Cardenden and further afield gathering in large numbers on Friday and Saturday evenings, the risk of fighting between individuals or rival groups of young people from different places outwith the village meant the presence of police surveillance units video-recording these crowds was not unfamiliar, and public space after dark was predictably likened by older residents to 'running a gauntlet' and an unsurprising 'moral panic' about young people was heard.

However, adults were not innocent of violence of course and the passage to adulthood did not necessarily mean more laudable behaviour. Hence, as it was my habit to spend many nights reading and writing until late in my attic study, I came to expect some incident or other to occur within earshot after closing time at weekends. On one particular occasion at around one in the morning, a peaceful night was interrupted by the noise of the drawn metal shutter and neon sign of the Caspian takeaway on Station Road having a brick thrown at it, while on another occasion at four in the morning I watched unseen from my attic study window as two locals methodically set about smashing the glass panels of the bus shelter opposite. As I watched I could see that, being drunk, each kick aimed at the panels required some concentration, and any particular effort that failed to produce the required effect meant each vandal took the time to steady himself in preparation for the next attempt. Once the job was done to their satisfaction, they did not flee the scene of the crime but resumed walking home with no change in gait. Such were the actions of two grown men.

On another occasion on a warm day in June 2001 when again in my study and with the window open, I heard from the street below a young girl's voice shouting: "Are you a paedophile?" I looked out onto the street to see five girls and two boys making their way to a local primary school sports day in the nearby park. I looked in the direction faced by the school children and saw the question had been directed at a young man waiting at the (repaired) bus stop. The man looked like he was in his late-twenties or early-thirties, and was being approached by the pupils who proceeded to congregate around the bus shelter and poke fun at him. As I watched it became apparent very quickly that the stranger was uncomfortable with this sudden 'publicity,' despite not reacting to the children and their remarks and questions that were being aimed at him. As I watched this scene unfold, it was as if the pupils were testing for any weakness and I watched as the man's head turned to look up the street every few seconds, signaling (I imagined) his mounting disquiet and desire for the bus to arrive. With their intended 'victim' refusing to react, the pupils next proceeded to poke fun at his clothes. As I thought about the initial shouted query that alerted me to this scene I remembered a conversation with a local history group member (Annie) who had informed the group at one of our meetings that the hotel fifty yards from the bus stop outside my window was "putting up paedophiles" as part of an arrangement with Fife Council social work department. I wondered whether this local rumour was the reason behind the girl's question, whether these primary school children might even unconsciously be attempting to protect the borders of their village from unwanted outsiders. After a few minutes more teasing an older man arrived to wait for the same bus to Kirkcaldy, and proceeded to ignore what was happening around him. The next question from the group addressed to the man that I could clearly make out was: "Are you on drugs?" After another minute or two, the young man suddenly walked off up the street away from his tormentors, at which the group of Denend Primary School pupils resumed walking to the park, laughing loudly and leaning into each other and exclaiming loudly among themselves, as if they had scored the victory they had wanted.

It is my presumption that such behaviours are viewed as unprecedented and the empirical cause of the 'moral panic' of an older generation, and such practices are held to have been 'impossible' and unheard of previously. However, when older informants themselves reminisce about when they themselves were young and describe themselves as "mad for the dancing," the fact is that while Cardenden had venues that meant dancing until two or three in the morning was possible every Thursday, Friday, Saturday and Sunday night, informants also admit when asked why the popularity of dancing is a thing of the past that "there was too much fighting and drinking" – even in the allegedly conformist nineteen-fifties and sixties. If the same working-class communities across the industrial and post-industrial divide then have always faced the issue of young people and violent disorder, there is undoubtedly the sense of a behavioural and generational divide, and in this regard I quote from an article which appeared in the Fife Free Press newspaper (12 October 2001) entitled *Villagers Seek Action to Halt Hooligans*:

> Cardenden residents say that they are living in fear after an upsurge in violence and vandalism on their streets. The village's active tenants and residents' association says that over the last six months groups of teenagers and young adults have been making lives a misery for others, particularly the elderly. And they claim it is only a matter of time before someone is killed in a drunken brawl.

This article included an interview with an unnamed local resident who was quoted as saying: "I have lived in Cardenden all my sixty-odd years and, in that time, things have never been so bad." Such views I found were common. Three weeks into fieldwork a retired couple who have lived all their married lives in Cardenden in Whitehall Drive told me that Cardenden is "a quiet wee place," but after a subsequent weekend where their windows were the target of a local boy high on drugs who had smashed windows while making his way home, they peremptorily informed me the next time we spoke: "This f****n place is turnin to shit." Something else that is undoubtedly new is that since most locals have bought their former Council houses they are alert as never before to behaviours which threaten their property and have taken to 'policing' the behaviour of others by forming Neighbourhood Watch schemes and, given their long intimate knowledge of their areas, could not be better informed as to the individuals and families in their area they openly say they would like to get rid of. In addition to the formation of Neighbourhood Watch schemes there were other associations such as the New Carden Residents' Association, which was another forum where locals came together and which attested to the centrality of housing conditions in locals' lives.

The first public meeting I attended during fieldwork was the Annual General Meeting (AGM) of the New Carden Residents' Association on 28th April 1999 in the Corrie Centre.[17] Unlike ordinary meetings held throughout the year, the AGM was publicised throughout the village and a sizeable number of residents had gathered to voice their opinions regarding various housing-related matters. Typically of AGMs, however, the business of the meeting was the election of members to executive positions within the Association, with the result that what actually happened at the meeting was residents came in numbers eager to raise their practical concerns about their specific housing situation while the office-bearers or 'managers' of the meeting insisted such concerns were not part of the agenda of the meeting. This conflict of interests and agendas was compounded by the physical separation of the tenants and office-bearers with the latter seated at a top table facing the tenants, and compounded by a procedural dualism so that the meeting proved largely ineffective from the outset and throughout. With the exception of the chairman (Wullie Duncan) who was a local resident, those seated at the table facing the tenants were neither known nor introduced to the gathered tenants and none volunteered to introduce or identify themselves, and this procedural omission meant that as the meeting progressed, the tenants' frustration led to the standing of the office-bearers (chairman apart) deteriorating and fuelled the assumption that the "three suits gittin payed tae be here" – as one tenant[18] beside me described the office-bearers – were not from the village but from the Council and were obliged to be present to be harangued by women complaining about bad joinery work.

Because what the tenants had come for was essentially a 'housing surgery,' two meetings were trying to happen at the same time: there was the official meeting that followed procedures,

---

[17] The Association was formed in 1986 with Mrs Ellen Guild as the first chairman.

[18] This tenant also informed me that her mother was a previous tenant at 51 Cardenden Road where I lived, and made a point of telling me she had been in my house far more than I'd been in my house.

raised points via a chairman and discussed in a set order the items on a pre-circulated agenda, and then there was an unofficial meeting, the substance of which was obviously unhappy residents armed with particular grievances and questions but, receiving no answers, resulting in a disgruntled and unhappy atmosphere for everyone present.

Among the residents there was no one agenda as some were present solely to raise particular 'private' points and had no interest in anything else but were simply waiting for the opportunity, for example, to talk about antisocial neighbours, while others wanted to concentrate discussion on housing repairs policy. As the meeting broke up there was a palpable frustration and over tea and biscuits it was only a matter of time before a tenant, who happened to be employed by Fife Council to carry out repairs to the local Council housing stock, observed that those in charge at an executive level neither lived in Council houses or Housing Association houses or lived in areas of council housing and were in no position to identify with Council tenants and their concerns. This opportunity for 'civic participation' in the shape of engaging with the Residents' Association, then, only served to make for disappointment at the level of response from Council officials in attendance; where a perception of lack of response meant the chairman admitted: "A lot of the residents have lost faith in us," and the attempt at public engagement only reinforced a sense of frustrated passivity that hardly encouraged future participation.

The process that begins with interested participation which then becomes an experience of powerlessness and ends up becoming a resigned 'privatism' or even convinced 'absenteeism' was also something I experienced at the first Community Council meeting I attended (20 May 1999) during fieldwork. At this meeting an item on the agenda was how the village would mark the beginning of the new Christian millennium, and when this question was put to members for discussion I had naively hoped this would open a window onto the 'realm of meaning,' but in the event no discussion that touched upon the millennium or local identity took place, nor any exchanges regarding a post-industrial vision of Cardenden or any discussion of an artistic commission to mark the new millennium or to celebrate the many centuries of Christianity in the local area. Instead, what the Community Council settled upon as the means to mark the new millennium was half a dozen hanging baskets on lamposts within the village – with the much-discussed proviso they be placed high enough to be out of reach of the local vandals. And, as if to confirm members' focus upon the mundane, the next item on the agenda was concerns over bus shelters still being covered in graffiti, at which the chairman explained that this work had recently been subcontracted to a private company and in this change-over, problems regarding insurance had arisen which was why there had been a prolonged delay. Finally, the last item on the agenda was a status report on a previous suggestion about erecting a public notice board in the village, with the chairman advising members: "Apparently it costs too much," and suggesting instead procuring "space in a shop window somewhere."[19]

At another Community Council meeting (April 2001) it was announced that the Number 1 Goth, the pub on Station Road, was to be mothballed for the foreseeable future in light of the new management team previously announced that would reopen the premises as a going concern had failed to materialise. In light of this unexpected development, ideas were solicited from those present at the meeting about how to save the Goth from closure.[20] As I was nearly three years into fieldwork by the time I attended this particular meeting, this felt like a familiar request to 'save locality' which was met with an equally familiar silence from residents as they tried to think of 'something from nothing.' From this particular silence came the suggestion by the local Labour Party councilor

---

[19] While both the local Tesco Express and local branch of the Co-Operative (the latter being a David Sands shop until 2012) have spaces that act as makeshift notice boards, in April 2013 a dedicated Community Notice Board was finally erected in the village at the junction between Station Road and Orebank Road.

[20] Two days after this meeting the windows on the Goth were boarded up. Until 2008 only the upstairs function room was used once a week by the local pipe band to practice and an upstairs room used for free beginners courses in computing.

(Mrs Doig) that the Goth could be used as a community resource "for single mothers," while another idea was to create a *Rebus Tour* where visitors to the village could retrace the "old haunts" of the fictional Rebus character from the novels of local author Ian Rankin. As I listened to members discuss this proposal I could not help but think how ironic to suggest the production of 'locality' and 'something' based upon a local émigré's literary career which has been founded upon the voluminous commodification of locality as 'absence' and 'nothing.' Whatever the merits of such proposals, each was met with no particular interest or enthusiasm by the dozen or so residents in attendance and, as if to add to the sense of impotence, the time available to discuss this item was brief as there were other items on the agenda to be discussed, such as the new police constable MacFarlane introducing himself and advising the Council "from now on there will be two police officers patrolling on foot throughout the village."

Not for the first time I left a public meeting feeling frustrated as a result of an encounter with powerlessness. I found such meetings humiliating 'conscientisations' to the fact that there has occurred a process of divesting localities of executive decision-making power thanks to the centralisation of power away from localities. In this regard Harvie's (1998, p. 141) observation that, "The abolition of parish councils in 1929 heralded forty years of indifference to local democracy" has meant the centralisation of power has effectively 'privatised' power and taken away the *raison d' être* of local democracy and the responsibilities and rewards of participation in locality. The 'depoliticisation' of locality then is the more or less inevitable result of political choices and impacts upon the different experiences of the different generations where 'society' as much as 'locality' has become privatised (Bauman 2001) thanks to power being relocated outwith the village, so that we might say that 'society' has replaced 'locality' and 'community' over the course of the twentieth century. If understandably the range of concerns ordinarily addressed by the Community Council was in keeping with the range of powers it possessed, the source of frustration was that whenever any issue was discussed in a substantive and unrestricted manner, all sorts of macro-social realities were implicated and discussants were more or less fated to feel our verbal exchanges had little 'exchange value' insofar as we came up against the realization that the power to meaningfully discuss change or recognise local realities lay outside Cardenden in the hands of others.

The experienced members of the Community Council had learned a realism that meant their expectations were aligned with their powers and so they addressed themselves to the 'trivia' they could influence and *without any obvious desire to challenge or reverse this lack of power over local affairs*. In contrast, those locals such as myself who had yet to learn this realism, naively imagined the Community Council to be the place to take their local concerns. Hence, at the April 2001 meeting a local woman attended her first Community Council meeting to share her concerns over the number of mobile phone masts being sited within the village, and to ask what the response of the Community Council should be. This young mother came to the meeting with a large brown envelope full of material on the possible dangers to health posed by mobile phone masts and was quickly given the opportunity to speak and was listened to. However, the only agreed action was to write a letter to a local newspaper signed on behalf of the Community Council as the Labour councillor present at the meeting pointed out that Fife Council had no authority in the matter of mobile phone masts, and from the councillor's comments it was clear that nothing would be done as a result of a resident bringing her concerns to the Community Council. My presumption is that this concerned mother went away from the meeting disillusioned about the merit of participating in local affairs and I would surmise that, generally speaking, the deliberations of the Community Council upon the local public realm mean little to locals who stay at home and are of the view that nothing is lost by non-participation or being unaware of the Council's deliberations. Such reflections on involvement in local affairs were consubstantial with data collected from other sites that afforded an opportunity to witness the same frustrating and fruitless clash of realities and powerlessness that seemed to define the experience of participation in the local public realm.

Insofar as locals are more or less powerless to respond to the macro issue of deindustrialization as a locality, the onset of the post-industrial era appears synonymous with the demise of the village. As a direct result of deindustrialization there began the steady decline in population and decline in frequenting local pubs and the end of miners having a drink after a shift before making their way home as the Number 1 Goth public house was a short walk from the colliery.[21] The end of coal mining has also resulted in a decrease in the significance of public houses as sites for the reproduction of locality and sociality as they increasingly become the preserve of a younger set of locals with an older generation only frequenting pubs or the local War Memorial Club at weekends or special occasions. The nine licensed premises within the village reflect the industrial era of the village and a cultural and social era before the advent of home leisure systems and satellite television and today's music technologies and generalised affluence which is allied to a new 'privatism' and withdrawal from locality.

In addition to the end of coalmining and depopulation, in February 1987 the local Rex Hall bingo venue, formerly one of three local cinemas, was closed and subsequently demolished with the space created made into a car park, and in July of the same year the village's Auchterderran Junior Secondary school closed. In 1997 the local Baptist church closed and on 11 June 2000 St. Fothad's Church of Scotland church (built in 1910) closed with both churches being demolished in November 2001.[22] In February 2001 the petrol station in Station Road closed and in February 2010 the last remaining petrol station closed. In addition, several long-standing businesses that had their beginnings in the industrial

---

[21] The walk home from the colliery would also take the miners past the swimming pool which they had directly financed from their wages and past *The Miners' Welfare Institute* building which in 1992 was post-industrialised and renamed The Bowhill Institute, although its original name remains etched in stone above the main entrance.

[22] The stain glass windows designed by local artist Alexander Gilfillan were rescued from St Fothad's church and placed in Auchterderran church.

past of the village, as well as more ephemeral business ventures such as local hairdressers, video hire shops, fish and chip shops, hardware stores etcetera have closed, so that local wisdom has it that when not being converted into private housing, business premises are replaced by other business ventures that last a matter of months before closing and resuming the process all over again, with the result that village commercial life is increasingly simplified to comprise of either general grocery-type shops that do most of their trade by day, or fast-food outlets that do most of their trade in the evening and night.

With the same number of pubs trying to attract fewer customers there has emerged the novelty of having to advertise events to attract customers such as the *St. Andrew's Night Extravaganza* organised by the Number 1 Goth at which the folk band Kinrik[23] provided the evening's entertainment. This evening was of particular interest because it consisted of a steady flow of songs referring to events of Scottish history, such as the Jacobite rebellion of 1745 with references to the "exiled king" and "the English butcher Cumberland" that hold a special place within the nationalist imagination, along with commentary from band members and shouted agreement from the audience. Indeed, throughout three years of doctoral fieldwork (and prior to the setting up of the Yes Cardenden group in 2012 in preparation for the independence referendum on 18 September 2014)[24] this occasion was one of the very few where an explicitly nationalist ideology was present and where the stage was literally set for the production and

---

[23] The Scots word for 'kingdom' and a reference to the tradition of designating Fife as a separate kingdom deriving from Fife having been one of the seven ancient Pictland kingdoms.

[24] At the 2012 annual summer fayre on 26 August, the nationalist Yes campaign for the 2014 referendum had a stall at which the local SNP councillor (Ian Chisholm) and campaign members from Cardenden were asking locals to pledge their support for independence and sign up as volunteers for the pro-independence campaign. To date, the local Yes Cardenden group have organised three public meetings. Firstly at the Corrie Centre where the launch of the Cardenden Yes Campaign took place on Friday 14 July 2013, and then on 30 April 2014 and 2 June 2014.

consumption of nationalist rhetoric. Having said this, however, even explicitly 'pro-Scottish' or 'anti-English' sentiments which one might presume indicate a *nationalist* viewpoint, are in fact compatible with political loyalism to the United Kingdom so that the 'nationalism' being performed on this particular night may well have been a cultural and non-political nationalism.

On the Sunday before the St. Andrew's Night I had sat drinking in the Goth after interviewing residents of Orebank Road and I began chatting with the bar manager (Geraldine Wallace) who told me she had arranged for Kinrik to play the following Friday, and that there was a more or less ongoing need to constitute a calendar of events to attract customers. Abstract ideas such as 'post-industrialisation' and 'the reproduction of locality,' then, concretely mean a bar manager having to 'think of something' to offset realities released by recent economic changes in order to maintain her job and her presence in post-industrial Cardenden.[25] If there has been a shift to a service-sector economy at a macro-level, there is a local struggle to sustain a local clientele and service-sector economy that results in the novelty of having to 'produce leisure' and import entertainment with the prospect of failure never far away.

As of February 2001 a notice of temporary closure was placed in the windows of the Goth advising the pub would reopen on February 26th under new management. In the event, however, the pub remained closed long after February until it was finally reopened, but only as a result of the management of the nearby *Central Bar* deciding to transfer to the premises of the Number 1 Goth. The closing of the Number 1 Goth was evidence for many locals of the failure of the local community to maintain itself as a viable 'going concern' and was seen as the latest failure in the attempt at reproducing locality in the post-industrial era and was significant as the Goth had been taken into "community ownership" only a few months before and had undergone a major refurbishment thanks to a substantial grant from Fife Council and

---

[25] Geraldine subsequently left Cardenden to live and work some 200 miles away in Oban (Argyll), after which she returned to the village.

the European Union. Being situated in a former mining area, the project had qualified for special funding and the rebranding of the Goth from traditional working-class pub to upmarket bistro had been the subject of positive media comment at the time[26] and, much like the Mining Archives, had been something of a show-case effort at investing in locality and, as evidenced by the many mounted photographs depicting scenes and local landmarks within the village from the early twentieth century, illustrated the desire to simultaneously adapt to the post-industrial era and remember the village's industrial past.

There is then an undeniable empirical reality that is inevitably seen as decline, and while it is also inevitable that the 'loosening' of practices of locality and sociality are much lamented, I will develop the argument in later chapters that what we might describe as the secession from industrial forms of collectivism has also meant a welcome freedom from the 'tyranny' of locality as occupational community, and that the advent of the post-industrial era has also been good insofar as it has more or less rendered obsolete a previous cultural and political status quo and forced the 1979 generation to free itself from a self-understanding and view of their locality that was forged in the industrial era and in the image of tartanry, Robert Burns and the Masons and within the all-British NUM and all-British structures which *tied the imagining of locality to Britain* and fuelled the reality and the 'imagining' of Britain. If the ethnographer must sympathise with informants he must also break with informants' self-representations where need be, and I have often had to criticise myself for falling into the 'mirror of production' (Baudrillard 1975) which imagines

---

[26] The publicity surrounding the commercial failure of The Goth drew criticism from Fife councilors representing middle-class localities such as Dalgety Bay who wrote letters to the local press complaining about Fife Council wasting money on 'dead-end' projects and which applied the neoliberal critique of ailing, non-profitable state-subsidised industries to ailing and non-productive localities such as Cardenden, as dependent upon state-funding to maintain their artificial state-subsidied existence i.e. locales which cannot survive on their own two feet in the free market, far less contribute to the common good.

the local industrial era of 1895-1965 as the gold standard by which to judge the health of sociality and locality and village life. I often characterised to myself this shift from (working class) 'collectivism' to (bourgeois) 'privatism' as the movement from the 'society of scarcity' to 'scarcely any society,' but events such as the prolonged snow and icy conditions in the winters of 2009 and 2010 revealed the superficiality of such privatism, and practices of community such as the local shops having lists of names and telephone numbers of locals to be called when bread was delivered, and the thick level of casual conversation in the crowded shop aisles made it abundantly clear that below the onset of a degree of 'privatism' there remains a traditional collectivism which easily resurfaces at such times.

## 1.4 The Fun Day (2000)

Every year in the village there occurs set-piece occasions such as the annual summer village fayre or the winter bonfire and fireworks display where residents come together to participate in these established events in the local calendar. In the summer of 2000 the village's Bonfire & Fireworks Display Committee organised a 'Fun Day' on 5 August, and this particular day began for me by being awakened at nine o'clock in the morning by the sound system in the local park that had been hired for the day blaring out the Vengaboys' pop song *We're Going To Ibiza* some hundred yards or so from my flat at 113 Station Road. By the time I had eaten breakfast and was making the short walk to the park, I was savouring the prospect of the day ahead as I was relishing the prospect of the day providing me with something for my research; a new idea, a good quote perhaps, or a new informant. As I approached the stalls that encircled an area that had been fenced off for the day I was introduced to local mining historian Dan Imrie. I noted the badge Dan wore on his lapel: *Fife Miners' Community Culture Group*. For a number of years since doing research on the miners' strike of 1984-85 I had meant to interview Dan and as I began to tell him about my research he peremptorily asked: "How come you haven't talked to me?" Dan's forthright

49

query almost made me confident enough to tell Dan the truth of the matter was that, as I was researching the Cardenden of today and there hadn't been a miner in Cardenden for twenty years, I saw no point researching the past. As Dan was deeply involved in the coalmining era of the village I was keen to get his views on how Cardenden might deal with the transition to the post-industrial era, and for a long time I had wanted to interview him about how he saw the present-day. However, Dan's firm conviction was clear: to study Cardenden was to study miners, and this necessitated contacting the recognised local historian of coalmining i.e. himself.

Despite not coming anywhere close to steering him towards my research interests, Dan was in good form and we began chatting and were soon joined by more men who were mostly former miners. Upon being introduced to each other, the topic of conversation turned to nicknames, which led to comments such as "all the local characters are gone" and which were met with universal agreement. The next topic of conversation turned to how funerals in the village used to be occasions that were "watched," and this led to Dan recalling how he had 'lost' three brothers. Halfway through Dan's recounting how his second brother was lost i.e. had died, I became anxious not to get caught up in the company of entertaining but didactic old miners, and I excused myself from the company and walked over to the fenced arena where Cardenden majorette group *The Suzettes* were being introduced to the crowd by the master of ceremonies (Wullie Duncan).

After the girls marched in formation into the arena with their shiny blue uniforms and took their positions, they waited until the music for their routine began and started their opening dance. After this first routine, one of the girls danced solo to the song *What a Feeling* made popular by the nineteen-eighties American television drama *Fame.* When the routine ended I resumed walking around the stalls along with everyone else who wasn't watching the dancing. Walking between stalls men greeted each other by the query, "Were ye oot last night, then?" and fell into brief conversations. After looking at a stall which had mounted displays of black and white photographs of Cardenden from the first half of the twentieth century, I noted a group of young boys arriving on their bikes and from their comportment it was clear they were not rushing to join the Fun Day as they surveyed the scene without dismounting, as if drawn to the park by the music and crowd but unsure whether the occasion was worth their while. I was then approached by someone fundraising, asking if I wanted to buy a shot on a scratch card. I handed over two pounds and put my name beside the football teams Hibernian and Dundee, and shortly afterward the fund-raiser returned with the news that Hibernian had won me ten pounds. As I milled around the stalls I overheard a woman complaining that there was no ice cream van or 'proper food' available, presumably unaware that this was not due to bad planning but, as the point of the day was to raise funds for the annual fireworks display, the catering was being done by volunteers to ensure all proceeds were kept local. Unfortunately, this meant the choice of food available was not up to expectations. Next, another woman whose granddaughter had just won the Bonnie Bairn competition complained there was no photographer from a local paper to take a photograph, and this was followed by further complaints that there was no bouncy castle for the children and, to top things off, the face painting stall had run out of paint to the disappointment of the parents and children queuing.

As I continued my circuit of the stalls I spotted a cousin's wife and began to make my way towards her to say hello. As I picked my way through the crowd, however, I began to suspect something was amiss, and started to doubt whether the woman was in fact Tess. As I carried on towards her I realised my doubts were because I couldn't see any of her family nearby, and this was the first time I had ever seen her without her family and this had made me doubt my own eyes to the extent that I made a point of shadowing Tess for a few more seconds just to satisfy myself it was indeed her before walking up and saying hello. As soon as I did this, however, I realised that Tess was with a woman whom I had never seen before, and realizing this I said hello and introduced myself to the woman, but she did not reciprocate and, significantly, was not introduced to me by Tess. I proceeded to chat with Tess as normal and after exchanging pleasantries we said cheerio.

I was not alone in wondering about the stranger accompanying Tess, and within a minute or two I learned from two female informants that Tess worked for Home Start which was an organisation that involved volunteers befriending (normally) women, and that in Tess's case this meant she was helping a mother by giving her a few hours free from looking after her young children. While my female informants mused between themselves whether Home Start volunteers were paid or not and speculated upon the identity of the woman and the circumstances that led to her needing befriending, I returned to the fenced-off arena once more where *The Suzettes* had finished their programme and the MC was announcing that coming up next was a young local band called *Cheap Day Return*. As the band made their sound check in the arena I wondered whether their name was a clever way of signaling they had formed themselves into a band just for the Fun Day and had come up with a suitably disposable name, signaling the band was 'valid' for one day only, or whether they were expressing something about 'core-periphery' relations that had to be negotiated by a young and upcoming band from a small village seeking recognition from outside the village. When finally ready they began playing, but halfway through their first song a problem with the sound system developed. With the sound cutting in and out every few seconds the MC stepped in and announced the band would have to stop due to the faulty PA system. As the band began to dismantle their equipment, the MC took the opportunity to announce to the disappointed audience, despite everyone about-turning en masse and making their way back to the stalls, that the band was available for bookings and functions. Shortly afterwards I was approached by one of the day's organisers to ask if I was interested in taking part in a tug-of-war competition. Reluctantly, I agreed as I had wanted to keep observing but didn't want to appear lacking in community spirit. As soon as I agreed, however, I was handed a pen and piece of paper and asked to get a team together.

Having completed a circuit of the stalls there was little else to see or do apart from revisit the stalls and so my wife Eva invited my parents and some neighbours home for coffee. As we left the park the MC called for a second team for the tug-of-war as only one team had been mustered so far. At this point the rain began and shortly afterwards I reluctantly left for home. As I left the park I noted Dan and the group of stertorous old miners still going strong on the same spot I had left them earlier. Back home, from an upstairs bedroom window I looked out from where a few hours earlier I had looked out after being woken by the sound system and all that remained of the *Fun Day* were a few seagulls circling overhead looking for scraps of food. At three-thirty in the afternoon the first sunshine of the day arrived and lasted for fifteen minutes until the next blanket of cloud arrived.

Returning downstairs, the first evaluation of the day came from Eva while we waited for the coffee. "That was rubbish! So boring!" Her comment seemed to sum up everyone's thoughts as it was met with no resistance, and while I understood such a comment was only a matter of time, the day had held my interest throughout because, as I had made my way to the park a few hours earlier, it struck me that I was about to capture not only a quote which, thanks to an interpretive effort on my part, could be construed as evidence of a decline in locality, but I was about to have laid before me *an entire language of decline*, and from that moment I felt that after more than two years into fieldwork I had at long last brought my consciousness into alignment with the field and its data, and that instead of fighting against the data, the real meaning of this day and the whole of my fieldwork had finally come into focus. I was looking forward to the Fun Day as a welcome opportunity to spectate "the absence of culture" and, if only for a day, be spared having to painstakingly construct my object of analysis and enjoy a brief escape into empiricism and escape the burden of thinking 'something from nothing,' as finally the 'nothing' was about to be empirically 'given' to me on a plate. The day, then, was full of meaning and interest precisely because I was not straining for traces or signs of 'something' because my perception or expectation of the day was free from the mirror of the industrial period: because I was expecting to see 'nothing' I was not disappointed.

My 'reading' of the day meant understanding it in its historical context and putting it into relationship to other *different* and successful Gala Days held throughout the industrial era of the village. What was 'there' to be seen was a comparative decline because such summer festivals were once grand set-piece occasions for the celebration of village life in all its industrial and communitarian fullness, where participants paraded into the local park and were piped around the athletics racing track by world championship winning pipe bands from the village; where printed and bound programmes of fifty pages and more were produced to list the various sporting competitions and their sponsors. Far from an overworked member of an organising committee acting as MC and having to press gang volunteers on the day to make up the numbers in a tug-of-war competition, such programmes detailing previous gala days had the names of each entrant for each of the many races printed in the programme with each race having its allocated starting time and its dedicated sponsor, normally a local business establishment, as well as notification of the prize money for first, second and third places, and with each event's sponsor being introduced to the crowd after each event and applauded when asked to 'do the honours' and present the prizes to the winners.

The Fun Day (2000) was significant as it acted to not only help me grasp what there is to be grasped but to find a language to frame what is ethnographically significant. As the purpose of the event was to raise money for the annual bonfire and fireworks display held every Halloween, which is the only other annual event where locals gather together in any great numbers, crucial to the day's success was the production of a sense of enjoyable community involvement, of spectacle and audience as in previous years. From the outset, however, the song which had awoken me to the day was already a summons to what Adorno would undoubtedly have called 'fake' post-industrial locality and its 'fake' communal or collective presence. The very title 'Fun Day' was a glaring indication of the derivative bricolage that signals deculturation and the advent of popular culture that is mass produced elsewhere and imported to locales of little cultural thickness and consumed by the flotsam and jetsum of deindustrialization and those without any culture of their own. I would go as far as to say that until this day 'Cardenden' had been unthinkable in me because its constitutional history had remained invisible or abstract or, perhaps better, what I had imagined Cardenden to be was put together by a *private language* or purely an idea of mine and so had lacked reality until that point. When walking around the various stalls, however, it was as if each stall took on its true form insofar as I viewed each as a failed performance of 'being a stall,' as if each became another 'word' to be added to a language of decline because each was a poor copy or 'fake' reproduction of a better and more 'real' practice of Gala Days and village fayres of yesterday.

The Fun Day, then, *de-privatised* my sense of 'there's nothing here.' In this publication of what had been private, even locals' participation was seen as a poor imitation or facsimile of the participation that occurred yesteryear insofar as, instead of actually participating in athletic events, the people had rather simply 'turned up' and were there not as participants but just to watch something or buy something or try their luck at some game or other to win a prize and in the process contribute to a local group's funds. Thanks to the dozen or more stalls doggedly manned by local volunteers for the purpose of fundraising, the 'nothing' had took form and become many little somethings, a stall of photos from the old days, a stall for the local mining heritage group, a stall for the local Brownies or other stalls selling home baking. Necessary for the triggering of this 'private' perception of mine was the conspicuous public empirical display of attempts at locality, the conspicuous public display of attempts at constituting a community and the conspicuous public display of attempts at constituting participation in the present. Whatever the practice, whether forming a team for tug-of-war, a highly pleased local mother successfully entering her child for the Bonnie Bairn competition despite initially remarking, "Ah widnae degrade ma bairn like that!," each was a shadow or poor facsimilie of the previous practices of previous local crowds, previous spectacles and previous participations that enacted these realities in previous years.

Because all of these enactments and social practices are traditional and a matter of learned practice that can be learned and so can be lost, the Fun Day 2000 for me was the public performance of 'forgetting' made empirically visible *in the very attempt at re-enacting or remembering: only the attempt at remembrance publicly revealed or enacted what has been lost,* and when viewed in this way each stall for example enacted and revealed in miniature a historical process that had culminated in the clear conclusion that constituting "the present as history" was *failure,* to the extent of being an embarrassment in locals' eyes to the extent that people were relieved when rain provided an excuse to leave. Like Heidegger's (1962, p. 98) insight that only the broken hammer makes the idea or essence of "hammer" present, so the failure of *communitas,* locality and spectacle made public everything that was failing to be present; *that what was there to be seen at the Fun Day 2000 was what was failing to be there and failing in public to be there.*

It would be something of a miracle if my account of the *Fun Day 2000* could equal the ethnographic accounts of local festivals such as Turner's study of *The Gala Day* in Cockenzie and Port Seaton in 1978.[27] Ironically, where a previous generation of ethnographers when describing Gala Days during the industrial era imagined they were capturing the local culture and traditions, only upon seeing and recognising failed attempts at 'sociality' and 'community' do contemporary ethnographers find their sight, and see what is there to be seen, become properly attuned to what is there to be seen. Only comparing this with prior gala days brought the present as history into focus and made 'decline' appear 'in person' and in public. By attempting to construct a communal event 'Cardenden' was made to 'say itself' out loud for the first time during fieldwork because its people were performing decline

---

[27] Robert Turner "Gala Day as an Expression of Community Identity" in A. Jackson (ed.) *Way of Life and Identity,* North Sea Oil Panel Occasional Paper No.4, [no date].

*in public* for the first time since I entered the field, so that what for them was a moment of collective and public failure was for me a moment of insight. Finally seeing decline being performed before my eyes, I was able to see what had remained private and invisible for two years. Despite all the data collected in interviews, I still felt vulnerable whenever writing of decline, as if each individual's testimony was only a private opinion that could be wrong.

In retrospect I see that each individual's testimony wasn't authority enough and that I needed a *public demonstration* of what individuals admitted to me on their doorsteps, and the Fun Day gave me this. While the 'ideology' of the day promised a reversal of normality via creating a sense of community where ordinarily there are privatised lives, the day only succeeded in highlighting this normality ever more clearly, especially among neighbours and friends and 'kent faces' who have not developed a vested interest in eliding failure when it comes. This day was cathartic, then, for me because I was freed from my private 'hermeneutical maze' thanks to my interpretations being publicly verified, and this experience also allowed me to see clearly that previously I had been alone in attempting to make locality put itself into words, and had spent two years attempting an impossible intuition of 'pure being' as a result of grappling with an experience of locality that gave little significations and representations of itself. Until this day I had remained trapped in "the agony of seeing" (Gadamer 1979, p. 536) insofar as 'seeing' a particular day or long-term realities such as 'decline' was only possible via recourse to a construction of historical context that had to be painstakingly put together and learnt.

Being local involves memories of growing up in Cardenden in the coalmining era and annual Miners' Galas and the annual event known as 'The Club Treat' [28] where everyone came with their family to the park and each adult and child received their white cardboard box of food and juice, and each family would choose their spot on the grass around the running track and camp there

---

[28] Bowhill War Memorial Club.

for the day, and would picnic and socialise and take photographs and enjoy the races and competitions until late in the afternoon. Because *communitas* is not something that can be sub-contracted to an outside firm or hired in for a day, the Fun Day was a rebranding of the traditional and successful aestival Gala Day attempts at *communitas* and revealed the present condition as history (Jameson 1984). If in analyzing the Fun Day we follow Victor Turner's method of taking specific events to reveal "a limited area of transparency on the otherwise opaque surface of regular uneventful social life" (1957, p. 93), the Fun Day was premised upon the attempt to escape the mundane and produce something extramundane as the stage was literally set for a spectacle. Indeed, successfully constituting the 'spectacular' is central to whether or not locality remains capable of mediating 'higher' realms of human experience such as *communitas* and the aesthetic.

If locality doesn't so much set itself the task of producing aesthetic experience or an experience of *mitsein* and sociality but, rather, locality itself only comes into being if these realms of experience become real, the concrete example of watching a local dance group may be a starting point. Hence, when watching the first dance of *The Suzettes* my initial enthusiasm soon waned, and while watching the second act which was a girl performing solo, I was struck by the thought that I was spectating a dramatization of my own predicament and 'performance' as an ethnographer: a young local attempting 'art' with an unlikely audience in an unlikely setting, so that her routine prompted a moment of mimetic recognition that just as she was 'nature' attempting 'culture,' so any analysis I might attempt was a local example of 'nature' trying to escape into 'culture' as the never easy task of dancing while throwing and catching a baton in time to music was made more difficult by the wind and uneven grass surface. As I watched, the baton being flung high into the air and waiting to see if the girl caught it was to see whether she succeeded or failed in reaching the aesthetic realm of experience and so the question for myself was whether any analysis of the data I might attempt would fall flat to the ground and, in the attempt, reveal my own inability to 'make it' in the realm of authorised representations.

During this solo routine I also made a point of looking at the gathered crowd as they watched and I was struck by the thought that it was not simply that the dancers were poor but the audience seemed fated to feel disappointed with performances of such obvious lack of polish as they were accustomed to dominant aesthetics of performance thanks to the massive importation and consumption of culture as a result of the communications revolution in the late-nineteen-eighties and the advent of satellite television. It seemed the girl's attempt at art was doomed and this added a pathetic quality to her performance.

By its very nature dance is an enactment of a pre-established sequence of movements i.e. a structural practice which imposes upon its practitioners the necessity of disappearing 'personality' in order to achieve 'impersonal' or subjectless intersubjective co-ordination (which applies even more so if the dance is part of a tradition such as Scottish country dancing as it then becomes a variation on a canonical theme). Because it is a structured reality par excellence the dance requires each individual achieves 'subjectless practice' (Bourdieu) so that 'individuality' is precisely what is not required *to achieve the dance* because to achieve the aesthetic experience within the audience presupposes the disappearance of the individual as an individual. Should any girl stand out the dance fails, and no aesthetic experience is available to the onlookers, and in the case of the dancer with poor technique or little talent, the onlooker sees someone who is simply energetic and enthusiastic and in a literal sense has no idea what she is doing; a leg or an arm jerks out here or there signalling the dancer doesn't know what she will do next. She is untamed 'nature' with no 'culture' and the movements of her body express nothing because they are *formless* because no idea informs her movements, and she is defined by something that doesn't exist in her, is trapped in nature and is unable to 'say' or use her body to articulate something because her body is preliterate and has yet to acquire language and so cannot transport its spectator to the aesthetic realm of experience.

As I watched the next performance of *The Suzettes*, then, insofar as the non-performance or absence of symmetry was on view, what became empirically present was the failure or absence of dance and as a result of this unsuccessful attempt to access the realm of aesthetics, the observer had no spectacle by which to constitute the aesthetic gaze and instead is burdened with the task of constituting 'something from nothing.' This absence of spectacle is the result of the onlooker watching the dance and, by bringing the remembrance of past successful dances seen elsewhere, he brings to mind something that is failing to be present and this constitutes what is present to be seen. The 'lived experience' of spectating the dance is informed by memory so that it is this remembered something as much as what is empirically present that provokes the audience's evaluation of the dance. Spectators of the dance bring to mind the reality of absence by remembering past days which act as *absent interlocutors* of the present-day insofar as they successfully instantiated the prized 'something' of spectacle and event and aesthetic experience.

In the case of dancers with technique and talent their co-ordination has an effect upon those witnessing the dance because an audience is able to come into being thanks to the practice of the dancers and, insofar as they maintain their performance, the audience as an audience is prevented from falling out of this particular kind of existence or *mitsein* and back into a collection of individual mothers, fathers, acquaintances and passers-by. The reason dance can produce this 'magical' or 'group-constituting' effect is because, as a visual spectacle, when any onlooker's eye comes to rest on any dancer it registers she is doing what any other dancer is doing so that the eye is not able to spectate individuality because it is not there as each dancer is dancing the dance. Likewise, insofar as each local girl is performing the dance she reaches the level of culture or aesthetic experience and escapes her identity as Jean Lowe's daughter, for example, and this allows the audience member such as her mother, for example, to escape being a dancer's mother and constitute another kind of relationship to her daughter-come-dancer and be immersed in another group reality or experience of *mitsein* i.e. audience member. Insofar as each individual onlooker enters this *mitsein* reality they are de-privatised in their *dasein* and taken out of their privatism and constituted as the 'we' of an audience and thereby experience themselves and their intersubjectivity differently.

In being caught up in this new identity as an audience member, what also comes into being among the audience is a new relation to time insofar as there is a qualitative difference between waiting for the end of a performance or 'killing time' and being made unaware of the passage of time. In the former case the dancers are judged as poor and will remain poor until the end of the performance while in the latter case the dancers take control of the onlookers' experience of time to the extent that the audience member is not waiting to see what comes next because he or she is carried along by every moment and the flow or 'prolonged now' of the performance. By controlling the audience's experience of time the audience's experience of themselves is also controlled, and so they do not hang around watching like youngsters on bikes waiting for something to convince them to stay because waiting implies the absence of something expected, anticipated or hoped for. With the successful performance the audience experiences no absence because each moment delivers the 'something' of collective presence so that the spectators are released from the 'agony of seeing' into the catharsis of *submission* to the authority of the dance and submission to the group known as an audience. The dancers take charge of the onlookers' perception so that the audience members are freed from the burden of consciousness or awareness and having to decide the merits of each moment, moment by moment, and are released from the mundane into the aesthetic realm thanks to the ability and talent of the dancers. This realm that is accessed is normally given the name of the aesthetic[29] and, among other qualities, it is characterised by a 'giving of self' made possible by the action of others; a certain ceding of autonomy that is authorised by the performance of others reaching a certain level of quality.

---

[29] The word 'aesthetic' derives from the Greek *aisthesis* meaning 'perception.'

Dancers taking control of what there is to be seen and taking control of the experience of perception, to the extent of rendering onlookers passive as their perception is taken out of their hands, is a power whose effect among the audience is a giving of self to the spectacle by each onlooker as each is lifted out of individual seeing into 'groupness' because each audience member is sharing in the same perception and the same experience of time, which is the intersubjective or 'objective' basis of the aesthetic realm. This aesthetic reality cannot be faked as its existence is based upon real 'objective' or intersubjective conditions that have to be met. Each audience member, then, is briefly but *really* taken out of their private and idiosyncratic seeing and released from 'having' to watch their nephew or daughter or neighbour insofar as the dancers constitute a *mitsein* reality among themselves. Both the collection of individual dancers' and the collection of individual onlookers' escape from the mundane to the aesthetic is dependent upon a cathartic process of de-privatising locality, *dasein*, *mitsein* and sociality so that, when the dance comes to an end the applauding audience is as much showing its appreciation for being given an experience of intersubjectivity it is unable to give itself as indicating their appreciation of the dance. This successfully instituting a particular *mitsein* via others' doing is not something that is contemplated or passively spectated but something *enacted* and felt, so that the audience's ceding of control is freely given. Because it is the dance that makes the audience, aesthetic experience is the public or intersubjective effect of the dance upon *dasein* and integral to the aesthetic experience it makes possible is the *local production of publicity*, so the question of reaching the level of culture is the question of locality being capable of producing a local public realm and, in this regard, alongside the power to bring *mitsein* into being there are powerful processes of individuation at work.

From the perspective of the individual dancer, to perform in public is to be tested, and should one fail, one fails in a public and very *personal* manner. On those occasions which fail to instantiate the dance there is a particular humiliating experience of self that emerges, so that a Fun Day that involves a collection of individuals being put together for a day may result in humiliation because of the lack of talent or technique or preparation to enact the aesthetic realm and withstand the possibility of making a 'spectacle of oneself.' Likewise, among the spectators, just as perfect subjectless practice opens the aesthetic realm to them, so this practice convinces the observing ethnographer he is witnessing culture rather than a group of friends having fun or messing about. For the dancer, then, when the aesthetic realm is enacted, this brings into being a particular experience of *dasein* or 'being there' which convinces each individual dancer that the identity of 'being a dancer' can be internalised because it has objectively come into being via having been publicly made real and validated. If the dance successfully comes into being the identity of 'dancer' comes into being for each of the girls, and the success of this identity coming into being has nothing to do with the private opinion of a critic as it is a public and social affair. To the extent the dancers are visibly synchronized with each other and the music, the audience witnesses a triumph and for as long as it lasts the audience is not given permission to dissolve itself back into an aggregate of individuals and pre-performance behaviours such as remarking on nice dresses and make-up. The audience is compelled to watch in silence as they too fall into their own form of subjectless practice and refrain from inappropriate behaviours that would break silence or break rank and thereby break the spell cast over them.

The source of this compulsion or 'coercion to convene' which is central to the successful spectacle is the gathered collection of onlookers escaping themselves and entering the 'realm of meaning' thanks to a successful constitution of language being communicated so that in the unsuccessful performance, the effort is said to collapse back onto itself and, far from achieving the shift to 'art' or 'meaning,' it is described as artificial, pretentious or even embarrassing. With the successful performance permission is granted to enter the realm of meaning where a story is told or a meaning is communicated, so that the girls are judged 'literate' and the fact that they 'know what they are doing' is evidenced by their ability to 'say' or signify something meaningful with their bodies which communicate a meaning that transcends their bodies as opposed to communicating a lack of preparation or their estrangement from culture. As Bourdieu (1977, pp. 1-2) has it: "[A]rtistic production is always also...'pure practice without theory', as Durkheim says" i.e. the meaningfulness of art is largely mimetic, a matter of physical imitation and kinesthetics, so that when local girls give an exhibition of their learning and control and skill and mastery of their movements, the spectators respond by freely allowing themselves to be 'mastered' into the *mitsein* of an audience which is held in existence until the dancers finish, upon which the audience dissolves itself via the practice of applause which is simultaneously the last act of the audience and the action which returns each audience member to a 'private' mundane individual again.

As the dancers take their bows there is the paradox where successfully performing 'subjectlessness' is a source of intense individuation and personal affirmation so that what can be achieved in such village festivals is nothing less than the enrichment of personhood, gender identity, locality, families and the national culture. Thanks to raw nature being disciplined by the talent and technique of culture, female dancers simultaneously perform 'being feminine' and bring into being for future reference their belonging to locality insofar as being applauded by one's 'home crowd' involves being uniquely recognised and individuated because it is one's first audience and perhaps the most difficult crowd to constitute into an audience because for one's home crowd one has until that point always been Jean Lowe's daughter, for example, so that to become a dancer in such eyes and for the 'magic' of the aesthetic realm to come into existence the girls must constitute this new identity and reality *ex nihilo* because one is performing in front of fellow locals, among whom are one's mother, aunts, cousins, friends, schoolmates and neighbours. To be recognised by one's locality is to know the power of the group to produce an affirmation thanks to this process of firstly nerve-wracking and then powerful experience *of affirmation and individuation which trumps all other realities* because it is not the result of a private opinion or some secret desire but *a public affirmation that is incontestable because to contest it would require other publicly* recognised *grounds to contest the affirmations the public realm makes but, of course, we cannot put the social into question as there is no point of view upon the social that is beyond the social realm.*

In February 2001, a meeting was held to discuss ways to ensure the disappointment felt at the Fun Day 2000 was not repeated and the result of these deliberations was that a Village Fair would be organised for 26 August 2001. However, in the Bowhill Centre Annual Report of 2001 the *Fun Day* was summed up in the following contradictory fashion:

> Once again this was a successful event run in August 2000 by the Bonfire & Fireworks Display Committee. Due to lack of volunteers and helpers this will be the last Fun Day organised by the Committee.

The trend subsequent to 2000 has been one of importing or buying in entertainment as the way to ensure something approaching a 'spectacle' is enjoyed by the crowds that gather each summer. This problem of reproducing a sense of spectacle and community, of course, is not confined to Cardenden as in many locales there is the same struggle for a sense of local identity and a 'new narrative' after the more or less enforced collectivism of the industrial era. The *Glenrothes Gazette* (Thursday, May 27th 1999), for example, reported the failure of North Glenrothes Gala which had only been resurrected the year before in an article with the headline *Apathy Kills Gala in North Glenrothes* and which quoted the Gala committee secretary:

> The public just don't seem to be interested in helping at a gala in North Glenrothes. They may have turned up on the day, as they did last year, but it requires a lot more commitment than that.

Now that much local industry and local jobs have gone there has emerged a generation that is stripped of the many bonding relations of locality as occupational community, resulting in the ongoing problem of constituting the positive meaning of locality and provinciality. Traditionally, annual miners' galas and village pageants have been an obvious source of local identity so that today there is a perceived decline in local culture and identity within small communities across post-industrial Fife and Scotland more generally. Local newspapers report small former mining villages alarmed at the 'loss of identity' and, taking the recent example of a Cowdenbeath May Queen being stripped of her crown due to it being subsequently discovered her home address was outside of Cowdenbeath in Lumphinnans,[30] and the subsequent decision to revive a pageant day for Lumphinnans as a means of addressing this 'insult' and reasserting local 'independence' from the encroaching towns of Lochgelly and Cowdenbeath, such episodes illustrate what Cohen (1985, p. 50; 70) terms the symbolic construction of community when perceived local identities are felt to be under threat: "[T]he symbolic expression of community and its boundaries increases in importance as the actual geo-social boundaries of the community are undermined, blurred or otherwise weakened...as a consequence of social change, so people resort increasingly to symbolic behaviour to reconstitute the boundary."

We may say then that summer festivals throughout post-industrial Scotland act out "a pervasive nostalgia for 'real' social relations" (Herzfeld 1997, p. 8), a nostalgia which is very much alive because the real experience of solidarity has been recently overtaken by the event of deindustrialization in the nineteen-eighties. These festivals and fayres and galas aim to maintain a tension between locality and modernity and in this effort face up to the challenges of anonymous forces upon the basis of their often beleaguered locality. Having begun to recognise this challenge of producing 'ethnography from nothing,' the next section looks at writers who have lived in Cardenden and turned their attention to

---

[30] A former mining village known locally as 'Little Moscow' as a result of its historic Communist Party sympathies.

the challenge of 'writing locality' where the problem of generating 'something from nothing' has been addressed.

## 1.5 The History of Writing Cardenden

### David Rorie (1867-1946)

During fieldwork I discovered the writings of David Rorie when I happened to leaf through Buchan's *Folk Tradition and Folk Medicine in Scotland: The Writings of David Rorie* (1994) which I had purchased three years previously, but which for all that time I had never dreamt contained a collection of ethnographic and folkloric writings on Cardenden stretching back to the nineteenth-century. To my surprise and delight, then, I read that Rorie came to live in Cardenden in 1894 as the medical officer for the Fife Coal Company at Bowhill Colliery and that Rorie, "was an ethnographer...the first folklorist in Scotland, and one of the first anywhere, to record the culture of an industrial community: that of the Fife miners" (Buchan 1994, pp. 5 & 11). I discovered that Rorie had a keen interest in collecting and commenting upon the practices and beliefs of the miners and peasants of Cardenden and its environs, and in his writings he drew upon the ethnographies of the Torres Straits Islands expedition of 1898 and the theories of magic articulated by George Frazer in *The Golden Bough* (1890-1915), and Rorie proposed a parallel between Cardenden farm workers' beliefs regarding diseases and their 'primitive' practices of treating illnesses via mimetic magical practices with similar beliefs and practices among native Paraguayan Indians.

However, having read the book I found there was no evidence of Rorie having set himself the task of articulating a 'native' point of view. At most, there is evidence that Rorie engaged in a form of 'salvage ethnography' insofar as his writing seems to have been motivated by providing interesting amusement for the reading public concerning the provinces and backwaters, something textually confirmed by a throw-away remark when reviewing a case of 'Second Sight' which touches upon the battle of Culloden, and where Rorie remarks that the case "has no romance in it"

(Buchan 1994, p. 188), and so is to be dismissed as of no interest to his readers.[31]

This concern to identify 'romance' ties in with a wider debate regarding European Romanticism's critique of industrialism and allegations concerning nineteenth-century Scottish literature's flight from depicting the new industrial order of the time, so that in attempting to identify what Fredric Jameson (1982) terms the "political unconscious" of Rorie's texts, a case can be made for the argument that his depiction of 'locality' is governed by two contradictory impulses: a search for the cultural survivals of a pre-modern outlook among the Fife peasantry so that Rorie can be described as part of a 'save the data' campaign, and secondly, a set of modernist assumptions which effectively prevented Rorie from developing a conception of his data that could be more than a romantic hunt for 'curiosities.' In this regard I am unclear whether Rorie's writing on the pre-history of medical science is a serious effort at recovering and recognising 'lost knowledges' or perhaps modernist condescension. I am unsure if a much-respected and high-status pillar of the community turning his attention towards coal miners and farm workers as sources of knowledge had to adopt a façade of condescension so that Rorie would not appear to his modernist 'scientific' readers as taking folklore too seriously. While I am unsure if Rorie deliberately wants to appear to trivialize the subject matter as a bit of fun in order to deflect the question why a qualified medical doctor would devote his time and attention to peasants' superstitious beliefs and practices, it is clear that Buchan is keen to press the claim that a 'native viewpoint' was captured by Rorie, despite the fact that Rorie (Buchan 1994, p. 12) himself tells his reader:

It is not pretended that all the customs, etc., mentioned were universal. Many of them were dying out, and many more

---

[31] At the time of Rorie's writing an indication of what was then popular with the reading public is given by Ian Maclaren's kailyard novel *Beside the Bonny Brier Bush* (1890) having the distinction of being the first book to top the first American best-seller list which had been established in 1895 (see Harvie 1993).

were referred to jestingly, often with the semi-apologetic remarks, 'that's an old freit [superstitious belief], that's what the auld folk used to say, or do.' But everything I have set down I have tested as having been at one time or other common in the district.

There is the assumption that there is a local or miner's viewpoint, and that it is something available not only to miners themselves but can be grasped by a medical officer turned amateur medical folklorist. However, there is no actual exploration of the notion, for example, that the 'viewpoint' of miners or peasants is something that must be constructed or pieced together because it is not suspected that this viewpoint can not be simply recorded or read off or reconstructed from house call notes as it is not something so conveniently 'given.' What is clear is that Rorie never produced an account of the conditions of nineteenth-century miners so that my initial sense of good fortune at discovering Rorie's works was to end in disappointment, as Buchan's claims that Rorie actually studied miners' culture is misleading to say the least. The quote from Rorie above clearly indicates that his informants were indicating their lives and consciousness lay elsewhere than Rorie's folkloric interests, that the data being requested of them was already obsolete so that we may say the more Rorie restricted his inquiry to 'medical folklore' the more a native point of view was being marginalised and missed, and what in Rorie's writings is glossed by Buchan as 'the native point of view' is in fact the afterlife of a pre-industrial era that was at an end.

This glimpse of the impending obliteration of the last remnants of a pre-industrial outlook is characteristic of pre-Malinowskian ethnography and understandable and laudable as Rorie conducted his research when various customs and beliefs were disappearing due to massive and sudden industrialisation. In this regard, there is a continuity between my ethnography and Rorie despite being separated by a century insofar as, whereas Rorie began his fieldwork at the point of the transition to heavy or 'total industrialisation' in 1895, my own research was conducted more than twenty years after locality had become post-industrial; where Rorie sought the 'survivals' of a pre-industrial folklore I found myself piecing together 'survivals' of the industrial period of 1895-1965, and while Rorie is rightly lauded for recording medical folklore among late nineteenth-century miners and agricultural workers, it is a matter of dispute that Rorie researched "the culture of an industrial community: that of the Fife miners" (Buchan 1994, p. 11) as Buchan claims. Perhaps a more accurate appraisal is that Rorie did not suspect anything in *industrial workers'* lives of particular *folkloric* worth and he was probably right to draw this conclusion in light of the rapid de-traditionalisation that was already ongoing in 1895.

## Rev. Archibald McNeill Houston (? – 1933)

If I contend that powerful forces more or less coerced or 'decided' the construction of what counted as data and which more or less rendered certain data 'invisible' and non-existent as candidates for representation in the writing of Rorie, this same 'political unconscious' is even more pronounced in the text left to us by the Church of Scotland minister the Rev. Archibald McNeill Houston who arrived in Cardenden nine years before Rorie in 1885 and is today remembered as the author of *Auchterderran, Fife: A Parish History* (1924). Rather than giving a parish history as we today would understand such a project, Houston's text is essentially a collection of events and 'eminent personages' with very little effort at constructing any meaningful connection between the data, save that they occurred more or less within the same locality. What is remarkable about Houston's history is not only the absence of a historical narrative but the author's success in 'emptying' locality of any historic significance thanks to his *suppression of history* thanks to his monotonous enumeration of kirk session notes charting the relentlessly 'remarkable' and 'faithful' line of local ministers and schoolmasters and their relentless progress in all their endeavours. The remarkable absence of any narrative or story throughout the four hundred and more pages paradoxically ends in a representation of locality as a place where nothing of historical worth happens because all political and historical dialectic has been removed, so that locality is made to participate in what Marinell Ash (1980) termed the "strange death" of Scottish history.

It is clear that Houston's history was written after history has come to an end. As with local history group members and old women who prefer to slam their door shut than talk of the establishment of the Scottish parliament to be discussed in Chapter 4, in Houston's text nothing enters his representation that would reopen or put into question the established order of things, so that even the recognition that the realm of political contestation and governance exists is off-limits; so that, if there is no 'cut and thrust' it is because the triumph of the British bourgeois Protestant order has brought all such drama to a happy conclusion and there are no more causes to be won. The significance or the intelligibility of the long durée of history is essentially constituted by the long gestation of Protestantism and what for Houston constitutes the meaning of history and historical continuity is deployed to close history and 'naturalise' the 1688 politico-religious constitutional settlement:

> It is, therefore, worthy of importance to note how the Reformers connected themselves with the Lollards and the Lollards with the Culdees, as the Culdees connected themselves with the Waldenses, and the Waldenses with the Apostolic Church (1924, p. 29).

Much as Latour has described French historiography finally grasping "the revolutionary reading of the French Revolution... had organised [French] historiography since 1789" (1993, p. 40), so Scottish historians highlight a particular era of Scottish historiography which was dominated by adherence to the Whig project of bourgeois Protestant modernism and support for the political union of Scotland and England. To read Houston as he wanted to be read is to play along with the Whig interpretation of Scotland and its post-Reformation history as progress and as the only credible hermeneutical standpoint. The 'political unconscious' of McNeill's text then consecrated the present social order with all other counter-imaginings of the past and present as in Catholicism, republicanism, communism, Scottish nationalism and socialism that *were* also present being rendered invisible. With the benefit of hindsight it is clear that throughout Houston's work an unstated 'politics of identity' is in charge of his framing locality, where the present is narrated as the Christian God's arrangement of Scottish history and to which the movement of centuries of history have been nicely brought to their providential conclusion (Kidd 1993). Whether via the reduction of the past to the degraded existence of 'romance' in Rorie or Houston's parish history, Cardenden is framed within the larger historical paradigm which Young (cited in Broun et al. 1998, p. 105) characterised as follows:

> Previous generations of scholars in the early twentieth century focused on a Whig interpretation of history, with history being fundamentally equated with progress, and viewed the Treaty of Union of 1707 as an act of liberation which civilised Scotland and freed her from the shackles of a barbaric past.

If Houston's history is void of interest because it has been washed clean of any drama, of successes and failures, intrigues, villains and heroes and great causes to be fought for and won or lost, it is also a history that is free of the realities of socio-economic forces, industrialism, wealth, poverty and social classes. In Houston's history the industrial revolution makes no appearance, nor does its transforming impact upon the local landscape, so that Houston's descriptions of particular aspects of the local landscape are done in such a way as to remove the land from the impact of history. Significantly, despite being written by a Christian, there is not a single sentence in the book that could be described as an instance of critical social commentary. This suppression of the story of how the present came to be means that Houston covers 'everything' with a pre-modern or 'end of history' *tensionlessness*, so that the text becomes interesting precisely because of what it suppresses and what cannot appear within the horizon of meaning that is at work; a horizon of meaning that can not resurrect history and its clash of ideas and interests.

The spectre that haunts this imagining of Scotland is the thousand years of Catholicism in Scotland prior to the 'invention' of Protestantism, so that integral to Houston's suppression of history is the myth of a non-Catholic 'Celtic Church.' In Houston's horizon of meaning, that which is allowed to appear and be recognised is only that which has a role to play in the emergence of the present established order of things. This need to find a Protestant navel within Catholicism (Davies 1992; Hudson 1994; Clancy 1997; Veitch 1997) seems to indicate Protestants were not psychologically ready to accept the *modernist* rupture that Protestantism represented and so the Celtic Church is the 'ballast' Protestants needed to suppress their original modernist revolution so that, ironically, the invention of the Celtic Church was a form of Catholic 'Protestantism' that suppressed the novelty of the Protestant Reformation and repressing the truth of what they had done.

In later chapters I will argue this suppression of history underpins the 1945 generation's British and Protestant identity and a political integralism and narrative or imagining of national and local history that is more or less fated to view the 'reopening' of Scotland's history thanks to the establishment of the Holyrood parliament as profoundly unsettling. I will argue that what prepares the way for '45 generation unionism is Houston's prior 'theological cleansing' of local and national history from local and national consciousness, and that this is isomorphic with a similar clearing of Scottish education and the removal of all political dialectic from Scotland and the reduction of the imagining of the future to the hegemony of Scottish unionism and the view that "1688 marked a grand turning point, when 'ancient superstitions' and 'the old theological spirit' *were* sloughed off, and the *'real* interests of the nation began to be perceived" (Beveridge & Turnbull 1997, p. 67). In the Protestant modernist imagination, then, the advent of Great Britain in 1707 was the great action of God in history that simultaneously marks the advent of the modern era and the political and religious liberation from the medieval Catholic era. In this salvific-come-historical event, localities are also 'liberated' into the great polity of Great Britain and are modernised and liberated from 'medieval particularism' into the larger modern organising formation known as 'society.'

While Houston shows us a neat way of having one's modernist cake and eating it, the fatal price to be paid is that at the heart of the political-theological unconscious 'governing' Houston's history and imagining of locality is the 'worship of facts' because *nothing fundamental is left to achieve or happen.* After the great salvific-come-historical exodus event and period of 1688-1707, events and localities are fated to suffer from the 'end of history.' It is the internalization of this symbolic order that acts to render the historic events of 'Scotland 1999' or the upcoming referendum on 18 September 2014 non-events for those elderly residents who align themselves with the historico-political-religious order articulated in Houston. Where the history of locality is only imaginable or able to appear within this horizon, the parish can only ever attain the 'romantic' status of an "old-world quaint corner of Fife" (Houston 1924, p. 12), despite Houston writing in the aftermath of the Russian revolution of 1917, the enfranchisement of the working class in 1918, the general strike of 1921 and the emergence of Cardenden as "the storm centre of the East of Scotland working class movement" according to the British Socialist Party's weekly newspaper *The Call* (1921 or 1922, page unknown).[32]

Because Houston was writing his history during the unprecedented emergence of class struggle and the contestation of established cultural and political power, his text evidences the 'dead hand' of a modernism that kills the living tension of 'being modern,' 'being local' and 'being-in-history;' a Protestant modernism that having successfully exercised a will to power at a certain point in the nation's history, thereafter became the creature and the captive of power and stopped being modern insofar as it succumbed to the desire to end the tension of 'being modern.' Insofar as Houston's imagination became petrified into this mindscape, his local history

---

[32] I have since lost the exact details of this reference.

petrified Cardenden into this image. However, if Houston's writing repressed the emergence of social critique and class conflict, the local miners who are absent from the texts of Houston and Rorie began to produce literary representations of their own, and with this development both Rorie's and Houston's texts and worldviews were fated to quickly fall into obscurity.

## Joe Corrie (1896–1968)

Joe Corrie was a coalminer-turned-author and part of an inter-war generation of working-class autodictats that emerged from a recently enfranchised working class in Wales, Scotland and England which elected the first-ever UK Labour government in 1924. This inter-war generation became 'producers of culture' and set about the task of representing their lives and localities and the political views of the twenty-one year old miner Corrie, like every politically-engaged working-class person, had been electrified by the 1917 revolution in Russia, and in his literary output Corrie pursued a conscious commitment to realism which sought to dispel the mists and fogs of the 'kailyard school' of the likes of Houston and Rorie that had obscured as much as revealed. Corrie's play *In Time 0' Strife* (1927) (see Corrie 1985, pp. 23-80) enjoyed international success while his other published poems and plays as well as unpublished manuscripts, represents the most credible and sustained attempt at representation of Cardenden as Corrie devoted himself to writing of the miners and their community during the years of the Great Depression. Importantly, Corrie's plays went through many productions not only in Cardenden but throughout Fife and Scotland, as well as the mining areas of England thanks to the theatrical group *Bowhill Village Players* which later became the *Fife Miner Players* in the nineteen-twenties and thirties.[33] As a committed socialist Corrie

---

[33] In the winter of 1930 Corrie was in Leipzig to see a production of his play *In Time O' Strife* (1927) and was aware of the rise of Hitler. For years after this trip to Germany, Corrie corresponded with the German translator of his play who was a member of the Communist Party. When Corrie learned from this

understood his role as a writer in terms of class struggle and saw the role of the writer as one of rendering the standpoint of mining communities. As he wrote in 1933 (Corrie 1985):

> I must write about the world I know best, the world of the working man and woman, their trials, loves, hates, suspicions, generosities and loyalties, I feel somehow that – well, it's a contribution – I am doing what I love best for a class that needs it now.

In Corrie's only published full-length novel *Black Earth* (1939) Cardenden appears as the fictional coalmining village of 'Brandon' and Corrie (1939, p. 88) pulls no punches in his depiction of Cardenden and its neighbouring hamlets:

> Until he passed through the little dirty hamlet of Whitgrange, still as dirty as ever, still as depressing, the same long unbroken row of small houses with the water barrels to catch the rain for the womenfolk to wash their clothes with, the same uncultivated garden patches with their rickety old sheds, pigeon houses and rabbit-hutches, and the same drawn faces looking through windows at the falling snow. Then his thought suddenly went back to the days of his youth. It was in Whitgrange that he had been born and had spent the best part of his life. He looked out on the little house where he had spent his hungry childhood and fighting youth. And he felt slightly sick for many reasons.

*Black Earth* (1939) is the tragic story of two marriages and two Brandon men: of how one is corrupted by power while the other is corrupted by powerlessness. In the opening scenes Corrie depicts the homely life of Jack Smith, a miner and his wife Maggie and their three children; a happy and hard-working family headed

---

comrade that the German Communists decided to support Hitler in order to defeat their rival Social Democrats, however, their correspondence came to an abrupt end. See Corrie (1985, pp. 175-7).

by a mother and father who, having been childhood sweethearts, were destined for each other. Despite this happy beginning, the novel becomes progressively darker as a result of Jack having an accident at work and eventually committing suicide in a desperate effort to save his family from poverty. While the opening chapters are dominated by the Smith family, the reader is introduced in due course to the other male protagonist, George Williams, who is the 'villain' of the novel and who is another local man also employed like Jack in the local colliery but has married an outsider to Brandon whom Corrie (1939, p. 49) describes as a woman who:

> [H]ated going to the pump...made no neighbours, and held no conversation with them. She had nothing in common with them, nothing at all. She hated them for their roughness, for their ill-manners, for their vulgarity, for their hopeless fatalism. They were low, in her estimation, very low. And to live among them was misery.

The character of Elizabeth is depicted by Corrie as having to endure local women's use of language which amounts to barely concealed aggression grounded in a deeply internalised and deeply defining *ressentiment*. Corrie depicts Brandon's women as viewing Elizabeth's petit bourgeois standards as a standing provocation which triggers an ongoing aggression within them as a result of Elizabeth's behaviours acting as a mirror in which is reflected back to the local women their defeatism and their resignation to their fate, so that Elizabeth acts as a scapegoat because these women heap upon her all of their resentments and bad conscience as a result of having settled for their lives with no thought of betterment. The outsider, then, is resented because her mere presence resurrects the long-dead hopes for a better life that local women have killed off within themselves. Elizabeth is provocative because she 'deconstructs' local women to the extent she is determined that she will not be mastered by her material conditions and to the extent she acts with a view to making things different for herself and her family. Corrie, then, uses his fiction as a means of exploring and representing working-class *dasein* and to capture the situation where material reality has been so pressing for so long that it has called forth within the human being living this reality so many chronic coping behaviours and accommodations that the slightest deviation from this repertoire of accommodation stands out; where the slightest 'deviancy' from this accommodation instantaneously calls forth within the breast of local women the whole force of their habitus as it rushes to defend itself in response to being symbolically challenged.

As Elizabeth endures her fate of being déclassé, her husband George enjoys promotion through the ranks of the local mine thanks in no small measure to the promptings of his ambitious wife Elizabeth; promptings such that she insists he take night classes to better himself, and which culminate in his being promoted to manager within the local pit. While her husband prospers, however, Elizabeth becomes increasingly mentally unhinged as a result of her years of having to endure the material and emotional and cultural poverty of working-class village life. As Elizabeth declines her husband George rebels against his formerly dominant wife and resurrects a sexual interest in Jack's wife Maggie whose decline into poverty as a result of Jack's failings has forced her to seek the help of the now-affluent George and draw upon the fact that they were once romantically linked as teenagers. In an atmosphere of suspicion and vicious gossip as to what is occurring between Maggie and George while Jack lies crippled in bed as a result of an accident down the pit,[34] the finale of the novel sees the heroine in her hour of need brought about by her husband who had turned to gambling in an ultimately disastrous attempt to provide for his family, become a fallen woman.

*Black Earth* (1939) then is as a novel that tells the story of how two marriages end in failure and how a working-class man makes his way up the occupational ladder and ends up becoming a petty tyrant; how power and powerlessness are related to material poverty, with the latter corrupting judgment and behaviour and

---

[34] My paternal grandfather who made common cause with Corrie in the local Communist Party lay for years in his bed suffering from the pneumonoconiosis contracted due to working in Bowhill pit until his death in 1966.

wreaking psychological damage. *Black Earth* (1939) is an 'anti-essentialist' sociological novel which, step by step, sets out to show the reader how material poverty tears at the veil of 'false consciousness' that surrounds the myth and practice of conjugal love. In a very real sense, the real protagonist of *Black Earth* is material poverty insofar as it slowly but surely deconstructs everything it touches – human relationships, love, friendship, ideas of womanhood and manhood and individuals' deepest beliefs about who they are.

For Corrie, poverty is the great source of 'conscientisation' insofar as the experience of becoming poor triggers the protagonists' breaking free of their previous 'humanistic' relationship to their selves and society insofar as poverty imposes an endless questioning of self that gradually moves further and further towards a nihilistic gloom as a once naïve trust in life and love is lost. Poverty destroys the soul and the fabric of society because grounds other than improved material conditions cannot be found to maintain basic beliefs and practices regarding self-respect and interpersonal relations. The beliefs and practices concerning love, marriage, family, fidelity and relationships etcetera are deconstructed over time to reveal they are in fact means for social survival, and it is only the desperately and chronically poor who are fated to arrive at this insight. *Black Earth*, then, is concerned with exploring the psychological condition of men and women and the reality and level of repression that accompanies poverty and how poverty traps and imprisons and determines the psyche, so that *Black Earth* (1939) is a novel about the clash or confrontation between the decentred reality of working-class masculinity and the myth of men being autonomous and centred, and how material poverty results in a psychological poverty of character and fragility that is only capable of imagining itself using one or two primary colours.

If this is the strength of the novel, a clear weakness is the tendency to reduce the representation of workers' *dasein* to those aspects of their lives that are work-related, a weakness shared with much agitprop literature of the inter-war years. This weakness results in characters lacking psychological depth and sometimes credibility. In this regard *Black Earth* (1939) is not comparable to Platonov's *The Foundation Pit* ([1929] 1996) or passages of Brierley's *Means Test Man* (1935). While I would never describe Corrie as being guilty of "the common reproach levelled by psychoanalysts at Marxists, that the latter speak as if a man has no psyche until he gets his first paycheck" (Sahlins 1976, p. 8n), Corrie is clearly on the side of the Sartre who writes, "the truth of a man is the nature of his work, and it is his wages" (1963, p. 93). Also, in the unpublished manuscripts of Corrie that I have examined there is a certain materialist 'flatness' of horizon which is devoid of any attempt to paint *dasein* with the colours of historicity or culture or nationality to arrive at an in-depth representation of the complexity of human *dasein* beyond the representation of the worker as dominated by capital in his consciousness and behaviour, and caught up in structures and events beyond his control. If this limited use of colour to depict *dasein* is a weakness it was not unrecognised by Corrie himself. As he wrote in 1932:

> It is a failing of mine, I believe, that I never enjoy a play which does not have a strong relation to real life. I know people who can go to the theatre and enjoy the technique of a play even if they scoff at the theme. I am not so fortunate. If the theme of a play is trivial, I immediately lose interest and make my exit from the theatre at the first convenient moment.
>
> (Corrie 1985, p. 183).

Despite this self-criticism Corrie's work endures as the articulation of a local and detailed standpoint which remains unprecedented in a Cardenden writer as there is no doubt that Corrie was committed to realism and locality and, as a result, representations of 'ordinary' people in their daily lives and so has produced a body of work of lasting ethnographic worth.

## Ian Rankin (1960 - )

The first writer that has faced the challenge of representing the post-industrial era of Cardenden is also the most successful local author by far, Ian Rankin. Beginning with his first novel *The Flood* (1986) Rankin has produced a substantial body of work of more than thirty novels, and in this body of work the dominant and perhaps only representation of Cardenden is one that is uniformly bleak, if not miserabilist.[35] In Rankin's texts the claustrophobic localism of Houston's (1924, p. 12) "old-world quaint corner of Fife" is gone and macro-economic forces and the cut and thrust of political difference and class contestation is present along with the musings of the private, lone individual Rebus[36] character who is more or less estranged from his natal village (1987, p. 3).

> He drove quietly, hating to be back here in Fife [i.e. Cardenden], back where the old days had never been 'good old days,' where ghosts rustled in the shells of empty houses and the shutters went up every evening on a handful of desultory shops, those metal shutters that gave the vandals somewhere to write their names. How Rebus hated it all, this singular lack of environment. It stank the way it had always done: of misuse, of disuse, of the sheer wastage of life.

As if his own testimony concerning Cardenden were not enough, Rankin's novel *Dead Souls* (1999) begins with the following

---

[35] This view of Cardenden is not reserved to native authors but is shared by architects to judge by the architectural magazine *Urban Realm* which in 2000 inaugurated the 'Carbuncle Award' to highlight the worst examples of architecture in Scotland. In 2009 Cardenden was nominated for this award, although the Fife town of Glenrothes was the eventual winner. In arriving at their choice the magazine editors explained: "It's a hard call when you get into the southernmost parts of Fife but since nobody other than characters from an Ian Rankin novel would dare step through the tumbleweed in Cardenden these days, the 'Plook on the Plinth' had to go to a place that was at least walkable and – more importantly – with potential to be salvaged." http://www.urbanrealm.com. Accessed 5 Aug 2012.

[36] The fictional detective 'Rebus' character is a native of Cardenden.

excerpt from the American novelist Kate Atkinson's *Behind the Scenes at the Museum* (1995):

> Once I caught a train to Cardenden by mistake...When we reached Cardenden we got off and waited for the next train back to Edinburgh. I was very tired and if Cardenden had looked more promising, I think I would have simply stayed there. And if you've ever been to Cardenden you'll know how bad things must have been.

A theme within Rankin's series of detective novels is some kind of reconciliation within the Rebus character of the metropolitan 'somebody' and the village 'nobody,' as Rebus is characterised by an ongoing psychodynamic of being troubled by memories from his past which come to haunt Rebus or surface and play on his mind, usually during a lull in the exigencies of solving a murder case and as a result of drinking too much whisky. In *Dead Souls* (1999, p. 55) we read: "He [Rebus] could see streetlights across the Forth in Fife. He thought of Janice and Brian Mee, who had never left their home town. He wondered how he'd have turned out if he'd stayed," and further on Rebus asks himself (1999, p. 197): "*If I'd stuck around Fife*, he thought, *not joined the army...what would I be thinking now? Who would I be?*" (italics in original).

The theme of unresolved questions of identity I read as evidence of Rankin's ambivalence towards his decision not to base his writing within and upon his natal locality; as if Rankin simultaneously wishes to recognise and pay homage to his natal village and set himself the task of making 'literature from nothing,' but also seeks to justify and never seriously engage with the self that has left his locality behind. Certainly, this suppressed alter ego or former self is not invested with sufficient substance to force this reconciliation, so that in place of a genuine engagement with the relationship between locality and writing and an engagement with psychological repression to maintain the fiction of a post-provincial self, there is instead the resort to a formulaic depiction of locality along the lines of 'there's nothing here,' and this reliance upon a readily available pat answer is more akin to a cliché that, because it is ready to hand, avoids the challenge of thinking an answer. After each brief sojourn in Fife, then, the fictional protagonist removes himself to the metropolitan centre as if admitting it is only in the metropolitan "somewhere" that a village nobody can have a life of meaning and participate in history, and the post-provincial writer can have a locality that can furnish material of literary merit.

Paradoxically, then, whereas Houston banished the movement of history and politics from his representation of Cardenden, Rankin, by following the very opposite strategy and recognising the full 'uglifying' impact of these processes, produces a depiction of Cardenden that is strangely similar to Houston insofar as both construct Cardenden as a place where nothing of any real import or consequence happens. In his debut novel *The Flood* (1986, p. 24), for example, Rankin locates significance and the movement of history elsewhere in nineteen-sixties Paris: "This was 1968. Far away there was talk of revolution and radical change. The world was slipping and sliding on the edge of a new era of communication. Carsden [i.e. Cardenden] slept longer and deeper than most." Rankin, then, reproduces the traditional representation of Cardenden as lacking significance, and whose inhabitants are in need of being rescued from their provincialism and insignificance. As Rankin has one of his fictional characters observe in *Dead Souls* (1999, p. 243): "He seemed really interested in Cardenden. I told him off, thought he was taking the mickey." For Rankin, then, significance and meaningfulness are unequally distributed and this hierarchical geography of significance structures Rebus's perception so that a kind of *spatialisation of modernity* cleanses villages and non-urban settings of significance so as to 'essentialise' and frame Cardenden according to an a priori template that is conveniently at hand, so that there is little reason, save some Rorie-like idiosyncratic curiosity in backwardness, for a young writer to look to his post-industrial village for anything of literary significance.

In this scheme of perception, the consequences for 'writing Cardenden' is that Cardenden is fated to be perceived and represented as a place containing 'nothing' populated by 'nobodies' and is unable to appear as anything more than a cipher for already highly-structured perceptions, so that the idea that Cardenden may be a source of literary merit or interest is a non-starter and never contemplated. As a result of this perception, 'being local' is a predicament and the only solution is to leave. In a purely speculative manner, then, we can say that insofar as Rankin sees 'nothing' in Cardenden, his perception of his locality has entered into his self-understanding as a writer so that the fictional police Inspector Rebus character is the compensating *somebody* or *alter ego* who lives in the compensating *somewhere* of Edinburgh. In this regard the words of Kavanagh (2003, cited in Glen and Hubbard 2008, p. xv) are worth recalling:

Parochialism and provincialism are direct opposites. The provincial has no mind of his own; he does not trust what his eyes see until he has heard what the metropolis – towards which his eyes are turned – has to say on any subject…The parochial mentality on the other hand is never in any doubt about the social and artistic validity of his parish. All great civilisations are based on parochialism…it requires a great deal of courage to be parochial.

If Rankin himself instantiates in his own life the predicament he ascribes to his fictional Rebus character, this predicament is something that has not featured as material for his fiction i.e. the struggle to produce literature from 'nothing,' and we may say that while belonging to the '79 generation and having seen the extension of the *cultural franchise* to the '79 generations thanks to affluence and which Rankin has clearly taken up in exemplary fashion, and while wholeheartedly sympathizing with Rankin's desire to run from 'the data' (see Chapter 3), he backs his writing into a corner where he must either stay and firmly base his writing upon this ethnographic reality of locality, or leave and 'write from plenty' and let his native cup as a departure point for writing pass him by. While Rankin pulls no punches and adverts to the 'nothingness,' from a strictly sociological point of view Rankin is regressive when viewed within the context of the post-British

'79 generational trajectory of 'producers of culture' such as The Proclaimers, Deacon Blue, Irvine Welsh, Gordon Clegg, Gregory Burke, Laura Hird, Andrew O'Hagan, Ross Sinclair and Alan Bissett etcetera, insofar as he is not part of the emergence of the new wave of working-class literature and culture and politics that took place during the nineteen-eighties and nineties, so that if Rorie and Houston failed to attain a conceptualisation of working-class *dasein* and the unique density of 'being local' in the industrial period, Rankin has reproduced this 'failure of representation' in the post-industrial era. While Rankin's depiction of Cardenden is typical of the '79 generation insofar as he does not shrink from a critique of local absence, Rankin's writing to date is fated not to have the sociological significance it otherwise might have.

Insofar as other writers, however, have taken up the challenge of producing a 'literature from nothing,' the playwright David Greig (in Billingham 2007, pp. 77-78) when asked why he had written his play *Europe* (1995) gave the revealing answer:

> There were two things concerned with the genesis of the play – one was travelling through Fife and the old Scottish mining villages there and realising that the trains didn't stop there anymore – they just went whizzing by. I suddenly thought: the really violent places aren't the inner cities but these deserted towns. I then tried to imagine myself living in them: I thought it would be intolerable. Why did these places exist, why did people still stay there, why didn't people just f\*\*\* off? I don't mean that aggressively to the people of those towns. So that was the central question that came to my mind: why were these towns deserted and who was still living there and why?

Like the great literary figures of Joyce in Ireland and MacDiarmid in Scotland, Greig is challenging himself as a producer of culture to assume the task of representing his people by taking upon himself the burden of their condition, and the merit of Greig's comments lies in his resolve to constitute his 'production of culture' via meeting the challenge of 'writing from nothing,' of rendering something of artistic and cultural merit *upon this basis*, as opposed to removing himself to the metropolitan centre and writing from its abundance. It is interesting to note that just as novelists, playwrights and artists face the decision of where to look for their material, social researchers likewise have to choose where to conduct their research and in this regard Nadel-Klein (1997) has argued that what little ethnography has been done in Scotland has predominantly been done in the Highlands and Islands, so that academic research has constructed Scotland along the received dividing line of the 'exotic other' of the Highlands and the familiar 'at home' of the Lowlands. As Condry has observed (in Wight 1993, p. 2):

> Too much attention has been paid to the islands and Highlands, and too little to the anthropological study of the Lowlands and the urban areas. Despite the theoretical rejection of the urban – rural dichotomy researchers have remained firmly encamped in rural fields in the far north.

Within the research literature on Fife this representational divide has been reproduced as it has been in the picturesque coastal villages of the East Neuk of Fife, as opposed to the mining areas of central and west Fife, that has attracted the attentions of researchers, so that still relevant are Harvie's comments (in Wight 1993, p. 1):

> An unlovely 'third Scotland' sprawled from South Ayrshire to Fife...old industrial settlements that ought to have been evacuated and demolished...but were preserved... Somewhat isolated, ignored, lacking city facilities or country traditions – even lacking the attentions of sociologists.

In a similar vein Nairn (1988, pp. 80-1) has neatly summarised how Fife is represented according to a well-established binary manner of imagining this old province:

> Eastern Fife appears in holiday brochures; middle and western Fife in the unemployment statistics. With its

abandoned mines and defeated or problem industries it is an area typical of Scotland's economic malaise...Not many foreign visitors turn off the prescribed Tourist Route to see this zone of dereliction... where else in Europe could one find a 'High Street' quite like Methil's, not marked but blighted from one end to another by closure and disuse? This is not aboriginal poverty, an ancient or customary deprivation. It is the wreckage of quite recent prosperity: a small, once confident world broken by its fall from modernity, and now condemned to the grey fungus of loss and second-best.

By definition, the author of fiction is at liberty to represent or reject reality, while the ethnographer or sociologist has to justify any decision not to engage with this phenomenology of 'nothing' in a sustained manner because not to do so is to be open to the criticism of ethnographic refusal (Ortner 1995). As with Houston where the paradox was observed that, being the 'captive' of a particular long durée view of history which prevented any serious engagement with the cut and thrust of history, so in Rankin there is this same lack of engagement with real subjectivity despite his voluminous writing. While Rorie, Houston and Corrie had the abundance of industrial reality to conceal the question of 'nothing,' Rankin is writing after de-industrialization and is clearly aware of this challenge, yet his many novels opt for rhetorical genuflections to 'nothingness' instead of meeting the challenge of transforming Nothing into a Story of Being, and so there is a 'flight from particularity' in Rankin and a turning away from locality so that Houston, Rorie and Rankin have produced a literature that condemns Cardenden, and by implication every industrial and every post-industrial locale, to an unthought and unrepresented existence. Hence, just as there are accounts of locality with all of its history and politics and 'thick' ethnographic particularity removed so that locality becomes a 'timeless' Brigadoon that is 'out of history' (Craig 1996), so even among '79 generation post-industrial era writers there is a surprisingly similar refusal to engage in particularity and which is alienated from anything approaching a holistic engagement with the realm of meaning upon the basis of a particular locality, and so do not even approach representations of localities with the realism and miserabilism of the likes of Irvine Welsh's *Trainspotting* (1993).

It is because not every writer has the vision of the likes of James Joyce and the talent to write a work of fiction such as *Ulysses* (1922) that the challenges of 'writing particularity' are long-standing within Western literature. Another signature challenge faced by the writer is the unavoidable 'alienation' from self the writer must endure in the use of language, thought and writing because the writer must suffer as he puts his shoulder to the task of translating a particular *dasein* into its adequate literary form. From Hegel we take the sharp sense that between 'being' and its 'representation' there is the gulf of language and conceptualization which are their own sui generic realities and which require their own specific labours and talent if the chasm that separates 'reality' and 'representation' is to be bridged. However, not every writer is defined by the desire to bring these two disparate realities or mediums into alignment through the practice of writing, and it is precisely because being and its textual representation are radically discontinuous that a writer is perfectly at liberty to refuse to align reality and writing. In this regard, then, insofar as Rankin is viewed sociologically he is defined by his misalignment with the signs of the times and is in no position to illuminate contemporary Scotland. Insofar as Rankin sees Cardenden only through the 'mirror of production' his literary depiction of locality can only see the absence of the industrial era.

To this structuring of perception I would add that Rankin only sees Cardenden through 'the mirror of Edinburgh' and that as a writer he does not show the necessary act of will to engage with the task of articulating a provincial or regional, or even parochial consciousness, so that in his *literary ontology* or landscape there is only oblivion outwith the metropolitan centre, and his literary consciousness not only offers no variety on the dominant metropolitan consciousness but extends its dominion to the provinces. While this sociological criticism of Rankin's fiction is inherently 'unfair' and does not detract from his undoubted abilities as a novelist, this criticism regarding the 'sociological purchase' of Rankin's oeuvre comes into play not only in light of the celebrated dictum of Alastair Gray that "if a city hasn't been used by an artist, not even the inhabitants live there imaginatively" (1981, p. 243), but insofar as Rankin strays into making sociological claims by stating his aim in his fictional writing is "to explain Scotland to myself, to fellow Scots and to the outside world."[37]

While representations of Cardenden in terms of decline are easy and readily available, in fact are clichéd because any village émigré relocating to any city at any point in time has these representations ready and waiting for him upon leaving local life behind for – pick one's cliché – metropolitan colour or urban energy, such representations of de-industrial decline act as a valid *departure point* for the task of articulating what kind of self-consciousness is now possible for post-industrial localities across Scotland. In addressing this question what is certain is that those who live in the national capital are hardly best placed to articulate this local form of historical consciousness. My aim in the following chapters, then, to paraphrase Marx and Heidegger, is to construct a local consciousness in possession of its unique ownmost self and tasks, so that the difference between myself and Rankin's representation of Cardenden is that I centre decline or 'nothing' within Cardenden itself and proceed to give an account of locality's ownmost tasks and ownmost consciousness that owes nothing to metropolitan ontologies and that is a trajectory that is uniquely its own and which is not readily available or conveniently 'at hand' because it is not copied from elsewhere.

The aim then is to construct Cardenden's own mirror by which its inhabitants may see their true selves and offer Cardenden its own density and free its residents from the modernist self-consciousness by offering a model of what post-industrial consciousness might be and what might be the consequences of this for their 'being local' and 'being provincial' at this time.

---

[37] See interview with Rankin on http://www.ianrankin.com/interview.htm (June 2001).

The aim is to make Cardenden 'coequal with itself' and bring post-industrial Cardenden to a sustainable self-consciousness that spans and encompasses the industrial and the post-industrial eras. In achieving this representation, the hope is to offer some ballast and resistance to any portrayal of locality where its very existence is the result of macro-economic forces which have the power to bring Cardenden into existence *ex nihilo* and have the power to end that existence. The aim is to resist the ontological violence of any imaginary whereby Cardenden has no 'secondary nature' of its own and where locality exerts no causality of its own, and so locality is void not only of its properly 'natural good' or perfection but has no literary or even transcendental worth to its inhabitants. From the standpoint of an 'integral representation' and an integral sociology that I will develop in later chapters, these views are unacceptable and are to be resisted.

What is clear from this opening chapter is that the industrial era has gone but its impact upon the local imagination is still felt. My task in the following chapters as another representer of Cardenden coming after this history of representation is to overcome its failures and address the omissions which I have identified and criticised. There is a textual history of engagement with working-class *dasein*, culture and locality stretching from 1894 to the present and these writings highlight the challenge which the ethnographer faces if he is to take his stance upon 'nothing;' a crucial problematic for rendering post-industrial working-class localities, *dasein* and *mitsein*. Perhaps the most salient point, however, is that with the exception of Rankin this tradition of writing is more or less unknown to locals themselves and does not inform their consciousness;[38] something that was brought home to me when going into Cardenden public library in October 1998 and, enquiring of the (English) librarian what the library held on Joe Corrie, I was met with the reply: "Who?" Furthermore, obtaining a copy of Corrie's *Black Earth* (1939)

---

[38] While Corrie's work is no longer performed, local nationalist MSP Tricia Marwick and the 7:84 Theatre Company were promoting a tour of Corrie's theatre works across Scotland in 2002. (See *Fife Free Press*, 31 May 2001).

involved having to request it on Special Loan from the Bodlean library in Oxford (England) and, upon its arrival six weeks later, I was not able to take the book out of the library so that, due to a combination of the part-time opening hours of the library and when I was free to go to the library, I could only consult the text for one hour every Thursday evening; and when the date for the book's return arrived I had to initiate the lending process all over again. When added to this is the absence of any of Rorie's writings in the local library, there is a clear failure at curating the history of writing about Cardenden so that, despite the existence of the elements to constitute a literary tradition, 'Cardenden' has no (literary) consciousness of itself.

In the following chapters my own commitment to locality involves the attempt to think locality using *local mirrors* and thereby accord locality its own place within a non-metropolitan geography or a non-metropolitan ontology of space, as well as a local conception and form of 'historical consciousness' adequate to the post-industrial era. To resort to 'the mirror of Edinburgh' and to resort to clichés colludes with emptying locality and reproduces the hegemony of an urban metropolitan imaginary in the provinces. While recognising 'absence,' 'failure' and even 'nothingness' is essential, the deeper intention is a ground-clearing exercise as a prelude to a new imagining of a post-industrial and local engagement with the challenge of 'being modern' and 'being national' at this unprecedented point in time. Informants advising "there's nothing here" is a challenge to think the condition of 'being local' without the clichés of industrialism and to produce a kind of writing that is stripped of the full, busy and thick industrial fullness of the 1895-1985 industrial era. However, the labour of rendering 'something from nothing' is just the beginning of redressing a long history of failure to give an account of the subjective structuration of working-class *dasein* and looming large in this endeavour is successfully rendering the 'world of work,' and it is to this task that I now turn as I explore working-class structuration by outlining the 'subjectless practice' of manual work where, unlike the failure to escape nature and reach the aesthetic realm discussed earlier, for example, the argument will be that there is a realm of reality and structuration infallibly achieved via labour where not only is it impossible for the ethnographer to postulate an escape from 'nature' but it is vital to imagine no such thing, if the ethnographer is to engage with lives lived immersed in nature and immersed in the body as sui generic realities that act as 'keystones' upon which is built an entire edifice of individuation and sociation.

# 2

# The Being Brought About by Doing

'One *is*' what one does.

Heidegger 1962, p. 283

## 2.1 Physical Socialisation: The World Made Flesh

While working as a manual operative with *East of Scotland Water* authority during fieldwork a routine maintenance task at the wastewater treatment plant in the coastal village of East Wemyss was hosing down a fine screen with a high pressure hose to remove the layer of scum over the screen's wire meshing. The meshing had to be regularly cleaned to allow the water to pass through to the next stage in the treatment process and, when sufficiently clean and compliant with statutory Scottish Environment Protection Agency (SEPA) standards, the water was pumped into the Firth of Forth estuary separating Fife and Edinburgh where it would be dispersed by tidal currents into the North Sea. To clean the steel mesh plating the drum, water was passed through a generator to produce sufficient pressure to blast the scum from the large rotating screen which filtered out solid human waste, rags, condoms, sanitary towels and various domestic and industrial waste products from the water entering the plant via the main inlet channel. The hose carrying the pressurized water was attached to a 'gun-piece' with a trigger which 'fired' the water at the steel mesh, and such was the pressure that the hose constantly vibrated under the force of the water rushing through, that two strong hands and the continual application of upper body strength was needed to keep the gun-piece under control when the trigger was pressed.

Because of the level of noise and health hazards from exposure to harmful levels of bacteria associated with human and industrial waste, this routine maintenance task was performed by one man wearing a special bodysuit and mask. Each week the task took approximately thirty minutes to complete and, having done the job many times previously, I was not expecting to be interrupted and as the only effort required was physical, I used the time to mentally switch off, letting the rotating drum pass under the action of the jet of water while my supervisor (Rory McNeill) busied himself checking instrumentation panels and taking various readings.

With the plant checked and maintained we signed and dated the log book and returned to the van to head off to the next treatment plant in Leven on our route that particular day (Monday 19th June 2000). As we drove off I intended to use the fifteen or so minutes driving time between East Wemyss and Leven to write down some thoughts that had occurred to me while working, and as I picked up a pen and shaped my hand to write, it suddenly began to shake uncontrollably. I immediately forcibly tensed my fingers, straightening and stretching them and then flexing my fingers by clenching my fist two or three times. At this, the shaking stopped. I shaped my hand to write again but, once more, my hand began to shake uncontrollably. Again, I stopped trying to write and straightened and tensed my hand, flexed my fingers and stretched and shook my hand and wrist for a few seconds. Once more I shaped my hand to write, and once more it began shaking uncontrollably. It then dawned on me that my hand was shaking because the writing position was mimicking the position required to hose down the screen, and that by assuming the writing shape my hand was triggering the 'memory' of work which was somehow still present within my arm and hand: attempting to write was evidencing the reality of embodiment and the content of embodiment, work.

I recall this incident as an example of *physical socialisation*, of how the body is affected by its practices and how in this particular context the external world or that which transcends the body, via practice, becomes immanent or part of human being or *dasein* through embodiment insofar as work structures the body of the worker; produces a physical structuration that in its being or ontology is independent of awareness or consciousness. In the same way as the body's production of sweat does not require awareness or permission from the worker, the body is an autonomous realm of reality and therefore socialisation or its own *medium of becoming*, so that manual labour is a source of structuration among those who perform manual labour; that the body or the 'kind of embodiment' of the labourer has its own *dasein* or being-in-the-world *which achieves itself within the worker* independently of his consciousness. In contrast to Castoriadis (1987, pp. 263-4) for whom, "The 'product' has to exist in and through the actual social imaginary before it can and in order to be 'real,'" the physical structuration of *dasein* that comes into being as a result of doing manual labour is in no need of recognition or discursive articulation to come into being, and the possessing of this physical structuration is not jeopardised by the absence of its discursive recognition. Finally, not only is the body its own autonomous reality and source of structuration but *the body is realistic* insofar as it encodes real objective experience i.e. does not construct or imagine the world but is passively constructed by the real world.

This agency of the world or the agency of practice upon *dasein* and the agency of one's practice in the world *upon oneself* illustrates Heidegger's point that " 'One *is*' what one does" (1962, p. 283) and critiques any ontology in which the environmentally 'ready-to-hand' is marginal or mere 'background' to understanding human being 'in the world;' that spectatorial or contemplative ontologies are fundamentally inadequate insofar as the power hose incident shows that ready-to-hand equipment 'answers back' and conditions *dasein*; the ready-to-hand *takes us 'in hand'* as much as we take tools and equipment into our hands. More particularly, an understanding of *human being* that fails to explicitly recognise this relationship between labour*ing* and be*ing* is not only unlikely to grasp working-class *dasein* but is likely to fundamentally misrecognise or misconstrue such being-in-the-world. In this regard the thoughts of Connerton (1989, p. 104) about "how bodies are variously constituted...the body is not seen equally clearly to be socially constituted in the sense that it is culturally shaped in its actual practices and behaviour...the body is socially constituted" are useful. Connerton (1989, p. 1) addresses the question of "how is the memory of groups conveyed and sustained?" and his answer is *bodily practices*.

Similarly, I propose that the life of manual labour is the 'mode of acquisition' *inter alia* of a linguistic habitus and a particular manner not only of being-in-the-world but a manner of comportment towards the world, a manner of interpreting and orienting oneself to the world or a kind of somatic hermeneutic. The natural body by becoming the socialised body via labour also takes its place alongside other labourers who have likewise become this socialised self previously, and have embodied this embodiment for various lengths of time; who have exercised their freedom and tastes and lived their lives alongside others upon the basis of this embodiment. Becoming this (embodied) self then is to acquire a particular means or medium of sociality or inter-personality, is to acquire an ontological likeness to others and to sow the seeds of the *dasein* and *mitsein* that the group has historically developed within the individual, and which the individual's own use of freedom and personal taste will develop throughout his life as he lives his life from within the medium of this embodiment. Across the generations and across the industrial and post-industrial eras and their changing occupational landscapes, then, the body and the life of manual labour is a medium of continuity and memory which can only be uncovered insofar as we highlight its consequences for language, comportment, mental and social life.

As a general definition or description, a life of manual labour is that which involves work – including unskilled, semi-skilled or skilled – which routinely involves performing short bursts of working until muscle exhaustion, followed by pauses or rests to allow the lactic acid built up in muscles to dissipate, before having to do more short bursts of work until muscle exhaustion sets in again and another build-up of lactic acid recedes by resting again. Any life where this is more or less performed on a daily basis is a life of manual labour and given this definition, a 'manual labourer' will include a skilled tradesman such as a bricklayer and such labourers will be acutely aware that, thanks to their practice of labour, there is a physical transformation of themselves as they notice that the body has to become accustomed to labour; that at first it is onerous and difficult and a continual subject of awareness and conversation with others, but also that the skin hardens and muscles become toned as the labourer becomes accustomed to work until, finally, his incarnation of his doing passes out of his awareness into the silence of his 'secondary nature,' the silence of the body accustomed to its social incarnation and the social practice of labour. If as a general statement we can agree that, "Neither our personal bodies nor our social bodies may be seen as natural, in the sense of existing outside the self-creating process called human labour" (Haraway 1991, p. 10), this is true in a pre-eminent way among manual workers insofar as their labouring 'in-forms' their *dasein*.

While there is a realm of reality brought into being by manual labour that exists outwith any reference to consciousness or the realm of meaning, this is not to imply "what it is that doing brings into being" (Castoriadis 1997, p. 168) is confined to the pre-linguistic biological realm of the body. Beyond physical structuration, then, the life of manual labour has consequences for the constitution and 'kind of psyche' that comes into being, has consequences for the *psychological being-in-the-world* of the labourer. If we extend the time-frame of performing work to include not only the few minutes after working with a high-pressure hose but a lifetime of work, and ask what other unsuspected consequences for *dasein* this enlarged period of time may entail, we might begin by noting manual workers evidence an earthy no-nonsense sensual 'immediatism' which it is not unreasonable to suppose is the result of the body being disciplined by performing labour over time, a disciplining of the body that includes a disciplining or 'repressing' of the psyche over time, and which is inevitably taken up by active freedom and choice to produce a particular structuring of 'personality.' If we take this 'immediatism' as an object of inquiry and ask what are its social grounds or its medium of acquisition (Connerton 1989), the answer is the life of waged labour and the body. The relentless physicality of work and its effects upon the psyche are taken up by the exercise of freedom and the play of circumstance where they 'in-form' the psyche and make the psyche into its image; a psyche constructed according to a 'homologisation' of physical and psychological selves that comes into being over time.

The dominant social practice of labouring, then, informs how the labourer relates to reality but is also a *gestalt* that is the medium through which the labourer constitutes his relationships and his realities.[39] While one can only speculate as to the many instances this 'informing via doing' will take over the course of a particular lifetime, in attempting to tackle the question of how the ethnographer can grasp the many consequences of performing manual labour and grasping the density and content of that which is embodied and its consequences for individuation and sociation, I propose that the self brought about by manual work or the 'worked self' is a *master of forms* and 'promiscuous' in its informing the *dasein* and *mitsein* of the worker thanks to it being enjoyed and taken up by freedom and the life of the group, and that the task is to capture something of its existential hegemony and 'promiscuity.' I argue that a particular human *dasein* that comes into being is the keystone that not only constructs a determinate ontology but must also be understood as functioning as a hermeneutical key for the consciousness and intentional life within the *dasein* characterised by a constant conforming of its

---

[39] In describing manual labour as responsible for brining into being a *gestalt* I define this term as a "configuration of sensations: strain, aches, and fatigue... thus, many physiological cues are involved, as well as memories of work situations and actual performances and the emotions associated with them... Motivation and emotions during the exercise may also influence perception and performance" (Borg 1998, p. 3).

'lifeworld' to the reality and exigencies of work. I argue that a process takes place within the individual that involves a reduction to an already long-established 'objective' working-class *dasein* and *mitsein* that is already established in others, and there is thereby formed a fundamental ontological horizon. Moreover, because human beings are reflexive and free, manual workers develop a *worked-self-based* consciousness which instantiates a kinship among its many behaviours and its many relations to a range of realities which includes the realm of meaning, and which impacts upon or in-forms the life of the psyche. If this is the abstract argument, the concrete ethnographic aim to verify this argument will be to reveal and capture a particular way of human being characterised by a series of nested realities or structurations or confinements to the real which involves:

1) a reduction to the body
2) a reduction to time
3) a reduction to social structure

Our opening anecdote from working during fieldwork confirms that "the past is...sedimented in the body" (Connerton 1989, p. 72) but is also evidence of how much that is real can quickly pass out of existence and leave no trace of itself. In this regard Connerton has written: "[I]ncorporating practices...are largely traceless and that, as such, they are incapable of providing a means by which any evidence of a will to be remembered can be left behind" (1989, p. 102). The effects of working seem peculiarly at risk of disappearing from the consciousness of the worker through time and in regard to uncovering that which is ordinarily subjugated, Connerton refers to kinaesthetic practice which is a kind of practice that (1989, p. 29) "is as nearly as possible without reflection," and a kind of doing or practice that may be described as a non-conceptual kind of knowing so that "it is our body which 'understands'" (Connerton 1989, p. 95) and this explains why in most situations in life there is no weighing up of alternatives and no reflection upon consequences for our habits of behaviour are not propositions to be learned, so that only by "living with people who habitually behave in a certain manner...[do we see] that neither the idea of a rule nor the idea of reflectiveness is essential to it" (1989, p. 30).

I begin from "labour process accounts of worker subjectivity" (Tanner et al. 1992, p. 439) and share "the insistence of labour process theorists that the point of production is the key source of worker consciousness in capitalist society" (Tanner et al. 1999, p. 439). However, while Braverman's *Labour and Monopoly Capitalism* (1974) and labour process theory has exerted a lasting influence upon the sociology of work, I also have much sympathy with the view of critics who assert the "labour process is incapable of theoretical growth because of its...fixation on the workplace" (Tanner et al. 1992 p. 439) because I share the view that a preoccupation with the 'extrinsic' question of whether or not the worker is 'exploited' and a more or less obvious agenda to reach political and policy conclusions, that was endemic to such literature prior to the fall of the Berlin Wall in 1989 and the end of Marxism as an alternative to the free-market economy, more often than not resulted in the inability to produce an adequate phenomenology of labour. If I have produced an ethnography of manual workers thanks to having worked full-time for a year and a half during fieldwork and because of the fundamental position that a focus upon the workplace is essential to the extent that ignorance of the workplace is fatal to the credibility of any subsequent analysis, I hope to avoid "the common reproach levelled by psychoanalysts at Marxists, that the latter speak as if a man has no psyche until he gets his first paycheque" (Sahlins 1976, p. 8n) as this is precisely the proposition that I want to explore: that the manual labourer's psyche is *formally* constituted as itself via the web of relations entered into via his paid employment, and the relations at least symbolised by the receiving of the paycheque.

I do not pretend to know whether the free-market economy is unjust or a particular wage-capital relationship is unjust. Likewise, the choice between a focus upon the workplace or a focus upon wider cultural considerations has always been for me a 'signature weakness' of traditional Marxist and positivistic sociology that I wish to avoid. My experience of work varies from day labour in a mechanised factory where I knew no-one to a workplace where work was mediated via 'thick belonging' thanks to family connections to fellow workers stretching back to childhood and school days and shared family/workplace relations with fellow workers stretching back to my father and the fathers of work colleagues. With the exception of working as a day labourer on potato-picking squads and a few weeks working at *Kettle Produce* in the summer of 1998, I never experienced a 'pure workplace' that could be described as free from cultural ties of kinship and locality. In this regard Tanner et al. (1992) have much right on their side when they argue the labour process approach has become sterile as a direct result of Braverman's original refusal to deal with the subjective aspects of class relationships. Hence, I take as my starting point Thompson's view (1990, cited in Tanner et al. 1992, p. 440) that inserting subjectivity and an adequate articulation of individuation into our accounts of workers is the "greatest task facing labour process theory" and align myself with those theorists of the labour process who frame the issue of worker subjectivity in terms of 'immanence' (Antonio 1981; Van den Berg 1988) as I too propose to take the path of immanence but not as a retrospective search for why a revolutionary working class has not appeared, but as preamble to a liberating act of self-understanding accomplished within language and thought, and then to subsequently consider this question in relation to a nationalist politics and as a basis for a Scottish modernity and, ultimately, as a basis for a renewed Christianity that is free from supernaturalism.

Prior to the fall of the Berlin Wall in 1989 and the triumph of neoliberalism in the nineteen-eighties, much ink was spilled in the attempt to explain why industrial workers across Europe and across the generations had failed to develop 'revolutionary consciousness.' Today, it seems no-one is interested in resurrecting this question, perhaps because history has given its answer and so it has been buried within the European imagination. However, those who remain interested in this question have a 'free run' at the problem and are free to take it back to its fundamental ground. In resurrecting this question I locate myself within what until recently was a mainstream concern of sociology, namely "The responses of workers – principally male manual workers – to industrial capitalism" (Tanner et al. 1992, p. 447), as I continue to share the "proposition that experiences at work and in the local community provided the raw materials out of which broader understandings of class-based inequality would develop" (Tanner et al. 1992, p. 447). However, while happy to locate myself within labour process theory and privilege "the confines of the workplace" (Tanner et al 1992, p. 448), I reject any idea of excluding other contextual information (generation, class, gender, nation etcetera) as non-empirical immaculate purism. Neither labour process theory nor every other theorist who has addressed himself to thinking about working-class *dasein* from Marx and Engels to Lukacs, Bourdieu and Charlesworth has produced a phenomenology of workers' consciousness or a phenomenology of labouring, far less an account of the worker's consciousness 'fully in act' thanks to a cognitional event of self-actualisation. While Lukacs's *History and Class Consciousness* ([1924] 1971) is the closest the Western mind has come to a proper estimation and articulation of this task, Tanner's (1992) failure to mention Lukacs signals Lukacs's failure and that of labour process theorists to provide such accounts. It seems to me, therefore, that the task of articulating the *dasein* brought into existence by labouring remains whole and entire.

## 2.2 The Reduction to Reality

> We call him Blister. He only shows up wance a' the work's done.
>
> Tim Colville
> Wastewater Worker

If the physical structuration of human being as a result of practicing manual labour is more or less straightforward to illustrate, evidencing in a convincing fashion how the *realm of meaning* as much as the physicality of working impacts upon the very constitution of embodiment is much more difficult, largely because those authorised to produce texts upon the body or embodiment are not more or less coerced or 'fated' to discourse upon embodiment because the freedom they enjoy to discourse and represent in the public realm is largely synonymous with the condition of being free from one's *body* evidencing one's (social) fate. When we read Marcel Mauss (1979, pp. 97-106) on 'body techniques,' for example, we find rather abstract considerations of something called *kinetics* and 'gesture systems,' while the edited collection *The Anthropology of the Body* (1977) sees ethnographers write about blushing, the skin, bodily products, female sexuality, dance, possession, initiation rites and bodily symbolism. Such themes and such texts do not contest but confirm the scepticism that meets the claim that *embodiment theory* is of real significance as, on the strength of such evidence, the reality of 'the body' is weak or marginal and certainly of insufficient importance to bear the weight of an entire ontology and to bear up the individual to his natural perfection, far less the supernatural life. It is the aim of this and subsequent chapters to make such an argument and erect an ontology upon embodiment, to articulate the being of embodiment and how physicality is structured by social structure, culture and freedom so as to form the 'cornerstone' upon which I will erect an account of a fully Scottish contextualised working-class *dasein* and then an account of this *dasein* fully 'in act.'

In affluent post-industrial societies the idea of economic activity as 'selling one's labour' has the feel of being a relic from the nineteenth century for more and more of the population, and so 'the body' becomes increasingly backgrounded for more and more people. Also, the body as the medium of repression and where one's social fate is registered and lived as one's destiny or fate seems likewise to be something of a relic insofar as 'the body' is seen as having been liberated from drudgery and necessity and scarcity, so that embodiment is increasingly experienced as the medium where we exercise choice, freedom, control and creativity.

The body throughout the 'dictatorship of scarcity' era was not only a fundamental medium of *dasein* but was a fundamental organising principle of politics and much of working-class political mobilisation owed its success to addressing the needs of the body because in the nineteenth and twentieth centuries the body-based politics of class gave materialist conceptions of class struggle not only their obvious and compelling legitimacy but their policy content. While the creation of the Welfare State and the political rise of the working classes and the Labour Party, as well as the social cohesion of post-war Britain relied upon the successful politicisation of the needs of the body in areas such as health and housing, this bodily-based coherence has been lost because affluence has made this 'body politics' obsolete thanks not only to the political agency of the working class but the free market's 'conquest of bread' (Kropotkin 1906). We no longer live in a society of scarcity but a society of affluence and a politics of affluence, so that our politics has lost its former coherence insofar as the working class do not politicise their cultural or geo-political conditions or mobilise upon the basis of symbolic goals.

This shift to affluence also fundamentally impacts upon sociology as labour or 'work' had been a standard sociological category in the investigation of Western societies throughout the twentieth century, so that the concept of post-industrial society means that an integral aspect of contemporary societies is the demise of manual labour from its former dominance. As McCrone has observed of today's occupational landscape: "[T]here are now more workers in the service class than in the manual working class for the first time in Scotland's history" (1992, p. 141). In this regard, I do not propose to contest such representations as there is no suggestion that this ethnography is relevant for the increasing percentage of the population that are far removed from the rigors and realities of the body and the life of manual labour. Similarly, having regularly sat in most of the local pubs and watched as local manual labourers send text messages back and forth to 'ex-pat' pipe-fitters from Cardenden and its environs working off-shore in Sierra Leone and elsewhere, for example, I am not oblivious to the evidence that the local is being globalised or that the "localisation of the context of proletarian life is radically in decline" (Schumann, cited in Offe 1985, p. 142). If the local is to be given its due density I recognise these 'de-localising' forces are at work.

Likewise, if I argue that work is a fundamental category of embodiment, it is not because I wish to negate the data but because I have conducted fieldwork among manual operatives and unskilled agricultural labourers, and this is the research context from which emerges observations that theorising the body without theorising work is theorising the body 'from nowhere' and is not theorising the body at all.

Also, by way of parenthesis we might note that what was once referred to as *the woman's movement* has similarly the feel of being another relic from a bygone age as this politics of identity that was founded upon embodiment and the reality of physical differences between men and women has come to an end, not because of any failings of its white middle-class leadership or any interior conversion or change of heart among men, but because affluence and women's entry into the post-manual occupational landscape has more or less swept away the objective social basis for the women's movement so that, once again, there is scepticism towards the idea that the (female) body today can be the medium of a 'secondary nature' or a standpoint for a hermeneutic and a standpoint or basis for a different politics.

If a dis-embodied feminism appears vacuous and wilful, and if feminism welcomes an 'immaculate' sexuality free from embodiment and the issues of pregnancy and maternity as fundamental structurations of female *dasein*, this is a feminism that is also alienated from class, poverty, manual labour and material conditions that is fated to become a cipher for an academic game reserved for middle-class white women reproducing a politics of identity which is more or less fated to lack sociological purchase and relevance, and which explains the crisis of third generation feminism and the exhaustion of the women's movement. In Chapter 5 I will argue that a (traditional) politics of class is alive and well in Scotland because of its 'post-materialist' alignment with a politics of nationality and its alignment with powerful geo-political events in the era of affluence. Similarly, it seems likely feminism can only survive insofar as it becomes allied with 'extrinsic' forces and until such alliances are formed the 'liberation' of feminism from the female body and the invention of 'gender' as a post-material re-foundation of the woman's movement will only convince those with 'metaphysical' tastes for non-empirical rationalist myths such as 'patriarchy' to retain some purchase upon the imagination.

More broadly, the exhaustion of the workers' movement and then feminism signals how the imagining of the European project of modernity in the era of scarcity, whether in the guise of class-based materialism or in the guise of feminism, or secularism or rationalism or socialism has run dry, so that the very survival and constitution of the project of European modernity requires a post-material or new holistic foundation that simultaneously involves a turn to culture and the return to an older conception of modernity that is more appropriate for the era of affluence. I will develop the argument that there is a close and more or less direct relationship between the recent decline in the social significance of the body and what is known as the 'crisis of the West' because convincing accounts of the body are exceptional today because those who live embodiment as their social destiny are hardly ever in a position to theorise this condition. As with their female feminist contemporaries, male academics instantiate a liberation from *the body as destiny* and their experience of embodiment is more the result of their private post-manual strategies than a fate they could not escape.

While the occupational landscape described by McCrone indicates the increasing dis-alignment of the world of work from 'the body' and a world of post-manual or clean labour, my fieldwork location meant I was more or less fated to argue that manual labour remains a fundamental explanatory category for individuation and sociation, and that an understanding of labour is an integral part of understanding other aspects of contemporary working-class politics and culture, and the world of work still dominates the day to day experiences and life of the villagers with manual labour of some description remaining central to this world, and it is upon this basis that I contest Lutz's (1988, p. 4) assertion that there is "no privileged route to some underlying and unmediated psychophysical emotional reality" as the world of work remains such a 'privileged route' because it is a necessary daily practice that informs the construction of affectivity.

Expressed more philosophically, in turning to *embodiment* I follow Gabriel Marcel's (2001) rejection of the Cartesian cogito and the 'philosophy of consciousness' tradition and reject approaches to the body which take the standpoint of an *attitude spéculaire*. If no-one can spectate another's being and so can not generate the categories by which to grasp another's *dasein*, this truism is all the more appropriate when the *dasein* brought about by the life of manual labour is the particular object of inquiry. More generally, occupying a position of power is often fatal for original thinking insofar as to refuse someone's particularity is to refuse the labour of thinking them in favour of a will to power which wishes to make every potential other into an already known image i.e. a prefabricated category. The method used to extricate my account of embodiment from the snare of power and the errors of pure reason and objectivism[40] has been expressed poetically by Whitman when he wrote: "I do not ask the wounded person how he feels, I myself become the wounded person" (cited in Hall 1968, p. 60), as my view is one can only generate the relevant data on embodied *dasein* by becoming that *dasein* and by experiencing this positionality and experiencing what there is to be experienced from this positionality.

However, in the previous chapter we saw that what may be termed the 'bourgeois gaze' is not exclusive to members of the middle class, as a working-class individual may well share the spectatorial 'bourgeois' gaze upon embodiment as there I argued Corrie illustrates how the task of representation is a sui generic reality with its own exigencies, so that simply being working class is not enough to ensure its adequate representation, even in a writer whose aim is to write about the world he knows best. It seems to me that to adequately orient oneself to this task of translation is to reproduce within one's own intellectual development Merleau-Ponty's rejection of the vocabulary of the philosophy of consciousness tradition and focus upon that for which there is no name in traditional philosophy (Lakoff and

---

[40] "Experience is not an objective fact. A scientific fact need not be experienced" (Laing 1982, p. 9).

Johnston 1999). If there is progress from Cartesian rationalism to embodiment theory, it is instructive that Lakoff and Johnston's *Philosophy in the Flesh* (1999) purports to achieve a turning to the body yet never frees itself from pre-sociological thinking about embodiment and reproduces the usual flight from particularity thanks to the absence of any consideration of work as a fundamental way of incarnating the reality of embodiment. Indeed, the same criticism may be aimed at Merleau-Ponty's category of the 'flesh,' as unless there is a turning to the labour experience, accounts of working-class *dasein* seem fated to remain stuck within a 'philosophy of consciousness' paradigm because the merely discursive disavowal of this paradigm is not enough.

Also, as a direct result of being fated to imagine itself free of social determination, the 'bourgeois' gaze is more or less fated to be tempted by the 'culturalism' of Geertz or the post-structuralism of Derrida (1976) that imagines *dasein* is akin to a 'readable' text whose meaning can be accessed cognitively via the act of decoding like the reader learning to read a new language. This idea that one can read an other's ontology is an illusion that is typical of every literati and is the antithesis to my own view that to learn the 'language' of working-class *dasein* one must instantiate the class relation to the totality over time before it can appear as data onto one's horizon. Because any contextualised *dasein* cannot be spectated, every kind of gaze remains inadequate even after the end of positivism and the embracing of reflexivity and the (rhetorical) end of universalism, as there remains the defining relation to the 'totality' and the fact that different relations to the real or 'totality' remain *class relations* so that the positionality of each class cannot be spectated and to propose to spectate, far less know, an *essentially non-speculative reality that is enacted via praxis* is the fundamental methodological error responsible for body-free and class-free accounts of reflexivity in much of the social science literature. As Sahlins (1995) and MacIntyre (1989) have argued, different classes mean different realities and different objectivities, rationalities and truths.

Hoberman (1984, p. 119) identifies a "renunciation of the body" among the academic left with Western social theory having simultaneously required for its very existence and having been disadvantaged as a result of being the product of a leisured relation to material conditions, and Claus Offe has questioned whether work remains "the key sociological category" (1985, pp. 129-150), and usefully draws our attention to the alleged decentering of work as a source of self. If I develop the position that work remains a key sociological category that must be accompanied by theoretical attention to developing the subjective category of the 'worked self' as a key phenomenological category of contextual *dasein*, it is because I spent much of fieldwork among manual workers.

Articulating the being brought about by labouring, however, is done without any wish to make universalist claims that the continuing centrality of work is true for every member of the working class, far less other social classes. Beginning from the minimalist position that manual work informs the manual labourer, the aim is to overcome the status quo long identified by Marx (1970, p. 121) when he wrote: "The chief defect of all hitherto existing materialism (that of Feuerbach included) is that the thing, reality, sensuousness, is conceived only in the form of the object or of contemplation, but not as sensuous human activity, practice, not subjectively," because, despite Marx having written these words in 1845, the fact remains that even a theorist and empirical researcher like Bourdieu fails to give a phenomenology of work, so that the long-standing failure of intellectuals to give an adequate account of working-class *dasein* remains. This failure is undoubtedly sourced in the fact that there is very little that is spectatorial or speculative about working-class *dasein* as fundamentally it is enacted via practices tied to a particular occupation of social space and can not be known speculatively either by the working class themselves or the observing onlooker.

It is thanks to reflection upon the practice of manual labouring that abstract points such as it is through practice that the external objective realm becomes internalised and subjective through embodiment or, thanks to embodiment existence becomes essence, become rather mundane statements of the obvious. What is less obvious and certainly not mundane, however, is to systematically develop the notion of *a worked self* where the body answers aporias of pure reason such as the binarism of the subjective and objective or the individual and the social. My opening anecdote concerning working with a high-pressure hose then is an ethnographic answer to Hegel's analysis of the hand and his question whether the hand is an object for me or is part of me as subject, and his conclusion that the "inner and outer in this way fall apart [as the body is] this mediating term uniting inner and outer" (1967, p. 343).

Recalling the incident at East Wemyss usefully illustrates the fact that whatever the being brought about by labouring is, it is not an objective reality that is objectively 'out there' for the researcher to come and see and 'gather' as data as he might pick daisies that are objectively there waiting for him in a meadow; the being brought about by doing is never observed and never known by the non-labourer as it is a reality that only exists to the extent that it is enacted, brought about at the end of a process, of acting or labouring over time. The body knows what hard work is like, and does not need a conceptualisation of it to know labouring is arduous. When one's body is tired and one's fellow worker is tired, there is the shared agreement to 'take it easy.' There is no 'objective' means of knowing the worker is hard-working or lazy as the body is the only means available to answer these questions or, better, because it answers these questions, they never explicitly arise as questions. Only thanks to his body does the worker know he has worked hard, so that when a boss tells him different, his body's knowledge robs the boss of the authority of knowing. The worker, thanks to his body, becomes something the supervisor doesn't know; becomes something the supervisor is not.

That the body has its habits, reflexes, processes and conditioned responses that never require consciousness in order to be is not disputed. But what does it mean to say that the body is a source of knowledge or that the body knows? Is there non-conceptual knowledge? And what is the content of such non-conceptual knowledge? For example, is the reality of 'being dominated' or 'being dominant' a condition that by definition is propositional or is it only known via embodiment? Likewise, if above and beyond the purely physical changes that come about as a result of working there develops a particular *psychological being-in-the-world* as a result of 'doing through time,' then this again will presumably not be 'objective data' objectively available to be observed and known by the non-labourer. As the next section will illustrate, the evidence for the existence of an embodied *dasein* or *worked self* is not sourced in having thought about cleaning a rotating drum in a wastewater treatment plant or from having watched my charge-hand clean the drum or having interviewed my chargehand about his work. If the *attitude spéculaire* is unable to suspect or guess at the being brought about by doing, so the body too is passive insofar as it can not conjure up what the hand both grasps and is grasped by. Because the body is the primary 'material condition' of labour, it is an autonomous source of structuration and has its own being-in-the-world and adaptation to the life of manual work *which achieves itself* because it does not become real because it is represented or recognised or brought to awareness as a *res cogitans*, but rather is embodied and sensuous i.e. "is embodied, not represented" (Calhoun et al. 1993, p. 54), and to empirically evidence this non-objective realm of data it is necessary to enter and describe the world of manual labour.

## *Kettle Produce, Back Shift (5 p.m.–2 a.m.)*

On Friday 30 March 1997 I am in Cowdenbeath Job Centre looking for work and spot an advert for workers for Kettle Produce at Orkie Farm beside Freuchie (Fife). I enquire about the job to a member of staff and am given a telephone number to ring and told to ask for Yvonne. I ring the number and ask for Yvonne but am told Yvonne is not there. I explain that I am calling about "getting a start," and ask if I can speak to someone. Initially, I am asked to call back in half an hour before the person adds: "It's a pity you didn't call a wee bit earlier as folk are getting picked up at half-three." Sensing there is an opening I say, "I have my car. Can I just arrive for five and talk to someone?" The person says that would be okay, and there follows details about how to

111

get to Orkie Farm some twenty miles away. After being given the directions I am told to turn up at quarter to five and speak to Happy. "Happy?"' I ask, to confirm I had heard correctly. "Aye, that's the boy's nickname," I am told. "And who am I speaking to?" I ask. "John Reilly."

At about four-fifteen I arrive at Orkie Farm and park in a large and rather empty car park. Once parked I look around to get my bearings and then go into a door to the right of a much larger doorway that is the main entrance to what I will soon learn to call 'the shed' where the vegetables are processed. As I enter the door I go up a flight of stairs and ask the first person I meet where I can find Yvonne or John Reilly. Both are not there I am told. I then ask where I can find Happy. "Don't know. Try in the personnel there," I am told. I go in the direction of where the person pointed and give my story to someone else, and am told to wait for Happy to arrive "in a blue transit van." Back outside I wait. After about twenty minutes a blue transit van arrives into the car park and a few workers get out. I look at the boy driving; it's a warm day and he has an open shirt, showing his chest, tattoos and sun tan. I approach and ask the question I had been trying to find a way of avoiding asking: "Are you Happy?" "No" he replies. I'm then told to wait for a blue transit van but this time one without windows, and at about ten to five a blue transit van with no side windows arrives into the car park.

As I follow the van to where it parks, I see a pair of feet with white socks and no shoes with jeans and calves hanging out the front passenger seat window, and the sight makes me think of a trapeze artist using the base of the window frame as a swinging bar. Once parked, I make my way to the driver's side and begin to explain my presence. The driver cuts me short: "You're Paul?" "Aye," I reply. The driver explained he had received a call to say I'd be here. "So, you're Happy?" I asked. "No, that's him there," the driver replied, motioning with his head to the owner of the two dangling feet I had spied earlier. At this, Happy, without moving or opening his eyes, told the driver (Jim) to look out a form for me. Jim then rummaged for and retrieved a form in the glove compartment and began looking for a pen, which he eventually located attached to the rear view mirror from which hung a pair of Rosary beads and other Catholic devotional paraphernalia. Jim handed me the form which as far as I could make out was from the Inland Revenue. In the space beside 'Job Title' Happy told me to put down 'Agricultural Labourer.' The 'Personal Details' section which the form indicated were to be supplied by the employer I was told to supply myself. As the form required my bank sort code details I took out my wallet to retrieve my cashline card and after reading out my sort code to Jim he asked: "Is that bank e Scotland, Main Street, Cardenden?" "Naw, St. Andrews Square, Edinburgh," I said. At this, one of the workers (Rab) seated in the back of the van asked: "What were you daen afore ye came here? Hope it wisnae Saughton." I replied, "Ah wis on the dole," to which Rab replied: "Oh its only lazy bastards that are on the dole." "It's better than work," I said. "No it f***in isnae. Nae money!" said Rab. Once the form was complete I was told to take it to Yvonne in the office. Back in the office, as I chatted briefly with one of the office staff about the need to fill in the form I was told: "It's law. There's no such thing as casual labour now. If there's nae paper there's nae payslip. Just check yer bank fir yer pay." I then asked: "For tax purposes, should I not send you my P 45?" "We jist put you on emergency tax code. If you send us your P 45 then fine. Otherwise you just have to claim it all back yourself at the end e the tax year."

When I returned to the car park I was handed a coat and hair net which Jim made a point of telling me as we proceeded to the main shed for the start of the shift were to be worn at all times. As soon as we entered 'the shed' I felt the cold air. Jim took charge of me and showed me up a short flight of steps beside a conveyor belt. At this particular time the crop being processed was carrots and Jim instructed me: "The split ones, the broken ones, the rotten ones etcetera, get rid of," taking a few examples of rejected carrots lying around on the floor between the silent machinery to show me the kind of carrots not wanted. In the minute or two left before the shift began, I looked around to see there were four belts and on each side of the belts workers had stationed themselves ready to process carrots, and to the left of the belts where the workers were standing were other belts and machinery that brought the carrots to the workers. At the far left of the building were large doors where lorries carrying loads of carrots would reverse and tip out their cargo into large vats of cold water where the carrots were washed before they were then placed by machine onto the black conveyor belts for distribution to the four belts to be processed by hand. At each work station the carrots had to be quality checked by workers before they fell into crates, with all substandard carrots being removed. After the carrots had made their way past the sorters they were belted directly into wooden crates situated to the right of the workers. When any crate became full, the conveyor belt changed direction and the sorted carrots were belted into an empty crate that was always already waiting in position alongside the full crate. Finally, the full crate was forklifted into what were referred to as 'the chills,' refrigerated spaces where the sorted vegetables were stored before the final 'bagging' stage before being transported to retailers across the country.

Just before five p.m. two supervisors appeared and made their way to a raised platform where they stood highest of all, and from where they surveyed the machines and workers for the duration of the shift, only coming down from their perch if there was a problem to be dealt with. A whistle was blown to signal the start of the shift and immediately the machines roared into life and the feeder machine and the platform I was standing on began to vibrate. From the starting-up of the machines to carrots arriving to be sorted at my belt there was less than a minute to wait. I began sorting at a frenetic pace. After ten minutes my back was sore as a result of having to lean forward to survey the moving carrots and having to work with both hands simultaneously, which meant my back taking all the strain. After twenty minutes or so I began to pick out the substandard carrots using only one hand at a time as this left the other hand free to lean upon the conveyor belt's metal casing, thereby taking some of my weight and relieving the strain on my back. After about another ten minutes I began to imagine it was *me* and not the carrots that was on a conveyor belt, and that it was me that was on a conveyor belt passing an endless shelf of carrots.

After two hours of non-stop work we stopped at 7 o'clock for a fifteen-minute break. At this point most of the workers headed out into the sunshine, with everyone either lighting a cigarette or eating a sandwich or having a drink before lighting up. After a few minutes some of the younger workers, teenagers or those in their twenties, began to throw a frisby in the car park. I went to sit in the blue transit van and rest my back. As I sat I listened as Jim and Jimmy talked. "…best tae get up north daen the landscappin, cuttin gress an pickin flooer beds. Braw min." I asked Jim if the job he was talking about was something completely separate from Kettle Produce. "Oh Aye. Ah'm only at Kettle cause ma contract fir the ither joab didnae come through this year." Presently, some of the younger workers who were throwing the frisby came over to the van to ask Jim for a drink of vodka. Jim refused point blank: "It's ma joab on the line if caught. So no vodka!" As they turned and headed back to their frisby-throwing, Jim explained to me that Friday nights meant the possibility of buying bottles of whisky or vodka for five pounds each from the lorry drivers who brought cheap alcohol from France.

During the second stint from seven-fifteen to nine-fifteen I struggled to maintain any conversation as my back was becoming more and more sore. During this period Jimmy told me that Happy was drunk and that that had explained his behaviour. I hadn't realised, nor did I know Happy was sleeping the drink off in a grass ditch beside the car park, only to emerge soon before 10 p.m. when he approached me, rather sheepishly, to say: "Sorry aboot that bud." During this second period a rumor spread that we might be finishing early as there were a reduced number of loads of carrots to be processed due to it being a Friday. While I welcomed the possible early release I didn't press for details beyond establishing it was a possibility. Half an hour or so later, the rumour of an early finish was confirmed and we were told the normal break at nine-fifteen would be dispensed with as we would work through until 10 p.m. to finish the last load and then head home. At 10 p.m. a whistle blew and immediately everyone stopped working and started to walk towards the exit. I staggered down the stairs, stiff and sore, stopping only to confirm with Jim that Monday at 4.p.m. at *The Auld Hoose* pub in Cardenden was the time and pick up point, before heading to my car and driving home. When I got home I went straight to bed, and as I lay in the darkness I became aware that my hands were tingling, became aware that it felt as if I was wearing gloves as my hands quietly tingled and began the process of callousing.

The following Monday at 4 p.m. I was standing opposite The Auld Hoose, and as I waited for my lift a local woman walked towards me on her way home from getting her messages. As we knew each other she stopped and we chatted briefly, and I explained I was waiting to be picked up as I had started work at Kettle Produce. At this she said: "Ah'd never heard e Kettle Produce until the miners' strike. A' the young boys wi nae money gaun there." When my lift came I got in the van and as we headed towards Freuchie in silence I counted thirteen workers. There was Rab, a young lad from Cowdenbeath; Craig, another young lad who was listening to a Billy Connolly tape on his walkman; another young lad called Goldie (because his surname was Gauld); Jim, the driver whom I would guess was in his early fifties; Happy, who was in his mid-to-late thirties; John, Jim's son; Annette, a woman in her late forties whom the younger workers liked to tease by calling her Miss Whiplash as a result of sometimes being given supervisory-type tasks to do; Jimmy, a quiet older man in his late forties or perhaps early fifties; Maggie, the soon to be ex-wife of Jimmy; Kelly, a young girl with a temper and who was to bloody Craig's nose in a fight later that night in the van on the way home; Rob, a man in his forties; Michelle, a young girl in her late teens or early twenties, and finally James, a young lad with tattoos on his forearm and one with a dagger through a skull with the emblazoned motto: 'Death or Glory.' As we passed through Auchtermuchty we stopped to pick up Karen, an older quiet woman and a young girl who was working her last shift that day before going to stay with her father in Dundee. In Auchtermuchty Jim also had to stop to hand in time sheets to someone and as he returned to the van he announced he had bad news, that he had been given a letter for employees to the effect that anyone found drunk would be dismissed. Jim informed us we were all to get a copy but no copy was handed out to us there and then. Happy, who as usual was seated alongside Jim in the front, took the letter and read it out to us: "Those who wish to purchase drink from the drivers must do so off the premises…" As Happy read everyone was quiet and after the letter was read no-one offered any comment.

On my first full shift I was on the second belt working with Michelle. As work started at the usual frantic pace, the noise from the machines was deafening as usual so that supervisors had to whistle to communicate above the noise, and when the relevant worker lifted their head upon hearing the whistle, the supervisor pointed instructions, such as for a worker to jump up to a part of the machine and free a blockage of carrots. Not long into the shift a supervisor pointed and shouted at me to put my hair net over my ears and to take my watch off. Some time later I saw for the first time there was a clock on a wall. Later I was told to climb up and free a jam of carrots in the feeder. As we neared the end of the first period Michele pointed at my fingers, and I looked and saw my middle and ring finger and pinkie on my right hand were bleeding. Such was the frenetic pace of the work that I hadn't noticed. I then noticed blood stains on the steel strip where I had been alternately supporting myself with each hand and I hurriedly wiped away every trace of blood. As we started our fifteen-minute break Michelle told me I would need to get an Elastoplast from a supervisor. At the break I see that the quiet Jimmy has also cut himself and seeing him get some tape from Happy I do likewise. Just before the break, Annette had come around and told us all to clean up around and below the belts and tidy up any black baskets lying around before we went on break. Apparently we were not tidying up after ourselves and the supervisors were not happy. From nine fifteen to nine forty-five we have our half-hour break and as we come out into the car park I see the sun about four or five inches from the horizon. Some of the younger workers are about to play skipping and will be joined later by some of the female supervisors, and as we head for our break we each get a slip of paper that has a printed text with the title: *Communication from Kettle Produce to staff*:

> It has come to our attention that workers have been caught drinking before coming out to work this is not acceptable. Any one caught at work whilst intoxicated will be dismissed. Also the purchasing of alcohol whilst at work will not be tolerated. If you wish to purchase drink off any of the drivers at KP it must be bought off the premises. or you will be dismissed.

Back in the van I watch the quiet Jimmy roll and light a cigarette, noticing his shaking hands as he does so. I then look at Jim the driver who, hunched forwards and with his elbows resting on his knees and lunchbox resting on his lap, takes a sandwich up in his left hand and his cup of tea in his right hand, and remarking in passing to Happy, between taking big satisfying mouthfuls of tea and food, about "some c**t daen nuthin," Jim makes light work of his first sandwich and, ready at hand, grabs his next sandwich without changing position. The van is quiet as everyone eats their crisps, chocolate, rolls or sandwiches and drinks their tea or juice before having a smoke. After a few minutes as people finish their food and light up, conversation begins and the first thing talked about is how many more weeks work they are likely to have left. Happy announces he'd be happy to get paid off as this will mean, "Ah'll be on the lettuce." The other workers express incredulity at this, as apparently this is back-breaking work. Michelle says: "What? You've got tae pu' them and yer no allowed tae kneel." Happy responds to this by saying: "F**k no that! Ah'll be on the big machine. Inside. Ah'll no be f**kin oot wi aa you c**ts pu'n them up. F**k that." At this, one of the younger girls tells the story of how the last time Craig was on the parsnips, and only after an hour of work, he had a sore back and the next morning as he rolled out of bed, had to get his dad to tie his shoelaces for him as a result of being so stiff and sore. Craig laughs and confirms the story is true. Michelle then talked of how two workers (whom I didn't know) were needing all the shifts they could get because they were getting married on 28th August. At this, Kelly then shouted out to another female worker (whom I later realised was the bride to be) in the car park about some man (whom I later realised was the groom to be) of whom she said: "He likes getting blow jobs but doesnae ken how tae use his cock. Doesnae ken what it's fir!" Jim then started another line of conversation by saying: "Ah got tell't we could be finishin at wane," at which Rab asked: "Who the f**k tell't ye that?"

**Happy:** Some e the day shift finished at twelve o'clock.
**Goldie:** Was it the cleaner?
**Happy:** No, it wis Maggie.
**Jim:** Maggie! Might as well be the cleaner.
**Happy:** No it's Eleanor tell't Maggie and she gets a' her info fae John.
**Rab:** So, then, Happy, what time are we finishin ye hink?
**Happy:** F**k knows.
**Goldie:** How many loads are there?
**Happy:** F**k knows.
**Jim:** Have they started unloadin yet?
**Happy:** F**k knows.
**Jim:** Ye cannae see it, no?
**Happy:** Ah cannae see f**k all fae here.
**James:** Whose got the time? How long have we got?
**Michelle:** Ten minutes.
**James:** Braw. Time fir anither fag.
**Happy:** Aye, cause ye'll no hae time tae scratch yer baws when that f**kin belt starts gaun. Some c**t'll need tae hae a word wi the f**kin fitters. F**k me!
**Jim:** F**k its jist hard work.
**Rab:** Aye, you're right. Bashin ma baws workin like f**k.
**Craig:** Ah'm no built fir hard work. Need tae get some blacks in.
**Rab:** They should shoot a' they bastards.
**Craig:** Cannae dae that. There'd be nae shops left.

**Rab:** Look at that fat bastard, eating his Pot Noodle and throwing a frisby. His f\*\*kin mither feeds um wi a shovel.

Five minutes into the third two-hour period from 9.45 until 11.45 I noticed three of my finger-tips had turned a dark purple colour, and I started to worry I will permanently damage them if I don't do something. I decide to hang on until the next break, periodically resorting to sorting the carrots with only my left hand and clenching my fist and pressing my nails into my palm to assure myself I can still feel my fingers and to force blood into them. Bleeding fingers are a problem because so frenetic is the gathering of spoiled carrots that the skin around the nail as one's fingers go to pick up substandard carrots is constantly hitting against heavy, cold and hard carrots that are tumbling onto the back of the worker's hands. Also, because after a while the skin becomes numbed to the pain of being hit by cold wet carrots, workers don't feel any pain and so don't suspect they are bleeding. While the obvious way to prevent this constant hitting of the back of one's hands by carrots that are falling and tumbling onto the belt is to only start sorting the carrots after they have come to a standstill and settled, this would mean waiting until they are so far along the belt as to leave the worker not enough time to identify and remove the substandard carrots before they tumble into the waiting crate. Also, there is a very high level of motivation not to let any substandard carrots fall into the crates as supervisors are invigilating everyone's work and will let any individual know in no uncertain terms and in front of everyone, if they are not doing their job properly, thereby giving fellow workers ammunition that you are a slacker, so that no fellow worker will want to work alongside you for fear of having to work harder to make up for your deficiencies.

At a quarter to midnight we stop for our last fifteen-minute break. As I walk out of the shed it is now dark. I ask someone if there's a canteen anywhere and am told to "follow them." I follow some of the other back-shift workers who are not part of our crew as they walk to the works canteen. However, as there are only vending machines I head back outside for some air and take off the tape around my fingers to let them breathe. I feel my finger tips tingle as the blood flows to them. Just before we resume work I tape them again, but try to do so not so tightly. Throughout the last stint from twelve until two I look at my fingers. They are still purple but I can feel them more. At two a.m. I finish my first full shift. As we pile into the van Rab announces: "Ah'm geld that's f\*\*kin o'er." To this Jim replies: "That you happy, son?" to which Rab then retorted: "Ah'm gled. No happy or any shit like that. Ah've got tae dae it a' again the morn."

As soon as the last person is in the van we speed off. There is fifteen of us crammed into the back and everyone seems to be smoking. We drop Karen and the younger girl off in Auchtermuchty and head for the M90 and then Cardenden. At about 2.45 a.m. I am dropped off at The Auld Hoose. When I get home the microwave clock tells me its 3.09 a.m. I go to the fridge, have a drink of cold milk and then go straight to bed. The bed feels wonderful and the backs of my fingers seek out the cool and comforting mahogany wood of the bedframe. In the quiet darkness I prepare to greet sleep with gratitude, only to realise in the silence and stillness there is a loud ringing in my ear, in fact there is a noise pounding through my head, a constant and loud sound. It takes me a while to find any words to describe what is not a natural sound. I firstly imagine it is like the one unvarying note a television makes when all the programmes are finished. An unchanging and endless "oooooooooooooo" that seems to get louder the more I consciously avert to it, and which goes on and on. I turn over once or twice to see if I can get rid of it but can't. It's in my head. My body has brought the workplace back home and I can't sleep for the racket of 'machine noise' sounding in my head. As fifteen, then twenty, then thirty minutes pass, I realise my eyes too have brought the 'point of production' home as, uncalled for and out of my control, mental images of endless carrots pass before my mind's eye and I even catch myself seeking out the blemished, the split, the misshapen carrots, as if exhibiting my Pavlovian conditioning at the point of production. As I can't get the image out of my head I have to open my eyes to stop the images coming. Eventually, I fall asleep. When I wake in the morning I shower, and as I do so I get rid of all the black nasal mucus that has gathered during the course of the previous day's shift.

Such were my first two shifts at Kettle Produce where I worked during April and May 1997. While the above descriptions of working I would venture to say are rather straightforward and a more or less universal kind of experience of such kind of work, beyond such empirical descriptions there is no such thing as experiencing working *per se*, and therefore there is no such thing as an intrinsic description of working *per se*. For example, then, an 'extrinsic' determinant of the experience of work might be the 'infinity' of carrots a worker sees waiting to be fed onto the conveyor belt. The sheer volume or number of carrots is something the mind does not know exactly so the mind 'instructs' the body to 'know' or 'register' the fact that all those carrots represent 'endless' effort and work until 2 a.m. The body may react to this knowledge by 'sinking' at the prospect, giving work an 'endless' Sisyphean aspect. While this reaction is likely to be universal, however, it is *not intrinsic* to work per se or inevitable, because the individual worker may have a different reaction to such a prospect because of a home situation that means they are happy to be at work.

Because the subjective experience of work passes through the filter of individual circumstances, wishing to write a phenomenology of work per se is an ideal that has to explicitly recognise this variation. What should be included in this 'ideal type' phenomenology of work is the experience of work where the worker looks and knows there will be no early louse or reprieve, and how this stabilizes the body or anchors the body to its work and configures the temporality of the seven-hour shift and informs the phenomenology of work. My experience was that the possibility of being tapped on the shoulder at any moment to be told, "You're finished," heightened awareness that we didn't have to be here; that 'being there' was contingent, was not set in stone, that we might not be there in another twenty minutes and this meant one couldn't settle quickly into the habitus as one kept either hoping one was going to finish or had to keep telling oneself not to think about finishing, while knowing everybody else was thinking about a possible early finish, so that one never really settled to the work as a result of thinking of a possible early end, as in this instance the mind does not switch off and let the bodily habitus take over because, with the possibility of an early louse, one is continually being forced to 're-present' oneself to the work at hand and 'start again' and keep deciding to keep working, which is draining.

In my experience, when a worker refers to him or herself as working hard when among his workmates, this might easily provoke a fellow worker to say in jest something such as: "You were working? What was wrong?" In my two months at Kettle Produce I never heard any such banter. At Kettle Produce the work conditions excluded the exercise of autonomy so that 'feet-dragging' or 'time-wasting' was not possible because such decision-making is out of the worker's hands. Also, the invigilation of time and space meant that whenever a worker looked up he or she was seen as the supervisors were looking over all of us from their perched position. Workers, then, keep their eyes down so that the workers' eyes and attention settle upon the belt and the carrots. In terms of reflecting upon these conditions and their consequences for the free conditioning of *dasein* by the worker himself/herself, I assert this hyper-invigilation of time is *learned and then internalised* by the worker himself, and the worker subsequently 'freely' uses this internalised discipline as a weapon against others who are not working to this standard. The worker also, of course, uses this same weapon against himself to keep himself working. As well as this frenetic immediatism there is the internalization of hierarchy, almost to military standards, with the result that workers can be easily interpreted as full of what might be glossed as 'free-market ideology' insofar as their use of language is 'programmed' or 'armed' with the attitude that is ready and armed to declare, "Work or want!" at the slightest provocation by those not deemed to be earning their way. As I will describe in the next section more fully, all of this conditioning and internalization of the labour process or 'point of production' comes out in workers' psyche and comportment and their use of language which may be described as informal, personable, affectionate, casual and a constant exchange of crude or rough intimacies insofar as language is their cipher of choice for their conditioning at the 'point of production,' and a dominated use of and relationship to language that means it is never allowed to wander far from empirical reality.

## East of Scotland Water

As part of fieldwork I spent four summers from 1997-2000 working as a manual operative with *East of Scotland Water* (ESW) authority from June to September as cover for permanent workers taking their annual leave. As the senior engineer (Brian Robertson) told me when being interviewed for the position at Craigmitchell House (Glenrothes): "Ah always say that instead of one extra permanent man Ah prefer to have four students in the summer to cover for holidays. Four of you students cost one man's salary."[41] At this initial meeting Brian also informed me that I would be sent to work wherever I was needed and with whoever needed a 'second man.' Brian also talked briefly about the basic statutory role of ESW: that it was responsible for the day-to-day running of two hundred and fifty plants, and the agreement with government was that only twelve plants in any one year could fail, but that in the event of an electrical or mechanical failure at a plant, ESW would contact SEPA [Scottish Environment Protection Agency] and they would agree not to come to that plant and take a sample.

## The Pool Squad

As a manual operative I was routinely assigned by my line-manager (Ivor Cox) to work with the 'pool squad' which was a three-man team tasked with those repair and maintenance jobs

---

[41] My weekly salary was £186.06.

that men with regular fixed routes didn't have the time or equipment to do themselves. The 'gaffer' on the pool squad was Paul Diamond, and Paul took pride in his range of knowledge and practical know-how. Along with Paul in the pool squad was Adam, also from Kirkcaldy, and one of the first jobs I was sent to do with Paul and Adam was to repair and replace the covers of oxygenating blades at Bowhouse wastewater treatment plant. As we drove to Bowhouse from our base at Pathhead works in Kirkcaldy, Paul informed myself and Adam that the aeration blades had been reported as hitting the covers and that on the previous Saturday some five days ago, Jimmy Melville, who was responsible for the day to day maintenance of Bowhouse, had first noticed this and so our job was to swap or move the affected covers. As Paul passed on this information to me he gleaned, perhaps from my expression, that I hadn't understood him and so once we got to Bowhouse he told me to follow him to a raised grassed bank in the plant beside the perimeter fence where he began the first lesson of the day to his student-come-apprentice:

**Paul:** Okay, what you have to understand first is that Bowhoose is a fu' treatment works. Ye'll hae other plants like Ladybank o'er there [pointing] but that's jist a pump station. So, at Bowhoose ye hae three pumps, three inlets. Ladybank. Giffordtown. Auchtermuchty [as Paul says the names he points in the direction of each location]. There's actually a fourth for Dunshelt but that goes straight intae the aeration ditch. Ah'll explain that in a minute. So, first stage is a' the rags an shit an grease and grit are taken oot e the flow, then it goes intae what ye call the reception well. That's that there [pointing]. It then goes into the ditch o'er there and it's there for a number o' oors. There's bugs in the ditch. And the aeration blades pit oxygen into it. It then goes o'er the weir and into the FST [final settlement tank].
**Me:** The sludge goes o'er the weir? Is that no a fail?
**Paul:** The f\*\*kin sludge doesnae go oot the weir! Treated inflow or dirty water goes oot the weir. The sludge is doon below cause it sinks in the tank and's only moved by turnin

valves and pumps. Which is where us boys come in. That's why in this joab yer ayeways doon ladders every day cause a' yer tanks and the valves are under the grund. The sludge sinks and goes back to the ditch. The RAS valves...

**Me:** The what?

**Paul:** Returned activated sludge valves. They're doon there [pointing] and they're only touched by somebody who kens the plant.

**Me:** Why does it go back?

**Paul:** The sludge?

**Me:** Aye.

**Paul:** Well, think aboot it. If ye didnae you would kill the ditch by takin oot the live sludge and only puttin in dead sludge. You have to keep the sludge alive.

**Me:** [laughing] What the hell is *alive* sludge?

**Paul:** Sludge wi bugs in it.

**Me:** Are you serious?

**Paul:** Aye! A' this, a' this yer lookin at relies on bacteria. Bugs. It gets a bit complicated but what's needed is a particular kind of sludge that settles and sinks and disnae disperse cause then it *will* go o'er a weir.

**Me:** Right okay. So it goes back, why?

**Paul:** Ah've jist told ye! Tae keep the sludge alive.

**Me:** If it wisnae returned what's the worst that could happen?

**Paul:** Ye kill the ditch.

**Me:** What?

**Paul:** Fir a start, right, if a RAS [returned activated sludge] pump is switched aff too long that means nae treated sludge will be returned to the [aeration] ditch and so it'll die. Also, the sludge, cause it wullnae be getting taen oot the FST [final settlement tank] and returned to the ditch, it'll jist gaither at the bottom and die completely and eventually there'll be that much of it it *will* jist go straight out o'er the weir and into a burn or river or whatever and fail. And then SEPA will get involved. Fines. Money. Folk gettin shouted at.

**Me:** Okay. Got it.

**Paul:** So that's why fae the FST tank the sludge gets returned back to the ditch. It's a circuit. Ye've got tae keep it gaun. That's the joab.

As Paul was instructing me on the basic layout of the plant an ESW electrician (Rab) drove into the plant, at which Paul dismissed me saying: "Right, f\*\*k off an get some work done. Typical student. Raither stand yappin than work." As I headed off to perform the routine manual task of scrubbing down the channels, Paul fell to chatting with Rab about how the fitters were getting their 'dirty money' and 'tool money' cut i.e. those amounts of money that the union had negotiated with management over the years in recognition and compensation for the men working in unsanitary conditions, and an amount of money to renew and or replace necessary work-related tools.

Paul and Adam then started to inspect the covers in the ditch, but as they did so they disturbed nesting birds and soon discovered two bird nests and called a halt to their work. Paul's view was that they should postpone the job until the young had hatched and flown the nest. At this, they turned their attention to Rab who was in the plant to look at a gear box. Rather than doing the job they were sent to do, then, Paul and Adam spent the next hour helping Rab to dismantle the gear-box used to turn the aeration blades. Once the job was done they chatted, and before leaving Rab told Paul and Adam of an incident that had occurred at the weekend when he was on 'stand by' i.e. a period of one week where the worker after completing his normal daily shift has to be ready to respond to any incident at any time of the day or night. "Ah got a phone call at half-two on Sunday morning and the guy said, 'There's a low chlorine alarm flashing at a plant.' 'And what am Ah supposed tae dae about that?' Ah said. So next thing Ah heard a rustle of pages and he says, 'Oh, it's the water inspectors Ah should inform.' So Ah says, 'Thanks for tellin me that!' an put the phone down." At the end of this anecdote Paul advised: "You should still put down for disturbance money on your timesheet."

After we took our leave of Rab, Paul asked myself and Adam if we had our dinner or needed a shop. We didn't need a shop.

"Right, then" Paul continued, "once we're finished here we'll go tae Ladybank and open the tanks." Adam then asked: "What are we daen there like?" and Paul explained: "Ivor wants us tae hose doon the storm tanks." As we made our way to Ladybank, Adam contacted the van that has day to day responsibility for Ladybank on the two-way radio that each van was fitted with to ask Jimmy Melville to confirm the two-inch pump we would need for the job was at Ladybank. When Mick Kelman answered the radio, Adam said: "Mick? Is that you? What the f**k are you daen in Jimmy's van?" Mick explained: "Shanny's oan holiday this week so Ah'm wi Jimmy." Adam then asked: "Have you got the two-inch pump?" and Mick advised Adam he would bring the pump from another plant to Ladybank within the hour. As we drove along I asked Paul and Adam which were the main sewage plants in Fife that they dealt with. Paul informed me:

> Well in Fife anyway Dunfermline is yer biggest sewage works. Then Ironmill Bay. Cowdenbeath's probably got the deepest storm tanks in Fife. Cowdenbeath's sewage used to be treated on site at Cowdenbeath before being pumped intae Lochgelly Loch. But noo it a' ganes doon tae Leven.
>
> **Adam:** There used tae be a belt press and dryer in Cowdenbeath, but noo Cowdenbeath's no a treatment plant any mair, it's storm tanks and a pumping station only noo.
>
> **Paul:** Talkin aboot Cowdenbeath, the three e us'll be shovelin grit in Cowdenbeath works maybe this week. A' the inlet channels are needin a guid scrubbing accordin tae Jimmy Melville and Shanny. So when they tell Ivor he'll gie the joab tae us.
>
> **Me:** What about Glenrothes?
>
> **Paul:** Glenrothes's sewage ganes doon tae Leven Screen Hoose.
>
> **Me:** An Kinross and Milnathort?
>
> **Paul:** Milnathort is a third stage treatment plant. That's Jimmy Melville's. Near enough drinkable. Cause it's pumped oot intae Loch Leven ye see and no the sea, so it his tae be guid quality as it's naewhere else to go.

**Adam:** Then ye've got Kirkcaldy Pathhead works. If it can get through a four mil screen it goes oot. Anythin bigger will be stopped.

**Me:** So Kirkcaldy isn't a treatment plant really?

**Adam:** Pit it this way, ye'll no see me gaun fir a swim doon there!

As we arrived at Ladybank plant I jumped out to unlock the padlocked gate to the plant and open the gates to allow Paul to drive in and park. We then proceeded to open the metal covers to vent the storm tanks that hadn't been hosed down for over a year. Once done, we headed back to the van for our dinner. It was a warm sunny day and we had the doors and windows open. Adam put on Talk FM on the radio and we fell to listening to Nicky Campbell interviewing the SNP leader Alec Salmond.[42] At one point the interviewer was heard to say: 'Well Mr. Salmond, I've been reading up a bit on all this nationalism and are you not afraid it'll all get out of hand?" At this point one of the men exclaimed: "Oot e hand ya f**kin spastic bastard! Out of hand! That makes me want tae jist punch f**k oot e that English c**t. Out of hand! What a f**kin bastard." At this point Mick and Jimmy arrived in their van with the pump and parked along side us. Once they had put the generator and hoses beside the tanks they returned to their van for their dinner. After our half-hour break (which ended up being more like forty-five minutes) we got on with the job. I moved the generator closer to the perimeter fence and started connecting the hoses, one of which I put in the small stream that runs beside the plant, while the other hose with the nozzle that will aim the water into the tanks being attached to the generator. As we were about to start and, no doubt because we had properly vented the storm tanks before starting to do any work, Mick recalled an incident to myself and Adam about how hydrogen sulphide had got Paul in North Queensferry plant some

---

[42] The Scottish National Party (SNP) is the main nationalist political party in Scotland in favour of independence.

time previously, and that Paul was lucky and could have been sacked for misconduct. I asked Mick to explain further.

> Paul went doon wi a squeedgie intae a big tank. Nae gas monitor or f**k all. So he went doon his sel tae move it, and must have broke the skin e it and aff course he released the gas. So he got a whiff e it. So he bailed. Got tae the tap e the ladder and then oot like a light. Fell back doon. He wis really lucky. Didnae kill himself or break anything. He'll no be sae lucky again.

As we started hosing down the tanks I looked inside, and when my eyes had become accustomed to the light, the scene below appeared to me like layers of mud and silt and sludge being loosened and peeled off like layers of ancient desiccated duffel coats being forcibly separated by the damaging action of the water. Soon, however, the pump began to stutter and the water pressure began to fail. Upon hearing the change in generator noise Paul exclaimed: "Oh what the f**k is it noo? Ah've changed the oil." Mick volunteered that perhaps there was something wrong with the oil. "It looks a bit watery, maybe petrol is getting mixed in wi the oil; maybe too much pressure comin back and burnin a seal an the petrol's gettin intae the piston chamber and seepin doon an dilutin the oil. Ken what Ah mean? So the oil's loosin viscosity and no coating the piston shaft with the result that yer gettin metal against metal an scorin the bore, the cylinder, and losin compression and f**kin the pump into the bargain."

It turned out that Mick's line of reasoning was far too complicated and the fault was entirely mine as I had failed to put an 'arse' (i.e. a metal meshed fixture) onto the end of the hose that I had put in the burn, and so little stones from the stream were able to get into the hose as it drew water. I found this out as I unscrewed the hose from the generator to look into the impeller of the pump and as I unscrewed the hose heard a stone falling out. After the inevitable slagging for "being a student" I corrected my mistake and from then on the pump worked fine. After two hours of hosing down to the bottom of the tank I got the job of going down into the tank to hose down those areas of the tank that could not be got at from above. As I got to the end of the job and all that remained were the larger pieces of debris that couldn't be broken down by the action of the water, I called for a bucket on a rope to be lowered down so I could start shoveling the debris into the bucket so that it could be lifted out. As I put my hands into the shallow soak away drain on the floor of the tank I lifted what turned out to be the corpse of a cat. I then put the cat in the bucket, taking care to have the head propped up over the bucket rim, so the cat appeared to be peering out of the bucket and so that Adam would be sure to see it when he pulled the bucket up.

As Adam began to pull the bucket up I stopped working and waited. Adam presently exclaimed: "What the f**k!" as soon as he saw the cat, and I went up the ladder to enjoy his reaction. At the commotion Paul and Mick walked over. Mick looked but was not impressed: "Ah've pu'd oot a lot f**kin worse than that."

**Paul:** Oh f**k Mick, dinna get started on what we've pu'd oot e drains. We'll be here a' f**kin day.
**Me:** C'moan then, what?
**Paul:** Ye dinnae want tae ken.
**Me:** Come oan! What?
**Mick:** Jim Smith discovered a newborn bairn in Ballingry plant. Jock, Paul's faither, went tae a choked drain an it wis an unborn bairn. A woman had gien hersel an abortion.
**Adam:** Gary Biel says he's come up against dead dugs.
**Paul:** Twice Ah've come tae a choke at a hoose an it wis drooned Alsatian pups. Twice. Tae the same hoose. Ah pu'd them oot e the drains. Folk had flushed them doon the toilet.
**Mick:** That's illegal.
**Paul:** Ah f**kin ken it's illegal. Ah says tae the women if it happens again Ah'll hae tae report it. So it did happen again. An Ah did report it. Dinnae ken what happened tae her like. Then there wis Jock McPhee an Davey at Cluny a few years back. They foond a women's body doon at Cluny. Cluny dip. She had topped hersel. Jock wis doon there wi the rods.

Davey wi the hawk. Next thing a shoe pops up. That wis that. It wis a' o'er the news before that thit the woman had went missin. There wis a big search for her. So Jock says as soon as him an Davey saw the shoe pop oot, the hair went up on the back e their necks. They jaloused right awa' that it wis her. Jock says he kent straight away. An they were right. That wis Cluny.

**Mick:** A mind last winter Ah pu'd oot a rat that was blockin a sewer. This wis doon in Leven. It looked like a cross between a fitball and a cushion. It wis blue. All the fur had fell aff it. It wis that bloated. Imagine the smell e that when ye burst it!

As we were packing up our gear after we had finished, Paul answered the radio and afterwards informed us that the following morning Ivor wanted us to head straight down to Kinghorn for eight o'clock and we were not to bother with the usual morning brief in Pathhead works (Kirkcaldy) as we were to start removing grit from the holding tanks in Kinghorn, and the tide would be in our favour at that time of the morning. The next day, however, I was instructed to pick up Rory McNeill and came with Rory as usual to Pathhead to help Rory with a two-man job before Rory would head down to Kinghorn on his usual route and drop me off to help Paul and Adam for the rest of the day. By the time we arrived at Kinghorn it was well after nine, and as we approached we could see Paul and Adam were sitting in their van with no sign of any work being done. As we neared the van Rory said: "You two on strike then or what?"

**Paul:** Strike! Might as well be.
**Rory:** How, what's up?
**Paul:** No got the tools fir the joab. A wanted a f**kin Hi-Ab wi a bucket. Two men at the bottom shovelin the grit in if need be. An what happened? The office sent a tanker. Jist two men. An they coodnae even go doon or nuthin. F**kin health and safety.
**Adam:** Aye, bit wait til ye hear the best bit.

132

**Paul:** The tanker arrives an guess f\*\*kin what? He's no got a hose fir it. So they cannae even suck it up. What f\*\*kin guid is that! One thousand pound a day. We'd tae f\*\*k off tae Pathheid fir the two inch pump. The [tanker] boy wanted tae go an find a water mains. F\*\*k's sake. Ah says tae him, Ah'm no stay'n here a' day daen this. See these boys this is their joab. They're maybe cumin it ye ken. Tae get their foo shift oot e wane joab.

**Adam:** Widnae surprise me. F\*\*kin tanker boys, eh? That's what f\*\*kin happens when they change fae a two to a wane man job. They're no prepared fir half the joabs they get sent tae. Eck Beattie blames Mick Coulson and Dan Oseman. Antisocial c\*\*ts that preferred being oan their ain which meant management got it intae their thick f\*\*kin heids that tankers could be done by one man. They didnae realise that they were arseholes and that naeb'dy liked them or wanted tae work wi them, but they thought that the job was a one man joab.

**Paul:** Aye, well. So they hid tae gane away tae dump a load e water an gravel an then fill it foo e water again. F\*\*k knows where they went tae dump it. Then they needed tae find water tae hose it doon, a' the gravel tae the hose. Ah wanted a Hi-Ab f\*\*kin lorry like Geordie McPhee's. That wid mean it wid only be an oor's wurk. Bit Christ! They never even dumped their silt. They were jist fillin up wi water. They could only use a wane inch pump. F\*\*kin hell. Take them ages. Ah'll tell ye it's a guid joab noo the bonus is a' the same. Hoo the f\*\*k could ye make a bonus waitin fir a tank tae fill up a' f\*\*kin day?

## The Daily Route

My line manager also often put me to work as 'second man' to one of the men who had a regular or fixed route and an assigned list of plants to get through either every day or checked at least every week. Often I worked with Rory McNeill (Kirkcaldy) on his route and, being assigned to work with Rory on a particular

Friday, this meant our first stop of the day was Kirkcaldy crematorium. Rory advised that the pump panel to be checked here was always done early so as not to arrive when a funeral was in progress. To ensure that the pumps were working, all that was often necessary was to open a pump panel (also known as 'switch gear') with a key and inside, usually, were three sets of circuits or one for each pump. More often than not, a pump would not be running at the moment it was being checked so each pump would be manually switched on so the ESW operative could be sure they were working. Normally, simply by listening to the sound of the pump starting up was enough to tell it was fine and, once running, the pump was switched off and the next one was checked. This particular day Number 2 pump was not working and so Rory asked me to take a note. "Need tae report that" advised Rory, "it might jist be tripped oot so might just need a sparkie [electrician] tae check it." Next, we headed to St. Marie's primary school grounds where we checked a sub-station and more pumps, before heading to Hendry Road where there was a 'hydro-break' and overflow chamber and screen rake. To check this, all that was normally required was to lift the covers and have a look inside. Next was Lauder Road.

Much like when working with Paul and Adam, Rory too could be expansive when we went out on the route together. As we checked Hendry Road he explained that coming down this part of Kirkcaldy was once an open burn which had subsequently been covered up, so that now it was basically a series of pipes that also, usefully, 'broke' or slowed the water down. Piping the burn using large pipes meant that if there was a surcharge of water, this excess was now able to be put into storm tanks that were built underground. Sonic sensors hung within the chamber and picked up any rising level of water, and once a certain level was reached the sensors automatically started the screening process or began pumps to move water to storm tanks, thereby controlling the flow. Explaining the screening process Rory advised:

> The screens here take a' the shite and condoms and nappies, tights, fanny pads, rags, women's things oot see. So's tae

make sure it's jist water that goes intae the burn. They spent a lot e money here. See originally if the sewers would overflow, which af course bein Scotland they always f**kin did at some stage cause e a' the heavy rain we get, that excess went straight intae the burn. A' the gulleys on the roads see are a' connected tae the sewers. So they hid tae stop that. Ye cannae hae bairns playin in shite and fanny pads and God knows what. So they've piped a whore e a burn.

Our next stop was Charlotte Street, followed by Buchanan Court which was just a pump panel, and so Rory sat in the van while I checked it. After Buchanan court we headed along the coast to Kinghorn. Our usual routine was to have our nine o'clock cup of tea after checking Kinghorn, which consisted of going down a dry well to check sump pumps and six rotork valves and taking a note of the inflow to the plant and replace the 24-hour flow meter recorder and "do the screenings" i.e. remove any larger items caught in the screen since the previous check the day before. Rory's routine complaint was that what we did at Kinghorn every day should all been done automatically, and that there should be no need to go down dry wells for half an hour turning rotork valves one by one to make sure the tanks' levels were as they should be. After Kinghorn we headed off further along the coast to Burntisland, and on the way we met an ESW tanker driver (Wullie Pollock) who flagged us down to advise us: "It's over-flowing at Pettycur beach." We headed off to look for ourselves and when we arrived we saw there was untreated sewage flowing onto the beach. Rory speculated that either a sewer had burst or the pumps installed to deal with the sewage from the new houses nearby had failed. Rory contacted Ivor:

We've got three manholes surcharging doon here at Pettycur. There's nae screening getting done. There's fanny pads everywhere. Ah'd say the pumps at the new hooses have failed. They probably cannae handle what they've got tae deal wi. If it's the actual sewer then we'll need the DLO [drainage direct labour organization] boys tae hae a look at this the day.

Ivor advised us to sit tight until he could arrange something, and twenty minutes later the drainage DLO boys arrived in their van and trailer. On seeing us in our van they parked opposite us and while their gaffer came over to us, his squad stayed in their van and took their morning break. After we had chatted and established they were here to have a look and see if they needed to repair or renew the main sewer, the gaffer headed back to his van for his cup of tea, and I asked Rory if he knew any of the men in the van. "Oh f\*\*k aye. There's Haggis on the left, Fortnight, Squeaky Baws, Jaffa, then Jock who'll be on the digger, an Tam Jamieson the gaffer we were jist talkin tae." "The guy's name is Jaffa?" I queried. "Aye," said Rory, "it's short fir Jaffa cake." As I was still none the wiser, Rory explained the reference was to the fact the boy had had 'the snip' (a vasectomy) which meant he 'fired blanks' i.e. was like the chocolate Jaffa cake biscuit that tasted of orange but had no orange seeds i.e. was seedless. Our next plant was Auchtertool which at this time was at a standstill because, as Rory explained:

> A pipe wis ripped intae. It's they New Works boys. That chinky boy [an ethnic Chinese ESW engineer] Ming, is it? Ming the Arsehole. Cannae dae their f\*\*\*in joab. Bit ye cannae fuckin tell them f\*\*\* all. So Ivor wants them tae pit in a temporary pipe. So we'll tell them today. Ivor wis tell'n me noo there's not to be treatment e the sewage at Kinghorn or Pettycur. So much fir it no longer bein able to be untreated and pumped intae the Forth. So much fir the year 2000. A load e shite.
> **Me:** Am no followin ye.
> **Rory:** If a place has a population o' less than ten thousand they can still pump oot untreated sewage.

As Rory tried to make contact with someone in the New Works department I got on with the usual routine of going down the dry well to manually check a pump before scrubbing down the channels, and then heading to the plant outlet that ran into the stream that flowed past the plant and scrubbing the area clean. Meanwhile, Rory took one of the insurance certificates he had in the driver's side door compartment inside the small building in the plant where he hung it somewhere prominent on display, "jist in case the health an safety boys pay us a visit" as he later explained. As we sat in the van once the plant was checked Rory advised:

That's Auchtertool and Cardenden and Leven screenhouse all getting done over.
**Me:** What's bein done in Cardenden?
**Rory:** There's new storm tanks bein built. Cardenden will never be flooded again judgin by the size e the tanks in there.
**Me:** That's guid. The play park in Bowhill is often flooded fir months on end at times. Ye ken Ian Rankin the author fae Cardenden?
**Rory:** Aye.
**Me:** His first ever book was called *The Flood*, and the title refers tae a' the floodin that Cardenden a'ways got.
**Rory:** Oh right.
**Me:** And what's the problem here in Auchtertool?
**Rory:** They're re-doin it cause it's failin. The quality isnae good enough. Apparently the set-up isnae regular enough. It's variable. If the vandals stop the sprinklers then the water isnae gettin spread evenly. So the New Works design team in Craigmitchell Hoose [Glenrothes] say we need a new way at Auchtertool.

As we sat and talked a car came down the track towards the plant, and on seeing the car Rory told me it was not an ESW employee but someone from Klargester. "Don't know if that's a Dutch or German company but obviously Klargester won the tender. Of course they'll sub-contract. They'll get on the phone tae the cheapest Scottish company tae dae the civil, ken the donkey work e digging an whatever. Civil engineerin is jist donkey work.

Machines. Movin this and that etcetera." Our next stop was Cluny which was only a pump station that required to be checked. Next, we headed to Kinglassie which was a pump station with large storm tanks and which took all the sewage from Kinglassie and, only screening the sewage as opposed to treating it, pumped it via a long rising main to the main trunk sewer which runs along the river Ore and which takes raw sewage from as far away as Kelty all the way to the river Leven and eventually into Leven screenhouse. After Kinglassie our next stop was Thornton, which in my memory is always associated with having to save frogs as a result of the fact that whenever it rained heavily during the night, for some obscure reason, this meant having to spend part of the following day rescuing frogs from various storm tanks and wells and Thornton plant in particular.

On this particular day I spotted two frogs struggling in the well and went to the back of the van for a bucket before heading down the well to rescue the frogs. The procedure at Thornton was to drain the well using the pumps until the level was sufficiently low, at which point the pumps were switched off and I could go down the ladder and wade through the water and get to the frogs. Safely in my bucket, I would give the all-clear to Rory to switch on the pumps again to pump out what was left in the well. Once a week we also had to thoroughly wash down the well, but on this particular day we hadn't the time. Before we headed back down the east coast of Fife to Dysart, we swung by Kirkcaldy works for some degreaser for the floats at MacDuff. At MacDuff [43] we cleaned the floats and level censors that hung in the chamber and which were attached to cables and picked up the level of the water by measuring the distance from the floats on the surface. The floats had to be regularly freed from thick deposits of domestic fat and grease that accumulated around the censors. Our last job before stopping for dinner was to go to Dysart harbor to check the

---

[43] Whenever I was lone working and was my own boss, I always tried to take my dinner break at MacDuff to enjoy its secluded peace and beauty and walk through the trees until I could see the sea, and then sit and eat while daydreaming and gazing out to sea.

pumps before driving to West Wemyss where we had our dinner overlooking the Firth of Forth. As we listened to the news on Kingdom FM, the newsreader used the phrase "the Scottish government," and I was struck by this phrase and said to Rory this was a change. "Aye…" said Rory in agreement as he looked over the water to Edinburgh, "we've oor ain government sitting o'er there noo." The next news item concerned allegations of the Indonesian army committing atrocities in East Timor, and as the newsreader reported how a UN peacekeeping force could be in East Timor by the weekend Rory commented: "We should get in there and kick f**k oot e they Indonesian c**ts. F**kin Hindu bastards." Next on the news came a report that a new European Commission has been approved as a result of the previous Commission having resigned *en masse* due to corruption, and this new Commission was to be headed by an Italian named Romano Prodi. At this news item Rory commented: "So what do they do? Elect an Italian. F**k me! An Ah thought Italians were a' Catholics? Some name fir a Catholic!"

After dinner we headed to East Wemyss plant, and as we parked the van Rory advised we had nine vents to clean for insurance purposes but this time-consuming job would have to wait for another day. East Wemyss plant was basically a screen-house with two large Archimedes water pumps taking raw sewage and screening it before it went to the outfall untreated. After East Wemyss we headed to the last group of plants to be checked that day. Our first stop was to check the Satic pump beside The Empire pub in Lower Methil, before heading to what was referred to as the RGC (power station) but which had been taken over by Kvaerner Oil and Gas. This meant passing through a manned security checkpoint and barrier in order to check three large pumps. The next plant was the nearby Leven Roondall into which most of Leven's sewage went, and from where it was gravity–fed to Methil power station (a.k.a. the RGC power station) and pumped from there to Leven Screenhouse, and then out to the Firth of Forth estuary. However, if there is too much inflow coming into the Roondall, the excess goes over a weir into another channel and from there is pumped untreated into the Forth where the trained eye can spot the two marker buoys indicating the location of the end of the outlet pipe. After the Roondall we headed to our final plant of the day which was Leven Screenhouse, a very large building with a very large capacity. From the plaque on the building I could see the Screenhouse was opened in 1952 by Lord Home, Scottish Secretary and was originally run by The River Leven Purification Scheme. Into this plant came all of the contents of the main trunk sewer that carried waste from as far away as Kelty, through Glenrothes and then Leven, before being mashed up by very powerful and very loud macerators before being pumped out into the Forth untreated.

As we headed inside Rory told me there was a problem with "too much shit" getting caught around the macerators as well as there being an ongoing problem with very large eels getting caught in the communators, with nobody being able to explain how they were able to get into the system. On this particular day one of the communators wasn't working, so we opened the storm channel penstock and then shut the duty penstock to put the plant on by-pass to give us a chance to get our waders on and go into the water and give the communators a clean, initially using long brushes specially made for the purpose but, as it was difficult to get sufficient purchase on the machinery when using such long brushes meant being four feet away, we ended up doing the job by hand and putting our hands beneath the water to feel around the macerators for any debris.

After cleaning around the macerators and having removed the larger items that had made it through we reset the plant and signed and dated the log book and headed back outside, where we met a SEPA analyst (Davie Black) who had come to take samples. As we chatted I asked him what he was looking out for. "Bad stuff" he joked. "What counts as bad stuff?" I asked. "Mercury, volatiles, iron, zinc etcetera. The pesticides farmers use. A sheep dip is probably the worst gaun aboot. Ye dinnae ken what yer eatin or drinkin. At Leven here Ah've found cryptosporidium. Bad if it gets into the water supply. Salmonella. E coli. Methane. Hydrogen sulphide." After a quick chat we took our leave and headed back to Kirkcaldy where I dropped Rory off at his house before heading home.

While these two brief excerpts from my participant observation of work as an agricultural labourer and a manual sewerage operative are included in order to communicate something of the concrete 'world of work,' when writing about working it is actually very difficult to actually write about working and avoid writing about conversations, incidents, in fact everything except working. It is actually extraordinarily difficult to write about sorting carrots per se as this would require describing particular hand, arm and body movements that, because they were so many and done without thinking or reflection, are beyond recall and therefore beyond representation in writing. Hence, if one attempted to describe digging a ditch by hand, unless one had a video recording of the process, it is more or less impossible to actually recall and describe in sequence the range and order of movements of one's body as, again, they will be 'innumerable' and so nuanced that the time and trouble and necessary wordage required to communicate them to a reader in realistic detail would be practically impossible as they are beyond recall because the body acts and the mind deliberates and reacts so spontaneously to its environment as one digs a trench that the labourer is simply unable to recall and represent his doing afterwards, even if he wished to do so. Perhaps the following description of miners working by Nash (1993, pp. 173-174) is the only option if one attempts to describe working:

> Manuel worked twenty seconds pounding, he stopped to measure the distance on the other side to see that it would line up evenly, then pounded the mallet one minute, rested fifteen seconds, breathing through the inhaler, worked another three seconds, paused, hammered another three seconds, stopped as another worker sidled by in the narrow passage...proceeded to work again, striking one minute, taking a five-minute break, striking thirty seconds with a thirty-second break, working twenty seconds...

When writing about working with East of Scotland Water it is difficult to resist describing everything but working because there is a dignified relationship between the men and machinery, between the men and their work tasks and the time allowed to accomplish them. At East of Scotland Water the men know and use and fix machines and working with Paul, for example, it was clear there was a received wisdom 'at hand' about how to go about every job; that each wastewater treatment plant had its own history which meant a wealth of experience within the worker was 'at hand' to be displayed when maintaining any particular plant. However, when working at Kettle Produce one is forgiven for saying there is no relationship to machinery, and that any sense of self as agent is lost to the experience of self as pure passivity, and that the sense of immediacy has implications for the lack of reflexivity and the non-conceptualisation of their selves and their work.

While rendering via writing the movements of the body while working is extremely difficult, the fact is without drawing upon the body and embodiment, one has no medium of knowing manual labour; that it is via the body that the reality of work is known long before it ever becomes a matter of words or conceptual knowledge – if it ever becomes these. The body, then, understands working, grasps what the mind forms no concept of, and registers what the mind finds uninteresting and pays as little attention to as possible. For the ethnographer, however, the impact of working upon the body must become an object of analysis. If the body 'feeds' reality to the mind or mediates particular realities to the life of the mind, this mental existence is another sui generic source and medium of reality which is responsible for unique human experiences such as meaning, insights and experiences such as ignorance and not knowing and the experience of the tension that is the discrepancy between seeing or 'taking a look' and 'knowing.' This radical difference between 'taking a look' and 'knowing' and the mental tension involved was a familiar fieldwork experience as I often looked at a diagram or flow chart describing a plant's process and could only 'gape' at this symbolic representation because I did not have a clue what it meant. Likewise, technical conversations among workers I could sometimes only listen to without understanding insofar as the meaning escaped me.

Another aspect of social behaviour that is of interest as an object of analysis is the use of language as it seems clear that workers have a very particular relationship to language, and practice a defining use of language which was often evidenced, for example, when driving from one job to another and I listened as the men enjoyed calling out to each other and assigning 'ontological labels' to the sights they passed by. For example, then, upon passing someone who, for whatever reason, was deemed to be wearing something unusual or had some kind of manner about him: "Look at that poof;" upon passing someone wearing large sunglasses: "Look at f\*\*kin Elvis Presley there wi the seventies shades;" on passing a young woman: "Quite tidy. Nice tits. Ah'd shag her fir a start;" on passing two women: "Ah dinnae fancy yours much Adam;" on passing a child wearing a Rangers football shirt: "That's a form e child abuse;" on listening to a radio announcer announcing the song *Heal The Pain* by the pop singer George Michael: "Feel the pain? Aye, the pain up your Greek arse loverboy!"

This *ad libitum* use of language was something that more or less went on all day every day, and just as with the internalization of a hyper-invigilation of self and others as a result of a frenetic pace of working discussed earlier, so this use of language was as often aimed at themselves as much as others.

For example, then, when someone happened to be working for a length of time with the others standing about talking, instead of any trace of ambivalence, far less guilt, there would be comments such as: "Ye've missed a bit ya daft bastard. Are ye blind?" Language geared to constituting and maintaining a particular *mitsein* meant 'having a laugh' was a routine affair so that when three or four workers gathered together, this often meant an audience to be performed to and behaviours such as grabbing a screen rake to use as a microphone and clowning about and dancing while The Divine Comedy's *Generation Sex* played on the radio with the dancing worker (and fellow sociology graduate) advising his observing workmates: "Heh boys, Ah'm tell'n ye, if they had done this dance on their video they'd have got tae number wane. Ah'm tellin ye. Brilliant, eh?" If

143

the reaction to such a show was a predictable chorus of guffaws and one-liners such as "Look at that c**t" (Mick)" or smiling wearily and observing: "F**kin students!" (Adam) and the worker-dancer retorting: "Superannuated slaves!," in recalling such scenes the aim is not to describe a worker dancing but the enactment of a form of sociality or intersubjectivity or *mitsein* that was integral to the experience of working.

It is clear that in describing the world of work there are many different kinds of realities that are potential objects of analysis, but if we wished to focus solely upon actual 'working' we might begin with the basic point of Wallman (1979 p. 4) who describes how: "In physiological terms each [worker] is expending energy and is therefore altered by the work effort." Regarding this socialisation of the body, then, insofar as the anthropologist participates in work, the ethnographer's "body may serve as a diagnostic tool" (Blacking 1977, p. 5) and insofar as he is reflexive he is able to conceptualise the physical structuration brought into being by doing. As a first attempt at arriving at such a conceptualisation of the basic physiological alteration of the worker as a result of the expenditure of energy by working, I introduce the notion of a *reduction*. Hence, just as when applying heat to a foodstuff in cooking it is said to become more concentrated or *reduced*, so the activity of working when conceived as expending energy can similarly be described as *reducing* the body to a more 'concentrated' or basic or simple version of itself, so the body too can be described as undergoing a process of being 'reduced' by work.

I conceive the worked-self or the *dasein* brought into being by doing, then, in terms of a physical and biological reduction effected by the expenditure of energy in labouring and introduce the term *reduction* as a way of conceptualising the particular embodiment of labourers or the labouring body. The semantic cluster of food, reduction, digestion, ingestion and assimilation are suggestive of a condition that comes into being as a direct result of the burning of energy via working and the somatic quality of this becoming, with the culinary metaphor designed to communicate the notion of a *dasein* not only made real as a result of undergoing a process but the visceral and bodily quality of becoming this *dasein*, as well as the quality of inalienability thanks to becoming this reality via bodily assimilation and 'ingestion.' The worker then instead of becoming something radically other than himself is better described as changing into a version of himself that comes into being via performing or 'suffering' the social practice of labour, with the culinary metaphor of 'reduction' suggesting the interior biochemical processes or physicality of this becoming that comes into being, and to indicate the processual nature of this becoming and to advert to the historicity of embodiment within the worker as a result of his practice of labour and to describe the labourer's embeddedness in his ownmost being.

The term 'reduction' or 'condition of reduction' is also used to advert to the worker's orientation to or anticipation of the future on the basis of this becoming; its dynamic and autonomous tendency and the decentred nature of the *dasein* of manual labourers as a result of this 'worked condition' informing the personality thanks to being taken up into the lifeworld through the exercise of freedom. The notion of a 'worked self' is used to conceive and indicate not only the historicity of embodiment but its dynamic orientation of the person towards his social environment and the future, an embodied and dynamic 'secondary nature' that informs behaviour and personality; hence, when viewed according to the lifeworld that is immersed in this class, what occurs is the *reduction to reality*, while for the outside observer a particular construction of a non-objective reality or 'secondary nature' is brought about.

If the notion of a condition of reduction allows us to "see the agent not primarily as the locus of representations, but as engaged in practices" (Calhoun et al. 1993, p. 49), it also suggests the impossibility of a 'spectatorial gaze' capable of suspecting, far less knowing, this kind-of-being that comes into being via working. If the effect of work is inalienable, there is a becoming that is intensely private and personal yet shared and 'objective' among manual labourers and which cannot be appropriated unless one practices this form of life. I propose this 'reduction' then as the basic universal category that describes lives of manual labour, so that anyone living this life will share in this ontology which spans the industrial and post-industrial eras. Also, while clearly not every working-class individual will share in this condition of reduction as their existential reality, those who are not manual labourers themselves can be described as being socialised in contexts heavily marked by the culture of manual labour and the *dasein* and *mitsein* such a culture or occupational community brings into existence. The *reduced dasein* is properly said to be for the worker only in whom it becomes a departure point for subsequent mediations and constructions of self.

The worked-self only exists as a personal *dasein* or a person's ownmost existence insofar as it is enacted, so that the condition of reduction is a contingent process and condition. However, long before any particular *individual* becomes this *dasein*, it is very likely they have been surrounded by it as a lived condition they themselves did not instantiate yet as the living form of their life. Prior to the advent of their labouring existence, then, they are shaped by it via socialisation and share the intentionality and use of language it produces, despite the fact they may have no direct experience of manual labour. This condition then objectively exists in others before it is enacted via labour in any particular individual, so that when it is 'becomed' via labour, the ontology of adulthood and the socialisation of childhood and adolescence are aligned and integrated in a living synthesis and their antepredicative group membership is 'thickened.' This is how I meet Bourdieu's characterization of the concept of a historicist ontology being "truly oxymoronic" (in Calhoun et al. 1993, p. 273).

If one of the effects of manual labouring for workers' *dasein* is "the extreme simplification of their situation [causing their]... environment to become condensed and uniform" (Sartre 1966, p. 707) and the establishment of a 'primitive' *mitsein*, this is not to imagine the burden of freedom is lost as the manual worker at some point during every Scottish winter is likely to recognise within himself the predicament of the systematic divergence between the life he is more or less fated to live and the life he would choose to live if he were free to choose. There remains a dialectic or tension between 'social determination' and the exercise of freedom, and in this regard I argue that there is a specific form of individuation that takes its 'social determination' as its medium and starting point for the exercise of freedom and choice throughout the course of a lifetime.

## 2.3 The Reduced Person

In our inquiry into the relationship between material and mental life we began by raising the question as to what extent we could describe the socialised body as a 'source of self,' and began with a simple anecdote to illustrate how the body is socialised and how the external world becomes immanent and 'made flesh' and informs the physical body. I now proceed to articulate a second level where the reality of embodiment is extended and is a medium for the constitution of the depths of intentionality and personality, and I begin by reproducing some of the testimony of a thirty-five year old worker (Dauvit Urquhart, Orebank Road) who at the time of interview in November 1999 began talking about his work while being interviewed about his views on the new Scottish parliament, and whose discourse on a first reading appears to be an example of how work is *not* a source of self but an example of Offe's (1985) assertion that, in the post-industrial era, work or occupational identity is no longer the dominating source of identity for workers that it once was.

**Dauvit:** Everythin revolves aroond money eh...

**Me:** Where are ye workin aboot?

**Dauvit:** Bukos. Supermarket trolleys an that, eh? Ah wis there an Ah left. This is ma third time back. Ah've been back comin up fir two year noo or somethin. Bit Ah mean the money's crap. Bit it's only five minutes o'er the road.

**Me:** Ah used tae work back shift at Kettle Produce, packin veg.

**Dauvit:** Oh Ah wis up there an a'. Ah wis the same a couple e Christmas' ago. In fact the wife wis wi us wane year. The bairn wis only aboot two or somethin, an ma faither said

'Ah'll watch it.' Couple e shifts o'er Christmas on the night shift. Cannae mind what we were. Twenty quid a shift or something the night shift, bit c**t ye've got tae dae it eh when yer skint. Ye've got tae dae it, eh? Aye, Ah've been up there a couple e times eh, jist sort e on the side an that eh, workin away bit. Plus Ah never want tae go back tae cause it's aye the winter months when everythin's happenin ye ken. It's f***in freezin ken.

**Me:** Ah see the tattie place in Cluny is shut.

**Dauvit:** In fact Ah went along, Ah wis strugglin aboot three year ago an a'. Ah went along fir a joab and what wis it fir, Ah wis back shift that first week Ah started. Ah done the Monday and the Tuesday and Wednesday. Ah come f***in hame. Went tae the portacabin, went fir a pish an the boy wis watchin the Liverpool game. An Ah said Ah'm no workin in here. It worked oot aboot twenty-one pound a night or somethin. Ken it wis say, four o'clock till twelve, or five o'clock till one in the mornin it wis. Bit it worked oot aboot a hunder an twa pound a week or somethin an Ah thought f**k, Ah wis desperate wi Christmas comin eh, wi the bairns.

**Me:** It's jist what ye can get. Last Christmas I worked six twelve-hour shifts at the Post Office a week for two hunder an fifty.

**Dauvit:** Terrible eh? Bit everybody's the same noo. Ah mean even wi the minimum rate an that. Ah wis oan four [pounds] sixty-three [pence] an oor there Ah think. Ah dinnae make bonus or that at ma work, eh? When Ah wis workin on the line operatin, Ah mean Ah wis getting o'er thirty-five pound a week bonus. Ah went hame wi two hunder an five, two hunder an six pound jist fir ma thirty-nine oors which wisnae bad. Bit Ah've got an easier joab noo, Ah jist drive a forklift an that an dinnae make nae bonus. Ken, bit four [pounds] sixty-three [pence] an hour an they're that tight these bastards.[44]

---

[44] In March 2000 the average weekly wage in the U.K. was £426, so that with the official government definition of poverty as less than half average earnings

**Me:** What's the union at Bukos?

**Dauvit:** Transport and General. Half e Cardenden's there. There's loads an loads e folk.

**Me:** How many's employed there?

**Dauvit:** Full time there's usually aboot two hunder an fifty or three hunder ken, bit like the noo Christmas, that's the rush. Ah think there wis four hunder an forty or something. They jist payed them a' aff there.

**Me:** So they take on folk especially for the Christmas?

**Dauvit:** Aye. Ah'm usually aboot July, August time, right up tae Christmas ken. Usually get aboot six month, eh? Some folk are jist there six weeks an get paid aff again. Christmas. That's a' the orders. Shite, eh? Bit it's a joab, eh? [45]

At no point in Dauvit's discourse is work described as meaningful and we might even say that there is in Dauvit's testimony a relentless unsaid advertence to the fact that his work is so meaningless that its presence in his consciousness is stripped to the bare minimum, that work is something that hardly merits being paid attention to and *hardly merits existence in language.* It seems clear that Dauvit's work does not relate him to the 'realm of meaning' and that his work is purely functional, so that in contrast to traditional sociological studies of 'occupational identity,' for example, Dauvit's relation to work is not sufficiently real or significant to him to generate a work identity, or at least one that merits being talked about. Also, however, Dauvit does not use the meaninglessness of work to highlight the meaningfulness of other realms of experience or contrast his

Dauvit is classed as living in poverty, although he himself describes his weekly wage of £206 as "not bad." In August 2001 a 30 year-old male informant showed me his Jobseeker's Allowance letter of notification advising he was entitled to £53.05 a week or £7.58 a day; enough to buy four pints of lager at £1.75 from the local *Railway Tavern.*

[45] As reported in *The Fife Free Press* on 4 January 2002, Buko Ltd, a Glenrothes-based supermarket trolley manufacturer employing 280 staff went into receivership in December 2001.

work experience to a non-work related world such as self, family, home or some leisure-time activity or interest, so that from Dauvit's discourse it seems his work experience is isomorphic with his relation to the 'realm of meaning' and it is likely that his work experience 'flattens' his experience of non-work realms or fashions other realms of experience into its image, as if his relation to the market informs his lifeworld insofar as there is no surplus left over that allows his experience to reach escape velocity from the structuration effected by more or less 'meaningless' work.

The task of articulating the relationship between material and mental life is less than straightforward insofar as a worker is concerned to keep his 'market objectivity' at arms length from his sense of self, and at some distance from his self-representation to others in language. However, the sharp existential preoccupation with maintaining a 'live' connection to the world of paid employment is the evidence for the inability to credibly imagine any manual labourer's consciousness and *dasein* being free of deep accommodations to the market place, regardless of linguistic self-presentations. When listening to East of Scotland Water sewage operative Rory, in his early forties, recount how he had been a miner, worked as a cook, worked in the building trade and now worked as a drainage operative as well as having been unemployed at one point for four years, it is clear that finding and keeping a job had taken continual effort because it is fundamental to constituting his identity and the social status of an adult to the extent that his other identities as a man, a father or a husband or a son and brother all fundamentally stand in relation to his being employed, and stand in a relationship of dependency to being employed, so that the free market or the occupational landscape is the mirror in which every man must continually look if he is to see himself as a competent adult. However, while every worker I have ever worked with more or less *accepted* the social order, I have never met a manual worker who *consecrated* the social order he accepted.

Similarly, workers do not consecrate their occupation or turn their string of jobs or constitute their history of relationship to the market into a 'career,' so that while Rory has done a string of jobs, he never imagines or represents himself as having one true vocation or path in life because his material conditions do not allow such a signification of his life; his manual-level occupational history forbids such reifications about himself, and for the truly decentred economic biography all such fictions are reserved for the elite caste of professionals, among whom the relation between material and mental life sees inflated mentalist theories of the self and personality which are isomorphic with consecrations of the social order thanks to the myth that one's occupation is the result of one's special vocation and unique talents operating in a just social order where talent and hard work are rewarded.

For all of Dauvit's impersonal matter-of-fact and even 'off-hand' manner of speaking about his working life that may mis-direct his interviewer into imagining a gulf exists between his material and mental life, it is clear how 'ready to hand' are not only the details of his hourly rate and take-home pay but *his inability to be other than his objective economic position.*
I propose Dauvit's testimony evidences his inability to be more than his relations and his subjectivity's inability to be impersonal or distanced from his objectivity because of the inability to construct any distance between himself and the world: his personality and discourse and comportment are always reducible to his objective social position. In Dauvit's discourse we have a self-assured telling of what 'half of Cardenden' would also no doubt have to say regarding their working life; a matter-of-fact relating how the impersonal practice of work produces *a highly personable lack of personality* or a 'subjectless subjectivity,' which instantiates the most personal relations with the most impersonal objective conditions so that Dauvit talks of himself almost in the third person. Under cover of matter-of-factly relating the matter-of-fact facts to an interviewer, far from an impersonal reality that has little significance for the self being talked about is the paradox of a person freed of any personal relation to the person he is; a person perfectly at ease with his alienation from his ownmost being.

The contextual *dasein* that comes into being via doing then is a complex reality because what comes into being is simultaneously the worker's ownmost being (Heidegger 1962, p. 307) insofar as the emotional life as a symbolic system is sedimented or embedded within the endoctrine system (Wilkinson 2000) of the worker thanks to the day-to-day necessity of 'selling one's labour,' yet there is no myth of personality that accompanies this deep becoming. Also, because of the relentless experience of being related to one's objective social position, using terms such as 'economic behaviour' is a false representation even of economic behaviours as these are never separate or free from social relations. Insofar as meaningless work does not make possible a meaningful family or social or inner life, the sociological imagination that posits the dualism of 'work' and 'non-work' is a flight from the reality of working-class lives because there is a relentless isomorphism. Indeed, one is tempted to write the lived experience of the economic is the extent of how they experience the *social* realm because the quality of their experience of 'society' has been more or less completely reduced to being dependent upon the purely 'economic' realm, so that there is no evidence whatever of the reification named the 'work ethic' because no ideological articulation of the necessary is necessary.

Listening to East of Scotland Water authority workers analyse and compare and discuss at great length the minutiae of their pay slips, and discuss the pros and cons of the immanent shift from weekly to monthly payment, was to become aware that these workers "have no margin of security" (Nash 1993, p. 102) so that an immanent absence of income for three weeks led to all sorts of pressures being felt, so that union and management took the step of making an interest-free bridging loan available to workers. This more or less permanent pressure acts as an existential horizon that acts to configure and confine the person to the real and explains another feature of Dauvit's testimony which is the absence of any space or room for interpretation. For Dauvit there is no possibility of misunderstanding or 'false consciousness' to enter into his account or representation of work. In his friendly and assured performance there are no euphemising mechanisms whatever so that whatever is, is perfectly on view: the relentless determination and the relentless lack of power to change this condition of being determined. There is no attempt to cover anything and there is no interpretation required from the ethnographer in order to attain a hidden or unsaid reality as Dauvit's discourse simply mirrors Reality, and there is no room to engage in interpretivism or perspectivism.

As the dominant relation in the experience of workers is the labour-wage relation, this relationship realises in an eminent manner the fundamental structuralist principle that *the real is relational*, and the daily obedience to and daily performance of this 'fact of life' safeguards against temptations to a substantivist self-understanding by workers themselves. For the ethnographer, then, any realistic representation of manual workers must fundamentally concern itself with how work configures the relation between the material and the mental as a necessary 'odedience' in the order of representation that mirrors the necessary 'obedience' to social reality which workers practice on a daily basis. Work is both structurally fundamental and existentially "f\*\*\*in crap;" is despised as the source of unhappinesses and frustrations but also the *sine qua non* of maintaining one's social identity and place in society. Because of this dual reality it seems likely that the manual worker will not invest time and effort in cultivating what is simultaneously his despised-yet-necessary identity as a worker, so that 'being a worker' seems fated to be the least likely standpoint upon which a worker would build a project of self-appropriation.

If workers ever do gaze into their 'lived experience' of the 'point of production,' what is clear is that they require an interpretive horizon to prompt them to suspect their 'point of production' experience can be a point of departure for something such as a project of self-appropriation, and isomorphic with this finding is the fact that there is no automatic or direct link between the workplace and (revolutionary) consciousness because no situation whatever causes a particular consciousness about that situation, and to imagine this is to be in profound confusion as to the relationship between material or physical conditions and their symbolisation or interpretation. Lived experience can either come alive or remain largely inert thanks to the "large cultural systems" (Anderson, cited in Bhabha 1990, p. 1) that are brought to bear upon its perception and interpretation, so that instead of assuming there is a univocal relationship between "life as physical existence" (Connerton 1989, p. 101) and consciousness, it is precisely this which requires painstaking investigation along with inquiry into the different cultural and symbolic material available to workers in any particular context with which they imagine their condition and bring their 'secondary nature' into the realm of language and consciousness. According to Tanner et al. (1992, p. 447):

> [N]umerous case studies, particularly in the British context, have consistently failed to document a strong connection between objective work experiences and working-class social imagery (Bulmer 1975)...in his study of American manual workers, Hallee (1988: 4) found evidence of 'multiple identity holding'. While work did provide them with a 'working man' identity (which governed their industrial behaviour), this co-existed with a non-work identity, based on life-styles and consumptive patterns.

Hence, experiences on the job are not automatically fated to have exceptional 'causal' effects upon workers who have other identities that are the source of other 'rival' experiences competing to 'cause' or determine behaviour and consciousness. With multiple identities being the source of multiple experiences, it is difficult to see why one identity and one source of experience should predominate over the rest, especially when the source of identity and experience is not judged pleasant or a matter of pride and self-esteem. It is because 'work experience' becomes caught in the realm of meaning where it is negatively evaluated (and the fact that *bios* as a sui generic realm can exist independently of *logos*), that explains why work as a source of self may not register in consciousness, far less be for the worker the identity that is to be privileged above all his other identities and experiences.

I argue it would be a grave mistake to imagine the presence of work in the 'life projects' of workers (Offe 1985) is becoming marginal and to take discursive disavowals of work at face value. What is clearly on view in Dauvit's testimony, but nowhere actually stated, is not just the constant presence of the need to keep reproducing week-to-week existence and the constant awareness that this is only possible via work and wages, but precisely because in such lives work's presence outside work is never far away because "everything revolves around money," Dauvit is inviting the conclusion that *meaningless* work renders 'everything' meaningless insofar as everything enters into its sphere of influence and becomes reduced to its image and likeness. This would seem to contradict the notion that the meaningfulness of work is derived from its making possible non-work realities such as social life or family life, so that a lifetime of doing meaningless work is the ultimate proof of the *meaningfulness* of the most meaningless forms of work in the free-market order.

It seems clear that both positions are true and in a frank existential manner Dauvit lives the truism that social order and the desire to belong and maintain one's place in society is what compels individuals to take up the practice of 'meaningless' occupations, and that the free-market society is integrated via the market (Hayek 1976) and a shared non-economic realm of meaning or a Durkheimian *conscience collective* is marginal to maintaining social order. The paradox is that both the following contradictory positions are true: it is non-economic goals and motivations that are the only motivation Dauvit has available to motivate his economic behaviour and these non-economic values bear the weight of maintaining his integration into the free-market order, an order which militates against non-market realities and motivations. Dauvit lives in a post-industrial economy that has been "disorganised" (Lash & Urry 1987) and his own imagining of his relation to work might also be described as disorganised, insecure and continually under threat, as both Dauvit's accommodations to and his resistances to the discipline of the workplace are fragmented, private and even chaotic affairs.

In contrast to the coalmining industrial era of his father and grandfather before him, there is little chance of this first post-industrial generation reproducing the rich 'workers culture' that developed across the generations until it came to an end in the late nineteen-eighties. However, even in such circumstances when not only is an occupational identity constantly under threat of dissolving into nothing and any attempts at worker organisation and empowerment via trade union activity is disorganised and flitting, Dauvit is unconcerned to hide or euphemise the omnipresent subjective consequences of his market objectivity as he knows all the evidence is stacked against any other self-representation, and his mindfulness of this fact results in his use of language which reflects his matter-of-fact acceptance of a defeat which in others can result in inarticulate rage.

## Poverty as Res Cogitans in The Number 1 Goth

Going in the *Number 1 Goth* on a cold winter afternoon I ordered a pint and took a seat at the bar. After being served I was approached by 'John' who peremptorily informed me: "Ma car's packed up." From his speech and movement I immediately saw that John was drunk, and several times he announced in a loud voice to no-one in particular that he was about to head home; was going home to check his gas meter to see if he had enough credit to allow him to put the heating on "withoot feelin guilty." As I sat on a stool leaning on the bar, John made a point of informing me he had twelve pounds and thirty-three pence worth of gas left in his meter. At first I thought that John was expecting me to start a conversation, and so I tamely asked: "How do you mean gas meter?" as at that point I hadn't known anybody poor enough to have to resort to this way of consuming gas in their home. My query, however, went unanswered as John suddenly shouted "F**kin braw!" as if three separate and distinct words in the general direction of the mirrored gantry behind the bar. At this outburst the barman who was busy setting tables looked up in our direction but said nothing, and resumed his work. Next, John announced he would go to bed and that he wanted to read the paper in a warm bedroom until he had to "face the music when the wife gets in fae work." John, however, didn't go home but went to the toilet.

I ordered another pint and in the brief interlude the barman sympathised with me on being accosted by a noisy drunk. Returning from the toilet, the next topic John suddenly fixed upon was the state of his marriage, as he began a fitful monologue or drunken lament in the tradition of Burns' *Tam O' Shanter* (1791) and McDiarmid's *A Drunk Man Looks at a Thistle* (1926). For about twenty minutes John performed a kind of masculine monologue of visceral abuse and venom that consisted of shouted words, half-formed sentences laced with descriptions of his wife as "that c**t," "cow," "stupid naggin bastard" and "f**kin arse;" as if each out loud expletive or half-sentence emerged from dark painful musings as he brought to mind some previous painful experience or harsh exchange of words between him and his wife. I made out comments such as, "She kens how tae lay it oan. F*** me! The car's f***ed! Aye, yer f***ed withoot yer car," and quickly surmised that being married for John was another means whereby the pressures exercised by the relentless isomorphism between material and mental life took another form and made his economic failure all the more promiscuous in its informing all of his other relationships.

I took John's ejaculations as evidence that 'everything' is problematised when one lacks sufficient money to repair a car, as this inability signals other consubstantial inabilities such as reproducing the behaviours that constitute the local model of male sociality such as frequenting pubs, buying drinks and running a car. After a further twenty minutes of John's company I left for home, where I reflected that as my encounter with John had progressed I had become unsure whether or not I had even been 'talked at' by John. At one point as John kept talking I maintained my silence to see if this would elicit some sort of recognition of me thanks to my lack of response on his part, but no recognition occurred. It seems by simply talking at anybody John found some relief from the weight of being reduced to his objectivity.

It seemed clear that, to paraphrase Shakespeare, it was ruin that had taught John to ruminate thus. Insofar as his economic failure – no gas and no car – signalled a man's inability to be generous and to practice the small behaviours that allow him to successfully meet and thereby fleetingly transcend his material conditions, and so fleetingly allow him to be more than be reduced to his market objectivity. My assumption (and it is clearly an assumption) is that underlying this local man's fractured and flitting discourse on one topic after another was a glimpse of the quality of his relationships; of how so many of his relationships were 'at risk' insofar as his relationship to money was 'at risk' because money mediated his ability to maintain (or not maintain) a range of social practices. I also assume that money mediated the quality of his presence to his own psyche as it was this relationship to money that was in charge of whether or not he was, in his own estimation, 'good to think' or 'be around' or present to; as if, because his psychological existence was relentlessly enthralled to social structure, for him to believe in himself was not in his own hands because his self-estimation or mental health was a radically decentred reality at the mercy of his material conditions and not something he possessed as he possessed the car keys in his pocket, for example.

In this interpretation behaviour is reliant upon self-esteem which itself is in a more or less direct and immediate relationship to money, hence the wisdom of Bourdieu's (1979, p. 40) observation that: "unemployment is so intensely feared only because economic deprivation is accompanied by a social mutilation" and unemployment entails the alienation from one's former grasp upon one's former psychological sense of self. In such a context, to ask what freedom or agency is likely from the psyche that derives real pleasure from having twelve pounds of credit for gas left feels akin to mocking the afflicted or asking the same foolish question of Edwin Muir (1935, pp. 142-3):

> Once on a summer afternoon, as I watched the young men wandering among the ranges of slag-heaps outside Airdrie, I was foolish enough to wonder how it was that no sage or Mahatma had ever risen among them, for they seemed to me to have nothing to do but think.

Muir's naivety was to wonder why the psyche immersed in material poverty could not be reflexive and 'think itself;' his foolishness was to imagine the 'life of mind' did not have its own political economy and was a universal natural endowment that was free or autonomous vis-à-vis social and material circumstances. While peddlers of 'pure reason' define Man as a rational animal so that it seems no set of material conditions could divest any man of his nature, the fact is that the 'life of mind' is caught in a social determination and, given a relation of dependency exists between the life of mind and material conditions, for the young unemployed men mentioned in the above quote from Muir to produce 'great wisdom' would require *not that these men overcome or transcend their condition of being ashamed of themselves as this is impossible, but that their relationship to their shame had become sufficiently free from shame so as to enable them to look at themselves and their shame 'freely,' and exercise the freedom to use their 'shame' (and material conditions) as a standpoint or point of departure for their thinking* i.e. would require them to have escaped the social determinism that dominates the symbolic order of the free-market realm of meaning that says poverty is 'shameful' and is not to be used as a standpoint for thought or an 'identity' to be represented because it is evil and not 'good to be.'

In the philosophy of Aristotle things are made up of two realities, their *matter* and their *form*; and Aristotle describes the human intellect as the measure of all things or the master of forms because the intellect grasps the intelligible or spiritual form or *eidos* (idea) of things, and so is said to be able to become all things in a spiritual manner. In an analogous fashion I argue that poverty is promiscuous in its ability to 'inform' all things and make every relation and every reality into its image. This is because when poverty enters the symbolic realm as a *res cogitans* it means that being married for John, for example, became another mediation of not having any control over no longer having any control; having no say in a spouse's reaction to a condition that must ordinarily wish to remain private, rather than yet another mediation of having to cede control over one's lack of control. Being married meant that the facts of John's objectivity or 'situation' were taken out of his hands *precisely when the wish to be autonomous and have at his disposal sufficient agency to privatise the fact of his poverty would be most psychologically determining of his wishes and desires.* As a single man the meaning of John's poverty is far more able to be his own private affair, but from the moment he becomes a husband, the constitution and meaning and living out of his poverty is taken out of his hands and the defining of himself as a 'failure' is fated to be interpersonally mediated above and beyond being simply objectively real.

John's discourse emerges from his awareness that he is fated to be relentlessly made aware of his objective worth or 'market value' as a result of being married; that in his *mitsein* or being-alongside-others, integral to being sensitive is being sensitive to the criterion others deploy in their coming to their judgments about us and so, being sensitive to others will include learning 'self-defence' behaviours so as not to be the occasion for others coming to less than flattering judgments about us i.e. this *dasein* will develop the disposition to remove itself from the field of perception of others. Sensitivity to others, then, means the active non-representation of their being what they objectively are as they cleanse not only their own psyche but their intersubjective interaction and localities of their presence. This exigence will also inform their relationships to language and thinking and will exert pressure to give highly-euphemised and highly-edited representations of themselves when among others because they know the judgments that await any objective or any free self-representation.

The excluded, then, collude in their exclusion as they are under pressure to internalise the judgment that they are not 'good to be or think' so that, insofar as they are social animals and are sensitive to others, this very sensitivity leads to them 'freely' practicing self-exclusion; means their campaign against themselves becomes what a Scholastic thinker would term *formally* dynamic because it freely enacts and puts its exclusion together, and they 'freely' do not produce true behaviours of their true selves when in the presence of others but rather euphemise, disguise and deceive and end up living what Rankin describes as "bitter, ignorant married lives" (1986, p. 148) thanks to such marriages being private and intimate spaces where market judgments are intimately and relentlessly present, so that marriages become private sites for confrontations with the public market logic and its merciless classifying power that is capable, as per Corrie's *Black Earth* (1939), of dissolving the family.

When a man is trained to see himself via the 'mirror of production' and he becomes unemployed, a series of psycho-social dynamics are released into the marital relation, routinely leading to the man's withdrawal from his marriage; something which is more likely and more swift to occur among poor men as they are the more likely to be married to wives who use the same 'mirror of production' to see and judge their husband. Similarly addicted to the dominant symbolic order, the wife and the espousal relationship mediates a husband's failure directly into his 'inscape,' and the husband-wife relationship seems fated to weaken as the man will psychologically retreat from the marriage and exclude himself from freely developing his relationship to his wife, and will instead practice withdrawal behaviours which will also inform his relation to his children so that in his fatherhood he will *practice shame behaviours* and withdraw from his children and this same psycho-dynamic will spread outwith the immediate family unit to his extended family and locality and will be 'freely' reproduced.

Baudrillard's (1975) phrase the 'mirror of production' is used as shorthand for the idea that the horizon of the worker's perception is limited to their occupation to the extent that they have no consciousness of their own outwith their industrial function. Examples of this are found in Corrie's *Black Earth* (1939, p. 3) where we read: "There were long threads from the pit fastened to every soul in Brandon. The faster the pit went the faster the souls moved. When the pit stopped so did life." Again, *Black Earth* (1939) opens on the morning of the elder son Jim about to start working down the pit for the first time and Jim is described as being glad to be going down the pit as it means becoming "a man at last and looking forward to the time when he would have a place of his own and make a real wage" (1939, p. 16). The common sense view that the labour-wage relation makes every other development of self or phase of the lifecycle possible means the 'mirror of production' gives the true image or the true picture of what it is to be a man, and that only by looking into the 'mirror of production' can a boy 'measure up,' or see the true image of being a man and, on the basis that this image is shared by others, it is only by looking in the mirror of production that he can imagine a future for himself as a grown up competent member of the community. Industry, in the shape of the local pit, then, is *the* mirror boys look into to recognise themselves by and constitute their likeness to their fathers by and their belonging to locality. In this respect it is interesting to note that Robert Burns' poem *A Man's A Man For A That* (1795) which describes 'an honest poverty' that 'dares be poor,' and how despite his poverty 'a man's a man for a that,' so that poverty can not remove this inalienable dignity, obliterates the relation between material and mental life and is innocent of a sociology of meaning insofar as it represses the capture of the meaning of 'being poor' by 'the rich.' My analysis rejects this immaculate universalist anthropology of pure reason and argues that a man's poverty informs his 'secondary nature.'

While any individual of any social class is characterised by their relations, the working class seem especially *defined* by their objective social relations so that there is a high degree of libidinal investment in the ordinary mundane relations of the marital, the familial and the interpersonal as to be truly defined by one's relations is to be always likely to be put 'at issue' or 'at risk' by minor changes in circumstances. Perhaps this explains Lutz's (1988, p. 65) observation that "it is the dominated members of this social system (such as women, children and the lower classes) who are primarily defined as experiencing emotion, both in general and to excess." Also, beyond the interpersonal realm the working class as a social group are also at the mercy of either having their lives defined in a collectivist manner as found among the '45 generation thanks to certain objective conditions, or being 'disorganised' as found among the '79 generation as a result of changed economic and cultural conditions.

As a result of this micro and macro-level inability to generate resistance to vulnerability, there is a particular social construction of the emotions at work so that the working-class person is someone who is libidinally immersed in his relations and the subject of Lutz's observation, unlike the figure of the dandy or the bourgeois personality who is fated to imagine and desire and experience himself as free of the immediate issues of survival, or free of being reduced to his objective structural relations. John, then, afforded a glimpse of the psychological 'wear and tear' involved in the internalisation of social structures, and the existential and psychological consequences of being placed in a hierarchically-ordered structure which 'roots' or embeds the person to himself and commands the undivided attention of his psyche, to the extent of 'determining' the psychological life of the individual.

## 2.4 The Isomorphism Between Material & Mental Life

In days gone by medieval theologians contrasted human nature with angelic natures by describing how the latter were creatures in full possession of their powers and potentialities from the moment of their creation, whereas human nature unfolded over time so that human beings first experienced infancy, then childhood and then adolescence before coming into possession of the full range and extent of their powers as adults. Human nature was conceived as having a set number of in-built ordered sequences that unfolded over time, and this human nature was objectively given and had its designated duration and was determined by the Creator so that no human agency or set of social conditions could change. Likewise, in Heidegger's fundamental ontology the universal temporal horizon of Man is described as something that is objectively given by nature and stretches between a basic thrownness into the world and a defining self-consciousness that Man is uniquely a *being-unto-death* (Heidegger 1962, pp. 290-311) because each man knows he is going to die and comports himself throughout his life accordingly.

This universal temporal horizon is not my concern here. My concern is the very particular and far from universal temporal horizon brought into being among manual labourers as a result of their ongoing doing, and the experience of time or the temporal

163

horizon among agricultural labourers in mechanised factories, for example, and how this informs their 'selves' and their intersubjective *mitsein* or 'fellowship.'

In my interpretation of John I described a close relationship between 'money' and 'manliness' and identified a certain psychodynamic that requires time to come-into-being. When 'being unemployed,' for example, is a newly arrived at condition as the result of a sudden event such as redundancy, the individual concerned draws upon his stock of accumulated symbolic and social capital and self-worth and dismisses with ease any crude materialist or sociological judgments that describe how self-esteem, for example, is a decentred reality as any reduction of the self to the banalities of *homo economicus* and *homo hierarchicus* carry little phenomenological weight because at this point in time there may well be very little felt relationship between subjectivity and objective social position. However, through time, the self is more or less fated to become *ashamed* of itself as a result of social interaction evoking judgments of shame not simply from objective contextual considerations of being immersed in the symbolic order of a free-market society, but from interpersonal interaction among those who once 'loved' the social actor before he became unemployed.

The unemployed man is fated to end up ashamed of that self which those around him 'teach' him is not lovable i.e. he is more or less fated to learn that to love such a 'redundant self' is unrealistic because it is not intersubjectively constituted as capable of being loved. He is fated to become ashamed of himself and repress himself, so that the longer the individual is unemployed the more he is fated to arrive at the kind of *dasein* that evicts itself from the ken of others *as the 'free' decision of habitus* as opposed to a one-off manoeuvre when confronted by a particular awkward situation. Finally, as the coup de grace, the individual is more or less fated *to evict this eviction of himself* from his self-awareness and that part of his psychological life he allows himself to recognise, so that he becomes incapable of learning from his experience and is more or less fated to instantiate a host of further consequences for the intentional life of the psyche as poverty over time effectively reconstitutes intentional life. Paradoxically, because he represses this repression of himself, the relentless isomorphism between *liebenswelt* and social structure leads to deviations from this 'rule' among those most disadvantaged insofar as they instantiate a disposition to illusion and escapism which becomes paradoxical evidence of objective social determination, so that this condition becomes an unknown and even unknowable *dasein* despite many instantiating this condition.

As I adverted to previously, an obvious criticism of this interpretation or analysis is that I cannot pretend to know John nor the state of his marriage, and I accept such 'empirical' criticisms without reservation. However, the argument that wives internalise and reproduce 'market judgments' in their estimations of their husbands, while unlikely to be directly articulated in an interview or conversation with an ethnographer, is hardly a wilful or far-fetched interpretation because 'being unemployed' is despised for very good reasons, and wives do not want to be married to men who instantiate this condition for very good reasons. If wives instantiate such judgments within the marital relation it is not because of any particular weakness or fault of women but, once again, it is because of the agency of time which is capable of deconstructing love. A wife will not inflict crude materialist judgments upon her husband the day after he becomes unemployed, so that any accusation she instantiates such judgments will have little psychological purchase upon her self-estimation, and she will dismiss such a crude materialist sociological analysis with ease. However, by simply adding the passage of time, it is inevitable that she will become separated from this first reaction and it is more or less inevitable that her comportment will slowly deviate from the self-awareness she allows herself because, just like her unemployed husband's sense of self, so a woman's 'wifehood' is a social and decentred reality that is never her private possession insofar as it is interpolated and informed by time and circumstance like her husband's self-esteem is interpolated by time and circumstance.

Also, the permission of self-consciousness is not necessary to instantiate particular attitudes and behaviours although, again over time, it is more or less likely that a wife will not only increasingly take an 'instrumentalist' view of her husband *but will take a stance upon taking such a stance.* The *dasein* of wives and the *mitsein* of marriages are structural realities within which the plausible denial of the existence of objective market attitudes and judgements is always possible and probable. Because the phenomenological data a person or a married couple have about themselves is not an exhaustive inventory of the truths about the person or the couple, there is always the unlikelihood of objective realities being caught sight of so that, viewed from the confines of awareness, the phenomenological data of the reality of being a self or a couple who instantiate such a hermeneutic in their marriage is always likely to be disappeared from their self-awareness outwith times of crisis.

Plausible denial is always sincere and always an option to the consciousness that nevertheless instantiates instrumental logics because denial rests upon conscious awareness alone, whereas a spouse's instantiation of 'free-market rationality' in her judgments of others is not conditional upon explicit awareness for its reality. Just as the 'worked self' is a real structuration of *dasein* despite it not being a matter of conscious awareness on the part of the worker, so the representations consciousness gives itself are always likely to approach a clean bill of health so that the most upright of self-concepts coexist with impersonal and objective social logics within allegedly private and intimate spheres such as marriage which we like to imagine escape all such instrumentalist considerations, but which in our behaviours are tightly policed and disciplined by such instrumentalism.

If there is *the agency of time* there is also *the agency of the symbolic order* that assigns poverty its meaning. Why a broken car opens a window onto an informant's ownmost self and reveals his inability to esteem himself is the result of the existence and internalisation of a *cultural system* that reads and evaluates poverty in a particular manner, and explains why being reduced to one's objectivity is experienced as humiliating rather than affirming or liberating. What is revealed is that 'esteeming' oneself and esteeming others is a social practice that has to meet objective criteria publicly set out, and thanks to John's internalisation (and everyone's) internalisation of 'shame' regarding poverty, a lack of money triggers the experience of being measured and being found wanting to the extent of mutilating an individual's sense of worth.

In my analysis John had *no cognitive capital* to resist this objective reading of himself and so had turned to the bottle and the first person to walk into the empty pub to 'share' this truth of his existence with. As a result of his poverty he was placed outwith this definition or construction of 'being a person' and was ashamed at no longer meriting this definition *even in his own eyes*, so that 'being a person' is revealed to be a social construct that he no longer had the means to maintain. Thanks to being reduced to his objective condition, John could not *in good conscience* summon sufficient 'heart' to engage with himself or me via his normal persona because this had been 'deconstructed' and put beyond his reach. Perhaps another aspect of John's anguish was that this decentering experience had allowed him to glimpse the fact that his previous attempts at personhood had been 'fake,' so that integral to the constituting of the moment was having to bear the weight of his long 'fake history;' that his 'manhood' was revealed as all along having been the plaything of circumstance, and it was because "Money and manliness became integrally linked" (Gilsenan 1996, p. 282) that the absence of money had such emasculating effects.

The intense emotion and *ressentiment* on display in John's discourse came from being reduced to his objectivity and his sensing the 'end of self,' belonging and participating. When one's personhood and worldhood are at issue the only adequate response is the strongest of emotional reactions, but what is also revealed in such moments is the symbolic or cultural resources (if any) one has available to draw upon to cope with such a crisis, or to act as ballast as one navigates a reversal of fortune. Being objectified it seems left John with only one credible sense of self i.e. abject, miserable and shameful because he (and his 'significant others') had insufficient symbolic capital available to resist this reading. If it is certain that John's car had broken down, it also seems clear that something else had broken and a veil had been torn in the fabric of himself to open a window onto his wider cultural condition; as if something changed from a state of potency to existence or a structured possibility had become an existential event.

If we make the reasonable assumption that this event was not adventitious or unique in John's experience, what is revealed is a highly determined relationship between psyche, social position and culture or status where the very sense of self is "means tested" (Brierley) and is at the mercy of being constructed and deconstructed by events. If we assume that this kind of event and the resultant existential awareness has happened before or has threatened to happen before, it seems reasonable to suppose that living with this reality over time will fundamentally mark the life of the psyche *even independently of such an event in fact empirically occurring*, so that a reality that doesn't actually empirically exist may more or less permanently exist within the individual's intentional structure, so that we arrive at Sartre's conclusion that human being is characterised as much by what does not exist as what does exist, and we may say that John's *dasein* has integrated within itself the possibility of its 'death' or non-existence, so that this *dasein* has its very dissolution integrated into its constitution because of its adaptation, over time, to precarious material circumstances, and this raises the question of the consequences for the psyche as a result of continually living on the brink of its dissolution.

What is certain is that the personality that bears no traces of these concessions to objective economic realities must appear unreal or childlike, and that the constitution of John's perception of others will emerge from his *dasein* being characterised by its confinement to his relations; to not being able to not be its relations i.e. being defined by its inability to escape its objective definition and always being an incident away from an existentialism that will act as a cipher for its social position, so that its bearer's consciousness is more or less fated to act as the 'mouthpiece' for its culturally-mediated material determination.

If such insights help to deconstruct the myth of our autonomy they also allow us to appreciate the fact that "the individual, as possessor of the contents of his own consciousness, as author of his own thoughts, as the personality responsible for his thoughts and feelings, – such an individual is a purely socioideological phenomenon" (Volosinov 1986, p. 34). However, as a final thought we might add that when faced with this emasculation, John was being authentic insofar as it took courage to refuse to mask his emasculation, and it took courage of sorts to refuse to fake 'personality' when one's truth is one hasn't got the heart for it any more. John was being authentic insofar as just as for the slave to be authentic he must "choose himself on the ground of slavery" (Sartre 1966, p. 703), so he was determined to make a stand by 'making public' to an ethnographer out for a quick pint on a cold November afternoon the isomorphism that exists between the objective and the subjective.

Having begun this chapter by illustrating how the body encodes and remembers "life as physical existence" (Connerton 1989, p. 1), I argue the socialised body is also a medium capable of registering and making present to the individual the realm of "meaningful social action" (Weber) because judgements of meaning are accomplished through the body and these enactments or realisations of meaning are routinely immediate and instantaneous thanks to the relationship or symbiosis between mind and body. The body, then, not only encodes the vibration caused by working with a high-pressure hose but the public realm of meaning so that embodiment is a medium of the social actor's understanding or *verstehen*, and in Chapter 3 I will argue that 'housing conditions' are embodied and the body registers or 'knows' what it is to live particular social conditions. Thanks to the symbiotic relationship between the mental and the physical, the body is to be privileged as the locus for emotion and an analysis of emotion is vital because it is the medium and the location of the lived reality of 'culture,' so that if a 'science of meaning' is of interest then the body is of interest as this is where meaning is immediately made available to social actors in their spontaneous reactions.

In terms of developing a contextual account of affectivity, then, I assert that the realm of emotions is often the extent of the psychological life of those members of a social group whose primary social condition is a permanent reduction to being their relations, to being stuck fast to their reality. However, I also argue that if there is a self produced in work, for example, that is objectively and more or less forced into existence, this self becomes reflexive and generates an intentional and emotional horizon that can encode free responses to an infinite number of concrete situations which the subject meets with in life. In terms of the worker, then, the objective world becomes isomorphic with the inner world but this latter is taken up as a reflexive project.

Every day the social actor is simultaneously grasped by the real and takes the real in hand, so that over time there develops a feedback system that is long sedimented in emotional responses as a matter of habitus. Moreover, because objective social structures are stable and enduring, emotions too are patterned and stable, and each class develops its own 'emotional geography' with members of each class having their own psycho-somatic signature and socialised encrinology (Wilkinson 2000). Because objective social structures are stable and enduring, emotional reactions-come-judgments are able to become somatised systems of class intelligence or distilled class ways of embodied knowing, and judgements of meaning are immediately and expertly enacted via the body. A 'sociology of feelings' is possible, then, because our responses to stable social realities also become stable and patterned and predictable and one learns how to behave and can anticipate the required behaviours for most situations, including how to feel.

Among manual labourers the order of intentionality is simplified and disciplined by and conformed to objective reality, so that conformism becomes reflexive and takes on a life of its own and it is in the body-mind relation as opposed to overt empirical behaviour that the reality of, for example, being dominated is most free to constitute the reality of the condition of 'being dominated;' is most free to fashion every realm of experience into its own likeness via the exercise of freedom and reflexivity, so that when reflecting upon particular individual lives we may ask whether the worker outside of work is free to be himself, or instead uses his freedom to reproduce his domination in every other relation he inhabits. The exercise of freedom and reflexivity then in a particular individual may collude in closing the mind to the realm of meaning by *freely developing the range and repertoire of its alienation* from realms of human experience, and in such an impoverished consciousness, intentional life is restricted to the bare existence of chronic worry and occasional release, and is more or less another experience of poverty by another name.

The isomorphism that exists between material and mental life is confirmed by research into health inequalities between the social classes which highlights the damaging biological consequences of chronic stress as a result of 'living in the moment' over long periods of time beyond the 'flight or flight' response. According to Wilkinson (2000) the raised resting or baseline levels of the stress hormone cortisol and the release of adrenaline and noradrenaline into the bloodstream as part of the body's natural 'fight or flight' response, is damaging to health and is exacerbated by living within a toxic 'realm of meaning' in the shape of shame, fear and worry and fright (Scheff and Retzinger 2000), as such emotional responses over time become embodied and biologised and brings into being a psycho-somatic 'secondary nature.' The body registers social realities but also registers the length of time it has been embodying the same social realities *so that time exists twice* because any individual's embodiment of time includes the embodiment of the length of time spent embodying time, so that the body cumulatively embodies its embodiment of time.

This temporal and socialised body, then, is the medium that registers social conditions and social realities such as domination and the reality of social class, and it is because of our *embodiment* or the alliance and alignment of mind and body that these realities are real and far more intimate realities than can ever be suggested by the blunt instrument such as how we answer the survey question about one's father's occupation. If the experience of time is socialised and is a fundamental structuring reality in any individual, there is the further question of how the experience of time, self and social conditions are transformed by *being experienced* time and time again.

If we can say of any experience that its nature or its phenomenological reality is changed insofar as it is experienced time after time, then we can also say that *dasein*'s experiencing of time as sameness is fundamentally altered insofar as this experience is self-aware or is reflexive. If we take the earlier example of an agricultural labourer in a mechanised factory working eight-hour shifts sorting vegetables and, upon hearing an unexpected noise looks up to see several tonnes of carrots being disgorged into an industrial vat from where they will make their way to the conveyor belt where he is working, an adequate understanding of how the moment is experienced *when the worker knows the future has been determined for him*, alters his experience of the moment despite the absence of any empirical difference. Knowing the future impresses the worker further and deeper into the present much more than the 'merely' present ever could, as time is said to 'fall heavily' as it is not experienced as the unfolding of fresh 'nows' but just more of the same, and knowing that the future will not involve any change in that situation alters how the situation itself is experienced, so that there is a specifically *temporal imprimatur* that puts its seal or mark upon *dasein*.

The labourer's *dasein*, like every human *dasein*, is relentlessly caught in time and social and cultural structures, but far from human being suffering an endless becoming that warrants a Sartrean declaration of the impossibility of any man 'founding' himself, the fact is because much of objective social reality is more or less unchanging, so contextual human being becomes *fixed* and 'comes to a standstill,' and the experience of time can likewise 'stand still' in lives where there is no perpetual Heraclitean flux because, insofar as time makes structures structure much more than mere structures could structure, the lived experience (*Erlebnis*) of *temporality itself is affected by the passage of time.*

Also, because secondary natures (such as the condition of reduction) are 'fixed' and static, this makes it possible for language to catch up with contextual human being and for *dasein* to be translated into consciousness and for consciousness to catch up with existence. Similarly, thanks to repeatedly performing work on a daily basis, the condition of reduction and the temporal horizon of immediacy become templates or patterns that are taken up by the body's chemistry, nervous system and psychological life as a result of being daily or serially enacted and more or less forcibly 'becomed.' Thanks to freedom, this secondary nature is also freely anticipated and taken up into consciousness and intentionality to become a 'code' or *gestalt*, so that in terms of the quality of *immediacy* as a feature of much behaviour, this quality of immediacy over time is *established as a code* within the working person, and is the result of determination and freedom and reflexivity and choice and establishes the *autonomy* of the condition of reduction, and this autonomy frees the body-subject from having to adapt afresh each new day to its environment and does away with the need to endlessly reconstitute itself *ex nihilo* as, once learned and established in behaviour, this code becomes spontaneously available to the body-subject so that the code is endlessly repeated in intentional and emotional life.

If my starting point in constructing the isomorphism between material and mental conditions is the 'moment of labour' there is also an isomorphism that comes to exist through time between the often frenetic pace of production line work imposed upon agricultural labourers in mechanised factories working to the speed of a conveyor belt or the internalised 'time is money' mentality of construction workers, for example, and the psyche and behaviours of the labourer outwith work. The moment, then, is an important object of analysis and an important medium of meaning so that in any 'archaeology' of the moment, the quality of intense presence that is often packed into the moment and the life of the socialised psyche must include an analysis of the freneticism of work, and to specify this relation I use the notion of immediacy to refer to this signature characteristic of the psyche of the labourer.

Being objectively disciplined to live in the present means coming under pressure from sociological forces to not attend to the future or the long-term, and Scheper-Hughes in *Death Without Weeping* (1992) describes the barrio residents in north-eastern Brazil living lives dominated by living in the moment because their poverty means an enforced existentialism due to the lack of psychological or cultural capital to establish any other relationship to time. This more or less coerced immediatism helps us recognise the instantiation of an 'end-of-tradition' tradition within the working class like no other class, and their alienation from any pretence to tradition and a common-sensical practicality that is often contemptuous of any attempt at a resentment-free relationship to the symbolic order or the 'realm of meaning' or time.

Furthermore, it is because the condition of reduction is taken up into the personality and intentional life that it is as a *res cogitans* that it is reflexive or puts itself together i.e. it is in intentionality that it is *formally* dynamic or a source of self which anticipates itself and comports itself to the present as itself i.e. as the condition of reduction. Workers' behaviour then is never a direct result of their particular practice that particular day as no human behaviour is so mechanistically produced. So it is that intimate relations, aggression, sexuality and that which requires individuality and freedom and intimate presence to self and an other is liable at its heart not only to be socially-mediated but co-constituted by the condition of reduction. It is not simply that in the midst of the interiority of psychic life there is an interlocution with the public realm but that much of 'psychic life' is constituted by this interlocution, so that a universal psyche or psychology does not exist and the psyche of the labourer is reflexively co-constructed via a dialectic that has two sources: the objective necessities of the life of labour and, secondly, the free decisions of a reduced self through time, so that it is in the interior and intentional realm, then, that is located and sourced a range of behaviours and data which will best reveal the promiscuous extent of the *dasein* that is 'brought into being by doing;' the extent to which the practice of labouring over time is able to constitute the reality of subjectivity and establish an affective-come-libidinal horizon.

If in unskilled workplaces such as Kettle Produce there is an obvious level of supervision and control of behaviour, a window upon the tight isomorphism that comes to exist between material and mental conditions are those social spaces characterised by workers having greater freedom to 'be themselves,' such as those social spaces removed from public view and outwith formal regulation. Often the being brought into being by doing can not be expressed in the supervised workplace, and if in the course of a working day there is the production of an 'essence,' it must postpone its expression as 'existence' in visible behaviour. Hence, workers will postpone their libidinal selves and *ad libitum* talk until they are in a suitable context. While the space *par excellence* to gather data on the consequences of work for *being-with-oneself* and *being-with-others* will be within the interiority of intentionality where the worked self is free to dominate the private moment and constitute an interior habitus of intentionality, this is hardly available to the ethnographer who must look to those social spaces and times, such as the daily journey to and from work, for example, or the daily twenty-minute break halfway through each shift, or the payday 'drinking session' in a local pub that are accessible.

From conducting fieldwork in such spaces it is clear that a characteristic of working-class *dasein* is its libidinal investment in language, and this is undoubtedly a consequence of their libidinal relation to their laborious being-in-the-world, and their characteristic lack of psychological distance from their subjectivity and their lack of psychological distance from their objectivity. This *immediatism* is the result of their chronic doing or practice under particular circumstances that, upon its internalisation, becomes reflexive and promiscuous outwith the objective demands of the workplace. When observing psychic lives characterised by immediacy, what is empirically given are views that are expressed with urgency and conviction, along with behaviours that are reactive, immediate, ad hoc and spontaneous as opposed to long-term, polite or strategic, along with a relentless cultivation of common sense at the expense of other ways of knowing; a matter of 'taste' that means a relentless bringing themselves and others to order should they stray too far from the practical and the empirical.

This signature development of common sense and practical functionality seems clearly to emerge from the more or less limited 'meaningfulness' of the work that is done. As per our previous analysis, Dauvit's discourse on his work involved coming to terms with the apparent 'naturelessness' of work and the 'naturelessness' of the self that does such work. Being thirty-four years old, Dauvit is a member of the first post-industrial generation and it seems clear that he has no 'occupational identity' worth talking about as even his identity as 'worker' comes in and out of existence as he is a worker one day and then without work the next, and with no change in his sense of self. However, the notion that Dauvit thereby escapes the 'mirror of production' and instantiates a post-industrial era authenticity insofar as his self-understanding is not fixed or essentialised as a worker is fanciful, as Dauvit does not have a mobile or liquid identity and escapes nothing as social forces remain just as thoroughly dominant of his life as they would have been for his father and the '45 generation of the industrial era.

In any analysis of Dauvit's testimony the notion of 'resistance' on the part of the individual to the dictates of the free-market economy is a forlorn hope, just as in our analysis of the Fun Day the notion that localities are able to escape the fate of decline in light of disinvestment by market forces is also a forlorn hope. Both the post-industrial individual and post-industrial locality cannot escape into substantive projects for the ethnographer to analyse in the style of Beck et al. (1994) and Giddens's (1990) idea of "reflexive modernisation" or in the style of Bakhtin for whom an aestival festival involves the symbolic re-imagining of social relationships. In the case of Dauvit, responding to reality is so occupying and relentless that mere survival is its own achievement, so that establishing any kind of distance from reality does not even reach an imaginary or symbolic level of existence. Such is the hegemony of structure that among the consciousnesses and existences of even those only fitfully caught up in it, simply the renewal of social existence becomes an event every time a new contract is signed, and Dauvit *celebrates* each six-month contract with Bukos because it means his enthrallment or domination can continue, because he knows that being free of the free-market order is no freedom at all for a human being in a free-market society.

Just as economic forces created Cardenden out of its agricultural-come-parochial life as a collection of farms and scattered households in the nineteenth century, and has now 'disorganised' the village life which the industrial era called into existence, a question for the sub-jective 'lifeworld' is whether the advent of the post-industrial era is a disaster or a liberation. Has working-class *dasein* been unfrozen from the inertia of poverty and heavy industry and, in its new 'liquid' state, become free to become something new, or has working-class *dasein* been disorganised out of existence?

While the occupational and much of the cultural landscape has changed, the power of the free market remains to exact an existentialism within workers; the relation to the cash nexus remains hegemonic in subjectivity across the generations, and across the industrial and post-industrial divide this relationship relentlessly constructs and produces no escape from the existentialisms it calls forth; a hegemonic structure that doesn't require the 'false consciousness' of a work ethic to ensure its hegemony in the lives it reduces to reflections of its hegemony as it requires no consciousness at all, which explains the quality of disinterested detachment that characterises Dauvit's 'voiceless voice' or impersonal persona, reflecting *his reluctant engagement with his own activity*. It is clear that for Dauvit there is no experience of the social realm that is independent of how he is economically positioned, or a realm of experience that is free of the influence of his menial low-paid work. Work makes non-working life possible but does not make it meaningful. In the last analysis, both work and non-work must be meaningful upon the basis of standing upon their own two feet.

There is then the 'material determination' of the mental life so that in working-class lives, family life, social existence and inner lives come under sustained and objective pressure to be 'dumbed down' to the same unskilled and menial level of their working lives. There is an unmistakable reproduction of economic realities at the level of symbolisation because rather than fuelling 'escape velocity' from material determination, one finds material circumstances pulling the symbolic level into its orbit, so that among the working class the doctrine of the determination of the superstructure by the base is a simple empirical truth. Asserting the isomorphism between the realm of work and interiority and intentionality, then, is an argument based upon empirical observation and does not rely upon any philosophical proposition such that the material base 'determines' the superstructure of consciousness. There is no resort to crude arguments that human behaviour is 'caused' or that freedom or agency are illusory. Rather, while clearly there will be instances of workers cultivating personal interests, the general argument is based upon the analyst disciplining himself to follow Dauvit's refusal of pretensions to meaningful work or occupational identity to the 'bitter end,' and to construct a Weberian 'ideal type' that remains valid even if in the case of Dauvit some details are not empirically true at a particular point in time.

There is a direct relationship between the 'mirror of production' and the 'realm of meaning' where the individual such as Dauvit learns a hermeneutic at his work that, if firstly an objective necessity, subsequently becomes a free principle of subjectivity with a life of its own which informs other relationships, so that the meaningless practice of the workplace habituates him to 'subjectless practice' so that other realms such as family life, social life, political life, spiritual life and intellectual life all come under the force of social determination to become characterised by underdevelopment. Dauvit's insistence that his work is meaningless when considered in itself and outwith its obvious functional utility, signals the fact that he endures 'famine' conditions because the self that performs meaningless work must in some way itself become meaningless in its own estimation and must impact upon the worker's relationship to the realm of meaning, indeed marginalise the quest for meaning within himself precisely to stop the question of his meaninglessness arising. This, then, raises the question as to whether a man can live on bread alone, or whether subjectivity can survive on objectivity alone.

If this is the psychological price paid for performing menial work over time, it seems a *famine hermeneutic* must develop over time and develop a life of its own in the psyche and behaviour of the worker in the sense that necessity is taken up by 'personal' taste and developed by freedom. Such is the grip of his relation to the job market upon him that *the objective relation to objective reality 'informs' or is reproduced in the subjective relation to his own subjectivity*: the same marginal or disorganised relation to work leads to the production of a marginal or disorganised relation to self, and the inability to signify menial work as meaningful leads to an inability to signify not only the self that does this work but the self when outside of work as meaningful. The self that is uninterested in the work it does comes under pressure to not be interested both in the self when at work and the self when not at work.

In terms of his interior life, how can there be a robust and dynamic self-consciousness when the reality of working is void of representations for consciousness to constitute itself in a robust and dynamic manner by? Again, if there is a permanent psychological absence caused by the absence of significant significations of work, must this absence inform or reproduce itself throughout the individual's inner life, family life, and intersubjective social life? If the worker does not give himself representations of his work, what likelihood is there for the consciousness habituated to such absence developing any kind of 'true consciousness' of his other realms of experience? Given a habituation to inertia and absence, how can the naturally dynamic desire to understand and the natural desire for experiences of love, beauty, truth or the transcendent and divine *be present to such a consciousness*? How can such desires and appetites fail to be drawn into an ethos of inertia and absence until they 'spontaneously' become interpreted as unreal and 'not for me'?

The post-industrial imagination or symbolic order has not found a place for working-class *dasein*, and both politicians and formerly left-wing political parties have fallen into line with this new symbolic order, and so have become another source for the production of the invisibility of 'working-class being' and the widely-held judgment that a politics based upon this *dasein* is unrealistic. Consubstantial to this new illegitimacy of class-based politics is the notion that this *dasein* as a standpoint to produce knowledge is likewise under pressure of being considered of no practical merit, and so we arrive at the conclusion that in society in general a trajectory based upon being this *dasein* or representing this *dasein*, whether in the arts or politics, is a form of artistic and political suicide, and that occupying any position of importance requires the negation of this being so that, ever realistic, the working class themselves when outwith their localities have no serious social or cultural use for their own *dasein*. Moreover, if it is true that a particular 'worked incarnation' cannot be spectated nor speculatively known in a contemplative fashion, it is also true that because the realm of representation is dominated by non-working-class interests, it is more or less inevitable that Dauvit, for example, is 'unthinkable' because his culture gives him no representations of himself (outwith the miserabilism found in literature) and gives him no room to exist in the symbolic order so that his being-in-the-world is unrepresented, unthought and un-presented *to his own consciousness.*

In these conditions of famine, so deprived is he of the adequate conceptual and linguistic vocabulary of his being that Dauvit is unable to appear to himself as he is, and insofar as his *dasein* is socially 'recognised' it is encouraged to improve or retrain but is never encouraged to be what he is, but thrown into trajectories of self-improvement and schemes and policies and initiatives sponsored by the State or its allies in the voluntary sector, and with all such schemes more or less considering working-class *dasein* solely from the point of view of economic functionality, so that 'working-class being' is the *dasein* society judges the most useless, unrealistic, dysfunctional and so its only space in the symbolic order is in trajectories that span all the options from dissolution to embourgeoisement.

Because the 'condition of reduction' is not objectively 'out there' and yet is the signature 'secondary nature' brought about by a lifetime of doing manual labour, attaining real conceptual purchase or knowledge of Dauvit requires a particular view of what is real as well as a particular understanding of what it is to understand. What must be simultaneously moved beyond is a positivistic understanding of the real as well as the idea and practice of data gathering as essentially 'taking a look' at what is 'out there' because in such an understanding of the process of knowing, the knower is never 'at stake' in generating his knowledge. When we think about Dauvit and note a lack of substantive representations of self is reflected in a linguistic silence vis-à-vis his 'work as work,' this isomorphism between the material and the mental is also a clue for the ethnographer of

Dauvit and has important methodological consequences, such as to come-to-know the isomorphism that is in Dauvit the researcher must come to suspect an analogous isomorphism in himself. In Dauvit coming to be what he is he has been 'at issue' or 'at risk' many times, and the idea that we can know this reality but in a risk-free manner is to fall into the illusion that Dauvit's 'secondary nature' can be spectated. The error of this view of knowing is the idea that all of reality can be spectated, or that all of reality is accessible to the researcher without the researcher having to undergo any change in order to suspect, never mind come to know, the existence of a particular reality. If the ethnographer faces the challenge of knowing how his informants are known in the field, the aim is *to know Dauvit as he knows himself* and the analyst can not know Dauvit if he does not arrive at the view that different realities can only be accessed or known through their particular mediums or 'modes of acquisition' (Connerton); that if one wishes to know, for example, a secondary nature brought into being by doing, one requires a non-objectivist epistemology in which *enactment* and *bios* are media of the real and coming to know the real.

Similarly, to know what it is to be confined to one's relations and to live this determination over time is to know that to know Dauvit is to share the point of view that emerges from this positionality, and to understand that this 'taking sides' is not a matter of morality or intuitionism or humanist solidarity but an exigence of understanding Dauvit at all, because the only adequate method of knowing Dauvit is the one he uses to know and become himself, so that by engaging in the life of manual labour one instantiates the same isomorphism, so that suspecting Dauvit's social determination is suspecting one's own. A consequence of this tight isomorphism between social position and the knowing mind is grasping the impossibility of the social researcher carefully 'extracting' knowledge of this isomorphism or the social determination lived by Dauvit (or an entire population) and avoiding being 'at issue' or 'at risk.' Hence the idea that the social researcher can remain objective while being committed to understanding a group or class is a faulty idea of what knowing is and an inadequate idea of what there is to come to know, and an inadequate idea of how to go about coming to know it.

In another similar context of menial or 'meaningless' work, Constable's (1997) ethnography of Filipino domestic workers in Hong Kong argues that it is kinship and culturally-defined obligations which determine their 'economic' activity as opposed to some reified conception of 'economic' rationality. Among the low-paid it is extrinsic cultural factors or the non-work 'realm of meaning' which allows economic activity to appear as functional and rational, so that Constable's unskilled informants instantiate in their behaviour the work ethic in a pure form i.e. they have a purely instrumental view of work with no conception whatever of having a vocation or special aptitude for the work they do. In their consciousness they are clear that work is about meeting the 'timeless' obligations of culture and kinship, and so in much the same way as the moon gives light to the earth though in itself it is dead and without life, so work has no significance in itself and is only meaningful when placed in the cultural context of the worker, so that the 'work ethic' is complied with behaviourally yet is utterly irrelevant in terms of providing the motivation and meaning required to ensure a lifetime of practice.

Much like Constable's informants, then, my own informants' work is full of non-work related meaning and given the caesura that exists between praxis and consciousness about that praxis or between doing work and its meaning, it seems that among manual workers Offe's (1985) argument that work today is becoming marginalised as a source of self is something that has always been true among those who have no trace of the elitist ideology of 'work as vocation.' However, should the occasion arise where there occurs a 'contest' as to the meaning of their work, the interpretation of work is tightly monitored or policed by workers in the sense that workers *stand guard* over the 'meaninglessness' of their work, and workers jealously preserve their hermeneutical rights to state its meaning and are alert to any misrepresentation of their work by those who occupy positions reserved for those who are more or less fated to conceive of work via the language of vocation.

Among manual operatives, for example, there were innumerable occasions when work was the subject of extended discourse as technical aspects of particular jobs were discussed among themselves on a daily basis. The most basic wastewater treatment plant or set of storm tanks or even the simplest pumping station contains a range of instruments for measuring and recording different sets of data that have to be attended to and interpreted, so that when anything malfunctions the plant operative is expected to realise this and to either fix it himself or advise the relevant person(s) what needs to be done. Without exception, then, workers were deeply interested in the minutiae of their plants and it was a matter of 'honour' that not only did nobody know 'their' plants better than themselves but that they demonstrated this expert knowledge. However, while discussing the purely technical aspects of work was more or less constant, such talk is resolutely different from any discourse regarding the 'meaning' of work, and I found a fierce resistance to management attempts at 'mythologizing' work.

Discourse vis-à-vis the meaning of work is associated by the men[46] with 'managers' and as evidence of a lack of experience, or a certain naivety they identify as peculiar to management and, as the next section attempts to demonstrate, a purely technical appreciation of work-related issues and a purely instrumental view of work is assuredly not in any way indifferent to struggles over definitions of being an authentic person, and that different deeply held views that are very rarely forced to become a matter of words and, owing to individuals' different positions within workplace hierarchies, deeply held views that are ordinarily fated never to meet directly in a face-to-face encounter, when they do in fact come together in the same space at the same time, much data that is normally unsaid is forced into the open, and opens a window onto deeply subjugated realities such as conflicts over the relationship between the 'mirror of production,' the class structure and the symbolic order.

---

[46] As they refer to themselves in contrast to "staff" who work in the company offices.

## Pathhead Treatment Works, Kirkcaldy

When working with East of Scotland Water in the summer of 1999, a series of meetings were held to allow a new manager based in Edinburgh to "get to know the men" and to communicate imminent changes in working practices. Hence, at 12 noon on Monday 16 August in the main waste water treatment plant at Pathhead (Kirkcaldy) the men gathered upstairs in their bothy waiting for the manager to arrive and the meeting to begin. When the new manager arrived he was accompanied by his young female assistant who carried a plate on which was a packet of biscuits and a packet of small cakes still in their packaging. While the pre-meeting banter was polite and friendly none of the men took up the repeated offers of a cake or biscuit. The meeting formally began when the manager took charge of proceedings by introducing himself at some length to us. In the course of his opening remarks he made a point of emphasising that, in contrast to previous "company culture" and management practice, he wanted to know "what makes you tick" and, to put these new ideas into practice, the new manager began by "sharing" something of himself and listing the various engineering and management projects he had been involved in beginning with Lothian Regional Council prior to his current position with East of Scotland Water.

As the men sat listening, we learned which Edinburgh public school our new manager had attended as a boy, and that he was a keen rugby player, as well as something of his university career and the opportunities and interests he developed while at university. After this, each of the men were 'invited' or more or less coerced into introducing themselves and to say something about themselves, which they did by each of them stating their Christian name, that they were married and the number of children they had, how long they had been employed with East of Scotland Water and which football team they supported.

The next phase of the meeting consisted of another lengthy discourse from the manager concerning his determination to put in place "a new company culture" and how central to this goal would be the "empowerment" of the men and the introduction of new working practices including "self-management teams" and "lone working within the waste water treatment part of the business." As an example of worker 'empowerment' the manager cited the novel proposal that the men assume responsibility for handling their own absenteeism[47] and that they assume responsibility for their "skilling up" on the job. Something also emphasised in this regard was the devolution of "continual professional development" and "all kinds of decision-making" from management to workers. In the course of this discourse the idea of workers' autonomy was presented as the latest in management thinking on how to make a company more competitive. In the last part of his discourse the new manager outlined the timescale for the implementation of the new changes and informed us that a series of worker-management forums aimed at updating the day-to-day running of the company would be organised.

At the end of the discourse the men were given the opportunity to raise any questions or clarify any points, but none chose to do so. Knowing the men I knew their silence had nothing to do with not having anything to say, but their shifting in their seats signalled they were impatient for the hour-long meeting to end so they could get their flasks and sandwiches out and get on with getting through their schedule for the rest of their working day. As the meeting broke up the men stayed in the bothy to take advantage of the opportunity to have their half-hour dinner break together, while the manager went downstairs to say his goodbyes to our supervisor before leaving with his PA and unopened biscuits and cakes for his next scheduled meeting with more of 'his men' in Cupar later that afternoon.

As the meeting had progressed I had felt tense at what increasingly felt like a stand-off that had begun with what I had felt was an initial refusal of politeness on the part of the men by their refusal of the gesture of commensality as this was something

---

[47] Far from any problem with absenteeism the East of Scotland Water employees that I knew were in the habit of not taking all of their holiday entitlement, and 'selling' them back to the company as a way of making some extra money.

I had never seen before among them. I had also grew increasingly tense throughout the meeting as I was convinced that the new manager's performance of middle-class distinction could only provoke the men, so that as the meeting wore on, the manager's flagging up his middle-class credentials would mean a 'retaliatory' performance of a normally unsaid working-class identity; that this manager's performance of his management identity would trigger an 'essential' proletarian identity within the men. At the same time, however, I was aware this may have been a misreading of the situation on my part, and I said nothing during and immediately after the meeting so as to wait and see if my intuition of 'muted conflict' was accurate or not. In the event I did not have to wait any length of time as immediately after the meeting a palpable sense of relief among the men was expressed, and as soon as the manager was out of earshot the views of 'his men' came thick and fast:

> What the f***in hell wis that? Wi her f***in see if ye can see ma fanny [vagina] skirt on. Coming in and shoving cakes on the table expectin something. What the f**k is that a' aboot? Some f***in tart wi a skirt half way up her arse. Treating us like f***in baubles. F***in prick. "Ah've got a f***in career!" Ya c**t!

The contempt expressed by Mick was followed in quick succession by similar expressions by more of the men, and even unfailingly mild-mannered older men revealed a very different and unexpected side of themselves. My considered view is that the reason the men were angry was because behind naïve and easily dismissed attempts at making work meaningful they saw a manager attempting to 'steal' from them their own consciousness; an example of symbolic violence (Bourdieu) insofar as the manager, in his company role, wanted to make an intervention into the lifeworld or symbolic order of the men and assume the role of 'teacher' to his 'pupils' *and more or less wanted to coerce 'his men' into joining him in his illusions*. What the men saw before their eyes was a new manager's performance of his misrecognition of himself, and their new manager's misrecognition of his practice and his misrecognition of 'his men.' Hence, because so many rules were being broken, the normal rule concerning the 'privatisation of meaning' whereby the men listen as employees listen to an employer in an ethos where each know their unequal place in which each side is more or less comfortable, was under severe strain.

What the new manager was proposing was that the men sign up to the fiction that a fundamental transfer of power from management to them was imminent, whereas the men knew that industrial relations between workers and management involve a basic agreed 'stand off:' management have their role and the men have their role and in which each have their freedom. Management is free to propose changes in practices to make efficiencies and savings, while the men have to listen. However, this new discourse was different insofar as the new manager wanted to de-privatise meaning by expecting 'his men' to misrecognise an established hierarchy and *believe* in this new 'discourse of equality.' What the men were accustomed to was having to 'lump' the fundamental difference in power between management and workers where neither side pretended there was equality, but under the new manager they were being asked to believe a state of equality and empowerment was soon to be upon them, and this was a provocation because the manager was thereby attempting to extract not simply the usual 'subjectless obedience' that power can command, but was asking the men to 'buy into' rather than tolerate the proposed changes; were being asked to believe the lie that these minor changes represented equality and empowerment, and so they sat 'fixed and furious' at the misrecognition of hierarchy the new manager was trying to achieve *within the consciousness of the men themselves.*

The men were angry and were fated to keep their counsel because of the differences in power the new manager pretended to be oblivious to, and thanks to their silence were colluding in reproducing *within the manager* the illusion that they were listening intently to his fairy tale of empowerment and equality, and thereby colluding in preserving the new manager's ignorance about how they organised their perception, and colluding in reproducing the manager's fairy tale that he was communicating with 'his men.'

This meeting was memorable as a social situation where the objective and unequal power relationships were increasingly 'excruciatingly' present in a meeting that, ironically, was devoted to equality and empowerment because this power differential was the only reality that was holding the meeting together or made it possible to occur at all, with the usual decorums and pleasantries failing to euphemise or mystify the reality of the situation. Such was the discrepancy between 'reality' and 'representation' that nothing was hid from view and nobody was 'taken in' as the men were aware the manager had power and they didn't, and they had no intention whatever of telling their new manager anything of themselves and so, on the one hand, their subordination was in plain sight to themselves while their rebellion in the realm of meaning was totally invisible to their manager and kept to themselves. If a casual passer-by (or manager) were to judge the men by their observable behaviour he would have seen evidence of acceptance of the relations in place and no evidence that a step too far into the symbolic order had been attempted and had failed and had caused resentment, because a basic principle of the men was that 'if as workers our behaviour isn't our own to command, our consciousness is our own to command.' Insofar as the new manager wanted to intervene into their symbolic order he revealed the extent of his 'bad faith' or misrecognition of himself and the extent of his power. If the manager was performing power and the men were performing their relative 'powerlessness,' as soon as the manager attempted to exercise power to extract more than the 'dumb' obedience of behaviour he became powerless, because there was no question whatever of the men adding 'inner' or 'authentic' or real subjective obedience.

If the men were acting out their habitus the manager too was acting out his fatedness to believe in his inflated discourse on changing 'company culture' while leaving the organisation of the company as an institution intact. As the manager's speech had progressed I became more and more uncomfortable at the level of miscommunication and the contempt that the new manager's misplaced confidence was fated to inspire in 'his men.' As the manager was getting into his stride I tried to imagine the early social separation that he must have been subjected to in order to imagine to myself the remote 'archaeology' of our brief encounter, and marvelled at the new manager's utter conviction about himself and his utter lack of conviction for his men; the utter lack of any consciousness about the level of non-communication going on, and the radical caesura between his being-for-himself and his being-for-others that seems essential to maintaining the social practice of management and the fiction of having 'my men.'

Did the manager believe his discourse at night with only himself for company? Insofar as the answer is 'yes' we see that each class's habitus is fatal in its hold upon consciousness, which is fated to be ignorant of how we are seen by others. Working-class men never believe in their work role in the way managers seem fated to believe in their work role insofar as every day of workers' lives their fellows lead them away from the temptation to believe their job is any kind of indication of their true self or vocation in life. The distinction between mere behaviour and unstated meaning is important for workers because the distinction between their mere 'economic behaviour' and who they really are is where they are free to exercise sovereignty over themselves.

If I marvelled at the manager's entrapment within the confines of his class habitus, the same was equally true of the men for whom exchanging their presence and words was one thing but engaging in a token form of commensality seemed off the table. Again, then, what was the 'archaeology' of the men's rejection of the new manager's new 'company culture,' and what made this rejection so easy and so readily available to them as a matter of habitus? Were these expert sewermen also expert at imprisoning themselves within a 'worker essence' that meant they never gave their manager a fair hearing, or was it that they realise change isn't permanent and soon enough their new manager would be replaced by another new manager with newer new ideas? Clearly their behaviour had nothing to do with having their own ideas on management theory and practice that were being discarded by the new manager, nor the result of any great investment into the best way to manage absenteeism or continual professional development of the average sewerman. By commanding the men's presence for an hour the new manager was drawing upon the organisation's existing hierarchy as was his right, but for the men to 'buy into' his discourse or even show goodwill by eating a biscuit, for example, was to symbolically *freely extend* their subordination to a level that is not necessary, and therefore was tantamount to betraying their interests, and to *freely legitimate* and extend within consciousness a merely objective and enforced subjection.

However, because the men have a practical and decentred sense of themselves that is context dependent and so depends for its 'live' existence upon 'triggering situations,' their resistance to both the man and his proposed measures was not necessarily a matter of holding clear and distinct ideas but was more intuitive and deeply felt. If we can analytically describe a life of labour as an existence-led *dasein*, this existentialism has long since become a matter of habitus or a pre-discursive antepredicative expertise which, when faced with the reality of the discourse of their new manager, means that two dialectically opposed habituses came into direct contact, and the men's instinctive 'incredulity' being proportionate to the cumulative reality of their enduring selves and relations so that the meeting was fated to appear as the dialectical conflict of one 'essence' coming up against another 'essence' that more or less determined their consciousness and comportment and the outcome, so that when the manager writes up his report on the meeting he believes it has gone well while the workers are 'fated' to see it as a waste of time.

While the new manager presented himself as changing 'company culture' and wishing to empower the men, the fact is the information the men would have been interested in, such as on what basis he was hired by the company or whether certain managers were being retired and replaced by 'hired hands' such as himself to prepare the company for privatisation, this level of equality was never open for discussion. Similarly, the men were given no account of what was meant by 'company culture' and whether the existing power relations between management and men were to be involved in this change of company culture. While such a devolving of power and such a sharing of information would have been of interest to the men and would have begun a real conversation, what the men got instead was their introduction to an absurdly artificial manner of introducing oneself by running one's CV by total strangers. In the main part of the manager's speech it was clear that by changing company culture and by the repeated use of the term 'empowerment,' the manager wished to intervene into the 'personality' of the men, but because the meeting from the men's point of view was an illustration of management power being set to remain a 'reserved matter' in the new company culture, the reality that was *practically* affirmed even as it was *discursively* disavowed, was that the workers were to spectate their 'empowerment' and continue to consume management discourse as rhetoric so that the net result was the re-affirmation of the status quo.

This explains the felt need among the men after the meeting to voice what they viewed as historic instances of the abuse of power by management, and so the men recalled that such was management's disregard for communication that when men who had been off sick had died, the company did not inform fellow workers, and this had resulted in workers failing to attend fellow workers' funerals and having to explain to a widow why no work mates of her dead husband had attended his funeral; how retirement collections for men who had retired five years ago and died four years ago were still sitting in an office drawer somewhere. As these recollections came thick and fast in the chat between the men before they left to continue with the rest of their day, it was plain the meeting had triggered a need for the men to reclaim their history; to tell it like it was, and thereby reject all hired 'modernisers' who could easily claim the past was dead in proportion to their lack of any knowledge of it.

Looking back with the benefit of hindsight, this meeting was the annunciation of the end of a way of working and the beginning of a new way of working. With the benefit of hindsight, the men viewed this meeting as the beginning of the end of an era for those men in their fifties and sixties who had enough years of service with the company so that the early retirement packages they would subsequently be offered made financial sense, so that they took early retirement although they had no desire to retire whatsoever. In my last months with East of Scotland Water in 2000, many of the men I had daily contact with took early retirement with many feeling apprehensive about the immanent changes in working practices. I remember one manual operative from Cowdenbeath in particular (Toaster Clerk) would always conclude any discussion on these changes by saying, "Aye, the job's f\*\*\*ed man!" and when I asked Mick[48] (quoted earlier) what he thought of plans to merge the three Scottish water authorities he replied: "We'll soon be runnin roond in vans wi Last o' Scotland Water an eventually f\*\*\*in Thames Water as the new logo" – a reference to the workings of the Competition Act which most ESW workers believed would mean the water industry in Scotland would be taken over by one of the larger privatised English water companies. Similarly, the men's derision of 'lone working' was because this was interpreted by them as a means not only of downgrading health and safety issues thanks to the prospect of there no longer being a second man for safety but cutting staff.

More generally, what was felt to be under attack as a result of the new changes was the very worthwhileness of the work they did. The men were responsible for the upkeep and maintenance of plants and it was clear that this was something they took seriously and took pride in, so that what were no more than pumping stations that in some cases were no bigger than a garden shed, were routinely spotless inside while the surrounding grassed area likewise was well-maintained. This level of attention to detail and maintenance meant even the smallest buildings were regularly checked by the superintendent with a record kept in a log which was signed and dated by the workers, and then again by the supervisor making his own inspection. On the days when I made the rounds on my own with no chargehand to supervise me, I liked to stop for dinner in the little pump station in Ravenscraig

---

[48] Not yet fifty, Mick took an early retirement package in October 2001, citing unacceptable changes in working practices. He now works for a supermarket delivering leaflets to households in Glenrothes and the surrounding areas.

Park (Kirkcaldy) and I often took the dust-covered maintenance logs from the shelves where they had lain undisturbed for years and look through them, sometimes noting familiar names and reading comments made, and taking a note of the very first entry made in the plant's first logbook. I took great pleasure in reading these entries made by men who were now long dead, and spotting one or two familiar names and noting names of men no longer on the plant side and asking about them later and listening to anecdotes and stories about dead men. All of this meticulously gathered and recorded data held a fascination for me, perhaps had a certain poignancy because this level of local detail seemed fated to end. It was clear that there had once been a meticulous attention to detail and a meticulous cultivation of locality and care for locations that the men, on the cusp of another modernisation of their working practices, were apprehensive about. Having said this, however, the men freely admitted that not all change had been for the worse, as they talked of how previously they were not supplied with gloves or overalls and had to supply their own working clothes, in stark contrast to today with their uniforms, safety clothes and working gear all being supplied free of charge.

Men openly voiced their fears among themselves and with those managers with whom they had a long relationship, that the new management in Edinburgh were preparing for the privatisation and the deskilling of their jobs. With the benefit of hindsight many of the men's fears have come true with the dissolution of East of Scotland Water and the other Scottish regional water companies being amalgamated into the new company *Scottish Water* in 2002. With the more or less enforced early retirement of many workers aged fifty and over there has been a reduction in personnel and there has been a reduction in the level of plant maintenance. Already in 2000 the men complained of plants not having their grass cut due to having to hire in machines and the time wasted in having them serviced and repaired, as well as getting the time to do the job in the first place. This particular aspect of maintenance was then sub-contracted to private tender, which effectively meant bringing in workers to do the job on the minimum wage. This opening up of part of the men's jobs to the competitive free-market tendering process was something deemed necessary by a senior engineer in one meeting (Brian Robertson) who advised the men it was necessary under the terms of the new Competition Act that had recently come into force. Managers at meetings referred time and again to 'The Competition Act' and the legal requirement to put jobs out to public tender, which many felt resulted in a race to the bottom in terms of prices, and thereby a drop in the quality of service.

In response to this new neoliberal reform, workers were expected to work 'flexibly' and 'skill up' on other competencies so that, among other things, students such as myself would no longer be required in the summer months as each job would be covered by a new 'flexible' worker. Among themselves the men referred to these measures as the new 'policy of neglect' as a result of one meeting where a manager (Roger Black) had replied 'Yes' when asked if the new management rhetoric was just the ideological justification for letting pumping stations and plants become nothing more than unkempt "shithooses," as had already happened in England where the privatisation of the water industry was complete.

Managers at meetings openly appealed to the need to be more cost-effective and efficient in working practices in order to "save our jobs," and when this bottom line was mentioned all objections tended, if not to fall away, then to lose their force as very quickly the ethos of meetings between men and managers shifted from a "them and us" ethos to one of "we're all in the same boat" as managers themselves admitted they too were at risk of redundancy thanks to the ongoing process of 'culture change' within the company. The criticisms, then, of the men were taken on the chin by an older management cadre as time and again it was explained to the workers that the water industry was in a process of privatisation and that "market forces" were the real managers of the company. The men's concerns about maintenance were usually dealt with by some generic reference to cost-cutting and efficiency so that, eventually, raising objections didn't make sense when management replied to objections that individual unemployment and corporate failure would be the only alternative should management proposals not be implemented.

In addition to the minutiae of changes to manual operatives' working practices, more large-scale changes were happening. After years of failure to up-grade existing treatment plants a new treatment plant was being built in Leven and, when completed, was to be run and maintained entirely privately, so that those taking early retirement packages were advised to put in for the upcoming jobs that would be advertised when the new private plant was on line. Also, for St. Andrews, a new plant was being constructed and a major up-grade was planned for Kirkcaldy, Auchtertool and Kinghorn thanks to the private sector's ability to attract millions of pounds of new money into the water industry, which was seen as the *raison d' être* and appeal of privatisation insofar as it delivered better public utilities at no cost to the public purse.

This view of the virtues of the free-market economy and the relation between 'public services' and 'private goods' goes back to Adam Smith's *Wealth of Nations* (1776) in which the village of Pathhead provided Smith with the opportunity to describe another new set of workplace practices in a pin-making factory, and allowed Smith to give to the world one of the earliest formulations of the principle that a greater division of labour in the manufacturing process means greater productivity. Despite the two hundred and twenty-three years separating these two instances of changes in working practices in Pathhead, Smith was alive to the question of the relationship between worker autonomy and efficiency, and did not disguise the fact that during the advent of capitalism the worker's autonomy did not feature in the drive to maximise productivity. Today, however, in the current era of 'disorganised' capitalism, economic productivity is now deemed best served by increasing as much as possible worker autonomy into the workplace. In this regard, Savage (1999) has discussed male manual work cultures and the advent of a 'new managerialism' and the "new individualism" (1999, p. 23) into the work experience to describe today's increasingly 'flexible' industrial relations where a much greater level of reflexivity is required from workers on the shop floor and which entails higher levels of decision-making and risk-taking for skilled blue-collar workers.

Undoubtedly, the new manager in Pathhead was attempting to introduce a form of "shop floor reflexive modernisation" among East of Scotland Water workers. However, while these changes represent the triumph of neo-liberalism and managerialism begun in the nineteen-eighties, in this latest re-organisation of the international free-market it is questionable if there is any fundamental change in the exercise or distribution of power at the shop-floor level as traditional power relations are not up for negotiation and are not devolved to the workers as part of their 'empowerment.'

As mentioned, in my account of the meeting with the new manager the usual power relations were in place as far as the men were concerned, and it requires the possession of power to talk with great conviction to workers about the devolution of decision-making and the empowerment of workers in a totally unconvincing fashion, yet command a show of attention. This 'capture of language' by power is something that is not lost on the men, and so when talking with Mick after the meeting he told me of previous occasions when his line supervisor had advised him he could 'have his say' so long as he didn't swear or "come across as aggressive" when talking to managers. Mick took delight in recounting how he was required to act as his own spokesman, to speak for himself or 'represent' himself as if he were absent.

Having to invent a polite persona to inform his managers about his 'absent' working-class self is something that is captured by Bourdieu (1984, p. 462) when he writes: "The dominant language discredits and destroys the spontaneous political discourse of the dominated. It leaves them only silence or a borrowed language... unable to express anything true, real or 'felt', dispossesses the speaker of the very experience it is supposed to express. It forces recourse to spokesmen." A contextual analysis of the use of language, then, opens a window onto the differential distribution and possession of power and status. In the discourse of Dauvit, Mick and John analysed earlier, there was an impersonal personalism in Dauvit, and with Mick there is a form of silencing because of being required to 'say himself' as if absent. With John there is a similar imitation of speaking as he stared into the gantry speaking a discourse that was evicted of personality because the 'who' or the subject speaking was 'absent,' as he too was forced to perform 'subjectless speaking' or fall silent.

In introducing the notion of a 'worked self' and the notion of a reduction earlier, physical labour was semantically connected to ideas of accessing or uncovering 'genuineness' or an underlying authentic reality as in the phrase "the salt of the earth" thanks to the salt being produced by the labouring and sweating body. More generally, the men discursively identified with their 'hands on' selves and an implicit discourse concerning human authenticity based upon this identification was voiced at particular times. The men would say they preferred manual work because they preferred 'being themselves' because they identified the loss of free speech as an occupational hazard among those promoted to white-collar positions, as if moving up a hierarchy *under these conditions* required 'selling out.' The refusal of pursuing a 'career' under these conditions was justified upon the basis of refusing to lose their identity as the men seemed to believe that being successful meant successfully competing against competitors in hierarchies full of others similarly hoping to be successful; that being successful would mean buying into a culture of not cultivating friendships or solidaristic behaviours as they might jeopardise one's ability to compete. My intuition is that the new manager was a model of inauthenticity thanks to his having 'successfully' negotiated his way through the occupational-come-institutional hierarchy and having instantiated a biography in which, along with solid material motivations for selfishness on the part of the individual, there would emerge over time an entire moralism and humanism to justify narcissistic behaviours. By refusing the treadmill of a career, then, the men were distancing themselves from an ethos of competition in favour of a more authentic and honourable way of working, and so they would relate among themselves instances of management favouritism and the practice of promoting inferior men to positions of greater responsibility, precisely because their relative incompetence vis-à-vis other men made them easier to control.

More concretely, I believe that the men were disgusted at the 'false consciousness' and narcissistic self-comprehension and self-representation of the manager, as well as his de-historicised and immaculate understanding of the company he worked for, and the danger such a 'free man' represented to them; a man *ex nihilo* with the power and will to make employees into his image.

We may speculate, then, that the order of representation in a class-divided society is more or less fated to be a society where the symbolic order is built upon various class-based existences that are fated to more or less deny the reality of other existences that are differently situated vis-à-vis the social whole; that in such a society and in every game of distinction (Bourdieu) each participant is fated to routinely attempt to totalise their positionality to become the measure of all things, and there will be a hundred and one 'objective' reasons to construct an entire realm of consciousness geared towards denying to oneself what one is objectively required to be in order to become a responsible and mature adult in such a highly competitive and hierarchically ordered society. If theory comes after praxis then, because they instantiate the trajectory through social space and biography of the inauthentic's practice of authenticity, they are fated to believe the 'lies' they are fated to tell themselves, so that while the 'semantic' work middle management must do is fated to be seen by the men as nonsense, middle management in their discourse is condemned to believe and be caught in the illusion and 'mythologise' or over-interpret their practice.

In our analysis of 'the worked self' we drew upon Gadamer's *Truth and Method* (1979) where the point is made that we cannot play at playing so that, for example, one can not play ironically or adopt a detached attitude so long as one in fact is playing, because to play at all one must be committed to or caught up in the action of playing so that self-consciousness destroys the reality or being of playing. With regard to our analysis of working, one similarly cannot 'play at' working because there must always be a surrender or giving of self to the work, so that to work at all means one can never opt out of the effects of working such as the sweat that forms on one's brow. The effects of work, then, are accomplished within the worker regardless of the intentionality or disposition of the worker towards his work i.e. regardless of the distracted, bored or concentrated state of mind of the worker, he is always delivered over to the effects of labour no matter if the task has been done a thousand times before because the body can not 'switch off' or absent itself from its working. Unlike one's attention which may be put elsewhere, such absence is impossible for the body as it is condemned to being present to its doing. For the manual worker, then, his work makes the reality of the body present in its own right and yet, given time, this presence becomes routinized via the formation of a bodily habitus, and so a paradox of working is that it integrates that which is thought to be antinomous i.e. event and structure or moment and habitus so that "determinism and contingency...freedom and necessity come to terms unceasingly – in nature, in history, in the destiny of peoples as in that of individuals" (Rondet 1972, p. 4). Finally, because there is ordinarily nothing more immediate, pressing and real than sweating and labouring, a pattern is established at 'the point of production' and this fundamental disciplining or simplifying of the person involves an habitual experience of being a self that informs other identities and practices such as being a father, son, brother and husband etcetera, but without suggesting that the 'point of production' determines all other identities but simply that it informs other identities or 'ways of being.'

Empirically, of course, it may well be that among the culturally dispossessed who have little traditions by which they may resist the self brought about by working becoming all there is to their *dasein*, and they may fail to resist a kind of ontological dictatorship forming within themselves. Indeed, perhaps a kind of proletarian version of Marcuse's one-dimensional man may be more or less normal in a market society and a free market in labour where people's experience of society is being effectively reduced to their economic functioning.

Taking informants' expressions of contempt for work as justifying the notion there is a separation between the real self and the self hired out to the labour-wages relation is an error. What informants say about their work and the changes work effects upon them must be distinguished. I reject the possibility of 'suspending' the self and reject any real dualism and argue the contempt workers routinely express for their work does not authorise the conclusion there is nothing brought about by doing, or the conclusion that there is no ontological transformation of *dasein* as a result of his life of labour, despite the worker not being interested in or wanting to be what he in fact is. Not only is a 'real self' produced via labour but at the 'point of production' there occurs a deep integration of self and world, and that it is here that a dynamic reflexive project comes into existence insofar as the condition of reduction is taken up by freedom, so that an initially purely physical condition leads to a Weberian 'ideal type' or a set of signature behaviours which are not produced mechanically or automatically or causally as, being human behaviours, they are as much sourced in human freedom as they are in objectively determining material relationships.

Once the appropriate physical and attitudinal accommodations are made by the novice worker, the work experience is free to reproduce itself not only in *bios* but in *eros* and *logos* and other areas of experience and this adds a certain quality of fatalism or *amor fati*. In this regard Willis (1977, p. 102) makes the mistake of taking his informants' 'humanism' as his guide when he argues: "In the end it is recognised that it is specifically the cultural diversion that makes any job bearable." I argue that it is *necessity* that makes any job bearable; it is because it *must be* borne that it is bearable and has little to do with "cultural diversion." The body, unlike the spiritual reality of mind and consciousness, is both incapable and capable of instantiating a 'forgetfulness of being' in order to negate the effects of labour. If the kind of work that possesses 'intrinsic properties' in Willis's estimation is not manual labour, it is because he fails to conceptualise the body adequately as a source of self, and source of psychological life and a project of *freedom* and so fails to give manual labour "its own properties" and reproduces an ontology and understanding of meaning that privileges semanticism.

While production-line workers incessantly appeal to cultural values or 'diversions' to make their work more meaningful, the ethnographer is not authorised to imagine work is ontologically insignificant unless his theory of human being is content to confine itself to the reports consciousness gives of itself. While in work an embodied self is made 'live' and present, the difficulty in grasping this self is due to it being embodied and fated to be 'betrayed' or lost in translation from real contextual *dasein* to its discursive representation. In any concrete research situation this 'worked self' will only be 'given' in moments or by events which 'trigger' it. As Bourdieu has written: "It is only *in the relation to* certain structures that habitus produces given discourses or practices... We must think of it as a sort of spring that needs a trigger" (Bourdieu & Wacquant 1992, p. 135). It is because of this radically non-substantialist manner-of-being that it is inevitable for a particular individual that is new to practicing introspection that he will search within for this reduced 'worked self' and reduction-based reflexive project and conclude there is no such self to find. If workers will always appear to discursively dissolve their work identities into other identities and will always refer to cultural values to find meaning in their work, none of this changes that which is brought into being by their doing, as nothing is forfeited by being forgotten or discursively disavowed. We may say that reality takes care of itself regardless of representational regimes, so that a lifetime of 'forgetting' to discursively constitute this level of *dasein* sits happily with the reality they are.

Attempting to analyse "what the being of doing is and what it is that doing brings into being" (Castoriadis 1987, p. 168) is unlikely if the ethnographer does not share in the daily life of manual work as part of his ethnographic practice, and he is unlikely to be able to report experiences with a trigger-hose that makes the previous point of Bourdieu's as real as it is ever likely to be. Without such participant observation the attempt at articulating a 'point of production' or a 'worked self' will probably be suspected of being essentialist snark-hunting, and in this regard Hill Gates has written of Chinese women's identity as workers as "always on the brink of dissolving into those of kinship" (in Perry 1996, p. 128), while women scholars have highlighted the difficulty of women thinking themselves sociologically thanks to the dialectical clash between 'being feminine' and 'being working class' (Walkerdine 1996; Skeggs 1997). In terms of the 'condition of reduction' within the lives and *dasein* of women manual labourers, one reads Macdougall's (1993, 1995) work, for example, on women manual labourers and finds no interest whatever in the question of the structuration effected upon women's *dasein* as a result of performing manual labour either in Macdougal or among the women workers themselves. It seems clear that the connection between men and manual labour is recognised in the symbolic order in a way that the relation between women and manual labour is not recognised, with the result that female manual workers will find it very difficult to articulate their 'worked self' and are likely to come under pressure from their culture not to allow the condition of reduction to become a free and reflexive project in their lives.

While a structuralist or relational view of reality and meaning implies a "break with the tendency to think of the social world in a substantialist manner" (Bourdieu 1998, p. 31), I reify or 'make something of' labouring subjectivity not by positing some unchanging essence over time but by thinking through their radical susceptibility to the world and the relentless condition of 'relatedness' to what are contingent social relationships but which are more or less stable over time. The embodied worked self then is a substantive reality notwithstanding the *relational* character of its constitution and its *continual* need of active constitution. Having paid our dues to the relational nature of reality I abstract a substance or 'secondary nature' i.e. the condition of reduction which in Chapter 6 will be taken up further as the *conditione sine qua non* of the intellectual life and an act of self-understanding that is available to manual workers.

This chapter has attempted to analyse the life of manual labour on its own terms and has argued that this life is one wherein self and world are integrated and this integration is effected via embodiment, time and intentionality which come into alignment to unite not only the self with the world and the self to itself, but provides the basis for the subsequent 'free' intersubjective development of that subjectivity. As Castoriadis (1987, p. 106) put it: "the support for this union of the subject and the non-subject in the subject, the point of connection between the self and the other, is the body...The body, which is not alienation...but participation in the world." This integration is pre-discursive and antepredicative and it is via work that is 'produced' within the labourer not simply a particular experience of being a person but, over time, there is also established ontological continuity with a working-class tradition and the existential triangulation of self, intersubjectivity and the realm of meaning that is unavailable any other way. While there is a period of life that is innocent of the 'condition of reduction' it is often a childhood and adolescence spent within the ambience of a working-class family, so that when one attempts to theorise the being brought about by manual labour it is always both something which is already objectively 'out there' and something which comes into being as a personal existential reality because the individual who becomes this condition has long ago been surrounded by it and socialised through it via his experience of sociality among those who already are this condition. Via work the youth not only becomes an adult but becomes working class as a matter of his *dasein* and destiny and 'secondary nature,' as opposed to merely symbolically or vicariously via his primary socialisation and family life.

This chapter has argued that the 'worked self' or condition of reduction is the product of the conjoining of particular relations and the socialised body that are sufficiently enduring to mean the resultant way of being merits an analytical category of its own. In establishing this theoretical category a fundamental element of working-class structuration is in place and it is upon this basis that other structurations that are present can be more fully understood and brought into focus. The next chapter, then, opens other lines of inquiry into contextual *dasein* via a threefold investigation of:

1) a phenomenology of a set of particular housing conditions and neighbour relations.

2) the major cultural changes that inform the lives of the 1979 generations.

3) the temporal horizon operative among residents as a result of 'being local.'

# 3

# Housed *Dasein* & a 'Politics of Identity'

Ye cannae speak tae them. She bawls and shouts at ye. She screams! And ye think tae yersel, 'Oh my God!' That's why Ah tend no tae approach them really. An the Council always says 'Would ye like to come and have a meetin wi them?' Ah says, 'Look', Ah says, 'Ah don't want to meet wi these people.' Ah says 'Ah don't speak to these people.' Ye ken what? It even affects me wise, even ma religion. It's like yer supposed tae love thy neighbour. Ah cannae love these people! Ah cannae even be civil tae these people! It's affected ma whole life.

Helen Sillar, Cardenden Rd, 27 June 2011

## 3.1 Fife Council Housing:
## 17 August 1998–7 February 2000

This chapter explores the impact of living through a particular set of housing conditions and a resultant 'politics of identity' that dominated much of my experience in the field which, from the outset, was dominated by living below an antisocial neighbour and the process of securing their eviction. If a central concern in understanding working-class structuration is the workplace experience of time (Thompson 1967) and providing an account of what Husserl (1964) termed "the phenomenology of internal

204

time-consciousness," the fieldwork event or set of conditions which highlighted temporality not only as a *sui generic* structuring force in its own right but as a structuring force that structures every other structuring relation, was my particular housing conditions for the first nineteen months of fieldwork.

In July 1998 I returned to Cardenden from my honeymoon spent in Vejer de la Frontera (Cadiz) and a few days later received a letter from a Mr. Donald Grant (Locality Manager) asking me to confirm that I was still looking for a tenancy. Having by that stage already been on the Fife Council housing waiting list for over a year, I was delighted as I knew this letter meant I could soon be able to bring my wife and daughter from Spain. Upon confirming to the Council that I was still very much interested, I was told a two-bedroom flat in Cardenden Road would be available soon and, sharing this information with some female residents, it was less than an hour before I learned the name and address of the person who was moving out, and so I went to speak to the tenant (Mrs Guild) who invited me in to see the flat for myself. As we chatted in one of the bedrooms, Mrs Guild gave some warning about noise levels of the neighbour upstairs but as she showed me the bedrooms and, after remarking on how her portrait of Pius XII was lit up by the afternoon sun shining directly into the bedrooms, she expressed her confidence that my family would "be happy here" as it was "a very sunny, happy flat." On 17th August 1998 I signed the tenancy for 51 Cardenden Road with a sense of relief at having finalised my living arrangements so that fieldwork could begin at long last.

After having painted and re-carpeted the flat, myself and Eva moved into our first home as a married couple. A few days after moving in, however, two Housing Investigations Officers from Fife Council knocked on our door and asked to speak with us, and proceeded to inform us that Fife Council was in the process of investigating our upstairs neighbour at number 57 due to a number of complaints regarding behaviour and noise. As we sat in our living room we learned that the standard Council procedure for dealing with antisocial neighbours was that, from receipt of a complaint, a process was begun which started with informal visits and, if the problem continued, formal letters and 'counselling sessions' being set up to resolve the issue. When I queried the track record of counselling sessions and "last warnings," the confident reply from one of the Council employees was: "We have the law, and nobody beats the law" (Stuart MacQueen). At this meeting we were also advised that while a process of evidence-gathering had already begun, the end result may not be an eviction as the tenant, when formally advised she *would be* evicted, still had the option of voluntarily giving up her tenancy, and therefore avoid actually being evicted by a court order. In the course of the meeting we were handed a supply of forms to be completed and which would be used "as evidence" by the Housing Investigation Team in a court of law, should Fife Council request an eviction order from a judge in the future. We were asked to help with the gathering of detailed information on our neighbour's behaviour as this was necessary to secure eviction by compiling a *Neighbour Complaint Incident Diary* which involved myself and Eva compiling information under the following headings:

1. Date & time of incident
2. Where did the incident occur?
3. Brief details of what happened
4. Who did it?
5. Any witnesses?
6. Do you have their names and addresses?
7. Did you report it to anyone?
8. If so who? (e.g. Area Office, Police)
9. Any other complaints?

As the two Council employees asked us if we had any questions and it became clear they were ready to leave, I asked why we were not told about this problem tenant before we signed the tenancy and moved in. The two Council employees answered that prior to signing our lease we had no right to know Fife Council was seeking an eviction order on the upstairs tenant. However, now that we had signed the tenancy and now that Fife Council was our landlord, we were entitled to know. While we had asked this question, however, it was not asked with any anger or exasperation as until this point we had not had any experience of the problem neighbour. In due course, however, it became clear I had made an awful decision in signing this tenancy agreement with Fife Council as the first nineteen months of our married life turned out to be more or less unhappy, unpleasant and sometimes desperate.

The problem soon manifested itself to us along with the specific behaviours that had led to complaints against our upstairs neighbour at number 57: communal front door buzzers sounding 'continually' through the night and awakening neighbours; routinely having to answer our intercom well after midnight as another unidentified voice who didn't know the correct flat to buzz asked to be admitted to the building (early on we learned to switch our intercom off at night);[49] smoke alarms sounding in the early-morning hours while unattended food that was being heated started to burn; loud music being played anytime from midnight until three, four or five o'clock in the morning, so that being awakened at night became a more or less expected and regular event, as well as a general 'continual' coming and going of individuals and small groups from mid-afternoon onwards. To convey something of everyday life at this time I reproduce an excerpt from my field diary for 18 November concerning one incident among many other similarly fraught incidents:

11.30 am. I go to clean the common stairs and entrance hall at my flat. I hear from the first floor above a neighbour's daughter who is about to leave her mum's flat complain "Oh who's a' this noo?" I look up. About to enter the main door are four young people making for number 57, the problem tenant. First to enter is a young woman whom I recognise from previous occasions[50] followed by three

---

[49] As the tenant was unemployed it is likely she was unable to afford a land-line telephone. Also, this was 1998 when mobile phones were not the ubiquitous commodity they are today.

[50] A single mother of two who had been recently evicted from her Fife Council tenancy in Cardenden.

young men. The first one I look at. He is gaunt with short cropped hair and two or three small round gold coloured earrings in his left ear. He looks old and he is thin. With a grin he says to me in passing, "A'right?" I don't answer. I look at the next one passing. Young again with fair hair with his Glasgow Rangers football club sweatshirt on. I get back to cleaning and listen to the mumblings that follow the silence of passing. When they reach the middle floor I hear the words, "He's a housewife" passed among them. The insult stings and reveals the muted conflict going on all around. A challenge has been made. I look up and am thinking to reply, "An Ah suppose you're a hard-workin man?" but this is too cruel, too thought-out and personal an attack, so I settled on my own counter-mumbling retort of "Idiot" in the direction of the middle landing, loud enough to be heard. Amid the ensuing mumble I realise my counter-insult had been heard and await nervously their response. I can only make out "...come doon there an f**k you." Nothing more is said. They go into number 57. I finish the stairs.

This journal entry was written at a time when I felt I had no reason, and certainly no desire, to conduct research into 'neighbour relations' or 'housing conditions.' While the incident was indicative of day-to-day living that was characterised by having to confront the continual threat of aggressive confrontation, and while these issues were very quickly occupying more and more space in my fieldwork journal and family life, it is clear with hindsight that it was with great reluctance that I began to come to terms with the fact that I was being more or less coerced into allowing this reality onto my research agenda, and thereby 'spoiling' my long-awaited fieldwork. In the end, transforming my miserable situation into 'data' and an object of analysis became a kind of therapy that helped me to cope.

Thanks to living directly underneath an antisocial neighbour, I realised very quickly that far from being 'open to the field' I shared in all of the prejudices against 'the underclass' as any 'middle-class snob,' but also that my prejudices ran deeper as all of the *ressentiment* that is a characteristic of much of the working class (and which I recognise within myself) was available to me to be mobilised against the problem neighbour. Far from the pieties of being 'open' to the field, then, it was beneath me to attend to this debased level of reality, and I strongly resisted condescending to give it my attention. I was shocked to find myself living with people who seemed to be "as tasteless and ugly as…could be" (Muir 1935, p. 166) and so involved was I in reacting to this situation that I began to no longer trust my interpretation of the data.

Realising the scale of the problem we became angry that the Fife Council local area office in Cardenden had no responsibility to inform us of the problem as it seemed incredible that a landlord in the process of investigating complaints against our immediate neighbour for over a year had a policy that meant prospective tenants to the downstairs property were unable to make an informed decision as to whether or not to accept the offer of a tenancy. Due to Fife Council tenants' rights to confidentiality and the police being "unable to discuss details," the only source of information was neighbours themselves who had no such 'ethical' or 'professional' concerns. What soon became clear was that it was only myself immediately below number 57 and the tenants living directly above number 57, Mary and Alan at number 63, who ever approached the problem neighbour in an effort to speak to her directly about the level of noise. Mary and myself bore the brunt of the problem and it was from talking to Mary that I learnt that, by the time of my arrival to the block of nine flats, the problem had been ongoing for a year, and when visiting Mary and her husband Alan for the first time, myself and Eva were informed that the police had raided the flat and lifted the floorboards searching for drugs; that the police were 'constantly' in attendance and that number 57 was used as a meeting point for other local problem tenants such as Rhona Sheed and her children; that number 57 was in effect a 'gang hut' for local unemployed youths. When remarking to a policeman entering the flats one day about his frequency in our building, for example, his reply was that number 57 was the first port of call when dealing with child order breaches which required minors to be with their legal guardians at specified times.

If much of the social interaction that occurred within the block of flats often involved picking over the details of the latest disturbance, it was not only number 57 that came in for criticism. When I would clean the common stairwell on the ground floor, Mrs Davidson from number 53 would often emerge from behind her locked door and proceed to talk to me about the long-standing failure of the cleaning rota in our block, or some other neighbour-related issue. In one sentence and with one accompanying movement of her walking stick she would point above her head complaining: "Her up there's just as bad," and with her stick now pointing at the door of number 49 tell me: "...and her over there, she never cleans. Ah've never seen her cleaning. And them up there...." Mrs Davidson was an elderly widow and made a point of repeating how she did not feel secure day or night in her home. Apart from her daughter who lived a few streets away and visited her more or less every day, her relations with her neighbours were non-existent, and she probably complained to me so often because I was the only neighbour in the block who made themselves available for her tirades against her neighbours and her complaints regarding her situation.

The first time I went upstairs to knock on the door of number 57 to complain about noise I spoke to somebody who was not the tenant, and on the second occasion when I knocked on the door to complain about the noise, the only response was a woman's voice in an irritated tone from behind the closed door telling me: "The music's been turned doon." On this occasion when I asked the person to open the door to speak to me, there followed a prolonged silence before she replied: "The door's locked an Ah dinnae have a key." At the third attempt at complaining about noise I managed to speak to the problem neighbour (Stacey Orr) and put a face to her name as only at the third attempt did she answer her door.

As the journal entry quoted earlier indicates, so disagreeable was the situation that neighbours felt unable to occupy the space between their door and the street with any sense of security and so tended to hurry through such spaces. This sense of threat when having to negotiate the immediate environs of the flats was brought home to me one day when, returning from work early at four-thirty in the afternoon, I found the door locked and, asking Eva why she had locked the door she replied: "I don't feel safe here." This sense of feeling displaced or 'homeless' when at home is also evidenced in the following letter of complaint from Mary at number 63 to the Fife Council housing officer dealing with our case.

63 Cardenden Road
Cardenden
Fife KY5 0PD
24th September 1998

Dear Mr. McQueen,

I am writing this time on behalf of Alan and myself and Mr. and Mrs. Gilfillan of number 51. We would like your advice on any possible further action we can take against Miss Stacey Orr of number 57 as at this present time we feel we would have more chance of sleeping in a crowded nightclub. The only word that we can use to describe our recent sleep patterns is non-existent. The last few nights have been 'hell.'

Both of our families comprise two adults and a young baby. We are all having our sleep disrupted nearly every night of the week with some noise or other from no. 57. Mr. and Mrs. Gilfillan's baby is very young and at this rate will never know when she is supposed to sleep due to unnecessary excessive noise from Stacey's house at all times of day and night.

Mairéad (my 19 months old daughter) was up three times during the early hours of this morning crying, each time following loud bouts of laughter, shouting, heavy footsteps, incessant use of intercom (which, may I add, is a problem with most of the tenants in the block) or extremely loud banging noises, all of which were of course from our spiteful neighbour. Another four hours sleep lost. A huge amount of stress caused by tiredness and frustration is being forced upon both of our families as of the former tenants. We cannot understand why Fife Council would rather put more and more new tenants through the same continuous hell, when the only person deserving this treatment is the uncontrollable, immature and totally inconsiderate tenant of no. 57.

Fortunately for Mr. and Mrs. Gilfillan, they heard nothing this morning, as after only three weeks (approx.) in their new house, they were pushed into spending a night or two with family to allow them to get at least one restful night. Only three weeks have this family had the tenancy for this flat and already they are desperate to be rehoused. Doesn't this go for anything?

As previously discussed with yourself, further action from Fife Council is to be taken to rid us all of this nuisance, but it is now becoming clear that no visit from either yourselves or the police will intimidate Stacey. She is not responding to visits or warnings, I feel there must be something that can be done soon on our behalf. The more she receives such telling offs, the more rebellious she is becoming. She has no care for anyone. How much must we hear of her being told off by the police or by Fife Council? Please accept that this does nothing at all in our favour. Police and Council visits to Stacey are frequent but not one visit seems to have any better outcome than the previous.

Due to the build up of sleepless nights recently, my husband's timekeeping at work is becoming very poor, and whether late or not, his efficiency level has dropped drastically, and unfortunately his place of employment consider this to be unacceptable whatever the reason. I would like to know if people losing their job because of nuisance neighbours, therefore unable to keep up rent payments, would be able to sit back receiving warning after warning for years with no severe action being taken?

I am nearing the stage of visiting my G.P. as I don't think I can tolerate much more pressure as I already suffer from anxiety caused by stress and tiredness. Without all this hassle, people like the Gilfillan family and my own family would lead such an easy and straightforward life. Please advise us of anything we can try until the Council at least find us other accommodation (just like they had to for the previous tenants). Unfortunately for you, this will not stop the complaint letters, it simply means they will be signed by another tenant.

I would not advise anyone to accept a tenancy agreement at either of our addresses in the future, or anywhere even close to Stacey Orr. Please advise by return of any suggestions you may have on how we may speed up this whole process of having her and her many noisy friends removed from no. 57 Cardenden Road.

Yours sincerely
Mary Mead

p.s. Mr. & Mrs. Gilfillan have read this letter and fully agree with its contents.

With effect from 4 November 1998 a *Notice of Proceedings* was issued by Fife Council against the tenant at number 57; a legal document which informed her that Fife Council had begun the process of seeking a court order to evict. In practical terms being evicted meant forfeiting one's statutory right to be housed and not being able to be on the Council housing list for ten years. However, as one of the housing investigations officers told me, because the process of eviction is so lengthy, the actual number of evictions compared to the number of cases of antisocial behaviour any particular housing investigation officer is dealing with is small because, more often than not, in order to speed up the process of removing antisocial tenants, Fife Council advise the problem tenant that because they *will* be evicted at the end of a legal process, the best option for the tenant is to sign a form voluntarily surrendering their tenancy as this allows the tenant back onto the Council housing waiting list after one year.[51] Hence, it is normally a tenant being informed of the start of the formal process of seeking an eviction that actually evicts antisocial tenants, and so on 7 December 1998 the tenant 'voluntarily' left her flat.

Upon the tenant's departure there came an immediate and collective sigh of relief as the residents in the block in every conversation celebrated with each other the return of peace and normality and the repossession of shared space. As we joked among ourselves at this time, it was *us* who had been re-housed

---

[51] However, when interviewing with the housing investigation officer involved (Stuart MacQueen) he made a point of emphasising that Fife Council does not "advise" any course of action to the tenant.

thanks to being able to take possession of our homes again. On the day 'the problem' left, I lay in bed at night *confidently* enjoying the silence and ended my field diary entry for the day with the comment: "At last I can begin fieldwork!" and for the next weeks we enjoyed a relationship to space which allowed us to have qualitatively better relationships among ourselves as neighbours.

It felt as if existence had suddenly been augmented as it became co-existence again, thanks to our lives being suddenly 'de-privatised' and released from our alienation from our shared spaces and each other. We felt able to breathe again thanks to the communal air being decontaminated of the toxic and threatening presence of the former tenant. This re-established relationship to space and time made the present moment all the more sweet as integral to the experience of the moment was the anticipation that every future moment to come would be equally peaceful; as if each not yet real but anticipated future moment added another touch of sweetness to the present moment's peace, as we were released from our individual bunkers and could constitute 'being neighbours' again.

During the month or so that number 57 lay empty I was able to get to know some of the neighbours better, and returning to my flat after a few days of peace and quiet I met the neighbour from number 59 coming out of the building, and she began a conversation by asking, in reference to the recent eviction of the problem tenant and the peace and quiet all of us were enjoying: "Enjoy a quiet night last night?" Before I could do more than smile in reply she informed me that her upstairs neighbour Siobhán at number 65 had a young boy who was "like a baby elephant when he runs across the room."

This was the first occasion I was able to have a real conversation with this particular neighbour, having had little opportunity to establish normal relations during the first four months of my tenancy, and it provided us with the opportunity to introduce ourselves and talk about ourselves, and so I learned she was originally from the nearby village of Ballingry but had moved to England where her two sons still lived and that: "They will not move up here tae Scotland. They're mair English than Scottish. They were jist young boys when they went doon. They even talk

English. They dinnae speak Scottish. They dinnae want tae come up." She then told me that when first married she was in a maisonette in Glenrothes and then progressed to a flat; that "every time" she would prefer a top-floor flat with nobody above her. At this I told her that Alan at number 63 had told me of how the police had ripped up the floorboards of number 57, to which she matter-of-factly replied: "It'll be fir drugs. That's the way it is these days wi young folk. They're a' intae the drugs noo here." She then told me about her mother who had lived in her Council house for forty-four years and had died four years ago; how as the daughter she had "put in" for her mother's house but didn't get it, that her mother had been the only tenant in the house which had originally been built for miners but now "the police have been in it; raided the place fir drugs. We still think e it as ma mum's hoose, ye ken."

After enjoying conversations that centred around our new and improved living conditions, the subject of conversation among us turned to whom would replace the previous tenant, and the opinion of neighbours as to who was at the top of the Council housing waiting list was that it was one of two single women, and the tenant at number 49 advised (prophetically as it turned out) that of the two candidates one "would definitely be quieter than the other." As it turned out, then, the relaxed mood among the tenants lasted until word spread that the tenancy had been given to another local young unemployed single woman (Randy Moss) who came from a large family from the nearby street of Cluny Park that was described by one neighbour as "pretty low class" and another neighbour as "a' rough as f**k."

The new tenant took up residence in January and so began our second phase of living with an antisocial tenant, with my first meeting with her occurring well after midnight when, unable to sleep due to the noise of wallpaper being scraped off walls and music from a radio, I went upstairs to explain to the new tenant that the flats had poor sound insulation and to ask her to "keep the noise down." After knocking on the door it was opened by a friend of the tenant who then leaned against the door, and the conversation that followed was conducted with myself standing at the door and the friend helping with the redecoration holding the door ajar while the tenant remained seated on the floor with her back against the far wall of the front bedroom with cigarette and scraper in hand. Taking a few seconds to realise the tenant was not going to stand up, her comportment and every sullen monosyllabic response of "Aye" and "Right" when I explained about the noise signalled to me an unwillingness to engage in basic conventions of civility.

I returned downstairs where Eva lay waiting to ask me about my first impressions of our new neighbour, and as I lay in bed replaying the incident in my mind it struck me that the tenant's resolutely monosyllabic agreement to keep the noise down seemed like a calculated way to maintain the maximum possible social distance, and that any notion of apology for keeping one's new neighbours awake because of noise after midnight through the working week was never going to be forthcoming, and that such behaviours meant the idea of introducing myself as her neighbour became absurdly formal and out of place.

This first meeting with the new tenant proved to be a sign of things to come and so at around two a.m. on March 27th I got out of bed to go upstairs and complain about the noise. I knocked hard on the door so as to be heard over the music and a few seconds later the music was turned down. I remained standing at the door waiting for someone to answer the door. After waiting longer than it would take someone to come to the door I knocked again. As I stood at the door I heard voices from inside, presumably discussing what to do. Because the hall light inside the flat was on I could see from the movement of shadows that I was being 'spied on' from the spy-hole in the door. Wondering whether I was better off just going back downstairs content that the music had been turned down, I decided to persevere and knocked again. Eventually a man opened the door and there was the following exchange:

> **Me:** Is the tenant there?
> **Man:** Aye. She's in the bathroom.
> **Me:** Could ye tell her Ah want a word?
> **Man:** Aye.

The door was then closed and he looked to the side, as if awaiting instructions on what to do next. The tenant then stepped from behind the door where she had been standing. The conversation was as follows:

**Me:** What's wi a' the noise?
**Randy Moss:** What noise?
**Me:** This is the second time the night you've woke us up.
**Randy Moss:** Ah'm seek e the police comin tae ma door every night.
**Me:** Ah've never called the police. Not once.

At this the tenant shut the door in my face. I took a step backwards in disbelief, before complaining: "What are you playin at? Look, open the door. Ah want a word." As the door remained shut I opened it to go into the flat but, after opening the door a few inches, it was shoved shut again from the inside. From the strength it required from me to turn the handle to open the door it was clear someone on the other side was trying to prevent me from turning the handle. In this trial of strength I managed to turn the handle enough to force the door open but, in the ensuing battle to open the door, my bare feet didn't allow enough grip to keep up the contest and I gave up. As the door stayed shut, each of us stood on each side of the door waiting for the next move. I returned downstairs without further comment and never spoke again to the neighbour.

The following week, however, the new neighbour's sister (Sharen) came to our door to explain there would be noise that night. Friday nights turned out to be party night and, in the only effort at ever acknowledging the problem between us, the older sister of the tenant had come, in her own words, to give us "fair warning." At this unexpected turn of events my first thought was to invite her into my flat to take advantage of this acknowledgment of there being a problem, but as she stood on my doorstep flicking her cigarette ash onto my doorstep and floor, such a gesture seemed absurd, and in the conversation that took place between us my complaints regarding noise in general and throughout the night in particular, and of having to endure listening to hours of videos of the American sitcom *Friends* and its endless formula of four lines of dialogue followed by punch line followed by canned laughter *ad nauseam* until six o'clock in the morning, were flatly denied: "Naw. Nut. Ma sister disnae dae that. Naw. Nut." While the sister of the tenant had come to warn me of noise, she was not there to apologise for anything as there was nothing to apologise for.

Reflecting upon these incidents highlights how human behaviour is more or less always surrounded by moral evaluations and social interaction is infused by our internalisation of the 'normal' and the 'correct' way of doing things. Menley's *Tournaments of Value* (1996, p. 104) observes that the etiquette of greeting a person has "a quality of moral compulsion about it," so that a direct corollary is that to withhold or fail to practice such etiquette is to immediately suspend social relations. In light of much ethnography arguing that greeting practices and the etiquette and aesthetics of hospitality are central to the construction of personhood, so that to violate or withhold such social practices is to insult an other person (Altorki 1986; Biedelman 1989; Myers 1993), it is easy to appreciate how in a context where one's lived experience of neighbour relations is characterised by a lack of hospitality and practices of recognition, an individual who has to deal with antisocial neighbours such as Helen quoted at the outset *become hard*, and are more or less fated to instantiate an attitude and discourse towards their neighbour that is a cocktail of indifference, alienation and resentment.

Hence, when cleaning the common stairs on a Friday afternoon (22 January 1999) Mrs Davidson at number 53 came out and stood on her doorstep for her usual chat with me when cleaning, and immediately announced without firstly saying hello or good morning: "This is a terrible place tae live. A terrible place tae live," and there followed a litany of complaints. After Mrs Davidson had returned inside the elder of the two sisters at number 59 came out of her flat and, seeing me cleaning the ground floor, we began chatting about the rotas for stair cleaning which the Council drew up and distributed to the tenants via the Council caretaker (Tam Barr). This neighbour was middle-aged and as on previous occasions when we had talked in the stairwell, she was personable and sympathetic in her conversation. On the subject of cleaning the stairs on her floor she told me: "Ah refuse tae dae it. Ma sister done it a'. Cleaned right doon the stairs bit they [the other tenants on her floor] never bother. See ye've got tae make yer mooth go." Two days later when chatting with the tenant at number sixty-five, a young divorced single mother who worked in the supermarket opposite the flats, she informed me that the evicted tenant at number 57 had informed the Department of Social Security about her working, with the intent of jeopardising her welfare benefits. Next, she told me that she had just been to look at her new Council flat in Kirkburn Drive and that: "Ah'll be oot e here in a fortnight!" From her comments on living in the block of flats it was clear she felt more or less compelled to leave.

During the time spent living beneath the second antisocial tenant the problem changed insofar as when living beneath the first problem tenant I felt she was indifferent to all of her neighbours, and so her behaviours were 'anonymous' or 'impersonal,' whereas the issue with the second tenant involved behaviours that were personal and directed towards me. On one occasion late at night, for example, I heard the sister who had simultaneously acknowledged and denied the problem of noise enter the flat upstairs and immediately begin playing loud music, at which the tenant asked her to turn the music down, and to which the older sister replied: "F**k um. F**k um" (which I interpreted as referring to myself). On another occasion in the early hours of the morning music was played at full volume only to be turned down, and then turned up again to the maximum *until my bedroom ceiling visibly vibrated.* This behaviour carried on for hours and when the police were called a patrol car from Glenrothes six miles away would be sent, and soon after the police had spoken to the neighbour and started back to Glenrothes, the music and noise resumed. This second phase of living with antisocial neighbours lasted until 7 February 2000 when we gave up our Council flat tenancy and moved into a private flat at 113 Station Road, which was inferior to what we had before and double the rent we had been paying at 51 Cardenden Road but solved our problem of living below antisocial neighbours.

## Learning How to Become Dominated

To live in the field I needed to obtain a Fife Council tenancy and, having been on the housing waiting list for over a year prior to being offered a tenancy, I was struck from the outset of fieldwork by the level of control that Fife Council and the local Ore Valley Housing Association[52] exercised over the ability to live locally. In contrast to stranded American novelists like Kate Atkinson referred to in Chapter 1 "simply staying" in Cardenden, the difficulties involved in simply being present in Cardenden to do my research highlights the fact that resolving the question of housing independently of local government bureaucracy in the nineteen-nineties was far from straightforward, as private renting opportunities were very few and far between as there was very little in the way of a local housing market and so there were very few opportunities to privately rent or buy property in Cardenden.

As a result of Fife Council's de facto control over local housing, then, shortly after the first tenant at number 57 left I arranged a meeting with a Council official in the Cardenden area office to request some thought be given to who was allocated the vacant tenancy. From my initial phone calls to arrange the meeting, however, it was clear that in requesting this meeting at all I was being presumptuous; was getting 'above myself' and breaking the normal 'rules of engagement' and inconveniencing busy individuals. In the event, the meeting went badly. Our request for some thought on the part of the Council was not at all welcome given the irritated and incredulous reception our request was met with at the meeting. It was clear the Council official was unimpressed *as a matter of principle* at our desire

---

[52] In 1998 the only other renting option was to apply to Auchterderran Housing Association (subsequently enlarged and renamed Ore Valley Housing Association) for a tenancy and so I had also applied for a house with this organisation.

to be part of the housing allocations procedure, and she was dismissive at our desire for a form of devolution of power to sitting tenants regarding having a role in who was to become our neighbour.

Also, in all probability, another contributing factor as to why the meeting went badly was my agenda to establish at the beginning of the meeting why I had not been informed of the ongoing situation of antisocial neighbours before I signed my tenancy agreement the year before, and why I was only informed of a problem after I had spent my savings furnishing the flat. To this particular query myself and Eva were told that what was or what was not happening with another tenant was a confidential matter, and *the Council official was not aware of having received any complaints about our previous neighbour.* At this 'revelation' I pointed out that neighbours at number 63 had informed us the problem had been ongoing for over a year by the time we signed our tenancy in August 1998, and the police had raided the house on two occasions. To this we were told: "Well, you're telling me that but I have no evidence. Who is to say what is unreasonable noise? I need proof." Again, I felt incredulous at this request by a Fife Council local area office employee for evidence of antisocial behaviour concerning the tenant at number 57 given her colleagues in the Housing Investigations Team had months before visited myself and Eva to advise us of an ongoing problem with the behaviour of our upstairs neighbour, and request we begin collecting evidence to be used in a court of law to secure an eviction order. In an increasingly fraught series of exchanges I told the Council employee: "We are here because if you can make a mistake once, then you will probably do it again!"

Although told in no uncertain terms that housing allocation policy meant whoever happened to be next on the waiting list would be offered the tenancy, we took comfort from the words: "We will do our best to make sure the person is suitable" in light of the fact that the idea of organising a rent strike within our block of flats, for example, to impress Fife Council as to the unacceptable lack of action in resolving the issues of noisy neighbours was out of the question, given many did not pay rent and therefore were not in a position to threaten to withdraw the monthly rent of £137.28. We felt coerced into pursuing what seemed like utterly dominated attempts at exercising some kind of agency to change our situation. The merest hint of complaisance from the Council was greeted with heartfelt relief, so that on our way home from this bruising encounter myself and Eva congratulated ourselves simply at having 'done something.'

Other pathetic attempts at agency that were related to me, such as when chatting to one of Auchterderran Housing Association's employees was local housing stock being used as "giro drops" i.e. the practice of individuals lying and presenting themselves to the Association as homeless, often presenting themselves as having split from their wife or partner and thereby qualifying for being deemed officially 'homeless' and therefore a new tenancy, which is taken but is not actually lived in so the house is simply used as a 'giro drop' (and also securing more giro money on account of being single as opposed to married or living with a partner). Unsurprisingly, this practice of seeking a tenancy purely as a 'giro drop' fuels a sense of resentment among locals as the practice is often known or suspected by locals, and the issue of social security fraud was a constant presence in letters to local newspapers, such as the following from the *Central Fife Times* newspaper (6th September 2001):

*Why do they get away with it?*

It is no wonder there are so many homeless people in Scotland. Here in Fife and elsewhere you have people living often as not with someone else. While the council house or flat lies empty, they get their rent paid by the DHS. They often do not pay council tax yet they continue to cheat and lie their way into keeping the council house that some genuine family or single person needs very badly. So why do the DHS and councils continue to let these spongers in society away with this fraud?

SOCIAL JUSTICE FOR ALL,
Cardenden.

Among locals it is well understood that 'working' the system is a spectrum, and while giro drops are extreme examples that are condemned, there are more or less accepted forms of exercising agency such as giving false or misleading information when form-filling in order to gain as many points as possible when completing a housing application form. Similarly, casual working while claiming unemployment benefit is another more or less acceptable form of dominated 'agency' among those who are often tacitly seen as unable to meet the standards of the majority. Related to new practices such as 'giro drops' is another novelty in Cardenden as regards housing which is the coming together or the 'alignment' of people on low incomes or the unemployed and Council housing, with the result that there is today a certain stigma attached to 'social housing' where previously there was none. As a result of the boom in former Council tenants buying their properties and becoming property owners from the nineteen-eighties onwards, there is today a distinction made between those who have bought their house and those who have not, often with the presumption that the latter have not bought their homes because they are too poor to do so, and so whether renting privately or renting a Council property from Ore Valley Housing Association, there is a strong association of renting and poverty or some kind of misfortune.

Hence, some five months after moving the few hundred yards from Cardenden Road to our new address in Station Road, new neighbours moved into the flat beside us which until then had lain empty. Our new neighbour was an unemployed single mother (Charlene) who had two young daughters. Every morning their two Labrador dogs would be let out to defecate wherever they could find space among the parked cars, children's toys and various patches of grass that served as gardens, despite the large public park being less than fifty yards away. On one occasion soon after our new neighbours moved in I came out of my flat with my two-year-old daughter and saw the two dogs were tied to the railings at the foot of the stairs we shared, while nearby Charlene was painting a used car tyre which she had salvaged from the rubble and junk lying in the property belonging to the Caspian takeaway next door or one of the untended gardens belonging to an absentee landlord. As Charlene painted the tyre her daughters smoothed multi-coloured gravel around the plant they had placed in the centre of the tyre.

Walking down the stairs I picked up my daughter and carried her, and as we approached the dogs I felt my daughter's body tense in fear as she gripped my neck with her two hands and buried her face into my chest as we descended closer towards the barking dogs who had become agitated at our imminent arrival to the foot of the steps. As we approached the dogs I asked Charlene if she could keep the dogs to one side for a moment, explaining my daughter was afraid of the dogs. Given that Marlene could see I had a bag in one hand and my daughter in the other, I was not expecting her to refuse this request, nor her reply: "She'll just have to get used to it." As things turned out, however, my daughter had only seven months to get used to the dogs as Charlene moved out in February 2001 as a result of the Department of Social Security refusing to pay the rent her landlord was asking, and upon leaving she left dozens of black plastic bags full of rubbish at the foot of the common stairs which the landlord, who lives in a large private bungalow in Cardenden Road, had not removed six months later when we ourselves left 113 Station Road. [53]

In August 2012 Fife Council began a programme of renewing the roofs on their housing stock within Cardenden so that by simply overlooking the village one can immediately tell from the bright orange coloured roof tiles the extent of houses in the village still owned by the Council, and I would estimate that about a third of local houses are rented. It is also clear from simply walking through the village that some streets are more wealthy than others with particular streets such as Hyndloop Terrace or a certain section of Derran Drive, for example, being known for

---

[53] The issue of who was responsible for the upkeep of the spaces at the back of the buildings was ongoing, with the general lack of any cleaning or maintenance of these spaces having led to a Fife Council Environmental Officer inspecting the area due to complaints of vermin.

housing tenants with little money and whose gardens and general appearance communicate a level of neglect going back to the 'dictatorship of scarcity' period.

Given Cardenden's SIMD rankings detailed in Chapter 1 it is undeniable that Cardenden suffers from levels of deprivation that are considerably above the national average. However, it is also true to say that for all of Cardenden's inhabitants there has been clear material progress with improvements in housing conditions to the fore of a tremendous change for the better. While Corrie's *Black Earth* (1939, p. 180) described a Cardenden where: "there was nothing better for them, for all the houses were the same. They were built cheaply by the Brandon Coal Company to house their workers," these original miners' dwellings which were built for the workers by the mine owners were demolished and the current houses seen today were built after World War two during 1946-47. At this time streets were given their current names as previously they were simply numbered First Street, Second Street etcetera. When I asked the local history group members why the streets had originally been numbered this way, I was told the presumably apocryphal story of how a Mr. Muir who in 1895 was the manager of Bowhill Colliery had saw to it that upon his return from honeymoon in America the American system of naming streets was adopted in Cardenden, and as Adam Ingram (25 May 1999) told me: "Once we discovered there was a Sixth Street in New York we felt better."

The following memory from Mrs Rollo (d. 1995) indicates something of the importance of housing conditions for improving the quality of life (Local History Group, vol. 5, p. 26):

In 1926 the Education Board opened a new primary school for the Roman Catholic children at the end of 17th Street. The Fife Coal Company built more houses at the end of 16th Street opposite the new school. These houses had a living room, two bedrooms and a scullery...their own gate and path to their door...a garden, front and back...Oh! What bliss!...hot and cold water laid on.

Despite these post-war improvements, however, it was not until the nineteen-nineties that most residents in Cardenden began to enjoy homes that could be said to have 'conquered' the Scottish winter, and had upstairs bedrooms warm enough to spend time in during the winter months as a result of the installation of gas central heating and double glazing windows along with new bathrooms and kitchens and new wiring and loft and wall insulation at this time. Thanks to this revolution in housing it was not until this time that the majority of residents enjoyed adequate housing. As one informant (Tom Henderson) told me: "The best thing that ever happened wis sellin' the council hooses. New doors, central heating, double glazing. The improvements are unbelievable. It certainly improved the schemes." Similarly, when talking to another informant (Mr Duncan, Carden Avenue) when the subject of the 'right to buy' policy of the nineteen-eighties came up, he remarked that this policy was: "The only thing Thatcher ever done for the working class." As per the remarks of Tom cited above, the widespread uptake of tenants' right-to-buy their council houses means the popularity of home improvement is ubiquitous throughout the village in the shape of conservatories, loft conversions and all manner of alterations to gardens.

We may say that *domestic space* has been further liberated thanks to being taken out of the hands of local government and is able to be a substantial 'something in itself' that literally creates space for a more expansive sense of habitation and more possibilities for individuation and sociation, thanks to the ability to habitate spaces that have been liberated from nature and a prior dependency upon the weather thanks to being sufficiently warm to be habitable. This progress in housing was extended further between 2003 and 2008 when property developers built approximately two hundred new private houses in Cardenden, while Ore Valley Housing Association built new 'social housing' properties for rent in Craigside Road, Whitehall Avenue and Bluebell Gardens.

Thanks to the shift from coal fires to gas central heating that occurred at this time, a whole series of practices came to an end, such as having to go outside for coal to put on a fire to heat a house, and no more "putting the blower on" in the fireplace to heat water, and no more having to endure winters with ice forming on the inside of bedroom windows as a result of the cold. To sum up this recent revolution in housing conditions we may say that whereas Muir described and lamented a Scotland that was "covered with tasteless council houses" (1935, p. 69), a young mother-of-three and lifelong resident in Cardenden could remark after visiting one of the show homes in the new private housing scheme in the Jamphlars area of the village that was built in 2005: "When yer in the new hooses ye dinnae feel like yer in Cardenden!"

Thanks to this revolution in their domestic spaces, the next section argues that a contextual "ontology of place" (Verran 2002, p. 165) must include the emergence of *the house as a new medium and mediation of 'territorial sovereignty' and control from the nineteen-nineties onwards*, in contrast to social theorists who propose a liberation from place; that locals' relationship to domestic space has been modernised and liberated from the 'feudal' relationship to the local State in which it had languished, so that the home has become a new site for the tasks and tensions of 'being modern,' and insofar as this new empowerment vis-à-vis space becomes reflexive it is taken up by freedom and developed into a 'doctrine' of belonging and dwelling in other realms of experience, such as the geo-political and constitutional and the question of national sovereignty.

## 3.2 The Task of 'Being Modern' among the '79 Generation(s)

In my meetings with both the local Fife Council employee described earlier and my meetings with the two members of Fife Council housing investigations team, I found myself up against individuals who were very guarded and more or less hidebound, with the result that very little information was forthcoming. However, when interviewing a Housing Studies student (Eddie, 17 December 1998) which I had arranged to try to get some background information on housing issues, I was finally able to speak with someone who was very much alive to the general issue

227

of Fife Council allocating tenancies to antisocial individuals and the deeper cultural question as to why Scottish localities were producing so many 'antisocial individuals' in the first place. As we began our interview Eddie began by telling me of a new initiative concerning young people and housing:

> Fife Cooncil have a scheme, Springboard Housing Project, where they assist young people in what they call independent livin. They gie them a tenancy an they show them how tae keep it. They teach them how tae look efter their hoose, how tae look after their tenancy. That's their joab. Jist show them how tae budget, how tae cook, how tae clean, how tae run a hoose. That's their joab. That wis set up in response tae the fact in the Templehall area [in Kirkcaldy] there wis a lot e young people gettin tenancies an abandonin it, 'cause they didnae ken how tae look efter it. They were up tae here in arrears, rent arrears. Their hoose wis a doss hoose, there were people in it a' the time that they didnae ken. This wis set up in response tae that.

Eddie's testimony alerted me to a wholly unsuspected level of dependency that I had no idea existed. While aware in a general and abstract manner of the neoliberal critique of the Welfare State such as Hayek's (1944) 'new serfdom' thesis where, as a result of the qualitatively new socialisation role being undertaken by the State, the family and individual responsibility are being replaced by the State and creating new levels of dependency or 'serfdom' among a fraction of the poorest members of the '79 generations, the information Eddie had at his fingertips was empirical evidence to safeguard against any temptation to imagine there is a new generation emerging from the industrial era with a clean pair of heels and that is capable of instantiating, for example, the new relationship to domestic space that has recently become possible and mentioned in the previous section, far less are capable of a return to a pre-industrial holism after the cultural and physical predations of industrialism. Having seen the many houses that are facsimiles of Corrie's "uncultivated garden patches with their rickety old sheds, pigeon houses and rabbit-hutches" (1939, p. 88), it is clear that such locals will never appropriate a post-industrial narrative. As Eddie told me when I asked him to give an overview of the main issues in managing Fife Council housing stock in Cardenden:

It's come doon tae the legislation on home ownership cause anybody that's in a decent hoose has bought their hoose. An a' that's left is a' the shite hooses an the people that cannae afford tae buy them. That's why it's now called Social Housing, because it's only the people that are on benefits that are in. It's what ye call 'residual housing.' That's a' that's left an it's usually a' the crap in hard tae let areas. If a'body in Cluny Park, Whitehall Avenue, Carden Castle Park [local streets] have bought their hoose and they flats [in Cardenden Road] is a' that's left, a' the dregs are gonnae go there, a' the dregs e society is gonnae git pit in the flats if that's the only Cooncil hooses left. That's the wrang term tae use obviously bit ye ken exactly what Ah mean. There's a big issue in housin at the moment in that they're wantin it tae take oan a more social role because it's a' poor people that they are basically dealin wi. They're wanting it integrated wi social work, housin and social work's the same department, because it's a' the poor people that's rentin, so they've integrated wi social work. That's why Ah'm daen a degree in housin. They're tryin tae make it a professional qualification.[54]

Eddie's experience of working with young people being in need of 'charity' and special welfare schemes to help them manage their tenancies relates directly to the closely-related crisis in such young people making the transition to being an independent adult insofar as the inability to keep a tenancy also implies

---

[54] Eddie was previously a pipe-fitter to trade but had subsequently completed his post-industrial "reconversion strategy" (Bourdieu 1984, p.125) and moved from skilled manual work to non-manual social work.

less-than-adult status in the eyes of the community. When talking with locals about their experiences of antisocial neighbours there was a sense of bewilderment and even *bereavement* surrounding a generational-fraction for whom effecting the transition to adulthood has become problematic. As one long-term resident (born in 1940) commented on the day of the eviction of a young single mother (Donna Reid) in August 1998 from Cardenden Road, after I had expressed surprise as until then I had never heard of anyone being evicted in Cardenden:

Evicted today! At the bus stop, the double block. Ricky Bell up Whitehall Avenue has got a key supposedly to the house. She's got two laddies. Young one's going in and out. Ah saw the bags. She's away tae a homeless place. She come fae Lochgelly.[55] They all got a petition signed. Saw their councillor an got a lawyer. Forced the Cooncil tae dae somethin. Ah dinnae believe in this silence crap. These Van Becks'll be next.[56] That Sarah pits her music oan. See they're a' oot e crap hames. Bit if ye jist sit an say nuthin they'll take o'er the place...One e the Van Beck's son-in-laws gave that Ricky Bell a doin. He got taen away in an ambulance but the next day he was back. Thought he had broken ribs bit the next day he wis pinchin wheel trims! Nae wonder everybody wants their ain wee bungalow. Away somewhere. Peace an quiet. See the Council's got a lot tae answer for. The lassies are the worst. The Cooncil's gien them a' hooses...Next door tae Wullie Doig, accordin tae Cathy (Whitehall Avenue resident), they were dancin naked oot the back. The RSPCA wis doon there fir the dug. Ye cannae take it tae a homeless shelter. See these folk cost the poll tax. Aye, they're a burden tae society. See they've nae faithers. Nae work. Cause it's ay been a decent area. Why let the thugs take over? An it's a' these wee yins, ye ken? Ah mean they're startin young nooadays...jist a continual gaun oot an in yer girden, a' the

---

[55] A neighbouring village.
[56] Tenants in Whitehall Avenue.

time Ah mean ye ken. Ah mean tae hell wi that...their ain girdens are like middens...you're workin tryin tae keep yer place braw...an they're gonnae...ye ken?...Och Ah mean when you were young it wis jist mischief...ye'd go in girdens, ye'd steal vegetables or what...a'bdies done that bit wi thame they're wicked some e thum noo. Bit ye see this is jist...see at sixteen year auld we were oot workin at fifteen year auld...bit noo they're runnin aboot like bairns, ken what Ah mean! Sixteen year auld we'd been oot workin fir a year...an noo sixteen year auld they're runnin aboot cryin folk poofs, ken what Ah mean? The mentalities jist no there, it's no there!

This informant's discourse is highly structured and highly 'available' to her, so that we may say her experience has structured her perception and speaking so as to bring about a 'social literacy' that enables her to quickly read any 'antisocial tenant' as a matter of genre or as a variation on a well-established theme, so that her analysis 'flows' and is readily available when interviewed because her discourse is informed by an already established *gestalt* as opposed to being dependent upon first-hand knowledge of the particular situation. Integral to this informant's perception is the fundamental notion that employment is the condition *sine qua non* of adulthood, so that she is baffled by behaviours and neighbours that are fated to appear to her as infantile and unsocialised, a concern that is shared by Eddie when he commented: "Young people are no mixin wi adults any mair...at work. They're a' on these trainin schemes."

In my nineteen months spent at 51 Cardenden Road the two problem neighbours were young and local single unemployed women, and while the particular set of housing conditions and neighbour relations within my block of flats is unequivocally not representative of Cardenden, they do share continuities with other more general behaviours observable on a daily basis. Hence, because the kitchens in the three blocks of Council flats in Cardenden Road were too small to fit a table, all meals had to be taken in the living room and so we ate breakfast overlooking the spacious enclosed grassed area for the use of the tenants of all three blocks of flats. More or less daily we would watch a tenant from the middle block of flats come out and lean against the same clothes pole and light a cigarette and let her Alsatian dog exercise for as long as it took her to finish her cigarette. Because we were a ground floor flat she could see us looking at her before she returned to her flat without cleaning up after her dog. This kind of mentality or 'privatised consciousness' that is oblivious to basic standards and oblivious to how their behaviour is perceived by others echoed the views of another informant (Ena Herd, Orebank Road, 14th November 1999) who had observed that:

> Young folk'll sit in a beautifully decorated living room and they'll no clean up their litter outside, young folk. They'll withdraw intae their ain wee bit and they'll no interact wi other people.

While informants refer to 'mentalities' that 'are just not there' and refer to a broken world of work, another theme that informants kept drifting back to was the reality of "broken families" or "broken homes." Both Eddie and another local social worker I spoke to who was involved on a daily basis with children deemed to be 'at risk' and young people in residential care units, and who supervised home visitations by young people 'in care,' it is clear that their work experience has led them to their own evidence-based 'essentialism' which they summed up in the truism that broken homes lead to broken children and then broken lives, in much the same way as apple trees produce apples. When enquiring about the background of the young people in the homeless unit Eddie worked in he replied:

> A lot e them come fae broken hames. Ah'd say the majority e them come fae broken homes. An they're stayin wi their mum or step faither or the ither way aboot an they cannae deal wi it. There's letters in the press every week aboot Lochgelly. They're sayin Lochgelly wis a dumpin grund fir bad tenants. A' the antisocial tenants are dumped in

232

Lochgelly. An that wis happenin in Cardenden fir a while as well. Craigside Road. That wis a dumpin ground...cause it is happenin! Ah used tae say, this wis afore Ah got interested in this line e work, when the Cooncil first started daen a' the hooses up, Ah used tae say aye it's no the hooses they want tae regenerate, it's the tenants they're wantin tae regenerate. Because they've got a' these braw hooses an then, ken, two weeks later some e they hooses are jist as bad. Broken windaes, ken? Three-piece suite lyin in the front garden, ken? So Ah think the problem has always been there; it's jist worse. The Snell family's [source of tension in Whitehall Avenue]been evicted fae somewhere in Kinglessie. Bit Ah'm no sure if the problem's jist movin roond aboot, bein displaced, or if it's growin. Ah'm no sure. Bit Ah ken Cardenden's no the worse place Ah can tell ye that.

After highlighting the lack of local employment and the demise of family life, my two informants with many years of experience of social work feel there is nothing more to be said in answer to the more general question as to why the various initiatives and services that are being put in place and provided by voluntary, local authority and State organisations were never required before.[57] When asked to comment on the differences seen today and previously, for example, Eddie's laconic reply was: "Well, that was when we had a family structure." This was typical of informants who routinely referred to the breakdown of families, absent fathers and young unemployed locals lacking financial resources being given tenancies as either causing or appeasing the rise of antisocial behaviour.

---

[57] Both informants had a vast repertoire of anecdotes and both told me their work load always increased during the summer months as a result of school holidays and parents having to be parents all day rather than just when their children were not in school; that such was the level of dysfunctionality that parents routinely looked to social workers to help them top up their mobile phones, rather than concern themselves with details such as shopping and having milk in the fridge for the following day's breakfast.

My informants' experience of dealing with individuals and families that have unsuccessfully negotiated the shift to the post-industrial era and the new service-based occupational landscape, meant that they have become trapped in new forms of dependency upon the State. This predicament allows these social workers a daily view of their clients' socialisation and individuation and reveals a deep dysfunctionality that is often 'inherited' from their parents; as if these '79 generation individuals have lacked from an early age the mental and cultural wherewithal to equip them to successfully negotiate the shift to the post-industrial occupational landscape and so they remain trapped in a pre-adult stage.

The fundamental impact of worklessness in the socialisation of young people into adult life is a clear theme among many informants, and in the discourse of the '45 generation there is a persistent signalling of the sense of caesura between the '45 and '79 generations and the fundamental fact of de-industrialization experienced during the nineteen-eighties. Traditionally, it has been the function of work to socialise young adults into their place within local society, and this had many other integrating consequences such as establishing psychological continuity between the generations and between fathers and sons and mothers and daughters. Prolonged worklessness, then, involves a loss of social ties and the loss of the means to belong, fuelling discussions of the creation of an underclass in deindustrialised areas throughout post-industrial societies. It is because the industrial era was characterised by a local world of work and a local public realm that their coming to a conclusive end in the nineteen-eighties means that, among the '45 generation, what is framing the 'present as history' is a more or less sharp decline in a sense of working-class cohesiveness and the sense of local community and the sense of a cultural tradition that no longer has a viable future.

Similarly, the '79 generation are more or less removed from the lived experience of locality and traditions of their parents' generation with the result that, as well as inheriting an undeniable freedom, they also inherit a vulnerability as they enter a new manner of 'being modern' and a new manner of being disembedded from the past and locality, and are at risk of instantiating a new level of 'traditionlessness.' I would not contest the assertion, then, that a class fraction of the '79 generation(s) is characterised by a 'tensionless' surrender to new social and cultural logics; that much as the first generation of peasants who experienced the rigors of a 'first modernisation' which saw the advent of the factory system and saw themselves become a landless and de-cultured proletariat, so a 'second modernisation' has taken place (that began locally in 1965 and ended in 1986), and which has seen the '79 generation(s) enter a second phase of 'traditionlessness' where localities and psyches are 'liberated' from traditional industrial narratives and the traditions and disciplines and beliefs of the industrial era, so that the world for the '79 generation(s) has been re-made insofar as they inhabit a 'disorganised' economy and a 'disorganised' symbolic order for which they have no preparation and little cultural ballast to ensure they maintain their course.

If younger generations face a qualitatively new economic and cultural situation, the changing role of women has been identified as fundamental (McCrone 2001) and I argue the dialectical position that while the social and cultural situation of women has changed dramatically since the nineteen-seventies, the idea that there has been a "liberation from the family" (Giddens 1973, p. 288) is simultaneously true and a myth. The number of female informants who could be described as freed from the rigors of raising children, for example, are statistically insignificant but it is true that women have increasingly become 'liberated' from the rigors (and supports) of forming a family and household with the men who father their children. A younger generation of women, then, are liberated from the traditional family but are still immersed in or weighed down by a host of conventional female roles and identities and disciplines. In this regard, mothers with young children remaining within the labour force has impacted localities insofar as there has been a drastic and defining loss of status suffered by 'women's work' among women of the '79 generation(s), which has led to the 'defeminizing' and deskilling of neighbourhoods and local space.

I would speculate that the absence of any 'female culture' in our block of nine flats in Cardenden Road was integral to accounting for the level of de-socialised neighbour relations thanks to women's more or less coerced retreat from a traditional habitual occupation of and domination of the domestic/public boundary space; that an intergenerational 'disappearing' of a domestic-centred female culture has occurred but, as a result of my inability to access the chat and conversation of women, I am only able to guess at specifically female forms of pressures and processes via informant's anecdotes; such as one informant's common-law wife and mother of two grown daughters and soon-to-be grandmother who, one day, when preparing food, had complained to him the recipe she was following required a litre of water. As related to me the exchange between my male informant and his wife was as follows:

**Wife:** How much is a litre?
**Man:** Jist use that plastic jug.
**Wife:** How dae ye mean like?
**Man:** The jug! That'll tell ye.
**Wife:** How like?
**Man:** It's got the measurements on the side!
**Wife:** What are ye talkin aboot?
**Man:** See they marks on the side e the jug? They tell ye a' the different measurements.
**Wife:** Oh right! Is that what they're fir? Ah never kent that!

When recalling this incident my male informant made a show of being incredulous that a mother could be so alienated from basic culinary competences, but did not offer any further comment or analysis. However, it was clear that his telling this anecdote was surrounded by an unstated moral evaluation of his common-law wife, and if we were to pass his anecdote through the sociological imagination, 'his' view was that this woman had been 'un-done' or 'un-made' by forces of modernisation. My own view is that it is clear that mothers in particular are subject to a range of objective social pressures that have come into alignment in such a way as to effect specifically female forms of deskilling, and that there is alienation from traditional female roles and a recent

236

alienation from a previous female 'realm of meaning' among the first post-conventional 1979 generation(s) whose members are interpolated by their new 'marketised' relationship to time and self, and which more or less coerces them into failing to reproduce the exigencies of child-centredness, the demands of domestic culture and the disciplines of family life. While this alignment of objective social forces (including a 'female friendly' post-manual occupational landscape) is often rightly celebrated as the real historical agent responsible for female liberation, not every woman is able to reach 'escape velocity' from their circumstances to take advantage of new economic and social conditions.

One evening (23 August 2002) while drinking in one of the local pubs with a friend, we got chatting with the barmaid Margaret whom we could see was pregnant. Margaret told us she was pregnant by her current boyfriend with whom she was living and that the baby was due in November, and that she was to go for a screen tomorrow and her young son Ian "is all excited about it." As business was slow and Margaret had time on her hands, she then asked us what we thought about the following scenario. Margaret told us she had a friend 'Mary' whose former boyfriend has two young children by two different women – one of whom is her friend Mary while the other woman lives in England with her child. Margaret then told us that Mary will not allow her ex-boyfriend to see his child; that "to his face" Mary denies the child is his but to the Child Support Agency (CSA) she names him as the father of the child. Margaret asked us if we think Mary's ex-partner should pay maintenance for the child, and whether the CSA should ensure he pays maintenance, and then asked us whether we think her friend has the right to prevent her former partner from seeing his child. To this last question we said no, that it seemed a question of natural justice that a father sees his child. Margaret then asked us to consider whether because Mary's ex-partner's name was not on the child's birth certificate this might be a problem for her friend persuading the CSA to pursue child maintenance from the father.

As we pondered this question, Margaret revealed that she had no such friend Mary, that she was talking about herself, that while expecting a baby by her current boyfriend, her son Ian was fathered by a former boyfriend, the boyfriend in the story who has one child in England and the other in Cardenden i.e. Margaret's son Ian. Margaret came clean and informed us that she was chasing the CSA to get money from her ex-boyfriend and father of Ian, but that because she did not put his name on the birth certificate, getting any maintenance was proving difficult despite the fact she had given the CSA: "Everything except his National Insurance number. Ah gave them where he works, who for, his address etcetera but the CSA a few months back wrote back saying they couldn't trace him and that was the end of it." Margaret was angry that the father of her son paid no maintenance for his son. Talking further, she told us her own mother and father divorced when she was three years old.

While Margaret's set of circumstances are clearly of her own making, they are also indicative of a wider predicament that may be described as a second *female modernity* specific to working-class women, but a predicament faced by young women that an older generation of women are aware of. Among older female informants whom I interviewed, then, many touched upon the crisis affecting family life. Interviewing Rose Anderson (Carden Cresent) in June 1999 she reported a profound sense of foreboding, and when pressed to explain replied:

> **Rose:** Things are definitely changin. People jist dinnae, ye ken... When Ah look aboot me Ah think we need a change...Ken look at the trouble that's gaun oan, ye didnae get that before!
> **Me:** What trouble do ye mean?
> **Rose:** Everythin! Ken it sounds silly, wee things...Bit families! Ah dinnae ken...somethin's went wrong some place...something's happenin tae oor country an Ah don't know what.

Similar concerns about family life were raised by my wife Eva from the outset of fieldwork. While we were painting our flat before moving in she had suddenly asked me: "When are we getting divorced?" Asking what she meant by this, her reply was

238

that everyone in our block of flats was either divorced or separated, that she had been struck by the fact that 'everyone' we talked to was either divorced or separated. This drew my attention to the fact that households headed by divorced, separated or unmarried mothers and their children formed half of the households in our block of flats, and my awareness of the endemic reality of family breakdown increased throughout fieldwork as locals themselves identified absentee fathers and single mothers as a sign of the times.

It was always with a little trepidation, despite being armed with the latest electoral register, when conducting door-to-door interviews that, having interviewed a woman on her doorstep, I asked if I could speak to her husband or partner as I quickly learned that asking to speak to a woman's husband or partner may cause some embarrassment when she had to reply, "He's no here any mair." Likewise, whenever a child answered the door I quickly learned not to ask if their mum or dad was in but to simply ask if I could speak to their mum.[58] As a result of these fieldwork experiences I made a point of keeping notes on matters of 'the family' and kinship relationships and individual case histories, and my practice was to freely write up all such information. While informants were often happy to 'tell me everything' not only about themselves but other families they knew intimately, the implicit sense of betrayal that would arise if I were to make public such 'family business' meant I freely collected this data but with no intention of publishing any of it.

What I was struck by was what appeared to be the *casual* nature of sexual relationships, and the casual manner of conceiving and either having children or aborting unwanted pregnancies. Informants casually mentioning in conversation for example while shopping in Bowhill or when collecting their children from school about some local woman having had 'another abortion' means that, as well as an upsurge in freedom, there has been an upsurge in violence as a result of the 'casualisation' of male-female

---

[58] Similarly, teachers in the local schools confided in me that they have discontinued the practice of having pupils draw their family tree as a result of the difficult issues this would raise for many children.

relationships and the normalization of the "liquidation of the subject" (Adorno, in Bronner 1994, p. 180) via the practice of abortion, and the fact that casual gossip about a woman having an abortion in a playground happens at all shows the social practice of speaking also participates in this casualization, so that "knowledge, however vile, is frankly expressed" (Muir 1935, p. 117) whether in the public park by teenagers or the playground by mums.

It seems safe to conclude that the '79 generation is the first truly post-conventional generation insofar as it has been the first to practice what was once quaintly referred to as 'free love,' and is the first generation *to practice* or experience primary relationships more or less always at risk of failing to exist as a result of the normalization of family breakdown thanks to ever-deeper capitulations to utilitarian evaluations of human beings as unborn human life and then teenage life are more or less fated to be drawn into the violent/liberating condition of 'being modern' and simultaneously liberated from tradition, only to be put at the mercy of objective depersonalizing forces.

Among '45 generation members in particular, then, there is the perception not only of industrial or economic decline but a wider *cultural decline* which is viewed as tearing at the very fabric of life and so is profoundly disorienting. The idea of the 'end of the family' then acts as a cipher for informants' concerns that previously untouched areas of human life, such as the family and the nature of parenthood, are being drawn into the dilemma of 'modernisation' and so in their own way they grasp the 'crisis of the West' and its signature 'crisis of knowledge' whereby convictions and beliefs and practices that were previously so fundamental that they did not need to be thought about, far less defended, are now 'at issue' and experienced as threatened with immanent privatization, if not obsolescence. I describe this condition as the radicalisation of the tension of 'being modern' and among the '45 generation this is a cause of an unprecedented 'cultural disorientation' or lament because it signals the ending of a shared symbolic order.

From a sociological perspective it is clear that the same objective forces that have 'disorganised' the free-market economy

(Lash and Urry 1987) and disembedded Christianity from the nineteen-sixties onwards (Brown 2001) are having a similar disorganising effect upon the family, so that it is among the 1979 generation that the family is simultaneously liberated and privatised, so that Marx's view of "the practical absence of the family among the proletarians" (Marx and Engels [1848] 1996, p. 31) becomes an empirical fact for many in the '79 generation. Informants such as Rose are concerned about the ongoing and unforeseeable consequences for individuation the 'post-family' contexts of early life are having as a result of sexual relationships and practices reaching 'escape velocity' from conventional norms. From a sociological point of view, then, we can say that in the younger generations where 'everything' has reached its escape velocity from public or conventional regulation, 'everything' such as family life requires the 'miracle' of the personal commitment to convention in a post-conventional era to survive.

Thus stated, it is relatively straightforward to anticipate various forms of conventional behaviour as being destined to decline, and from the nineteen-seventies onwards the sociological constant behind the massive intergenerational economic and social and cultural change is that one set of conventions has been quickly replaced by a new set of social determinisms, so that the 'post-Christian' and 'post-family' individual is the new convention or socially determined lifestyle of choice, with the notion of the 'free autonomous individual' remaining just as strong and just as blatantly mythical among the post-industrial '79 generation(s).[59]

An older generation of informants also raise concerns regarding what might be termed a sharp rise in 'behavioural nihilism' characterised by casual linguistic violence, drug use and pro-miscuous sexual relationships which they see coming in the wake of fractured biographies and family life. These may be seen as new conventions or social determinisms signaling a new typical 'individuation trajectory' which severely handicaps or disempowers

---

[59] The 2011Census found that the most common type of household in Scotland at 35% (of 2.4 million households) was one adult living alone. See Release 2C. www.scotlandcensus.gov.uk.

informants such as Margaret from attaining any real autonomy or occupational mobility in the post-industrial market economy as she is a member of a generation and class fraction for whom the post-industrial 'second modernity' or second modernisation means suffering the double blow of deindustrialization and cultural disorganisation, which leaves them without the resources to master or successfully negotiate the socio-economic determinations that are operative in their lives.

When to the absence of a 'sacred canopy' (Berger 1967) is added a tradition of low-income employment and a traditional low level of educational attainment, it becomes unremarkable for young men and women to become fathers or mothers without any thought or prospect of constituting a household or family unit for their child insofar as they are free from any normative symbolic disciplinations that might regulate and order their lives. Paradoxically, then, human sexuality and behaviour are anything but a purely private affair but are rather highly socially-determined illusions of choice or examples of a socially-determined 'privatism' that is the new conformism.

This social determination of behaviour and consciousness and freedom, then, interpolates individuation so that the most fundamental forms of sociation such as male-female relations are added to the list of candidates for 'modernisation as liquidation,' so that this class fraction of the '79 generation are vitiated with the 'crisis of belief' or the 'crisis of the West' because 'everything' in second modernity reaches escape velocity from convention and the materially and culturally poorer elements of this generation are more or less fated to painstakingly put their lives together by trial and error because their *reason and freedom have become modernist* and, lacking any kind of symbolic or economic ballast, are more or less left to fend for themselves and fabricate answers *ex nihilo* to exhausting predicaments such as what it is to be a human being, whether to marry or not, whether to have children or not, whether to believe in anything or not, and then how to practice via parenting behaviours their makeshift beliefs about self, family, children and questions of ultimate meaning.

This generation, then, lives the trauma and triumph of 'being modern' with a new intensity and lives the demise of earlier answers to the predicament of 'being modern' (found in rationalism, secularism, materialism etcetera) because their existential and social condition demands answers to all of these questions because social convention no longer provides any answers. In this generation eighteenth-century Enlightenment rationalism comes to an end in a new and urgent manner because 'pure reason' or de-traditionalised reason (MacIntyre 1988) either gives no answers or gives prefabricated answers articulated for a different era, so that in this generational and class fraction an irrationalism reaches epidemic proportions and the dialectic and tension of 'being modern' fails to be caught sight of.

Since 2008 more children in Scotland have been born outside of marriage than within and in light of the rapid rise in divorce since the late nineteen-forties and since 1970, it is clear that commitment to a primary family relationship stands a much better chance of enduring when this social practice is immersed in an objective cultural ethos and does not rely upon the 'miracle' of a free-standing choice of each individual grounded upon values. Primary family relationships that require daily effort to maintain are vulnerable to being put 'at risk' by changing social conditions, and the class fraction of the '79 generation that is 'free' and 'poor' is simultaneously 'liberated' and 'lost' by the increasing absence of socially-sanctioned structures of commitment and kinship relations, and becomes a casualty in the 'casualisation' and privatization and disorganisation of culture and lose the structure of the family as a source of individuation to such an extent that the poorer elements of the working class are tacitly exempted from the expectation of reproducing traditional family life.

If we take the much-discussed example of fatherhood and absent fathers, because this primary natural relationship is also a conventional social practice and institution, it is increasingly caught up in a social determination and increasingly required to become a stand-alone substantive value 'in itself,' simply to survive among the 'canopy-less' 1979 generation(s) and with predictable results i.e. widespread decline because the continued existence of fatherhood among this generation is increasingly dependent upon that rarest of sociological creatures: an interpersonal relationship exercising a form of agency over a lifetime that runs counter to a series of social determinations.

If there is a crisis in the reproduction of family life, then, it is because there is the more fundamental reality of the advent of the freedom to be post-conventional and to live outwith conventional wisdoms. There is the widespread collapse of family life because *kinship conventions* in a post-conventional culture are *fated* to have to do their own work to survive upon what, sociologically speaking, is the worst possible basis: the free choice of the free individual, and among those least able to work the substantivist 'miracle' of commitment to the conventional 'value' of family life in a post-conventional society. Reproducing realities such as family life and religion are more or less fated to decline because when Paul VI pronounced "the split between the Gospel and culture is without a doubt the drama of our time" (1975, p. 20), this split rests upon the same sociological predicament faced by the family which is similarly exposed to the full brunt of second modernisation with the result that the family realm is added to the list of items that have been 'privatised,' so that being a single mother or absent father is a new form of social determination and a new 'post-conventional' convention.[60]

The older generations, then, have a sharp twofold conviction: firstly, in terms of material living standards they have never had it so good, while secondly, they enjoyed a far richer or 'denser' experience of locality than that available to the younger '79 generation, so that between the two generations, locality as a source

---

[60] I do not for one moment imagine illegitimacy was a 'discovery' of the 1979 generation or imagine the '79 generation as being somehow less 'upright' as the unpublished manuscripts of Corrie held in the National Library in Edinburgh are full of hints at more or less 'anarchic' family formations and 'natural bairns' i.e. children born outside of marriage. I also accept that previous generations may well have been alienated from much of the symbolic order just like a fraction of the '79 generation(s). However, previous generations were disciplined in their behaviours by poverty and all of the exigencies that follow from not being a contracepting population.

and locus for meaning, intersubjectivity and belonging has declined to the extent that their reflection upon 'locality as history' includes reflecting upon empirical data such as local shops being fitted with metal shutters and video cameras being installed outside the local hotel, and their voicing their fears of being aggressed upon in their old age if they are in local public space after dark. I speculate that the vicious linguistic and textual data referred to in Chapter 1 emerges from individuations occurring within a very particular set of social and cultural and economic conditions.

In an abstract manner we can say that young people being subject to the public realm as themselves for the first time involves a *rit de passage* where childhood days of play and freedom from self-consciousness when out in public are left behind, as the advent of self-consciousness brings awareness of one's being-for-others and the first steps to grasping oneself objectively and particularly in relation to the free market in labour. While this truism can be said of any generation at any time, I propose that from adolescents of the post-industrial generation's first interrogation by objectivity and their first experience of being tested by the public realm, and finding themselves lacking credible or imaginable futures to comport themselves towards and which act as ballast for their behaviours and decisions, they are at risk of being caught in a social determination that may seal their fate. Some in these teenage years have not learned to obscure the fact that this interrogation is happening and so they may be said to give themselves away or betray themselves cheaply, insofar as being in public without the protection of unself-consciousness or a trajectory into the future means it is experienced as an interrogation, and so they are led into risk behaviours that may or may not include petty vandalism or a range of antisocial behaviours.

We might describe such behaviours as mindless or the result of bad parenting but they may also be sourced in coming to realistic self-awareness, and their failure in social comportment may be the result of the meeting that takes place for the first time in their consciousness between their long history of failing to prepare a future for themselves and the dawning of awareness of the lifelong consequences of this lack of preparation. Ordinarily it is the young teenagers from poorer or most 'disorganised' families who are most unable and most unprepared to contest this interrogation when in the public realm, and so it is the teenagers from these families who wander unsupervised on the streets and resort to 'risk behaviours' as if answering back the symbolic violence involved in being confronted with the more or less clear sense of their objective lack of worth.

I would venture that in proportion to the number of times a sixteen year old will be asked the question what they will do after leaving school there are an equal number of ways of avoiding this question, so long as it remains futural and at the mercy of the disposition of the maturing teenager. However, immediately upon leaving school the context of this question changes, and it is forced upon awareness and existence whether the school leaver likes it or not. At this point there takes place an interrogation that cannot be avoided, because in the public realm of Western free-market societies and economies every young adult is required to submit evidence of his place within the occupational hierarchy and must give an account of his trajectory into the future of that society and economy. Those young people with a credible projection into the future will also have a history of preparing for this trajectory and their imagined future, whereas those who cannot answer this interrogation are continually made to register their lack of a future because, unable to resist the objective demand that they be of some social and employable use, they are continually interrogated.

Faced with this continual interrogation, some are tempted to give away their failure for free, whether seeking the safety of numbers in a gang or the brinkmanship and bravado of a leader and 'risk behaviours' because they have nothing else to wager or resist this silent and unspoken interrogating experience as they register they are free of projective trajectories and resort to getting into trouble for the most trivial of reasons, thereby making public the 'private' drama they instantiate. The free market in labour, then, exacts a form of psychological obedience as it reads an individual's rejection of the school system, for example, objectively by handing him its objective consequences and thereby forces upon those about to attempt to enter the job market the fact that they fail to instantiate cultural capital in the post-occupational community employment market.

For Bourdieu, "the unequal distribution of linguistic capital... is an aspect of the class system" (in Jenkins 1992, p. 154) and the young person's use of language and manipulation of the symbolic order puts before him two choices or trajectories: firstly, the prison of conformism and conventions where social determination prevents the use of language because, perhaps coming from a family or level of educational attainment where language-use remains submerged in the 'dictatorship of scarcity,' the advent of a 'free' use of language does not come about so that there is a failure of freedom to take the second option, where the self opens onto the horizon of his autonomy thanks to an 'affluent' relation to language which becomes the means to an unknown and unsuspected individuation.

A teenager apprehending for the first time the absence of any credible means to imagine their autonomy by, and apprehending their fate as one of lifelong low-paid employment that their history of inattention or rebellion has sealed for them, *is a source of individuation* because this confrontation with their objectivity forces onto consciousness what they may have no desire to bring to their attention: their relationship to their use of freedom, and their history of decision-making and its fateful consequences. Insofar as this 'terrible knowledge' becomes a source of individuation it becomes reflexive and is taken up into intentional existence, where it teaches a new literacy or reading of the role and influence of others in their young lives as parents and friends and family members are 'implicated' or read in relation to this confrontation with their objectivity. When being stripped of all credible trajectories through social space becomes reflexive it is fated to imagine the future as more of the same, and this experience within any young consciousness must impact as a wound upon awareness and engender an experience of 'pure being' or 'nothingness' because, much like philosophical exercises of 'pure reason' that attempted to imagine substances or natures stripped of all accidental qualities so as to leave behind the 'pure essence' or nature of the thing, so the young adult without a socially recognised trajectory is likewise stripped to his bare human being or 'pure being,' so that the arrival of post-industrial society is the sociological underpinning to a relentless structurally induced confrontation with 'pure being' or social invisibility among a class fraction of the '79 generation.

In suggesting a process of individuation based upon this existential predicament, it seems reasonable to conclude that if there is a structured coming up against the experience of *dasein* as 'pure being,' the internalising of the experience of never being positively signified within the public symbolic order must eventually form some kind of structuration of *dasein*. If we ask what this structuration will consist of, it will include as an integral part of itself the condition of never being signified or recognised; a condition which, by definition, will appear unthinkable because it is not verbally or conceptually registered insofar as it is stripped of social recognition, and the only discipline to match this description of reflection upon the experience of being-qua-being is metaphysics, so that we might conceptualise this condition as a *metaphysical callous* insofar as it emerges from the chronic condition of constantly 'rubbing' against 'pure being' despite having clear social grounds.

This unsignified 'excess' adverts to a part of youthful *dasein* (that may extend into adulthood) unable to be captured by the representational nets of language, so that integral to this condition is the related difficulty of 'saying' this condition via the social practice of speaking once we accept: "The structure of experience is just as social as is the structure of its outward objectification. The degree to which an experience is perceptible, distinct, and formulated is directly proportional to the degree to which it is socially oriented" (Volosinov 1986, p. 87). While the metaphysical callous is real and not a product of pure reason, this *dasein* is characterised by a 'linguistic deficit' insofar as the words do not exist to express this condition as the poverty of the language 'at hand' to express working-class *dasein* is so poor, precisely because language is a socialised medium and this aspect of 'working-class' *dasein* has remained unsaid. The 'metaphysical callous' then is more or less fated to be experienced as a purely private reality because it is socially invisible and even unthinkable.

An adequate social ontology then challenges Hegel's claim that to exist is to be recognised and Derrida's (1976, p. 158) claim "there is nothing outside of the text," and acknowledges that regardless of that which society has taken the trouble to classify and recognise in language, there are realities that remain real, however unrecognised. Also, the bearers of this objectively-induced experience and metaphysical condition do not live this condition imaginatively or artistically or aesthetically, but are left to themselves to fend off the symbolic violence that says they are 'nothing,' because society and language has not developed the categories to render what they are and to make it possible for them to constitute a 'consciousness of their own' upon their ownmost being, or understand the soteriological worth of their *dasein*. Society then simultaneously creates and negates this condition; makes it appear only to disappear its public or symbolic appearance by submerging it within the swamps of subjectivity and removing it from thought and representation, and thereby weakening its phenomenological reality insofar as the world is will and representation (Schopenhauer).

A busy society that has normalised the 'total mobilisation' of its energies and resources for economic productivity is unlikely to take the time and trouble to recognise and think about, far less celebrate, those *daseins* that are marginal to such concerns, and this structuring of perception is more or less guaranteed when the imagination is immersed in *modernism*. This *cultural control* of thinking and representation implies the lack of impetus to think working-class being insofar as this (and every other) historical *dasein* in the modernist imagination is more or less timetabled for 'dissolution.' Berman's (1983) description of a city's inhabitants as not being allowed the time to grow fond of their buildings before they are torn down and replaced, can be applied to 'secondary natures' and every human *dasein* that is under the spell of a modernist hermeneutic that works to render unlikely the translation of these *daseins* into language, consciousness, culture, literature, philosophy and theology. A culture infected by modernism will fail to take the time to know and give itself representations of the selves and communities they are, and to the extent one's consciousness shares the modernist attitude one is unlikely to set oneself the task of thinking or loving a condition fated to disappear, or put in place a conceptualisation of what this *dasein* is capable of at the apex of its powers as part of a project of self-appropriation.

This modernist control of thinking and imagining is isomorphic with the modernist imagining of history, as found in the eighteenth century Scottish Enlightenment's myth of progress and its unionist and 'anti-Scottish' agenda (Kidd 1993) insofar as it is from this point that Scottish *dasein* is not imaginatively lived as sovereign and a destiny, but as a stepping stone to another identity, so that the bearers of modernist consciousness are made into 'tourists' towards their own being and *are deeply ambivalent about being themselves* (so that the task for a fully contextual performance of self-appropriation as individuals (Lonergan 1957, 1967; Bourdieu and Wacquant 1992) or as a people (van den Bruck 2012) is to recognise and resist this coerced spectatorial relation to *dasein* and *mitsein*).

If we return to our teenager and ask from within the perspective of this young *dasein* what possibilities there are of finding one's ownmost voice through language, we can say that even apparently 'mindless' language-use which would indicate an unfeeling insensitivity to others is grounded in a deep internalization and sensitivity to the negative public evaluations of themselves *which their lack of a credible trajectory into the future means they cannot resist*; that their relationship to language reveals they know what they lack and so are fated to attempt 'revenge,' so that if the young vandal defaces the public realm about him it is because it has firstly 'de-faced' him, as it is here he comes face-to-face with his lack of worth and his anonymity and objective uselessness. His inability to resist despoiling virginal space by writing his name over and over again seems an attempt to rescue himself from the lifelong anonymity he suspects awaits him; his behaviour is mindful 'mindlessness' because *his anonymity within the objective public realm individuates him* and his dominated attempts at agency with his 'useless' *dasein* confronts being-qua-being and can not credibly resist *in its own eyes* this judgment because of his lack of any 'private' credentials of his own.

Today's post-industrial working-class adolescent is by definition at risk of this individuation if he is unable to break, for example, from an older generation's anti-learning ethos as he makes his way within the post-industrial occupational landscape. For whatever 'private' reason, a boy who fails to imagine a future is objectively condemned to an existential condition characterised by always being at risk of being pinned back to experiencing himself in a very particular way because of his lack of a credible route either to the prefabricated realm of jobs, careers, markets and apprenticeships or the lack of resources to fashion one of his own making.

In the young person's project of self-appropriation there will be the paradox that, integral to discovering and appropriating their ownmost voice will be the practice of introspection which will discover that their speaking routinely amounts to being a mouthpiece or cipher for the particular relations they are immersed in. In analyzing their first use of language outwith childhood and institutions such as the family and school, the confrontation between their freedom and their social determination takes place. While in school or at home the use of language is able to avoid the question of their use of freedom as it is immersed in their always-already established identity as son or daughter or pupil, so that their use of language can easily remain conventional and, geared to the tasks of playing their 'institutional' role, language-use among peers is where they encounter this dialectic between freedom and determination so that when talking with their fellows alone as a group, their use of language can take its first steps in freeing itself of constraints insofar as the group is a space for freedom and invention where they are able to take their first steps outwith the 'prison' of their identity.

However, even outside of the formal setting of school there is ordinarily the reproduction of a more or less clichéd relationship to language in the peer group where language is heavily policed by, for example, levelling practices should 'big words' be used so that accusations of getting 'above oneself' which amount to a symbolic breaking of ranks are avoided by policing one's language. All such trespassings from 'determined identity' to 'freedom' are routinely prosecuted by youths when in groups, so that any individual instantiating a new relationship to language, reading, writing or speaking is seen as putting at risk or re-negotiating their identity and membership of the group, and re-negotiating not only their class identity but asking questions of those who remain 'behind' in that identity and relationship to language and expression.

Such adolescent psycho-dynamics are the consequences of the internalization of the hierarchized symbolic order wherein the free use of language is reserved for higher caste groups, and while the use made of language as an idiom of freedom is undoubtedly minimal insofar as this potential idiom of freedom in practice often only becomes a new idiom of conformity, so that rather than speaking being the one practice where individuality emerges, intersubjective language-use is characterised as hackneyed and cliché-ridden and playing safe, language remains a standing provocation or opportunity to develop their ownmost habitus in an original direction.

I privilege linguistic practices as disclosing a dialectic between 'determination' and 'freedom' and with Willis (1977) I identify a class fraction whose relationship to language and meaning is conformed to their fixed place in the world thanks to a doxic obedience to an 'industrial mirror' that is internalised as children and adolescents; a habitus which is a breeding ground for a hackneyed 'anti-learning' attitude that gives itself no tasks because it only sees the fate of endless conformity and domination awaiting them. This unimaginative and constant self-understanding via the external authority of parents and teachers endlessly fuels their rebellion against conforming to rules and regulations, and makes them incapable of suspecting their rebellion is sealing their fate and sealing their being-in-the-world and their being-for-others. For some individuals their relationship to language really instantiates the alienated relationship to the realm of meaning they were always likely to have, while, phenomenologically, this 'free' domination may be experienced as rebellion against authority, and if there is every appearance of rebellion and autonomy until the day they leave school, that day reveals their 'authenticity' or 'rebellion' was only ever functional to sealing their fate of only ever having low caste positions of employment available to them. Language, then, is a privileged site where a dialectic between social determination and freedom occurs and is also a privileged medium or window onto domination that has been taken up by freedom and choice.

## 3.3 A Politics of Identity

I suddenly encounter the total alienation of my person:
I am something which I have not chosen to be.

Sartre 1966, p. 672

At the heart of our time spent living with antisocial neighbours was the problem of noise. The central complaint of neighbours was noise during the night and being deprived of one's normal self through lack of sleep. To understand the problem, then, requires a turn to embodiment to evidence a particular quality of lived experience which grounded the change over time from mere annoyance to the construction of difference and intense animosity. An enforced sense of lacking agency led to an enforced choice between resignation or 'arming' oneself in preparation for a fight, so that frustration among neighbours seemed as much to do with having reached a multi-faceted impasse vis-à-vis objective social conditions and local Council bureaucracy and national building regulations regarding sound-proofing specifications, as much as the problem tenant herself.

Informants were aware of the widespread nature of the problems of anti-social behaviour in many locations throughout de-industrial Fife. But if they read local newspapers and conclude: "It's the same everywhere," this does not alleviate an existential problem or prevent them calling problem neighbours "scum" and "parasites" and calling for their eviction. Such words clearly signal a 'hardening' of perception which had occurred over time and such 'hardening' is evidenced by the following quote from owner-occupier Helen who lived two blocks up from myself throughout my time at 51 Cardenden Road and who was going through something very similar to myself, and who told me that: "Often Ah feel, Ah say tae masel, 'Helen, you're really hard, you're getting really hard an the way yer thinkin, yer life.' Ye ken what Ah mean?" As per the above quote from Sartre, Helen's testimony adverts to her sense of alienation from herself and becoming a different person as a result of living in a context characterised by conflict, and evidences how *conflict acts as a source of experience and knowledge and a source of becoming and being which, just like working, cannot be known by 'pure reason' or speculation.*

Given the behaviours of both tenants at number 57 mentioned previously, a silent unspoken antagonism had come into existence where eviction was the only remedy and in any eviction, whether the antisocial tenant leaves unnoticed by neighbours under cover of darkness, with only items of household furniture and black plastic bags left behind to be blown and scattered along a street, or whether it involves the dramatic event of defiant gestures with police and Council officials in attendance with neighbours at their windows watching every moment, a long series of experiences of dislocation and disruption for those involved will have preceded the day. The 'event' of eviction is constituted by what has gone before, such as practices of deliberate daily exclusion that had to be learned and subsequently freely practised by neighbours; the daily eviction from normal conversation and bringing unguarded friendliness to an end, as behaviour geared to negate a sense of belonging are learned and practiced and culminating in the day of action taken by the State and judiciary whose agents understand themselves as representing a force which "nobody beats."

When neighbour relations become poisoned in this way there is also the inability to escape various knock-on effects as a result of living in the same block of nine flats, or sharing the same street or even the same village and amenities. Feeling unsafe when making one's way to and fro meant neighbour relations were under pressure to be minimised due to the coerced practice of not tarrying in communal spaces when returning or leaving home. If under normal conditions, when hearing an upstairs neighbour coming out of their flat to go out one might tarry so as to let them descend, so that one has the opportunity for social interaction and to exchange pleasantries, such behaviours were avoided as the person coming down the stairs might well have been an unwelcome stranger and someone one did not wish to meet at all.

Such micro-behaviours were the result of a particular way of thinking about communal spaces and a particular imagining of space that involved the sharp distinction between 'inside' and 'outside,' or between private and public space as safe and unsafe space. Such classifying of space resulted in the minimalisation of boundary 'softening' practices, such as neighbours fulfilling their obligations according to the stair cleaning rota at the same time as neighbours on another level, or leaving one's door ajar or unattended so that domestic practices are opened to observation and comment by neighbours or visitors, and can become the occasion for social interaction.

This 'feedback loop' between one's being-in-space and one's being-for-others was further contextualised by locality and the symbiosis between these three relations that means there is a very intimate and affirming experience of 'thick belonging' under normal conditions. In our particular case, however, this triangulation resulted in what felt like an imprisonment, thanks to the inability to access different social situations that allowed some variation in social interaction and the playing out of different roles with different others to vary the experiencing of self solely by reference to the same limited range of social interactions with the same protagonists. Having to share the same social space with a problem tenant, always being liable to see them and be seen by them, having to do one's shopping in the same shops, always being liable to pass each other on the same street or pavement, having one's conversations with neighbours and friends and family overheard, continually 'standing guard' in one's mind by having to anticipate and prepare oneself to face 'the problem' just when thinking about going outside or returning home when out, meant one problematic neighbour began to dominate other relationships. To communicate the lived experience of such a situation then is to render individuals frustrated at not being free of their circumstances, of being confined and defined by the daily battle with the same circumstances that are continually present and continually problematic.

Other evidence of other local lives that were similarly blighted by antisocial neighbours appeared in the local *Fife Free Press* newspaper in an article with the headline 'Pulled Air Pistol on Youth:'

> A Cardenden man tortured by noisy youngsters flipped after one youth threw a snowball at him, a court heard this week. Kirkcaldy Sheriff Court was told how John Campbell (51) then collected an air pistol from his home and threatened to shoot one of his tormentors. Campbell, 22 Whitehall Avenue, admitted that on December 6 he assaulted a 15-year-old boy, repeatedly presented an air pistol at his head and threatened to shoot him.

At first glance, threatening to shoot someone in the head for throwing a snowball is an over-reaction by any standards. However, insofar as such an 'over-reaction' is not a reaction to an event but to a history of more or less similar events, the emotional response to any particular event does not emerge *ex nihilo* but from a habitus that is 'thickened' as a result of an add-on 'temporal' effect that is sedimented within subjectivity. I would interpret the event adverted to above, then, as an example of 'structure' becoming 'event,' insofar as it adverts to a history that preceded this incident. In order to communicate behaviour laden with historicity the resort to the word 'flipped' indicates the absence of an adequate vocabulary to represent the fact that emotions or emotional states are never simply the response to a particular situation, and so as not to fall into "the occasionalist fallacy" (Bourdieu and Wacquant 1992, p. 145) we must recognise that what has preceded the occasion explains the occasion; that responses to events are heavily interpolated by time from two directions.

When faced with a situation for the first time, the emotional response that is available or 'at hand' if often ambivalent and certainly not a matter of habitus. Something that is new often has to be experienced several times for us to know how we should feel about it. Responding to a familiar situation over time, then, means we already know how we feel and so the appropriate emotional response that becomes immediately available and ready as one's 'spontaneous' response in fact emerges from a history of responding. What must also be factored into the emotional response of the moment is the weight or existential 'density' of the structured situation being responded to. For example, then, insofar as one is responding to a situation that has no end in sight, the moment being responded to is not unforeseen or unsuspected but is more accurately described as another incident in a history of similar incidents, and this means that included in the reality that is being responded to is one's powerlessness and the history of one's powerlessness to 'do something' about changing or resolving an ongoing set of circumstances.

Hence, contained within responding to the moment is the weight of a history of having responded to a particular situation and an indefinite future of similar incidents and having to respond to such incidents, so that defining the moment and the self responding to the moment is the intentional grasp of a history that is past and a history that has yet to happen but which, by being anticipated, adds more weight to the burden of the moment thanks to this set of circumstances being taken up by intentionality, where it becomes reflexive and structures intentionality. Hemmed in by the past and the future, the moment's emotional discharge is the product of these two pressures, so that in such instances, perhaps, individuals do not overreact but respond in a rational fashion to what is another mediation of their being at the mercy of events, of which there have been many and of which there will be many more to come.

As regards the ongoing situation referred to in the newspaper article, locals living in this street advised this problem stemmed from a family which had already been evicted from the neighbouring village of Kinglassie and had been re-housed by Fife Council; and that from this point onwards neighbour relations took a turn for the worse as antagonism towards the new family occurred, and trouble among erstwhile peaceable neighbours and their extended families also began, and which had ended in violence and hospitalisation, followed by the involvement of police and a court appearance and conviction and imprisonment and another broken family. When interviewing a committee member of the Neighbourhood Watch scheme which had been formed to deal with the 'problem family' in Whitehall Drive, she prophetically warned of the likelihood of something similar to the incident reported in the local newspaper above:

They started hasslin Kenny. Noo they were oan dangerous grund there...cause if they git um wi a pint Ah mean he'll kill them ken what Ah mean? They were hasslin him fir a while. Rhona [next door neighbour] says she wis feart tae gane oot the door or tae say onyhin. Noo that's...so we says we're stoppin it ye ken?[61]

In my interview with Eddie this particular neighbour dispute was mentioned, and in light of Eddie's experience of working in a unit for young homeless people in Kirkcaldy who require emergency accommodation,[62] I asked him for his views on the effectiveness of various Fife Council and voluntary sector initiatives to deal with the issue of antisocial tenants:

Whether they make any difference or no Ah don't know because it's a trend. It's a trend fir a' these young folk. Tae be rajes.[63] There's mair an mair e thum showin up a' the time. Take Whitehall Avenue for example. Noo Whitehall Avenue's always been a dead quiet place. An that guy Ronnie Snell... that family's [64] moved in, and noo the police are up there two or three times every week. This is happenin a' o'er. Some e them are total rajes.

---

[61] Despite this rhetorical flourish signalling agency on the part of neighbours, Mr Campbell was evicted by Fife Council in September 2000. One might say he was punished for publicising his intolerable social/housing conditions which Fife Council were responsible for creating in the first place by housing an evicted family nearby.

[62] Eddie could only remember three men from Cardenden who had been referred to the homeless unit where he worked. One had been evicted for "drinkin," another for "interferin wi bairns" and the other for "bein wild."

[63] Slang term for young person(s) deemed to be more or less antisocial, wild or out-of-control.

[64] The family was subsequently re-housed again by Fife Council out of the village.

Living particular social relationships over time 'fixes' human being, so that we may say time has the power to change people, and there arises the paradox that the inability to overcome having to continually cope with particular relationships *becomes habitual and routine* and a matter of unconscious habit over time, resulting in a kind of *temporal imprimatur* upon *dasein*, which explains 'subjectless' behaviour and the paradox of individuals who seem the most likely to mobilise upon the basis of the fundamental realities responsible for structuring their lives are in fact predisposed to 'forgetting' these social conditions, precisely because these issues become subject to *routinisation* and *forgetting* over time because they are the most real and most present.

As we argued in Chapter 2, *time exists twice* so that the condition of being relentlessly subjected to time itself, over time, becomes determined by time and this relentless interpolation of human being by time is what transforms the blatantly antisocial into the normal, turns stupid behaviours one would never dream of practicing into normality and in the case of Helen, turns one into a person one doesn't recognise. If we recall our analysis of Dauvit in Chapter 2 where I argued his ability to esteem himself was at the mercy of time, that one can credibly strike attitudes of indignation or incredulity to oneself and others when one's poverty is an event or a recent happening and ponder one's condition with a certain detachment, I argued the passage of time transforms all such responses into shame at one's very being, and we see that the routine social determination of human being more or less forces the abandonment of distinctions between that which is 'subjective' and that which is 'objective' or extrinsic, because such lives are evidently determined by objective restraints so that whatever dispositions such individuals exhibit they can scarcely be described as personal as they are clear "submissions to necessity" (Bourdieu 1984, p. 376).

I would argue that in some individuals what becomes distinctive about them is the degree to which such submission has reached, and in this regard, when thinking about the incident referred to earlier concerning Charlene and her dogs, the more I observed Charlene the more I could never wander far from concluding she was living a form of social determinism that had achieved something approaching 'subjectlessness' within her that had been brought about by the exigencies and disciplinations of deprivation and raising two daughters on her own. What also struck me was the challenge of representing behaviour that was not the young wilfulness evidenced by the second tenant at number 57 but was behaviour that had the quality of the absence of deliberative consciousness, so that to describe any behaviour of Charlene as "rude," for example, would be to misrecognise it by implying deliberation, or that I was the object of Charlene's intentional acts.

Instead, to adequately represent Charlene is to recognise a subjectless behaviour and consciousness insofar as she had become a 'mouthpiece' for her structures. These same characteristics were also something I recognised in the evicted tenant when on one occasion I asked her why she couldn't understand the level of noise created by her playing loud music was unacceptable, and rather than giving an account of herself, she had shrugged her shoulders and lifted her two hands up in the air to communicate she had had enough and about-turned and left me standing holding the door. It was being on the receiving end of such 'subjectless practice' that provoked my conscientisation to the structuring effect of temporality and convinced me I would have to move out or she would have to be evicted, as I saw a depth of domination from which there could be no recovery until she became immersed in another set of relations and another experience of time brought about by some new reality in her life such as employment or parenthood.

In *The Gift* (1990) Marcel Mauss demonstrates how the practice of exchange implicates the parties involved into a system of reciprocity and that sociality is constituted upon this basis, so that the purpose of withholding reciprocity is to deconstruct the conditions for becoming a neighbour by aborting the moral imperative at the basis of gift-giving and being-with-others (*mitsein*). In a block of Fife Council flats, then, the denial of giving and receiving conversation and simple chatting produced ignorance of one's neighbour and, over time, desensitises the individual to moral and social exigencies. In antisocial tenants this disposition has become defining and systematic to the extent that it can legitimise behaviours such as that recalled to me when (10ᵗʰ January 2000) playing cards at *The Auld Man's Shelter* card school and, chatting with a young local unemployed man, he informed the company that he leaves his vacuum cleaner on in his flat "sometimes for an hour just to annoy the old woman downstairs."[65] While I doubted the truth of his assertion it is revealing that it was not only said expecting to be believed but was felt unlikely to arouse disapproval. Even if a complete fiction, its mere utterance evidenced a level of regression and a subnormal 'politics of identity' that is possible among neighbours and in which the repression of recognising there is a problem at all is an integral part of the problem itself.

In terms of the issue of recognising the very existence of a problem, it is revealing that over the nineteen months I spent at 51 Cardenden Road I never spoke about the problem with either tenant at number 57. During both phases the problem 'dissolved' into the day-to-day routine of minimalizing relatedness, leaving only the bare minimum of physical proximity, which was productive of a wider ethos of mere endurance of others which clearly impoverished the experience of social interaction, and created the paradox whereby the absence of social relations came to characterise the experience of social relations.

In the incident with the problem neighbour referred to above, any attempt to address the problem only triggered denial of the very existence of a problem as admitting to a problem would be to implicate or commit oneself to recognising and practicing reciprocity and their attendant moral and social responsibilities, the very things that must not be allowed to emerge as this leads more or less directly to being accountable and recognising the need for a change of behaviour. Instead of the free development of reciprocity, then, there is regression to a form of 'autism' or an

---

[65] Andy was over thirty years old and locals told me he has two young children by his ex-wife whom he sees each Sunday when his ex-wife drops them off for the day at his mother's house; that he also has children with his current partner but that: "He hisnae worked in years cause the Child Support Agency wid make um contribute tae the maintenance e his bairns."

'infantile' consciousness that cannot face its own behaviours nor its interlocutors who challenge such behaviours, and which resorts to 'magical' responses such as: "The door's locked and Ah dinnae have a key." However, the real work which such 'magical consciousness' does is to effect the disappearance of one's neighbour and the consequences of one's behaviours and thereby achieve the illusion of an immaculate relationship to one's social context. Viewed from the perspective of the consciousness of the antisocial neighbour, when asked to turn music down this request falls like an arbitrary will-to-power by an unknown 'other' and, in true existential style, provokes heartfelt resistance as if authenticity were at stake, with the result that an invincible alienation from reality occurs thanks to a politics of identity.

Bourdieu has remarked somewhere that every habitus is equally fatal, and as a rule we can say that as a result of what Adorno termed 'identity thinking,' identifying with one's social position is perfectly normal and inevitable. If we also recognise the "role of feelings in indexing the true self" (Lutz 1988, p. 7) is often decisive in telling us who we are, and that the "role of culture in the experience of emotion is seen as secondary, even minimal" (Lutz 1988, p. 3), we can see that dominated individuals (and the socially dominant) easily make the mistake not only of identifying with their objective domination but, thanks to the exercise of freedom, *make a reflexive project out of their domination* with the result that they do not see themselves as being caught in a social determination to be overcome but imagine instead they are defending their 'true self,' so that there is a fine line separating the authenticity involved in the slave "choos[ing] himself on the ground of *slavery*" (Sartre 1966, p. 703) and the inauthenticity of imagining one's being a slave is one's true self to be defended against all-comers.

Rather than becoming free of particular relations, then, there is an internment into and collusion in de-humanising relations as to truly admit one's neighbours into one's self-construct is to open oneself to being a self in relation to others. However, in a consciousness addicted to not cultivating these relationships and seeing a form of authenticity in this refusal of reciprocity, becoming a neighbour can only appear as a form of capitulation to an oppressive other.

This eviction of the other within the consciousness of antisocial individuals via a refusal of representation, however, was not one-way traffic as among neighbours there was a refusal to call the problem neighbour by name, as if a form of 'eviction from language' to achieve distance in spite of spatial intimacy. Neighbours' reification of the problem into the "neighbour from hell" was only a matter of time; an 'othering' or reification in thinking about the other expressed in the damning shorthand diagnoses that readily came to hand such as: "She's rough as f**k. The hale family's rough as f**k."

If *dasein* and *mitsein* are integrally linked it is because existence is always co-existence, so that being a good neighbour is an integral part of locating and constructing the self and being recognised as an adult and competent human being. In a situation, therefore, where the law intervenes and declares any person unfit to be housed, a host of other declarations of failure are made public at this point. For example, then, because being a mother is an interpersonally maintained social identity, recognition or verification of such an identity may be withheld, so that when a mother is declared unfit to be housed this is simultaneously to be declared unfit to be a mother. Furthermore, because in a village context an individual relentlessly encounters the world in terms of how other locals view him or her, any tenant who is evicted has little resources to *credibly* combat local definitions of themselves. Of any individual who is evicted the question will be raised as to whether they possess the necessary wherewithal to qualify for the social identity of 'mother,' given that access to such identities is something that requires being able to 'pay' the admission price of conformity to social conventions and a number of competencies in order to belong to the imagined identity of 'mother.'

Similarly, the same extrinsic competencies and conditions that have to be met for others to ascribe the identity of 'mother' to an individual apply to a woman being able to understand herself as a mother, because an individual requires 'social permissions' to internalise and identify with that identity.

263

Subsequent to being evicted from 104 Cardenden Road a young single mother would arrive with her two young children every morning at eight o'clock to 57 Cardenden Road, so that I was able to see on a daily basis something of the lives of pre-school children subject to parenting that was void of the deep practical resolve or the condition of being immersed into an imagined future that is the fundamental prerequisite for practicing the discipline of being family-centred and child-centred, and the creation and daily reproduction of a domestic realm. As if these conditions are not demanding enough under normal circumstances, when life is characterised by struggling alone in the absence of fathers and meaningful employment and meeting the pressures of day-to-day survival, the demands of family life are a mirror that reflects back one's objectivity and a continual call to deconstruct prior learned behaviours and put in place new behaviours in accordance with the demands to decentre oneself and become child-centred, because a parent's behaviours must be more than a cipher for wider socio-economic pressures and realities. Being a single mother, then, involves instantiating a dialectic between the two poles of social determination and freedom insofar as a mother simultaneously is defined by her material conditions but must also 'transcend' them or not be mastered by them for the sake of creating an adequate environment for children.

If we ask what are the prospects for a successful project of self-appropriation when one's energies are exhausted in coping with objective structural realities, it seems that insofar as there is a profound fatalism or acceptance of one's objective life-chances, a kind of 'defence mechanism' that prevents any obedience to new and 'higher' demands and new and 'higher' behaviours seems inevitable; as if by refusing the development of self there is a 'psychological budget' being adhered to, and the avoidance of cognitive dissonance and maintaining a psychological immediacy frees the individual of the burden of having to psychologically finance other possible or potential identities. It is here, then, that the social realm is reproduced within the psyche as it is precisely here where a symbolic revolution must take place in order to resist settling for the socially determined self that one already is; it is precisely here where a dialectic of struggle between social determination and freedom is relinquished as a result of 'identitarian thinking' that settles upon one's true self being this social determination devoid of an impulse to transcend itself.

In my account of 'living with difference,' a particular set of housing conditions have not been described along the lines of differences that arise as a result of sharing the same space as one shares a street or where instances of difference are confined to a shared space that can be occupied at a time of one's choosing, so that interaction with difference can be a 'contemplative' affair that more or less occurs at one's discretion. What has been required is an account of difference as a contact sport, and a non-contemplative experience of difference and conflict which seeps into one's self so as to forcefully trample upon one's possession of one's self and one's intimate spousal *mitsein* and relations with others, so that we may describe contemplative theories of 'difference' and contemplative theories of pluralism as sublated forms of segregated housing conditions which afford detached and private relations to neighbours and purely contemplative accounts of difference.

In my account of *difference as conflict and a contact sport*, the house is a site for a struggle over the exercise of *sovereignty* because housing conditions put schemes of perception of self, other and territory to the test, and thereby raises the question of sovereignty which under normal circumstances lies inert because *there can be no normality unless the question of sovereignty is settled*. Talk of the house as a site of sovereignty then is fated to be viewed as merely rhetorical until it is challenged by the advent of conflict. In this regard, history shows millions of people accommodating themselves to what historical hindsight imagines to have been 'intolerable' conditions. In breaking with established practices of accommodation, the advent of conflict is often what proves decisive in transforming accommodationist strategies into all-or-nothing battles over sovereignty. Where the condition of sharing sovereignty with others becomes intolerable, it can only be brought to a decisive end via an *exclusive* integralism that is no longer prepared to share sovereignty with an other, and so

I propose an analogy between the housing conditions described in this chapter and the wider historical and geo-political questions; an analogy between two periods of conscientisation fuelled by 'contact and conflict:' one that occurred at a geo-political level between 1979-1997, and another that occurred at the micro-level of housing relations between August 1998–February 2000.

I argue that, as a rule, both the 1945 and 1979 generations lack the symbolic and intellectual resources to break with their collusion and collaboration in the coercive ideologies of powerful social classes, but that this aporia has come to an end thanks to a new 'politics of identity' and the awakening of the question of sovereignty as a result of the combined effects of the advent of affluence and political and economic events during the period 1979-1997 which has liberated an inert historicity and long-inert possibilities for agency among the 1979 generation, thanks to the political and cultural defeat of prior accommodations throughout the 'society of scarcity' period. If the 1979 generations are objectively freed by the arrival of general affluence from the nineteen-eighties onwards, the '45 generation were largely confined to 'scarcity thinking' and a symbolic accommodation in the form of a more or less coerced pooling or sharing of sovereignty with England, and the difference between the two generations is the difference between two conceptions of sovereignty and two different levels of freedom, which lead to two differing estimations as to what is realistic and two differing estimations of what should be done about the divergent electorates of Scotland and England from 1979–1997 and 2010–2015 and beyond. The same alignment or 'fit' between the personal, local, social and national that in the previous '45 generation led to a British identity is re-cast in the post-1979 and 'post-conflict' era of affluence into the *practice of exercising sovereignty* that discards the zombie category of 'Britain' as a relic from the 'dictatorship of scarcity' era.

Underlying the struggle between nationalism and unionism, then, is the struggle between two competing imaginings and practices of sovereignty, and in the next two chapters I will argue a range of social and cultural and economic forces for a sovereign Scottish State are in alignment as never before, so that among the '45 generation the following fivefold alignment or integralism held until recently:

1) Housing. As Council tenants, housing conditions were a site for dependency as they did not have the power to exercise agency or 'sovereignty' (ownership) over their housing conditions.

2) Locality. Locality was founded by the owners of the means of production, and as the children of the first in-migrating miners the '45 generation do not have the symbolic resources to re-found and re-imagine locality.

3) Class. As a class they remain defined by economism and 'scarcity thinking' and did not have the level of material development to secede from all-British solutions in their pursuit of a political project to challenge their domination within the free market.

4) Nation. As a people and nation they lacked the political difference from England to mobilise their historicity or geo-political positionality to begin a politics of identity, and exert the agency of securing a sovereign Scotland.

5) Culture. The imagining, producing and consumption of 'Scottish culture' remained enthralled to scarcity-era all-British formats ('folkism'/inferiorism).

While among the '79 generation(s) the following fivefold alignment or integralism is upon us:

1) Housing. As owner-occupiers freed from local authority control, the house has become a site for the imagining and practicing of agency and sovereignty, with a younger generation empowered to become intolerant of antisocial behaviour and who act to secure evictions.

2) Locality. A younger generation begins a new 'imagining' of locality free of industrialism and modernism.

3) Class. As members of an affluent working class they keep faith with a post-1979 centre-left politics of class or redistribution.

4) Nation. As a people and nation they pursue a 'post-materialist' politics of identity to bring an end to sharing sovereignty with England, and break with the '45 generation's collaborations and accommodations to dependency and will vote for independence on 18 September 2014.

5) Culture. A new affluence-based imagining and practicing of cultural agency emerges, which breaks with all-British cultural formats in the pursuit of developing the projects of a purely Scottish culture and modernity.

In coming to the above depiction and description of the 'present as history,' perhaps the key to remember is it emerges from *using conflict as an essential part of data-constituting and data-gathering*. When daily life takes the form of contestation due to the fact of sharing the same housing-come-living space, this space becomes the site of the production of difference, leading to a 'zero sum' game that involves the process of eviction *in an effort to exercise sovereignty* vis-à-vis their homes and shared domestic spaces, so that the process of eviction is a *politics of identity* and a struggle against an other who is to be expelled from a particular territory. In this regard I posit an analogy between large-scale geo-politics and the micro politics of eviction insofar as a particular *housed dasein* becomes reflexive and a principle of interpretation so that there occurs a structuring or 'hardening' of perception over time (and which 'contemplative' social ontologies and hermeneutics are incapable of suspecting – far less knowing), and which aligns its reading of its neighbour and its locality and its nationality; a localised class and housed-sensibility to antisocial practices of neighbours that is isomorphic with and aligns with wider social and geo-political practices of inequality in the multi-national State of the UK.

In a scene from the film *Crash* (2004) the character of police officer John Ryan confronts his younger partner, who has only begun working as a policeman, with the words: "You think you know who you are? You have no idea." These words are spoken in rebuke of the younger man who, through lack of experience, has judged Ryan's actions as morally indefensible. The words are spoken to convey the idea that even intimate and unique realities such as who we are or who we become are in fact at the mercy of events and time, and that what we become in life is not something that is immaculate and immune from the many contexts our human being is immersed in. Likewise, with the passage of time the effects of social structure upon human being become 'secondary natures' or 'essences' and insofar as the condition of being dominated is reflexive, it is perfectly capable of pursuing its own micro-politics of identity all the way to the bitter end of eviction thanks to the processes that transpire within the confines of a block of nine flats.

In this micro social space, tenants 'fix' other tenants into an essence so that they are thereafter deemed essentially incapable of change *because of what they are*. 'Giving up' on one's neighbour is comportment towards an essence based upon the well-founded judgment of the impossibility of an individual exercising agency, and is a judgement which produces fatalism or resignation and the judgment that such an individual can only be evicted. *Only by 'giving up' on one's neighbour as capable of agency does the ethnographer acquire the idiom of his informants and learns "to get used to it"* (as per Charlene's advice), and only by giving up does one reproduce their 'being-there' and reproduce their own history of having given up on the attempt at agency. In making essentialised judgements on one's informants, then, one is becoming alike and finally learning that until one did so one was fated to remain a stranger to the *sui generic* structuration effected by time upon consciousness and behaviour and the essentialist politics of identity that follows.[66]

---

[66] If I managed to accomplish Whitman's advice quoted earlier, I did so despite myself and as a result of not being in control of the field or the data.

## 3.4 Overcoming Objectivism

Meaning, of course, is ethnographically problematic. It is not susceptible to objective description, but only to interpretation.

Cohen 1985, p. 98.

In asking to meet with a Fife Council representative, myself and Eva were breaking the 'rule' that states tenants should not presume to arrange a meeting in order to question their landlord or attempt to instantiate *a non-dominated relationship to the condition of being dominated.* In order for us to exercise agency, this required nothing less than a reversal of Fife Council's housing allocations policy, and for our point of view to be more than a private attitude on our part would require Fife Council to cede authority to us and accept our interpretation of events and solutions i.e. either sound-proofing their properties or admitting their housing allocation procedures were at least partly responsible for tenants experiencing the problem of antisocial neighbours. For myself and Eva as Council tenants, then, not to instantiate a dominated relation to our being dominated required nothing less than the hopeless presumption that Fife Council housing policy would change because it did not happen to suit our 'personal' circumstances. Instead of any of this happening, of course, what did happen was what was fated to happen when the subordinate attempt to contest the established bureaucratic procedure of the dominant i.e. nothing.

Among local area office Fife Council employees I found a culture defined by an etiquette of euphemisation that was unable to recognise me as one of its tenants because it was unable to recognise the reality of my housing conditions insofar as it failed to recognise its responsibility for creating unacceptable living conditions, and break with the euphemisation practices deemed integral to public service culture and which disempowers locals and locality and effected a 'dumbing down' of tenants or 'service users.' Being on the receiving end of this bureaucratic 'managerialism' meant it was we as Council tenants who were eventually coerced into becoming the 'victims' not only of antisocial tenants but the policies of our local Council. This local authority culture and practice, then, is directly relevant to the phenomenology of 'council housing' as it impacts upon the experience of those tenants living such housing conditions.

If a fundamental principle of the 'sociological imagination' is that for something to be real it has to be intersubjectively agreed as being real, a problem I faced when trying to communicate our housing conditions was that it was a situation which was never forced to an openly shared or intersubjectively agreed representation of itself by informants or neighbours or the professionals involved. A major factor defining the phenomenological reality of my 'neighbour dispute,' then, was the 'invisibility' that surrounded it. At a formal and official level it seemed to 'disappear' as a result of the 'professionalisation' of the problem by Fife Council insofar as the persons involved are reduced to the legal and contractual status of "tenant" in the name of bureaucratically defined objectivity.

During the time of the second tenant at number 57, no formal complaint was made to the Council and, because the Council never enquired as to our views of the new tenant, it seemed as if the only level of existence available to this lived experience was the private realm; as if the only space available to register the reality of the problem was the 'private body,' as the other agencies involved 'privatised' this reality into a bureaucratic world of professional discourse so that, thanks to the "splitting of subjectivity from objectivity" (Taussig 1992, p. 96), to keep track of the lived experience of this reality meant resorting to the practice of 'bodily reflexivity' as a means of data-gathering and as an interpretive key for analysing an aspect of subjective structuration that would never be verbally evidenced, and so meant breaking with objectivism and the embrace of "the swamps of subjectivity" (Levi-Strauss).

Hence, just as with the 'condition of reduction' brought about by labouring discussed in Chapter 2, what I have described as 'housing conditions' are not objective realities 'out there' that one will find in local authority housing officers' reports or in the curriculum followed by Housing Studies students because they are not empirical realities that the casual passer-by can spectate and describe and discuss. As a result of this caesura between 'reality' and 'publicity' there was a more or less coerced interiorisation of 'living conditions' where intentionality and embodiment bore the full weight of reality, and consubstantial with this 'invisibilisation' and somatisation is the silence towards these realities by those intimately living these conditions. In this regard I was struck by the fact that informants seemed to have learned not to invest any great effort in discursively naming their reality, as if they had learned the fundamental impotence of language; as if the social conditions required for speaking were absent because to speak one's reality via language was not just to say the same thing yet again, but was to deliberately invite an experience of cognitive dissonance insofar as it raised to intersubjective reality once again their failure to change their unchanged reality yet again. Paradoxically, then, the veracity of the Scholastic doctrine that language affords reality a more perfect medium of existence (O'Callaghan 2003) results in a refusal of language when the reality in question is simply too painful to mention.

When real social problems are not addressed by public institutions then living with the accumulating consequences of this unresolved reality over time is liable to engender a particular habitus over time among those affected. A particular reality, then, when it first 'begins life' is one thing but when time and powerlessness are added, this can enforce an alienated and even 'hysterical' relation to this reality as a result of objectivity being systematically 'privatised.' What is clear is that a context where real social problems are not resolved engenders a context for that problem that is not characterised by *free communication* or *the free use of language*, and I would venture that neighbours' inner psychic space was alienated from the free articulation of their experience because to 'speak their situation' was to trigger an entire temporal structure that weighed heavily upon their relation to language; as if in this inter-psychic realm there had developed a default position of avoiding anything that would trigger discourse upon the situation, so that their silence revealed the fact that their powerlessness through time informed their relationship to language.

If the public face one presents to others about one's situation arises from the demands of maintaining a show of normality and avoiding conversation about it, *the body* can play no such language games and is fated to register and encode its world, so that embodiment becomes a sui generic site of reality as the body and psyche are the media par excellence that register and live the meaning of events and relations. In the case of one neighbour, then, the privatisation of her living conditions were medicalised in the form of an addiction to Prozac, while my wife's answer came overnight in somatic form when she developed dozens of little yellow spots the length and breadth of her back and shoulders which exhibited a striking uniformity and perfect equal spacing, as if expressing a mathematical formula and which I took to be a remarkable somatic speech act 'saying' her living conditions.

This triangulation of housing, embodiment and the psyche reveals the fact that so intimate is the relation between the home and *dasein* that it is difficult to begin to think about this relationship which for most of us most of the time remains firmly in the background of our awareness. The home may be viewed as the first space or medium in which we come to awareness of ourselves and learn the fundamental truth that our existence is co-existence, as the space of the familial 'little society' is not simply that which conditions *dasein* and *mitsein* but rather the house and home is the medium within which and through which our *dasein* and *mitsein* come-into-being and maintain their being. The house and home is the existential space where relations and 'deep selves' are created and maintained; the place where social interaction first takes place and is nurtured and the place *par excellence* for experiencing privacy, tranquility, stability, convention, meaning and where there occurs the deep and remote preparation for the exigencies of adult life.

It is at home then that our ownmost selves come about, and something of this link between authenticity and the home is captured in the rhetorical expression, "What's that when it's at hame?" which locals use when asking someone to explain something or clarify what something means, as the presumption is that being 'at home' is where things are what they really are, that when at home we remove masks and lay down our 'extrinsic' identities and all of the artificial role-playing associated with the world of work, as the home is where people are their real or true selves. As Corrie (1939, p. 30) put it: "In the pit he is a brute – only brutes could survive there – in the home, rough and all as he is, he is a man once more." If domestic space humanizes it is because the home is surrounded by a cluster of meanings which associate the domestic with notions of authenticity and truth, while the public realm is associated with notions of affectation, appearance and inauthenticity. However, living amongst antisocial neighbours involved the deconstruction of naïve notions of autonomy, with the more or less coerced 'revelation' that *dasein* is never an island unto itself and this truth extends to the domestic realm where the myths of privacy and autonomy are most cherished.

The lack of control that one concedes in negotiation with the social world, then, is resented when 'extorted' in the intimacy of domestic life because it violates a cluster of symbolic meanings, and in adverse circumstances one is fated to begin to resent this fundamental human condition of existence as co-existence or *relatedness*, and to resent the fact that because all human living is at the mercy of its relations, one is always at the mercy of others to behave well in order to allow oneself to live well. Living the process of eviction, then, reveals how much we are invested in a normally unstated and unsaid code of *dwelling* which is naturalised to the extent that a theory of 'correct dwelling,' for example, is a redundant notion as the presupposition is that, because dwelling is defined in association with notions of goodness, to dwell at all is to dwell 'correctly' and it is impossible to dwell superficially or badly or inauthentically.

Over the course of our nineteen months as Fife Council tenants the house became the space, medium and *conditione sine qua non* for registering the illusion of privacy, the locus for the forceful ending of the illusion of autonomy insofar as these months involved a decentering process that more or less forced my thinking about the social conditioning of human *dasein* and *mitsein* to go back to the drawing board. Far from a space for an oasis of privacy, the house became the medium *par excellence* that allowed 'society' to effortlessly find me 'at home,' and my housing conditions more or less coerced me into taking seriously the fact that there is a relationship between housing and individuation and sociation; that much like the being brought into being by doing manual labour discussed in Chapter 2, so housing conditions have the power to deconstruct *dasein* and familial *mitsein*, and re-make them in its image independently of the consciousness and will of those immersed in these conditions. Our nineteen months as Fife Council tenants taught me that 'being dominated' is a structural reality that has little to do with an individual's personality or psychological make-up; that what there is to be communicated is the reality of people being lived by structures; a situation where *dasein* is 'epiphenomenal' to impersonal structure.

Over the course of nineteen months spent living at 51 Cardenden Road I came to this 'extreme' structuralist point of view as my response to my housing situation underwent the process of beginning with fighting to resistance, then to silent tolerance and then to subordination, and then surrender and finally flight. If my housing conditions forcibly taught me the unreality of any idea that I could privatise my living conditions *these same conditions also taught me that not only data-collection but the interpretation of data is a contact sport*, as they forcibly brought to awareness the realisation that any idea that I was conducting research as a delocalised academic was disingenuous bad-faith. Prior to this nineteen-month period of 'rough wooing' I had devoutly attempted to write and represent the field in a way that would be perceived by others as fair and objective, and I also found that this involved pretending to some imaginary future reader that I was following some kind of special sociological or anthropological method while in the field, and that it was this method which was responsible for my data and insights, while the truth was both my data and my analysis emerged far more from having lost control of the field and lost sight of where it might lead me.

Living with problematic neighbours was firstly a novelty and a surprise that soon became a source of more or less constant preoccupation which only came to an end when we resigned our tenancy and moved out. It was because my experience of housing conditions for the first nineteen months of fieldwork was so problematic that the reality-constituting power of relationships became the focus of my attention, and I was coerced into understanding that something as 'unreal' as a relationship could be powerful enough to construct or deconstruct apparently substantive realities. From being immersed in the swamps of 'substantialist' thinking I caught up with Marx's characterisation of the human being as "the ensemble of the social relations" (cited in McLellan 1977, p. 157), and as I constructed a map of social actors and their social space and the relevance of housing conditions as a point of departure for understanding their structuring role for individuation and sociation, what I was deeply impressed by most of all was *the reach* of social relations' *determining* of *dasein* and individuation.

Living with antisocial neighbours means the normally unmarked and unsaid relationship between self and space becomes an object of inquiry and conscientisation, to reveal the extent of how those affected experience embodiment and live their house and are lived by their house; how antisocial neighbours structure what we like to imagine are *personal* spaces. Neighbours' complaints that: "Ye cannae relax! Yer hoose is no yer ain!" refer to the fact that we normally *dwell* in our bodies as we normally dwell in our houses so that our sense of self too is 'housed' in our bodies to the extent that, when such social spaces become problematised, there is a consequence for *dasein* and nothing can be taken for granted; that unless one controls one's housing conditions one cannot even control one's being oneself insofar as one's *dasein* is opened up to the mercy of relations that have the power to deconstruct a once-solid sense of self. In the case then of Eva developing a stress-related outbreak of spots across her back, then, "her body provided an alternative standpoint from which to tell an unsanctioned story" (Farnsworth-Alvear 2000, p. 207), and in light of such data there is the need to develop an embodied reflexivity that takes the body as the privileged place for 'fielding difference,' where "bodies are physical field sites upon which the world inscribes itself" (Nast 1998, p. 95) due to the body being an involuntary site of structuration or a site for the 'inscription' of social conditions due to the natural process of the bodily inscription of the world. Hence the salience of the attempt to use the experience of living in a situation of everyday near-conflict and confrontation as a:

> Cultural and material context for understanding reflexivity not as a voluntaristic and leisured process of the mirror, initiated and/or controlled by a subject through mental exertion [but] as an embodied process wherein the body is itself a field for registering and negotiating difference.
>
> (Nast 1998, p. 107).

Nast's (1998, p. 405) focus upon the "ways in which places are experienced through the body, and how the body is experienced through places" is a useful model for thinking about living with antisocial neighbours, and breaking with objectivism to 'save the data' and significance of neighbours complaining: "Ah'm at the end e ma tether; Ma nerves are shot tae hell; Ah'm gonnae loss the heid; Ah cannae stand any mair e this. Ah'm gaun aff ma heid." This discourse which draws upon embodied metaphors points to "the integration of mind/body experience" (Low in Csordas 1994, p. 145) and informants' speech, which reflects their embodied experiences and challenges reflexivity to break with objectivism and cognitivist biases in favour of an embodied reflexivity that can capture the bio-psycho-social or mind-body-world integration that characterises informants' experience. If Cohen (1978, p. 6) is correct that "one has to acquire the idiom of the locality, and then learn within it. The acquisition of the idiom is the starting point for investigation," then, having shared in their housing conditions, I argue the many different relations constituting locals' experience informs not only my 'conversion' to a structuralist standpoint and the practice of a *non-objectivist ethnographic reflexivity*, but also allows me to properly *see what there is to be understood* and how housing conditions condition not only embodiment but *the range or extent of what there is that is embodied.*

This embodied reflexivity (Scheper-Hughes & Lock 1987; Jackson 1989; Stoller 1989; Nast & Pile 1998) emerges from being more or less constrained to draw upon an embodied sense of being-there and living with indeterminacy over time and becoming one's own informant in order to by-pass a context characterised by the refusal of discourse, and to access such intangibles as 'bodily comportment' and a context that more or less coerced me into realising that to omit the bodily realm would be to miss important data as the body is a *sui generic* evidencing realm of the consequences of living a particular set of relations and housing conditions that other research methods and 'contemplative epistemologies' would entirely miss.

If a basic insight of structuralism is that particular *relation-ships* bring particular realities into existence, then relationships characterised by conflict and contestation bring additional realities into being. When an exasperated neighbour says: "Nae wonder everybody wants their ain wee bungalow. Away somewhere. Peace an quiet," they are expressing this ability of relationships to bring 'war' or 'peace,' and is affirming it is the fact of *sharing* the same space, often due to a lack of sound proofing, as opposed to the person or lifestyle of a particular neighbour *per se*, that is the conditions for the possibility of conflict and strife.

Insofar as neighbours are largely indifferent to what others do behind closed doors so long as this means being done in private, it is the fact of not being able to have privacy and having no control over hearing noise or witnessing certain behaviours that constitutes the problem; the inability to avoid 'being related' makes indifference impossible and sets the scene for the emergence and contestation of difference and the rationale behind the strategy of evicting others or 'evicting' oneself to another address. Living in a poorly sound-proofed block of Fife Council flats beneath an antisocial tenant then meant the inability to privatise one's relationships and living a certain being-for-others that was out of one's control, and the inability to live on one's own terms and at a time of one's choosing, so that the constitution of one's *dasein* and one's being-for-others was experienced and known to be out of one's control.

The obvious escape from all of this coerced becoming such as moving house, however, is often unavailable to locals until they are re-housed by the Council normally after years of waiting.

Many locals who are either young or new to the housing waiting list 'game' see themselves at the bottom of the housing hierarchy and accept a tenancy in a flat while immediately putting themselves back onto the waiting list again, and specifying their desire for a semi-detached cottage or put an advert in a shop window in the areas of the village to where they would like to move advertising they would like to swap with another tenant. Such are the strategies of those without the financial resources to buy a house and buy themselves out of the problem of antisocial neighbours and buy themselves out of the 'full constitution' of the reality of antisocial neighbours.

To arrive at a full statement of this particular set of housing conditions is to understand how living them impacts upon other relations that are present such as kinship relations. Allowing these further mediating structures into the picture reveals how 'problem neighbours' are transformed into a *total fact of living mediating the experiencing of the whole social structure*. Ideally, then, a systematic structuralism would require not only a sensitivity to the many social forces at play in a particular situation but a multi-faceted reflexivity (mind and body) in order to register these many forces. Hence, opening onto the embodied nature of reflexivity is only the beginning because the systematic nature of both structuration and the systematic nature of the reflexivity that must accompany it in the informant *should be reproduced in the ethnographer also*. Both must be systematically developed to include awareness of what further mediates and constitutes the experience of, for example, antisocial neighbours so that an adequate practice of reflexivity will give an account of all other mediating influences present.

More concretely, then, my sharing in the same relations and difficulties of neighbours was further made possible by my family life insofar as this immersed me further into the construction and living of the reality of antisocial neighbours as having this reality mediated or co-constituted via one's family heightened and revealed what was at stake. Fundamental, then, to this aspect of fieldwork and fundamental to my data-gathering and data-interpreting was being married, as I was not simply an apprentice ethnographer taking notes on antisocial behaviour but a husband and father, and these identities as much as any other identity constituted the field and its data. The condition of being married had implications for how the experience of antisocial neighbours was constituted and mediated via this interpersonal relationship, and also informed my practice of reflexivity insofar as 'being married' was a 'structuring structure' impacting upon how housing conditions were experienced due to its structuring the structuring structure of embodiment.

Being foreign in terms of class, national identity and culture and not having working-class dispositions, Eva was also more or less coerced or weaned from her established *dasein* or habitus and underwent a nineteen-month process of acculturation, thanks to having to face the fact that she had to face being disturbed by neighbours as a matter of routine; had to form a habitus in relation to the constant disruption and expectation of disruption. When analysing our relationship over the course of this period, the psycho–somatic reactions developed over time in response to noise levels or disturbing phenomenon eventually became stable and fixed as part of our own structuration and our reactions became highly determined over time until our reactions to events were not invented afresh in response to a passing tracasserie between neighbours, but were constituted and dominated by a history of reacting and a history of the lack of agency, so that the 'secondary nature' that was triggered on any particular day by a particular disturbance was something that had taken months to construct; a *history* was triggered because a history of responding had formed into a psycho–physical reaction already constituted and available and waiting to be triggered by an event.

Any particular response then to any particular event emerged from our institutionalisation within our *mitsein* condition of 'helplessness' or the condition referred to as 'being dominated,' and when responses to a spouse or a neighbour are so heavily structured or determined, there is little freedom to respond to a fresh event simply as that event, because it triggers a highly structured response which bears a resemblance to the structure of hysteria found in psychoanalytic theory where the hysteric is someone whose condition results from a traumatic event and who is unable to be free of his symptoms until he 'integrates' the original trauma into his psyche. Further, if Erikson is correct that the word 'patient' "denotes a state of being exposed to superior forces from within and without which cannot be overcome without energetic and redeeming help" (cited in Kakar 1996, pp. 147-48), then a particular set of social conditions could be described as traumatic where the trauma would not be an event that comes and goes but a structure that remains, and so there can be no moment of catharsis until the objective social conditions are brought to an end.

One of the challenges of 'writing culture' (Clifford and Marcus 1986) for much of my fieldwork was how to make the data of antisocial neighbours interesting or sociologically significant. My 'sociological imagination' at the outset of fieldwork was unable to see any such significance and so my initial reaction to my data was panic when faced with a younger generation whose "existence seems to take place on the brink of nonsense" (Charlesworth 2000, p. 293). My initial reaction was of a doctoral student whose research project was slipping through his fingers, and being left with the task of trying to shore-up my data against descending to greater levels of trivia in light of a sixty-eight year old informant describing to me her support worker son's new job consisted of "teachin young folk how tae use a knife an fork an that." Unable to see anything of significance I felt condemned to play the role of recording the minutiae of a post-industrial dystopia and a post-industrial generation so traumatised by the industrial era that it was entering a new era in need of attending State-sponsored courses to learn how to eat properly.

Upon reflection, however, I came to realise my panic had in fact far more to do with the *personal* nature of my data, and that it was to avoid disclosing what was happening within my family life that was the force behind my reluctance to write about antisocial neighbours or local housing conditions, even to the extent of being prepared to carry out the sham of omitting the dominating facts of the field as I had in fact experienced it. *My predicament was how to write about what was happening while avoiding disclosing the fact that I had fallen into the swamps of subjectivity* (Lévi-Strauss).

Living at 51 Cardenden Road made me confront my own unexamined assumptions as to what was 'good' and 'bad' research and what counted as 'good' and 'bad' data, and what I was forced to recognise was the extent to which my own structure of perception was dominated by socially dominant judgments as to what was to be considered 'serious' data and what was to be considered 'trivial' data of no serious import. Reflecting on my resistance to take my own field experience seriously as a source of data, I was compelled to recognise I had no 'working-class consciousness of my own' insofar as my own positivism insisted that, insofar as I was generating the data and I was one of the protagonists, this was the antithesis of sound research. If the question I kept turning over in my mind was what sociological good could come out of Cardenden, my answer was that, based upon much of the material available to be gathered, there was nothing of sociological worth; that in fact my data was farcical thanks to anti–social neighbours who seemed to be involved in the active pursuit of helplessness.

I also realised that pursuing such data seriously would mean I was not engaging in grounded theory or reflecting any empirical data but instead engaging in a form of auto-ethnography, and this was the beginning of my journey away from positivism and objectivism as my living conditions convinced me of three things: the importance of time in structuring structuration, the need for the practice of reflexivity in order to aim at explaining all relevant structurings' impact on any one structure in order to fully explain *any particular aspect* of reality such as housing conditions and, finally, to not rest content with a turn to reflexivity but to develop an auto-ethnography in order to think the data beyond informants themselves.

Only thinking I was free to put the experience of antisocial neighbours behind me in the days after the first tenant left on 7 December 1998 did I feel sufficient mental 'distance' from the problem for it to become a matter of reflection and words and part of my research. But for the second tenant arriving to number 57 in January 2000, it is likely that I would never have seen the impact of *temporality* upon lives, or the new reality of the house as a new site for the imagining and practicing of territorial sovereignty, and a 'housed politics of identity' which I now see as fundamental. While no tenant has any control over the particular building specifications that result in poor sound insulation allowing the transmission of noise through floors, and has no control over a Council's housing allocations policy, so as a father and husband I could not choose the phenomenology of my living conditions nor control how the problem of antisocial neighbours appeared or presented itself. My personal details informed the constitution of the field and the data, so that there can be no *one* existential truth or one adequate representation of antisocial neighbours to make available because the structurations the researcher brings to bear are necessarily different for each researcher, because the data of the field is co-constructed by the field and the particular situation of the researcher.

My journey from positivism to embodied reflexivity and auto-ethnography may never have happened but for poor sound proofing in a block of flats. Similarly, important insights into how it is that it is our relationships that locate and fix us and generate much of the reality of our lives, would probably never have occurred to me with such force if I were not married, as to truly grasp the reality and reach of the structuring force of temporality and social structures I had to trace these forces to the most personal level and to do this I had to become my own informant if I was to escape the criticism of Jules Henry who saw "everywhere the human disciplines run away from the humanity of human beings" (in Bauman 1999, p. 140).

In seeing with some clarity the fact that data-gathering and the interpretation of that data is something of a contact sport, I also see with some clarity that there is a price to be paid: because contextualized *dasein* can never be caught in the representational nets of what Bourdieu terms the scholastic gaze, the only adequate methodology is a reflexive approach to oneself until one closes the gap between self and informant to the point of realizing one would be exactly alike if faced with the same realities. However, learning such truths requires the unlearning of certain illusions about oneself one has been 'lucky' enough not to have been made to let go off; means the deconstruction of a euphemised relation to oneself and a thoroughly de-mythologised self-understanding and awareness of one's position in the social hierarchy and the depth of one's ongoing commitment to one's internalization of one's social position and its constitutive role in one's individuation and sociation. Because understanding is not simply 'taking a look' it is not free, and a full awareness of my own conditioning and *ressentiment*, for example, was some of the price I had to pay if I was to understand; having to reproduce or having to reconstruct for oneself one's own social structuration and being made to see its fatal hold upon oneself, as only when this is in place are we allowed to begin to understand and appreciate the same reality at work in others.[67]

I practice writing and representation, then, from the very bottom of the 'slippery slope' that began innocently enough by practicing reflexivity, but which has led me to the 'pure subjectivism' that haunts the positivist imagination; the non-scientific fate that awaits anyone who allows 'subjective' or private and idiosyncratic realities to become part of their data and methodology. What the 'positivist imagination' fears is the end of any kind of verifiability or reproducibility of data and research findings, and insofar as this criticism is largely fair, a break with objectivism as an ideal of knowledge becomes necessary and inevitable. What also has to be broken free from is the notion that the empirical data *in itself* (whatever that might be) was able to appear to me in a pure or unmediated manner, as it was the objective conditions and events coupled with my own situatedness that forcibly brought unforeseen aspects of structuration into view, as well as forced me to abandon the fiction of the identity of 'ethnographer' and any simple notion of objectivity.

---

[67] In May 2013 the former tenant at 51 Cardenden Road moved back to the village and when we met I told her how shortly after moving into her old flat back in August 1998 I was asked by Fife Council to collect evidence against the upstairs tenant. At this, she told me how the police had raided number 57 looking for drugs "wi dugs an everythin." Fifteen years later, I still had a mind to ask her why she hadn't told me this when showing me her flat all those years ago.

Having a family and being unable to escape my housing reality was what more or less forced the issue of antisocial neighbours into its full structuring potential. If I had been single or simply a 'researcher' (whatever that might be) I could easily have elided much of the problem during the second phase where the worst of the problem occurred at the weekends, so that the issue of housing and antisocial neighbours may well have merited no more than a footnote or one or two anecdotes. A related point to make having broken with objectivism is that it would be vain to attempt a formula or Weberian 'ideal type' of working-class structuration that would have universal relevance, or would enable the social scientist to 'calculate' or assign inputs or values to each structuring structure identified upon an 'ideal type' working-class *dasein*, as the part played by any structuring relation changes over time, and may only becomes part of the whole at a given stage in the person's life-cycle (such as marriage) or never become relevant, so that to look for a one-size-fits-all 'structuration formula' is to ask each researcher or field situation to be the same.

If the initial opening up to an embodied reflexivity was done in the hope that my conditions of learning would further approximate and reproduce informants' conditions of learning and solve a problem of 'data-gathering' about an issue that was not freely discussed or accessible, the price to be paid was to be more or less coerced into abandoning objectivism, because the only way to know the extent of working-class structuration is to allow (or be coerced into allowing) it to happen to oneself, and not pretend one knows this structuration other than by imitating how locals themselves come to be their being. If our methods are to secure the data that is there and capture the story of human being and what happens to it under certain conditions, then a fully-contextualised and fully-socialised social ontology should govern our views on epistemology and what constitutes an adequate methodology. A turn to embodiment, then, also highlights the aporias of pursuing inquiry into 'private spaces' upon the basis of 'purely private' evidence, and it was because my data lay in these spaces and media that it was necessary for me to be coerced out of my contemplative objectivism.

By drawing upon the nineteen months as a Fife Council tenant I have attempted to articulate the *processual* and structural logic of the structuration of human *dasein* and how it happens, and argued that such structuration is not only compatible with the exercise of agency but the *situated* exercise of reason. In Chapter 5 I will develop the analysis begun here concerning a micro-politics and how this same pattern occurs at a national and historic level, and explain how among the '79 generation in particular this is relevant to explaining the rise of working-class nationalism. In preparation for this argument the next chapter deals with some of the generative themes of the '45 generation and how these have influenced their responses to the recent historic political developments in Scotland, by turning in particular to the *historicity* of *dasein* and drawing upon material gathered while attending the local history group for two years. Having begun an analysis of the *sui generic* structuring effect of time, the next chapter then develops this theme by turning attention to the site *par excellence* that reveals the importance of the signification of temporality over the long durée i.e. the relationship to History and Nation.

# 4

# The 'Present as History' & the Return of the Repressed

The appeal of independence remains – at bottom – what it was in the late 13th and early 14th centuries.

Kidd (2012, p. 9)

I see no point in reviving medieval kingdoms in order to actually make sure that we are all rather smaller on the world stage.

Ken Clarke, Conservative MP
BBC *Question Time*, 16 February 2012

## 4.1 The Local History Group

The place-name Cardenden consists of two parts where 'den' refers to the geological feature of a den or glade, typically consisting of a length of landscape hollowed out as a result of a retreating glacier cutting a groove through the landscape at the end of the Ice Age, with the local den having a small stream or burn called the Den Burn running through the village, and which separates the areas of Bowhill and Cardenden. The earliest reference to *Carden* comes from a royal charter of King William in 1165 referring to the granting of land to MacDuff "except for my forest of Carden" (Taylor and Markus 2006, p. 91). This twelfth-century reference describes the area of Carden as a royal hunting ground with the lands of Carden (*Cardone* or *Cardenni*) forming part of the coastal parish and royal domain of Kinghorn until 1642, when these lands became part of Auchterderran parish which itself dates from the medieval sherrifdom of Fife and king David I's (1124-1153) original "modernisation [of Scotland] by invitation" (Bartlett 1994, pp. 78-79), and his organisation of the Church into parishes and the creation of the parish of Auchterderran (*Urechehem* or *ecclesia de Hurkyndorath* or *Hurhyndemuch* or *Ochtirdere*) at this time. According to Taylor and Markus (2006) the earliest known reference to the parish church in Auchterderran is from a document written in Gaelic which records the gifting of the parish church to the community of monks living on the nearby island of St. Serf in Loch Leven, which was famed for its library and school of translation dating from before the twelfth-century (Ross 1958, p. 5).[68] More generally, however, the lack of historical records from the late-medieval and early-modern period is lamented. As McNeill-Houston (1924, p. 145) has written:

> It is one of the sorrows of our Church that there is no record of those who served this cure from the time of St. Fothad, 1050, to the consecration of the Church by De Bernham in 1243, when, even then, no incumbent's name is given. From this time on to 1452 all is silent again. Reference is made to the "parson" before the Reformation. His presence still persists through his title in the old but now disused lint mill, 'Parson's Mill,' a little farm now bearing that name.

While historical records of the abbeys and monasteries of Fife detail a local coal industry flourishing from at least the twelfth century, the parish of Auchterderran's largely agrarian character more or less survived intact until the late eighteenth century, at

---

[68] Gaelic was spoken in Fife in "the late thirteenth century, if not later" (Taylor & Markus 2006, p. 7).

which time the parish minister wrote in the Old Statistical Account of 1791: "The pasture, including sown grass, comprehends four-fifths of the parish" (cited in Taylor and Markus 2006, p. 92). This agrarian past of the local area is evidenced by the area of Bowhill within Cardenden being derived from the Scots words for 'Cattle hill,' while the street of Kirkshotts Terrace is a reference to the twelfth-century duty of villagers to practice archery at designated times of the year within the precincts of the local church, to ensure their readiness for military service at the time of the Wars of Independence when William Wallace (1270-1305) and king Robert the Bruce (1274-1329) secured Scotland's independence from England.[69] In the 19th century, however, a period of unprecedented industrialisation began with Cardenden becoming a 'pit village' from 1895 until 1965.

To explore locals' historical consciousness and the historicity of *dasein* I joined the local history group during fieldwork, and so on 19 January 1999 I walked the short distance to the Corrie Centre hoping to join the group. As I arrived well before the meeting was due to start, I took the opportunity to look around: to the right of the entrance was the largest room in the building which was familiar to me as it was the venue for a Mothers and Toddlers group which I had attended several times with my eldest daughter (just as I myself had attended the pre-school nursery in the same building in the late nineteen-sixties). To the left of the entrance was a space given to advertising the various user-groups of the Centre and a range of literature advertising upcoming events, such as a seminar the following Saturday in Kirkcaldy on the topic of Problem Neighbours. As I browsed through this literature members of the history group began to arrive. I introduced myself and expressed my interest in joining the group, at which Wull

---

[69] An example of locals' consciousness of this iconic period in Scottish history came during the winter of 2010 when local authority road gritters were unable to clear the roads of snow and ice and residents had to make their way on foot to the shops, and as I made my way to the shops I struck up a conversation with Margaret Snell out walking her two terrier dogs, which she had named Wallace and Bruce.

informed me there were in fact two groups, the afternoon group which met at one-thirty p.m. and the evening group which met at seven-fifteen, adding jokingly that if I was "interested in gossip" attending either group would be ideal.

As I had thought the local history group was an obvious place to do ethnography on locals' historical consciousness some sixteen months after the 11 September 1997 referendum that established a mandate for the restoration of the Scottish parliament, and four months before the first elections to the new parliament, I hadn't given any more thought to joining the group so when all the assembled members were sitting around a large table facing each other in one of the side rooms, I suddenly realised that, as I was not joining the group as just another local interested in local history but to do research, I suddenly felt unprepared as I realised I needed to gain the group's permission to attend their meetings and switch from informal chatting as "Dauve Gilfillan's laddie" and say something about my research. After my improvised summary of what my research was about and why I wanted to sit among them, one hard-of-hearing eighty-nine-year-old member turned to Mrs Doig (whom I learned made a point of sitting next to her octogenarian friend's 'good ear') to ask her to explain what I had just said. "He's here tae study us Jenny!" replied Mrs Doig looking straight at me.

With no-one objecting to me joining the group I very quickly felt at home and enjoyed attending every Tuesday evening, and soon learned that both history groups had met every week since 1989 despite the groups being originally established as a one-off course only meant to run for ten weeks. Both groups were organised by the Workers Educational Association (WEA)[70] and came about as a result of the interest in local history generated by the Corrie Festival held in the village in 1986 to commemorate the opening of the Corrie Centre in 1985. Over those ten years the groups had produced texts on Cardenden in the shape of pictorial booklets, calendars and a five volume series of

---

[70] The WEA was founded in 1903 and was part of the movement for independent working-class education.

reminiscences begun in 1989, and through this 'memory work' the groups enjoyed a certain contemporeity and status in the village as a result of their calendars being much in demand as Christmas presents, and their five volumes of local history having been well received.

While I attended a few of the afternoon group meetings it was the evening group that I attended regularly for over two years, and from the beginning I enjoyed the group as it was a site that was free of any frustrating search for 'something,' as the members were able to draw upon an abundance of material via their collective backward glance to the past. There was a relaxed and informal atmosphere among the group and if I was a novel presence thanks to my continual note-taking throughout meetings, being a local and the only young person to have joined the group helped members feel comfortable, as to judge by the comments passed and the views expressed throughout the two years, I am confident members kept very little from me.

At any particular evening meeting the average turnout was about ten or twelve members who were all in their sixties or seventies, with the WEA tutor (Roisin Nesbitt) taking the initiative by proposing a subject-matter for discussion and regularly providing reading material. Some of the topics covered included the history of St. Andrews, the East Neuk of Fife and Abbot's House in Dunfermline, and because of the informality of the group and the freedom it gave itself to range over any period of history and set their own agenda, and the absence of anything resembling a curriculum, it was after the tutor had read one or two pages of text aloud that the group would begin chatting about a particular topic that was related or, sometimes unrelated to the text. Hence, when after a reading a particular topic emerged such as suicide, for example, members would thematise the topic by recounting stories about who in the village had killed themselves, so that the group eventually proceeded to list known cases to each other, and then divulge or speculate upon the reasons for particular incidents so that a conversation could range from local men caught avoiding conscription at the time of the Great War of 1914-1918, to the more recent case of a young soldier from the village killing himself after a tour of duty in Kosovo.[71]

This procedure of giving free reign to local knowledge meant these discussions were an invaluable means of accessing and appreciating local knowledge, so that the members were as much sources of information about daily events in the village as of information of historical interest thanks to their habit of chatting about any significant happening, such as a death or burial that had occurred in the village since the previous meeting. Regular topics of conversation were any items of interest raised at the Community Council meeting (thanks to Annie Laird's attendance), or incidents where the police had been called to in the village. Having remarked on one occasion to the group that they seemed to know everything going on in the village, one member immediately retorted by asking me: "Dae ye ken there's seven paedophiles in the village?" At my incredulous reaction, a discussion then ensued for half an hour of the individuals (including names and addresses) living in the village who had been convicted of paedophilia or sexual abuse of children, which was followed by a discussion of other local instances of sexual perversion that had become public knowledge among the members.

In 1986 when the history groups first began, the members undertook research such as going to Kirkcaldy public library to access the records from the first census of 1841, and copying information about Cardenden and bringing it back to the group meetings to stimulate discussion and to build up an archive that was kept in a cupboard in the room where the group met. At this time the group were also instrumental in helping to preserve the site of the medieval ruin of Carden Tower[72] and marking the spot in the wood where the last duel in Scotland was fought in 1826, as well as mounting a plaque to commemorate the local landmark

---

[71] A former province of the former state of Yugoslavia which declared its independence as a sovereign nation-state on 17 February 2008.

[72] For this work the group was awarded second prize in a UK-wide conservation competition, with their plaque hanging on a wall in the room where the meetings take place.

known simply as *The Big Tree* that had been felled in 1933 as a result of road improvements.[73]

As the years have passed, however, such research and conservation activity has more or less come to an end, and what remains is a group of friends who meet together to chat about days gone by and enjoy an experience of community and conviviality. To achieve this, the normal focus of attention was memories associated with their lived experience of Cardenden and Scotland and further afield during the industrial era when Cardenden was a pit village i.e. from the 1920s until the 1960s, and from listening to their weekly discussions it clearly emerged that a primary experience for members was a previous material poverty and, as a direct consequence, a deeply internalised sense of belonging to the first working-class generation to have known a level of affluence and material security unknown to their parents and grandparents. As one member (Nan Pearson) described the lifelong material struggles of her neighbours:

> She wis that mingin she sold her soap coupons in the shop. And she hid twelve bairns. Ah mind ma sister wis a rent collector, collectin wages. An one day Ah saw him, Jimmy Ritchie, sittin in the scullery wi a hammer breakin his plaster after his broken leg tae get back tae his work earnin money. Mrs Gardner she hid sixteen bairns and she stayed in a single end.

Similarly, Mrs Doig recalled to the group her grandmother, born in 1873, and the start of her working life:

> She went tae work in the Leslie mill fae six in the morning til six at night at ten years auld. Prinlaws mill in Leslie.[74] A flax mill, for the manufacture e linen. When she was twelve she did it full time. Before it was wane day at school, the

---

[73] The Community Council (established in 1978) intended to commemorate this tree by planting another tree in what was a derelict space until 2002, when it was made into a Community Garden.

[74] A village about seven miles to the north-east of Cardenden.

next at the mill. The system e half-timers wisnae abolished 'til 1936. A jute mill is the dirtiest place on earth.

Another member (Anne Mead) recalled local events such as the annual 'School Treat:'

> All the children made their way to their school about lunchtime on the Saturday in July. The local bands, pipes and drums and brass, turned out to lead the procession. The children from Denend School waited patiently at the Sweet Shop at the foot of Station Road and joined in the procession as it passed by, then on to the Goth[75] to collect St. Ninian's school and Auchterderran School pupils. From there the procession went right up to Woodend Park (the one just below the Golf Club)...The streets were lined with mums and dads, brothers and sisters, and aunties and uncles all cheering as the children marched past waving wee flags and balloons.

The quote from Anne above evokes the conspicuous enjoyment and consumption of local spectacles, and if we focus upon the words "all cheering" and think about cheering as a social practice, there is a sense of 'effervescence' (Durkheim) and a local society recognising and celebrating itself, as to cheer involves the idea of something that is present in abundance, a spectacle in which nothing is lacking and a belonging to locality and the present where an abundance of children also evidences that this village and this belonging to locality is set to endure thanks to its pipe bands, its schools and streets where the generations come together in annual rituals, games and parades. There is an evocation of abundant life and an abundant local population and families with aunts and uncles and the extended family present to locality;

---

[75] There are a number of pubs in Fife in former coalmining villages and towns named 'The Goth' as a result of the importation of the Gothenburg public house system from Sweden, where the profits of local licensed premises were retained in the local community to fund local projects.

a non-contracepting population and place where locality is inter-familial and free of privatism and villagers' individuation and sociation was localised so that time is spent locally, so that on any particular day everyone was in the village for all-village gatherings and practices, as this is the era before the mass consumption of motor cars and private mobility. 1945 generation informants' recollections indicate the rich presence of the past, and this effortless ability to recall a substantive past makes the local history group possible. As already highlighted, however, the descriptions of the 'present as history' among the '45 generation seems fated to be narrated in terms of decline.

> **Hugh:** When the pit and Co-Op shut, a' the wee things, a' the pictures shut. You go up Bowhill noo an it's always like it's half shut. You had movement e people all the time.
> **Nan:** When you had the pictures, when the pictures came oot and you were drivin you had to go like a snail because they never walked on the pavement, they were on the road.

Other 'wee things' adding to the texture of village life included the display of wedding cakes during the week prior to the day of a wedding in the bakery window, and practices relating to death:

> When a death occurred in the village, intimations were posted throughout on a black and white card approx. 9" by 5" giving all information as to time and place of the funeral.

Until the late nineteen-seventies a notice board stood outside the entrance to Cardenden library and the Registry Office in Cardenden Road,[76] and on this board and other sites such as telegraph poles around the village, locals were literally 'kept posted' of local births, deaths and marriages so that the reproduction of locality and locals in the pre-internet era was a daily spectacle. Hence, on the day of the burial of a local notable at this time such as the

---

[76] The building which housed the library and registry has since been demolished and the space today is taken up by a large private residence.

local GP Dr. Cranston or parish priest Fr. Smith,[77] the centre of the village would come to a standstill as local police cordoned off the roads to traffic to allow the funeral procession of hundreds of locals to make its way to the cemetery. Throughout this period the spectacle of death and the practice of mourning was a public and local affair. Today, however, as a result of the local cemetery becoming full, the spectacle of death has increasingly become a private familial affair that takes place outwith the village five miles away in the crematorium in Kirkcaldy. Previously, then, "all funerals were to the cemetery – there was no crematorium in those days" (Local History Group, vol. 2, pp. 17-18) and the spectacle of death and locality coming together to practice solidarity with the bereaved was a constituent part of village life, which only required the short walk to the cemetery and attendance at a grave-side ceremony in contrast to having to make a journey of some miles outside of the village.

Until the nineteen-eighties, then, death was a local and public affair and integral to learning what it meant to belong to a locality. While residents who have already purchased their burial plot will be buried in the village, the ongoing failure to make long-term provision for local burials is a scandal for many residents who complain bitterly at Fife Council's failure at local planning; a failure that continually makes itself present each time a local is buried outwith the village and is not accorded the local burial they wanted for themselves. The intensely meaningful and intensely local spectacle of death, then, has been expropriated and relocated outwith the village, and the disappearance of this meaningful social practice from the life of the village was an ongoing source of resentment and complaints from history group members.

As mentioned, the group members exhibited an expertise in local knowledge and what may be described as an expertise in belonging to the village. When a particular story was about to be related to the group and a particular protagonist was unknown to any of the

---

[77] Both men were well-known and long-term residents within the village, in contrast to the doctors of today who live elsewhere and who normally have no non-work presence to the village, while the parish priest since 2009 is a Polish national.

members, for example, the anecdote was put on hold until he or she was normally identified via kinship or address, after which the story could proceed. This work of remembering and identifying individuals via recourse to a long gone time and space was itself a performance or enactment of knowledge, and the evidencing of the reach and reality of kin-based and locality-based knowledge that constituted the group dynamic and kept it going over the twelve years by the time I joined. Members' reminiscing was person-oriented, event-centred and overwhelmingly biographical and local, but certainly not parochial (in the pejorative sense), as the great motif of all of their lives and the subject to which they returned again and again was their working lives and the Second World War of 1939-1945, and as in the following testimony of Bien Bernard, how the two were combined in their lives:

> See me, Ah started tae fire fae Ah wis five year old. Ah remember the very first word 'strike.' Ah wis soon tae learn what it wis a' aboot because Ah hid an achin' belly. Noo if ma belly wis achin' fir the want e grub what like wis ma parents? Bit there's the thing. Ah listened tae pit talk a' ma life, at the fireside, Ah could smell the pit afore Ah went doon it...an' a lived wi it, it wis in ma blood. Ah lived wi' it. Ye ken Ah wis oot in the Mediterranean in 1942 on HMS Brocklesbury durin' the war an' Ah wis still spittin' black, Ah wis still spittin' black. We hid fower scabs in this village, an' they'll be scabs tae the day they die, an' they'll always be remembered as scabs, they'll be scabs. An' when ye come intae the village here one time up at the Jamphlers there at the gable end wi' the eleven scabs, the 1926 strike, their names wis on there; they were there fae 1926; they were there fir thirty year.

While in the main their anecdotal and person-centred 'memory work' only briefly and infrequently reached the level of discussing the history of ideas, the question of the meaning of the past was invariably never far from their discourse about events which were pregnant with politics and history. This emphasis upon individual memoirs but from a shared era and shared locality, touches upon

Halbwach's investigation of collective memory which in the view of Connerton (1989, p. 37) was the first to demonstrate that "the idea of an individual memory, absolutely separate from social memory, is an abstraction almost devoid of meaning." The group, then, studied local history in the manner it established *communitas* among themselves i.e. upon the basis of shared memories of locality as opposed to cultivating a shared interest in studying history *per se*, so that integral to the group's practice was recalling the details of people, places and incidents from their past, whether funny, sad, tragic, remarkable or quotidian.

Members' identification with the experience of locality as industrial occupational community was not an insular affair as Cardenden like many towns and villages throughout central west Fife and central Scotland were creatures of 'primitive industrialisation.' From Ireland and the West of Scotland and the Lothians, many miners and their families settled in the late nineteenth-century and early twentieth century within the Fife coalfields. This industrial era also had its accompanying culture or 'sacred canopy' that structured members' discourse on post-industrialisation which identified the high watermark of locality with the industrial coalmining era, in particular 1895–1965, and listening to the experiences informants remembered was to form the impression that they belonged to a time so imbued with community that it produced near-identical interests due to the highly homogenous reality of the single-occupational community, and a level of community which, when remembered within the group up to seventy years later for some members, *reproduced again* this experience of *communitas* despite the fact that the objective conditions that made this *communitas* possible no longer existed in the post-industrial era.

Reflecting upon this ability of the group *to make communitas exist twice* and reconstitute this 'thick togetherness,' I often said to the group that I doubted whether locals from my generation in fifty years time would have enough material and memories in common to be able to come together and reminisce for twelve years about the Cardenden of the 1980s and 1990s, as I was often moved by members' ability to make an unknown past come suddenly alive and present to me as I sat listening among them.

Today it is difficult to appreciate the Cardenden of a population of over ten thousand residents, and its dozens of clubs and societies and branches of national and international associations which characterised village life at a time when "You had movement of people all the time" (Hugh). When Buchan (1994, p. 11) recalls Dr. Rorie resigning from the twenty-two positions he held on various local committees upon leaving Cardenden in 1905, we catch a glimpse of a 'thick' local civic culture, and the density of the experience of locality that was a matter of opening one's eyes to see the spectacle that was physically there to be seen and which is impossible to reproduce today.

As a result of being accepted into the group, however, something else that became clear to me was that the group members were part of a generation that was living through a series of 'endings:' the end of locality as occupational community, the end of the industrial era, the political end of Britain among the Scottish working class, and the ending of a level of cultural cohesiveness characteristic of a pre-affluent era and a pre-privatised working class that had not yet undergone embourgeoisement (Zweig 1961). This older generation was witnessing the 'privatisation' or pluralisation of a once-shared symbolic order, and insofar as the group's recollections focussed upon the era prior to the arrival of affluence to the working classes from the nineteen-seventies, their ability to educate me about my own past was something I found new and intriguing, to the extent of making me reluctant to break with the spell they cast over me. Such a break, however resisted, was inevitable as the members emphatically and unself-consciously revealed to me their alienation from the present-day in general and the historic event of the restoration of the Scottish parliament in particular.

## 4.2 The Political Consciousness of the 1945 Generation

Ah'll no be voting.

Hugh Young (77)
Retired Miner
19th April 1999

At the second meeting I attended (3 February 1999) the tutor Roisin began by reading a paper entitled *A Brief History of St Andrews* which she had downloaded from the internet and [78] which culminated in the destruction of the great twelfth-century cathedral of St. Andrews, and the advent of the sixteenth-century Protestant revolt in the ecclesial centre of Scotland.[79] As the tutor narrated what for myself was a familiar tale, I waited with my notebook and pen ready to record locals' views on this epochal event in Scottish history, confident that an explicit engagement with the *long durée* of Scottish history, and an engagement with fundamental questions of identity and belief and 'being in history' were about to fall into my lap. As I waited for Roisin to finish reading I looked around: a long-established group of friends ensconced in their regular comfortable chairs in pleasant and familiar surroundings, and a young and enthusiastic history tutor narrating their national history, and it occurred to me that even at this early stage of fieldwork my research might hinge upon the discussion to follow, some ten weeks before the first elections to the new Scots parliament in May 1999, and how fortunate I was; that of all the possible research topics and of all the possible ethnographic sites available to me, I had chosen the right topic and at the right time, and felt that the data I was about to gather would share in the significance of the moment. After Roisin finished reading I recorded the following exchange:

**Wull:** What's a Culdee church?
**Roisin:** Ma friend Sharon's a pagan. She's gonnae get married in a field. She says that's the true Scottish religion.

---

[78] The material used in the group was normally downloaded from the internet by Roisin at home and photocopied for the group. Roisin advised this practice was due to the WEA wanting to avoid any possible legal problems regarding photocopying copyrighted material.

[79] In the summer of 1999 I listened to an interview with Richard Demarco on Radio Scotland, which included details of his initiative to restore St. Andrews cathedral to its former glory as a "new national symbol for the new Scotland."

**Jim:** Ma brither wis an atheist. And what aboot a' these nations that worship totem poles?
**Hugh:** Where does Roman Catholicism come fae? Does it come fae the Romans?
**Wull:** God only knows.
**Moira:** Ah dinnae ken.

From the above exchange it is clear that no revealing discussion occurred, and no engagement with the meaning of Scottish history fell into my lap. Indeed, far from gathering data reflecting a generation's historical consciousness, what I learned was that this exchange was typical of the history group meetings as a whole, and firmly put onto my horizon the task of trying to understand why a local history group failed to discuss both the history of their nation and the history *they were living through*.

If such were my initial attempts at conducting an ethnography of 'working-class nationalism,' my first reaction was that I had made a blunder to have imagined such a thing as working-class nationalism existed, and so the meeting was a salutary lesson as it was clear that I had imagined my informants as I wanted them to be and not as they were. Insofar as it seemed clear that there was no political dialectic left in this generation, my intention was to make my excuses and leave the group as it was hardly an appropriate space for research on working-class nationalism. In the event, however, I continued attending the group as a valuable source of background material so that, having tempered my great expectations, I wasn't surprised when at the meeting immediately after the first elections to the new Holyrood parliament on 5 May 1999, the only comment on this reversal of two hundred and ninety-two years of Scottish history was: "Ye can argue aboot politics till yer blue in the face and ye'll never get anywhere" (Jim Russell).

This 'comical' show of indifference to the new parliament, which was greeted with a show of approval from members, was consubstantial with other indifferences, bordering on hostility, such as that shown to the new millennium of 2000, and so I began to suspect there was a *ressentiment* against history insofar as each historic event seemed to open a window upon informants' indifference-come-hostility. Hence, regarding a recent spate of job losses in Fife in the spring of 1999 which was widely reported in the media, there occurred the following rare exchange that touched on the new Scots parliament:

> **Annie:** Ye jist wonder how many joabs'll be left once it [the parliament] gets gaun.
>
> **Jim:** Ah'll tell ye, a hunder an twenty nine joabs.[80] That's how much. See when they get somethin, what dae they dae? They go and build a big posh buildin. An look at the money bein spent on a temporary building. A temporary building! That's sick.
>
> **Moira:** Ah jist switch aff when it comes tae politics.
>
> **Annie:** Me an a'.
>
> **Jim:** Bit we cannae solve our problems wi the parliament we've got the noo! Where's a' this money gonnae come fae?
>
> **Me:** Where do you think it has come from, this new parliament and nationalism?
>
> **Jim:** What started it all was that film Braveheart.[81] And what did that prove? That Scotsmen couldnae agree wi theirsels! This Scottish parliament is jist anither talkin shop. What else can it be?
>
> **Nan:** Ah dinnae hink there'll be many SNP aboot here. Ah've ayeways voted Liberal.
>
> **Hugh:** Ah've voted Labour a' ma life. A monkey could stand an Ah'd vote for it.[82]

The above comments were very much representative of the discourse I heard and recorded during two years of meetings and

---

[80] The number of members elected to the Holyrood parliament.

[81] A film directed by and starring Mel Gibson about the Scottish Wars of Independence and the historical figure of William Wallace (1270-1305) which premiered in Stirling in 1995, and which has since passed into the popular national consciousness in Scotland.

[82] By this phrase Hugh means that such is his devotion to voting Labour that even if the Labour candidate in an election was a monkey he would vote for the monkey, rather than vote for another candidate from another party.

while I quickly learned to expect it, I was still capable of being surprised by their level of estrangement from the times they were living through, or their level of being 'out of history' (Craig 1996). At the history group meeting on 19 April 1999 that was just a few days before the first election to the new parliament, for example, I informed the group that as part of my research I intended to conduct door-to-door interviews to ask people what they thought of the new parliament. At this, Roisin (whose husband was a policeman) hurriedly advised me: "If ye dinnae hae permission and folk complained ye could get done fir breach e the peace!" and in the exchange of views that followed Hugh emphatically announced: "Ah'll no be voting!" with Annie advising she too would not be voting in the election to the new parliament. In light of the hostility of the group towards the new constitutional settlement and what seemed like their boycott of Scottish history, and the fact that they were always prepared to make clear and unequivocal statements to this effect, an obvious question was what this said about their twelve-year study of local history.

The group members were born in the 1920s and 1930s and belonged to a generation that experienced the historic high-water mark of the domination of politics by class interests, and the experience of locality as occupational community. All members exhibited a default unionist nostalgia for the *status quo ante*, and throughout the two years I attended, I garnered not a single instance of even pro-'home-rule' sentiment, far less nationalism.

If the content of members' discourse on constitutional matters was largely settled, something else that was settled was their manner of expression, along with the relevance of Bernstein's (1971) description of language codes, and how the working class's relationship to language as 'restricted' as opposed to 'open.' Many of the exchanges I noted were forms of rhetoric that emerged from a very specific habitus that was operationalised 'without thinking;' as if such was their settled habit of self-expression that it seemed their use of language had fallen into cliché and was no longer capable of being open to new realities, so that what was sayable was only that which was firmly held and had been arrived at long ago, so that any expression of any opinion was rhetoric and liable to an exaggerated degree of decisiveness. Certainly the verbal exchanges showed a predilection for one-liners, and a linguistic habitus or relation to language that did not encourage long pauses or long sentences but what may be described as a defining 'in and out' use of language, where talking is not practiced in order to explore something even in a group devoted to talking for twelve years, but is more akin to a 'smash and grab' functionalism. While members were free to talk about any subject they chose and for as long as they pleased, there was a characteristic hurriedness to the contributions and a hurriedness to contribute one's piece when the opportunity presented itself and before the group's attention moved on; almost as if their use of language betrayed an insecure relationship to the realm of meaning, with this latter being none of their business, so that there was no question of a leisurely, unhurried use of language and time to explore and engage in an intersubjective process which could allow the significance of unprecedented historic and political events and new opinions to emerge.

In the brief exchange quoted previously concerning the new parliament, for example, we see that both what informants have to say and the manner in which they say it are settled matters of habit; that their expression of hostility is sure of itself and ready-to-hand, and what it is sure of is that the return of Scottish history is unwelcome and easily dismissed but for the expensiveness of it all. These '45 generation members, then, are not in the business of imagining a break from the constitutional status quo and so are alienated from the movement of contemporary Scottish history and indeed *resent* the return of Scottish history, so that *a hermeneutic of resentment* is developed to 'read' events within and outwith Scotland.

The first election campaign for the new Holyrood parliament coincided with the NATO bombardment of the former Yugoslavia and the Kosovo crisis, and the daily reporting of alleged 'ethnic cleansing' that was being practiced by the Yugoslavian armed forces and provoked among group members their view that ethnic conflict is inevitable because people are what they are and their defining 'whatness,' whether conceived in terms of ethnicity, religion or nationality, cannot be changed and is real enough to have inspired Jim to ask "How do you change human nature?" after a discussion that came after the following exchange:

**Jim:**[83] The British flag as such is steeped in blood.[84] In Palestine they shot Arabs left right and centre. The Middle East has been fighting since the Bible days. Ah think it'll get worse here in this country. All these ethnic folk comin in an eventually they'll take over. There'll be war between them an the whites. In aboot twenty five years we'll be the foreigners.
**Annie:** We're the foreigners already. Look at a' the hooses in Cardenden an Bowhill, they're a' owned by other folk.
**Nan:** What are we needin tae split this country fir?

If I am correct in presuming that Nan, as a self-confessed lifelong Liberal voter, was referring to the splitting of Scotland and England as a result of the creation of the Scottish parliament, it is interesting insofar as it reveals how the advent of the Scottish parliament was viewed as adventitious, as if it had emerged 'from nowhere' for Scots with a British national identity or for those whose Scottish identity played no part in their politics. While the new Scottish parliament had clearly emerged to deal with a long-standing sense of a democratic deficit since at least 1979, I do not believe Nan was engaged in bad-faith but rather her *one-nation British unionism* was sufficiently structuring her perception to 'disappear' from her view the political difference between Scotland and England. More generally, I argue that this sense of Britishness is integrated with the 1945 generation's experience of the high-point of locality as community, is highly integrated with an enduring and defining connection with the idea and the practice of a convincing Britishness thanks to the Second World War.

---

[83] Jim had served in the British armed forces during the Second World War and it was common knowledge among the group members that he never talked of his war-time experiences.

[84] During fieldwork I heard the Union Jack flag referred to as the Butcher's Apron by nationalists among the younger '79 generation.

In addition to this high-point of Britishness is the creation of the Welfare State which remains the high-point of British politics for the '45 generation, and which is deeply defining of their self-understanding and deeply consequential for their constitutional politics. Hence, because there is a *doxic organisation* of their consciousness upon a British basis, even eighteen years of Conservative Party minority rule in Scotland between 1979 and 1997 is not enough to alter their views or dissuade Hugh from voting for a "Labour monkey." My '45 generation informants, then, made a show of freely presenting themselves as impermeable to the constitutional arguments that have dominated Scottish politics for a generation, and their indifference-come-hostility towards the nationalist triumph of 1999 was by no means restricted to local history group informants as a number of elderly locals, especially women, were angry and upset at the restoration of the Scottish parliament, and were clear that the return of Scottish nationalism represented the defeat of their deeply held 'unionist' views and sense of British identity. Indeed, such was their antipathy that a number of would-be informants could not bring themselves to talk to me about the creation of the parliament and preferred to slam their door shut after I informed them on their doorstep of my research interest.

During the first weeks of interviewing such sentiments were not uncommon and, just as with my initial encounter with the local history group, they left me at a loss as to how to make sense of this data. What became clear was that I needed to move beyond my preoccupation with politics and history and realise that my informants' sense of having nothing to say or contribute about unfolding historical and political events was something which merited inquiry in its own right. As I reconciled myself to the loss of my imaginary construct of 'working-class nationalism,' I started to take note of the choicest expressions of indifference or hostility to events such as the State opening of the first session of the Scottish parliament which took place on 1 July 1999, and began to search for ethnographic value in encounters which occurred when beginning interviewing locals such as seventy-plus year old retired coalminer Bert Lister (Woodend Park, 11 July

1999,) who after I had introduced myself and my research project of locals' thoughts on the establishment of the Scottish parliament, and ten days after "the most important political event in three hundred years,"[85] and who while eloquent on "that f***in bastard Winston Churchill" and his decision in 1921 to "send in the tanks against the Scottish miners," told me that as far as the new Scottish parliament was concerned: "Naw, Ah'm past a' that. Ah'm past a' that."

Many would-be informants, then, clearly had no sense of the new parliament being 'theirs' or the result of semantic or political struggle on their part, and they were not about to represent themselves as having harboured a desire for Home Rule all along now that it had arrived, and the question they firmly put on my agenda was how was it that the Scots had just created a parliament thanks to thirty years of constitutional agitation and yet my informants were more or less hostile to the whole affair?

As already stated, the continued existence of a British identity among older residents has freed them from any need to engage with the constitutional politics that has gradually emerged among the central belt working class since the famous nationalist victory in Hamilton in 1967.[86] Informants' hostility-come-indifference to contemporary developments and events was not wilful, but had 'real presence' and depth because it emerges from early and primary identity-formation that has lang syne become doxic or unexamined so that, while sourced in a set of political and material and cultural circumstances that have largely disappeared, has been taken up by freedom and become autonomous as a 'politics of identity' from its conditions of emergence.

I also propose that the absence of the politicisation of their 'inert' Scottish identity is isomorphic with their limited politicisation of class. My elderly informants' political identity then is based upon the two co-ordinates of nation and class i.e. being

---

[85] Scottish Television's political pundit Bernard Ponsonby advertising the television programme *Vote 99: Scotland Decides*, aired 22 April 1999.
[86] The Hamilton by-election of 2 November 1967 when the SNP's Winnie Ewing won with 46.1 % of the vote.

British and being working class, an integralism which, while in the aftermath of World War two was responsible for new and laudable achievements such as the Welfare State, today results in a political inertia and a certain alienation from the 'present as history.' Because the '45 generation had such a strong experience of locality and class cohesion and an enduring sense of belonging and *communitas* through their British identity, they neither then nor now feel any need to politicise their Scottish identity as they still identify with a period when belonging to locality as occupational community and the imagined community of the nation was unproblematic, colonial and even imperial and triumphalist.[87] Something of the 'density' of being British is indicated in one elderly informant's remembering (Local History Group vol. 4, p. 25):

> There were many traditional customs in the local community which have disappeared completely and others which are rarely seen nowadays. One that comes to mind from my youth was the flying of a flag, usually the Union Jack, on a house chimney which was to signify that there was a young man in the house about to be married. The flag was usually erected by one of his workmates and the custom was to reward the person who had scaled the rooftops, secretly and generally at night, with a bottle of whisky.

Among my elderly informants class is permitted to be politicised to the 'reasonable' extent of adherence to the Labour Party, and their Scottish national identity is permitted to be politicised to the 'reasonable' extent of decrying 'Thatcher' and 'England' on occasion, but the further politicisation of these identities as in

---

[87] I remember my paternal Uncle John (1932-2008) posing to us children the trick question: "If ye wernae British and ye could pick any nationality in the world, which wane would ye be?" In this scenario the not-so-clever child's imagination roams over the world trying to decide which country is second-best after Britain, while the clever child is the one who realises the terms of the question mean he or she is not British, and so is free to answer "British."

the socialist demand for a redistribution of wealth or the further politicisation of Scottish national identity as in the call for the exercise of national sovereignty via independence is judged beyond what is practical or prudent. I also suggest that attempting to uncover why my informants felt it presumptuous to politicise class and (Scottish) national identity is isomorphic with their refusal to politicise history and their reluctance to freely engage with Scottish history because the free discussion of the long durée and historic geo-political relations between classes and nations would require a break with or a loosening or subversion of the doxic organisation of their consciousness, and a real engagement with the new events and the new developments they are living through.

Socialised in the 'dictatorship of scarcity' era and born into the British Empire, their inability to break with their internalisation of what might be termed their 'scarcity British subject imagination' is the heart of the matter,[88] and in this regard an analogy may be drawn between British unionism and the liberal imagination insofar as, just as the liberal accords no place for religion in public life, so the national question for these working-class unionists is something to be privatised and play a very limited and inoffensive role in political and public life.

If human being is deeply historicised and socialised so that it is simultaneously in-history, in-society and in-nature, the expression and recognition of this integral contextualisation of human being or *dasein* is kept under control insofar as 'being Scottish' is policed among those who must 'budget' their human being, who must exercise a 'psychological prudence' so as not to indulge in 'luxurious' or deluxe models of integralism that are imagined to be outwith their material and symbolic means. What working-class unionism also evidences then is the controlling of reason, thinking and speaking and politics via processes of socialisation among this generation as they stand guard against 'expensive' self-understandings as much as expensive buildings (Hugh), and

---

[88] "What happens if they faa oan their arse? Dae ye beg tae go back?" Mr. Davie (New Carden Farm, South Cottage) on the prospect of independence.

so such a socialised consciousness must keep within a dominated estimation of reason and human being.

We may say then that even prior to affluence and Zweig's (1961) embourgeoisement thesis, the working class were already bourgeois insofar as they had internalised and practiced the privatisation of their *dasein* or 'being Scottish' as per the quietist Scottish middle classes. We may also say that Scotland until 1999 remained ruled by unionist elites who managed every institution in the land and dominated every official or mainstream imagining of Scotland, and both the middle and working classes were thoroughly offended by the idea of practicing Scottish sovereignty and founding the project of modernity upon a purely Scottish basis. This 'privatisation' of Scottish identity and embarrassment-come-hostility towards the return of Scotland from its repressed existence may be viewed as the signature 'success' of the liberal peace which is likewise embarrassed-come-hostile towards any moves to a Scottish integralism or *holism* in politics, education, public life or within *dasein* itself because, fundamentally, the liberal imagination and its middle- and working-class bearers are embarrassed-come-hostile to thinking human being outwith the discipline required to retain either their social hegemony or social subordination, and so remain incapable of 'painting' Scottish *dasein* with a full palette of colours even in conditions of affluence.

In the next section I will argue a previous eighteenth-century Enlightenment narration of 'being modern' which justified stripping the altars of human being to the bare minimum of being functional to the reproduction of market society and the political submergence of 'Scotland,' has filtered down to the non-elites and made every other Scot more or less ignorant of their history and illiterate and uninterested in the question of their own sovereignty and self-understanding and self-interest; and that a new and older understanding of 'being modern' is at hand, and which is reversing this unionist modernity and thereby resurrecting the project of a Scottish modernity upon the basis of a new Scottish sovereignty.

However, returning from the abstract realm of ideas, is it fair to describe elderly informants' views as evidence of, for example, domination? In this regard I concede without equivocation that an equally reasonable interpretation of my elderly informants is that their views reflect a perfectly acceptable desire to retain their British identity. However, I also argue that *in the practice of interpretation, context is king or is sovereign*. Interpretation is not a contemplative or philosophical affair but a contextual social practice that must take its cue from objective structures and events so that interpretation in the realm of politics is a 'contact sport.' My interpretation of a dominated unionist psyche makes no pretence at being objective in any philosophical sense. Rather, my interpretation is immersed in the same context it wishes to interpret and must be judged according to that context. I make no claim that a British identity is unreasonable or that a non-nationalist point of view is unreasonable *per se* (whatever that might be) but *because interpretation is not a spectator sport I make the claim that such views at this point in time and in this place* collude in the reproduction of the constitutional status quo and, in the context of the long event of 1979-1997 and 2010-2015, is 'guilty' of *interpretive quietism* and subordination. My position is this is evidence of working-class consciousness being interpolated by the liberal imagination which wishes to privatise *class* just as it wishes to privatises the *national* question, just as it wishes to privatise the question of sovereignty and religion and the meaning of *history*, until we arrive at Schmitt's (2005) position and conclude that it wishes to remove the question of human being from politics and public life.

Such is what I believe is a fully-contextualised interpretation. In direct contrast, however, if one were to consider a decontextualized interpretation done in accordance with 'pure reason,' one could plausibly argue, for example, that far from being dominated my informants are so confident and their sense of and possession of their Scottish national identity is so secure that they feel little need to constitute their politics by this identity, so that the notion that one's 'authenticity' as a people and nation is at stake insofar as one refuses to politicise this national identity is quite non-sensical, wilful and far-fetched.

Faced with such dialectically opposed interpretations of the same data, my view is that as soon as one steps into the real historical context of Scotland today, all purely contemplative or leisurely interpretations fail because *the historicity of human being* or 'being in history' is not a private reality to be contemplated or cultivated at one's leisure as one sees fit because the periods 1979-1997 and 2010-2015, for example, do not allow for a contemplative or leisurely relation to Scottish national identity, because the period 1979-1997 and 18 september 2014 sees the Scots being more or less coerced by the force of events to chose, for once and for all, whether Scotland or Britain is to be the organising basis for their lives. The resurrection of this constitutional decision as to who is sovereign in this land is today unavoidable, and has been more or less forced upon many 'unionist' Scots who would much rather that such fundamental questions be privatised again as soon as possible, and indicates the Scots' context of 'being in history' and at the mercy of relations, so that the Scots did not take up nationalism as the conclusion of a timeless theoretical debate but from a context of geo-political weakness that was revealed in the periods 1979-1997 and 2010-2015.

With no need to peer into anyone's soul and pronounce upon their authenticity, then, non-nationalist opinions *because of the extrinsic historical context* evidence a double domination: (1) the acceptance of Scottish political subordination to England and (2) a dominated consciousness insofar as a dominated relation to the de facto acceptance of geo-political subordination denies to itself a clear grasp of the extrinsic contextual truth about itself. If from Bourdieu and Wacquant (1992) we learn that society exists twice i.e. objectively 'out there' and intersubjectively within consciousness, then my 'unionist' informants' domination exists twice i.e. geo-politically and insofar as the straightforward recognition of their accepting their national subordination is denied at the level of consciousness. This double subordination which dominates elderly locals' political horizon is not confined of course to a few members of a local history group, as from the field interviews in 1999 and again in 2014, it is clear there exists a generation whose members are antithetical to any meaningful engagement in the current political developments, so that the ethnographer of Cardenden 1999 or 2014 would misrepresent the facts if he were to write "we are all nationalists now, to some degree or another" (McCrone

1998, p. ix). It seems more accurate rather to recognise it is in fact a profound consequence of ten generations of symbolic and material domination, and as something utterly predictable among the '45 generation working class so that the idea we are all nationalists now is unsociological insofar as it postulates an immaculate relation to history or a *dasein* free of history.

I do not think it reasonable to hold the view that unionism (Seawright and Curtice 1995) among the Scottish working class in 1999 or 2014 is free of complicity in geo-political (national) and class subordination. Indeed, unionism appears today as the 'cipher of choice' among the dominated (elderly or young) and a form of contextual false consciousness. However, what I interpret as a dominated relation to 'being in history' is not confined to the political realm or the question of sovereignty as, while fieldwork offered opportunities to record how locals view the long durée, what emerged instead was the opportunity to record an antipathy towards unwelcome 'events' such as the new millennium, which served to highlight a population who do not 'do meaning' insofar as they opened a window onto hostility towards engaging with the meaning of history and 'substantive events.' For example, then, early on during fieldwork the following item appeared (November 27, 1998) in the *Fife Free Press* newspaper:

> Ideas Wanted to Mark 2000 by Cardenden and Kinglassie Community Council. To request info. call community council secretary Mr. D. Taylor 7 Kinglassie Rd. Woodend.

Three months later at the history group meeting of 2nd March 1999, a letter from the Community Council which had been sent to every user-group of the Corrie Centre was read to the history group giving details of a meeting to be held on 16th March to solicit ideas about how the village would mark the beginning of the third (Christian) millennium. After the letter was read aloud to the members, the response was far from enthusiastic. "An excuse tae spend money!" was how one member responded, and which sparked further comments about 'millennium hype' that members deemed prevalent in the media, and likewise during another brief exchange regarding the millennium at another meeting, one informant could opine without the least self-consciousness: "Well Ah hope there's somethin bloody decent oan the telly."[89]

While resistance to media manipulation is undoubtedly to be welcomed, what is also operative here is a context of communication where the 'realm of meaning' is a thoroughly 'private' and individual affair, with the result that any group or public context is felt to be an inappropriate space to divulge one's 'personal' views, so that the ethnographer is in the dark as to the very existence of any such views. As with the non-discussion of historical events such as the Reformation in St. Andrews described earlier, the advent of the new millennium acted to reveal informants' well-honed relationship to the realm of meaning and their indifference-come-hostility to the constitutional debate which was consubstantial with their alienation from any discussion as to whether members participated in any meta-narrative concerning history. I was struck by what appeared to me as their highly-determined lack of relation to the realm of meaning, so that the signification of History and events was fated to be left to the media or the idiosyncrasies of the individual and locals' discourse as a rule was not tempted by events to reach 'escape velocity' from quotidian discourse, with the result that it is not simply that internalised 'rules of linguistic engagement' prevented substantive discussion of the meaning of the millennium but an underlying tight control exercised over language, thought and imagination was always at work.

The apparent failure of baptised Christians and church-goers to articulate a 'freely available' Christian interpretation of history raises the further question as to whether this inability to mobilise their Christian identity is consubstantial with their refusal or inability to mobilise their class and national (Scottish) identities.

---

[89] If there was a poverty of 'millennium meaning' there were also idiosyncratic assertions of meaning at the millennium Hogmanay, such as one sixty-seven-year-old retired miner telling the assembled company: "Ah'm delighted tae see this day [1 January 2000] cause no male member of the race has ever reached sixty–seven year auld;" by which he meant he was the first male member of his family to reach sixty-seven years old.

It seems that beyond or deeper than these 'identities' is an all-powerful social determination or perhaps deeper cultural ethos that is at work which forbids their Christianity from structuring their use of language in public and their self-representations even among themselves; *a strict or integral privatism* or internalised liberal censor that does not 'do meaning' or does not 'do history' and does not 'do God,' so that to deploy their Christian identity in order to 'read' the millennium would be to break from their integral privatism that strictly polices the expression of their human being and all its identities, whether 'being Christian' or 'being working class' or 'being Scottish' or 'being in history.'

If interpretation is a contact sport and context is everything, then the rush of events and the unforeseen context of 1 July 1999 (and even more so 18 September 2014) also mean unforeseen judgments, such that there is among the 1945 generation a fourfold domination insofar as the four identities or structurations of *dasein* of class, nation, religion and historicity are not freely mobilised at this point, so that future writers in an independent Scotland are more or less fated to judge the action or inaction of those living through the events of today as evidence of a fourfold subordination. In the event of independence after 2014, the generation that refuses to constitute itself upon the fourfold basis of religion, class, nation and history will be taken as evidence of an integral subordination where a free integralism was contextually or historically called for, and such a conclusion will form part of a more general argument that the working class collude in their subordination and are ashamed of being or practicing themselves beyond the limits set for them by privatism. As a corollary of this interpretation, it seems clear that a *return of the repressed* in a younger working-class (and middle-class) generation must coincide with the overthrow of privatism.

As with the structuring reality of poor sound insulation being the necessary condition for mediating and constituting the reality of antisocial neighbours, so the creation of the Scottish parliament and the 18 September 2014 referendum are conditions that reveal a normally unseen and unsuspected aspect of an older generation's mental structuration by more or less forcing their privatism

to 'show itself' in public. Whether it is housing conditions characterised by poor sound insulation, and the political union
of Scotland and England or the creation of the Scottish parliament, each reality does not possess its meaning or adequate
interpretation *within itself* or in a manner that is immune to its
context. Because each is a fundamental structuring reality, each is
able to disappear from social actors' consciousness while setting
the parameters for contests over the meaning and interpretation of
events, to the extent that this basic background structuring role
is not revealed until some exceptional circumstance occurs to
highlight their presence. Because the creation of the Scottish
parliament was a unique historic event, the local history group
provided a unique ethnographic opportunity to elicit the depth of
indifference-come-hostility towards Scottish history that had been
reached by the '45 generation and, to my mind, so accustomed
had they become to the absence of Scottish history, and so accustomed had they become to their own acceptance of this state
of affairs, that not only were they taken by surprise by its
re-emergence but resented the sudden advent of their immanent
politico-cultural obsolescence.

Generally speaking, the constitutional debate in Scotland has
been ongoing since the 1979 referendum so that expressions
of 'alienation' from set-piece events such as the creation of the
parliament in 1999 meant my informants' long-invisible 'condition
of domination' was turned into a spectacle to be seen, and revealed
their long-undisturbed indifference-come-hostility to 'being in history' and how this structuring force has produced deeply dominated consciousnesses that are unable to respond to events. Events,
then, not only reveal domination or make domination show itself
but cumulatively add to this domination, so that if the Thatcher/
Major period revealed the domination of the 1945 working-class
generation thanks to their constitutional quiescence, by the time of
'events' such as 1999 or 2014, what was once an understandable
reluctance to respond to events by 'unconstitutional' means has
become an invincible reluctance to respond at all.

Events, then, but also the profound symbolic failure to either
imagine a new unionism or a new engagement with 'the present as

316

history' to free themselves of their indifference-come-hostility to 1 July 1999 or 18 September 2014 or to align themselves with a younger generation's response to being ruled by England (Thatcher, Major and Cameron) via the politicisation of Scottish national identity, reveals the dominated condition of the older generation and allowed me to see how locals' relationship to history and the nation *is a cipher for their class and cultural condition.*

Integral to the historicity of human being or 'being in history' is *not* being free to decide the terms of engagement or the criteria by which actions are judged; that not only is the condition of being dominated not an immaculate condition 'in itself,' but is at the mercy of events mediated and constituted by geo-political contexts and events that are not of one's choosing or timing. Hence, when I argue in the coming sections for the emergence from domination among the '79 generation, it will not be upon claiming a miraculous 'free' relation to reality but rather a qualitative shift in the recognition of reality that allows a qualitative shift in response to that recognition in comparison to the more dominated relation to 'being working class and Scottish' that prevails in the '45 generation. If some members of the '45 generation practice a 'thick' hostility to unfolding political events, it is not because of a peculiar generational inability to participate in history but because participating in the 'present as history' is difficult for them as the meaning of the present is the defeat of an historic long durée which the '45 generation identify with, and the ending of a symbolic ordering of space and time (Scotland and its history) which the next section identifies as responsible for how it is that an older generation have gone from participating in unthinking hegemony to being the unthinking 'enemy' within a Scotland on the cusp of independence.

## 4.3 Liberalism, Protestantism, Unionism & Modernism: the Four Horses of Hostility to History & Holism

When first announcing to the members of the afternoon group my research concerned politics and present-day Cardenden as opposed to the history of Cardenden, the afternoon group tutor

(Anne Mead), a 1945 history graduate from St Andrew's University told me:

> Oh we're no interested in politics and religion! Two things. And that goes back to nineteen eighty-six. And we were all retired then. We didn't talk about that as that was too much trouble and division.

I immediately interpreted these words of Anne as evidence of the long history of sectarian strife in Scotland since the Protestant revolt in 1560, and the long history of intra-Protestant strife and its ongoing toxic legacy of division among Christians which my elderly working-class informants were as familiar with as they were familiar with life itself, so that in their weekly meetings it may be said they reproduced miniature versions of the wider Scottish public sphere thanks to their avoidance of politics and religion. Clearly, however, this doxic fact of life which, while it responds to liberal sensibilities and embarrassment at 'public' discussion of what should be a strictly private affair so as to keep 'the liberal peace,' is something of a problem for a history group insofar as politics and religion are integral to history.

As I became aware of informants' studied avoidance of issues which seemed to cry out for attention, I began to realise that they were the hermeneutical heirs of the Rev. Houston in their practice of the study of history, and any talk of a 'symbolic poverty' among my Protestant pensioners was wide of the mark because, for all of their denials, they were in fact immersed in their own 'politics of identity' and politics of knowledge and recognition. The advent of 'home rule,' then, was a provocation that opened a window onto the "large cultural systems" (Anderson, in Bhabha 1990, p. 1) which elderly informants had internalised and identify with; a Liberal-Protestant-British-Modernist doxic organisation of consciousness and identity which, if it once signalled belonging to an empire upon which the sun never set, is today seen as evidence of a condition of symbolic subordination that the nationalist project not only brings to an end but more or less declares to have been a long mistake and wrong turning point.

The fact was that their participation in a certain *hegemonic* consciousness was coming to an end, and they were unable to bring themselves to recognise the 'present as defeat,' and integral to their defeat was *a defeated relationship to their defeat* insofar as informants preferred to effortlessly produce signs of indifference or hostility to politics instead of bring themselves to a clear statement of themselves as that would be to objectify themselves and break from their long enjoyment of 'being British,' integral to which was never having to acknowledge that integral to this identity was the existence of rivals over whom they had militarily prevailed. As noted previously, the former soldier Jim had said: "The British flag as such is steeped in blood."

Reflecting upon the fact that whenever the subject of politics or the constitution arose, there occurred a sudden lack of generosity and the evaporation of the normal bonhomie and good humour, it seems that to even recognise and admit the defeat of Britain was to admit to having long enjoyed success over rival nations, so that at the heart of the flight from historical reflexivity among elderly history group members was the following existential dilemma: insofar as they were reflexive, this felt akin to drinking from a poisoned chalice as it meant having to recognise the loss of the exercise of symbolic, constitutional, political and civil hegemony in Scotland i.e. they could not face up to their prior hegemony because that would have been to publicly admit among themselves that the defeat they were feeling was upon them was something they had made many other native populations feel.

Members of the local history group, then, were unable to participate in the spirit of 1 July 1999 because they were unable to perceive the present as other than decline thanks to their deeply personal British and unionist assumptions which structure their perception and which are part and parcel of a *fides implicita* and a once successful integration of economy, locality and (British) nationality, so that insofar as this integralism becomes a thing of the past thanks to the successful rise of a younger and rival integralism in the shape of Scottish nationalism, the present can not be *theirs*.

Such were informants' fears of conflict at the prospect of Scottish independence that even attempting substantive discussion of independence proved futile, as not only history group members but many locals proved incapable of allowing it to emerge as a theme in itself without it being immediately surrounded by issues such as Irish nationalism, ongoing events in Kosovo, the evils of ethnic cleansing or 'Protestant' bigotry.

Back in 1999, then, the question of independence remained trapped in historicity and social and cultural conditions and an apprehensive intentional horizon, and this is what explains the remarkable fact that within the cosy confines of a local history group, a group of pensioners who met regularly in a local centre named after a local miner-turned-author who wrote of the struggle of their mothers and fathers during the Great Depression, and whose existence as a group is the result of a Workers Educational Association initiative, remain devout 'liberals' who practice an integral privatism and are convinced that politics and religion are taboo subjects beyond discussion. In order to explain this strange state of affairs the proposal of Anderson (in Bhabha 1990, p. 1) is suggestive:

> What I am proposing is that Nationalism has to be understood, by aligning it not with self-consciously held political ideologies, but with large cultural systems that preceded it, out of which – as well as against which – it came into being.

If the advent of the modern era entails the two-part conundrum of (1) being modern and (2) remaining a 'community' (people or nation), the ideology which modernity has had to overcome in Scotland is any which, insofar as it put its shoulder to the task of imagining a 'modern community,' has imagined the public or civic order in which sovereignty lies *outwith* the nation and its people, and in which the constitutional question of the relation between nation and state has been successfully resolved in such a state of affairs, and in this regard the term 'civil society' has simultaneously been liberalism's great achievement and a toxic fiction.

If the socialist answer of internationalism to the problem of 'being a people' and 'being modern' came to an end with the Great War of 1914–18 and again with the fall of the Berlin Wall in 1989, and if the political Right's answer to the conundrum of 'being modern' and 'being community' came to an end in Europe with fascism in the nineteen-forties, the Scottish nationalist imaginary has to succeed where liberalism, socialism and fascism have failed, so that the nationalist task of constructing a post-liberal modernity resolves itself into whether another modern form of human community can be built from the ruins of fascist Statism, socialist internationalism and bourgeois liberalism. In this regard, 1945 generation members voiced concerns about opening the Pandora's box of Scottish history, and this concern is a blood relative of the eighteenth-century liberal and unionist constitutional settlement which sought to prevent the return of a previous era's geo-political organisation of politics and modernity upon the sovereign Scottish nation.

Neo-unionism's concern to retain the liberal settlement into the twenty-first century seems regressive in light of the fact that, with the advent of relative affluence to working-class populations and the present already being described as post-secular (Habermas et al. 2010) and Scotland's 'pre-modern future' being characterised by Mulholland (2011, p. 206) as "*neo-medieval* self-reflexiveness," the future of the past in a post-affluent stateless nation like Scotland is more or less fated to loom ever-larger because a sociological consequence of affluence is the rejection of the symbolic patrimony associated with the 'dictatorship of scarcity' (Beck) as found in 'scarcity era' liberalism (Oroussoff 1993) among social groups that have been suppressed by these imaginaries. Affluence fuels being-in-history escaping the confines of the 'dictatorship of scarcity' period of the modern era, and in this return of the repressed the first casualty will be the liberal settlement and the modernist myth about modernity as a great historical caesura, thanks to the advent of a more balanced and holistic view of human being and a more relaxed view of the tension of 'being modern' and a post-secular and post-liberal public sphere.

If there is to be a 'return of the repressed' in this new era of 'affluent modernity' then, a re-evaluation of the Christian legacy (Zizek 2000) and Protestantism in particular will be integral as the latter has been *the* 'large cultural system' that has played a crucial role in imagining Scotland in a non-sovereign manner, and which largely owed its success in Scotland to the prior success of Protestantism in England and England's military might. Only such long durée perspectives explain comments by the Grand Secretary of the Grand Orange Lodge of Scotland (Jack Ramsay) who, when replying to the question what would happen if Scotland were to end its political union with England, said: "The Orange Order would become a paramilitary force...a spy behind enemy lines...It obviously implies a recourse to arms" (Sunday Herald, 8 July 2001).

If within the Scottish Protestant imagination the union with Protestant England has traditionally been seen as a political necessity to safeguard its position as the established Church, the fact that various Scottish Catholic prelates publicly favour independence and that since 2005 the Catholic Church has the largest number of practicing members than any other church in Scotland for the first time since the Reformation period (Brierley 2011), it seems that Ramsay cannot be accused of 'false consciousness' as to what is at stake.

If the Catholic nationalist understanding of Scottish history is summed up by a writer such as Scott-Moncrieff (1956), the notion that the Protestant reformation of 1560 was more or less disastrous for Scotland's modernity and sovereignty is a view shared by many historians such as Peter Hume Brown for whom: "1560-1603-1707- these three dates are connected by the strictest law of cause and effect. Without the Reformation the Union of the Crowns would have been impossible, the Union of the Parliaments unthinkable" (cited in MacColla 1967, p. 192). Similarly, in explaining why Scotland's nobility voted for political union with England, historian Tom Devine (1999, p. 12) has described how the Scottish Protestant church's initial opposition to union with England was 'bought off' by the Presbyterians being guaranteed a position of power in the new State that was about to be created:

Basic to their successful strategy was the elimination of the threat posed by the Kirk...By an Act of Security of the Church of Scotland of November 1706 the historic rights of the church and the Presbyterian system of government were guaranteed as a basic condition of union.

Of course, whether such historic actions are regarded as shameful and unprecedented acts of betrayal, or are to be lauded as great progressive strides is a matter of interpretation, but what can be agreed is that the dominated over time can be more or less coerced into accepting what previously was unacceptable, and the sin of 'high treason' can be subsequently covered over by the powerful with the myth of progress so that, while the exiled James Stuart in his *Declaration to the Scots Nation* promised to restore Scotland's independence and its parliament and end Scotland's union with England (Devine 1999, p. 17), perhaps more powerful than the 'empirical' military defeat of the Jacobite cause in eighteenth-century Scotland was the symbolic victory in the realm of meaning, and the myth of the inevitability of the defeat of the Stuart cause at the hands of the Hanoverians in order to secure material progress. Insofar as this became the myth that socially made it (Lévi-Strauss), O'Ciardha (cited in Zimmermann 2003, pp. 5-6) has put the matter neatly: "Hindsight is the worst enemy of Jacobitism."

If the weight of evidence is that Scottish Protestantism has always been more aligned with securing Britishness rather than imagining Scotland's independence, this geo-political coherence was not mirrored by any doctrinal coherence as for generations the fundamental ecclesiology of the new dominant religion in Scotland was far from settled. "In the 130 years following 1560 the reformed Church of Scotland went through periods of Presbyterian and episcopal church government. Not until 1690 was the Kirk finally settled as Presbyterian" (Macdonald 2010, p. 89), and if we add that a return to 'rule by bishops' in the Church of Scotland and the threat of Anglican domination was only removed in 1706, when the English Crown guaranteed Presbyterian government for the Church of Scotland to secure the Church of Scotland's acquiescence to political union with England in 1707 as per the quote from Devine, we see that from 1560-1843 (and even after that) the notion that the Protestant revolt of 1560 led to an empowered laity or a democratic way of 'being church' is *another myth of progress* as Christianity in Scotland's 'national Kirk' has been more or less dominated by ecclesial sectarianism and self-inflicted secularisation if we add Macleod's (2010, pp. 25-6) observation:

> The Act of Patronage of 1712 deprived the Church of her independence in the most crucial area of all, the election of her ministers, and invested in 'heritors' (usually landlords) the right to present ministers to vacant charges, regardless of the wishes of congregations. The results were disastrous and long-lasting...Control of the Church passed, as Hugh Miller bitingly remarked, to 'Scotland's acres.' Patronage replaced episcopacy as the way to secularize the church, and as the years went by, the lairds took full advantage, giving preferment to men who would serve their own social and political interests.

The historical events referred to above allow the reader to make sense of many pages of Houston's (1924) parish history discussed in Chapter 1, which are otherwise inexplicably devoted to narrating the details of heritors and their control or 'period of guardianship' over the local parish church. What we are inadvertently allowed to see is that the Church of Scotland at a parochial level has not been allowed to be an otherworldly call to transcendence situated in the midst of secular society, thanks to the corruption of Scottish Protestantism by secular powers, and in terms of imagining a sovereign Scotland, given the sudden and massive decline in Church of Scotland membership since the nineteen-sixties and nineteen-seventies (Brown 2001), and the rise of Scottish nationalism from the same period, it seems Scottish nationalism has come into being *against* Scottish Protestantism which was foundational for giving the new fledgling British state the 'sacred canopy' (Berger 1967) it needed to cover the opportunism of its instigators.

If the great failure of medieval Catholicism was its attempt to subjugate the secular to the sacred as per various forms of Catholic integrism or supernaturalism/fideism, which the Franciscan reform set about over-coming via Scotus's reconfiguring the Catholic imagination by his opening to the theonomic value of 'secondary natures,' the sixteenth century project of the new Protestant religion also had to grapple with the conundrum of 'being modern' and 'being Christian,' and the role of secondary natures. However, from the outset of the Protestant revolution a template was laid down that allowed for a purely fictive solution to *the tension of maintaining holism under modern conditions* by creating a new imaginary in which the need to achieve a synthesis between the natural and secular with the supernatural (once the original policy of liquidating corrupt 'secondary natures' as of no theonomic value was discarded) became over time a purely private affair, and where the task of aligning Church and State more or less disappeared. Subsequently, of course, when such ad hoc half-measures were not deemed sufficiently modern and radical, simply liquidating the tension altogether between the 'old' and the 'new,' as in Marxism and aggressive forms of rationalism and secularism, were added to the long line of historic failures to return to the task which twelfth-century Franciscans had begun (and which Francis I is attempting to re-align the Church with once again).

If Protestantism, then, bequeathed to secular liberalism an original 'signature embarrassment' at Catholic holism and Catholicism's theologically-sanctioned embrace of the secular and the secular embrace of the sacred, if the current 'present as history' is to be post-liberal it must also be post-secular if it is to embrace holism because a twenty-first century return to an integral vision of *dasein* is more or less fated to take the earlier Catholic period, that not only embraced holism but invented it, as a historic reference point. A key component in this configuration of a new Scottish symbolic order, then, will be the view that affluence does not mean the symbolic order reaching 'escape velocity' from the 'material base' but rather the symbolic order being properly and integrally aligned with the material base, and seeing its impact upon ownmost *dasein* in a holistic way that is free of supernaturalistic Catholicism, tensionless Protestantism, liberalism and modernism. This is a 'task of freedom' that has been released by affluence among the working class (and the already affluent middle class) who are liberated by literacy and free to reproduce their symbolic subordination or secede from each of these symbolic-system 'errors.' A new generation is more or less fated to erect a superstructure of its own and instantiate *its ownmost* relation to the still 'determining' material base.

In this regard, the advent of affluence from the 1970s and the post-industrialisation of the 1980s are the sociological keys that have 'disorganised' or unlocked Pandora's box. The return of the repressed and the de-privatisation of culture and the meaning of the long durée that is being discussed in the public realm thanks to Scottish nationalism and the 2014 Referendum, has broken the 'sacred canopy' of Britain, Protestantism and modernism; has broken the ideological backbone used to imagine the political construct of the UK among younger and older generations.

If the success of the Protestant revolution in both Scotland and England is the obvious basis for the historic and ongoing alignment of Protestantism and political unionism in both countries, and is a psychological and cultural continuum dating from the eighteenth century (Greenfeld 1992), a founding 'Protestant integralism' which integrated the local parish with the wider national self-understanding and culminated in the founding of the new state of Britain, then *it is the lack of religious or cultural secularisation among the history group members that makes them impermeable to the 'spell' of nationalism,* and it is because local history group informants remain immersed in these traditional long durée symbolic structures that have been able to resist the shift to the reclaiming of Scottish sovereignty movement and the depoliticisation of their Protestant identity insofar as they have also resisted the de-protestantisation of Scotland since the 1960s (Brown 2001).

If the current state of the symbolic order is 'disorganised' it is also an unprecedented opportunity. If a new Scottish state requires a new symbolic order or imaginary, what should that new order or constitution be? If previous alignments between the religious and the constitutional such as that of the integral Protestant Ramsay are more or less obsolete, what new alignments between the sovereign nation-state and the Christian legacy are possible today? What 'narrative of redemption' or 'sacred canopy' can be wrested at this time from Scotland's history? In an a priori sense we can say that what is required is a synthesis that is fully modern yet resists the temptation to abandon an ancient worldview and more or less fall into nihilism. While these are some of the divisive and contentious questions that will be addressed in any future written Scottish constitution, present-day concerns about conflict between religious organisations in an independent Scotland were expressed by informants, and are a window upon "a limited area of transparency on the otherwise opaque surface of regular uneventful social life (Turner 1957, p. 93).

As already highlighted, when the word 'religion' is uttered in Cardenden its semantic context means it is often a euphemism for the long durée struggle between Catholicism and the various Protestant churches for control over Scotland and how it is to be imagined, and so remains a delicate subject 'in mixed company' that is routinely avoided as a topic of conversation to keep the liberal peace. Thanks to the unresolved past which weighs upon Scottish *mitsein*, there was little likelihood of any discussion among the local history group members of the Reformation in Cardenden despite volume 2 of the *Auchterderran of Yesteryear* series adverting to the destruction of the residence of the Catholic clergy in Auchterderran at this time, nor any discussion of local history as revealed in the *Second Statistical Account* by Rev. Andrew Murray, minister at Auchterderran referring to the Catholic Emancipation Act of 1829 which lifted a number of anti-Catholic laws in 1832:

> About fifty years ago, we persecuted the papists and burnt their chapels; now our enmity has ceased, and Catholics are admitted and have a right to the privileges possessed by Presbyterian and Episcopalian fellow-subjects (cited in Houston 1924, p. 427).

However, in one-to-one conversations with locals there was the frank admission of this problem, and in a lengthy interview with a young non-Catholic married couple in Carden Castle Park (Mr and Mrs Paterson, 5th October 1999), both expressed fears of anti-Catholic bigotry in an independent Scotland:

> The boys that work aside me, if it wis total independence the way they talk they would start ethnic cleansin. It wid

start aff wi foreigners and wance they'd got rid e a' thame it'd start. Ye'd have Scotland right doon the middle. Ye'd end up wi, dependin oan what religion took o'er, ye'd end up wi the ither wanes either getting forced up the way tae the Highlands or doon the way tae England.

When non-Catholic locals express fears about Protestant bigotry in the event of Scotland becoming independent, one has to conclude that the Catholic and Protestant violence in Northern Ireland that has been daily televised into Scottish homes since the late nineteen-sixties with the Catholic Civil Rights movement's contestation of sectarian practices in Northern Ireland, and the violent 'return of history' from 1969-1997 that occurred in Ireland in the form of the Provisional IRA after the Northern Ireland riots of 1969 until the IRA ceasefire in 1997, all of this has provoked fear and apprehension among many working-class Scots. Hence, I recall after discussing the work opportunities for construction workers in Ireland with two bricklayers in the *No. 1 Goth*, the conversation turned to Irish politics and one of the bricklayers remarked: "God made Catholics. The Armalite made them equal."[90] Similar concerns over sectarianism were also voiced by Ian Rankin in a *Sunday Times* newspaper article (3 October 1999) where he characterised his upbringing in Cardenden as follows:

I was brought up surrounded by bigotry and segregation, yet barely noticed it, my own myopia compounded by the fact that the society I lived in seemed to accept the condition.

When conducting my door-to-door interviews in the aftermath of the establishment of the Scottish parliament, the presence of Ireland within the consciousness of some locals acted as a conduit for their fears for what might happen in Scotland:

**Me:** In the elections to the parliament did ye bother voting?

---

[90] The Armalite was the firearm associated with the armed struggle of the IRA for a united Ireland. I have since traced this bricklayer's expression to Gerry Adams's *Before The Dawn* (1996) where it featured as a Catholic nationalist slogan in Belfast.

**Heather:** Naw Ah didnae.

**Me:** You had problems with it in the first place?

**Heather:** Well aye cause Ah've never thought that it was such a guid idea tae divide a wee island like this. Well we're bad enough o'er in Ireland bit tae start dividin us a' up, where's it a' gonnae stop?

Heather Stewart<br>
Carden Castle Avenue

**Me:** Do you think the new Scottish parliament is a good idea or a bad idea?

**Rachel:** Ah think it's a bad idea.

**Me:** Did ye bother voting in the elections fir the parliament?

**Rachel:** Aye Ah voted.

**Me:** D'ye mind if Ah ask how ye voted?

**Rachel:** Ah voted against it...Ma husband's English, Ah'm Scottish, and Ah would almost say I'm sure that within aboot twenty-five years we'll be another Northern Ireland.

**Me:** You think so?

**Rachel:** Yes.

Rachel Sims<br>
Carden Castle Avenue

The above extracts from interviews reveal the conviction that there can be no 'return of Scotland' without a 'return of the repressed,' and that for many what has successfully been repressed until now are pre-liberal struggles between Christian denominations. Interviewing residents upon their doorsteps I found that, without fail, when any particular individual expressed this fear of a return of repressed antagonisms, it was expressed as if it was something uppermost in their thoughts, and it was never suggested to me by any informant that an independent Scotland would see the outbreak of a repressed 'class war' or an outbreak of anti-English sentiment. Always, informants' imagining of violence was internal to Scotland and centred around the spectre of the politicisation of religion in the shape of the sectarianism of Northern Ireland. In this regard Gallagher (2013) has argued that the present moment in Scotland is ripe for recognising the extent to which the weight of the past lies heavily upon social interaction within the liberal public sphere in Scotland, and that it would be to practice social analysis as Protestant pensioners practice local history not to advert to a fear of deep rivalries lying beneath the liberal surface.

In this regard the question of anti-Catholicism was an ongoing debate in the media throughout fieldwork thanks to the Catholic composer James Macmillan's speech to the Edinburgh Festival in 2000 in which he castigated Protestantism's effects upon Scottish culture[91] and which resulted in the edited collection *Scotland's Shame? Bigotry and Sectarianism in Modern Scotland* (2000).[92] Also, in 2011 there occurred a number of high-profile incidents of anti-Catholic bigotry where the Catholic manager, players and high-profile supporters of Celtic football club, as well as a member of the Scottish parliament (Patricia Godman), were sent bullets and parcel bombs, so that in 2011 the Scottish parliament passed the *Offensive Behaviour at Football and Threatening Communications Bill* which aimed to criminalise expressions of anti-Catholic sectarianism.

If anti-Catholic sectarianism remains part of life for some parts of Scotland, it is also true that recent historic events signal the fact that 'large cultural systems' are changing in a profound manner. The sight of former IRA members such as Sinn Fein's Martin McGuiness, for example, becoming the Minister for Education in the new devolved government of Northern Ireland, was a spectacular victory of working-class nationalism in Ireland, and such peaceful developments were directly relevant to my own

---

[91] The castigation of Protestantism for its alleged disastrous effects upon the Scottish psyche, culture, politics and religion used to be something of a past-time among non-Catholic intellectuals and artists prior to the de-Protestantisation of Scotland since the 1960s. One thinks of figures such as Edwin Muir, Neil Gunn, Hugh McDiarmid, Sorley MacLean, George Mackay Brown and Fionn MacColla (1967, 1975).

[92] In February 2001 fears of Protestant bigotry among Catholic politicians were sufficient to force the cancellation of a visit by the Irish Taoiseach to a Catholic shrine in Carfin in Lanarkshire to commemorate the victims of the Irish Famine of 1845.

ethnographic context insofar as informants back in 1999 imagined Ireland might to be a sign of things to come should Scotland become independent: "We'll end up jist like Ireland" (Anne Penman, Muirtonhill) as one informant put it, so that at that point in time Northern Ireland clearly inhibited the development of nationalism in Scotland, despite the historic changes that were occurring.[93]

An ethnography of working-class nationalism in Scotland has a highly comparable context in Northern Ireland, where another working-class nationalism has emerged since the nineteen-sixties to contest the British state. While both Scottish and Welsh nationalists contest the idea and practice of Britain, it is in the armed struggle in Ireland where a working-class nationalist consciousness and armed practice has taken its most radical form. Much like Banquo's ghost, the contestation of the British state from the standpoint of class, nationality, religion, culture and history as found in the struggle of Sinn Fein[94] and the Irish Republican Army (IRA) until recent years haunted the *imagining* of Scottish nationalism, and it was no accident that the Labour Secretary of State for Scotland Tom Johnston (1941-45) chose to characterise the Scottish nationalism of his day as "a sort of Sinn Fein movement" (Lynch 1992, p. 436) to persuade the prime minister of the day (Winston Churchill) to concede him special latitude when Secretary of State for Scotland. Interviewing locals on the cusp of the 2014 Referendum, however, and after fifteen years of peace in Northern Ireland, news reports of bombings and violent clashes between Republicans and Loyalists have quickly faded from people's minds.

In terms of the question of the relationship between Scottish Protestantism's auld alliance with British national identity, it is clear that these once near-identical identities are in the process of

---

[93] During the doctoral period of my fieldwork there occurred the first meeting of the North-South Irish Council (13 December 1999), where the Irish cabinet met with the Northern Ireland Assembly members; the first meeting of the Irish–British Council (16 December 1999), and the first public handshake between Sinn Fein representatives and the British Prime Minister (Tony Blair).

[94] A predominantly working-class political party, in contrast to the more moderate and middle-class nationalist Social and Democratic Labour Party (SDLP).

being loosened from each other, and for some elements within Protestantism such as the Orange Order this is a betrayal of Scottish Protestantism's legacy. However, if the relationship between religion and the State is fated to remain a divisive issue and if the Orange Order poisons parts of Scotland and aspects of Scottish culture, I argue that something of importance for Scottish *dasein* and the nationalist project is attempting to emerge and must be allowed to freely develop despite some toxic false-starts. Despite the fact that the rapid and ongoing de-Protestantisation of Scotland from the nineteen-sixties in particular is well-established (Brown 2001; Voas 2006; Brierley 2011), so that anti-Catholic organisations such as the Orange Order appear fated to die out with the death of its '45 generation members, *something of ontological worth fuels anti-Catholic bigotry in Scotland i.e. the desire to remain integral and the resolve to resist the liberal settlement* wherein "only citizens committed to religious beliefs are required to split up their identities, as it were, into their public and private elements" (Habermas, in Mendieta 2005, p. 332).

The liberal establishment, then, wishes to institutionalise the modernist desire to rid the State's constitution of the religious ghosts of the past and is seen in the comedian Billy Connolly's anecdote about flying from Scotland to Belfast and the passengers upon arrival being advised to turn their watches back three hundred years so as to adjust to local time, a reference to the supposed 'failure' of the local population to privatise their religion and secularise their politics so as to keep to mainland British time. The joke, however, seems to be on Connolly and all those multi-national states who keep modernist time as it is they who suffer 'false consciousness' insofar as they believe the liberal settlement is a permanent solution, and not the makeshift 'scarcity era' fix that is more or less destined to come to an end in the era of affluent modernity.

I would argue that what must be resisted is the temptation to apply the usual liberal balm if a new understanding of 'being modern' is to emerge, because liberalism is a failed solution to how the Scots will resolve the tension of being modern. I also propose that no matter how toxic, examples of Catholic or Protestant or secularist integralism afford the opportunity to break with modernist assumptions because they model the re-imagining of how the cultural/symbolic and the socio-economic order might yet relate to each other in an original synthesis in an independent Scotland. After 18 September 2014 it may well be that the present moment offers the opportunity to escape a 'disciplinary liberalism' and to renew both culture and consciousness: to unlearn Catholic supernaturalism and Protestant liberalism and modernism, and to re-learn how to be modern and have children that understand the names of their mountains (Macdonald 2009).

## 4.4 1979 Generation Catholic Historical Reflexivity

Honorius, bishop, servant of the servants of God, to his dearest son in Christ Alexander, illustrious king of Scots, and his successors for ever. Considering the reverence and devotion towards the Roman church which we know you and your predecessors to have had from times long past, we most strictly forbid that it be permitted to anyone... to publish a sentence of interdict or excommunication in the kingdom of Scotland, because *the Scottish church is subject to the apostolic see as a special daughter, with no intermediary.*

Bull of Pope Honorious III, *Filia Specialis* (1218)
Cited in Souvenir Masss book of vistit of Pope John Paul II, Glasgow 1st June 1982.

During doctoral fieldwork (1998-2001) and during 2013 I carried out a number of interviews with local Catholics and Protestants to find out whether their Christianity impacted in any way upon their understanding of Scotland and its history and the question of sovereignty. In conducting these interviews I was very much aware of the social context of Christianity in Scotland is one of declining church attendance. For example, between 2005 and 2010 the Church of Scotland's membership declined by 25% and by 2015 it is estimated to decline by a further 31% to 283, 912 members (Brierley 2011, p. 3). However, the 2011 census reported that some 1.7 million Scots (32% of the population) identified with the Church of Scotland and such findings are reflected in my fieldwork where, while I have had discussions with men in their forties about religion and their experience of religious education in Cardenden's local non-denominational Auchterderran Secondary school (which closed in 1987), and while some were married in the local Presbyterian church, I personally have never known a friend or acquaintance of my generation who was a member of any Protestant congregation, and I am struck by the conclusion that, if 'being Protestant' involves coming together liturgically with others, I have never actually known anyone from Cardenden who was a Protestant.

If there is evidence of a more or less precipitous decline in Protestantism, a similar fate has befallen the local Catholic population. Up until the nineteen-seventies the Catholic church in Scotland was thriving, and being a Catholic in Scotland was very much a working-class affair (McCrone 1992) so that in a former pit village such as Cardenden, one is liable at any Sunday Mass to see Celtic football shirts worn, and a parish priest from a central belt working-class locality telling jokes on the altar about the difficulties faced by Jesus trying to cure working-class cripples on social security benefits.[95] Indeed, one might say that Catholicism is the

---

[95] At Christmas midnight Mass in 2001 the parish priest told the following joke to his congregation from the altar. An Irish cripple went into a pub and asked the barman for a pint of Guinness. Taking a sip of his Guiness, he had a look around and then asked the barman: "Is that Jesus o'er there?" The barman said "Aye," so the Irishman said to the barman, "Gie him a pint e Guinness." Next, a lame Scotsman came into the pub and ordered a pint of Special. Taking a sip of his drink, he too had a look around the pub and then asked the barman: "Is that Jesus o'er there?" When the barman gave the same reply as before the Scotsman also said to the barman, "Gie him a pint e Special." Having finished his drinks, Jesus walked over to the Irishman and stretching out his arm said: "Rise up my son and walk!" –at which the Irishman was healed and danced a jig in delight. Jesus then walked over to the Scotsman and raised his hand, but before he could say a word the Scotsman said: "That's far enough Jesus. Ah'm on invalidity."

most working-class religion in Scotland. While the 2011 census reported that since the 2001 census the number of Catholics in Scotland has remained the same with 800,000 Scots or 16% of the population identifying themselves as Catholic,[96] this figure masks real numerical decline. At the beginning of doctoral fieldwork the Catholic population of Cardenden stood at 750 according to the *Catholic Directory for the Archdiocese of St Andrews and Edinburgh* (2000), and according to the 2012 edition, the local Catholic population has declined to 400, and in May 2014 only two children from the local Catholic school made their First Holy Communion and the following Sunday, of the thirty-one candidates for the sacrament of Confirmation from three adjacent parishes, 19 candidates or 61% were Polish, so that while there has been a massive decline in native Catholics the large influx of migrant Poles have kept Catholic numbers 'artificially' constant.

Throughout doctoral fieldwork I attended the local Catholic parish's prayer group that met weekly in a member's home (Josie O'Kane) and, interestingly, I found that in contrast to the local history group, views upon Scottish history were far more developed, and their views on Scottish history and its alignment with their faith was a very conscious affair. I recall from one meeting a discussion on the Stone of Destiny which in 1997 had been returned to Scotland, leading to two members of the group to recall for my benefit the story of Scotland's crown jewels; of how the Scottish sceptre was made in Italy and gifted by pope Alexander VI to James IV in the fifteenth-century, while Scotland's Sword of State was a gift from pope Julius II to James IV, and how the Scottish crown jewels were the oldest in the British Isles and had lay hidden for many years to prevent the English ruler Oliver Cromwell melting them down as he had the English Crown jewels.

As with previous occasions when informants had educated me in what was my own history, I expressed my great interest and

---

[96] According to the findings of the organisation Christian Research there are more Catholics attending Sunday Mass in Scotland since 2005 than there are Protestants attending Church of Scotland services for the first time since the Protestant Reformation of 1560. http://www.christian-research.org/

confessed my ignorance of these events, and this encouraged my two female informants to recall how although the Crown jewels were rediscovered by Walter Scott in 1818 they made no appearance in the coronation of Elizabeth II at Westminster abbey (England) in 1953, and when the newly-crowned queen travelled north to Scotland to be presented with Scotland's Honours in Edinburgh, at no point did she wear the Scottish Crown or hold the sceptre. However, by far the greatest insult to Scotland for my two female informants was that the queen did not wear her royal robes but ordinary clothes.

This small group of Catholics, then, evidenced a knowledge and reading of Scottish history very different to that of the local history group, and this was no doubt in no small measure due to not a few of the members of the prayer group being highly educated as, in addition to housewives and tradesmen, the group included a retired doctor, a school teacher and two university students. The group members rejected the 'invented' traditions of a 'Celtic Church' as found in the Rev. Houston and were clear that their tradition was that of the two local saints (Ss. Ninian and Fothad) who were the first missionaries that had brought the Christian faith "straight from Rome" as one retired doctor and group member (Bernie Cranston) said.

Within the consciousness of this group, then, their imagining of their relationship to the past encompasses the longue durée stretching from the first evangelisation of Scotland in the fourth century onwards to the present-day eve of independence, and this relates to another feature which struck me as I sat among these educated Catholics, which was that they talked of the history of Scotland in a manner that clearly indicated that *it was their history and that they held the keys to its proper interpretation.* In contrast to the insecurities of Protestantism in Scotland discussed in Chapter 1, which must discover a navel for itself somewhere in Scotland's Catholic past, the Scottish Catholic imagination welcomes the return of the repressed, whereas the Scottish Presbyterian imagination as evidenced by Houston's cleansing of his imagining of much of Fife's Catholic identity and history, is more or less coerced into finding a way to heal its relationship to the formative Catholic period of Scotland if it is to embrace and participate in the return of the repressed.

A few days prior to the inaugural Holyrood elections in 1999 the Catholic Bishops' Conference of Scotland issued a pastoral letter entitled *Make The Cross Count* which was read at Sunday Mass on 2 May 1999 throughout Scotland. This was widely perceived as pro-nationalist and pro-SNP due to its endorsing three of the SNP's policies on student grants, nuclear weapons and Catholic education, and came six months after a speech in Brussels by Cardinal Winning (1925-2001) in which he welcomed the likelihood of independence in the near future, and characterised Scottish nationalism as mature, democratic and progressive. More relevant, however, is that the local Catholics I spoke to agreed with the pro-SNP interpretation put on the bishops' address and there is evidence of a shift to a nationalist position among Scottish Catholics. Nairn (2000) has also pointed to the significance of Catholics shifting their allegiance from the unionist Labour Party to the nationalist SNP, a change which he describes as "'Class' was being transmuted into 'Nation' before our eyes" (2000, p. 196).

Similarly, the 2011 Scottish Election Study (SES 2011) found that for the first time ever Catholics voted for the SNP (43%) in greater numbers than they voted for the Labour Party (36%), and more generally it is perhaps hardly surprising that Scottish Catholics today, overwhelmingly of post-Famine Irish descent, move to support Scottish independence given the track record of political nationalism and anti-British sentiment among the descendants of Irish Catholic immigrants (see McCrone & Rosie in Boyle & Lynch 1998, pp. 67-94; Gallagher 2013; Kehoe 2013). As the historian Tom Devine reminds us: "The Catholic Irish in Scotland campaigned vigorously for a restoration of an Irish parliament" (1999, p. 490). [97]

---

[97] I recall one occasion in 2012 when taking my children to school I spotted Mrs McCutcheon who was chaperoning one of her grandchildren to "the Irish school" as I heard her say i.e. the local Catholic school; an expression which reveals the perception of an older generation who equated Catholicism with an immigrant Irish population.

Aside from these macro intergenerational shifts in Catholic voting behaviour, evidence of the political consequences of the Catholic view of Scottish history (Schmitt 1996) came when interviewing the pass keeper of St. Ninian's church (Chum Wallace) about his views on the Scottish parliament. When I asked Chum for his views on the new parliament he began laughing, and I asked why he laughed:

> Well, isn't it funny? They think they have a parliament. It's fitting that a puppet parliament should be sat in the General Assembly building of the Church of Scotland. One makes it obvious it has no idea how to be a real nation and the other has no idea how to be a real church. They've nae idea of power and nae idea of government. It's a farce.

This testimony seems to point emphatically to the conclusion that Chum is a Catholic in the sense identified by Carl Schmitt (1996) that insists there is among Catholic populations an analogy between the exercise of authority or sovereignty by the Church and the exercise of authority or sovereignty by a people or nation; that just as the Church exercises authority that it can not devolve to any other institution (State, Nation or Parliament for example), so a nation exercises sovereignty and cannot pool or cede or share this sovereignty with another nation. In the 'Catholic opinion' of Chum, then, 1 July 1999 does not deliver sovereignty to Edinburgh or the Scottish people and he laughs at 'Protestant Scots' whom he characterises by the inability to imagine and demand sovereignty and who can settle for the exercise of the mere appearance of Scottish sovereignty.

If I were to interpret Chum's words beyond what he actually said, I would propose he is saying that Scottish Protestants make excellent Britons but second rate Scots; that both history and the present-day provide evidence that Protestants are not very good at being Scottish when it comes down to deciding between 'being Scottish' and 'being British:' that if the political form of Scottish Catholicism is the exercise of sovereignty, the political form of Scottish Protestantism is unionism and that Protestant Scots are divided in their identities because of their defining Protestant ecclesiology which eschews the exercise of sovereignty because it is agonistic about its divine foundation as an ecclesial community, and this ecclesiastical ambivalence is reproduced in the Protestant population vis-à-vis the question of the Scottish sovereignty, and so Protestants are divided in how they imagine their being together as a nation and divided in their interpretations of their history, and divided in their vision of how to imagine and organise their future.

In making this argument I, of course, freely admit that Chum himself made no such claims, and am equally confident that Chum had no knowledge of the 'social contract' theory of sovereignty found in Duns Scotus (Harris 1994; Wolter 2001) which was enshrined in the famous *Declaration of Arbroath* of 1320. However, what struck me about the testimony of Chum was that it was delivered in a deliberative and emphatic fashion. Chum identifies the location of sovereignty as the heart of the matter, and he scoffs at the 'puppet show' of 1 July 1999 because the categories organising his perception of where sovereignty lies is his Catholic view that sovereignty, whether that exercised by the State or the sovereignty exercised by the Nation or the sovereignty exercised by the Church cannot be borrowed or loaned from another 'more sovereign' authority. Chum is not making a philosophical or theological or 'contemplative' argument from 'pure reason' that there is some intrinsic connection between Protestantism and unionism but is making an empirical observation that the nationalism of 1 July 1999 is not real nationalism but a typically Scottish Protestant affair, because it involves the same refusal of sovereignty at a political level which Protestantism in Scotland refuses itself at the ecclesiological level. I July 1999 then reproduces this Protestant tradition of 'Scotland as puppet show,' as both the unionist political parties and self-styled national church have come to a deal with English power and reproduced their ambivalence vis-à-vis sovereignty, and reproduced their political subordination all over again.[98]

---

[98] Having conducted a number of interviews with local Catholics (and Church of Scotland members) in early 2013 for a paper delivered to the annual BSA conference, my data clearly evidences that there is no single 'Catholic view'

As already indicated, at the time of my doctoral research the ongoing peace process in Northern Ireland was a significant development, and when walking through the village it was interesting that graffiti in support of the Irish Republican Army or the loyalist equivalent was physically fading, as if indicating sectarianism was also a fading reality. Similarly, the drastic decline of any numerically significant kind of religious practice among a largely once-Protestant population is another important development insofar as the decline of Protestantism is viewed as a condition for the re-politicisation of Scottish national identity in a pro-independence direction which is free of anti-Catholic sentiment. In this regard it is safe to say that integral to the Scottish Catholic imagination is a consciousness of having been systematically excluded and oppressed and marginalised over generations by "Knoxian barbarism," so that integral to their imagining empowerment is the decline of that 'large cultural system' that presided over their subordination (Ross 1959; Goldie 1991, pp. 35-45; Durkan 1994).

When interviewing a local convert to Catholicism and now a priest within the archdiocese in his late thirties who was raised within the Presbyterian Church of Scotland, I noted how he casually referred to the influence and legacy of Protestantism in Scottish history and society as "a force of darkness," as if this was a common-sense truism among Catholics. When I asked how his views squared with the fact that he had, at least nominally, been a Protestant, his reply was: "I was brought up to nothing," implying a trajectory and biography whereby the conflict and contestation of four centuries can be resolved via the exercise of late-modern freedom. However, while his quip about the Protestant legacy was announced as a truism available to one and all, it is of course not an interpretation that is available to one and all, but only to someone rich in symbolic capital and with degrees from St. Andrew's and Oxford and not those who are unable to casually and confidently engage in long durée matters.

If there is a movement towards nationalism among Catholics I do not mean to suggest any kind of equivalence between Scottish

---

regarding what Schmitt termed *the political form of Roman Catholicism*. Also, there is no one view of Scottish history among Catholics who are divided according to generation, class and level of education. See Gilfillan (forthcoming).

Catholicism and *political* nationalism. If it is clear that Chum draws upon his Catholic scheme of perception in support of independence, this is not to imply every Catholic holds his views as it is also abundantly clear that the unionist Labour Party commands support among working and middle-class Catholics, and there is little doubt that a perception of Protestant bigotry has kept the political unionism of Catholics alive and well. My view, however, is that a positive identification with being British is increasingly rare among Catholics of the '79 generation(s) as I found no *positive* identification with being British but a certain anti-British tradition *despite* their tradition of electoral support for the unionist Labour Party. Catholic informants told me about their practice of rushing to switch off the television every night at the end of the day's broadcasting rather than listen to the British national anthem, so that it seems clear that their de facto political unionism is no substantive value 'in itself' and is artificially kept alive by a long-standing contestation of Protestant bigotry, so that as soon as the latter is perceived to end, so will the former.[99]

## 4.5 The Historical Consciousness of the 1979 Generation(s)

In light of the fact that the 2011 census found that only 16% of the Scottish population are Catholic, their historical consciousness is unlikely to be decisive in the 2014 independence referendum. That role belongs to the historical consciousness of the 32% of Scots who identify with the Church of Scotland, and the 37% of Scots of no religious affiliation. If an older working-class generation's constitutional views are more or less settled and even impervious to the democratic deficit of 1979-1997 and the current 2010-2015 period of not only unrepresentative but anti-representative government, among a younger generation these

---

[99] One 35 year-old Catholic informant told me of how his history teacher at St. John's (Perth) advised pupils, when choosing which questions to answer in history exams, to 'play safe' and avoid answering questions that might excite the anti-Catholic prejudices of the marker.

years have seen the politicisation of Scottish national identity due to English Conservative leaders' dismantling of what remained of a *fides implicita* in all things British that a younger generation inherited from their parental '45 generation. However, while I have characterised the return of Scottish history as a 'spectre' within the consciousness of some older locals, it is important to balance this representation by adverting to their clear paradoxical awareness that they felt themselves akin to a "people without history" (Worsley 1982) as a result of the formal education they received. Their comments on Scottish history during meetings amounted to remarking upon its total absence from their education, so that I found unanimous agreement that the history they were taught at school contained "nothing about Scotland," with the following exchange being typical:

> **Adam:** It's one thing Ah regret when Ah was at school, Ah never learned a thing about this village.
> **Anne:** We never learned a thing about Scotland when we were at school. Even at school we never ever done anything but English history.
> **Adam:** It's something that didnae bother me then but it does now. We were taught about England but never Scotland. And never the history of Fife.

What I found was that both the '45 and '79 generations share in a lament for a knowledge that the education system failed to provide them, and this critique of the education they received was said as a matter-of-fact; that nobody taught local or national history or culture was not a contentious claim but the common experience that nobody ever contradicted. As historian Michael Lynch (1992, p. xv) confirms: "Scotland, until the introduction of the Standard Grade syllabus in 1990, was one of the few countries in Europe where a nation's own history was not a compulsory part of the history curriculum in its schools." Despite the older generation's clear awareness of this, however, I never witnessed any discussion of the possible reasons for the absence of Scottish history from the school curriculum. If there is an obvious irony where the '45 generation laments the absence of Scottish history while simultaneously exhibiting an absence from 'the present as history,' it seems likely that the one is related to or is isomorphic with the other. Among younger generation informants, however, the demand to know the reasons for the absence of Scottish history, as well as speculation as to the motives behind its absence, was something which did come through loud and clear as a theme. As a concrete point of reference for my argument that among the 1979 generation a politics of identity and a politics of knowledge *is* being constituted via Scottish nationality and the rejection of 'Britain' as an organising category of experience, identity, politics and territory, I reproduce the following testimony from Peter, a thirty-nine year-old Fife Council bricklayer whom I interviewed on his doorstep.

It's a' mair or less persecution. Ah think we've been kept at that level [lowers palm towards ground] a' the time. Ye wernae tellt anythin' aboot Scottish history because it could have caused trouble. An a' they fitba matches wi Scotland an England in the seventies it wid ha been even bigger bloodbaths cause it'd jist be like the English comin up tae Culloden or Stirlin Bridge an a' that f***in cairry oan a' rolled intae wane. That's a lot e the reason why they never tellt ye f**k all e it tae. Ah mean that thing in the paper the day aboot learnin bairns Scottish history; [100] when we were at the school, that'd be what, 1972, wane e the teachers[101] we got he wis SNP. He used tae turn roond tae ye an say right then, when wis the battle e Hastings? An every c**t says 1066. Right then; when wis the battle e Culloden? Nae c**t kent. So he'd tell ye. So fir a hail week when we got Modern Studies he wis tell'n us aboot Scottish history until wane day he come in an says eh 'Right, Ah've been gien a

---

[100] A front-page *Sunday Mail* newspaper article (24 October, 1999) highlighting the lack of knowledge among Scots of their own history.
[101] At a Hogmanay party in 2012 I learned that the Auchterderran Junior high school teacher referred to here was Brian Hill.

ticken off.' He'd been pu'd up by the heidmaister who said 'You're no here tae learn bairns, you're here tae learn them what the O level's aboot, no what's happenin roond aboot them.' And this is a' comin tae light noo, twenty year doon the f***in line. Bit Ah mean really, we should ken mair aboot what's happenin. Then again if ye gane doon the street and say tae some e they boys, 'Eh, aye, dae ye ken aboot this happened up in the Highlands five hunder year ago?' 'Oh f**k off we're no interested in that.' There's a certain time when, if ye dinnae get learned it at school there's a big period in between until you come tae yer senses an say well really Ah should be payin attention tae that, an Ah should be takin mair tae dae wi that. But there's that space in between when yer mair likely, mair f***in like half e they c***s doon there smashin bus shelters an pissin the drink against a wa' or gaun fae this pub tae that pub, ye ken? Bit there'll come a time when a lot e they boys sittin doon there'll be sayin 'Ya c**t Ah wonder what happened?' What sticks in yer mind when ye were at the skill? It's 1066, King Harold getting the f**kin arrow in his ee, that big tapestry f**kin thing, Guy Fawkes f**kin settin fire tae the ... tryin tae think e something that happened in Scotland at that same f**kin time an ye widnae ken.

If one were to change a few details in the above testimony it would be indistinguishable from the discourse of formerly colonised peoples reflecting upon the education system put in place by their colonial masters, so that we might interpret the above as a lucid critique not simply of Scottish education as the central institution in the reproduction of a disabling ignorance of history, but a wholesale betrayal of a nation and a critique of the failures of powerful elites who established and maintained this educational *status quo ante*. However, what I want to highlight is *the sheer availability* of Peter's analysis to himself. The above quote is the last three minutes of a ninety-minute interview and I propose that the key to Peter's interpretive lucidity, in contrast to the silence of the Rev. Houston, for example, lies in the fact that his reading of Scottish education is informed by his class position so that, leaving aside the question of 'empirical' accuracy, he is lucid in his critique of an education system that produced a 'people without memory' because he is 'doing class analysis' by drawing upon his internalisation of social structure which not only structures his perception but structures what comes into his horizon i.e. structures his *field of perception* and what counts as significant knowledge.

We may say that Peter can read so much history using one basic interpretive key because so much of the history of schooling and education in a stateless nation is taken up by the work of repressing history, so that *he is lucid because his mental structures of perception are structured by the structure of history which is itself structured by the reproduction of the geo-politics of stateless nationhood.* Having grasped this basic interpretive key, then, allows the members of the stateless nation to narrate historic events and incidents *ad libitum* because, whatever particular field is under consideration, the same structure or pattern is reproduced and the same interpretive horizon is able to read it as a matter of habitus. Finally, because his mental life is conformed to this truth there is a characteristic 'libidinal' enjoyment and catharsis in identifying instances of this isomorphism, and a characteristic 'libidinal expression' that emerges from this habitual reading and which is a characteristic of working-class men's use of language.

Peter can read history effortlessly or *ad libitum* because he knows via habitus in a pre-conceptual manner that the social structure at any time reproduces itself over the course of history and events, and the sheer availability of his analysis is his clue to the ethnographer why the survival and victory of a historic long durée, long marginalised and apparently defeated for three centuries, does not evidence an incredibly resistant oral tradition. He is also advising the error of the modernist fiction that 'all that is solid melts into air' because the Scottish managerial class has always throughout its time in charge 'stood down' the historic patrimony of Scotland and has faithfully failed to exercise leadership and lead the nation's secession from Britain, so that Peter is castigating the Scottish bourgeoisie for its perfect modernism insofar as throughout its history this class could always be relied upon to leave all of the 'nonsense' of history firmly behind and nowhere in the education system. What is also nicely revealed is that the contestation of the meaning of historic events such as 1 July 1999 reproduces the same contestation that much of Scottish history is constituted by, so that the ethnographer of 'the present as history' cannot propose 'objectivity' or a "view from nowhere" (Nagel 1986) but more history; more of the same dialectically opposed paradigms re-joining battle. As Bourdieu (in Faubion 1995, p. 34) explains:

> The *habitus*, a product of history, produces individual and collective practices – more history – in accordance with the schemes generated by history. It ensures the active presence of past experiences, which...tend to guarantee the 'correctness' of practices and their constancy over time, more reliably than all formal rules and explicit norms. This system of dispositions – a present past that tends to perpetuate itself into the future by reactivation in similarly structured practices... is the principle of the continuity and regularity which objectivism sees in social practices without being able to account for it.

Peter in his testimony, then, is also explaining how the liberal establishment can accommodate itself to 1 July 1999 because a devolved Scottish parliament does not challenge the social structure, so that subordinates such as Peter can be allowed to signify history and the nation according to their ownmost contextualised *dasein* and the Scottish middle classes can once again exchange exercising no cultural leadership of the nation (unlike every other national bourgeoisie) for their continued social dominance which remains intact. In contrast to the Rev. Houston's 'petrifaction via power,' Peter is made articulate by his subordination, and is free to recognise the empirical facts just as Houston is compelled by his 'disciplinary liberalism' to remain silent on the cut and thrust of Scottish history while Peter speaks out. This contrast is a clue that reveals the repression that results within the liberal consciousness conformed to reproducing social structure, a conformism that cannot recognise and celebrate *the meaning of* 1 July 1999; and why only the consciousness not tied to *reproducing* the social structure can recognise and celebrate the cut and thrust of history and historic events.

1 July 1999, then, can simultaneously signify the symbolic reversal of four centuries of Scottish history and the castigation of each elite-yet-subordinate generation throughout that history for their failure to politicise their historicity or being-in-history, as well as signify no change whatever of the social structure which remains intact, so that 1 July 1999 for '45 generation unionists is an expensive duplication of resources and for '79 generation nationalists is a great leap forward for an emergent sovereignty and escape from three centuries of self-colonisation, semi-modernisation and semi-sovereignty. Insofar as Peter's hermeneutic or manner of reading history is a matter of habitus and is shared with previous working class generations, something new has re-invigorated this hermeneutic with new hope as it has become electorally significant; as if what has finally been thrown off by the '79 generation is a de-politicised hermeneutic of hopelessness thanks to the ending of the suffocating 'sacred canopy' (Berger 1967) of Protestantism and unionism.

A final observation regarding Peter is that he is affirming the basic principle that interpretation is a social practice that may usefully be described as a 'contact sport,' insofar as there is an isomorphism between the geo-political analysis of nationalism and class analysis, so that if one should choose *not* to interpret Scottish history *at this time* as a long cultural and geo-political struggle for control over Scotland, such a view *at this time* would almost certainly be consubstantial with a refusal to interpret the social realm and its history as a long struggle between social classes, so that one may predict with some confidence that anyone who interprets Scottish history via the recognition of geo-political conflict would also be likely to read the social realm via the recognition of inter-class struggle. If this seems a sane interpretive principle given the national or geo-political realm and the social realm are ruled over by the same elites, so that it would be a flight from reality to view the history of society and the history of the nation as not shaped by the same interests, what clearly requires an explanation is why the working-class's imagining of socialism and Home Rule has been so unsuccessful for over a century and has been so successfully subordinated to the imagining of Britain.

The fact of Peter's lucidity, then, is sourced in his breaking from a 'double domination' at a class and a national level which allows him a clear view, and allows us a clear view of how political union with England is unlikely to survive the critique of a contextual class analysis insofar as a younger generation critiques the '45 generation's discourse on Scottish history and Scottish culture due to the latter's consciousness being 'doubly dominated' as a result of a British identity preventing a 'proper' interpretation of society and nation and history and the present moment.

When attending the funeral of a retired miner (Mr McLean) during fieldwork at which some of his Bowhill Burns' Club friends and members of the local history group were present, the marked cultural difference between the generations was evident in the dated genuflexions to Burns in the oration, which felt symbolic of an understanding of 'being Scottish' and 'being working class' that is obsolete among the '79 generation, so that this scene acted as a metaphor for the death of a certain idea of Scottish culture held by previous working-class generations. In this regard, the local institutions from the Bowhill Burns Club (founded 1912), the Mining Archives and Masonic lodge are of a time and culture that the younger generation have already abandoned. Likewise, their benign bemusement towards what Chapman (1978) has called 'the Gaelic vision' in Scottish culture as evidenced in their more or less incomprehension at the annual televised Mod, for example.

Likewise, at Hogmanay parties and brief exchanges regarding 'Scottish culture,' '45 generation members view televised Scottish country dancing as their idea of Scottish culture, while their sons and daughters laugh and are clear this is not their culture. Again, when passing among ourselves a collection of Fife poetry in Scots at one of the history group meetings, I often had to ask for a translation of the Scots words used in the poems, and the older members were incredulous at my Anglicisation and loss of culture and why I could not understand what for them was my language. All of this signals the younger generation's task of imagining their selves and localities free of industrialism and obsolete cultural forms is already a task that defines them.

I propose that if increasing numbers of working-class individuals are free to instantiate reflexive projects thanks to deep literacy and affluence, then charting the 'present as history' will involve charting the release of three reflexivities: a Catholic reflexive project, a Protestant reflexive project and a non-Christian or pre-Christian reflexive project that will each seek to construct a new symbolic order in their image. If each of the three options available to the '79 generations are likely to unite in important aspects such as the embrace of the 'return of the repressed' and a post-liberal vision of Scottish *dasein* and *mitsein*, perhaps a common 'purely natural' reflexive historical consciousness will prove decisive.

What all can agree upon is that historically-informed *dasein* is being released from its traditional confines, and integral to the modernisation of the symbolic order in Scotland today is *not* simply the notion of a liberation from the past but a release of historicity or 'being in history' from traditional answers and more or less coerced accommodations made throughout the 'dictatorship of scarcity' period which lasted until the nineteen-eighties. What will prove decisive is whether a 'purely natural' direction of travel and pre-religious estimation of Scottish contextual *dasein* and *mitsein* can be found. While it seems likely that the *modernist* interpretation of 'being modern' is fated to wish to see 'modernisation as privatisation/liquidation' continue, it will be rejected in light of its historic alignment with the subjugation of history and integralism and the national question. A new 'purely natural' '79 generation position then will take as its departure point the rejection of the liberal settlement and the modernist experiment of Great Britain which seem more or less fated to be viewed as examples of 'scarcity thinking' and 'scarcity praxis.'

## 4.6 The Post-Affluent Ending of the Modernist Experiment of Britain

Informants' perception remains fixed upon realities and relationships and deep symbolic divisions that the Scottish liberal and modernist imagination and public realm is reluctant to recognise. However, recognising such divisions is fundamental to recognising the desire not to live by bread alone and to face the challenge of 'being modern,' which involves being a people rather than merely a population. I will argue that this desire to be symbolically united, something which the liberal imagination can neither recognise nor rectify, also helps us to understand informants' fear of the return of something which union with England has successfully repressed; that underneath the eighteenth-century construct of Great Britain lies an essential 'medieval' reality that has not only survived but lies ready and waiting to 'take over.'

Crucially, however, what makes such intimations command our attention and forbids us from dismissing them is the fact that something else to be explained and another something which modernist and liberal understandings of modernity fail to explain, is why it is that after three centuries there is still no British *nation* in sight; why it is that the symbolic patrimony that the first post-industrial and post-affluent generation mobilises in order to imagine and constitute its politico-historical consciousness by is a species of what the modernist Lenin might have described as 'medieval particularism,' and its resurrection of a twelfth-century project of political freedom and return to a more Catholic and holistic conception of *dasein* and *mitsein* (Chapter 8).

If we are to get closer to an explanation of the 'present as history' we require an understanding of modernity that is stripped of the hackneyed fictions concerning *dasein/mitsein* and the nation that liberalism/modernism likes to tell itself; a new understanding that recognises, but does not reduce ourselves to, the pressures and conditions modernity undoubtedly brings about; a more mature understanding of modernity characterised by living with a series of tensions, rather than the superficial and tired idea of having to choose between binary oppositions. In making sense of the fearful apprehensions of locals we cannot rid ourselves of this issue by conveniently imagining they are living three hundred years in the past for some reason; rather, we must overcome a fiction that we have been telling ourselves for three hundred years, and that in contrast to the purely imaginary cleansing of the present of all traces of the past, the social ontology of liberalism has always had little purchase upon fully-contextualised human experience; that the past is not only not past but none of the 'big questions' – such as *what historical consciousness is possible in Scotland today*, and what kind of community is possible, and which constitutional form should the community (nation) take, and how are we to be modern and constitute a community among ourselves and what 'narrative of redemption' is possible for Scottish *mitsein* today – ever found a satisfactory answer in the eighteenth-century geo-political settlement. The great questions of meaning which liberal unionism imagined it had successfully answered or organised all now return, as 'to restore a medieval kingdom' is to turn back time and is the time to raise these fundamental questions and de-privatise or re-nationalise the realm of meaning and take it out of the cold storage in which it has lay since 1707.

From the nineteenth century social theorists such as Saint-Simon clearly saw that the very timbre of human being in free-market industrial societies was being forcibly brought into alignment with economic function as Western societies underwent 'total mobilisation' in the search for economic growth and material wealth, and while this remains just as true today as in the nineteenth-century, a crucial difference between the pre-affluent era and the post-affluent era is that in the former period modernity was conceived as the great event and condition in which 'all that is solid melts into air,' so that the modern era was imagined to be qualitatively different from all previous eras, and the new 'laws of motion' of capitalism fundamentally separated free-market societies from all previous social formations and historical periods. In the affluent era, however, the manner in which 'being modern' is imagined has changed insofar as *the reality of the past is no longer thought to be dissolved but liberated as never before*, so that 'affluent modernity' releases the original twelfth-century invention of modernity in its original integral or 'ontological fullness' which the 'scarcity period' of modernity denied itself.

This liberation of the past, coming in the wake of general affluence since the nineteen-seventies (Galbraith 1969), inaugurates nothing less than a revolution in the symbolic order. Insofar as the liberal imagination or, perhaps better, the 'scarcity imagination' that had more or less successfully privatised Religion, History and the Nation sees all such questions flooding back into the post-secular (Habermas 2010) Scottish public sphere, this represents the death-knell for those 'scarcity-era' rationalist philosophies of the eighteenth-century that had confidently imagined religion and the task of reconciling the territorial and the historical in religious myths of salvation as more or less over with the arrival of the modern era. The nightmare scenario for the modernist imagination, then, is that it itself has been modernised because all such views that imagined questions of historical and ultimate meaning were epiphenomenal window dressing to 'being modern' or 'human being,' are themselves regressive and obsolete 'scarcity era' thinking that refuses to think human being and history with a full palette, and so have become relics from another era.

If eighteenth and nineteenth-century political economists were caught up in 'scarcity-period thinking' because they had no idea that affluence was around the corner (Polanyi 2001), so we can say that many conceptions of modernity had no idea that Tradition and History were set to reach 'escape velocity' and be released as never before *precisely in those societies which were first to imagine that Tradition and History and the questions and tensions first sighted in twelfth-century thought and culture could be liquidated.* Paradoxically, this classical liberal mindset has been rendered obsolete by the very affluence that the free-market economy generated, and which liberalism paid so much homage to (von Mises 2012). In this regard, Jacques Maritain has written somewhere of great truths being held captive by great errors, and we might apply this observation to *modernist* understandings of modernity as, while no-one could fault modernists' wanting to be equal to the signs of the times and to have consciousness 'catch up' or aligned with contemporary socio-economic conditions, we cannot follow them by cleansing our consciousness and lives of the problematics and concerns of the pre-modern era as if they were of no further relevance or help in the task of 'being modern.' If the modernist imagination, then, is something of a 'ghost train' whose only remaining passengers who still keep the faith and who still believe they are heading towards the future are septuagenarian Marxists and Secular Society members, those who have alighted from the modernist error can still acknowledge that modernism's great founding insight was the sometimes heroic effort to turn to the purely social or the purely 'secular' and cleanse it of all supernaturalism. Indeed, as an ethnographer of the working class, I feel close to the modernist error as who cannot read the early Marx and fail to marvel at the effort that is underway, and who cannot but admire the many nineteenth-century modernists who, like the twelfth-century originators of the modern era, wanted to turn to the world and succeed where the twelfth-century had ultimately failed?

The modernist rejection of the wisdom of the pre-modern era is all the more incredible in Scotland today because the unresolved inherited tensions transmitted from its history are precisely what must be resolved on 18 September 2014 and thereafter, and which can not be repressed any longer, and the recently released desire for a symbolic order that can form the new basis for an independent Scotland can only be built upon adequate answers to these foundational questions. In coming to these answers, then, what must be avoided is the error committed by modernists as they began the same task of fitting themselves with a new symbolic order for the modern era, which was to imagine the modern era would privatise or abolish the Christian legacy and the need for a sacred canopy by conveniently imagining such needs and tasks and tensions had been privatised or liquidated by modernity.

Modernism's campaign of forgetting Scottish sovereignty and Scottish integralism stands revealed as a fiction that imagined it had privatised or liquidated a set of historical problems that dawned around the twelfth century, which concerned the invention of the social contract theory of government and the discovery of the categories of Nature and History and the (Christian) task of integrating the secular and the sacred. In preparation, then, for a second era of Scottish independence, it is imperative that 'the Scottish mind' is cleansed of the metaphysics that lies at the root of the modernist misunderstanding of the modern era in the sense of modernist given by Ardener (in Overing 1985, pp. 46-69) as the belief in "a once and for all break with the past."

That apprehension regarding sectarian prejudice is alive and well in the experience of a younger generation is evidence that engagement with questions of identity and a new resolution to Scotland's troubled history are also alive and well, so that to retreat into the ready and waiting clichés of the liberal imagination would be to repeat the errors from which we are trying to emerge, and to 'betray' the data insofar as these local concerns reflect a post-liberal and late-modern concern to reopen history and de-privatise the 'realm of meaning' and address the question of what should be the fundamental 'depth presuppositions' that may be shared among Scots and act as the basis for national life. The 2014 Referendum is the opportunity, then, to ask what 'deep imagination' might be agreed upon if we are to share a territory which has been the subject of struggle by rival traditions and erroneous or inadequate imaginings, and a way forward is the post-liberal solution of rejecting the privatisation myth regarding the separation of 'personal' beliefs from one's public office, and its blood-relative of secularism that wishes the privatisation of religion and imagines the modern era has forever resolved questions of ultimate meaning by 'liquidating' such concerns. The liberal-come-secular settlement then is a charter for 'bad faith' where only agnostics and atheists can participate in public life with integrity, so that insofar as a nation adopted the liberal myth as a solution because of never-ending strife, the time is now to discard this fig leaf which must always be threatened by the return of the repressed.

While confident that the data supports the thesis that there is an emergent break with the modernist settlement or 'experiment' of Britain, to pursue the further argument that this is *a conscious break* with abstract ideas such as modernism, secularism or liberalism, and that this is integral to a younger working-class generation's breaking from their condition of symbolic subordination, would be to repeat the mistake made at the beginning of fieldwork vis-à-vis an older generation as it would be to imagine a younger generation through my own prejudices and categories of perception, rather than sticking to what the ethnographic facts allow for. I do not imagine, then, for one moment that the lucidity of Peter quoted earlier is the norm among the '79 generation, and the proposition that there is an emergent project of imagining Scotland free of modernist assumptions is abstract and might yet be still-born, even among younger generations in light of the ongoing reality of symbolic domination. The very ability to appropriate the condition of working-class historicity or being-in-history and to practice a fully-contextual use of freedom depends upon one's simultaneous *immersion within* and *freedom from* this condition (thanks to its existing twice or in two realms), and upon one's immersion in and understanding of Scottish history and the long durée because this is the timescale and this is the semantic material at play in imagining an independent Scotland.

I argue that integral to the working class wishing to achieve a 'consciousness of its own' is its desire to imagine a sovereign Scottish State of their own, and to make that State in the image of their ownmost *dasein*, so that their nationalism is an integral part of the process of their recognition of and liberation from symbolic domination, while articulating their own theory of being modern is dependent upon their thinking of their being-in-history and the recuperation and recapitulation of long suppressed historical exigencies. In contrast to Nairn's description of nationalism as "the elites inviting the masses into history" (1981, p. 340), then, I propose Scottish nationalism is more accurately described as the release and resumption of twelfth-century exigencies and symbolic resources among a younger generation, and if we are "to separate the quite spurious 'national' and 'natural' justifications and explanations of nationalism, from the genuine, time and context-bound roots of it" (Gellner 1964, p. 151), this requires we abandon modernist and liberal understandings of 'being Scottish' and 'being modern' if they are to catch up with and adequately represent 'the present as history.'

Insofar as Nairn is correct to characterise nationalism as the elites inviting the masses into history, this explains why nationalism failed to happen in Scotland until the nineteen-seventies. According to Gellner (1964) and Nairn (1981), nationalism is the reaction to the arrival of modernity and uneven development which acts to generate 'catch up' modernisation via nationalism, with the latter based upon the invention and mobilisation of a proto-national culture by local intelligentsias. However, when industrialisation or uneven development arrived to Scotland, a British and modernist imagination was already in place among its elite, as was the modernist assumption that union with England meant Scotland's early modern programme of becoming modern on its own sovereign terms had been 'liquidated' for ever, and this prevented Scotland from becoming nationalist in the nineteenth-century. Insofar as the original task of gaining Scottish independence was itself sourced in the original twelfth-century turning to immanence across Europe, and exemplified in the project of articulating a new vision of the relations between the sacred and 'secondary natures' or immanence and transcendence (Negri and Hardt 2000, pp. 70-74), the modernist consciousness is only overcome to the extent that it is apprehended that twenty-first century Scottish nationalism is not simply about re-establishing political independence but retrieving an original programme of modernisation that disappeared with Scotland's political independence. The success of the Reformation in Scotland meant the overthrow of the Catholic and Scottish project of articulating the soteriological value of secondary natures, while its blood relatives of modernism and liberalism liquidated or privatised such 'quaint' old-fashioned concerns. The success of these errors, then, came at the price of liquidating Scottish independence and reducing modernisation and progress to the exigencies of *homo economicus* and arresting the development of Scottish culture through such notorious State-sponsored violence as the Statutes of Iona of 1609, while a host of historic identities and localities were taken 'out of history' (Craig 1996).

To secure this status quo, then, a foundational modernist 'sell out' of an original Catholic integralism has been reproduced by every generation of managers in Scotland since the eighteenth-century and so, if theorists of 'subaltern nationalism' describe local elites replacing the colonists at the top of the social hierarchy and using the spell of nationalism to convince the masses there is more at stake than reproducing a hierarchical social structure in which they will remain at the bottom, none of this understanding of nationalism as being a form of 'false consciousness' was necessary in Scotland *because from the point of view of the bourgeoisie, who were already in their managerial places, they had nothing to gain and everything to lose by becoming nationalists* and ending the experiment of Great Britain and tearing up the liberal peace; they were already too modernist and already too symbolically de-territorialised and de-nationalised to reopen the Pandora's box of history. Being good assimilated North British Protestants, they had no symbolic material with which to ignite any nationalist fires within themselves, far less the lower orders, so that their cultural assimilation to England on the cusp of industrialisation in 1832 was more or less complete. As the local Protestant minister (in Houston 1924, p. 417) wrote at this time:

> Those who are partial to the old dialect may think the language has changed for the worse, but fashion and our schools, and our close intercourse with England are transmuting us every year, every month, to the general standard of the empire.

Nationalism has been the great ballast peoples have mobilised to counteract the trauma of the advent of industrialisation in each European national context, and signalled the resilience of nations and peoples *to become modern on their own sovereign terms and refusal to become modern on any other nation's terms*, so that by the end of the First World War in 1918 the nation-state had replaced the myriad variations of the multi-national State that had existed in Europe as the new norm. In this prolonged period of upheaval, each nation's 'third estate' or bourgeoisie mobilised in order to practice sovereignty within their territory, and this political and social and cultural mobilisation saved them from believing, far less implementing, the excesses of modernist rhetoric, so that modernisation in practice if not in ideology meant the modernisation of medieval structures and localities and identities despite 'year zero' modernist rhetoric concerning the liquidation of the past and the advent of the new industrial age.

The Scottish middle classes, however, did not mobilise to exert control over a sovereign Scottish modernity but took instead to theorising everyone else's sovereignty by producing a universalist theory of modernity in the likes of Hume, Ferguson and Smith, so that beneath the sophisticated modernism that rejected every vestige of 'period costume' such as language, religion, history, tradition and parliament etcetera lay the fundamental fact of Scotland's suicide insofar as these Enlightenment figures theorised a more perfect liquidation of the past than any other European bourgeoisies ever dared imagine, far less practice.

In his instructive journey from Marxist internationalism to advocating Scottish nationalism, Tom Nairn has journeyed from being a Hume-like Enlightenment figure and typical zealous 'modernist Scot,' to his current position of arguing the reason why Scotland and England are half-modernised nations is because both languish in "British backwardness" (Nairn 1994, p. 62), or a constitutional arrangement that prohibits the full constitution of modernity in both countries. Nairn, then, has caught up with 'the people' and the facts as they have emerged since Hamilton 1967, and in the process has imagined or aligned modernity upon a purely Scottish basis. The modernist view of liquidating Tradition and History in order to be fully modern is the 'sacred canopy' (Berger 1967) and meta-narrative or long durée meaning which modernists give themselves and has long fuelled the 'immaculate anthropology' and the embarrassment at integralism of many educated individuals, convinced they had escaped from the holism and the tasks that result from embracing being in nature, history, territory and the question of transcendence. This modernist imaginary, however, has itself been liquidated and is at an end in an objective and sociological sense, although in many biographies it undoubtedly has a lifetime ahead of it.

Like Nairn I understand nationalism as functional to advancing a particular practice and view of modernity, but an older and original vision of modernity that I propose as an understanding of the modern era that meets the needs of today's post-affluent generations and the challenge of understanding the 'present as history.' A proper or integral or sovereign Scottish modernity has lost ground not only as a result of union with England but *as a result of the ultimate failure of the original project of modernity in twelfth-century Scotland* that I will detail further in Chapter 8. If the signature of 'being modern' is maintaining a tension between the view *sub specie aeternitatus* and a turning to the contingent and always-changing social and economic conditions characteristic of the free-market economy and society, the signature error to resist is a superstitious capitulation to the new that dissolves the very tension of 'being modern.' More concretely, if becoming a working class is part of the trauma and truth of 'becoming modern,' the mistake of modernists is not allowing this trauma and truth to fully or integrally register and impact all of *dasein*.

All 'materialist' anthropologies are more or less in alliance with the modernist error which renounces any pretence whatsoever at continuity with a fuller self-definition of human being that transcends the onset of the industrial era. A more adequate view of modernity is the release of historicity and human being from the confines of the medieval era and the 'dictatorship of scarcity,' rather than imagining a decisive break with the past and the liquidation of fundamental aspects of *dasein*. Whereas modernists like Nairn are embarrassed and out of their depth at the return of the fancy dress or period costume of twelfth-century particularism, this lifting of repression must be embraced, so that instead of drawing our understanding of modernity from the usual suspects of the Enlightenment and the French Revolution, Scottish nationalism ought to align with the modernity first caught sight of in twelfth-century Europe, which sought to escape from the 'dictatorship of supernaturalism' and which has only been released as a popular possibility thanks to the arrival of affluence and the escape from the 'dictatorship of scarcity.'

In light of the 'miracle' of affluence that has been worked in our midst, our estimation of the possibilities available to working-class *dasein* and *mitsein* must be re-thought, and integral to this is to re-think the long durée symbolic order. If a post-affluent generation identifies a symbolic poverty among the '45 generation as evidence of a condition of subordination, this can not be explained exclusively by the complex process of an agrarian population having had to become a landless proletariat. Beneath the self-serving reductionist rhetoric of Marx concerning the miserabilism and penury of the workers under capitalism, and claims of religion being opium and the working class having no country and having no family life and the worker having nothing to lose but his chains, Weber (1989) saw that an event prior to industrialisation was responsible for subsequent materialist philosophies to emerge i.e. the Protestant Reformation, and this is why Weber argued that Presbyterian Scotland evidenced an elective affinity with the rise of monochromatic or non-integral reductionist anthropologies such as *homo economicus*. When in 1790 the local Presbyterian minister (Houston 1924, p. 411) answered the *Old Statistical Account* inquiry whether "your people [have] any holy-days for recreation or merry-making?", his reply that: "Just one in the year, called Handsel Monday, and even the manner in which this is employed shows the sober-mindedness of the people," evidences modernity as 'iron cage' and the condition of disenchantment was already in place among the local population. Likewise, another glimpse of the local advent of Weber's iron cage comes from the Rev. Dr. Murray's response (Houston 1924, p. 411) from 1790 in reply to the inquiry: "What sports have your people?"

> Scarcely any after they are grown up. Amongst the infinite advantages of Reformation, this seems to have been one disadvantage attending it that, owing to the gloomy rigour of some of the leading actors, mirth and sport and cheerfulness were decried amongst a people already by nature rather phlegmatic. Since that, mirth and vice have in their apprehension been confounded together...so that the people must either dance by themselves or let it alone.

If late twentieth-century affluence ended the material 'dictatorship of scarcity,' then twenty-first century nationalism must escape metaphysical forms of miserabilism if it is to imagine and paint Scottish *dasein* with a full palette of colour. Weber's (1989) thesis concerning the *symbolic* (Protestant) basis for the arrival of the

New Man of *homo economicus* is a warning that the realm of culture exerts its own causality, and insofar as Scottish nationalism envisages the overthrow of symbolic complexes such as a disenchanted Protestantism or a purely secular *homo economicus*, it must put in their place a symbolic order that embraces and systematically develops those 'secondary natures' and those fundamental aspects of *dasein* that have been systematically marginalised because failure to do so opens the door to the same errors to slip into the new era of independence.

For example, then, when Nairn argues that nationalism is a better modernising force than unionism, we must be careful not to replicate the argument of earlier generations of Protestants and unionists who sacrificed Scottish independence, culture, politics and history for the sake of what they imagined 'being modern' to be i.e. the progress of the Protestant Reformation and, then, purely secular definitions as found in the Enlightenment and then the anthropology of *homo economicus* that served the rising commercial classes (Douglas and Ney 1998). Each of these historical 'ideal types' of the Protestant, the Enlightenment intellectual and the Entrepreneur did not have symbolic systems that brought enough ballast to enable their pursuit of 'being modern' avoid them 'selling out' *inter alia* their national sovereignty. I propose, then, that only the constant alignment with the original Catholic holistic conception of modernity and *dasein* gives sufficient ballast against the force of the new and the temptation to slip from being modern to being modernist.

Talk of a late-modern restoration of a twelfth-century patrimony must undoubtedly baffle many pro-independence voters insofar as they fail to see that the political sovereignty they seek for Scotland is only a fraction of the possibilities being released in late modernity, and insofar as they fail to see that to renovate the Scottish symbolic order they must go back to that period when integralism or the value of 'secondary natures' was first invented in the twelfth-century articulation of a purely natural beatitude that is proportionate to human nature and another beatitude that was super-natural or above nature (Chapter 8). I propose that in signifying the 'present as history' in this way, we avoid the idea that by rejecting three centuries of unionism we are thereby clearing the way to begin 'from scratch' and avoid an even-more cleansed modernist *dasein* that is once again characterised by caesura, liquidation and rupture from the past. Faced with the vertigo of the new, the sane choice is to embrace both the 'tasks of freedom' and that thick or 'heavy historicity' that gives ballast to the project of reversing four centuries of the Reformation/Enlightenment/Modernist paradigm in order to resurrect the revolutionary developments in twelfth century society and thinking which wished to renovate the relations between the new society developing at this time and begin the free and full development of 'secondary natures' and to follow wherever this development leads.

## 4.7 Re-imagining the Kingdom of Fife

In light of the fact that both '45 and '79 generation informants recognise they have been subject to the systematic neglect of Scottish history and culture as a result of the decisions of educational policymakers throughout the twentieth century, there is an abundance of 'material' available to anyone with a determination to politicise this 'educational deficit.' An article which appeared in *The Scotsman* newspaper (4 February 1999) reported the Scottish Consultative Council on the Curriculum's recommendation that more Scottish history and culture be taught in schools, as part of a drive to give lessons a greater "Scottish flavour." However, in the opinion of one member of the original review group (Robbie Robertson), the Council's findings were supressed with the result that fifteen of the eighteen members of the Council had written an open letter deploring the suppression of their report which had advised that 86% of people questioned wanted a "fairly or very well pronounced" Scottish theme to education, with Mr Robertson quoted as saying the revised report was less radical and took too narrow a view of culture, adding: "The Scottish people have been conned." In light of the fact that when asked to comment the then SNP education spokesman Nicola Sturgeon was quoted as saying: "It is impossible to escape the conclusion that the report has been watered down," it is clear that these skirmishes represent the return of the repressed and announce a new era of the 'politics of knowledge' or the politicisation of knowledge within education has arrived, and integral to this return of the repressed will be the re-imagining of Scotland and its historic localities and regional identities that have more or less lay artistically and aesthetically 'inert' throughout the modernist period of suppression.[102]

As was narrated by the tutor Roisin at the history group meeting of 3 February 1999, the region of Fife emerged in tandem with the emergence and history of the nation, so that like the nation this particular regional identity and history has suffered decline at the hands of a liberal or modernist social ontology, and the loss of national independence and the re-location of Scots' imaginations and their political sovereignty to London (England). In this respect, the medieval Kingdom of Fife is an example of the decline of sub-national identities insofar as they became locations for delocalisation, and the delocalising or deprovincialisation of the imagination of local populations in the name of modernisation; the disembedding or misalignment of locals and their locales, which has resulted in the decline and disappearance of 'regional consciousness' within regional populations, with sub-national identities effecting a weak structuring of perception, identity and culture (Glen and Hubbard 2008, pp. xiii-xv).

Beginning with the Protestant Reformation of 1560 and culminating in the union of Crowns in 1603 and union of Parliaments in 1707, the cultural importance enjoyed by locations such as St. Andrews and Dunfermline declined and came to an end as a result of this relocation of power, prestige and patronage outwith the nation, with the result that representations of Fife have become reduced to either a tourist attraction insofar as its coastal areas managed to escape the trauma of industrialism, or has become a symbolically inert non-space insofar as its hinterland experienced the full impact of the industrial era and

---

[102] To address the long-standing absence of Scottish history and culture from the curriculum in Scottish schools, the SNP administration from August 2014 have developed the new optional subject *Scottish Studies* which schools may offer their pupils.

now suffers deindustrialization. In terms of the Fife imaginary, then, inhabitants' symbolisation of Fife remains stuck between the end of coalmining and a post-industrial identity that is yet to emerge, and insofar as these two representations exhaust the 'mirrors' Fifers have to recognise their provinciality by, the imagining of Fife outwith those locations which have retained something of their historicity and something of their hold upon the imagination of their inhabitants echoes James V's description of Fife as "a beggar's mantle with a fringe of gold."

Wightman (in Hassan and Ilett 2011, p. 196) has described the Lanarkshire parish of Carluke as a locale in which "there is no institutional memory; there is no governance; there is no body with any real power," and as with the *Fun Day* discussed in Chapter 1 where only the attempt at community makes present the normal failure of *communitas*, so it is only the attempt to constitute an interest in locality and its history that reveals how in post-industrial locales such as Cardenden inhabitants can remark: "Nuthin ever happens in Fife" (Hugh Young) *as if nothing has been said*, because regionality does not exist as a medium of its inhabitants' imagination and does not mediate meaning or structure per-ception, so that 'being provincial' is a medium or mediation of *meaninglessness* and another source of the 'nothing' discussed in Chapter 1. Insofar as the consciousness of the inhabitants of regions have 'opted out' of their regional contexts, a regional consciousness has become a private affair and these localities and regions and their populations have seceded from the tensions of being modern (as opposed to have become modern) as a result of not having the categories to resist a global cosmopolitanism, so that 'regionality' has little reality left in the tenth generation since the Act of Union, and fails to act as a bridge to a deeper historical consciousness and a more holistic conception and practice of the tension between the metropolitan and the provincial.

Why this matters today is because the absence of regional identity means the absence of a source to model a post-industrial vision or trajectory for their localities and, paradoxically, it is the '45 generation which is least engaged with nationalism that is most able to speak of their locality and regionality in a *substantive* manner because of the richness of the many local relationships characteristic of the occupational community and which were repeated throughout Fife.[103] The younger generation is unable to draw upon this dense experience of local identity as they are the generation that has experienced deindustrialization and the 'thinning' of locality. While both experiences of locality across the generations share the same fate of being articulated by external structural forces, in the '45 generation such forces actively 'thickened' locality, while among the '79 generation the same forces during the nineteen-eighties in particular acted to disorganise or thin-out the experience of locality as 'occupational community.' Today, then, a younger generation is confronted with the question whether 'cultural forces' are able to constitute a regional identity by resurrecting Fife as part of its social ontology and part of a renewed imaginary, so that a Fife identity or 'regional consciousness' becomes integral to re-territorialising freedom and sovereignty and modernity.

The unprecedented opportunities afforded by affluence means opportunities to resurrect suppressed regional identities. In October 1998, for example, the first all-Fife radio station Kingdom FM began broadcasting to a Fife audience and soon became the most popular radio station in Fife, and I propose that this mobilisation of regional identity is a blood-relative of the task of re-imagining locality after the industrial era and re-imagining Scotland after the era of union,[104] and that a range of realities and identities after a Yes vote on 18 September 2014 are more or less set for a period of re-imagining, and integral to this will be recuperating much of the medieval cultural patrimony that

---

[103] When the Royal Commission under Lord Wheatley outlined the reform of local government in Scotland in September 1969, it proposed the end of Fife as a political and administrative unit of regional government. However, a campaign to 'save Fife' succeeded in 1971 when the Heath government's White Paper included Fife as one of the proposed regions of local government.

[104] An example of 1979 generation re-imagining of Fife that owes nothing to the industrial era and borrows from Tolkein and blends the mythical, musical and nonsensical would be Gloryhammer's symphonic rock album *Tales From the Kingdom of Fife* (2013).

throughout the years of hegemonic Protestantism, modernism and unionism was either physically destroyed or imaginatively neglected. If the unionist period saw a revolutionary historical and imaginary break with the medieval and early-modern period, the current late-modern nationalist present is more or less coerced into inaugurating a similar revolutionary break with the Protestant/unionist/modernist/liberal period in favour of returning to the Catholic era to break with the modernist fiction of being able to break from the past, because it is this earlier period which first sighted a break from supernaturalism and universalism was necessary to arrive at the value of particularism and a proper estimation of the value of 'secondary natures' which acts as a bulwark against the myth of 'liquidating' being.

What is set to emerge, then, is the antithesis of the imagined future proposed by Mill's *Considerations on Representative Government* (1861, p. 300) where we find the liberal argument that, insofar as small European nations become independent from larger nations, the fate that awaited the freshly-independent native would be the freedom to "to sulk on his own rocks, the half-savage relic of past times, revolving in his own little mental orbit, without participation or interest in the general movement of the world." Mill's rhetoric nicely illustrates how the modernist imagines the relationship between place and time under the conditions of modernity, and while no-one would contest the movement of modernity often acts to disembed populations from their places, Mill fails to articulate any kind of dialectic between the local or provincial and the metropolitan, so that his imagining of modernity fails to suspect that belonging to localities establishes their inhabitants' relation to the historic long durée, and their belonging to localities and provinces establishes a central tension of the condition of 'being modern' which is the tension between the urban centre and the provinces. Mill's casual symbolic violence upon non-metropolitan populations also acts as a pure cipher for power and capital insofar as it consecrates the view that, when any location is deprived of the movement and attention of capital it is more or less fated to cease to have significance even to its inhabitants.

If we recall Alastair Gray's memorable point that a place's inhabitants must live their imaginatively as well as physically, a place's inhabitants' imaginative and psychological manner of living in their locality is impoverished by the liberal imagination by definition, as the liberal imagination does not relate to locality in a deep manner because it does not relate to the long durée via locality or provinciality in a deep and 'thick' manner. More concretely, then, if authors bring this sensibility to their fictional representations of locality or provincial life, these locations *can only appear as places of little significance and of no aesthetic or literary worth.* Finally, having divested localities of any real relation to the long durée, such authors are also more or less coerced into imagining locals too as having no real or imagined relationship to history, and any such relation which locals feel they have must be 'backward' and of marginal interest.

As the earlier quotes from Adam, Annie and Peter highlight, the suppression of national history in Scottish education is consubstantial with the absence or suppression of regional history, so that if Scotland has long been a largely 'unimagined community' (Anderson 1983), then the provincial or regional identity of Fife has been similarly unimagined and has lain inert and remained largely latent as a source of identity. Even more difficult, then, than achieving national political independence may be the provincial and local task of imagining these sub-national identities free of modernist assumptions and outwith the 'mirror of production' characteristic of the industrial era.

When interviewing one resident (Ena Herd, Orebank Road) on her views of the new Scottish parliament, at one point she reflected:

> Actually, what Ah'm talking tae ye aboot, you're talkin tae a 56 year auld woman that is gien ye her view on life in 1999 before the millennium. So this is bound tae be, can go somewhere in what you're daen.

Ena adverts to two aspects of herself which are her being-in-society and her being-in-history, and this raises the question as to whether it is more accurate to describe late-modern social actors as dominated by the return of history and the return of the repressed, or whether it is more accurate to advert to a dislocation from historicity or the end of 'being in history' thanks to social forces creating more and more privatised self-understandings that are more and more divorced from long durée communal frameworks. My own dialectical view is that both points of view are true, and that to pose the question whether a collective working-class *dasein* is finally capable of being released, only to be deconstructed and privatised, is to misrecognise the structuralist constraints that inform the exercise of freedom and reflexivity.

The view that late-moderns are in possession of reflexive selves that allows them to free themselves from a traditional identification with such 'accidents of birth' as class and national identity betrays the class-provenance of such views, and I propose that the predicament-come-opportunities faced by the '79 generations directly contradicts 'contemplative' and decontextualized assertions which are consubstantial with other fashionable assertions, such as the narrative meaning which nations give themselves are largely mythical. According to Hobsbawm and Ranger (1983), for example, the short kilt is a nineteenth-century invention and is not traditional Scottish dress, so that nationalist movements are often based upon spurious history. According to this point of view national identities are much like the meanings late-moderns give to their individual biographies i.e. are fictions that are fated to be 'deconstructed' by the exercise of reflexivity.

As a rule I would contend that social theorists who fail to include in their understanding of reflexivity the structuring impact of class, nation and history are fated to produce representations that are more or less enthralled to the theorist's 'privatism.' If we take the example of Hobsbawn and Ranger (1983) mentioned, we are invited to imagine the (Scottish) nationalist as prone to being duped into irrational loyalties, as if the nation is a reality to be identified with and remain defined by because the flag-waving nationalist lacks the symbolic capital to develop a middle-class historian's kind of reflexivity; as if the working class are the last class able to appropriate the post-substance identity paradigm and so are judged yet to reach 'high-modern reflexivity,' and so remain fated to order their political mobilisation via obsolete communal categories, and are eternally condemned in the contemplative bourgeois imagination to play 'catch-up' to the realities and practices already enjoyed by the bourgeoisie. I would argue that despite the rise of individualism working-class *dasein* remains structurally constituted and determined by 'the mirror of production' and tied to its positionality within the hierarchical social structure, as well as tied to and defined by its 'being in history' and its 'being national.' However, in terms of consciousness, there is the possibility of producing a symbolic break with a historic long durée paradigm at the level of imagining via a usage of literacy (Hoggart 1957) and reflexivity in a post-British generation and a 'making of history' that embraces integralism and that is free of modernism.

Like nations, the reality of social classes is held together by their relations with other classes so that the 'class system' consists of the enduring hierarchical nature of the social structure while the transitory details of the empirical make-up of the occupational landscape changes. Similarly, the exercise of reflexivity and freedom is determined not by the conclusions arrived at by 'pure reason' as it contemplates 'society,' but by living in the space one occupies in social space and living that space's relations to the other positions in social space that are occupied by other social actors. The notion of the embourgeoisement of affluent workers, then, is of course true in its trivial sense of meaning an increase in privatism and individualism etcetera, but a fiction insofar as it is a structural impossibility for the working class to instantiate a middle-class relation to the social order because this would require the working class to experience their relation to the social structure the same way as the middle-class experiences its relation to the social whole, and in the absence of a social class below them to constitute the bourgeois relation by, there can be no reproduction of the middle-class experience, and therefore no embourgeoisement of the working class in this sense. If while interviewing an abject working-class female tells me she votes Liberal Democrat and describes herself to me as being middle class, such self-representations are fictions that do not change her position in the social hierarchy, nor make her the possessor of the experiences and habitus and consciousness of a real middle-class person.

Importantly, then, dispensing with the fiction of embourgeoise-ment allows into view the proposition that the high-modern exercise of class-based reflexivity involves an unprecedented *deep-ening* of class-based *dasein* and a deepening of being Scottish and being-in-history. This late-modern affluence-led project of reflexivity is very different from Riesman's (1961) analysis of the lonely crowd in which there is a privatised relation between structure and knowledge, in favour of recognising the free devel-opment of the homology between the two. As ever, the modernist representation of 'the present as history' fails as it presents the false understanding of being-in-the-world as either being 'mired in the past' or facing the future as a *tabula rasa* as the result of the liquidation of any historical ballast; and explaining the firework display of 1 July 1999 by resorting to the 'period costume' metaphor, where social actors 'dress up' their actions in the false consciousness of historical fancy dress – the usual metaphors by which the modernist imagination misrecognises the contemporary and its inability to think at a level that is equal to the times being lived through, as liberalism itself fails to suspect it is an example of what may be described as theoretical 'period costume' as its obsolete modernist parentage cannot integrate the *person-in-society* and the *person-in-history* and the *person-in-territory*.

Having sat with locals in Bowhill Park on many Thursday evenings during the summer months listening to the local pipe band practising and with many band members wearing the tartan, and conscious of the history group's collection of black and white photographs of local pipe bands often including their forebears playing in Moscow at the invitation of the former Soviet Union, this evidencing that national and class realities have worked hand in hand in the activities of the *Friends of the Soviet Union* societies that proliferated in Fife after 1917, for example, also evidences that Hobsbawm & Ranger's (1983) critique of tartanry, which they imagine capable of deconstructing Scottish nationalism, involves misrecognitions piling upon misrecognitions. The idea that being part of an impromptu audience watching one of the local pipe bands practice is supposed to strike the ethnographer as 'invented tradition' and a kind of false consciousness, is in fact convincing evidence of the failure of academic objectivism as a route to *verstehen*. If one can not, then, settle for indulging in objectivist critiques of the many errors of particular historians such as the Rev. Houston, it is far better to recognise that objectivism itself is a form of 'false consciousness' insofar as it imagines the alleged recent coinage of tartanry and the short kilt are relevant to underpinning Scottish nationalism.

More seriously for the historian, the analysis that suggests locals' appropriation of national identity and national dress is 'fake' is the real impostor as the objectivist understanding of authenticity or tradition is evidence of naivety regarding the nature of social and historical reality and how history is made. This naïve faith of academics as to the powers of objectivism is evidence of having little grasp of how people, whether a medieval peasantry or a post-industrial proletariat, make their history. Pace Karl Deutsch's remark that a nation is "a group of persons united by a common error about their ancestry" (1969, p. 3), systematically getting one's history 'wrong' in this academic objectivist sense is the glaring clue as to the post-objectivist or *interpretive* nature of historicity or history-making, and that historical error is pressed into the service of 'history making' and the historical work of reproducing and contesting hegemony and legitimacy in hearts and minds.

While no student of Scottish historiography can fail to be sympathetic to a 'social constructionist' position given the long history of historians' interpretation of history being revealed with hindsight to be immersed in and therefore more or less a cipher for the prevailing beliefs, the point is not to rest content with 'objectively' pointing to the fake nature of it all but to learn what Bourdieu (1977, pp. 1-71) terms "the objective limitations of objectivism," as at any time in any history the issue is one of identifying the relevant and contested relationships that social actors are engaged in reproducing or contesting, and these forces are routinely the same old forces of class, nation and religious identity so that the same old "period costume" is always in fashion.

When Nairn argues (1997, p. 184) that: "Modern patriotism has no natural persona in Scotland. Our old clothes are romantic rags, yet – embarrassingly, inexplicably – none of the new uniforms seem to fit either," it seems a backward glance in the constituting of Scottish nationalism is inevitable because it is in the past that we lived in 'community' as opposed to our current experience of living in a 'mass society,' but Nairn fails to conceive of historicity as integral to *dasein* and *mitsein*, so that nationalism is not a species of 'false consciousness' but a particularly effective way of addressing and solving in its confused way *the specifically modern dilemma* of how to imagine community in the open society, and this is why "the rhetoric of nostalgia" (Herzfeld 1997, p. 111) is deemed part of the DNA of nationalism, and why it has proven itself to be the cipher of choice for those who "desire to become a people rather than a population" (Geertz 1993, p. 237).

I propose that the modernist reading of history-making and peoples' historicity fails to realise that the actors involved are 'in history' and are more or less fated to 'dress up'[105] their present-day 'history making' in dated period costume because the 'modern' costume (whatever that might be) worn to address the present-as-history doesn't quite fit because what is to be expressed at any particular time of historic importance is the present moment's deep historicity and immersion in the past. If social actors dress-up structural realities in 'period costume' it is because structural realities are historical realities and the person-in-society is also the person-in-history, so that for intellectuals such as Hobsbawm and Ranger to persist in objectivism is to persist in their failure to understand they reproduce the intellectualist misrecognition of real historical *dasein*, and impute to their insights a deconstructive power they can never possess.

What historian of Scotland after 1979-1997 and 2010-2015 could fail to realise that for anyone to imagine Scottish nationalism is a form of fake 'period costume' is guilty of falling into what

---

[105] While Hobsbawm and Ranger (1983) claim the kilt is a ninettenth-century invention, historian Michael Lynch affirms that: "A cult of 'tartanry' at the royal court briefly flowered in the 1680s" (1992, p. 299).

Bourdieu (Bourdieu and Wacquant 1992, p. 144n) calls the "occasionalist fallacy," and is also manifestly failing to take the first steps in appropriating the 'historical imagination' as the plain fact is the period 1979-1997 or 2010-2015 is not simply the empirical event of 1979-1997 or 2010-2015 that comes and goes, but the latest instance of a long durée set of geo-political relationships that date from 1707 at least, so that this period of nineteen and five years are just the latest iterations of similar periods going back to the medieval period and the relations between Scotland and England practiced then.

Instead of taking aim at nationalism with the usual objectivist point-scoring that never hits its target because it fundamentally misrecognises what there is to aim at, social theory that is open to being-in-history should measure itself by its capacity to articulate the fullest statement of the historicity of human being that is emergent at this time. Is social theory capable of this deep recognition, or will it reproduce the long modernist flight from the real? Far from being discarded via the alleged disembedding effects of affluence or individualism, these forces in fact help these collective or group identities of class and nation within the '79 generation to emerge and further condition the reflexive project of (working class) nationalism, which is a blood-relative of the general emergence at the superstructural level of the underlying structures of contesting classes, nations, ethnicities and histories that have always been present and that have always been in need of repression.

With the post-colonial order and the end of universalist Enlightenment trajectories and the emergence of plural modernities, a plurality which appears as an epidemic of 'medieval particularism' in the modernist imagination, the modernist timetable of history is torn up and so *the modernist imagination within social theory should be brought to an end* insofar as social forces liberate historicity and tradition from their historic and traditional confines in the era of 'scarcity modernity' and 'scarcity thinking.' In Chapter 8 where I attempt to outline an *integral sociology,* I will propose that we are witnessing an unprecedented emergence of the real in all its historicity and density, and to find his or her bearings the social theorist, just as the social actor participating in this drama, is caught up in this process and is more or less coerced into asking himself whether his presuppositions allow him to recognise what is emerging or disappear it from view.

If much of the interpretive confusion surrounding articulating 'the present as history' stems from the great modernist illusion regarding having to choose between the 'end of history' (Fukuyama 1989) thesis or the release of history thesis that I am proposing, another source of confusion is whether advanced Western societies are becoming 'classless' societies, or whether social class is as real as ever thanks to social theorists after the fall of Communism and the triumph of the neoliberal world order after 1989 having finally given up any hope that anything can be done to change the class-based nature of free-market societies. If the modernist consciousness is fated to see the end of history and the end of the class system in every twitch, it is because such beliefs are ciphers of the middle-class habitus.

Given the rise in material affluence since the nineteen-seventies the '79 generations are able to become free behaviourally as well as ideologically from traditional working-class symbolic systems and certain traditional identities instantiated by the '45 generation. However, this freedom from prior conventions does not mean freedom from historicity or the social structure per se or what Baudrillard (1975) terms 'the mirror of production,' so that rather than the dissolution of the isomorphism between objective social position and subjective mental structuration, there is greater freedom than ever before to recognise the deep homology between mental and social structure *upon their own terms*, as opposed to having this homology and this relation to history pre-packaged by another class or generation. What is released is working class being in all its suppressed and unimagined temporality, historicity, sociality, locality and provinciality, so that a proper understanding of the present involves the need for a sociology that is capable of recognising the release of integralism or all of the colours of human *dasein*, and a 'springtime of structure' that is emerging into the cultural realm free from mystifications and a taking charge, for good or ill, of signification and a new symbolic order.

I propose, then, that a Scottish contextualisation of the 'reflexive modernisation' process associated with Beck and Giddens (1994) means the rise of the affluent society coupled with a freedom from modernist thinking equates to a 'high modern' age characterised by a return to an older project of modernity. After the firework display of 1 July 1999, and with no need to wait for May 2007 or May 2011 or 18 September 2014, modernists have been more or less coerced into conceding some kind of return of the repressed and a fuller conception of *dasein* and *mitsein*, and the exercise of political sovereignty is fundamental to solving the problem of how a nation and a people organises their being-in-the-modern-world. However, this coerced recognition is fated to lapse back into modernist misrecognition of the present insofar as 1 July 1999, or sometime after 18 September 2014, simply means instead of being modernist *on English terms Scotland is free to pursue being modernist on purely Scottish terms*. The new Scottish imaginary that I am articulating, then, argues against such a half-hearted understanding of the constitution of the Scottish nationalist project, as the point of recalling the Scottish parliament and regaining sovereignty is to not make the same mistakes that the British modernist project made but to recuperate a far older holistic understanding of 'being modern' and 'being Scottish.'

If what is possible is a vision of working class being or a holistic materialism free from modernist prejudices, what must be affirmed in the same breath is that freedom reveals as never before the *cultural poverty* of the working class, and their vulnerability to every kind of interpolation due to their symbolic domination. Having argued the emergence of a new integral 'dialectic of class' is possible, I also recognise that now that a series of forces has meant the working class can begin to systematically appropriate or reject every aspect of Tradition and turn their attention towards erecting a new symbolic order, far from finally emerging and constituting itself via this long-awaited task we see that much of the working class are not fit for this purpose. Paradoxically, *only now* in the era of affluence do we see the extent of the working class's incapacitation precisely *because* it is freer than ever before to manifest its capacities but also its incapacities. What is routinely revealed is not a pent-up ambition finally liberated but a profound lesson in the effects of domination.

When interviewing in Carden Castle Avenue (26 April 2014) I had the following conversation with a woman in her late-sixties, after I had asked her how she would vote in the upcoming referendum and she had said she would vote 'no:'

**Mrs. Clemiston:** Ah'm happy with the way things are really.
**Me:** But you won't be happy with this Tory government?
**Mrs. Clemiston:** Oh no, Ah'm no happy wi that!
**Me:** Are you happy with Scotland voting for policies and parties at elections and getting the opposite of what they vote fir?
**Mrs. Clemiston:** Ah ken what you mean.
**Me:** ... and having an unrepresentative system of government?
**Mrs Clemiston:** Well no, Ah'm no happy wi that.
**Me:** So why are you at your doorstep sayin yer happy wi how things are?
**Mrs. Clemiston:** Well, Ah don't know really.

In the same street I chatted with women who simply told me: "No, Ah'm no interested" and "Ah dinnae really ken anything about it, so Ah dinnae ken," and so the conversation ended. Similarly, I chatted with many locals who alighted on a particular material or monetary issue and who did not engage with 'the bigger pictiure,' such as an elderly man whose wife is disabled and who wanted to chat at great length about how there was no information regarding what would happen to the UK government's Motability Scheme (i.e. would he still get a free car) in the event of independence. From my door-to-door conversations I have a wealth of data that could easily serve the argument that my characterisations of *dasein* involving being national or being-in-history are insignificant when compared with the argument that informants are more or less solely motivated by material or economic values.

In spite of this counter-evidence I argue the '79 generations are being structurally coerced by deindustrialization, history and political events to take up a series of challenges which reveals the poverty of prior generations because deindustrialization and the collapse of ideological universalisms requires that working class to imagine itself free of economism and the industrial era which was too poor to uncover what cannot now be concealed i.e. the inability to articulate and imagine its own self, far less its ability to compete against other hegemonic producers of culture. Via their parents the '79 generation are heirs to localities and a culture betraying a prior material scarcity, and the enduring structural facts of life mean most may not catch sight of the trajectory I have laid out but remain prone to living some form of 'dependency consciousness,' or a kind of nihilism kept fresh by a never-ending supply of *ressentiment* that might be viewed as the 'cipher of choice' of the working-class habitus, so that a class fraction of this generation will not develop the freedoms their generation has 'objectively' inherited.

While arguing that a long-delayed critique of modernism among the younger generations is underway, I concede not only the fragility of this project but that it is far from being free of rival and competing interpretations and representations. I recognise the ease with which one could argue that, rather than a sighting of an original twelfth-century project, there is instead an ongoing 'Americanisation' of Scotland's youth and a flight from history and historicity; or that what is emerging is a form of nihilism and a more radical break with the past than even most modernists would be comfortable with; an emergent globalised identity among *the millennium generation* i.e. those born from the mid-1980s, given their unprecedented importation and consumption of world culture and who have come to political consciousness with no memory of there not having been a Scottish parliament. I recognise, then, that out of such data one could easily argue that 'Scotland' has returned too late, and that while structural requirements are in place to allow a project of retrieving and developing a long suppressed historical narrative, *the same forces* that gave birth to such a project have already rendered such a project nostalgic, backward and impossible.

While conceding a plurality of interpretations, then, I identify an emergent conception of 'being modern' that historically failed and that was subsequently lost sight of, and yet is fresh from having overturned much of the imagining of Scotland throughout most of the modern era. If we are all nationalists today (McCrone 1998, p. ix) it is because we are all 'medievalists' today because socio-economic forces have liberated a collective historicity and dissolved the modernist fancy dress costume that is too small for our needs. What is happening is not a 'retrieval' of the Middle Ages but an emergence *of the present in all its historicity*, and the task of the ethnographer is to interpret the emergent historicity of the present freely and systematically. Ironically, if we can agree "all that is solid melts into air" it is on the understanding that what is melting is the long campaign of repression and forgetting that was modernism.

Something else that can be agreed upon is that to be modern is to be reflexive about being modern, and the view that the modern era was a caesura from the past is the first casualty of this reflexivity. Thanks to affluence and deep literacy and driven by the long event of 1979-1997 and now 2010-2015, a more adequate description of the reflexivity of the '79 generation(s) is that there is a simultaneous release of sociality and historicity that is so far-reaching that only the twelfth-century advent of modernity can act as a precedent. To the query why just go back to the twelfth-century and not the tenth or eighth century or the pre-Christian era, I answer that prior to the twelfth and thirteenth centuries there had yet to ocurr the first turning to the natural and social worlds; there had yet to occur the invention of the mundane secular realm as distinct from the supernatural, and there had yet to occur the invention of *natura pura* or purely natural (and purely social) realities that were to be studied and known in their own right, and in this transcendence of supernaturalism an integral conception of *dasein* (and understanding of modernity) that was innocent of any desire to reduce or liquidate or privatise its full expression and exploration first emerged. This is why in looking for a non-reductive and post-materialist symbolic order that paints human being with a full palette of colour, this '79 generation turns to the twelfth century in the twenty-first century for ballast as it articulates its ownmost ontology and ownmost tasks.

Advocating the resurrection of the twelfth-century Catholic advent of modernity is to argue that the only basis for an inclusive modernity is one where each discussant subscribes to a holistic understanding of the purely natural-historical-social realm (and not that one becomes a believing Catholic). Upon the basis of such a common ground, the dynamic view of human *dasein* as articulated by the atheist Sartre (1966), for example, is compatible with the Catholic mind's understanding of human *dasein* and agreement upon this dynamism can act as the basis for a new imaginary in an independent Scotland. To be properly modern and to have a properly inclusive understanding of being modern is to have a *proper tension* between Man and his historical and social context, and to recognise this tension means refusing the errors that either cannot recognise these tensions, such as supernaturalism or militant secularism which each in their own manner seek to liquidate. The philosophical anthropology of nationalism then will consist of disallowing any metaphysical presuppositions that in terms of the natural-social-historical realm effectively destroys this tension by claiming to know in an a priori manner the potentialities and intelligibilities possible for 'secondary natures,' such as typically found in 'pure reason' positions (naturalism and supernaturalism) that claim to already know the nature and fate of contingent secondary natures.

Attending the local history group for over two years provided a privileged insight into an important point in time among a particular generation, and it is to the history group that I owe much of my grasp of the historical context of Cardenden; of the *something* that Cardenden was, and that afforded me an insight into the rich texture of local life that Cardenden once had for its residents. Perhaps it was meditating upon the distinctive 'density' of the older generation that helped me to identify the 'dense' tasks faced by a younger generation. Rapid social change produces a sharp awareness of separation or distance from the past among those who have lived through such change, and such a process is behind the opening words of the first Local History Group booklet: "Now, more than ever before, people are becoming aware of their heritage, especially those who have emigrated. Many did not realise they had a heritage until they had left the home shores behind them" (Local History Group vol. 1, np). Whether leaving native shores or coalmines and the experience of locality as 'occupational community' behind, the sharp sense of distance or separation as a result of deindustrialization has produced a powerful incentive among locals for discovering they have a history and a heritage, and in this regard I often noted the members' ability to frame the present as 'merely current' through the sheer longevity of their presence to Cardenden by evoking their early lives. As Ball (in Shields 1999, p. 78) has it: "A critique of the everyday can be generated only by a kind of alienation effect, insofar as it is put into contact with its own radical other, such as an eradicated past."

Reflecting upon the history group members, I propose that such is the isomorphism between mental structure and social structure that a strong identification with a passed conjunction of locality and self-identity means the members know Cardenden as they know or imagine themselves, and organise time and locality as they organise their self-knowledge: like the village they have had their youth and maturity when the village was still a substantive industrial coalmining 'something,' and they took their identities from this industrial period of the village, so that now in their dotage the post-industrial present of the village is marginal to their identity. Finally, as a direct result of political and cultural change from the nineteen-eighties, their identity has become petrified, resulting in the absence of categories to construct an engagement with the present political events so that their identity and experience of locality is simultaneously a paradigm and a prison because the categories which history gave them by which to have meaningful identities, a subsequent history has taken away and made obsolete.

Looking at the old photographs from past local events hanging on the walls in Bowhill Centre such as an annual dance or any communal celebration, the once ubiquitous Union flag bunting has long gone, and in proportion to the disappearance of the acceptability of the Union flag the Saltire has grown in popularity as a decorative feature to any social or civic occasion. The '45 generation's Cardenden and Britain have been 'retired' by history and so they experience the present not as the unfolding or development of their identity but as its rejection or repudiation, because according to their generational identity *1 July 1999, far less 18 September 2014, was never supposed to happen,* and so they constitute themselves as a local history group in their retirement and cast a 'backward glance' at a 'heritage' that is gone. What is gone is not simply locality as occupational community but their imagining of Scotland and their lifelong and committed participation in Britain, and it is because of this resilient British identity that among older informants there is both a hostility to the new Scottish parliament and independence, as well as a lament regarding the 'educational deficit' they experienced. This de-alignment of class and nation and their quietist acceptance of the disappearance of Scotland at the political level even when free of a prior economic necessity to which this generation learned to appeal in order to justify its acceptance of domination, means they only take the first steps in the project of reflexive self-consciousness, as even in retirement when financially comfortable a 'discourse of poverty' is mobilised to justify their inability to imagine a post-materialist reflexive look over history or the future.

In this regard the lucidity of Peter referred to previously highlights the defining tasks and the defining differences between the '45 and '79 generations. However, given the 'alienating' educational system informants of both generations allude to as a matter of course, popular or non-consecrated imaginings that break with dominant assumptions can only be successful 'against all the odds,' yet Peter illustrates this conscious break from modernist symbolic domination is happening. We may say the working class's acceptation of modernism was always the result of their lack of symbolic capital, and their long immersion in an imagining of 'being in history' that was divested of some of the primary colours of human being (Douglas and Ney 1997), so that even among the '45 generation their modernism was a more or less enforced and involuntary affair exacted in conditions of material and symbolic scarcity. The '45 generation's *fides implicita* in their unionist British paradigm has come to an end in their children and in articulating the 'present as history,' the task of constituting and understanding this intergenerational change is fundamental. Because of their generation-specific structuration the history group members pursue their caesura and are complacent in this. Because of the release of history and the return of the repressed, one can describe them as the last unionist and modernist generation and describe their meetings as taking place in the shadow of the Minervan owl of nationalism which they dismiss and which dismisses them, even as it accords them their final historical significance.

As of April 2001 the afternoon history group had effectively ended due to "a lack of numbers" and because people were getting too old and were not being replaced. Only the evening group survives, although without a tutor since April 2001. I last visited the group in June 2011 at which time the only surviving member of the group from the time of my doctoral research was John. The '45 generation stand as a permanent critique of any future naturalisation of independence and it is important to state 'for the record' the caesura that 1 July 1999 was in the consciousness of the local history group members as they are the end product of ten generations of a depoliticised national identity that will never be repeated as of 1 July 1999.

On this day, after three centuries of the modernist experiment of Britain *the medieval kingdom of Scotland* proved too strong to suppress itself any longer, and while the desire for Scottish independence and the restoration of its parliament is an old affair, what is new is not so much the politicisation of the nation but the social class that has politicised the nation. If eighteenth-century middle-class Scots went along with being North Britons, it was the nineteenth-century rise of the working class that ensured this identity was only a stop-gap or flag of convenience that came to an end with the advent of literacy and affluence. The victory of a late-medieval or early-modern template has had to wait for affluent conditions to liberate the working class and to allow them to flex their 'being in history' and overcome the modernist and British mind-set *among themselves*. In this process, the 'event' of 1979-1997 was crucial and a more detailed examination of this pivotal period and its aftermath is the subject of the next chapter which argues the unfinished project of a free Scottish modernity is the driving force of contemporary Scottish politics and history.

# 5

# A Scottish Modernity

The Scottish Parliament, which adjourned on March 25,
1707, is hereby reconvened.

Winnie Ewing SNP MSP
12 May 1999

## Ironmill Bay, 1 July 1999

The morning of 1 July 1999 began as usual with the few miles
drive to Kirkcaldy for the eight o'clock team brief at Pathhead
wastewater treatment works. Our orders for the day from our
superintendent (Ivor Cox) was to renew the worn scrapers in two
final settlement tanks in Ironmill Bay treatment works some
fifteen miles along the Fife coast beside the Firth of Forth estuary.
At the team brief we were advised we would have to clean the
bell-mouth in each of the two tanks as there had been problems
with poor-quality water going over the weir and into the river
Forth, making East of Scotland Water authority liable to what is
termed an 'instant fail' and a fine of five thousand pounds; an
amount which increased substantially with every subsequent fail.
At this time I was working with Paul Diamond and Adam Sharp
in the 'pool squad', which was a two or three-man team assigned
those longer repair and maintenance jobs the choke squads or
those men with a regular route did not have time to do.

When we arrived at Ironmill Bay some half an hour or so later,
we unpacked our waterproofs, tools, ropes and the cutting
equipment we would need before we would stop for our nine
o'clock tea break. As we were readying our gear we were joined by

383

Bill Allan who was responsible for the day to day running of the plant, and Paul quizzed him about the details of the inner diffusion drum and the valves which controlled the inflow to the two tanks we were to work in, while Adam and myself began measuring out the cuts needed for the dozen or so replacement scrapers for each tank before heading to the van for our cup of tea while Paul, once satisfied with the layout of the plant, joined myself and Adam and Bill headed off to resume his morning duties.

After our break we got to work. While both tanks had been emptied the day before and the sunshine had dried the walls and floors, Paul gave each immobilised rotating arm a high-pressure blast of water to remove the remaining in-grained scum, before we began handling them and removing the worn scrapers. As each of the scrapers was individually fixed to the arm, I began removing each of the scrapers with a spanner so that Adam could have room to take measurements and begin cutting the new replacement scrapers from the one-inch thick sheets of hard blue plastic to size. Meanwhile, Paul busied himself cleaning each of the two bellmouths at the centre of each tank and clearing the debris that had become stuck thanks to having fallen into the tank over the years.

As we each settled to our tasks we soon worked up a sweat as a result of the heat and no breeze reaching to the bottom of the tanks. It was a beautiful summer day with a clear blue sky and we were happy to be working outside in the sunshine. Twelve o'clock came round quickly and we began thinking about finishing the particular tasks we were doing before getting cleaned up and taking our dinner break. As we downed tools I walked off to find Bill to ask where I could wash before eating, and returning ten minutes later, Paul and Adam were already eating their pieces and drinking their tea in the van. As I went to the open side-door of the van and reached in and put my bag onto the back seat, Adam put the radio on and we listened to a live broadcast covering the State opening of the new Holyrood parliament in Edinburgh, and the excited radio presenter telling his listeners that the Royal Air Force Red Arrows display team and the Concorde aeroplane were about to fly over Edinburgh, and was encouraging listeners to look skywards to see the fly-by.

I ran and climbed onto a bridge that stretched across one of the tanks to take in the view over the Firth of Forth and the road and rail bridges, and looked up and saw Concorde. I suddenly felt connected to the gathering across the water in Edinburgh to mark the opening of the parliament and the beginning of a new constitutional era. After a minute or so I returned to the van, and we listened as the radio presenter described the details of the day, such as the parade of the one hundred and twenty nine politicians of the Holyrood parliament and their families processing up the Royal Mile, accompanied by school children from every constituency in the land. Paul informed us that Geordie Malcolm from Leven was the only East of Scotland Water employee he knew of who was in Edinburgh to be part of this historic day. [106]

As a result of 1 July 1999 Scotland was rescued from the no-man's land in which it had languished for nearly three centuries, and this day saw the resurrection of Scotland from its political suicide after two hundred and ninety-two years of liberal modernism which fancied that history was on its side and which had confidently left behind the younger 'medieval' solution to the question of the nation's being-in-the-world where the nation was sovereign, in favour of the modernist *pax Brittanica* and its pseudo-modernisation of human *dasein* as *homo economicus*. Thanks to 1 July 1999, then, Scotland was not simply turning a page in its history or turning back a page or two so much as tearing out several chapters of its story as long errors. Prior to this day Scotland had long ceased to exist as a political reality so that the idea of 'Scottish society,' for example, far less its reality, had been problematic as Scotland had been confined to a kind of half-life or merely intentional existence. Thanks to 1 July 1999, however, Scotland not only became real again but became the heart and organising principle of political life and the basis for the exercise of power as a result of a decisive defeat for the modernist imagination's organisation of geo-political space, territory, and history. What had been largely intentional became real, public and

---

[106] Tragically, Paul died suddenly at the age of 47 on 26 June 2010.

sovereign, and in the scramble among headline writers to express 'the present as history' *The Herald* newspaper (7th May 1999) captured the power of nationalism to inaugurate a new public realm and constitutional era: "Died 1707 ... Born 1999."

1 July 1999 was both an historic day and just another work-day, and the relationship between mundane class realities and 'historic days' such as 1 July 1999 was a central research interest in light of research findings that has found that, "Support for a Scottish parliament has been higher in working-class than in middle-class groups in every survey that has ever asked the question" (Brown et al. 1996, p. 153). However, while it seemed clear that some kind of relationship existed between class and nationalism, how national identity existed and was experienced, imagined and practiced outwith politics and 'special' contexts such as elections was not so clear. To explore this question, then, I take as a starting point a scene from fieldwork four months after the creation of the new parliament, a game of football played on 13 November 1999 between Scotland and England to decide which of the two teams would qualify for the Euro 2000 finals.

## 5.1 Integralism: Nature, Nurture & Nation

An hour before the start of the game I made the short walk to the Railway Tavern pub on Cardenden Road on what was a warm and sunny day. As I entered the pub I stood in the doorway to the lounge bar, allowing my eyes time to adjust to the dark smoke-filled interior as the curtains had been drawn to block out direct sunlight. I was immediately struck by a noisy and colourful and crowded scene: national regalia and bunting were displayed everywhere; flags, saltires and lion rampants hung on walls and the ceiling, with faces painted white and blue and most of the crowd with football scarves draped over their necks and wearing hats and replica football shirts. Along with this visual spectacle came a constant noise from the large group of local men (and a few women) crowded inside. The noise came from an incessant exchange of banter and anecdotes going on; shouted greetings and conversations, orders for rounds of drinks being arranged in loud voices and a relentless cacophony of conversations and news, stories and anecdotes and 'one-liners' being told and enjoyed by anyone within earshot.

After a few moments I was able to make out my hosts sitting along the wall on the right-hand side who motioned to me to join them, and as I squeezed into the gap opened for me Dauve asked what I wanted to drink, and then shouted to one of our company being served at the small lounge bar halfway along the left-hand side: 'Billy! Two mair pints!' while pointing at me in explanation. Perhaps to anticipate my asking why he ordered more than I asked for, Dauve explained: "Ye need tae order two roonds at wance. It's f***in mental gettin a roond in." Buying multiple rounds of drinks seemed to be the done thing to avoid having to waste time queuing at the bar as most of the small tables were rapidly, if not already, full of pints of beer and lager and spirits, thanks to the constant stream of individuals carrying trays of drinks and picking their way carefully to and from the bar to their table. On the far wall was what was soon to be the centre of everyone's attention – a 'giant screen' television on which football pundits were airing their views. Amid the noise and movement, an individual would suddenly stand up and begin to sing. Being instantly recognised, the song would be taken up by one and all and anecdotes being told were put on hold mid-sentence as the chant was taken up until it ended and the anecdote could be resumed.

After saluting everyone in the company I listened to Vickie, a thirty-five year old mother-of-three describing how earlier in the day she had telephoned her English brother-in-law and played the national anthem of Scotland down the telephone. After pulling this 'stunt,' she told us her brother-in-law had matter-of-factly asked if Vickie wanted to speak with her sister, before she concluded: "He never even mentioned it! Imagine daen that o'er the phone and he never even mentioned it. Of course, he's English." Next, I chatted with Drew, a joiner with Fife Council, who was speculating as to the probable identity of a local who had appeared in one of Ian Rankin's novels. Drew informed me the fictional character had sang REM's song *Losing My Religion* in the same lounge in which we were sitting, and he felt confident the individual Rankin was referring to had to be Stevie King. Next, Drew absent-mindedly remarked to the company: "I see Leena Zavaroni left millions when she died there." Thinking the conversation had taken a serious tone I asked: "Is that right? I never heard that." This allowed Drew to deliver his punchline: "Aye, apparently she left a few million in dinner vouchers." [107]

As the focus of the day was the long durée contest between Scotland and the 'auld enemy' (England) it was only a matter of time before the conversation turned to politics and so, after Drew came Dave, a local father of two in his mid-thirties who informed the company he had been working in England the previous week and, affecting an upper-class English accent for the company, informed us how he had "been gettin it all week...Oh the Jocks this and the Jocks that."[108] Dave then described to the company how he had established common Labour-voting ground with his English colleagues as a means of minimising the difference of national identity in the run-up to the play-off game between the two countries, before adding: "Aye, we'll see how they f****n like it when we a' vote SNP." Dave's final comment sparked more comments from the company which were brought to a conclusion by a thirty-six-year-old warehouse worker: "The English are no happy unless they're oppressin somebody"– a comment said without fear of contradiction and which signalled a shared horizon of meaning which I found operative in other contexts, such as the workplace where I was able to note many casual and incidental incidents such as the following where *East of Scotland Water* workers began talking about the construction of a new wastewater treatment plant in Leven which was a hundred yards or so from where one of the men lived.

**Gary:** Aye ye'll be getting disturbed wi a' the noise.
**Dauve:** Ye'll get a reduction in yer poll tax.

---

[107] The joke referred to a once-popular singer who suffered from anorexia nervosa and had died the previous month.
[108] The expression 'Jock' is a colloquial term for a Scotsman.

**Ivor:** Ah'll be oot there wi ma binoculars seein what's goin oan.

**Rory:** Jist like that English c**t in Kinghorn. Always phonin tae say 'Ye can smell it fae here.'

**Dauve:** Jist in the place. Jist in the toon an they're takin it o'er.

**Ivor:** Aye, ye get that.

As the two football teams prepared to walk onto the pitch all attention was directed to the television screen and events being transmitted live from Hampden Park in Glasgow, and with the volume of the television now tuned up so everyone could hear, an already excited crowd was fed fresh stimulus for shouted comment and adrenalinised analysis, and an already excited atmosphere began to reach fever pitch, so that when the Scottish national anthem was being sung by the players and spectators in Glasgow it was being sung 'to the rafters' by everyone in *The Tavern* in Cardenden.[109]

At half-time the company discussed who was playing well and reviewed the highlights of the game with each one giving their opinion. Reflecting on the discussion it is clear that one of the reasons that football is so popular is because it is a rare example of a 'meritocracy in action' in the sense that it is a competitive social activity whose outcome is not 'socially determined.' Each team faces the same set of material or empirical conditions and their shared task is to co-operate with their team mates to change that empirical reality to their advantage, and engineer a situation that is to their advantage. The idea then is that football is a rare example of an individual and a group's agency being unhindered by inherited social disadvantage because the starting point and rules of the game are the same for everyone, which is why football

---

[109] The national anthem of England is the British national anthem *God Save the Queen* because Britain and England are largely synonymous, and when the British/English naional anthem was being booed by the Scots in Glasgow it was being booed by everyone in *The Tavern*. For the non-Scottish observer then there is the strange scene of people booing their own national anthem.

was once famously described by the coalminer turned footballer and manager Bill Shankley (1913-1981) as the only practical example of socialism.

A more concrete source of football's popularity is enjoyment at the skill on display and enjoying how a player's consciousness and practice displays an awareness that is more complex than the binary opposites of *absence* and *presence* insofar as his awareness and practiced are characterised by what might be as much as by what is and what is not; by the *possibilities* in the present that his footballing skill might provoke or 'make real.' The creative footballer's perception and practice, then, is always dominated by being able to see before his opponent something that is not yet empirically given, by seeing what can possibly happen, so that the creative and 'dangerous' football player is the one who shows the audience who stare blankly at a particular situation something emerge 'from nothing' before their eyes thanks to the action of the player on the ball. The gifted footballer is simultaneously immersed in empirical reality yet transcends or frees himself and his team and the spectators from the merely real or empirically given.

Such was an enjoyable afternoon that was full of humour, verbal improvisation, bawdy sensualism and relentless improvised ad libs performed *ad libitum*. If I had hoped to observe a performance of 'national identity' as habitus I was not disappointed, as the day acted as a shibboleth of identity and belonging. What I found remarkable was the relentless energy and emotion; the at-hand availability and intensity of emotions which seemed to involve the 'total mobilisation' of *dasein* and *mitsein* in order to produce a total immersion in each moment of the game. From the gestures and language and emotion it was plain locals 'are Scottish' in an embodied manner, and they relished these occasions as opportunities for the practice of *communitas* and locality.

In this regard an example of a practice of *dasein* 'at-play' is the blatant constructions of 'difference' via deliberately hapless reifications and essentialisations of particular locals and localities within the village, so that at such gatherings locals regularly excoriate those from Dundonald as "mountain men" (because it is held to sit highest in the village) who are made the subject of songs titled *Feed Dundonald* sung to the tune of the Band Aid charity song *Feed the World*, with more cultural bricolage seen in adapting Elvis Presley's song *Heartbreak Hotel* to the characters and events in the local Central Hotel pub, and the alcohol-fuelled one-liners such as one wit when in The Caspian take away (re-christened *The Taliban* by locals) who, after quietly waiting his turn to be asked his order by the immigrant employee, asks for "a single hard on and a bottle e chips, please" so that he and the other queuing locals can enjoy the employee's confusion and the outbreak of hilarity.

As a first step in an analysis of the day's events then, if we take the view that "[t]he nation is primarily a psychological or symbolic concept; in Mackenzie's words 'is not merely a statement of fact; it is a state of feeling" (cited in McCrone 1992, p. 204), it seems that uncovering the heart or the social ontology of 'working-class nationalism' requires answering the question as to *what are the social conditions of this passion, or what is the idiom or the means of acquisition of this passion?* In answering this question I begin by observing that locals constitute and perform their locality and nationality through the idioms of kinship, residency and, importantly for working-class men, "life as a physical existence" (Connerton 1989, p. 101) i.e. through the idiom of manual work and propose that this nationalised *dasein* is a performance of and extension of the 'condition of reduction' discussed in Chapter 2 or 'embodied social being,' as the 'structure of feeling' present on this particular day is something I have witnessed many times before among manual workers. While the nation is being imagined and constructed, membership of the national group is a matter of feeling via a class-based habitus and performing in all of their sensual, visceral and bawdy idiom, practices of identification.

Throughout the afternoon a repertoire of non-verbal embodied gestures and paralinguistic communication and expression was on display, along with the use of the vernacular Scots which made for a 'community of embodiment' characterised by all manner of spontaneity and exuberance, including one individual jumping onto a table and exhibiting his 'manhood' all the better to perform his shouted insult at a televised 'other' on a screen.

If there was a kind of spectacle that football is able to put on view, there was also an obvious libidinal and stylised aspect to much of their behaviour so that the afternoon was a cathartic experience due to the release of libidinal energies, and there seemed to be what one might describe as the alignment or triangulation of id, identity and ideology as behaviours are drawn from *the embodied integration* of being-social and being-historical and being-national which meant they could have a fuller experience of their human being. On this day, throughout the nation the same processes whereby an integration of id, identity and ideology was effected, meant each local congregation was reproducing and celebrating their own locality and their own integration with the nation and in light of such empirical data, what is required of social theory is an emphasis upon the body as a locus of meaning, and in this regard Connerton's view on how bodily practices are able to bear meaning is useful:

> [I]ncorporating practices depend for their particular mnemonic effect on two distinctive features: their mode of existence and their *mode of acquisition*. They do not exist 'objectively', independently of their being performed. And they are acquired in such a way as not to require explicit reflection on their performance (1989, p. 102).

Similarly, reviewing the history of hermeneutics within the social sciences Connerton (1989, p. 101) notes:

> [T]he communication of meaning...could in principle include the body in its domain but did so in practice only peripherally. The object-domain of hermeneutics was defined in terms of what was taken to be the distinctive feature of the human species, first consciousness and later language. When the defining feature was taken to be consciousness... the life of human beings, as a historical life, is understood as a life reported on and narrated, *not life as a physical existence* [italics mine]. When the defining feature of the human species was seen as language...bodily practices are acknowledged, but in an etherealised form.

Much like Chatterjee's (1993) conception of the sourcing of (Indian) nationalism within a particular human interiority i.e. the (Indian) 'self' which was the one *hinterland* the colonising British were unable to penetrate, and so could become a resource the nationalist could mobilise as an uncontaminated source of Indianness, so in my identifying the social ontology of Scottish working-class nationalism in the relationship between the being brought about by labour and a subsequent mobilisation of this *dasein* and *mitsein* in the direction of political nationalism, I propose the following dialectical position: starting by explicitly denying the existence of a subject or subjectivity free from capitalist penetration, I deny a Scottish self or subjectivity untouched by capitalist relations having any place in any conceptualisation of locals because they are thoroughly penetrated by capitalist relations and the cash economy, so there is no Scottish subjectivity 'out of history' (Craig 1996) which nationalism can mobilise or which the ethnographer can imagine in order to arrive at a 'native point of view' or non-social sourcing of nationalism. However, precisely because of this deep historicisation of *dasein*, there does emerge over time a secondary nature or working-class 'hinterland' sourced in the life of labour that does indeed become an inaccessible sourcing of a Scottish nationalism that is not the civic nationalism of the SNP leadership and which is not sourced in bourgeois fictions such as civic society.

By this 'secondary hinterland' I mean to indicate an element of working-class *dasein* that is not national or local or provincial and yet very much included in any real instance of this 'secondary hinterland' is belonging to real geographical locations; that integrated to working-class *dasein* is 'being local' which is brought about by belonging over generations to localities such as Lochgelly, Kinglassie, Cowdenbeath, Ballingry, Lochore and Kelty etcetera and which has its own density. I propose, then, that working-class nationalism be viewed as a form of embodied meaning whose medium of acquisition is that of manual labour so that the mobilisation of national identity is the politicisation of a particular kind of human being, a performance of embodied (social) being, so that informants perform their being national via their embodiment, and their visceral nationality is sourced in their embodied class habitus which is itself emergent from a particular physical existence and its ability to produce a likeness of itself in the being and the performance of being national.

Because the day allowed an intense performance of solidarity, sociality and locality, *The Tavern* was a space where individuals can be themselves and a place where their Scots language and their gestures and mannerisms are not out of place, so that the day revealed what might be termed the deep 'hinterland' of working-class *dasein*. Such set-piece occasions are enjoyable because they are occasions of integral expression and affirmation which informants routinely advise is denied them in the post-trade union workplace and in post-Thatcherite New Labour politics and the middle class dominated public sphere. If this interpretation of the structuration of emotion on display is not entirely incorrect, the psychological work that visceral nationality accomplishes is the pleasure of being integral, and the catharsis effected by being national and its signature embodied practices is to restore the imagined and experienced caesura between self and stratified society, to heal or restore the imagined and experienced caesura between the nation-state and subjectivity when mobilised and deployed as a politics.

In terms of locating the social foundation of working-class nationalism, then, I do not locate it in any ideological or doctrinal proposition of reason or knowledge, nor in any extrinsic event or 'trigger' but in something more real and primitive and natural i.e. in the social ontology that emerges from the life of labour. Men draw upon their lives as physical existence for their performance or enactment of being Scottish, and so an object of research is to understand how the 'condition of reduction' is able to act as a template that is able to inform the constitution and expression of belonging and identification with the nation, and how this works *in practice*. Kellas (in Harvie 1998, p. 19) has observed that "working-class nationalism is generally related to culture and football," and in the pre-devolution era before 1999 this idea was repeated in the romantic notion that the massed football supporters at the national football stadium of Hampden Park acted as a kind of surrogate national assembly. While I am sympathetic to dismissing such notions out of hand, it does usefully recognise the idea that national identity *must be a matter of performance and must be practiced*.

In localities across Scotland and among men in particular, the prevalence of football within male society and sociality means it often mediates local and national identity. Young boys' experience of belonging to a particular sub-locality within Cardenden, for example, is 'performed' via annual aestival football tournaments such as the Johnny Thomson tournament held every September for youngsters from each area of the village, so that when performing national identity or performing their belonging to locality as men, *from a socio-ontological point of view* they are not doing anything different so that local, provincial and national identities always already feel part of or integrated with the 'worked self.

The key to understanding how locals *are* their national identity, then, is understanding the socialised body as the medium through which all these identities must pass if they are to appear at all within the working-class psyche and its field of perception, so that to appear at all is to already have a certain ontological kinship with other phenomena which appear and which are similarly constituted and expressed. Just as the 'worked self' is able to inform non-working life, so 'the nation' has a promiscuous ability to be itself in other realities, and this is what makes it possible for the working-class habitus to make connections between what, at least formally, are separate and autonomous realities i.e. the objective and extrinsic nation and the workers' sense of self, and what subsequently makes it possible to politicise this 'being national' and speak of a *working-class* nationalism. The net result then is the conclusion that the being of 'being working class' mediates the being of 'being Scottish' insofar as the former involves an affective matrix which reads the current moment and the long durée; life as physical existence becomes habitus and a template which is taken up by freedom and choice and reason and the wider culture to inform intentional life and thereby model the experiencing and the meaning of 'being national,' and provide a 'libidinal vocabulary' to express the nation.

The 'unionist' and the 'nationalist,' then, share the same *dasein* with the only difference that the unionist lives through 1979-1997 and 2010-2015 and still accepts Scotland's union with England, while the nationalist lives through 1979-1997 and 2010-2015 but applies his established class-based structure of perception to the nation and to his reading of politics and history, and politicises history in favour of independence. Because the class condition mediates national identity, locals are able to change their politics or party allegiance from the unionist Labour Party to the nationalist SNP *without* this requiring any great transformation of their being or consciousness i.e. without any great renovation of their already in-place 'structures of meaning' because nothing about *dasein* has to change.

From the frenetic scenes and behaviour seen on that afternoon in the Tavern, it is plain locals on such occasions come alive to a preferred but normally unavailable experience of themselves; as if in a televised confrontation with some 'other' what is required and what becomes possible is their favoured subjectivity and favoured experience of locality, so that such occasions highlight the decentred nature of identity, and such conspicuous displays of identity were attractive and enjoyable because, unlike the *Fun Day* discussed in Chapter 1, they provided locals with the opportunity to celebrate their integral selves; their gendered, localised, classed, and embodied nationalised selves. In this regard the importance of locality comes into its own as it is the possession of a locality that means by definition one is able to practice belonging as one's locality is both a passport to belonging to the nation and the certificate that legitimises one's sharing in the national identity. The notion that the nation "must be imagined by its members - in order to exist" (Eriksen in Olwig & Hastrup 1997, p. 106) is well-established, but such localised events not only set the stage for an imaginative coming together of the nation but *enact* and express a *dasein* and *mitsein* that is already constituted and integrated with the nation, so that locality is always also nationality, just as *dasein* is always already *mitsein*.

If as a general principle anyone's sense of belonging to his or her particular natal place is not something 'in itself' but is *inter-localitively* constituted, this being-in-space is not only a means of learning how to practice belonging to locality but is a medium through which an intersubjectively constituted imagining of the nation occurs, such as when the fan travels to his team's away fixtures every season in the company of other fans. As a general position we can also say that the class condition 'makes sense of' or mediates being national while being careful to say class *does not constitute* the nation or national identity *ex nihilo*. If locals are members of a social class they are also members of a people and the Scottish nation, and it is the ability of each identity to be a cipher for each other that means the unsubstantial or under-determined nation is made substantial and is intersubjectively 'quickened' by a thousand other identities, and this allows the nation to be promiscuously real and 'at home' in the most diverse circumstances.

While the nation pre-dates the rise of class society, the identity and reality of being working class mediates the identity of 'being Scottish' or gives it its salt, as being working class involves an affective structure which 'flavours' both the current moment and the historic long durée; alters the flavour of being and experiencing 'being national' as well as providing a libidinal or kinaesthetic 'vocabulary' to express this reality and identity during set-piece occasions. What gives nationalism its existential purchase upon members of the nation then is not the doctrine that the nation and the state shall be congruent, as this useful distillation of what nationalism 'believes' is not real enough nor does it possess the power to structure subjectivity or produce a 'structure of feeling' via the alignment or triangulation of nature, nurture and nation. Rather, the ability of a class-based habitus to make the nation into a cipher for its energies and insights and grievances is the key to its reality.

In coming to understand the politicisation of fully-contextualised *dasein* what must be avoided is any suggestion that for this politicisation to happen there is required a particular point of view on a particular issue in order to perform or enact nationality. What is to be avoided is any suggestion that locals require a consciousness of Scottish history, for example, in order to 'trigger' their national identity or to construct their visceral nationality by, as such a historical consciousness is not the 'bloodless' basis for this politicisation of national identity as in this cerebral case 'being national' would never amount to much among the working class, as the world of meaning that the student of history inhabits is not the idiom of mediation of national identity for the average working-class person.

When asking from whence comes the force of national identity if not from reason, knowledge or extrinsic events such as something as episodic as a football match, I propose the substantiality and vitality of nationalism emerges from the strength and vitality of *social ontology*, with the important qualification that if the nation can be a cipher for class-based realities, the symbolic quality of the nation does not mean it is a *tabula rasa* or blank page upon which each class and each man can write or project their private fantasies. It is clear that the football match both brought about the full subjectivity of locals and allowed for the expression of an already constituted *dasein* and *mitsein* and allowed their total immersion in the moment *on the basis of their ownmost dasein*, so that it was not simply that the locals in the Tavern identify themselves with their team's cause but that this practice of 'identifying-with' is instantly available to them as part of their emotional habitus, so that their observation of the events unfolding on the pitch was anything but passive as it was an activity based upon an already constituted immediacy reacting to a series of events on a football field. Once we assume the quality of immediacy of their relentless identifications with each kick of the ball is the acting out of an already learned immediacy and an already learned responding to the moment, it is a small step to conclude this responding draws upon the prior disciplining and training of affectivity and the disciplining of attention to the moment that is learned outwith such set-piece occasions in their mundane lives, such as in the workplace for example.

Much of my argument concerning the ontology of historicity and what might be termed the 'sociality' of nationality is concerned to emphasise the structural 'objectivity' of the nation and the structural objectivity of its history that cannot be imagined or manipulated at will. The nation is real because it is able to satisfy a desire for self-recognition that is continually being reproduced in the daily reproduction of locals' embodied habitus, which is characterised by the ability to produce a 'likeness of itself' and a connection to the nation. This inter-ciphering between the class-based social ontology that comes about via labouring, for example, and national identity is what makes a *working-class* nationalism possible and pleasurable. If we take the prescient remark of Herzfeld (1997, p. 19) that: "In constructing ideologies of national identity, it is the task of nationalist movements to present and appeal to...a culturally and politically powerful model of the self," we can say that to the extent that any form of nationalism (such as the respectable civic nationalism of the SNP) *that does not mimic or make appeal to this class mediation is fated to be unsuccessful among the working class.*

In this conception of the phenomenological ground of (working class) nationalism it is a politicised social ontology that cannot be easily recognised, far less mobilised and manipulated by liberal elites for their political ends. Because of its grounding upon an existence-led self that is sourced in the physical life of manual labour and the iso-morphisms it constitutes in the psyche of this subordinate class, this manual sourcing of nationalism means it may be described as a 'politics of being' involving a highly aligned and structured ontology characterised by a decentred openness to time, history, locality, society and physical work which mobilises to have Nation and State congruent, but without any need to resort either to 'blood and soil' ideology or to bourgeois forms such as the 'civic nationalism' of the SNP leadership.

This existence-led decentred *dasein* also means national identity is never a private possession to be enjoyed 'outside of history' or cultivated at one's leisure. The events of 1979-1997 and 2010-2015, then, do not allow for a contemplative or unhurried private relation to Scottish national identity because during these periods the Scots are more or less forced to choose whether Britain or Scotland is to be the organising category of their history, politics, culture and imagination. It was not any prolonged intellectual contemplation of the merits and drawbacks of political union with another nation that is responsible for Scottish nationalism, then, but the exasperating and 'never-ending' fact that Scots vote one way and the English vote another way, so that the defining experience of politics for those generations born since nineteen-sixty and who came to political and historical consciousness during and after the nineteen-eighties was that politics was mediated through two nations and two electorates fundamentally at odds with each other. In contrast to unionist claims about Scotland and England being 'better together,' the lived experience of political union has been that it is not fit for purpose from the point of view of Scottish democracy. It was the *difference* of political ideology, then, that made the relation of political union problematic during the years 1979-1997 and again during 2010-2015, a political or ideological *difference* that was more or less based upon class-based differences in political choices made at the ballot box and in this concrete context, to make politics meaningful again has meant firstly imagining and then re-constituting the political playing field upon a purely Scottish basis. In these circumstances, then, the nation became a class issue and so Scottish nationalism became a politics of class and Scottish nationalism became the pursuit of a class-based 'politics of being' all the way to an independent Scotland should the Scots vote 'yes' on 18 September 2014.

If this is the social and ontological and historical grounding of the working class's desiring and achieving political independence, the expression 'politics of being' adverts to the fact that much more is involved than simply a new constitutional arrangement insofar as the expression of history, locality and nationality are being imagined and practiced free from the old modernist 'inferiorism' (Beveridge and Turnbull 1989) and tired industrial narratives; that a younger 'medieval' patrimony is being mobilised to the horror of unionist modernists for whom this 'return of the repressed' signals the end of the hegemony of a cosmopolitan liberal elite over the imagining of the nation, so that the liberal cosmopolitan elite sense in this 'fundamentalist' integralist politics of class and nation a threat to their privileges and the end of their long 'suppression of being.'

## 5.2 Interpretive Sociology, Interpreting Scotland

On the cusp of 18th September 2014 there can be no doubt that the task of *interpreting Scotland* is being undertaken by unprecedented numbers, and on an unprecedented scale across every media format across the length and breadth of Scotland and further afield. As a preface, then, to interpreting my interview data it may be helpful to recap some earlier observations and re-state the hermeneutic or the 'rules of interpretation' that I follow. As a generalisation, the standpoint I take is generally known as *interpretive sociology* or a position that is often described as a post-objectivist or qualitative way of doing sociology. The basic principle of interpretivism is that in trying to understand the meaning of something, it is the particular social context of a text or discourse or a practice or an event that settles the question of its meaning i.e. not only does context decide meaning but decides the range of *competent interpretations* that can be reasonably considered.

In any concrete situation, then, social actors bring to their social interaction *schemes of perception* that are used to read or interpret a situation or behaviour, and the task of the interpretive sociologist is to discover what schemes of interpretation 'natives' bring to bear on situations. For example, then, if we think back to the exchange between sewer men cited in the previous section, an Englishman who might easily and reasonably be judged or interpreted as doing a good deed on behalf of his neighbours by telephoning in order to report foul smells from a wastewater treatment plant in the hope that something be done, we see that he is instead interpreted *according to an established code that is imposed upon his behaviour*; that it is not as a result of his actions that he becomes interpreted as a 'white colonist' (Jedrej and Nuttall 1996) but rather it is his English accent or being English that triggers his behaviours becoming interpreted by a latent structure of perception that is operative among the workers i.e. their Scottish nationality and its historicity, and so the English man as he is 'in himself,' and other perfectly reasonable interpretations of his actions disappear, and instead are effortlessly or 'without thinking' made to appear in accordance with an already established interpretive frame, where they become another instance in a long series of instances of an imagined historic English 'essence' with a track record of colonisation of foreign lands and usurpation of natives and their localities.

Another example of how different schemes of perception lead to very different interpretations of the same set of empirically given data came towards the end of doctoral fieldwork (Friday 8 December 2000), when myself and my family attended the Christmas pantomime *The Hunchback of Notre Dame* at the Bowhill Centre. The pantomime was an enjoyable family show and played to a packed hall with the pantomime villain being particularly memorable as the children quickly learned to hiss and boo his every entrance and exit. In perfect contrast was the virtuous and poor street-seller Esmeralda whom the villain blackmailed into marrying him, thereby thwarting the happiness of the hero Quasimodo who had fallen in love with the beautiful Esmeralda. The pantomime was an all-ticket event and a great success, and the audience were youngsters of primary school age who participated enthusiastically throughout by singing along with the actors to pop songs that were cleverly inserted into the storyline so that, by the time of the final scene, a hundred or so youngsters were out of their seats dancing and singing at the front of the stage along with the cast to the song *Reach for the Sky* by the pop group S Club Seven.

While aimed at children, however, there was also something for the ethnographer of nationalism out for an evening's entertainment to see; the unconscious performance of history and nationality as the priest character of Notre Dame cathedral was played in a caricatured asexual or effeminate manner, with exaggerated Irish accent and unfailing hysterical mannerisms and opinions. As a concoction of enthusiasm, naivety, stupidity and internalised inferiority, this pantomime character was an instantly recognisable Anglo-Scottish construction of the 'Daft Paddy' for those audience members whose 'scheme of perception' is aware of this trope from the English/Scottish literary tradition.

However, if the role of the fool or court jester was assigned to Ireland, the role of 'family pet' within the British 'family of nations' was played by the only animal character in the cast, a crocodile named Jock (i.e. Jock the Croc), whose role it was to provide comic relief. While the hero, heroine and villain were established as de facto 'English' thanks to their accents, it was some minutes into the pantomime upon realising the actor playing Jock the Croc was playing his part in a Glaswegian accent that I understood the stage was set for a performance of Kravitz's (1997) "subaltern Scot," and Zizek's (2000) reading of the *Jar Jar* character from George Lucas's film *The Phantom Menace* (1999), where the de-humanisation or de-personalisation of a national group is symbolically realised via 'animalisation.' A Christmas pantomime, then, suddenly became an allegory of England and its geo-political relationships with the Celtic fringe (Hechter 1975), with the latter reduced to providing comic relief while the responsibilities for the 'serious' matter of plot and narrative became an exclusively English affair.

Having spoken to the proud creator of the production[110] I have no doubt she would be very offended by what I am sure she would see as my wilful, perverse and incompetent interpretation. Also, when I put my interpretation to my Spanish wife Eva later that evening, it was clear she simply did not see the sense of my interpretation of the show. In defending my interpretation, then, I concede from the outset that it breaks with the author's intentions and the actors' interpretations of their roles, as well as with the audience's interpretation of the pantomime. If my interpretation is 'wilful and incompetent' it is because a scheme of perception I am able to bring to the pantomime places it into a context that the author did not share, and a context that fundamentally changes its meaning. My interpretation or reading of the 'text' is also indifferent to any desire to raise to consciousness that which is unconscious in the author, as I am happy to concede the 'subaltern Celt' motif did not objectively exist in the text, nor does it exist in the consciousness or unconsciousness of the author, actors or audience.

---

[110] Margaret Gary at M & M Theatrical Productions (Ayr).

My hermeneutical procedure, then, is to remove the data from the context of their creator's consciousness and their Christmas consumption, and re-locate it to a context or 'structure of perception' they were never intended for, and this new context is a context for judgment and interpretation outwith the control or ken of the author or audience i.e. the objective social 'realm of meaning' where the interpretation and truth of words and actions are judged in the public sphere where meaning is decided, and it is in relation to this sphere that the work of interpretation is settled, rather than in the privacy of the artistic or aesthetic or festive consciousness and context.

Interpretation, then, can be something of an ethical dilemma for the ethnographer as it can be an 'unjust' and offensive affair that is happy to dismiss the interpretations of an author or social actor, and in the following section I will demonstrate this offensive hermeneutic at work when interpreting some interview data and scenes from fieldwork.

While a unionist hegemony has come to an end in Scotland, 1 July 1999 is not the Independence Day the nationalist seeks and an essentially British 'social mindscape' (Zerubavel 1997) remains pervasive among many. Despite the power of nationalism to renew or make reality, 1 July 1999 also served to highlight the 'business as usual' dispositions of many locals, and provide empirical evidence that would put to rest any suggestion of 1 July 1999 involved the renovation of mental structures or any change in the symbolic order, with only 60% of the Scottish electorate voting in the September 1997 Referendum held to prove the 'settled will' of the people for a Scottish parliament. As an illustration of the confusion as to where national identity lies after 1 July 1999 and how it enters into everyday life, I recall an afternoon spent in The Auld Man's Shelter pub in December 2001 where, as usual on a Sunday at that time, there was a quiz in the early afternoon after the card school finished. On this occasion the card school put a team in for the quiz, and not long into the quiz came the question: "What was the name of the first foreign manager to win the F.A. cup?"[111]

---

[111] The Foootball Association cup is an annual football competition in which every English football league team is entitled to participate.

After a few seconds it was clear that there was some confusion among the teams as to what was meant by the word 'foreign.' The first request for clarification came from a member of the card school who asked: "Does that include Scottish managers?" At this, the compère showed annoyance, and replied by defining foreign as "non-British." After another few seconds, from another table someone asked whether an Irishman was to be considered as being British or a foreigner for the purpose of answering the question. At this, the guidance given was someone from the Republic of Ireland was to be considered a foreigner. This anecdote indicates the break-up of a shared 'realm of meaning' as a result of the ending of the cultural and political hegemony of Britain within the Scottish imagination since 1 July 1999, and this is a development that also means the end of interpretations of Scotland that can pretend to be objective.

My first examples of dialectically opposed interpretations of the same data, as a result of the social actors involved possessing different schemes of perception, come from two English men living in the Bowhill area of the village who illustrate how national identity heavily structures or even 'imprisons' perception and interpretation. As usual, my opening question was to ask each informant their views on the new Scottish parliament:

**Mr Tims:** They're a bunch e bloody hypocrites, that's what they are.
**Me:** What do you mean? Your wife is worried it could become another Northern Ireland in twenty-five years.
**Mr Tims:** Oh Ah've said that all along!
**Me:** Do you think it's divisive this Scottish parliament?
**Mr Tims:** Of course it is! Of course it is! It'll be another Northern Ireland, bound to be! You've only to hear them talking in the parliament, Scottish nationalists talkin, Ah mean they've only one idea! Ah mean they've got peace in Northern Ireland which is a good thing, they've got a sort of peace in Northern Ireland but at what expense? The governments said oh we'll never negotiate with the IRA when they've got guns and now they're invitin them into

parliament; give them an office which again is gonna cost the tax payer millions of pounds over a few years... And what will they do? They'll invite all their pals an sit an discuss it all in our parliament.

**Me:** Where did this parliament come from? Who wanted it and why?

**Mr Tims:** It's these pressure groups, that's why.

**Me:** Do you think it's not so much people that are wanting it but that the political chattering classes for whatever reason...

**Mr Tims:** They're just a talkin shop and it'll just run itself into the ground, of course it will. That's the unfortunate part about it, it's gonnae cost...the cost of building this parliament.

**Me:** You're wife said to me you're an Englishman.

**Mr Tims:** Aye.

**Me:** Do you feel as if because this parliament has been created that somehow it has put you in an uncomfortable position?

**Mr Tims:** No it doesnae, but as I say my family will see it. And Ah mean you only have to go up round about where the SNP are really...shall we say...got the swing, up round the north east coast area, that type e thing, to see all the anti-English slogans that are already there.

**Me:** In the elections to the Scottish parliament did you bother voting?

**Mr Tims:** Oh I voted!

**Me:** Who did you vote for because all of the parties were more or less in favour of the parliament so you'd be stuck wouldn't you?

**Mr Tims:** I was in a way.

**Me:** Who did ye vote for?

**Mr Tims:** The Conservatives.

**Me:** Was that the lesser of the evils?

**Mr Tims:** Of course it was. Of course it was. No doubt at all about that. Ah mean Ah've lived up here now for fifty odd years...Ah've no complaints about the people about here, Ah mean I get on well with them all... and they get on well with me. Ah've no complaints about them. An that's been goin on for fifty odd years.

**Me:** So why do you think it's come about just now? Ah mean is there somethin different from before?

**Mr Tims:** Oh aye, it's come about cause the nationalists have spent a tremendous amount of money. And they've brought in people... the likes of this clown that they've got...

**Me:** Salmond?

**Mr Tims:** No. That actor boy who doesn't live in the country.

**Me:** Sean Connery?

**Mr Tims:** Aye! People of that calibre walkin in. That's why they've gained so much. Ah mean I was a representative for the union, for the management of the coal board. And we used to go to Labour Party conferences and that because the union were part of Labour sort of thing like ye ken.

**Me:** Were you in the coalmines?

**Mr Tims:** Ah started at Comrie and then Ah came here. Ah was a chief engineer at Seafield Colliery in Kirkcaldy until I retired. Bit Ah mean Ah saw what went on at those conferences...An it's even worse now under this Blair because he's dictatin now in the Labour party.

**Me:** Aye he's got them on a tight leash.

**Mr Tims:** Ah'll tell ye somethin. I seen the same thing when I was a youngster. That's how it started in Germany. The very same thing! A wee bit here an a wee bit there. And then they started all these youth things, got the youth on their side. Exactly what Blair's doin. Now that's how it all started in Germany. And ye ken what happened in the end.

Next door to Mr Tims lived another English man in his forties and owner of a small local business whom I asked his views on the new Scots parliament:

**John:** Personally, it doesn't really affect us in any way whatsoever. Having a Scottish parliament is rather like joining a trade union, it's just somebody else to tell us what to do... so basically...I think it really has no effect whatsoever on me personally bit Ah feel for a lot of people yes it could do because it's somebody else to tell them what to do.

**Me:** Why do you think it is we have this parliament now? Is there anything in particular we can point to?

**John:** I think the Scots are a funny race. Very strange race. We'll bleet and bleet and bleet about something, we'll want it and want it and want it and when we've got it we'll totally ignore it.

**Me:** That is a bit of a paradox.

**John:** That's what the Scots are like. You know once they've got something oh that's it we've got it now we can forget about it. Let's face it, I don't think the parliament will be used, respected, referred to, as much as everyone thought it was going to be.

**Me:** Why will an initial enthusiasm die?

**John:** I think the Scots as a nation are quite an aggressive mob and want to fight for something all the time. They've got to be fighting. Scots love being underdogs. They like being oh way down there. They like to be able to fight and struggle and, of course, ma dad did it and ma grandfather did it, and it all happened in years gone by and so the only way to beat the system is tae fight! And oh, the Scottish parliament that's a great idea! Ah'll fight for that!

**Me:** So you think it's like some collective chip on the shoulder?

**John:** Yeah Ah think there's an inferiority complex through the nation personally anyway. Having been born in England, lived most of my life in Scotland, some of ma life in England, Ah've been all round the counties in England so Ah've actually seen the way certain parts of England treat themselves, you know, and Scots have definitely got this inferiority complex. They've got this attitude of being an underdog. Ah think the English tend to look forward more, the Scots live in the past. The English tend to go forward.

**Me:** Where has this parliament come from?

**John:** The idea of the Scottish parliament is very good. We had the Tory government for nearly twenty years, you know, and for the Scots...this was a very good idea to have

their Labour, their own personal government you know doing things for them. That's fine. At the end of the day it can't be nothing more than a huge expense to us all. Really.
**Me:** So you think it was a disenchantment with the Thatcher years an that the Labour Party had to be seen to be doing something?
**John:** Yeah. Ah think that's how the Scottish parliament came to be. It's just in case the Conservatives got in again. And it would be the Labour stronghold which central Scotland is and always will be. It's the usual joke, if an ape was standing for Labour he'd be voted in. It's a traditional vote, it was wanting to be represented which Ah don't think a lot of Scots felt they were being represented for many many years of Conservative government.
**Me:** What of the future?
**John:** Ah think the Scottish parliament is going to be a fairly weak affair in the future. It's gonnae be a fairly spineless body. It's not gonnae have the representation people thought it would have. Especially if it finds it has to raise taxes in order to survive. It's gonnae cost an awful lot of money this and its got to come from somewhere. It's only ten percent of people that are Scottish and really that's an awful lot of money that has to come from each individual person to support the very expensive parliament.
**Me:** Do you think if people realise their parliament is only a talkin shop they are gonnae want more powers or do you think it will end up a glorified council?
**John:** The Scottish parliament won't exist. It'll be got rid off as soon as Conservatives run the Scottish parliament.
**Me:** Do you think they will get rid of it?
**John:** If Labour runs England, if it swaps round, nobody in central Scotland will want the Scottish parliament; they'll want rid of it. Ah really think that's the whole cause of it in the first place.
**Me:** In the elections to the Scottish parliament did ye bother voting, did ye think it was worthwhile?
**John:** I did yes. I voted Conservative.

I have reproduced these lengthy extracts from these two interviews to evidence the rather innocuous proposition that social actors bring schemes of perception to bear upon their interpretations of events, but also to draw the 'offensive' conclusion that it is clear that these two informants being English Conservative voters is not unrelated to their 'wilful, capricious and incompetent' interpretations of 1 July 1999. While the first informant has lived in Scotland for more than fifty years and is clearly integrated into Cardenden, it is also clear that he is not at all integrated and *never will* be integrated, and is more or less fated to never know he is not integrated, nor know his estrangement from a proper or competent interpretation of 1 July 1999, and I would speculate that perhaps part of the reason for his shrill views is his anger at having been more or less forcibly made to suspect that his view that he is integrated into Scotland is a self-serving fiction.

Speculation aside, clearly Mr Tims interprets events in Scotland 1999 in the light of his generational lived experience, and in this regard he is an example of how following one's 'native point of view' outwith one's native context can be a recipe for interpretive incompetence or hermeneutical error insofar as his 'lived experience' does not in fact illuminate the data, but traps the social actor into inept interpretations. The structure of perception or the light this informant uses to illuminate the data in fact obscures the meaning of the data from his view because, in the absence of a shared historicity or access to the shared cultural background out of which 1 July 1999 has emerged, Mr. Tims interprets events in an 'infantile' fashion, or as they appear to him as a 'foreigner.'

Likewise, Mr. Tims's neighbour's interpretation evidences the distorting effects that an English historicity or identity has upon his perception of Scotland 1999, so that his having an English point of view ("It's only ten per cent of people that are Scottish") makes him unable to participate in the meaningfulness of 1 July 1999 and so, again, 1 July 1999 is freed to be interpreted according to private caprice, despite his astute observations as regards the Scottish parliament being created to prevent a repeat of the Tory minority rule of 1979-1997. The impoverishment of interpretation that results, then, is not the result of having a view from nowhere (Nagel 1986) or having no historical baggage or identity but rather from having *a view from elsewhere* or having the 'wrong' kind of historical baggage that leads to de-contextualised and therefore incompetent interpretations.[112]

## 5.3 Saved by England: Doxic Subordination and Its Interpretations

If the meaning of 1 July 1999 is in the eye of the interpreter, this does not mean that all interpretations are equal. Also, even when the 'interpreters of Scotland' share in the context and bring fully-contextualised 'schemes of perception' to the work of interpretation, reaching a consensus is often agonistic to say the least, and reaching agreement upon highly-charged judgments and interpretations such as domination, subordination or equality in relation to the history of Scottish-English geo-political relationships seems fated to be caught in endless disagreement insofar as one man's 'insufferable subordination' is another man's 'best of both worlds.' In this regard, the following excerpt from an interview with Ryan Wilson (Woodend Park) who was in his early thirties and who was the only informant to mention the word 'unionism' in all of my interviews, gives a useful illustration of the dialectically opposed interpretations of Scotland operative today.

> Ah'm no fir nationalism or that. Ah'm pretty much up fir the unionism eh? They're watchin Braveheart an a' that shite eh an they think aye that's the way tae go. Naebody's interested in it eh? It's jist eh...go wi the flow eh? What's in the papers,

---

[112] If perhaps the inability to recognise they are in Scotland and not 'greater England' is the animating principle, this need not be the humourless affair of the two informants cited above. The only other Englishman living in Cardenden that I interviewed (Stephen Robins, 24 Orebank Road), while evidencing the same interpretive incompetence or whimsy, did so not without humour: "Ah voted once in ma entire life so far and that was for Screaming Lord Sutch, Monster Raving Looney party when Ah stayed in England. The one day working week, that'd do me fine. And free national drink. At that time that was his policy."

what's oan the telly eh? Ken, they'll go wi that. Ah think everybody wants it [independence] bit it's fir the rang reasons eh? Ken what Ah mean? They jist want it fir the sake e it. Ah dinnae see any reasons fir it. Ah dinnae see any point in it. We're jist a wee country, eh?

What is striking about Ryan's discourse is that it is a litany of 'knowledge claims' and, as with our earlier analysis of Peter in Chapter 4, if we take Ryan at his word he has an abundant supply of knowledge that is readily available to him and which he deploys easily and spontaneously. Also, like a good Heideggerian, Ryan rejects the inauthenticity of 'the they' as, unlike everyone else, he knows and defends the truth. So certain is Ryan of his interpretation that he has no need of evidence to support his claims, so that there is a doxic organisation of his political consciousness that is impervious to counter-evidence because 'they' are immersed in false consciousness. In light of the lack of evidence and Ryan's certitude, it is clear that habitus or an already established 'scheme of perception and interpretation' is making the world in its image to such an extent that Ryan is oblivious to the fact that he is interpreting and selecting among different views, so that we may say his political views are immersed in naturalism. Scotland is "jist a wee country" and not being equal in size to big countries means being weak and vulnerable, and one's small size becomes a natural source of regret.

According to this scheme of perception, retaining the political union with England is a 'blood relative' of recognising the objective facts of nature that are 'out there' and that can not be changed, *so that unionism becomes a truth of natural science* because the landmass of Scotland is a fact of nature that cannot be changed. Union with England, then, is a natural and eternal necessity as Nature itself is Ryan's evidence, and nature has decided the question of how Scotland organises its being-in-the-world. Just as a monkey with a red Labour rosette will secure Hugh's vote, so a thousand years of democratic deficit and domination as a result of union with England are not only to be endured but *are to be preferred* to a relapse to Scotland's natural state.

Ryan, then, is more unionist than professional unionists and politicians such as David Cameron and Alastair Darling who concede that an independent Scotland is economically viable, and it is clear that there can be no counter-evidence or events that could challenge his reading of the data. In his own estimation, Ryan is a realist and he erects his politics upon recognising the 'facts of life' will not change and his recognition of the facts empowers him to see through any un-natural media hype which has corrupted 'everybody,' while his own political analysis is perfectly conformed to objective reality, so that there can be no room for debate or discussion of options or possibilities as Ryan's views are not interpretations but objective reflections of the way reality really is. What is revealing is that Ryan does not argue that Scotland could survive as an independent country but is well-served by being part of the UK, because this is the clue that what in fact lies behind Brian's unionism is not any kind of economic analysis but *something that does not make an appearance in his discourse*. Another clue that an unexamined scheme of perception is in charge of Ryan's discourse is the claim that everyone's pro-independence views are sourced in the media and a film released three years previously, rather than nineteen years of unrepresentative government with no democratic legitimacy. Ryan's resort to 'magical' thinking is the clue that reveals the lengths he will go to rather than examine his scheme of perception which is doxic or beyond discussion.

What, then, prompts this infantile resort to magic? To answer this question I begin by noting an interesting feature of Ryan's thinking is the work of repression that it accomplishes; the work of holding back and holding firm against all the reasons 'everyone' except Ryan has found to at least question the wisdom of continuing Scotland's political union with England. What is interesting is *the constant act of will required to maintain his discursive certainty* when all about him have lost theirs. It seems, then, that the social ontology that is the ground of 'the unionism' is a magical frame of perception or doxic subordination that reads the geo-political 'facts' in the image of this subordination, and so imagines Scotland's economic inadequacy where there is none. This doxic subordination, then, is responsible for the 'metaphysical' belief that the nation needs something added to it from outwith itself to become sufficient. On this interpretation, unionism among the working classes is the conviction that Scotland as it is is not good enough, and once this despairing view is learned and internalised, it is taken up by freedom and becomes an autonomous scheme of perception so that any proposal that the nation make its own way in the world as an independent nation is spontaneously deemed irrational, so that unionism is a disguised theory of salvation where England saves Scotland from itself.

The psychological reality that underpins Ryan's unionism, then, is internalised inferiority that stems from a class position that is unable to break from itself, despite being more or less coerced to do so by the events of 1979-1997 and the advent of affluence since the nineteen-seventies. Within this unionist informant's imagination, the mobilisation of any symbolic material to attempt to end the union would amount to a flight from reality and a hopelessly romantic mystification of the hard facts about Scotland and 'being Scottish.' Having described in Chapters 2 and 3 an intentional horizon confined by a financial and social precariousness, it is inevitable that among the dominated there is a more or less coerced 'metaphysical' quality to their surrender before empirical facts, and insofar as one 'worships' reality there is an imagined swift punishment meted out to any ambition that commits the sin of being unrealistic. If I have singled out Ryan, his views in this respect were certainly not unrepresentative as the question of the financial and economic feasibility of Scottish independence was a decisive objection to independence for many informants, and appeal to 'the facts' of Scottish-English relations was a consistent theme during interviewing. From Orebank Road, then, I reproduce two views (Mr Hindley & Mr Bowson) expressing doubts about the financial feasibility of independence:

Well Ah know people's campaigned a lot and Ah wanted to see it myself, Ah wanted to see Scotland make its own decisions but you know you don't go over the top because money's got to be found for this. Ah mean this'll change everyone's mind and they'll want it reversing like a lot of African countries want it reversin because they can't find the capital. At the moment Ah think we cannae really live withoot England. Ah honestly think that a' big business really comes through England Ah believe. Ah know we've oil an a' that bit...nah! Ah think a' the big business runs through England, and we have tae live that way. Ah really think that's the case.

And:

**Me:** If we did have enough money d' ye think independence could be a guid idea?
**Mr Bowson:** Aye, cause there is ither wee countries in Europe that show us the way, if we could follow. People are faired Ah think. Better the Devil ye ken. Scared. People are scared. It's a'right fir Sean Connery an a' the likes e that sayin aye come oan let's dae it. He could get oot any time he likes. Bit fir the ordinary guy on the street it's no as easy as that.

Similar concerns were raised when chatting with a couple to arrange an interview, and as we sat we listened to the BBC evening news programme *Reporting Scotland* covering a visit of the then (4 February 1999) leader of the Liberal Democratic Party (Paddy Ashdown) to Aberdeen, followed by a report on a speech in Glasgow by the then Prime Minister Tony Blair criticising Scottish nationalism. Alongside the Prime Minister was Donald Dewar and both men were shown on the news bulletin unveiling a billboard poster warning against the dangers of "Divorce," in reference to the separation of Scotland from England. At this, the couple began an exchange critical of Scottish independence. "We want oor pensions..." the woman told me, before adding: "Ah'm a' fir mair say in oor ain affairs bit Ah'm no fir this total..." Before she could finish, however, her husband interjected: "What aboot defence? What aboot some Arab rogue eejit? Whose gonnae pay fir it a'?"

In light of these concerns, nationalists and unionists wage an *information war* in the media to structure how the electorate perceives Scotland's economic prospects and, famously, the Scottish National Party in 1972 launched an electoral campaign with the slogan: '*It's Scotland's Oil*' in light of the discovery of oil in the North Sea, and this was to prove successful in both general elections held in 1974 because the discovery of oil gave credibility to the feasibility of independence. With Ryan in mind, we might say that despite Scotland's unalterable landmass, Nature had compensated Scotland in the shape of natural resources in its territorial waters so that alongside Ryan's naturalisation of unionism, the nationalists too can naturalise the political choice for independence and claim Nature itself as an ally.

The question of the affordability of an independent Scotland throws into relief informants' relationship to knowledge and information which is very much 'out of practice' and not free, as informants do not read books and economic reports and come to knowledge and a decision upon that basis. Rather, their relationship to knowledge is so dominated that they rely upon the media and their habitus to make up for the 'information deficit' they feel and which they are complicit in. Instead of accessing official figures contained in a GERS (2012) report on the performance of the Scottish economy, for example, informants resort to their dominated habitus which often acts as a cipher for a 'superstitious' *economism*, where an alleged Scottish 'poverty' vis-à-vis England trumps all other considerations when thinking about the best constitutional settlement for Scotland.

This free reduction of themselves to *homo economicus* and their free reproduction of their dominated relationship to the realm of knowledge opens a window upon subordination or the condition of symbolic domination, as it was ample proof that my informants were much more a proletariat than a people, so that in contrast to Nairn's (1981) account of the rise of Scottish nationalism being due to British economic decline, at no time did any informant suggest to me that Scotland was materially poorer than England *because of* the union. By far the clear majority judgment was that England is the richer country and Scotland can only benefit from union, and so *the reason why the conviction that national identity or "Braveheart an a' that shite" can not contest economic reality is so strong is because it borrows or partakes in the strength of habitus.* In terms of interpreting the fact of this consensus as evidence that informants' *inferiorism* is the basis for their *economism*, I begin from the basic position that this consensus is evidence of social determination at work. While a post-materialist 'politics of identity' and a more holistic *dasein* can generate a symbolic structure that is sufficiently real to produce the "ninety minute nationalism" (Jim Sillars) of football supporters, it is not real enough to generate the real nationalism of independence, which for many informants is a politicisation of national identity too far.

One instance of this inferiorism-come-economism that I came across during the first election campaign to the Holyrood parliament was when interviewing in Whitehall Drive (29 April 1999), and I began talking politics with a man and wife as, not for the first time during interviewing, I was invited to stay and have my tea at the end of conducting an interview. Both were lifelong Labour voters and had never voted for any other political party, and both told me they had no desire for Scottish independence, although both had voted 'Yes' in the September 1997 Referendum. As we sat we watched a news report on English attitudes to Scottish devolution and we listened to an interview with an 'ex-pat' from Dunfermline living in England who declared himself against setting up the Scottish parliament, which was followed by the views of some pupils from an English public school who were shown discussing Scottish Home Rule. Like the ex-pat from Fife, the pupils were also against Scotland having a parliament, with one pupil saying: "Scotland still needs England to support it." As the young boy continued to air his views I sat wondering if my informants would be tempted to react, and as if on cue the woman informant pointedly remarked: "Of course ye could change yer mind."

I did not ask her what she meant by her remark as I knew exactly what she meant, and did not want to embarrass her as I was now a guest in her home about to be given a meal. It was clear from her tone of voice that her comment was not light-hearted or an invitation to begin a conversation. Clearly the public schoolboy giving his opinion had provoked a reaction within her because we had both just seen the anti-independence views she had just finished defending in our interview being *in collusion or alignment in producing the precocious conceit of an English schoolboy*. When placed in this new context, her views were suddenly ripped from her habitus and placed in their geo-political objectivity, and thanks to this re-contextualisation, the same views suddenly went from being justifiable to being embarrassing.

This woman, who had no post-16 education, had undoubtedly thought about Scotland's constitutional crisis over the 1979-1997 period and was firmly against independence, yet it seemed as if the results of her reflection dissolved in seconds thanks not simply to them being the same as what any English schoolboy knows about Scotland i.e. that Scotland cannot survive without England's charity, but because *her views colluded and played their part in sustaining this English schoolboy's perception of Scotland*. When placed in this English context, my informant's views changed *for her* from being reasonable to being in collusion with an insufferable arrogance. Because the English schoolboy's views were based on nothing but his participation in a wider English cultural knowledge, his very innocence was able to dissolve or deconstruct my informant's unionism because the confident schoolboy revealed her views were not confidently held at all but were based upon the reality of her lack of self-confidence that suddenly became externalised for both of us to see; as if having subordinated herself to a fourteen-year-old boy and colluding in her subordination were not enough, her subordination had escaped its private individual existence and had suddenly become public and made a spectacle of itself.

My informant's *economism* then was trumped by her *shame* insofar as the schoolboy revealed to the observing ethnographer the woman's 'freely-chosen' subordination. Precisely because the boy knew nothing of political economy, his judgment emerged from his nation's exercise of hegemony; a hegemony that can produce such doxic views in its pre-pubescent youth. The English boy's 'violent' objectification of the woman's views dissolved the pretence that the woman's views had anything to do with 'political economy' or factual knowledge. The boy, then, put the woman's views and her herself 'in her place' and she was shamed; a boy had revealed her 'objective' being-for-others and had humiliated her opinions in front of the ethnographer who had just wasted his time by recording them – opinions that were now devalued, prompting her to recognise this by conceding: 'Of course, ye could change yer mind.'

On the question of whether Scotland could afford to be independent, the boy revealed that the truth of this question is not a transcendent reality 'out there,' but a judgement about Scotland that is freely available to any English schoolboy. While a judgment or interpretation is not to be rejected because it happens to aggrandize the conceit of a schoolboy, I propose that the schoolboy handed this woman a glimpse of her objectivity and subordination, and my evidence is the fact that my elderly informant did not dismiss the boy out of hand but was clearly embarrassed, so that *her shame was the clue that revealed her symbolic domination,* and the basis for my interpretation that her unionism and economism are masks worn by this normally hidden condition that, just below the surface, knows it has no business or judgment in this matter. The dissolution of 'firmly-held views' shows how easily a new social context or interlocutor can prize such views from ourselves, and how our views are often not really ours at all but are rather masks worn by our position in a hierarchy.

Underpinning the de facto unionism of Mr Bowson quoted earlier is the familiar economism where the perception of economic realities structures the perception of politics because the former necessitates the exercise of political restraint. If, as a class, they can not afford the experiment of socialism, it seems that as a people they can not afford the experiment of independence, and so there is a flight to 'scarcity era thinking' so that locals' pronouncements upon economic matters have less to do with economics than a dominated imagination sourced in their long durée adaptation to material inequalities and long durée inequalities of representational or cultural power between classes and nations; an habitual 'scheme of perception' which combines symbolic inferiority with material domination which spontaneously shapes or constructs the economic 'facts' into a likeness to its dominated perception. Economism then is a cipher of inferiorism, or a species of magical thinking among the socially and culturally dominated.

Interestingly, fourteen years later in 2013, I met this woman again and she told me that in the 2011 election she had voted for the SNP for the first time in her life, and when I met her again in July 2014 she told me that although worried about her pension under independence, she was thinking about voting 'yes' in the 2014 referendum.

Although I have no direct empirical evidence, I propose that just as subordination is silent and invisible and does not normally give direct representations of itself, so the beginning of breaking with subordination is silent and unspoken, and therefore very difficult to evidence. However, I propose the principle that more or less integral to working-class people being in favour of independence is the desire to recognise and break with subordination, whereas more or less integral to working-class people being against independence is the decision to keep on not doing anything more than recognising subordination as a fact of life. In proposing this generalisation I emphasise that I am not making a philosophical argument that people who vote 'no' on 18 September 2014 are happy to reproduce their subordination or are risk-averse while nationalists are more authentic. Rather, I am making the highly context-specific claim that insofar as an elderly working-class woman decides to vote 'yes' she evidences she wishes to break with her own long acceptance of subordination.

Despite an obvious economism among the poor, however, what must be adverted to is the clear desire for independence that is thwarted due to perceived economic realities, so that there is an unmistakable tension between what is culturally desirable and what is economically affordable, and I argue that the balance of power in the relationship between a risk-averse 'scarcity era economism' and an integral 'politics of identity' is shifting across the '45 and '79 generations. Although each generation provides evidence that the economic facts of life translate into a constitutional caution or gradualism, across the '45 and '79 generations the strain involved in accepting the tension involved in culture and identity pointing one way while economic concerns point in another has increased markedly, to the extent of a mounting pressure for a post-materialist politics and the realignment of culture and politics upon a purely Scottish basis. What is clear to nationalist and unionist alike is that a new legitimacy and mobilisation of "all things Scottish" has occurred, so that there is an increasing psychological tension in Scottish popular culture, and Scottish culture and unionism in Scotland are increasingly pulling in different directions.

My informants are not economists and never will be, and so if they judge that Scotland can only benefit economically from union with England, this judgment is fated to be an example of *fides implicita* that takes this signification of the economy of Scotland on trust because ordinarily this will not be an informed personal judgment. Because of what might be termed the 'fog of war' and the resultant *information deficit* on this crucial point, this crucial question is fated to be handed over to the media and socially constituted experts but, again, which expert judgment one believes *becomes a social practice* and must ordinarily become caught up again in non-economic social determinisms. The fact is it would be exceptional if any housewife, postman, sewage operative, taxi driver, shop assistant, bricklayer, nurse, warehouse worker, labourer, care assistant or joiner took the trouble to personally verify whether or not his or her material standard of living would be significantly altered if Scotland became independent.

Those with no non-vocational education are often at the mercy of the social forces at work that either favour the reproduction or the overturning of *the traditional dominant perception* of the Anglo-Scottish relation which has been inherited from the 'dictatorship of scarcity' period, and which holds that Scotland is too poor to survive as an independent sovereign state. Being in a position to understand the economics of independence presupposes having the exceptional agency to act independently and take the initiative to find out a series of facts. Also, in proportion to anyone having such resources to make competent and complex economic judgment, the less likely they would be pre-disposed to frame this issue in static 'yes' or 'no' terms, as this way of understanding the issue as wagering the fate of a nation upon a bookkeeping exercise is indicative of rigid and unsophisticated thinking.

The imagining of unionism by Ryan is dominated by *economism* and *naturalism* and is highly unlikely in a highly educated consciousness. Among the working class it is those who recognise within themselves more colours than the mono-chromism of 'scarcity thinking' who are least likely to turn to a unionism characterised by economism, as they are least likely to view themselves exclusively through the 'mirror of production' (Baudrillard) and hang their constitutional politics upon the outcome of a bookkeeping exercise. Among the dominated, however, there is always an ear for peddlers of 'scarcity thinking' as it calls to something of their ownmost *dasein* as there is a clear isomorphism or 'fit' between consciousness and politics, because this fundamental obedience dominates their everyday thinking and their everyday experience of reality. Both unionism and national-ism then are able to find strength within working-class *dasein* with the former appealing to and replicating a *laissez faire* accommoda-tion to and acceptance of subordination, and the latter represent-ing a class-based desire to recognise and put an end to such accommodations to and acceptations of subordination. The heart of the matter is how the symbolic level is lived among the domi-nated; how a condition of symbolic domination becomes aligned with political unionism or mobilised to resist this condition.

The truism that a class or a nation may desire socialism or independence but material necessity means such projects are unrealistic, is a familiar quandary to any working-class generation. However, the cultural sphere of the '45 generation included a strong British identity and British culture that meant 'Scotland' as a medium of culture, politics and the imagination played far less of a part in constituting the cultural sphere and symbolic order, and therefore less of a place in the disjuncture between the desirable and the possible. Among the '79 generation, however, the balance of power has changed thanks to the arrival of the affluent society and the cultural 'revolution' of the nineteen-seventies, so that when coupled with the long event of 1979-1997, a political programme *is* constituted via the cultural level which *has* increasingly jettisoned Britain as an organising category of the imagination. Affluence then has fuelled an escape from the dominance of economics over culture, and as affluence releases the cultural level to become stronger and no longer merely epiphenomenal to economic structure, a far greater recognition of symbolic domination at the cultural level is possible, so that today there is a tension between structure and culture in younger generations which was not there before. Finally, in this new context, unionism is increasingly stripped of its cultural content or legitimacy and is only imaginable by reference to an alleged relative material 'poverty' vis-à-vis England.

Hence, while among the '45 generation there is the clear victory for the view that economic reality determines the rationality of political unionism, even '45 generation informants cite fears over the economy as the *only* barrier to the Scottish independence they otherwise would prefer. If money, then, is the only imaginable reason left to tolerate the union, it seems logical that the arrival of affluence can only result in the problematising of the union among a generation that is able to afford a post-materialist politics and who are affluent enough to imagine and pursue a post-materialist politics of national identity. Also, of course, if the only credible reason imaginable for political union with England is an increase in material prosperity, the logic of unionism seems to imply the union must come to an end when, and it can only be a matter of time for the unionist, political union with England produces the affluence unionists claim the union provides and they claim they seek.

However, as the name of the *Better Together* campaign launched in 2012 to persuade Scots to vote against independence in September 2014 implies, the rationale for union with England would remain if it did not deliver the material benefits its advocates say it delivers, because 'being together' is deemed better *as a matter of principle* i.e. regardless of political difference or economic performance, so that union with England becomes 'philosophical' or even an ethical imperative in the sense of being an intrinsic good. For this unionism, then, resistance to independence is akin to a political faith position that is not susceptible to being challenged or brought to an end in light of poor economic performance or inconvenient political truths such as the democratic deficit that results from being 'together' with England for better or for worse.

If once upon a time unionism imagined it had the movement of history on its side, neo-unionism has had to become metaphysical in order to by-pass the realms of culture and politics and history and economy that are increasingly becoming aligned with independence, and the fundamental reason for this is the ongoing absence of an identifiable British nation and culture to pull Scotland and England together. This is why unionist political parties are more or less coerced into cultivating a perception of Scotland's relative economic poverty vis-à-vis England to prevent Scots voting for independence, so that if the Better Together campaign is obliged to search for a post-materialist rationale for unionism, much of its leader's (Alistair Darling) career was dedicated to sowing the seeds of doubt concerning Scotland's ability to afford political independence.

As part of the Labour Party's Holyrood general election campaign in 1999, for example, Alistair Darling in his capacity as Secretary of State for Social Security claimed at a press conference (24 April 1999) that was carried by both evening news programmes in Scotland that there would be a two hundred million pounds National Insurance contribution deficit should Scotland become independent, and given the quote earlier from a lifelong Labour voter ("We want oor pensions!"), this New Labour message that the Scots cannot afford independence, and that an independent Scotland would mean pensions of less than the £67 per week under New Labour in 1999, aligns with a dominated imagining of the economy among Labour Party voters insofar as housewives and pensioners construct their unionism via recourse to an economism based upon a dominated or dependent relation to the realm of knowledge.

Interestingly, when we inquire into who imagines unionism, the case for unionism is almost exclusively made by professional politicians and rich individuals who have been successful in business, and the weeks and months prior to the first election to the new Scottish parliament supplied a steady flow of revealing speeches and newspaper editorials and articles such as the following, which appeared in *The Scotsman* newspaper entitled 'Gloves off as Holyrood Campaign Launched:'

> The Prime Minister will open the election campaign today with a passionate defence of the Union...in a speech at Strathclyde University today....He will claim that the Holyrood election will be a battle between social justice and separatism...Mr Brown...has already made a series of speeches and published a pamphlet.

The article went on to quote the Prime Minister (Tony Blair):

> I will be emphasising that there is also a choice, if you like, between social justice versus separatism...Ultimately, politics is about more than identities. It is also about ideals, and that is why in the coming months, the principled politics of social justice will overcome the narrow politics of identity.

Commenting upon this speech, Murray Ritchie of *The Herald* newspaper observed that the Prime Minister had argued that Labour's delivery of devolution had safeguarded the distinctiveness of Scotland's civic institutions, so that the Prime Minister could conclude: "The Nationalists can no longer argue Scottish nationhood is under threat." This unionist rhetoric fails to recognise that Home Rule has not resolved the 'democratic deficit' of 1979-1997 (and 2010-2015), and reveals unionism's signature weakness which is its integral alienation from or mis-alignment with integral reality i.e. not only its inability to respond to and solve a series of problems but that the union itself is the cause of a democratic deficit and the discrediting of democracy and participation in politics; is mis-aligned with Scottish culture to such an extent that it is simply aligned against the very movement of history. All of these realities unionism is unable to publicly recognise because to do so is to publicly recognise there is only one solution. While it is abundantly clear in light of the almost daily breaking of ranks of Labour Party members to publicly join the 'Yes' Campaign, and the fact that many traditional Labour voters voted for the SNP in 2007 and 2011, that Labour politicians understand the weakness of unionism and the appeal of independence and that the continued existence of the UK puts Scottish democracy at risk, it is because unionism cannot recognise and resolve these integral problems that the signature weakness in New Labour unionism is that it proposes to solve a problem that doesn't exist in the hope that it will appear to solve a problem that does exist. For example, then, proponents of unionism such as Gordon Brown and Douglas Alexander in their pamphlet *New Scotland New Britain* (1999, p. 18) argue: "With the creation of a Scottish Parliament, no longer can it be claimed that Scottish nationhood or its civic institutions are at risk" and that (1999, pp. 11 & 47):

It is therefore a serious mistake to portray it as some sort of half way house, a mid-point between the status quo and separatism... the real battle in Scotland in May 1999 will now be between those who put the politics of social justice first, and those who practice the politics of national identity above and before anything else.

Despite the fact that the multi-national state came to an end in 1918 with the collapse of the Austro-Hungarian empire, New Labour unionism imagines not only that Scotland and England are 'better together' but that the multi-national state of Britain is a template for what might be called a 'global unionism.' In the speech of the Prime Minister delivered at Strathclyde university he called for Scots to back his vision of a new Scotland in a multicultural, multi-ethnic and multi-national union with England, while for Brown and Alexander (1999, p. 31): "Our opportunity is to forge probably the first successful multicultural multi-ethnic and multinational country." The new unionism of what used to be called New Labour, then, is not presented as a matter of political expediency or securing the future of the United Kingdom, but as the only and best means of securing nothing less than the advance of modernity and history, as Brown and Alexander argue the future of modernity in Scotland will be threatened should it become independent; that modern economies operate beyond the confines of "the sheltered national economics of the past" (1999, p. 47) and so, by definition, if not by performance, any nationalist political party is guilty of resisting the movement of history and the process of globalisation and dragging Scotland 'backwards.' Once the imagining of Scotland, then, is safely returned to its modernist moorings, Brown, Alexander and Blair conceive it to be their New Labour modernising duty to urge Scots not only to stick with union with England but to prepare for a new era of global modernity; for yet another modernist experiment of a *globalised Britain*, rather than turn the clock back and attempt the nationalist route of a purely Scottish modernity.

I propose that this 'new unionism' involves the systematic misrecognition of reality insofar as re-heating the treadmills of unionism and presenting multi-culturalism and multi-national internationalism to the Scottish working class as the New World Order is more chewing upon the old eighteenth-century modernist cud; the usual liberal fantasy sourced in the usual elite and privileged relationship to social conditions, and clear evidence that what escapes New Labour's imagination and policies is that its misrecognition of working-class Scottish *dasein* is contributing to the nationalist dialectic in Scotland and that if Scotland, moves from devolution to independence after 2014 it will not be due to a 'slippery slope' but the same class and nation-based realities of difference and conflict that remain real but deliberately misrecognised by the unionist political imagination.

However, if this utopian liberal middle-class fantasy is too rich for working-class voters more responsive to economism, the familiar resort to the eternal fact of Scottish poverty is never far away from unionism's imagining of Scotland, so that just as the Conservative Party had insisted prior to the devolution referendum of 1997 that Scotland could ill-afford devolution in monetary terms, both the old materialist unionism of the Conservative Party and the new multi-cultural 'better together' unionism of the Labour Party combat Scottish nationalism by appealing to 'economic realities,' and in their political discourse construct rationality in terms of *homo economicus* which, unsurprisingly, integrates with 'Big Business' whose interests were routinely represented in the print media as threatened by the risk of independence. Hence, with the then Secretary of State for Scotland Helen Liddle described the SNP as an "anti-business party" (Liddell 1999), there was little surprise to read a *Scotland on Sunday* newspaper article entitled *Big Business in Secret Bid to Save Union: Key Figures in Commerce and Industry line up to Oppose Independent Scotland* informing readers: "A secret summit to plan a 'Save the Union' campaign featuring leading figures from the Scottish business community will take place this week. The talks will centre on...business fears about independence."

On 9 April 1999 there appeared in *The Scotsman* newspaper an article entitled 'Economists Back Independence' which reported on a study by the David Hume Institute which claimed that independence would be better for Scotland from an economic standpoint. The *Report on the Economic Aspects of Independence* argued partial sovereignty to Scotland would lead to political instability in the UK which "will not help economic policy." In response, Donald Dewar, the soon-to-be first First Minister in the new Scots parliament, raised doubts as to the integrity of the report saying: "It has been produced for the election and that is for sure," while Jim Wallace, then leader of the Scottish Liberal Democrats and soon-to-be deputy First Minister, was quoted as describing the report as "nonsense" adding: "Going for independence would be particularly damaging to the Scottish economy because of the uncertainty it would create."

While such views may be likened to advocating a policy of starvation because of the inevitable expense involved in buying food, the revealing truth that is being repeated time and again is the risk-averse nature of unionism, and the appeal to the Scottish people to be afraid to take risks and to be afraid to break from a dominated relation to their geo-political subordination (Gilfillan 2009). The unionist message seems to be that it is not in the best economic interests of the working class to break from their political subordination. Interestingly, an editorial from *The Scotsman* newspaper commenting on the David Hume Institute report provided a rare example of imagining a non-monetary basis for unionism in the run up to the first election to the Scottish parliament:

> Independence is possible, especially within the union of Europe. But is it desirable to end a Union which has served the purposes of both Scotland and England and resulted in so much miscegenation and cross-cultural enrichment that only a deranged anthropologist would dare distinguish between ethnic – as opposed to native – Scots and ethnic English?... Scots, so proud of Hume and the other scions of the Enlightenment, voted for devolution, not separation, and the think-tank named after him would do well to remember it.

In the run-up to the May 1999 election it was widely felt that Scotland's union with England was in danger of coming to an end, so that unionists were forced to put down their heaviest anchors to weather the nationalist storm, and what is revealing in the above editorial is its raising the spectre of a Scottish *ethnicity* and its invocation of 'unionist saints' to protect the constitutional status quo in its hour of peril, and the bizarre description of the Scots as "so proud of Hume" and the editor calling upon the Scots to return to the faith of their eighteenth-century Enlightenment fathers to ward off the threat of independence.

This invocation of the Enlightenment is a revealing window upon the long durée 'scheme of perception' that is used to interpret Scotland's history and the present moment, and is a rare sighting of modernism having to rouse itself from its hegemonic slumber and arrive at a conception of itself beyond economism. What is usefully revealed is how it is assumed that the 1707 union with England is still seen as progressive despite the fact it is anti-democratic and results in a democratic deficit and unrepresentative governments; as if progress is somehow the result of union with England and could not have happened without union with England. Unionism, then, is a more or less thoroughly materialist theory of national development that has been more or less coerced into becoming a 'metaphysical' theory that inspires loyalty in the face of its political and democratic failure, and this having to become a 'faith position' in its own way evidences how empty the unionist cupboard is, and how threadbare are the rags (or period costume) it wears today.

Another example of how the symbolic material that unionism is able to draw upon to appeal to the popular imagination is at an all time low is the appeal to anthropologists to do their duty and defend the Enlightenment, the union and Reason itself from the spectre of an alleged ethnic difference between the Scots and the English. This foray into anthropological theory is made despite the fact that anthropologists argue "the degree of an individual's ethnicity is a structural matter" (Williams 1989, p. 415), so that an anthropologist may well argue in light of differences of income, social status, job satisfaction, deprivation, crime, educational attainment, physical and mental health, life expectancy, cultural capital, social mobility, housing conditions and various opportunities throughout the life-trajectory (Harding 1995; Reid 1998) that it would hardly be 'deranged' to propose that such thick-layered difference within and between nations might be classified as approaching 'ethnic' difference.

The editorial's argument of course is that centuries of inter-breeding means there is a biological impediment to claiming any ethnic differences between the Scots and the English, and so *independence has no biological or ethnic basis*. This adventitious resort to biology is revealing for its 'anything but class' and 'anything but democratic deficit' strategy. Having dispatched the claim of biological or genetic differences between the Scots and the English, the editorial spends all of its time nicely avoiding the very real differences that the period 1979-1997 revealed to exist between Scotland and England.

Finally, as a parenthesis, it is worth noting that it is anthropologists who have taught us that the invocation of the spectre of the 'primitive' (Kuper 1988), as well as the denial of ethnic difference and the refusal to recognise political and cultural differences, is an established practice of misrepresentation of elites who invent liberalism in order to have subordinates misrecognise social and cultural injustices and grievances (Tibi, in Hutchinson and Smith 1996, pp. 174-179). Williams (1989), for example, argues that in many political contexts the hegemonic ethnic-come-class grouping always seeks to mystify itself and obscure its social make-up, and spread a *liberal fog* that is a 'flight from particularity' and social context wherever it is able to do so. This political strategy of mis-recognising reality so as to better ensure the status quo also de-legitimizes any attempt by a rival class-and-ethnic group to gain power on the basis of mobilising and recognising class and ethnic realities as 'backward' i.e. those in control of the public realm wage a campaign against realist classification systems.

I would argue that a case could be made for the proposition that the concept of *ethnicity* is preferable to the concept of *social class* given the often sterile economistic connotations associated with the latter term, and its inability to suggest multi-layered non-economic differences. In this regard Ronald Cohen's (1978, p. 394) argument that "ethnicity may be of such positive value to members that lack of stratification and possible incorporation with loss of identity can produce counter-movements to revive and reverse the cultural distinctiveness being lost," is relevant to the situation in Scotland under Margaret Thatcher, John Major and now David Cameron as it was to prevent a cultural distinctiveness from being lost and to prevent incorporation into England's neoliberal project that the Scottish working class produced a counter-movement to revive boundaries via their politicisation of nationality, in which *a series of historical insights and inequalities and grievances were released from the liberal settlement and their modernist invisibility, to be mobilised in the current creation of a post-liberal future.* This brings into view the fact that informants' perception *has its own unique historicity* and density, so that many use the Thatcher period as a key to open and read British history and conclude the English upper classes and the assimilated middle classes have always been in control of the British state and always will be, so the only rational theory and practice of development is to secede from this straight-jacket by voting 'yes' in 1979, 1997 and 2014.

In explaining how the semantic sea-change from hegemonic unionism to being on the eve of the 2014 Independence Referendum has came about, the crucial element is the fusion or alignment between class and nation. If we consider the year-long miners' strike of 1984-1985 in a former pit village such as Cardenden, there occurred something approaching the contestation of the State at the everyday level as a result of miners and their families, neighbours, friends and localities being drawn into the many issues raised by this year-long event. Practices of picketing, monitoring movements of coal, monitoring fellow-miners' observance of the strike, organising food kitchens, rallies, trade union activities and fundraising events that were touched on in Chapter 1, formed part of an everyday resistance to what was gradually perceived to be an anti-trade union and anti-miner and anti-working-class English government, not to mention the struggles against the forces of law and order (police and media) deployed to enforce and defend government policy. At the time of doctoral fieldwork, many families were still marked by the strike of 1984-1985 and I recall one former miner telling me that only at having reached sixty-five years old and receiving his state pension in 1997 was he able to replace his household furniture because of the level of debt incurred as a consequence of the strike that had ended twelve years earlier.

If the effects of the 1984-1985 strike were long-lasting for this individual and many others, the same can be said of the poll tax which was introduced in Scotland on 1 April 1988, despite the Conservative Party suffering its worst general election result in Scotland since 1910 the year before, and which saw a third of Scots from the outset refusing to pay a tax that was introduced to appease predominantly middle-class home owners faced with increased local authority property rates to raise revenue to pay for local government services. Significantly for the future direction of the politicisation of young working-class people, the poll tax meant thousands of '79 generation members having lives that included a long drawn-out game of 'cat and mouse' between them and their Labour-controlled local authorities and sheriff officers hired to pursue unpaid taxes. Among young single working-class people living in the parental home there was widespread civil disobedience, so that for many this campaign of non-payment was the intergenerational 'handover' of their parents' 1984-1985 fight, and the psychological continuation of a level of politicisation that, again, reached the everyday level of young people's lives.

As a result of such events it became more or less impossible not to politicise nationality among the working class, and insofar as this happened this period saw the end of constituting politics and responding to events purely upon a class basis, and at this point voting for the Labour Party became 'disorganised' and problematic for many, as this was to respond to the 'signs of the times' upon an all-British basis and to pool their resentments and sovereignty with an English working class which had failed to resist Thatcher. This mobilisation upon a more integral basis meant a 'post-class' or 'more than class' mobilisation as a people upon the basis of historicity and nationality, so that in the period 1984-1989 the British State lost much of its legitimacy among the younger generation and a consensus was reached that identified the British State as the problem by the end of the nineteen-eighties.

The Scottish miners and working class had mobilised against Thatcher via local, class and occupational identities and this mobilisation not only failed but failed publicly and incontestably. Thatcher took on the working class and won handsomely and publicly, so working-class Scots' political mobilisation after their defeat in the nineteen-eighties was re-structured upon a clear grasp of their geo-political weakness and upon the basis of *recognising their defining structural realities and relations.* The Thatcherite revolution which discarded the post-War consensus politics meant governing from a position of strength, so that a retaliatory 'politics of weakness' became necessary, and integral to this new politics was breaking with the 1945 generation post-War consensus politics of their parents and mobilisation outwith the parameters of Britain and the Labour Party. Working-class nationalism, then, involved drawing upon hitherto non-politicised reserves of difference that were of no interest to their unionist political representatives; a politics that because it emerged from a class with a sharp appreciation of its condition of domination was thereby clear-sighted about what had to change to end its subordination – a politics constituted upon the *free articulation of their geo-political subordination* and that wanted a political party and political representatives who recognised this domination and promised to put an end to it.

It is significant, then, that the SNP at this time began to appeal specifically to the working class and to position itself as the political party that could canalise and best express this sense of a people being subordinate, and with the benefit of hindsight it is clear the Labour Party lost control over the political expression of class, and thereby lost their traditional role of proposing solutions in light of their inability to recognise the problem. As a result of the miners' strike, the poll tax and the secession from the post-War consensus politics of their parent's generation, there ultimately emerged among a younger working-class generation *a break from their dominated relationship to themselves*, so that the period 1979-1997 was a point of reflexivity which saw a sea-change in their self-understanding.

In the earlier quotes from Brown and Alexander (1999) I proposed that these are examples of *misrecognition*, as well as attempts to structure perception that are more or less fated to fail because this unionist politics of perception conflates Scotland with 'civic' Scotland, and fails to recognise working-class nationalism has nothing to do with safeguarding civic institutions from which they are excluded anyway, and the remnant of Scotland (church, education and law) that negotiated its survival during the 1688-1707 settlement period is of marginal relevance to informants' 'being national.' Their kind of nationalism is a class-based rejection of political union with England that is indifferent to whether 'civic Scotland' is accommodated or not in a new constitutional era, and by persisting in clichés such as being "proud to be Scottish and British" and Scotland and England being "better together," unionist thinking announces its inability to recognise, far less liberate, Scottish *dasein*, and announces its inability to recognise, far less address and resolve, the history of conflict and struggle these two nations and identities are responsible for. The unionist position fundamentally chooses to avoid a realistic grasp of 'the present as history' and is thereby more or less fated to imagine a constitutional position that misrecognises the present and what is needed. The flight from integral *dasein* is seen in the desire to reduce the ferment of the period 1967-2007 to the effort to preserve a nation where it is a movement to restore Scottish sovereignty.

Scottish unionist political parties, then, are handicapped by their inability to embrace the 'return of the repressed' as this would mean recognising and representing the integral interests of Scottish working-class *dasein*, and so they are more or less fated to fail to realise that throughout the 1979-1997 period, far from being in jeopardy, the nation was never more secure or awake, and that 'civic Scotland' is irrelevant to (working class) nationalism and the 1979-1997 (and 2010-2015) period was a godsend for a new and deeper politicisation of working-class *dasein* and a new and deeper exercise of reflexivity. Throughout the Thatcher/Major period the Scottish middle classes had their opportunity to reject Thatcher and mobilise resistance via nationalism but failed to do so because neither their class interests nor the civic Scotland they oversee and manage was in any jeopardy, and so much like Gordon Brown handing out packets of cigarettes to striking miners in Cardenden during the 1984-1985 strike, New Labour unionism that imagines that, with the advent of a devolved parliament the Scots have no reason left to be nationalists, is simply too little too late. Instead of embracing the release of Scottish working-class *dasein* and *mitsein* and championing its recognition and its possibilities, the Labour Party leadership's attempt to reduce politics in Scotland to the choice between 'nationalism' or 'social justice' is a hapless example of 'scarcity thinking' in the affluent era.

The heavily policed and very limited recognition of the reality of geo-political subordination that must characterise unionism explains why it cannot articulate a satisfactory 'anthropological turn,' and why unionist Labour politicians seem characterised by a desire to 'disappear' working-class nationalism from its policy-making process and pursue a strategy of non-recognition. Hence, in a televised hustings on 23rd April 1999 during the first election campaign to the new Scottish parliament, the Labour Party representative (Wendy Alexander) was asked three times if her fellow-Labour Party MP George Robertson was correct to claim that: "Devolution will kill nationalism stone dead." With opinion polls reporting the SNP and Labour parties neck-and-neck in peoples' voting intentions, Ms Alexander refused to concede that nationalism was obviously alive and well, despite being pressed by the programme presenter and the studio audience's clamour for her to give a straight answer to a straight question.

This behaviour evidences the struggle over representation; that what is at stake is not reality itself but the *public recognition* of reality, and that struggles for recognition are vital because "there is nothing outside the text" (Derrida 1976, p. 158) or nothing is real until it is publicly recognised, so that this unionist politician was prepared to become the object of ridicule rather than publicly concede nationalism was alive and well. What the viewers in the studio audience and at home saw was public proof that Labour politicians cannot bring themselves to publicly acknowledge that Labour politicians cannot publicly recognise contemporary Scotland. If unionists pay the price at the ballot box for their refusal to represent fully-contextualised Scottish *dasein*, a price paid by everyone during the nineteen-nineties was a toxic political atmosphere where the very phrase 'Scottish nationalism,' when recognised at all, could provoke in Labour councillors and prospective parliamentary candidates descriptions of nationalists as "sewer rats" and "racists."

Given this toxic atmosphere it is unsurprising that when interviewing I came across instances of the misrecognition of Scottish nationalism as a form of racism that undoubtedly acted to prevent individuals from voting SNP. For example, then, when interviewing one informant (Miss Muir, Woodend Park) she advised that she was worried that to vote SNP was to endorse a racist ideology:

**Me:** Who did you vote for if you don't mind me asking?
**Miss Muir:** SNP.
**Me:** Aye?
**Miss Muir:** Bit Ah wish Ah didnae really.
**Me:** Why?

**Miss Muir:** Ah think we should jist probably be a' one really, Ah think. It's probably a bit racist.

**Me:** What did you say?

**Miss Muir:** Well, the Scottish against the English...it's true though [embarrassed laughter].

**Me:** Do you think if you vote SNP folk will think...

**Miss Muir:** You're against the English.

**Me:** You think that's what it's like?

**Miss Muir:** Aye, a bias.

In light of the above testimony and to give a more in-depth appreciation of the up-hill struggle that the independence movement has undergone, I will analyse three 'moments,' the 1992 British general election, the issue of the Scottish Six and media coverage of the inaugural Scottish general election in May 1999.

### 1992 General Election

On the morning of 10 April 1992, the day after the British general election, I remember coming downstairs bleary-eyed as a result of having stayed up late the previous evening watching the coverage of the results, to find my father watching the news headlines before heading to work. "Who won then?" I asked. With the words hardly out of my mouth I could see the answer to my question from the television pictures of Conservative politicians and supporters celebrating their fourth consecutive general election victory. As my question hung in the air, I waited for my lifelong Labour-voting father to say something. Finally, in a weary and bitter voice he said: "Makes ye wonder why ye bother votin at a'." On that morning the view that participation in politics was futile achieved the status of a self-evident principle in Labour-voting households across Scotland. On that morning, even unionists felt the terrible truth that there was a blatant democratic deficit in Scotland and that *political union with England was the problem*.

As of 10 April 1992, the relation of political union with England became the entire political problem of Scotland. 10 April 1992 saw no complaints about a lack of democracy or a lack of political representation among Labour Party voters, as they had voted for and elected a remarkable fifty members of parliament out of a possible seventy-two. However, a few days later the then Labour Party leader Neil Kinnock, after visiting Scotland to congratulate party workers on their success, resigned as party leader and was replaced by John Smith. In many ways, then, one of the reasons why the relation of union became a working-class issue was due to the Scottish working class having for so long and so clearly chosen *not* to mobilise politically via their national identity, but almost exclusively via their class identity in the shape of voting for the Labour Party. Hence, the sense of defeat and futility at pursuing such a strategy was all the more stark and keenly felt on the morning of 10 April 1992, and this day more or less forced upon many Scots a new exercise of freedom insofar as after this day there occurred a moment of historic reflexivity and re-alignment of class and nationality that resolved that, in any subsequent election, the problem would move on from the relation of union to what the working class were prepared to do about it. The problem was not the Labour members of parliament they elected with their votes as they had not reneged on any policy commitments and the people had got the party and politicians they voted for. Ultimately, the lesson was the working class had to resolve to put an end to their own complicity in their geo-political subordination as a result of voting Labour.

The 1992 general election meant the need to defect from Labour to the SNP became a straightforward common sense observation. The relation of political union with England had become problematic because of *class-based differences* between a Labour-voting electorate in Scotland and a Conservative-voting electorate in England, so that the shift from Labour to the SNP was *not* a strategy to bring a halt to a lack of political representation but to bring a halt to a *powerless* political representation, so that nationalism is a power strategy that seeks to reconstitute the political field upon an *exclusively Scottish* basis as a direct result of having learned that voting Labour as a politicised expression of class interests was ineffective because of a vastly more numerous English electorate which returned a Conservative government. To make being working class politically efficacious again, then, meant *re-constituting the democratic political process without England*.

The relation of union with England became problematic not because it prohibited the free and democratic expression of political beliefs, but because the union prevented the Scots' political will from being translated into political power, into the hegemony Labour-voting Scots in their localities and regions had come to expect. In this situation, *since the nation cannot change and since one's class cannot change, the only solution is to make a new State* to ensure the two pillars of *dasein* (nation and class) can exist untrammelled by the eighteenth-century constitutional straight-jacket that the 1707 Act of Union is. Insofar as political union with England more often than not severs the link between democracy and government, the re-alignment of these two realities can only be secured by ending Scotland's political union with England. Nationalism, then, is a response to a specifically Scottish problem of a Conservative-voting English electorate, so that the Scots are more or less coerced into creating their own state so that Conservative-voting can become a purely English affair that affects the English only. If there is the 'return of Scotland' it is because the political mobilisation of the nation is a politics of class that uses the nation as a cipher to achieve its ends.

It was the success of the working class in entering and transforming the public sphere and experiencing taking control of local government via their elected representatives that made possible the subsequent sense of 'disenfranchisement' and democratic deficit of 1979-1997; only a prior empowerment meant a subsequent disempowerment was felt to be intolerable. After the set piece of the miners' strike in 1984-1985 and another two Conservative general election victories still to come in 1987 and 1992 and the introduction of the Poll Tax in 1988, an already anti-Tory prejudice became evermore entrenched, so that we may say it was the Scottish National Party who won the miners' strike and benefited from the eighteen years of 1979-1997, as through this period of more or less open conflict, Thatcher's infamous statement *"there is no such thing as society"* was equivalent to claiming *there was no Scottish nation*.

In the Scottish (working-class) symbolic order the advent of neoliberal market culture and society through the nineteen-eighties and nineteen-nineties were perceived to be an essentially middle-class English project foisted onto the Scots thanks to the union, so that nationalism became a retaliatory 'proletarian' response. Already in 1987 the Labour Party's record number of Scottish members of parliament had been labelled "the feeble fifty" by the SNP leader Alex Salmond,[113] and it was from this paradoxical defeat-in-victory that the Labour Party converted to supporting a Scottish parliament as the irony of these historic successes of the Labour Party in Scotland was that they were ample proof that voting Labour in Scotland was silly and ineffectual. The 'nationalism' of Home Rule then was designed to resolve unionists' embarrassment at the glaring powerlessness of Scotland within the UK, and was a more or less coerced conversion to shore-up the credibility of the unionist parties in the eyes of the Scottish electorate and media.

While there has clearly emerged a political divide between Scotland and England since the nineteen-seventies, it is significant that the standard sociological work on Scotland (McCrone 1992) devotes more than half of its pages to arguing the point that *sociologically speaking*, Scotland is not particularly different from England, so that it seems only a geo-political or historical-cultural approach can shed light on this political divergence. The end of heavy industry and coal mining in the nineteen-eighties in Scotland was part of a wider process of neo-liberal globalization, and a new international division of labour that has impacted upon traditional all-British industries and all-British trade unions, and this transition to a post-British or globalised economy has had a decisive impact upon the fortunes of Scottish nationalism. To highlight the long-term unforeseeable political consequences of deindustrialization within a multi-national state such as the United Kingdom, Siegelbaum and Walkowitz's (1995) study of Ukrainian miners

---

[113] Or as one wit put it in large red paint on a gable end in the Craigmillar area of Edinburgh after the 1992 general election: "Vote Labour For Fifty Useless Bastards."

has persuasively argued that, like Thatcher in the UK, Gorbachev in the USSR oversaw a massive retreat of the state from industry in general and national coalmining industries in particular so that, just as the mass strike in July 1989 by Ukrainian miners protesting against central government economic policy was followed by a withdrawal of support for the Soviet state, which paved the way towards Ukrainian independence in 1991, so an analogy may be drawn with the miners' strike in Scotland in 1984-1985 insofar as a similar withdrawal of consent among a deindustrialised population from the State has meant the emergence of nationalism as a response to the neoliberalism of the political centre.

This shift to a post-British economy has also unsettled or 'dis-organised' the established relationship between trade unions and the Labour Party. On 25 October 1998 there appeared an article in the *Scotland on Sunday* newspaper titled *Unison Branch Demands Union Donate Funds to SNP* which reported a trade union branch demanding Unison begin funding the SNP, and how a unanimously carried motion argued the SNP offered policies more in line with the interests of trade union members than the Labour Party with Alex Dingwall, the assistant branch secretary in Glasgow city saying:

> There is a general recognition within our membership that given the changing nature of Scottish politics we have to have a voice in other political parties, arguing the Unison case.

Two further examples of the alignment of 'labour and nation' and the end of 'Britain' as a category of the political imagination came in November 1998 when the Scottish Socialist Party was formed, which indicated the end of British socialist parties and a process of seceding from all-British formats within left-wing parties and the adoption of the nationalist policy of Scottish sovereignty and political independence. On 1st May 2001 the Scottish Workers Party merged with the Scottish Socialist Party, which consolidated the alignment of 'labour and nation' and represented another defeat for all-British formats within the Scottish Left. Much of the rationale for the 'eleventh-hour' conversion of the Scottish Left to

441

nationalism was to take advantage of the new platform of the Scots parliament, as prior to 1999 much of the political Left had understood itself via the prism of modernism and had viewed nationalism as a divisive ideology that distracted from the international struggle of workers against capital and, insofar as they viewed nationalism as "that outlook which gives an absolute priority to the values of the nation over all other values and interests" (Hroch *in* Eley & Suny 1996, p. 62), many socialists in Scotland saw nationalism as a kind of 'false consciousness.' However, with the advent of a less extreme understanding of nationalism in Scotland as a *national movement* (Hroch 1993) rather than 'blood and soil' chauvinism, the socialist Left have completed a journey from opposition to enthusiastic embrace of Scottish independence.

Similarly, in my conversations with lifelong Labour voters I found there was a sense that independence was something approaching inevitability in the same way that, for example, the end of the mining industry had also been talked about as inevitable; as if the desire for independence was being brought about without any 'ideological' contestation or confrontation with 'unionism.' It seems, then, that during the nineteen-eighties and nineties, something passed into the political common sense of the Scottish working class that was not present in the pre-Thatcher era. During the nineteen-eighties and nineteen-nineties the process described by Marx whereby "the struggle of the proletariat with the bourgeoisie is at first a national struggle. The proletariat of each country must, of course, first of all settle matters with its own bourgeoisie" (1996, p. 24), seems to have became more or less complete. When reading the tortured history of Scottish nationalism (Finlay 1994) from its beginnings in the Scottish Home Rule Association (1886) and over the course of the twentieth century, it is clear that there is a socio-economic mediation of nationalism, and that it is constituted differently among the different social classes and across the different generations.

According to Finlay's account, for example, over the course of the SNP's history there has been what I term a middle-class 'purist' or substantivist conception of nationalism which prevailed among the leadership of the SNP until the nineteen-eighties, at which point a more 'working class' and younger leadership began to occupy leadership posts. I propose that so long as the SNP wanted the pure appeal of independence to attract support from each social class, it only succeeded in attracting those with sufficient 'cultural capital' to take an interest in pure or substantivist nationalism, but thanks to the nineteen-eighties shift in SNP leadership there came the understanding that the project of independence had to step down from its purist pedestal and become fully contextualised in social realities, and this meant it had to appeal to the working class. In this regard, theorists have articulated the need to recognise the complex nature of nationalism as a movement of particular social classes and groups that has political aims and which mobilises a symbolic or cultural patrimony i.e. nationalism is a social and political and cultural reality, and none of these forces can be identified as the 'real reality' underpinning the other or as the real being of nationalism. As Gellner (1983, p. 121) has it:

> Only when a nation became a class, a visible and unequally distributed category in an otherwise mobile system, did it become politically conscious and activist. Only when a class happened to be (more or less) a 'nation' did it turn from being a class-in-itself into a class-for-itself, or a nation-for-itself. Neither nations nor classes seem to be political catalysts: only nation-classes or class-nations are such.

Similarly, Wallerstein (in McCrone 1992, p. 56) has remarked that: "I believe 'class' and what I prefer to call 'ethno-nation' are two sets of clothing for the same basic reality. However, it is important to realise that there are in fact two sets of clothing, so that we may appreciate how, when and why one set is worn rather than the other." These theorists of nationalism, then, accord nations or 'ethno-nations' equal importance with social class as historic forces, with the term 'class' referring to the global capitalist economy and the term 'class consciousness' essentially being a national and local culturally-specific phenomenon. In contrast to unionist politicians foisting the fabricated choice of social justice or independence, then, Wallerstein (in McCrone 1992, pp. 56-7) points out that the social revolutions in Russia, China, Vietnam and Cuba have been social and cultural and national.

> It is similarly not at all accidental that oppressed lower strata in core capitalist countries (Blacks in the United States, Quebecois in Canada, Occitans in France, etc.) have come to express their class consciousness in ethno-national terms.

Confirming this McCrone (1992, pp. 56-7) has written, presumably with Scotland and New Labour in mind:

> One can see the recrudescence of ethno-nationalisms in industrialised states as an expression of class consciousness of lower caste groups in societies where the class terminology has been pre-empted by nation-wide middle strata organised around the dominant ethnic group.

Finally, Herzfeld (1997, p. 6) criticised theorists of nationalism such as Benedict Anderson for failing to acknowledge the need for immersion into local contexts, to allow ethnographic research into the various forms of nationalism to uncover its social ontology:

> He [Benedict Anderson] does not ground his account [of nationalism] in the details of everyday life – symbolism, commensality, family, and friendship – that would make it convincing for each specific case or that might call for the recognition of the cultural specificity of each nationalism. In that respect, like Gellner (1983), he seems to assume that nationalisms are fundamentally alike in their debt to a common (European) origin and that they thereby represent the imposition of an elite perspective on local cultural worlds.

This new awareness that nationalism is endemic and integral to 'being modern' represents a major advance over a previous theoretical consensus that imagined nationalism to be merely epiphenomenal to the advent of modernity, and fated to end after the tensions and traumas of 'becoming modern' ended. This advance also guides us to view the original Scottish nationalism of the twelfth and thirteenth centuries, for example, as being similarly the means of becoming modern *on their own terms*, and that twenty-first century Scottish nationalism involves recuperating this original 12$^{th}$ century advent of the modern era and recuperating a holistic way of 'being working class.' This emphasis upon class, then, remains crucial because the fact is that the older generation of locals who remain Labour voters were never interested in the New Labour project that emerged after 1992 to make the Labour Party electable in England, and their children remain ideologically 'old Labour' or left-of-centre but upon a purely Scottish basis or from a *nationalist* position that is concerned with creating *for the second time* a Scottish modernity on purely Scottish terms.

## The Scottish Six

During doctoral fieldwork *The Scotsman* newspaper (20 October 1998) reported that the British Broadcasting Corporation's board of governors had decided to not allow Scotland to have its own six o'clock news programme after the advent of devolution, which meant Scotland after 1999 would continue to receive its main evening news programming from England. Commenting upon this decision, journalist Matt Wells concluded: "Now, many will feel that the BBC...already unpopular and distrusted among Scots... will be seen as the English Broadcasting Corporation," while an editorial of the *Daily Mail* (11 December 1998) had this to say:

> The depth of anger felt about the decision to turn down Scotland for its own programme was summed up by Nigel Smith, former chairman of the Broadcasting for Scotland lobbying group: 'What do we have to do? Burn ourselves to death on the steps of BBC Scotland to achieve this?'

As "control and manipulation of public information and discourse is an extremely important part of the activities of every regime" (Barth 1994, p. 21), this decision of the BBC preserved the *status quo ante* across two constitutional eras, and was seen in Scotland as more evidence that the BBC was an elitist and authoritarian and anti-democratic and anti-Scottish institution. This failure of the BBC to match political devolution with 'broadcasting devolution' was fated to be seen as perpetuating English-rule and English cultural hegemony in Scotland, and confirm the perception that such centralisation and reserving of cultural power in England also meant the continued underdevelopment of Scottish culture.

More generally, because post-affluent societies witness an explosion in the production and consumption of culture, the control and management of State broadcasters is of huge importance in every nation-state, and even more so in a multi-national state context. Similarly, the question as to which social groups populate media corporations and exercise control over broadcasting content is important, and it would be difficult to over-state the importance of the media (television, radio and newspaper) in the political process. While the BBC no longer enjoys a monopoly over television and radio broadcasting, as the State broadcaster *the BBC produces the daily reality of England within Scotland twenty-four hours a day*. Unsurprisingly, then, thanks to being an England-based organisation there is a widespread perception in Scotland that the media in the post-1999 era remains dominated by English interests and English perspectives and English programming, and this perception has become markedly exacer-bated in the post-1999 era because, as a result of so much power having been devolved to Edinburgh, far more news content broadcast into Scotland is only of relevance to English and Welsh viewers, and so this 'broadcasting deficit' is a daily spectacle and only fuels the general conviction that an independent Scottish broadcaster is the only possible solution to this cultural inequality.

The media then is an important ethnographic site because a daily struggle to structure perception occurs, and a significant event within the media came in the run up to the 1992 general election on 23rd January when *The Sun* newspaper splashed over its first sixteen pages its conversion to the independence cause, in direct competition with its unionist tabloid rival *The Daily Record*. This stunning development delighted nationalists as it gave them for the first time a direct means to spread their message by "targeting a largely young, male, working-class market with a nationalist message" (Bennie et al. 1997, p. 19). While nationalists welcomed the novel experience of a newspaper on its side, this pro-independence stance proved short-lived, and so Scotland is that rarest of national movements in that it has not a single newspaper or television broadcaster in favour of independence.[114]

If we assume that a 'representational deficit' exists, this raises the question how this impacts upon the 'schemes of perception' of Scottish audiences across the generations. When *Scottish Television's* newsreader Angus Simpson promises viewers "in a packed programme" at lunchtime news of "the new Keanu Reeves film where he plays a serial killer," and BBC Scotland's *Reporting Scotland* presenter Jackie Bird promises viewers another national news programme full of reports to the procurator fiscal "plus all the sport and a full weather report," we can share Harvie's view of television in Scotland as "a tundra" (1998, p. 153), and ask whether in Scotland there is a population that, insofar as it is also a television audience, is more or less coerced into accepting its subordination?

In this regard the only data that I gathered during fieldwork came when conducting an interview (April 2000) in the Dundonald area of the village with a woman who worked as a care assistant in a local nursing home, and as we sat watching the evening news bulletin *Scotland Today* my interviewee peremptorily complained: "See this Scottish news, it is absolutely pathetic!"[115] What is the effect upon mental health as a result of daily disgust at television programming that provokes the reaction of resentment? If as a

---

[114] In June 2014 the *Sunday Herald* became the only newspaper to adopt an editorial line in favour of independence. More generally, the internet and the new social media it spawns is the only media where the nationalist voice not only has parity with unionists but tends to predominate.

[115] Interestingly, much like the pensioner from Whitehall Drive discussed earlier, this informant voted for the SNP at the general election of May 2011 for the first time in her life at the age of 72, after a lifetime of voting Labour and advised me she would probably vote 'yes' in the 2014 Referendum.

rule the dominated are ordinarily fated to have a dominated relation to their condition of being dominated (Gilfillan 2009), I propose the media reproduces and reinforces such a relation among its audience, and in the following exchange with Kenneth Anderson (127 Orebank Road) I speculate whether something of the isomorphism between the quality of broadcasting in Scotland and the quality of confusion and defeatism is evidenced:

**Me:** Do you mind if Ah ask how ye voted in the elections, if you did vote?

**Kenneth:** Ah cannae mind.

**Me:** Cause there's been that much e them!

**Kenneth:** Aye. Eh...Labour.

**Me:** One question I'm asking is why do you think it is we have this parliament after all these three hundred years; why do you think it is?

**Kenneth:** Well Ah would rather we got complete independence really. Ah don't vote SNP ye ken bit Ah'm prepared...

**Me:** How no if ye want independence?

**Kenneth:** Ah don't know. It's strange. Ah jist dinnae...Bit Ah wid...

**Me:** Would you rather ca canny first? Get a parliament first and then...

**Kenneth:** Well Ah wid rather go home rule right away sort e thing.

**Me:** But the Labour party don't believe in independence.

**Kenneth:** Well Ah know bit that's jist the way e ma thinkin just now.

**Me:** Do you not trust the SNP or something?

**Kenneth:** Well Ah don't know what it is. Ah jist...well they're no gettin there nae mair any quick eh? They're really no quick enough.

**Me:** But they'll need your vote!

**Kenneth:** Well Ah'm actually a Tommy Sheridan...Ah'd really go fir him ken. But they dinnae get backin an a' this stuff ye ken. Everybody in Scotland's that pathetic. Ah'm the same of course. Naebody just seems to really care.

Much like our earlier discussion of an education system that is criticised for producing a people 'without memory' or history, I propose that in light of news programming being described as "absolutely pathetic" and informants describing Scotland as "that pathetic," a 'representational regime' is able to make a nation into its image. While my minimum wage care assistant informant did not proceed to draw any political conclusions, it is clear that in the nationalist imagination BBC Scotland helps achieve the crucial political function of keeping Britain imaginatively together, and the ubiquity of England and English-based programming and the normative middle-class bias in television schedules after 1999 is why the issue of a Scottish Six opens a window upon the ongoing struggle to structure perception that is played out in the media.[116]

## 5.4 Politics and the Question of Being (Whole)

Until May 2011 Cardenden was part of what used to be described as the Labour Party's 'heartlands,' as the Labour Party has exercised a virtual monopoly over political representation at local and regional and national level for at least three generations.[117] Because of the importance of the Labour Party I had hoped to attend the monthly meetings of the local branch as part of fieldwork, and talking in January 1999 with the branch secretary

---

[116] The BBC2 programme *The Referendum Debate* broadcast from Kirkcaldy on 18 March 2014 saw a remarkable level of criticism of the national broadcaster's news programming. When audience member Sandy Steel asked: 'Does the panel believe that the BBC have been impartial on their coverage of the Scottish referendum?' many audience members burst into spontaneous applause, indicating their judgment that BBC Scotland serves unionist interests. [http://www.bbc.co.uk/iplayer/episode/b03yq66n/The_Referendum_Debate_18_03_2014].

[117] I recall on one occasion hurrying from work to vote in a local Council election, only to find the Corrie Centre polling station empty and locked. After a few minutes wondering what everyone knew except myself, it dawned on me that the local Labour councillor must have been unopposed so that no electoral contest was needed.

(Wendy Fleming) about whether this would be possible, Wendy's response was positive, and she asked me to write a letter to the branch saying something about myself and my research. In the letter Wendy advised it was important that I stress I was not interested in the party political or ideological aspects of local politics, but was simply wanting to observe a significant site as an ethnographer of the historic year of 1999. During our conversation I also had to address Wendy's concern that I may be "an SNP infiltrator." While I wrote the letter as advised I was not allowed to attend any of the party meetings, and the reason given was that only party members could attend. However, after the first election campaign for the Holyrood parliament I managed to interview Roberta Catherine (Orebank Rd, 14 November) who was an office-bearer in the local Labour Party, and having invited me into her house Roberta proceeded to give me an interview which I cite extensively as it is representative of many other interviews conducted during fieldwork.

**Roberta:** Ah widnae say Ah dinnae like Tony [Blair] because Ah mean Ah've got a photo taen wi Cherie [Blair] an that an they're nice people but they're Tories.
**Me:** You think so?
**Roberta:** Ah think so.
**Me:** You're joking me! You can say that?
**Roberta:** Ah can say there's a part e Tory in them. Aye. Come on noo! They're rotten wi money. Where's an auld Labour like ma dad, who went doon the pit on his hands and knees and voted Labour and a union member all his life; what does he have in common wi Tony Blair?
**Me:** You're talking heresy.
**Roberta:** Ah know! Ah know! [Roberta begins to laugh]. Ah know. Ah know it's no right but we've a' Ah suppose got they kind e feelins.
**Me:** Maybe Ah'm bein naive but is that no a contradiction?
**Roberta:** Well Tony Blair's faither wis a Tory. And at the Labour Party conference, Ah wis at the Labour Party conference, and Tony's faither wis sittin doon. He was still

a Tory but he was at the conference. He changed tae a Labour Party member noo. Ah could never change. Ma husband could change. Ma husband could faa oot wi Labour an say "That's it; Ah'm no votin any mair" bit Ah couldnae. Ah'm one hunder per cent Labour!

**Me:** Why do you no vote for the Socialists? The Workers'...

**Roberta:** Nut. You're no tellin me Tommy Sheridan's a man worth voting fir?

**Me:** Well what Ah'm sayin is you said it, no' me. You said yer leader is a Tory.

**Roberta:** No Ah never said. Ah said he has...

**Me:** A bit e Tory in him.

**Roberta:** Aye. Ah widnae say he was a Tory. He's still for the working people but he's for middle England as well. He has to be of course or we would never have gotten in, if it hidnae been for middle England. Scotland alone could never get in, if it hidnae been fir middle England. Scotland alone could never get in under the Labour government; they have to have middle England. If we don't have middle England we wouldnae've won the general election! Because ye could vote a hunder per cent Labour in Scotland but it takes middle England tae get ye intae power. That's true.

**Me:** Do you think Tony Blair's really Labour but he's just pretendin in order to win middle England? D'ye think he's jist being clever?

**Roberta:** Ah think he's got Tory values! Three year ago, Ah stood oot on the streets in a' the villages in Fife. Ah went up tae Inverness an Ah went right up north, an especially in Cardenden itself this jist gien ye one village, at that particular time, Ah could have got a hunder per cent Labour vote. Ah could go oot in the streets today an Ah'll only guarantee you twenty per cent e a Labour vote.

**Me:** Ah thought Cardenden was quite solidly Labour?

**Roberta:** Aye, but they're auld Labour. And they're left. Ah could name ye a few people e this village who've been Labour voters an members e the Labour Party a' their lives but are weary! Ah shouldnae really be sayin this tae you, Ah hope yer no gonnae be sayin that Ah said this! Ah'll get shot fae Gordon! [Gordon Brown, Cardenden's MP] Ah'm only sayin what people have come tae me an said, aboot how they're disillusioned. They expect different things, even fae the Scottish parliament.

**Me:** So what do you think they're thinking noo? D'ye think they're a' busy sayin Ah'll vote fir the SNP noo? They're sayin we're scunnered wi Labour, we're gonnae vote SNP noo?

**Roberta:** Nut! They would never vote Labour,[118] they would rather form a Labour Party.

**Me:** Ah heard there was some folk in Cardenden were tryin to have a new sort e Labour party but it fell through because there wisnae much interest.

**Roberta:** A lot e the people, let's be honest, a lot e the Labour voters, they'll only vote, they're no politically minded. They'll vote Labour because, an Ah hate tae say this, bit if ye were pittin a monkey doon there, in this village, the village e Bowhill would vote Labour. Because it's part e a tradition. They dinnae ken any better.

**Me:** So you think only twenty per cent?

**Roberta:** There's a lot e people disillusioned.

**Me:** And you don't think the disillusioned vote is going any place in particular?

**Roberta:** Nut. They would just stay home. Ye'd bound tae watch the polls at the elections fir the Scottish parliament, how the drop was.

**Me:** When Ah wis growin up ye voted Labour and that wis it. There wisnae anybody else tae vote for. So where did the Nationalists come fae?

**Roberta:** They're an organised party noo.

**Me:** But take some of the headlines in the run up to the parliamentary elections; the Nationalists were runnin neck and neck wi the Labour Party.

---

[118] I assume Roberta meant to say SNP.

**Roberta:** They're a stronger party now because old Labour have disappeared. Although new Labour has got us intae power, it's middle England that got us intae power; it wisnae the auld red Labour. The auld red Labour has went by the wayside but there's still a lot e them there.

**Me:** But it's this agreed reliance on middle England that maybe the Scots, the Labour voters in Scotland, got tired of. That's why independence for Scotland became more popular no?

**Roberta:** But do you no think, Ah mean Ah'm Labour one hunder per cent so ye'll maybe see why Ah'm contradictin masel again, but if the Liberal Democrats had a better leader, everyone of us is a bit e a Liberal Democrat; there's a bit e Tory and a bit e Labour and a bit e Scottish National Party in every human being. Because ye want tae get on in life an ye want money and when Labour was Labour years ago everybody was the same. Everybody's no the same noo. A' tryin tae keep up wi the Joneses. So that's the Tory part e ye. The Labour part e ye is yer still wantin tae see, yer wantin yer national health, yer social security; and SNP is the Scotland at heart. Ah believe in ma country. Ah dinnae believe in independence bit Ah believe in Scotland. Ah ken that's maybe contradictin masel again.

In this refreshingly honest and revealing interview I gave Roberta every opportunity to euphemise her biting realism, but this seemed to encourage her plain-speaking and her determination to give as many hostages to fortune as possible and as quickly as possible. Roberta shows a remarkable commitment to voting Labour and a willingness to concede the concessions required in order to keep imagining herself as part of Britain, despite being clear she has good reasons to do no such thing. Roberta is also fully aware of all of the contradictions and electoral gymnastics that have to be gone through as a result of being Scottish, working class and left-of-centre; the contradictions of someone who is "one hunder per cent Labour" and who has "Scotland at heart." When surveying the political field, Roberta exhibits a sure touch and verbal command but, alongside the assured delivery of her no-nonsense views, is her clear awareness of a number of blatant contradictions as she depicts the Labour Prime Minister Tony Blair as "a Tory," yet "Ah widnae say he was a Tory," and as someone who has "Tory values" yet is "for the working people." Roberta also recognises the new alignments that are afoot in Scottish politics and the pressures to abandon the New Labour project as she openly acknowledges that her husband "could change." Her difficulty is that she sees the sense in actions she is not happy with, and even identifies with those making hard choices: on the one hand there is the Roberta that sees Blair as a Tory but another Roberta recognises the shift to the right by the Labour Party was necessary to win middle England. She can see New Labour is 'a necessary evil' to win middle England, so that *New Labour was an English solution to an English problem* as no invention of New Labour was necessary to win Scotland and, to the extent that this new direction involved all of the Labour Party, is an example of the Labour Party in Scotland accepting its subordination as a prerequisite for New Labour to become a party of power.

If winning political power was dependent upon a rearticulation of English hegemony within the Labour Party, this is something Roberta nowhere explicitly mentions, and something else she is consistent in is her refusal to recognise any connection between the rise of the SNP and the demise of "old Labour," and working-class people feeling disenfranchised or "weary" with New Labour in the nineteen-nineties. With the benefit of hindsight and the 2011 election when the SNP came close to defeating Labour in her own constituency, when Roberta advises that disillusioned Labour voters would not vote SNP but "would rather form a Labour Party," she is clearly reluctant to recognise the full extent of the re-alignment that was happening between class and nation.[119]

If we were to ask the real Roberta to stand up we see her difficulty as she has constructed four conflicting 'selves.' Roberta

---

[119] At the 2011 election to the Scottish parliament the SNP reduced Labour's majority to 1,247 votes. Helen Eadie (Labour) gained 11,926 votes while the SNP's candidate Ian Chisholm received 10,679 votes.

454

opts to be realistic, and therefore becomes untrue to (part of) herself. Rhetorically, she restores her integrity by saying she is "one hunder per cent Labour" and "could never change," but in the same breath admits she is "contradictin masel again." She admits many have left the Labour Party because they – like herself – identify with old Labour, but also says old Labour has "disappeared" and has "went by the wayside," only to contradict herself by recognising "but there's still a lot e them there." She disappears old Labour by being pragmatic and justifies its disappearance at the hands of New Labour because "it is middle England that got us into power." Her realism demands she marginalises her ownmost *dasein* and in the process accept and produce her subordination in order to belong to a party in power. As an office-bearer we may say she disappears her disappearance of Old Labour and this is what makes her "fit for office" as a New Labour office-bearer.

It seems clear Roberta knows she is walking a tightrope where the need to be realistic is continually at risk of becoming flagrant subordination insofar as it endorses the forfeiting of real representa-tion for *some* representation; in the end subordination is exacted because the alternative to Scotland accommodating itself to English Labour politicians' New Labour project is the political oblivion of joining former colleagues by "the wayside," or joining those who have changed their allegiance to the SNP. When Roberta advises "it's middle England that got us intae power," she sees clearly the reality of being 'Better Together' is that it takes middle England to deliver a left-of-centre government in Westminster, and it is not the Scots who exercise sovereignty over themselves but middle England, and if this arrangement is acceptable then one is a unionist and if it is not acceptable then one is a nationalist.

In a purely speculative manner I propose that there are two voices or 'two consciousnesses' present within Roberta during this interview. There is the Roberta interviewed at home, and there is the public Roberta who is a Labour Party official that accounts for the hesitation and the 'loss of voice' that occurs during the interview at certain moments. Roberta knows the Labour Party in Scotland has de-prioritised its core working-class voters to gain power because only in England did the Labour Party need to move to the right in order to be electable in England. Being part of an all-British political party means, for a realistic working-class Scot, one's political realism has to trump one's preferred option to have a politics that truly represents one's core voters. Being 'better together' means a duality instead of an integrity ensues, and so Roberta must construct a 'second best' politics and more or less spectate her real self in the name of a practical realism. Roberta realises very well that faced with this predicament, integral Scottish *dasein* becomes 'weary,' 'disappears' or 'stays home' from where politics becomes something that is spectated and perceived as unreal and unrepresentative.

Moreover, in this situation it seems likely this *dasein* over time will no longer represent itself *to itself* insofar as it has given up the aspiration that such a self will be represented in politics. If one assumes that to spectate one's being is in an important sense to already cease to be that being, one postpones representative politics because one has already in one's own consciousness failed to represent oneself so that one compounds an already objectively subordinate class and national positionality. The reality of being 'better together' is that Roberta must privatise herself and keep her "Scotland at heart" or keep it within the domestic realm and firmly out of the public and political realm.

If as a result of her national identity Roberta must accept a certain amount of subordination, as a working-class woman she is also clear that the 'class system' has infiltrated the Labour Party and that the middle class has taken over. During our interview Roberta spoke of the widely held view that the Labour Party leadership was "rotten wi money," and insofar as New Labour distanced itself from traditional working-class identity in the name of modernisation, this removed traditional symbolic 'signposts' for identification among working-class Labour voters. In this regard, the revelation of the first First Minister of the Holyrood Parliament being a multi-millionaire in the aftermath of his death did not go un-noticed or commented upon. When discussing the corruption of politicians in the aftermath of the Conservative peer Lord Archer's being jailed for perjury in July

2001 one East of Scotland Water manual operatives (Mick Kelman) commented:

> How the f*** is he [Donald Dewar] supposed tae represent us the workin class eh? A f***in Labour MP and he's supposed tae represent the workin class in, where is it, Anniesland in Glesgae an he's a f***in multi-millionaire! What the f**** is that a' aboot? Ah bet they Glesgae c***s in their two thoosan pound cooncil hooses must feel like f***in muppets votin fir that c**t. Ah mean how the f*** can somebody be a multi-millionaire an be a f***in Labour MP? How the f*** is that possible? [120]

This concern with a social elite enriching themselves was undoubtedly helped by the long-running 'cash for questions' affair that began in 1994 when Westminster politicians were found guilty of taking money from wealthy individuals to ask questions in parliament (and was to erupt on a new scale in 2009 in what is referred to as the Westminster parliamentary expenses scandal). At the other end of the social hierarchy, a constant theme that exercised the materialism of locals was that of unemployed locals living off state benefits; which for many amounted to a shameful refusal to constitute life authentically by responding honestly to the facts of life by working. For example, I recall in the kitchen of an elderly couple I was interviewing a notice board of family photographs and mementos and souvenirs as well as the following clipping taken from the *Central Fife Times* newspaper:

## A Shocker

I enclose an extract from a letter carried in the Courier and Advertiser.

---

[120] Mick was drawing upon the caricature of Glasgow as being synonymous with poverty and that Donald Dewar was the Labour MP for Glasgow Anniesland which had received media attention for being one of the poorest constituencies in Britain. The reference to "two thoosan pound Cooncil hooses" refers to media coverage at the time surrounding the proposed privatisation of Glasgow City Council housing stock, and the average market value of a Glasgow city Council house being reported to be less than £2000.

"A 65 year-old man who has worked all his life and paid national insurance and income tax for the past 50 years was entitled to a retirement pension of £115.40 per week for himself and his wife. Meanwhile, a similar couple who have lived off state benefits and have never paid a penny into the system all their lives are entitled to £140.55 per week plus rent, rates and all other handouts available." These figures were apparently provided by and guaranteed correct by an official of the DSS in the Dundee area. Now one could just imagine the dismay and shock experienced by our local MP The Right Hon Gordon Brown when advised of this completely immoral and bizarre situation. Indeed Mr Brown was so upset he found himself unable to reply to letters concerning this apparent anomaly.

SPION KOP, Lochgelly. [121]

When I asked the householder who had taken early retirement in 2002 after forty years of continuous employment why he had pinned this letter up in the kitchen, he told me coyly: "Jist a reminder." Along similar lines was the following short exchange that I noted prior to interviewing a Labour-voting man and wife while watching the evening news on the day of the first Labour budget for eighteen years (17 March 1998):

**Wife:** So long as they hammer the rich Ah'll be happy.
**Husband:** They never do, they'd be daen it tae theirsels.

As with Roberta and Mick and this retired couple, there is a deeply-felt awareness of the absurdity of rich people representing the working class and the working class voting for such

---

[121] Spion Kop is the name of a battle site in South Africa where the British army in 1900 was defeated by Dutch farmers. To explain the defeat of the British some reports adverted to inept military leadership, perhaps indicating the author is referring to the inept leadership of politicians to address the situation his letter refers to.

representatives, and we may say that there is a double domination here where the working class are unable to produce representatives from within their own class, and so are represented by middle-class representatives who possess the linguistic and cultural resources for public life. This embourgeoisement of the Labour Party signals a crisis of identity for a party that was founded in the 'era of scarcity' and which now seems to find itself at a loss as to how to negotiate its way in the 'era of affluence.' In Scotland, of course, this difficulty about what to do about the working class is compounded by the difficulty of what to do with the national question, and insofar as the Labour Party cannot solve these two issues it seems fated to decline while the SNP seems fated to rise. If the SNP is fated to become more attractive to voters, some were able to pinpoint a particular experience that helped inform their shift to a pro-independence stance. During the very first interview I conducted during fieldwork (Mr Ronaldson, Kinglassie Rd, 7 June 1999) my informant recounted the following incident:

> Ah mean if ye cannae stand up fir yer ain country...Ah mean okay, Ah'll gie ye an instance e what Ah felt. Ah wis talkin tae a guy wane night, Ah wis at a do, an there was a Dutchman there. An Ah've worked in Holland, Ah know how they think, how they work, how they behave an a' the rest e it...an this Dutchman was makin a fool e his sel, he wis enjoyin his sel, having a good time, an somebody wis sittin, they were all Scotch people, and he turns an says "You're nuthin but a f***in arsehole" an he says "Aye, maybe Ah am..." he says "...but Ah govern maself. There's a difference." That summed it up. That summed it right up.

As with the previous discussion of an elderly informant being made to feel ashamed insofar as her unionist views were revealed by a foreigner as colluding in their own subordination, something similar is being adverted to above, as central to this testimony is recognition of the fact that devolution is still subordination because the devolution settlement of 1 July 1999 does not amount to the sovereign self-government of independence enjoyed and practiced by every other nation. Also, when the existence of the nation is long settled within the imagination of its members, there is no need to raise the formal 'doctrinal' definition of nationalism (i.e. that the nation and the state shall be congruent) to explicit conceptualisation in order for independence to be attractive, because such is the structuring of perception that the individual simply 'looks' and draws the 'obvious' conclusion:

> Bit Ah mean Ah'm a' fir Scotland bein on its ain ken. Ah mean, likes e, if ye look abroad, a' the wee countries they're a' independent. An Ah mean they're a' joined up tae ither countries ken. So Ah'm a' fir Scotland bein oan its ain.[122]

As a result of the universal organisation of geo-political space according to the nation-state template, any Scot can draw the nationalist conclusion by simply "looking around" and seeing smaller and poorer European nations voting massively in favour of independence throughout the nineteen-nineties (Armenia, Azerbaijan, Belarus, Estonia, Georgia, Kazakhstan, Kyrgyzstan, Latvia, Lithuania, Moldova, Tajikistan, Turkmenistan, Ukraine, Uzbekistan, Bosnia and Herzegovina, Croatia, Macedonia, Serbia and Montenegro, Slovenia, the Czech Republic and Slovakia). Free from concerns about the long durée, the *modernist* nationalist can imagine his nationalism emerges more or less *ex nihilo* insofar as he need only draw upon thirty or forty years of history to draw the nationalist conclusion and so needs no resort to 'medievalism.'

The ethnographer constructing a 'native point of view' that has a national identity component, then, must advert to its real and imagined relations with other nations and how they resolve their being-in-the-world. As per Roberta's testimony, a Scottish working-class identity, for example, is aware of other identities such as 'middle-class England,' so that each particular individual's construction of their being-in-the-world borrows much of itself from neighbouring identities. Put simply, seeing how others imagine and

---

[122] Andrew Peebles, South Dundonald Cottage No. 2 (East).

practice their identities is part of the process of learning to imagine and decide whether or not to politicise one's own. Because existence is always coexistence, the existence of other nations naturalises the mobilisation of national identity and the desire for independence and, as in the quote above, it is often contact with other nationality groupings that is the occasion for evoking a nationalist response, although this inter-national 'spectre of comparisons' can also provoke a risk-averse unionist response. Hence, asking one local (Mrs Penman, Muirtonhill Road) for her views on the reasons behind the Scottish parliament, she answered:

> Ye always have the rebels who want these kinds of things, you know. And I really dinnae approve e pittin a line at a' through a country cause when ye see what's happening oot in Kosovo at the moment, and there are people who are gonnae fight wi each other like Ireland. And these kind e things Ah think are absolutely terrible. Ah really think that people should really try tae pull together and no go back.

Because this informant's country is the United Kingdom, 1 July 1999 brings three centuries of 'pulling together' to an end and the return of the repressed is "absolutely terrible," and so she is more or less bewildered by the politics of identity that is ongoing in Scotland (and Ireland and Kosovo). In contrast to the non-appearance of 'Scotland' in her discourse, another theme touched on by many informants was the perception of *cultural differences* between Scotland and England, with informants more often than not pointing to cultural difference, in addition to the obvious political difference, as part of their justification for supporting independence, although on the issue of cultural differences between Scotland and England next-door neighbours could express opposing viewpoints:

> You know Ah really think we're quite different from doon south as well in a lot e aspects you know.
>
> Mrs McGlaughlin
> Orebank Road

461

No. Ah definitely widnae want tae see us bein independent. Ah jist think we should a' be wane United Kingdom. Why can we no be wane? Ah jist think we're a' the same. Ah mean years ago they voted Scottish Nationalist because there was a big thing.[123] It was a young person's thing and ye were young an ye wanted tae vote fir them, bit Ah think in hindsight it was a bit silly and it never done any guid anyway.

Mrs Reilly
Orebank Road

If in light of the electoral victories of the SNP in 2007 and 2011 it is rather certain that we will never hear such views again as they were uttered on the brink of spectacular historic successes for the SNP, no hindsight is needed to realise the view that voting SNP in the seventies did not achieve anything was wrong even when they were first uttered as this married informant in her late-thirties seems oblivious to the fact that the nationalism she thought was a spent force *had just reconstituted the basis for politics in Scotland*. On the wider question of cultural differences between Scotland and England, Gellner in *Nations and Nationalism* (1983) argued that the emergence of Britain as a cohesive nation-state required the forceful homogenising of what were two markedly different cultures in Scotland and England, so that the successful emergence of Britain required the suppression of Scotland, Catholicism, Jacobitism, Gaeldom and the Scots and Gaelic languages, and this programme of cultural repression was functional not simply to the emergence of Britain but the emergence of industrial civilisation and modernity.

However, I would propose Gellner misrecognises nationalism when he describes it as "a phenomenon of *Gesellschaft* using the idiom of *Gemeinschaft*" (1997, p. 74) because this formulation fails to realise that, due to the creation of Cardenden (and any number of localities in the central belt) as an occupational community, working-class nationalism needs no backward glance to a long-lost

---

[123] Mrs Reilly was referring to the late 1960s and early 1970s. By 1968, for example, the SNP had the largest membership of all political parties in Scotland.

*Gemeinschaft* or experience of community in order to constitute nationalism by as, such were the rigors and the homogeneity exacted by the industrial occupational community, that working-class nationalism can equally be described as *a phenomenon of Gesellschaft using the idiom of Gesellschaft* as it does not need to resort to the 'period costume' of *Gemeinschaft* because industrial *Gesellschaft* is up to the job. Simply on the basis of their identity as a proletariat, only mobilising the timeframe of 1967-1997 (and leaving aside the historicity of their *dasein* altogether) there is conceivably enough to constitute a nationalist project by. Indeed, one might go as far to say that only the '79 generation are emerging into Ferguson's 'civil society' or Tonnies's *gesellschaft* because up until the dotage of the '45 generation locals had been living a form of modern industrial *gemeinschaft* in their couthie occupational communities and sharing in their undisturbed 'sacred canopy' which still burned brightly in their hearts and households until they were disorganised in the late nineteen-eighties.

Interestingly, regardless of their particular party affiliations and opinions about the cultural differences between Scotland and England, locals saw 1999 as a time of deciding once and for all the national question. While some locals wanted the status quo ante and some wanted independence, all seemed to agree this question had to be decided either way, so that in contrast to the devolution scheme created by border-crossing professionals for whom the constitutional settlement of 1 July 1999 is not "some sort of halfway house...an unstable mid-point between the status quo and separation" (Brown and Alexander 1999, p. 11), I found this is exactly how many locals viewed the new constitutional arrangement of devolution; and it seems clear that this view is sourced in the fact that they see other nations agitating and struggling for sovereign parliaments and not devolved assemblies, and so locals view independence and not devolution as the only imaginable end result for Scotland.

This uncomplicated view of Scotland's options and scepticism towards makeshift compromises worked out by unionist politicians signals that nationalism is a social practice embedded in localities and follows a different logic to that of the reified public political sphere. The concrete stuff of class and culture and 'being European' is the social grounds or the social ontology that gives nationalism its substance, and this is why ethnography for Herzfeld (1997, pp. 11-12) is particularly suited to uncovering the reality of nationalism.

> [Anthropology]...through its resolute insistence on the signifi-cance of the particular, is thus able to document how nation-alism is understood (and sometimes recast) by living social actors...The fact that such processes [of reconstituting the past] often use bodily and kinship metaphors is not evidence of some cultural inability to think beyond immediate social experience but simply shows that members of local communi-ties think about the state through much the same categories as those through which state officials woo local opinion.

Neither a reified 'thing' called 'the union,' nor any prolonged meditation upon something called the 'British constitution' is the ground of Scottish nationalism, but the much more embedded and 'thick' state of affairs where the Scots vote one way and the English vote another and opposite way in the lived experience of the generation that came to political consciousness from 1979 onwards. Insofar as devolutionists conceded that there must be 'Scottish solutions to Scottish problems,' this was something of a hostage to fortune insofar as Scotland's problem was not a 'democratic deficit' per se but that *exercising political power comes on English terms* i.e. access to the exercise of power is mediated through two electorates or nations fundamentally at odds with each other for a generation, so that no form of devolution can ever solve this Scottish problem. Again, the problem was not the unequal relation of union between a smaller and a less populous nation (Scotland) and a much larger and much more populous nation (England) per se because this had been the case since 1707. The problem, rather, was the *difference* between Scotland and England during 1979-1997 that meant the *relation of union* became a class issue.

We should be clear, then, that this political difference was not caused by the union or caused by difference in national identity as the political union with England does not explain the divergence in voting. Whatever the grounds of these differing voting patterns between Scotland and England, they were not caused by the union or the British constitutional settlement. It is political difference then and not the political relation of union that is the source of the '79 generation's rejecting the relation of union, and only when the relation of union with England became a class issue did the need to politicise the nation become the issue for the working class, and so the imagining and constructing of working-class nationalism could begin in earnest thanks to the never-ending fuel of a geo-political union with the right-of-centre English electorate. Despite the respite of a Labour government during 1997-2010, then, and the new devolved settlement of 1 July 1999, the reality of these two nations being 'better together' resumed normal service in 2010 when most Scots voted for a left-of-centre government, only to get a right-of-centre Tory-Liberal government they didn't vote for.

After their enfranchisement in 1918 the working class in Scotland quickly weaned itself from Liberalism to re-align itself with the Labour Party in their politicisation of their social conditions. Despite a brief period of 'class and nation' integralism during the nineteen-twenties when the likes of Connolly and Wheatley advocated Home Rule for Scotland, it was only subsequent to the advent of Margaret Thatcher on 4 May 1979 that this earlier twentieth-century integralist politics was resurrected, after having been forgotten throughout the post-war period of consensus politics, and by the end of eighteen years of Tory rule the Conservative and Unionist Party were thoroughly discredited in Scotland.[124] Hence, when interviewing Dauvit quoted earlier in Chapter 2, and noting his *Scotland Forever* tattoo on his arm which is something unremarkable among local men, I asked his views on the creation of the parliament:

That f***in Thatcher reign jist kill't everythin aff ken. Ah mean it's gonnae take some rebuilding like. It's got tae the

---

[124] Thatcher herself observed in her memoirs: "There was no Tartan Thatcherite revolution" (1993, p. 618).

stage noo ken people's jist sayin tae theirsel well, c**t it'll no maitter tae us if it's Tories or Labour or whoever's in ye ken. People jist dinnae seem tae be interested nooadays ken...Ah mean it is like a Labour f***in community ken, bit anybody that is switchin their vote Ah mean, it'd hae tae be an idiot anybody that f***in votes Conservative ye ken. Ah cannae see anybody gaun that wiy eh...any body that changes their vote it's gonnae be SNP ken. The SNP gets stronger an a'...ken there's mair people, Ah think they're gaitherin votes here and there....As Ah say aboot here naebody really talks politics a lot eh...naebody seems tae gie a toss. If we had an independent Scotland it cannae be a bad thing. Ken Ah mean oor haunds were f***in tied there fir a while ken, at least noo we can f***in speak fir oorsels ken. Pit oor side o'er.

If in Thatcherism the English commercial class produced its champion and provoked a rise in Scottish nationalism among the Scottish working class, there is a deep historical truth behind the assertion that 'Thatcherism' rescued an early twentieth-century 'integralism' or alignment of class and nation which had come to a standstill insofar as Thatcherism taught working-class Scots a lesson in their own history as much as a lesson in class-based politics by making a spectacle out of the impotence of lionised middle-class institutions such as law, education and the Protestant church which New Labour unionist politicians imagine constitutes the Scottish nation. The lesson that Thatcherism taught was that weapons more potent than 'civic mindedness' were required to defeat Thatcher; that without a State of its own to represent and protect Scotland from Thatcher or Major or Cameron, it became necessary to make one, and insofar as the professions-based civil society and trade unions were refusing the leadership task of imagining Scottish sovereignty, they were fundamentally inadequate to the task of meeting the needs of the nation. The net effect was to produce a discourse of difference that by the time of fieldwork had passed into locals' common sense. As Mary Gibbons (Orebank Road, 12th December 1999) told me:

Ah dinnae believe we're a' wane country. There's definitely a Scotland England divide, big time Ah think! Proved it time and again. Proved it! So, Ah think if we got oor independence it would have tae be Scotland, oor independence. Forget aboot the rest e them Ah think. What's Britain done fir us? Ah mean look at the unemployment up here, you know. Ah jist, nut. Ah blame Thatcher's government for the downfall, for the way things are the now. Ah blame her reign.

It is significant that no informant I interviewed obtained any satisfaction from criticising the Conservative Party, and I propose this was because this particular institution hardly registered in their imagination as *ab initio* it has been long perceived as irrelevant to their politics and their imagining of Scotland. For many, then, it was those institutions such as the Labour Party that had long been believed in and that had long held power in Scotland that were punished for the growing debacle of the 1979-1997 period. Hence, when all of Scotland's seventy-two Westminster constituencies rejected the Conservatives in May 1997, all of Scotland was expressing the same anti-Tory 'common sense' that understood this party did not even attempt to recognise, far less offer a rival imagining of working-class Scottish interests. Because of the political and cultural irrelevance of the Conservatives it was the Labour Party and the political establishment in Scotland that was the target for criticism. Hence the prescience of Anthony Smith's remark that: "the main battle of the nationalists is so often fought out within its chosen ethnie against the older self-definitions" (in Eley & Suny 1996, p. 124). Some locals by the end of the nineteen years of 1979-1997 had become so frustrated by the reluctance of the Scots to solve their own problem that one informant (Alistair McLelland, Woodend Park, 18 July 1999) even accorded England the decisive role in the process of Scotland achieving independence:

Ah'm for it, for the parliament. Ah'm very for it. Ah still think it should be everything. Ah believe that Westminster shouldnae enter intae it. Hopefully it'll come in the future.

Hopefully the English will see sense and do it for us, because Ah don't think we've got the guts to do it. But certainly Ah'm all for it.

Because locals endured a long period of 'democracy without *dasein*' and the misalignment between democracy and government, the rise of a new politics that restored the fit between politics and power was inevitable. If Thatcher's myopia concerning her own English nationalism more or less forced a reluctant Scottish working class to resume the 1918 generation's politics of 'class and nation' integralism, and resume a politics of human being that would perform a second break with liberalism, it seems they saw in Thatcher their nemesis but borrowed the weapons she herself wielded i.e. an unapologetic integralist approach to advancing the interests of class and nation to the exclusion of all others, so that Thatcherism was a problem that came with its own solution. The combination of affluence and a certain freedom to imagine their secession from the '45 generation's consensual way of 'doing politics,' then, ended the hegemony of voting Labour as many of the '79 generation feel they *can* afford a politicisation of class and history via nationality, in contrast to those of the '45 generation who still imagine Scotland can not afford the real nationalism of independence. If once poor and through voting Labour they transformed their social conditions by creating the welfare state, they are now affluent and able to afford to politicise more holistic imaginings of themselves and so move from Labour to the SNP, and on this trajectory will move from Home Rule within the United Kingdom to independence within Europe after 2014.

Reflecting upon the period 1979-1997 it is clear that one's class identity structures the 'lived experience' (Dilthey) of the nation. The identities of class and nationality are distinct and not reducible to the other, so that to say class mediates national identity is not to say Scottish nationalism is a simple 'superstructural' expression of class conflict as this social ontology gives far too little recognition to the reality of historicity and nationality within contextualised human being. Attempting to understand the dialectic of class and nation but without reducing one to the other has been a feature of the work of Gallagher (1991), Wallerstein (1979, 1980) and Hechter (1975, 1976) who have applied class-based analysis to Anglo-Scottish relations, and view Scottish nationalism as a form of class struggle transposed to the level of the nation. In this regard McCrone (1992, 1998) and Nairn (1997, 2000) have argued that Scotland was never a colony or a 'proletariat' to a ruling English 'bourgeoisie' but rather the junior partner in a political union and the adventure of Empire, as the evidence is clear that many thousands of Scots over the generations have directly benefited from union with England and the British empire. However, while objectively it may be inaccurate to assign a colonial status to Scotland, my informants were not academics so that objectivist accounts were of limited concern, so that many imagine Scotland as dominated by England. As Mr Paterson (South Dundonald Cottages) told me: "As far as Ah'm concerned England rules us."

In the struggle over how Scottish nationalism is perceived the role of history looms large, and if in the working-class national-ist's imagining of Scotland there is a history of struggle against English ambition and the conviction that the 1707 Act of Union only ever happened because the English crown and the English parliament wanted it to happen, the very idea of Britain is imag-ined as the invention of an Anglo-Scottish nobility that was sub-sequently managed and run after 1832 by the native bourgeoisie. If the working-class nationalist is able to prove to his satisfaction the 'proletarian' credentials of Scottish nationalism, the anti-nationalist working-class 'loyalist' socialist is similarly able to mobilise history and prove to his satisfaction the essentially 'bour-geois' character of nationalism. While each dialectically opposed position constructs reality to its own preferred image and likeness, what each position shares is the triangulation of symbolic struc-ture, social structure and the nation's history. As a rule, of course, each class is disposed to identify with those representations of national history which suit its interests, so that when watching football or a film such as *Braveheart*, for example, the same 'nested structuration' of perception will be at play so that when at the time of the cinema release of *Braveheart* there were newspaper reports of incidents of violence between Scottish and English people, (and I recall one tradesman telling me how after watching the film he had, "Wanted tae punch f**k oot e some English c**t"), there is nothing surprising or anomalous about a vegetable packer or warehouse worker identifying immediately and passionately with twelfth or thirteenth-century Scots peasants, as what is happening is a mundane social practice that has nothing to do with the warehouse worker's grasp of the *Lebenswelt* of Scots peasantry but everything to do with his own everyday experience, which includes being subjected or positioned in a social and geopolitical hierarchy, and so finds catharsis via identification with cinematic representations of national resistance as they are a cipher for his mundane social and geo-political experience.

Much of the strength and vitality and appeal of nationalism is its ability to draw upon and integrate or morph itself into intimate aspects of *dasein*, such as being-in-history or the worked-self. Also, working-class nationalism is able to participate in a large economically and socially-grounded 'return of the repressed' so that among the '79 generation there is an emergent integration of politics, culture and identity where Gellner's (1983, p. 1) definition of nationalism as "primarily a political principle, which holds that the political and national unit should be congruent" fuses with what Kravitz (1997) has identified as that which is defining about contemporary Scottish literature's transcending the 1920s literary renaissance's trope of the divided "British Scot" in favour of a self congruent with itself, and accompanied by a fully contextual literary production.[125]

If this integration of class and culture and nation and history (Mulholland 2011) has precedents, it is also fundamentally new because of the new economic and social forces that give this project a far greater social grounding than previous attempts at imagining this integralism into existence in the nineteen-twenties and nineteen-thirties (MacColla 1967). I argue the imagining of

---

[125] This view of a self 'congruent with itself' echoes Gellner's definition of nationalism and Heidegger's: "We want our Volk to fulfil its historical mission. We want ourselves" (in Wolin 1990, p. 86).

sovereignty is today aligned with powerful forces released by affluence and education and the event of 1979-1997 so that Scottish nationalism is not only about achieving something for the *second* time but something greater, and succeeding where the twelfth and subsequent centuries failed: a sociologically-informed account of the capacities of human nature upon a purely natural basis and giving a new and original account of integral liberation, and an inclusive foundation for an appreciation of the apotheosis of fully-contextualised *dasein* insofar as achieving this purely natural perfection readies *dasein* for its supernatural destiny (Chapters 6 and 8).

When McCrone writes "We are all nationalists now" (1998, p. ix), he is correct despite the fact that the September 1997 Referendum to establish a democratic mandate for the Scottish parliament only saw 45% of the electorate participating, and despite the fact that the unionist architects of devolution confidently predicted that devolution would "kill nationalism stone dead." [126] McCrone's words tell us unionist politicians suffer a form of 'false consciousness' if they imagine they can avoid the title 'nationalists' simply because they have so far prevented independence, as the fact is political parties and politicians are 'all nationalists now' as the agreed forum for politics is the Holyrood parliament, and each must be a nationalist 'more or less' if they are to avoid political oblivion. To paraphrase Hegel, we might say that a cunning 'medieval' long durée has used its opponents to bring its victory nearer insofar as the Labour Party has danced to the nationalist tune and many Scots were in favour of a Scottish parliament to the extent they were Labour voters and have subsequently become nationalists after 1999.

In this regard, locals seem to be correct in their political instincts when they report that 'nationalism as devolution' is a contrived affair that has been misrepresented as the people's 'settled will,' in opposition to more radical imaginings such as the nationalism of sovereignty that locals see other former stateless

---

[126] George Robertson, former Nato Secretary General and former Labour MP for Clyde and Cumnock (Ayrshire), and now the life peer Baron Robertson of Port Ellen.

European nations achieving. Hence, when interviewing on people's doorsteps I found a degree of suspicion regarding the Labour Party's motives for establishing the parliament. As an example I reproduce the following exchange with an elderly couple (Thomas Shand, retired miner, and Helen Shand, Whitehall Crescent, 24 October 1999):

**Me:** Why do we have a parliament now?

**Tam:** Because the English folk Ah think they're wantin tae break away. It's no us that's wantin tae break away. Ah think the English folk are wantin their ain country because they see it. If it's onything tae dae wi Scotland it's British bit if it's onythin tae dae wi England it's English. Whaure could ye get a union if they're gonnae be like that?

**Helen:** Well Ah dinnae ken actually. Ah didnae think we wid ever get it, the way the Labour went an everythin.

**Tam:** Ah think it's through the nationalists, the nationalists! They're the wanes that pressed an...

**Helen:** Aye that's right!

**Tam:** ...they have, they're at the bottom e getting the Scottish parliament. It's no Labour! Labour would have went along the way they were gaun...

**Helen:** Aye.

**Tam:** ...sittin doon there!

**Helen:** Couldnae care less!

**Tam:** Bit the nationalists got the parliament up here.

**Me:** Dae ye think it's jist tae shut them up, keep them quiet?

**Helen:** Ah think so.

**Tam:** Could be. Bit Ah don't think it'll quiet them.

**Helen:** It'll no quiet them.

**Tam:** Bit Ah mean if they keep at it they could get in theirsels ye ken.

Similar suspicions came from Ena Herd (Orebank Road, 14 November 1999):

Ah dinnae think much e Tony Blair like. Ah dinnae like him. He's a control freak. He's just like, Ah think they're a' jist like big brother is watching you. So Ah dinnae ken what his reasons are for letting Scotland get their parliament and get power. Ah dinnae ken what the *reason* fir that wis. There must have been some reason. Ah mean jist suddenly come up an says ye can have yer ain parliament jist like that you know. That jist doesnae jist happen itsel. Ah honestly jist think it's a set up. That's what Ah honestly think. Ah dinnae really think that the parliament is daen us much guid, because Ah dinnae think it's allowed tae dae much guid. They've a' got tae get in there an be there but they're bound tae ken theirsels that they're only jist puppets, eh? That's how Ah feel.

Again, from the same street Mr. Proctor (68 Orebank Road, 14 November 1999) told me after I had asked why after so long Scotland had a parliament once again:

It's a mystery tae me. Ah still think we will never get away fae England cause there's too many MPs doon there…they cannae even f***in tell the truth among theirsels. They're always fightin each other. There's that many lies gaun aboot. Ah joined up when Ah wis fifteen an was in the Middle East before Ah wis seventeen. Ah'm eighty-two noo.

And, finally, Susan Steele (Woodend Park):

Ah dinnae think the government'll let that go…easily. An Ah think they'll say right you've got yer parliament, give us a wee bit power and we'll think we're alright, we've got what we want but we dinnae really cause they're still in control. Really at the end e the day they've still got the say and the last bit e control. Bit they've given it tae us because there's too much rumblin about independence and stuff like that ye see. It's been gaun on and on and on and gie them a parliament and they'll think they're comin oot lucky sort e thing, eh? That's what Ah think. That's ma thoughts anyway.

Many informants are of the clear view the Labour Party's implementation of Home Rule is a matter of political expediency, and that the real direction of travel of history is not fulfilled by the schemes of the Constitutional Convention set up in 1989 but lies with the nationalists who walked out of this convention because it refused to consider independence as a constitutional option for Scotland. We might say, then, that the real 'historical subject' driving devolution lies outside itself because the devolution of the Constitutional Convention was conceived *ab initio* as a means of preventing the 'real nationalism' of independence. In the above testimony of Ena, for example, there is the view that unionist Holyrood politicians have to more or less pretend they are nationalists in the hope that the electorate do not see through the pretence, and Tam and Helen likewise know that devolution is not sovereignty and that Holyrood is not a real parliament because the Westminster parliament remains in charge or sovereign. To my mind, then, these informants express the 'integralism' which unionist politicians are afraid of, so that in contrast to Donald Dewar's fact-finding trips to Catalonia or Labour MEPs travelling to federal Bavaria as they construct Scotland's future, this is not where locals look to for models of their nation's being-in-the-world because these do not provide (in the words of my English informant discussed earlier) "their own personal government."

Many informants were open in their constitutional views to the extent that even if they voted SNP or Labour, this did not automatically imply an *ideological* commitment to unionism or nationalism. Unlike the two English interviewees quoted earlier for whom voting Conservative was an option, this was not the case for Scottish locals no matter how much they may have disliked New Labour. As a rule, locals vote SNP or they do not vote at all if they do not vote Labour, so that the unionism of locals would never go so far as voting for the Conservative and Unionist Party as this would require negating a far stronger class identity, and so this has resulted in a situation where many individuals with no real engagement with the constitutional question will 'go with the flow' rather than oppose devolution because such a position would be to ally with the only political party to oppose the creation of the Scottish parliament i.e. the Conservative Party, so that instead of devolution being the 'settled will' of the people, the settled will is whatever the Conservative Party opposes. As the following interview with retired local (James Reid, Whitehall Crescent, 24 October 1999) shows, while there is anger because "fir years we've been ruled by Conservatives," there is also a political fluidity between the unionist Labour Party and the nationalist SNP to the extent that an apparently solid lifelong commitment to voting Labour does not seem able to last a five-minute interview:

**Me:** How did ye vote?

**Jim:** Ah've always voted Labour.

**Me:** Do you think we really need this parliament?

**Jim:** Course we need it!

**Me:** Tell me why.

**Jim:** Well fir years we've been ruled by Conservatives and this is the first break we've ever hid. An' now we'll have to make good.

**Me:** Why do you think we have this parliament now?

**Jim:** Ye can take it all the way back. Fir years and years and years and this is the only chance we'll ever get of putting our thing right.

**Me:** Right, we need a parliament. Are you in favour of independence?

**Jim:** Yes.

**Me:** Is that not treasonable talk if yer a Labour man?

**Jim:** Ah am a Labour man!

**Me:** But the Labour Party doesn't want Scotland to be an independent nation.

**Jim:** Ah tae hell! It's times everythin was changed. Everythin else is changin and it's times this was changin also.

While James would be at home with the *Labour for Independence* group that emerged in 2012, we already see in 1999 the intuition that devolution is not something stable or that it is something that has difficulty 'being itself' because at its heart is an unsatisfactory compromise, so that just as locals view New Labour as a peculiarly English phenomena or an English solutions to an English problem of its working classes voting for the Conservative Party, so they view the devolution settlement as a unionist solution to a problem that only nationalism can solve. However, if the invention of New Labour is to the credit of the English political Left insofar as it is an attempt to address an English problem, this only serves to highlight the fact that the Labour Party in Scotland has only managed to dance to the nationalist tune, and this is a truth that many '45 generation Labour-voters (such as Thomas and Helen Shand) freely admit, while the Labour MPs they elect cannot freely admit.

Given the class, generational, historical, cultural and party political forces that already in 1999 were aligning in favour of a new imagining of Scottish sovereignty, the events of 2007 and 2011 were perhaps not entirely unpredictable given that the political party that cannot align itself with these forces is fated to be marginalised. In this regard, another instructive example of how the people were ahead of unionist parties in 1999, and which added to the sense that devolution in 1999 was already a kind of interregnum period, was when the media began using the phrase "the Scottish government" in their coverage of the affairs of the restored parliament, only for that phrase to be discontinued by the media sometime after July 1999, so that much to their surprise the people discovered that they did not in fact have a Scottish government but something called a "Scottish Executive." Watching the news programme *Reporting Scotland* on 10th November 1999 the phrase "the Scottish Executive" was used but only to be subsequently discontinued in favour of "the Scottish government" when Henry McLeish readopted this phrase upon becoming First Minister in October 2000. Finally, according to media reports, McLeish was instructed by English Labour MPs not to use this phrase and so it disappeared once again from the media until May 2007 when the SNP formed a minority government and officially adopted the phrase 'the Scottish government.'

Once again, what we see is the struggle to structure perception, and this struggle over who is entitled to describe themselves as 'the government' added to the sense of an unstable constitutional settlement having been foisted upon the populace. The spontaneous belief of having a government as opposed to something called an executive betrays the confusion as to what exactly devolution is, so that even immediately after 1 July 1999 informants did not have a sense of a series of problems having been resolved once and for all. Instead, as events have proved, the only thing that was settled on 1 July 1999 was that the constitutional question was set to be fought over every four years at every election to the Scottish parliament.

## 5.5 The Public Emergence of Reality: 1967-2007

Today for most people is the first day of reality.

Roseanna Cunningham SNP MSP
12 May 1999

Let's be honest, some of us hoped that we would never see this day.

David McLetchie Conservative MSP
12 May 1999

The above quote from Roseanna Cunningham adverts to the long struggle to reconstitute politics in Scotland upon the basis of the nation, and while nationalists celebrated the return of the Scottish parliament, the Labour First Minister Donald Dewar had his own narrative to meet any suggestion that 1 July 1999 was a nationalist triumph, or that the return of the long-repressed sovereign 'medieval kingdom' of Scotland was under-way. For Dewar, 1 July 1999 was to be celebrated because it established a *democratic* parliament which was without precedent in the long history of the nation. In his address to the new parliament on the occasion of its official opening, the First Minister delivered a paen to democracy, despite the fact the Scots had enjoyed democracy since universal suffrage in 1918 and 1927. In his speech Dewar gave no recognition whatsoever to the view that nationalism was responsible for 1 July 1999. While every schoolboy knew 1 July

1999 was about reversing an error made nearly three centuries previously, Dewar's description of the 'present as history' turned to the tried and trusted modernist myth that the Scots needed to wait for the French revolution of 1789 and the late eighteenth-century *Friends of the People* tradition to be taught to desire their political freedom – perhaps the greatest ever public act of 'repression of history' and the greatest insult ever delivered to Scottish history.

This opening speech of the de facto political leader of the nation was ample evidence that, in his self-understanding, Dewar was not a nationalist and had no truck with the very non-liberal and non-politically correct business of making sovereign States out of stateless nations. Insofar as Dewar's claim that the meaning of 1 July 1999 was that on this day the Scots successfully democratised an idea from eighteenth-century France, this is a tried and trusted modernist trick of burying the past, and how for the modernist there can be no admission of historical wrong-tunings such as the union of 1707 because to condemn three centuries of Scottish history as a fatal error is to bury the Enlightenment myth and modernist doctrine of 'history as progress.'

Remarkably, despite the fact that the previous thirty years of Scottish politics had nothing to do with establishing democracy in Scotland as this had arrived in 1918, by only emphasising the new parliament was democratically elected, Dewar misrepresented 1 July 1999 as a victory for democracy so as to suppress his suppression of history, and the fact that political union with England had been the problem 1 July 1999 was created to solve. Dewar's speech was carefully designed to kill off any suggestion that more history was to come or that there was any more history still left to be corrected or fulfilled, because in the Enlightened liberal imagination there can be no more ghosts of the past weighing upon the politics of the present. The resultant de facto 'end of history' narrative of unionism inevitably means a lack of depth to politics and the reduction of politics to 'eternal managerialism' insofar as the future is imagined as perpetual undisturbed liberalism.

Such are the tales unionists tell themselves, and it is clear they remain far from a holistic understanding of modernity and a fully-contextualised *dasein* and *mitsein*, so that the two unionist parties who were in favour of the devolved parliament (Labour and Liberal) were more or less fated to be seen as the uninvited guests at a party they were officially hosting insofar as Scottish nationalism was a social movement neither party could bring themselves to recognise and understand, far less celebrate and embrace. 1 July 1999, then, was a snapshot in time that captured the confusion in Scotland today that is sourced in the signature ambivalence of unionism which is evident in the Scotland Act (1998) in which the government published its intention to legislate for a Scottish parliament, and in which not a single nationalist flourish or crumb of long durée rhetoric appears, despite being written to bring about nationalist ends and amend historical wrong-turnings. This modernist document *par excellence* announces *ex nihilo* that: "There shall be a Scottish parliament" and is cleansed of all traces of history; a creation from nowhere of no lineage.

Despite these criticisms of modernism it is clear that nationalism has a modernist form insofar as it is dismissive or embarrassed at historical 'period costume,'[127] and has an integral form that freely embraces its source in the historic long durée. Despite these divergent understandings of the place of the past in the present, what unites both forms is that the nation must be sovereign regardless of whether the nation is a twelfth-century creation (Broun 1999) or an eighteenth-century invention (Davidson 2000), and both agree the nation is the medium through which they organise much of their political perception, so there is no need to imagine the nationalist as guilty of 'false consciousness' or backward-glancing even when the twelfth-century version of nationalism is opted for, because *the twelfth-century is contemporary* or 'fit for purpose' because the project that emerged at this time and first imagined and first achieved and first practiced the nation and first imagined and first achieved and first practiced *sovereignty*, 'condemns' every subsequent imagining and practicing

---

[127] My preferred form of modernist 'false consciousness' which I have to keep mysef from falling into is the period 1967-1997.

of this project to repeat, restore, recapitulate, retrieve or resurrect this original era. Contemporary nationalists, then, need not be self-consciously 'medievalist' to be aptly described as resurrecting a twelfth-century project of national freedom and modernity as this twelfth-century 'politics of being' (as opposed to the twelfth-century 'mode of production' or the twelfth-century level of technology) is what remains defining of the 'present as history.'

If desiring and achieving and exercising and enjoying national sovereignty is what the present is about then, by definition, 1 July 1999 and 18 September 2014 represent the return to a 'medieval' project that achieved this national sovereignty first. In any nationalist project then the 'medieval' must always be 'in fashion' or must always be perennial (with the only time that Scotland reneged on this patrimony being the brief eighteenth-century 'North British' identity developed among Enlightenment figures and the modernist experiment of Britain). The 'medieval is perennial,' then, only insofar as the nation is mobilised or imagined or desired as the locus of sovereignty, so that whenever political sovereignty is not imagined or not desired in this way, then for that era the medieval is clearly not a template and the medieval ceases to be perennial. On the cusp of 18 September, then, I propose the '79 generation's 'tasks of freedom' consist of transcending the Reformation/Enlightenment/unionist/modernist/liberal/secularist imagination, and a class-based recuperation of the long durée *from below* that is comprised of two elements:

1) a late medieval or early modern cultural-ideological complex, and

2) post-industrial class relations in an advanced affluent market economy and society.

What is emergent today is 'repressed reality' in all of its 'never-been-modernist' fullness (Latour 1993), and the metaphor we might use to express this might be that fully-contextualised working-class *dasein* in all of its 'heavy historicity' or in 'full period costume,' is one of the social carriers of this symbolic complex that has survived the long durée of 1707-1999 and its long defeat among social elites in Scotland, and is emergent thanks to affluence and the new relationship to the symbolic order among the working class and the event of 1979-1997, signalling the end of the modernist imagining of Scotland.

If this description seems to privilege the concept and role of 'social class' I am happy to entertain the position that 'historicity' and 'nationality' are finally emerging in their fully modern 'period costume' form of social class. While I have emphasised class I am clear, then, that this category can not do all the work that is required. If we take the case of a working class that was unable to mobilise via nationalism during the years of neoliberal triumph 1979-1997, such as the English working class, we see that no matter what historic timescale we allow this population to organise and re-imagine their class mobilisation, they can never mobilise their class interests via nationalism because the 'symbolic stuff' is not only shared by another class but has already been mobilised and monopolised by another class, and so cannot be mobilised against that same class.

For this population, then, to construct a route to class mobilisation via nationalism would require a truly modernist ontology and involve imagining northern England, for example, seceding from the rest of England and its inhabitants imagining this piece of England a distinct nation from the rest of England. However, being too English and 'medieval,' what is only ever really available to the English working-class '79 generation is the same 'Scottish project' of imagining itself free from modernist assumptions and developing its own free imagining of English integral sovereignty. However, even the purely philosophical question as to whether the modernist conception of nationalism is possible is ill-conceived, as even if the population in the north of England imagined a nation for themselves and seceded from England, this would require mobilising medieval realities and categories to achieve this allegedly 'modernist' scenario. More accurately, modernist theories of *dasein* and nationalism will only become plausible the day Afro-Americans, for example, imagine a country of their own on that continent and secede from the United States of America. Until such events happen, nationalism among the working class in Scotland must be understood as the operationalisation of a 'medieval' or twelfth and thirteenth-century national inheritance and tradition *and is impossible without this symbolic order or patrimony.*

While I have emphasised class throughout I also recognise that insofar as "the nation is the medium" of our imagination (Craig 1999, p. 32), then the Nation can be considered the real agent of contemporary Scottish society and politics insofar as *it is the Nation that has mobilised the working class to resurrect itself and more or less coerced the working class to break from its accommodations to affluence and post-War consensus.* Likewise, on this structuralist view, it is not social actors who imagine 'the nation' back to life but, rather, it is the nation that vivifies the imagination of social actors, and gives them the tools and the symbolic material with which to think their 'present as history.' The two pillars of 'class and nation' then animate a radical view that is fully alive to the importance of social class and embraces the nation as the medium of their hopes, as it is the nation that vivifies and gives life and gives context and ballast and a territory for their imagining of a new future.

Among the liberal commentariat in the media, an imagined freedom from territory and the routine denial of fundamental framing realities along with an imagined escape from historicity is something of an epidemic given their disposition to imagine themselves and their views as free of 'vulgar' social determination. This liberal misconception of human being was also fashionable among dominated working-class political activists for most of the twentieth century, and so the history of working-class political activism in Scotland is full of the confidant dismissal of "Braveheart an a' that shite," and full of the conviction that any turn to history was backward. Reviewing the history of Marxism, for example, it has clearly prided itself upon its theorisation of modern industrial class-based society, and yet is also a clear example of the modernist fight from real human being. As the brilliantly antinomian *Communist Manifesto* ([1848] in Howell 1986, p. 4) famously put it:

> The workers have no country. No one can take from them what they have not got. Since the proletariat must first of all win political power, must make itself the ruling class, must raise itself to the position of a national class, must establish itself as the nation – it is, so far, still national, though by no means in the bourgeois sense of the term.

In this extract the working class are made into Marx's image of what it is to be modern and are a modernist's dream come true as, on this description, they are the storm troopers of 'pure revolution' as they incarnate Mankind liberated from all culture, custom, religion, history and nationality as a result of the 'ontological cleansing' effected as a result of 'becoming modern' (at least according to the modernist imagination); are reduced *in their very being* to the immaculately modern social and economic forces that brought them into being *ex nihilo* in the late eighteenth and early nineteenth-century. This modernist proletariat, even after the advent of affluence and leisure and higher education, are forbidden to turn to history, nationality or Christianity to imagine or paint themselves using these colours or develop these aspects of *dasein* as their 'full period costume,' because they are imagined to have been reduced completely to their social conditions and all trace of such pre-modern superstitions have been wiped clean from their ownmost selves. As so often with Marx, an unprecedented recognition of the real sits alongside a tremendous modernist flight from the real and this has meant that, if informants have come to expect a more or less systematic neglect of all things Scottish and working class from the political Right, the response of the Left has not been much better, prompting the former Marxist (and now nationalist) intellectual Tom Nairn to observe that nationalism is "Marxism's greatest failure" (1981, p. 329).

The fundamental failure of Marxism is having articulated a theory of the working class that *ab initio* was infected by modernism and an anthropology irreparably scarred by 'scarcity thinking.' These errors are responsible for Marxists's inability to theorise 'secondary natures' and embrace fundamental aspects of contextualised human being such as culture, the nation and the historicity of working-class *dasein* in particular, thanks to its modernist contempt for history and anything other than purely natural sociological forces. A faulty doctrine of Man, then, lies beneath a tremendous *turning towards* Man, and is a fault which the current age of affluence exposes.

The Marxist legacy then affords ample evidence of the misrecognition of Scotland, such as Davidson (2000, p. 4) who has argued: "The Scottish nation was only formed in the late eighteenth century." As a devout Marxist, Davidson argues that purely capitalist-era processes created Scotland so that it was only after the Highlands came to an end as a distinct and separate region that the two sub-national regions of the Highlands and Lowlands came together as one united national territory with a shared market, language, religion and a shared consciousness of their identity. However, Davidson concedes the existence of the Scottish state prior to the commercialisation of Scottish society and before the industrialisation of Scottish society and identifies something called 'regnal consciousness' in the twelfth and thirteenth century Wars of Independence, and acknowledges that it was in the twelfth century that there was established a sovereign Scottish state, while taking care to retain his thesis that the arrival of a Scottish *nation* is a purely eighteenth and nineteenth-century affair.

Davidson, then, argues that the twelfth- and thirteenth-century nobility and clergy and peasantry fought and died for a sovereign Scottish territorial state, but had no concept of a Scottish nation and had no national consciousness. The Scots fighting at Bannockburn, then, had no 'national consciousness' but were merely doing their medieval 'regnal duty' when they fought and died for Scottish independence. In a repetition, then, of Weber's (1976) argument regarding France i.e. that having created France the next task was to create Frenchmen out of peasants, or Garibaldi's quip that having made Italy the next task was to make Italians, so in Scotland's case the twelfth and thirteenth centuries made Scotland and the next task was to create Scots – something which only occurred in the eighteenth-century.

In making his argument Davidson makes the usual modernist moves when he states that Scottish national consciousness *as we understand it today* wasn't around in 1296 or 1320, and this kind of equivocation is repeated in *Scotland: Class and Nation* (1999) where we have, at the eleventh hour, the tried and trusted Marxist hermeneutical principle of dichotomising 'class and nation' to discredit the legitimacy of nationalism as a working-class politics; hence the following from a member of the Socialist Workers Party (1999, p. 1):

> The history of Scotland I learned from an early age was that the Scottish nation stretched back to the dawn of time. In this version Scotland was one of the oldest nations in Europe. But this was false. Far from there being a seamless evolution of the Scottish nation, modern Scotland was created by a series of convulsions stretching back just a little over two and a half centuries.

Instead of providing evidence that Scotland is not one of the oldest of Europe's nations, Bambery states the hardly insightful proposition that "modern Scotland" does not stretch back to the dawn of time, and because this point is so trivial, Bambery is of course unable to provide evidence, for example, that the Scots or the French or the Irish believe modern Scotland or modern France or modern Ireland stretch "back to the dawn of time." As a result of chewing upon the old Marxist cud, then, the antinomian mind reproduces misrepresentations of the real so that the ideologist might play the starring role of 'bringer of enlightenment' and 'materialist liberator' of all those under the spell of nationalism. Similarly, Davidson's claim to know the consciousness of the twelfth-century Scots peasantry is only matched by his incompetence at knowing the twentieth-century Scottish working class when he writes that "over the last 20 years there has been a greater flourishing of Scottish culture than at any time since the 1920s and 1930s...Yet this has not been accompanied by any significant or sustained increase in support for the Scottish National Party" (2000, p. 2).

Already in 1999 these words were evidence of Davidson's ideologically-driven lack of judgment which, in light of the fact that the SNP went on to win the elections of 2007 and 2011, is all the more evidence of his lack of judgment. Davidson's inability to suspect these immanent developments which many working-class Scots knew were likely is evidence that Davidson is no guide to the national consciousness of working-class Scots today, far less the consciousness of twelfth and thirteenth-century Scots peasants. Indeed, what also seems clear is that Davidson has misread twelfth and thirteenth-century Scots in the exact same way as he has misread twentieth and twenty-first-century working-class Scots i.e. just like his imaginary medieval Scots peasants who had no 'national consciousness,' so in 2000 Davidson imagines the Scots working class have only very recently taken up nationalism so that Scottish Marxists like Davidson cannot be accused of failing to see what wasn't there to be seen.

The truth of the matter, however, is that unencumbered by 'historical materialism' the Scottish working class became nationalists while Marxist intellectuals like Bambery and Davidson remained mired in their brilliantly antinomian Marxism that was unable to anticipate, far less participate in, the historic developments they are living through. Insofar as these Marxists want their readers to imagine they are a guide to the consciousness of a medieval peasantry living seven centuries ago or the present-day working class, they are like so many Marxists who are made blind by the "polished folly" (Yves Simon, in Hellman 1991, p. 459) they imagine makes them able to see.

To propose that every twelfth and thirteenth-century Scots peasant who fought for their Scottish kingdom and its independence from a predatory English sovereign and nobility did not have national consciousness because the nation (arbitrarily defined as a unified territory with a common market throughout that territory with one religion and one language) did not exist yet, is clearly to load the definitional dice in favour of a particular outcome. Indeed, *given such rigorous criteria for what constitutes a nation, it is tautologous to argue we only find such evidence in the more recent past.* To say that medieval Scots peasants did not have such a national consciousness similar to the national consciousness of today is likewise tautologous given our media-saturated age. On this question, I am open to conceding that upon the basis of the four criteria laid out for national consciousness by Davidson Scotland did not meet such criteria until 1800 or 1900 or 2000, or indeed might never meet this criteria as his hopelessly homogenised criteria for the existence of a nation would mean the Scottish nation would have to vanish if he came across Hebridean Catholics, for example, with no desire whatsoever to share in the language or religion of the Lowland Protestant.

However, if we choose to define the nation using Seton-Watson's (cited in Davidson 2000, p. 9) definition: "A nation exists when a significant number of people in a community consider themselves to form a nation, or behave as if they do," then on this criteria historians have concluded that the Scottish nation existed in the twelfth century, and that medieval peasants possessed a form of national identity that can meaningfully be described as the direct ancestor of our contemporary national consciousness.

Davidson's argument that the twelfth and thirteenth century population living in Scotland wanted an independent and sovereign 'Kingdom-State' and that they had a 'Kingdom consciousness,' which is different from 'national consciousness' and the desire to have a nation-state, is semantic game playing. If we choose to define nationalism, for example, as the desire of a people to have a state of its own we can have nationalism but without any need for a nation or national consciousness. If there were a 'regnal doctrine,' for example, that stated every kingdom shall be a sovereign state of its own, this is clearly a direct ancestor and source of the nation and the nationalist consciousness that when politicised states that every nation shall have a state of its own, with 'regnal consciousness' being the direct ancestor of national consciousness.

The truth of the matter in such 'definitional dances' is that in the pre-devolution socialist imagination, nationalism was routinely judged to be a bourgeois fiction foisted upon the working class, so that anti-nationalist socialists such as Bambery could write "John Maclean was not a nationalist" (1999, p. 29). In the Marxist imagination the nationalist is not simply someone who wishes to have the state and nation congruent but is someone who is prey to all sorts of mystifications that blind him to his class interests. Such clichéd 'schemes of perception' look in the wrong places for the reality of Scottish nationalism and disappear the embedded reality of nationalism and betray an inadequate social ontology as well as ignorance of the working class.

However, with a purely Scottish political context upon them, the Scottish Socialist Party was created and began wearing the 'medieval' nationalist clothing of independence at the eleventh hour, although their then leader Tommy Sheridan betrayed his antinomianism and opportunism when he refused to admit he had become a nationalist when interviewed on television.[128] It is because of this traditional 'flight from reality' that we have the long-standing criticism of Marxists in Scotland: "They have built around themselves a paper wall of English books; no wonder the common Marxist cannot see Scotland" (MacColla1927, cited in Finlay 1994, p. 54).

Another ideological position that routinely fails to understand Scottish nationalism is liberalism, which may be viewed as another major carrier of antinomian 'flight from reality' insofar as it is *the* 'ideology' of choice among the powerful middle classes. I argue that to explain why nationalism and not a political form of liberalism is increasing in popularity among the working class (and indeed even the middle classes) is to explain why liberalism is another alienation from working-class reality *as a matter of liberal principle*, and to outline this argument I take as a representative liberal text the former leader of the Liberal

---

[128] Perhaps the Spanish language offers a way out for the anti-nationalist socialists as the word *independentista* refers to someone in favour of independence and the doctrine of the nation and state being congruent, but has none of the fascist and 'false consciousness' connotations associated with the word *nacionalista*.

Democrat party Charles Kennedy's *The Future of Politics*, which characterises the 'present as history' as follows (2000, p. xiii):

> The old verities have become a bonfire of the political vanities, and the joyous collapse of the Berlin Wall was to socialism what Black Wednesday became to Conservatism. There are no more glad, confident dawns. A good thing too. This uncertainty defines the territory upon which the Liberal Democrats now operate. Society seems to be defined by near-instantaneous flitting images; as a consequence we have to be fleet of foot politically.

According to Kennedy, who describes himself as "an open-minded, pro-European, moderate-thinking Scot" (2000, p. xiii), the 'signs of the times' require us to update ourselves so as not to remain mired in old loyalties, and to move ourselves on from "voting on purely tribal lines" (2000, p. 170). However, this 'moderate thinking' is itself mired in 'tribal liberalism' and the old verities of modernism in its imagining a new post-class and post-national era is upon us. Faced with ever-changing society, the moderate thinking Scot must keep up with the times and must become post-Labour and post-SNP in his voting habits so as not to suffer from obsolete 'false consciousness.' Thanks to this construction of the 'present as history,' then, the same old refusal to recognise social class is legitimised because such realities, in true modernist style, are imagined to be passing away, so that under the guise of recognising the emerging new, thick historical and social and national realities (in the spirit of J. S. Mill) can be dispensed with for the sake of progress.

Because of this flight from the real, political liberalism remains marginal to working-class politics due to its threefold lack of mediation via place, class and nationality, and this absence of emplacement in real time and space means liberalism rules in neither the inner-city nor the countryside, so that the question as to where Liberalism is located is more than a question of location on the political spectrum. Paradoxically, liberalism's only success in Scotland is in those parts of the Highlands where it has established a tradition and a loyalty in a particular locality.

Instead of making a 'bonfire of the political vanities,' then, we can say that Kennedy reproduces all of the traditional liberal defects such as its traditional inability to come to terms with the rise of class society and class politics after 1918 which ended the long hegemony of political liberalism in Scotland.

Also, Kennedy's denunciation of 'political tribalism' echoes *The Scotsman* editorial discussed earlier that warned against "deranged anthropologists" describing the Scots and English as two different ethnies. This deployment of the 'primitive' trope to discredit fully-contextual positions, and any kind of politics that would recognise such integralism, is in fact integral to how liberalism constitutes its apparent 'moderation.' Hence, when the then Liberal member of the Westminster parliament Paddy Ashdown came to Scotland during the election campaign to the first Holyrood parliament, and was questioned about Scottish nationalism, he replied with a textbook discourse on the evils of nationalism citing events in the Balkans and Yugoslavia as evidence of the inherent evils of nationalism; and thereby gave an exemplary indication of the spectres and fictions of 'tribalism' and 'fundamentalism' that haunt the liberal imagination.

In the new conditions of affluence and deindustrialization, then, Kennedy pitches for a new relevance of a political Liberalism that is fully aligned with the times thanks to advocating the undesirability of constituting politics upon the old-fashioned lines of class and nation. This desire to constitute politics 'without any period costume,' then, repeats the history of liberalism insofar as Liberals have a long pedigree of alienation from class and nationality-mediated reality, having split on the issue of Irish nationalism in the eighteen-nineties and having disintegrated even further upon the issue of class after 1918. There is clearly, then, a deep principle at work in liberalism that results in its being perennially 'unreal' or a class ideology which is afraid of engagement with class and national identity; as if liberalism is designed to mask from *liberals themselves* a determined lack of engagement with these fundamental realities.

Insofar as the liberal is shocked by the nationalist 'will to power' and the nationalist's recognition of the territorial imperative in politics, nationalism easily appears as a form of authoritarianism or fascism, so that we may say nothing has changed since Bruck observed: "Liberalism is the death of nations" (2012, p. 100). That liberals have been marginal to Scottish politics since 1918 because of the rise of class-based politics yet refuse to bring this to clear consciousness is indicative of a doxic 'scheme of perception' and an unconscious dogmatism that means they are more or less condemned to constitute politics as 'enlightened' to the extent that it is divorced from reality. While political liberalism and socialist internationalism share this antinomian flight from reality, and despite the few working-class socialist activists who remain at their modernist posts, this confident neglect and depoliticisation of Scottish history and *dasein* is at an end as a 'medieval' patrimony is mobilised to the horror of cosmopolitan liberal commentators.

The greatest obstacle in the way of achieving thinking that is free from modernism and 'paintings' of ourselves free from the black and white palette of the 'dictatorship of scarcity' is the liberal imagination. I argue because the twelfth-century saw the advent of a new level of technologisation and urbanisation across Europe, where incipient 'spheres of life' existed in their own right and far from being imagined as being fated to 'liquidation' or privatisation as a result of the onset of modernity, the task of 'being modern' was to reform and renew and integrate these developments and new 'life spheres' within each society's 'sacred canopy' (Berger 1967), and I propose that this remains the only adequate way to imagine the task of being modern in the twenty-first century. If such is the original and perennially valid understanding of European modernity then, what has to be perennially resisted is the always-present temptation whenever there is a new step-change within modernity (such as the advent of the post-industrial era) to resort to the clichés of liberalism or modernism and imagine our historical ballast must be thrown overboard in order to be fully coeval with the times.

Because of the 'dissolving' pressures of modernity it is precisely those modern urban affluent societies that teem with people more or less fated to struggle with the question whether or not they should liquidate their historicity and nationality and locality and begin *ex nihilo* both as individuals and as members of a people or a nation. This signature tension of 'being modern,' however, needs the ballast of the long durée if it is not to degenerate into the clichés of modernism. Also, thanks to affluence and education, this tension is no longer the reserve of an elite but increasingly the general condition, so that even working-class populations face these issues as they are released into the dilemma of 'being modern' in their own right, rather than having this tension being submerged in material disadvantage. Today, then, we are all more or less modern and live this tension as even repentant modernists like Nairn recognise that romanticism or the need for holism was an integral aspect of modernity rather than a regression from it (1997, p. 209), and is finally able to recognise that Scotland is a nation where "the road not taken haunts the one actually followed" (1997, p. 209). The link, then, between the 12th and 21st centuries stems from the fact the '79 generation has been recently freed to re-think and reinvigorate and renew the integration of their social conditions and their historicity and nationality, and in the twelfth century there is an historical precedent for this contemporary situation that allows us to simultaneously turn to the new social conditions but on the basis of a holistic understanding of our integral selves.

## 5.6 Thinking Modernity & Thinking Human Being

It seems tae hae been oor generation that started it and they're gonnae finish it off. Ma mum an that, she thinks we should get it [independence] noo, bit when Ah wis growin up she jist voted Labour. Whereas noo they see us, me an aa ma mates vote SNP so we're startin it. We've got the parliament and the ones that are growin up they'll hear it mair fae us than we did fae oor mum and dad, so they're gonnae pick up on it.

Steven Haggart
38 Muirtonhill Road
25 July 1999

The above quote captures many of the themes to emerge from fieldwork and is as precise a summary of an emergent working-class nationalism as I could have hoped for from an informant. Steven speaks of historical and political processes and the shift in allegiance across the generations in the intimate idiom of kinship, and reveals the self-understanding of his generation as that which achieved the Holyrood Parliament and, in due course, will achieve independence some time after 2014. An integral part of this self-understanding is a critique of the '45 generation as Steven is clear that his mum and dad "jist voted Labour." This advertence to the intimate intergenerational family context signals a critique of any account of nationalism that fails to understand the importance of class, and which one is responsible.

If we take Nairn, for example, there is a long-standing uncertainty as to which social class is the 'social carrier' of nationalism. On the one hand (1997, p. 189):

> All comparative studies of nationality have underlined the crucial place of such professional strata in generating the identity shifts behind nationalism: it is teachers, clerics, lawyers, journalists and loose screws who cause the trouble, far more than landlords, bankers, manufacturers or trade-unionists.

And on the other hand (1997, p. 187):

> [T]he awful, paralytic truth is that an upper-servant class may find it far harder to take such a decision ['to rule, rather than to merely administer'] than those who are genuinely below stairs – the outcast or dispossessed whose life chances have, suavely or brutally, been defined for them. The latter may quite easily tell itself there is nothing to lose. The Scots managing class has not been brought up to think that way at all; and it has permeated the nation with its caution.

For the young pre-nationalist Nairn (1977, p. 334) the origins of nationalism were: "located not in the folk, nor in the individual's

493

repressed passion for some sort of wholeness or identity, but in the machinery of world political economy," and it would be difficult to find a more different approach to nationalism than that of ethnographers such as Kapferer (1988) and Herzfeld (1997) who set themselves the problem of understanding the popular class-based appeal of nationalist discourse. For Herzfeld (1997, p. 3) the metaphors of belonging deployed in the construction of locality, for example, are an integral aspect of belonging to the larger community of the nation.

> I suggest that the model of cultural intimacy is a particularly apt concept for anthropologists to contribute to the study of nationalism (as well as to other idioms of identity formation), because it typically becomes manifest in the course of their long-term fieldwork, a site of social intimacy in the fullest sense.

Cardenden then affords scope to articulate the 'iconicity' between local and national identity, as both draw upon an ideology of 'sameness' which is used to mark boundaries of belonging, so that nationalism may be seen as a bounded community of meaning that draws its reality from the 'social intimacy' of small communities. In Cardenden the expression of belonging is largely through the idiom of kinship so that a person belongs because, like his mother and father, he was 'born and bred' in Cardenden so that kinship and residence are the medium through which belonging is imagined and comes about. Also, however, because an adequate explanation of working-class nationalism must include an adequate account of how people experience being a certain class, an adequate explanation of 'being Scottish' must explain much more than national identity if it is to avoid the reification of national identity. To give an integral explanation of experience then is the challenge to give an integral explanation of the experiencing of nationality and class and other relevant relations, and how each of these identities mediate and influence each other. This is why before the subject of nationalism was broached directly I spent the first three chapters dealing with apparently unrelated issues in order to convey to the reader how the quality of 'being national' is not something heaven-sent or transmitted intact through the ages, but is informed by a fully socialised ontology i.e. is shaped bodily, has an ingrained somatic coding and quality one would expect, for example, from a retired sixty-four year old miner (Bert Lister, 25 July 1999, 39 Woodend Park) who declares: "Ah'm Scottish through and through!"

Claims about the self such as Bert's derive their onto-substantive quality from an unequivocal class experience, so that the 'national self' is consubstantial with the worked-self, and such discursive claims (which are never uttered by a middle-class 'moderate thinking Scot') emerge from the triangulation of id, identity and ideology or nature, nurture and nation described earlier. There is a lived identity that is not fragmented or decentred but a *substantial* enduring quality which Bert's 'Scottishness' presents itself to him as having; a national identity that is not the result of choice or deliberation but necessity. While the 'social constructivist' position maintains there is nothing 'natural' about the existence of nations or persons 'being national,' once we allow that the self is socially mediated and allow for the play of time and place upon human being, social constructivism is compatible with recognising a miner will experience not simply national identity but his body in a determinate manner, and that when key social relations endure from generation to generation, a constructivist approach to identity must accede to talk about structural constructs becoming *substantive* realities that are able to lead a life of their own, leading to a social ontology of essences or stable 'secondary natures.'

Such a social ontology, then, can have its cake and eat it insofar as it rejects the ontological universalism that imagines human being having essences or as being "self-identical entities persisting during all changes in time and possessing the same qualities or properties" (Rapport 2002, p. 176), and transfers this classical Aristotelian view of essences onto the 'secondary natures' of class and nation and the 'secondary essence' of the 'condition of reduction,' for example, described in Chapter 2. A social constructivist sensitivity then does not involve championing the idea of a postmodern 'liquid' self precisely because it must take account of temporality and historicity and their structuring or 'fixing' impact upon the *dasein* of social actors.

If we take seriously the thesis that social stratification and mental structuration will come to exhibit an isomorphism that will endure over time, there is still the matter of establishing the particular empirical details which change over the generations as a result of social and economic and historical change. I propose, then, that the '79 generations are capable of greater reflexivity as, previously, the "dictatorship of scarcity" (Beck 1992, p. 20) held subjectivity and reflexivity in a particular stage or level of development. Because there is a homology between social conditions and mental habits, the development of society leads directly to the possibility of a new lived experience of the mind within younger working-class generations; leads to new mental achievements that previously were not possible.

More concretely, then, with the end of pure *laissez faire* politics towards the end of the nineteenth century, the State intervened directly into the condition of the labouring classes firstly via liberal paternalism and then via political parties constituted upon the basis of representing the interests of labour and capital and exercising political power. As industry and the local coal company were displaced as providers of non-workplace benefits such as schooling, housing and gas street-lighting, there occurred what Bourdieu (1998) names the 'uncoupling of fields,' so that the worker was able to free himself from the company's omnipresence in his life. Insofar as the company withdrew from its domination of local public space and retreated from its paternalist welfare role to become simply a coal company, something similar was able to occur within the worker insofar as, in proportion to this retreat from the extra-economic role of 'patron' the worker divested himself of his dependency upon the company and began to think his existence and emerge 'in himself' in his own consciousness.

As the worker could divide his experience as worker and as a free self, a space emerged into which the worker could begin to recognise submerged aspects of *dasein*; as if his 'worked self' only became visible because it was different from other selves he was now able to become. Because he now inhabited a structurally changed relationship to the organisation and experience of social space and this led to a new relation to himself, he could even dare imagine and constitute a separate politics based upon objectively being structurally released to begin the same 'turn to the subject' that is continued and evermore released among the '79 generation(s). With no need to "keep in with the gaffer" as one of Corrie's songs expresses it, or cue at the private doctor's house and pay for treatment at the point of delivery because his health care was out of middle-class hands thanks to the nationalisation of health, the two classes could each go their separate ways. When we add to this the advent of affluence and deep literacy, the '79 working-class generations inhabit social conditions that more or less coerce them to break with the '45 generation and resume the integral politics of the 1918 generation, and turn to subjectivity in all of its colours, so the current challenge is that of exploiting the opportunity to think working-class *dasein* and *mitsein* free of the 'dictatorship of scarcity' and modernism.

The current generation's 'politics of being' then may be viewed as the third stage corresponding to the third stage of capitalism (Lash and Urry 1987) where the first round was the transformation of politics after the enfranchisement of 1918 and exemplified in the likes of Connolly, Wheatley and McLean, and round two was the inauguration of the welfare state after 1945 and, thirdly, the contemporary emergence of working-class *dasein* laying claim to think itself and its free development free of modernism, materialism, supernaturalism and secularism, and which in the realm of politics means the pursuit of its own nation-state. In this regard it is significant that since the nineteen-eighties representations of class and nation have become integral to what Kravitz (1997, p. xix) views as a new kind of literature in which prior literary representations of the "subaltern Scot" have been replaced by representations of Scots as "whole, not split people." Kravitz's assertion evidences that working-class *dasein* is expanding its repertoire of colours and its self-definition to include post-material realities and to contribute to musical and literary traditions as working-class interventions into the symbolic order, which is in line with the emerging exigence of cultural self-determination identified by Mulholland (2011). Class then becomes culture as well as nation, so that opposition to 'Thatcherism' and now the drive to independence in 2014 becomes as much cultural as political, as evidenced by the organisation *Artists For Independence* in the wake of the 1992 general election and the host of contemporary groupings such as *National Collective* founded in 2011.

If the SNP are the main political beneficiaries of this movement to holism there can be little surprise as the SNP through much of its tortuous history was defined by the fact it wished to represent and advocate that which formerly dominant unionist parties sought to repress. According to Finlay (1994), the SNP was created because firstly the Liberal Party and subsequently the Labour Party failed to enact the Home Rule legislation they claimed they wanted for Scotland. In the history of the SNP also, there has been a long and tortuous history of grappling with the question of how best to mediate the appeal of nationalism i.e. via 'secondary natures' or not, and this has resulted in a number of *mediation battles* having to be successfully negotiated before it could credibly appeal to the working class.

It is because the SNP until the nineteen-eighties favoured a purist disdain for the messy and divisive particularity of 'secondary natures' that it long delayed re-constituting itself on the basis of nationality *and class*, so that the great mistake of the nineteenth-century nationalist movement was its failure to come to grips with the ontological revolution in *dasein* that went hand in hand with the industrial revolution. In each step-change in the modern era 'secondary natures' or real contextual *dasein* is made into the image of the times, so that a new relation to *dasein* has been recently made possible and a traditional relation to Tradition has been abolished so that Tradition and historicity and nationality (as well as sexuality and artistry and creativity etcetera) have been liberated from their traditional confines within the 'dictatorship of scarcity.'

Crucial, then, to the post-1979 phase of nationalism has been the decisive defeat of an 'immaculate' nationalism that has aligned with the fully-contextualised nationalism of a new generation of nationalists, symbolised by the left-wing '79 Group which was crucial to preparing the shift of the working-class Labour vote to the SNP after 1987 and 1992. If the SNP leadership finally constituted itself via class and nation, this does not mean working-class nationalism occurred once a political party finally sorted out its electoral identity. Rather, after the nineteen-eighties there began a fitting together or alignment of SNP leadership and policy and a renewed electoral appeal among the working class. The crucial shift has been the realisation that, because *working-class* nationalism must 'mediate or die' because it is a socialised and historicised phenomenon that required the event of 1979-1997 to constitute itself by because it does not have the resources to operate at the level of 'pure reason,' there is nothing paradoxical in the view that unless it is deeply mediated or even dissolved 'into other things,' working-class nationalism has difficulty existing, far less being able to stand on its own two feet and dominate the political scene. If a Labour government had been elected in 1987 or 1992, who is to say the Labour-voting Scottish working class would have shifted to the SNP so that instead of an Independence referendum in 2014, the cause of nationalism today could still be faced with the task of contesting Westminster general elections on an all-British basis.

If for nationalism to succeed politics had to become a politics of class and nation, then the nineteen years of 1979-1997 was the necessary 'event' to resurrect this integral political project. The nationalist hope is that nationalism becomes "not a mere by-product but the very stuff of social change...not its reflection, its cause, its expression, or its engine, but the thing itself" (Geertz 1993, pp. 251-2), and no longer at the mercy of relations and events for its being, and I would propose that if Scottish nationalism were a middle-class project then independence would have been achieved long ago given this class's control of all major institutions and most of the sites of cultural production. The kind of momentum that we see in Scotland where a dominated class has achieved a degree of leadership can only happen in exceptional circumstances, whereas a middle class can expect to exercise political leadership under normal circumstances.

Because Labour won 'middle England' in May 1997, working-class Scots were spared yet another debacle, and how much worse it would have needed to become before nationalism became a substantive stand-alone reality among the working class we will never know, but we do know that the period 1992-1997 was the high-point in the disjuncture between politics and reality and an integral politics was resurrected. In this regard, having successfully constituted itself as left-of-centre the Scottish National Party has reaped the benefits of the system of proportional representation put in place for the first Holyrood election. As Bennie et al. (1997, p. 16) observed: "the SNP has consistently had most to complain about" as they had consistently been penalised most by the first-past-the-post electoral system, and the working-class SNP vote in the central belt had the greatest increase in representation thanks to the introduction of proportional representation.

As of 1 July 1999, then, there has occurred a far greater alignment between representation and reality at the national level, and a further alignment of cultural and class reality at the local and regional level of government occurred when a more proportionate voting system was adopted at regional elections in 2007, and from this point onwards the already established reality of SNP/Labour contestation at the national and European parliamentary level has its full public emergence at the local and regional council level and, unsurprisingly, at the May 2007 regional elections the Labour party went from controlling thirteen Scottish Councils to controlling two, while the SNP went from controlling one regional council to forming ruling coalitions in eleven councils, and the Labour Party's domination of local government in Scotland came to an emphatic end.

Nationalism is so powerful in the modern era because it is the best solution to the predicament of 'being collective' and 'being modern:' how to produce a real sense of community after the rise of mass society in hugely-populated free-market societies, so that integral to the modern drama is the fear of losing authenticity and identity, and so integral too is the question of *cultural authenticity* which is the objective impulse for nationalism because, as seen by Eriksen (*in* Olwig & Hastrup 1997, p. 109), national identity's "great emotional power, and its unabashed linking up with the intimate sphere, suggests one important sense in which nationalism has more in common with kinship or religion than with, say, liberalism or socialism." In the endeavour to uncover "the social bases of nationalism" (Gellner 1983, p. 113) the very human being of social actors is implicated because of nationalism's ability to morph with and draw upon what Geertz has called 'primordialist sentiments' because the nation can symbolise and canalise our ownmost *dasein*. It is because symbolic constructs such as the nation are 'empty' enough that they can receive everything thrown at them by 'secondary natures,' and this means they can be spontaneously interpreted by the individual or social group with meanings that are *only available to those individuals and social groups*. As Cohen (1985, p. 21) has written:

> Symbols are effective because they are imprecise. Though obviously not contentless, part of their meaning is 'subjective.' They are, therefore, ideal media through which people can speak a 'common' language...without subordinating themselves to a tyranny of orthodoxy. Individuality and commonality are thus reconcilable.

If nationalism is able to appeal to integral human being, we now turn to thinking 'being human' and 'being modern' upon the basis of Special Ontology, or upon the basis of certain performative accomplishments that we now turn to in order to explain some knowledge-claims that have been made in passing but without having given any details of the developments of *dasein* that justify them. We proceed then to outline the 'perfections' of fully-contextualised Scottish working-class *dasein* that are possible among the '79 generations, and I do so upon the basis of firstly having accomplished them within myself. If such an outline is to be given or if *dasein* is to be capable of painting itself (and others) with a full palette of colour, the artist must firstly have a full palette of colour available to him. Hence, upon the basis of particular developments that add the finishing touches of colour, the final three chapters give the performative detail that grounds what I describe as an affluent politics of holistic *dasein*, not only 'in full period costume' but at the very apotheosis of its natural powers and even beyond these natural powers as the question of transcendence and the supernatural comes into view.

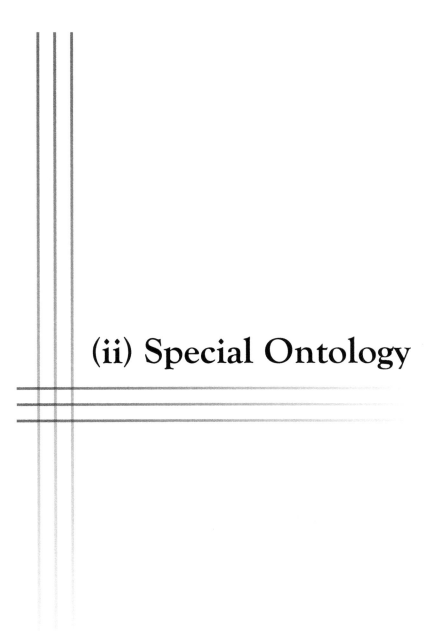

# (ii) Special Ontology

# 6

# The Natural Apotheosis of Contextual Scottish Human Being

> Reflexivity...can be a means of examining a field problem, that is...the study of the 'Natives'' reflexive acts.
>
> Myerhoff & Ruby 1982, p. 17

> An a priori study of man's nature is impossible. The only way we can know it is by studying its acts.
>
> Bettoni 1961, p. 73

## 6.1 The Worker & Self-Appropriation

In my account of the integral development of contextual *dasein* the structuration effected by *truth* is a privileged event, and in light of the transformation brought about within the worker-inquirer by a particular act of understanding, it is necessary to speak of the unique 'agency of truth' that structures the *dasein* of the worker-inquirer in a unique manner. Ever since Aristotle's observation that "falsity and truth are not in things...but in thought" (in Barnes 1984, p. 1623), truth has been recognised as a modification that occurs within the knower and not in the object or thing that is known. I propose then to describe an intellectual development within the worker and draw upon the Aristotelian-Thomist tradition and the work of Lonergan's (1957) philosophy of self-appropriation and develop an emphasis upon the intellect in the shadow of Marx's (in Arthur 1970, p. 61) 'scarcity thinking' point of view which famously declared "liberation is an historical and not a mental act." While I have much sympathy with this view, the fact remains that to develop *dasein* in a holistic manner is to develop a specifically intellectual or cognitional 'performance' or 'act' to the extent that we will argue *liberation is above all a mental act*. This stance presupposes an integral account of *dasein* must concern itself with achieving an integral self-understanding, and how this understanding is achieved is important not only because a series of cultural and social conditions stand in the way of the individual worker-inquirer achieving this act of self-understanding, but because by giving an account of this specifically cognitional or intellectual development, this presupposes a situated performance of cognitional structure,[129] and to achieve this *cognitional agency* the strategy I propose will be the appropriation of that part of the self which the worker-inquirer cannot fail to be interested in i.e.

1) the incarnate self immersed in and transformed by the mundane world of work, and

2) the symbolic self emergent from 'at risk' moments where the interface between 'self' and 'society' is made existentially real for the worker located in the occupational hierarchy.

While an emphasis upon the world of work and the workplace has a long history in social research and theory, the desire to integrate the workplace and questions regarding the possibility of 'revolutionary consciousness' among workers has a decidedly

---

[129] I will use Lonergan's *Insight* (1957) as a roadmap for the worker-inquirer achieving self-understanding by drawing upon his account of cognitional structure in which there are nine steps: (1) presentations to the senses, (2) attention to the empirical data, (3) imagination, (4) the drive to understand, (5) insight, (6) conception, (7) reflection, (8) grasp of conditions for understanding and (9) judgment.

pre-neoliberal 'new world order' feel today. Previously, mainstream texts such as Blauner's *Alienation and Freedom: the Factory Worker and His Industry* (1964), Edwards's *Contested Terrain: the Transformation of the Workplace in the Twentieth Century* (1979) and Gordon et al.'s *Segmented Work, Divided Workers* (1982) analysed workers in light of theoretical expectations that they could and should respond oppositionally to capitalism and develop a socialist alternative, and so these texts took up the search for the obstacles and blocks that impede a development within workers as a result of their immersion in the labour process. This rich heritage of empirical studies of a wide range of industrial contexts and workplaces, however, not only took place prior to the decisive shift away from positivism to interpretivism within social theory, but prior to the decisive neoliberal 'triumph' of the nineteen-eighties, symbolised by the Thatcher and Reagan eras so that, if intellectuals throughout the nineteen-seventies failed to answer the neo-liberal charge that "the poor get in a competitive market economy more than they would get in a centrally directed system" (Hayek 1985, p. 67), perhaps the greater failure of many of these studies is that they read as complacent and unsuspecting insofar as their focus and range of theoretical concerns were 'pre-Heideggerian' in their negligence of fundamental questions of *dasein* and 'being working class,' with the result that any relevance they might have had has been swept away by the advent of the post-industrial era.

If we take the approach and concerns of Burawoy's *Manufacturing Consent* (1979), for example, which seeks to explain why workers are compliant and which is concerned with identifying aspects of the labour process that are involved in producing complacency, I believe such an approach to be quite sterile. Similarly, Burawoy's *The Politics of Production* (1985) assumes that the naked appearance of surplus value in the eyes of the workers must inevitably create radical conflict, and that workers' subjectivity has become integrated to capitalism and shop-floor behaviours such as game-playing that relieve boredom and tension seduce workers into accepting their work conditions as inevitable, thereby defusing opposition. Tanner et al. (1992, p. 443) have usefully commented:

> While the incorporation of worker subjectivity into labour process analysis reflects an increasingly optimistic approach...there is no guarantee that re-introducing subjectivity will substantively create a hopeful picture. Indeed, the ironic upshot of Burawoy's and the segmentationists' revisions of labour process theory is that workers are portrayed as increasingly incorporated throughout the twentieth century.

With the benefit of hindsight, a weakness of much of these studies was the fact that in the sociological literature dealing with industrial workers there was no emphasis upon turning to the 'life of mind' upon the basis of a prior reintroduction of subjectivity, or turning to the self or *dasein* constituted at the 'point of production.' Whether writers from this era give optimistic or pessimistic estimations of the 'revolutionary possibilities' of the labour process, none used the labour process as a means and medium to lever an interior event within the worker himself. This omission is fatal, insofar as the first consciousness that needs converted or awakened to the reality and significance of the *dasein* brought about by the social practice of labour, and any implications this might have for political action, is that of the worker himself, and if he is not intellectually convinced of this then any project of politicisation upon the basis of self-appropriation upon the basis of this 'worked' *dasein* is more or less at a standstill.

This failure of 'labour process theorists' can be traced back to Marx himself who similarly believed that the production system was the seedbed for the workers' consciousness, but failed to show how shop-floor behaviour or 'trade union consciousness' becomes revolutionary consciousness. The absence of any accounts of such a process, which must have included a purely cognitional or intellectual component which must have stood in some relation to an account of proletarian Man's 'purely natural end' or beatitude, has haunted Marxism throughout its history, and for this omission many have criticised Marxism for being a secular version of an idealist metaphysics insofar as its 'materialist theory of history' and 'proletarian revolution' were never remotely ethnographically or cognitionally grounded in a historical context, or at the level of the individual proletarian via an act of cognitional agency. In light of the absence of any kind of performative verification, Marx's theory of labour, for example, was fated to remain full of philosophical a priorism and he, like his followers, never committed to integral contingency and where it might lead. Typically bourgeois, such was his biography that he was never able to suspect, far less theorise, the reach of thinking upon the basis of the contingent being brought about via labouring, so that Gorz (1997, p. 16) could rightfully point out:

> Marx's theory of the proletariat is not based upon either empirical observation of class conflict or practical involvement in proletarian struggle. No amount of empirical observation or practical involvement as a militant will lead to the discovery of the historical role of the proletariat...On the contrary, only a knowledge of this mission will make it possible to discover the true being of the proletarians. Consequently it is of little importance to know what proletarians themselves think.

Gorz neatly brings into view the fatal weakness of Marxism which was its inability to perform *die anthropologische wende* because the real subjectivity of the 'subject of history' (the proletariat) is more or less irrelevant to the truths of Marxism; truths which are free to become a set of propositions independent of any contact with any working-class population, and so Marxism as a set of doctrines was itself more or less fated to be accused of being another nineteenth-century product of Germanic 'pure reason,' and certainly not built upon or emergent from any kind of living relationship between the particular human being of the working class and theory. Indeed, instead of offering a vital living synthesis between the two there is a mutual alienation that has been integral to Marxism from the outset.

In contrast to this legacy my procedure is to begin with the worker himself, and to think contextualised human being by firstly stripping my own thinking of prefabricated categories or hackneyed linguistic signifiers and attempt to confront this *dasein* at the level of being-qua-being in the fashion of Husserl. In this task the all-important element is the beginning i.e. effecting the shift from *worker* to *worker-inquirer* and this will be done by imagining and conceiving the self brought about by manual labour and by *staking everything* upon the conviction that, because the worker is convinced of the reality of his 'situated self,' this is the ground upon which the project of self-appropriation is most likely to succeed.

This initial step is all-important because while clearly manual labourers are immersed in their contexts and realities in a practical and pre-theoretical manner, simply being a determinate 'worked self' does not automatically imply the existence of any kind of imagining of this self, or any kind of conceptualisation of what in Chapter 2 I referred to after Castoriadis (1987, p. 168) as the being brought into being by doing. Men who know what it is to work hard and have the calloused hands to prove their long experience of labour are likely to have no interest in a project of self-appropriation, or a development of their intellectual nature beyond the specialisations of common sense, or the particular range of technicalities necessary for their working and domestic lives. Ordinarily, an intense identification with work is perfectly compatible with the absence of asking questions that one associates with developing political or class consciousness beyond a limited range of practical concerns, and this divorce between the life of labour and the life of mind is doubly applicable to a project of self-appropriation to the extent that it is liable to be still-born insofar as it will require overcoming a certain anti-intellectualist bias, as well as a bias against any appearance of narcissistic self-absorption, not to mention the obvious obstacles of lack of education and free time to conceive and desire such a project.

This gap, then, between 'being' and 'thought' is the defining tension within any kind of project of self-appropriation by the manual labourer as it is the tension between two very different worlds and two very different aspects of the self: one aspect of self that is dominant over all other developments of the self, and another aspect of self which routinely even fails to exist. The difficulty, then, is that the self to be appropriated is the situated labouring self that may care nothing for intellectual inquiry and, on the other hand, the self to be appropriated is "the rational, intelligent, experiencing man" (Lonergan 1990, p. 193), so that the individual worker is faced from the outset with this paradox: in order to embark upon the intellectual pursuit of himself via a project of self-appropriation he must break with a firmly established 'immediate' relationship to himself if he is to effect the change from being a worker to being a worker-inquirer.

## 6.2 Labour and the Psyche: Justification

In Chapter 2 we set the task of articulating the lived experience of physical labour and noted that, in addition to the obvious physical effects of labouring such as sweat and muscle strain etcetera, something else a worker may come to awareness of are certain psychological effects that come about as a result of working. Ordinarily, introspective reflection is able to advert to the fact that part of the data available to be brought to explicit awareness is a particular effect upon the self that may be described as the psychological experience of *being justified*. In contrast to elitist doctrines surrounding manual labour as dehumanising the worker such as we find in the slave-owner Aristotle, or descriptions of manual labour as alienating the worker from himself and others as found in Marx, the fact is that thanks to his working the worker at a basic level is justified in taking up or occupying and *being in social space*, is justified in 'taking up room' we might say, is justified in being in a particular public place at a particular time. The worker is *spatially justified*, then, because any occupation of social or public space requires a publicly or socially recognised reason or justification, and thanks to his performing work the worker in social or public space is not 'out of place.'

Also, in his being-for-others, whether a workmate or his chargehand or a casual passer-by or even to a *purely imaginary other*, the labourer's doing work might be described as a passport legitimising his being in public in the eyes of others. Thanks to 'being there' (*dasein*) because he has work to do, the public place in which he works becomes 'owned' and *personalised* thanks to being taken up and freely developed by the life of intentionality and freedom. This kind of reflexive being in social space is the opposite of the kind of 'being in space' experienced by the stranger or the new-comer, as social space in this case 'interrogates' the social actor and demands to know the reason why he or she is 'there.' Performing work, then, removes this interrogation and the threat of being alienated or estranged from a place, and prevents a place becoming strange, and removes the threat of the self becoming a stranger or someone judged as being 'out of place.' Performing work then makes us 'at home' and is an obvious source of social inclusion and allows the worker to experience his 'being there' in a particular way. More than simply having permission to be somewhere, the worker feels he has earned the right to his 'being there' thanks to his working.

Similarly, another two media or mediations of the experience of 'being justified' are *temporality* and *embodiment* insofar as the sweat on the worker's brow witnesses to how the worker has spent his time in public space, and so signals his possession of a particular relationship to time that justifies him. In contrast to elitist existentialist doctrines of the self being 'at issue' (Heidegger 1962), part of the data about himself that is available to the worker is the fundamental experience of not being 'at issue' because the worker enacts or brings-into-being his justification *in time, in space and via the body* insofar as he is routinely literally covered in evidence that he has used time to good effect. The outcome of work then is not simply a trench dug to uncover a wastewater pipe to be repaired but a certain justification in relation to the use of time, resulting in a particular experience of 'being in time,' and a certain individual and interpersonal *reflexive justification* in relation to self, fellow workers and others.

Faced with the 'interrogation' of time and space and his body and any potential interlocutor, the worker not only has an answer but *is* his answer as he embodies this condition as his very *dasein*.

Finally, beyond these spatial and embodied and temporal mediations of justification via the practice of work are the many issues of social integration that are resolved by working; issues of 'identity' insofar as, above all else, one's relationship to money – the *ens realissimum* of labour for the labourer in a free-market society – is secured as money accesses a material realm of consumption as well as a symbolic realm of identity as paid employment resolves one's relationship to oneself as a man, husband, father, brother, uncle and local etcetera, and one's participation in a series of symbolic communities. In the free-market society paid work is the source *par excellence* of psychological and social individuation and social integration.

## 6.3 Labour & the Psyche: Alienation

While the body is constantly conditioned by its practice in the world and if performing the tasks of the world constantly leaves traces upon the body, another question is whether the structuring significance of performing manual labour for *dasein* is exhausted by the short-lived or long-standing physical effects of working with a high-pressure hose, for example, or whether the effects of performing manual labour extend beyond the physical socialisation or physical re-structuration of the body to become, for example, a sui generic 'source of personality' or source of self. If the fact that physical *dasein* is structured by the social practice of labour is hardly a novel discovery, perhaps a more interesting and involved question is whether and how the realm of meaning or the cultural context of performing labour also informs the very way embodiment is among manual labourers.

My argument will be that the 'brute fact' of physical labour is not only passed through the medium of the human body but the media of time and culture, or the objective 'symbolic order' and intergenerational 'filters' or contexts; indeed is passed through an infinite number of media that feedback onto and effect the lived experience of work. Hence, in addition to a biological universal connecting labouring humanity around the world and across generations in a universal or fundamental ontology in Heidegger's sense, and that can be studied by students of human anatomy and bio-chemistry, the *dasein* brought about by doing is also fated to be refracted through the medium of culture.

More concretely, then, among the 1979 generation, for example, this laboured *dasein* will be informed by "the liberation of the instincts, the revolution of desire" (Pefanis 1992, p. 105) that occurred thanks to the rise of affluence in the West in the latter twentieth century. More generally, as a result of being passed through culture, "not even the simplest, dimmest apprehension of a feeling – say, the feeling of hunger not outwardly expressed – can dispense with some kind of ideological form...one can apprehend one's hunger apologetically, irritably, angrily, indignantly etc...Outward expression in most cases only continues and makes more distinct the direction already taken by inner speech" (Volosinov 1986, p. 87). Finally, in addition to the filter of culture, *the 'self' brought about by doing is enjoyed and taken up by freedom and reflexivity* to become an endless source of informing of the person beyond the merely physical.

As a result of being taken up into the intentional order and the intentionality of the worker, the reality or significance of work from the point of view of the worker is not something fixed or definite once and for all, as its meaning and impact changes as the personal circumstances of the labourer change, with some meanings only coming into being through the play of time and circumstance. In itself, work is physical activity involving the expenditure of energy but as a social practice manual labour *within a market society* is related to an occupational structure that is ranked according to a cultural judgment or according to prestige or status and through this to a public realm of discourse, representations and meanings. Within this hierarchical division of labour the manual labourer is located towards the bottom of the occupational and class structure, and in highly stratified social orders there is universal consensus that manual labour in every such society is performed by members of the 'lower orders.'

Similarly, in the public symbolic realm of meaning and representations, not all social practices are equal as they have different values attached to them and these judgments have a structuring effect upon the psyche of the labourer just as real as the physical structurations of the body of the worker. Manual work then exists twice: firstly as a physical structuration and, secondly, as a psychological or mental structuration. In a society fundamentally divided into different classes whose members perform different social practices, it is reasonable to imagine these are the fundamental realities configuring the consciousnesses of its members so that a question is, if a high-pressure hose can structure the body after thirty minutes, what structurations of the psyche will be present in the unskilled or semi-skilled low-paid manual labourer as a result of occupying his particular social position over the course of a lifetime?

To begin to answer this question I return to the thirty-three-year-old informant Dauvit employed by the local supermarket trolley manufacturer Buko quoted earlier in Chapter 2, who began talking about his work:

> Everythin revolves aroond money eh. If you've no got a wage e money comin in Ah mean life's shit ken. Ken, what can ye dae wi nae money? Nooadays eh? Somethin tae live oan. Ah mean Ah've got a joab there the noo bit it's f***** crap; the money's crap. Bit it's only five minutes o'er the road, eh. Bit the f***** money's shite an a'. Ah mean Ah'm only comin in wi a hunder an seventy pound a week. Crap, ye ken. Bit there nothin better.

The above testimony adverts to the fact that the exercise of agency among the working class is caught in the grip of a social determination insofar as the disciplinary power of low-paid work means that any particular exercise of agency such as party political activism, civic engagement, some form of volunteering or the decision to practice a more healthy lifestyle or attain a greater level of educational achievement, will require a disproportionately greater exercise agency among the low-paid, so that ordinarily this will mean a predictable lesser involvement in the political process, a virtual boycott of public life, a significantly lesser life expectancy, a much inferior level of educational achievement and a subjective relationship to the realm of meaning that is dominated by objective domination. It is also clear from the above testimony that within the intentional and emotional life of the worker, an existential preoccupation with objective reality takes up much of subjective life; that intentionality is forcibly conformed to objective reality as a matter of mundane habitus, and a disciplining that is beyond the formal behavioural requirements imposed by the employer-employee relationship occurs, so that when intentional and affective life is dominated by market conditions, the coming into being of a particular mental habitus or intentional horizon is more or less inevitable.

It is in 'free consciousness,' then, and not simply behaviour that the extent of the reach and reality of the structuring of the market society upon human being will be registered and played out; it is in the intimacy and privacy of intentionality that will be found a forum for a dialectic of agency/constraint within what Baudrillard has termed 'the mirror of production' (1975). From Dauvit's testimony it seems clear that he would not distinguish which spheres of his life are dominated by his relationship to the free market in labour and which are free of its gravitational pull, because the words 'everything' and 'life' are his choice of words to describe what is conformed to objectivity. It is in consciousness, then, where the domination of the market society is most free to colonise and 'inform' the lifeworld and fashion every realm of experience and every non-production relationship into its image, so that a question for the worker-inquirer who sets out on the journey of self-appropriation is whether he is ever, phenomeno-logically speaking, 'outside' of work or free of the 'mirror of production;' whether there exists a meaningful space within him that is psychologically outside of work and is something other than a manual labourer; whether he has experiences beyond the reach of this determination, or whether as a result of his inter-nalisation of objective determination, he in fact freely extends the structuration of the identity and *dasein* sourced in his objective occupational-based relationship to the market society into his every other relation.

Such a question of course can only be answered by the practice of introspection which will attend to the data of justification discussed earlier. The worker-inquirer as he proceeds in his journey of self-appropriation will also recognise that this justification experience is serial, *is patterned* within his experience as it acts as a source of self and freedom in his behaviours and relationships to others. However, as well as the data of justification being brought into being by his doing, introspection will reveal something else, a particular dialectic that will also be seen to characterise the worker's consciousness and behaviour, thanks to the reality of work being far more than what it subjectively is for the worker. Thanks to work's relationship to a social hierarchy, the practice of *introspection will reveal the following 'dialectic' at work in the worker-inquirer's intentional life* as a result of his coming to awareness of data that can be organised according to two 'ideal types:'

1) a realm of experience that has the reality of justification or inner integration as the departure point for his identity and the exercise of agency, behaviour and social action.

2) a realm of experience that emerges from the objective reality of his *being-for-others* and a patterned set of experiences characterised by being 'at issue' or 'unequal' as the departure point for his identity and the exercise of agency, behaviour and social action.

The worker will be familiar with the reality of labour as a source of how he experiences his body and how this experience is something he shares with other workers, and how a certain inter-subjectivity and solidarity is established among his fellows. However, out of this camaraderie and fellowship and free recognition of himself, part of the data available to introspection is awareness of being 'read' by very differently placed subjectivities and very different lifestyles and institutions. There is awareness, then, not only of other codes but awareness of more powerful and more prestigious codes that operate in wider society and in powerful metropolitan centres that more or less coerce the worker into coming to terms with "symbolic violence" (Bourdieu and

Passeron 1977), or non-physical forms of domination that are present in the media and realm of representations.

The manual worker is aware that outwith his fellowship with his fellows is a social context and a cultural context that reads him as occupying a lower or subordinate or less prestigious position. To the extent the worker-inquirer is conscious of these schemes of interpretation, he is aware they are an integral part of his 'social awareness' which also recognises *a psychological tension* in his behaviour and consciousness that has already been behaviourally operative in his life and, subsequent to reaching this awareness, also recognises there is a duality or dialectic (a 'split' *dasein*) in his life as a worker-inquirer insofar as he understands that there is an integrity and freedom 'in work' which is more or less fated to be put 'at issue' by the public realm of meaning,[130] and coming to this awareness is a defining moment in his journey of translating or aligning his being with his consciousness.

Upon the basis of embodiment the worker enjoys an experience of integration and integrity. However, there is a second natural environment proper to human being that is the symbolic and cultural, so we can say that each adult social actor 'swims' in a semiotic 'sea of signs' and the labourer is always related to this objective realm of meaning, and in a historically class-divided society, this realm of meaning reflects this history of division and inequality and is just as hierarchical and stratified and real and powerful and present in its judgments as the unequal distribution of material and monetary resources is real and powerful and present in the judgments it makes upon social actors' lives. We can also safely say that the socialisation processes of such historically divided societies involve the internalisation of the dominant meaning systems among both the dominant and the subordinate social classes via schooling and parenting, for example, and

---

[130] Important ethnographic testimonies of the suffering among working-class persons that arises as a result of being trapped in their *being-for-others* is provided by Simon Charlesworth (1999), while Toni Morrison (1999) provides a memorable literary treatment of the same phenomenon in terms of race/ethnicity.

are just as real in their disciplining of bodies, behaviours and consciousnesses.

When attention is focussed, then, upon the stratified order of meaning, the practice of introspection uncovers an emotional terrain occupied by the worker-inquirer and his family and even locality, and each of their histories as a result of living the position of subordination through time and its accompanying feelings of resentment, anger, shame and embarrassment, as well as the memories of living through encounters where this subordination became existential, such as moments of realisation one's likely trajectory through social space is severely limited, or moments of being accused of 'trespassing' beyond one's class fraction by self, friends and family, or moments of trespassing onto another class's territory or trajectory. Crucially for the journey of self-appropriation is that introspection grasps that there is something available to be grasped in this range of experience, so that exploring this psychological terrain becomes a matter of the worker-inquirer recognising his psychological reality and history.

For the worker-inquirer this introspection includes thematizing his being-for-others, and reflection upon his relationship to the socialised realm of meaning and its ongoing structuring effects upon behaviour and psyche, so that he wages a campaign of recognising within himself his resistance to and his acceptance of the Geertzian 'webs of meaning' which class-based societies spin; either suspending him into behaviours and thoughts of subordination, or triggering behaviours and thoughts of resistance to his social fate and his allocated trajectory through social space. For the worker-inquirer who successfully carries out the project of self-appropriation there must come a point when he comes to a systematic awareness of his *being-for-others* and comes to awareness of this defining tension in his consciousness and behaviour, this tension between his being-for-himself and his being-for-others that is likely to lead to an ambivalence when in the company of those who do not share the same class position and habitus.

The worker-inquirer who uncovers this data about himself also uncovers an emotional life that may be described as a cipher or 'mouthpiece' for this dialectic, so that the project of self-appropriation recognises that much of the affective charge or 'cut and thrust' of social interaction as well as introspection lies in the fact that the working class is the social group least likely to articulate its condition via discourse and introspection because the closer an individual approaches this basic structuration as the existential data of himself, the less likely he is to voice this condition as, ironically, the closer one comes to one's psychological, emotional and intellectual condition of insecure being-in-the-world *as an existential event*, the less one is likely to translate these experiences into explicit awareness in an open, deliberate and 'leisurely' fashion because the psychological resistance one has to overcome within oneself to do so is considerable.

This Gordian knot of self-representation and self-recognition seems impossible to cut insofar as emotions of fear and anxiety become the 'live' data of oneself once this dialectic becomes the focus of introspection, leading to recognising the patterning and history of fear and anxiety, the history of one's being-for-others and its related behaviours and its related patterns of comportment that bring to awareness new vistas upon one's biography. Outwith practicing psychological techniques such as the 'healing of memories' or what *gestalt* psychotherapy's Friedrich Perls terms "the safe emergency of the therapeutic situation,"[131] this data only becomes real when one's structural objectivity is existentially apprehended and, in a cash economy, this normally only occurs in conditions of vulnerability because in secure financial conditions such 'moments of danger' do not arise, and so financial security disappears the 'data' of one's self. As per our discussion of Dauvit in Chapter 2, only failure and crisis triggers the emotional patterning and the shame and insecurity that is in fact already *in situ* as essence, if not forcibly present as existence.

Because the necessary condition for sustained reflection upon this data is the 'cut and thrust' of occupying a dominated life or a position of more or less 'failure' as read by the dominant code, what becomes clear is why working-class consciousness has been

---

[131] https://www.youtube.com/watch?v=8y5tuJ3Sojc. [Accessed 18 April 2014]

incapable of a phenomenology of itself, despite the fact that one social reality and one social practice that is not insecure but exists in abundance is material and symbolic insecurity. The paradox then is that should the task be to produce an ethnography, a culture, a literature, a psychology or a self-understanding, having the leisure to carry out this task will mean the disappearance of the data of oneself, which prevents the worker-inquirer or 'slave' being able to "to choose himself on the ground of slavery" (Sartre 1966, p. 703) because being successful necessarily means becoming distant from the raw existential data which can furnish consciousness with the phenomenological data of itself. There is, then, an objective determination in place affecting the disappearance of a phenomenology of working-class *dasein* and which answers Edwin Muir's wondering why unemployed Lanarkshire miners failed to write texts that plumbed the depths of human being.

The passer-by Muir in his *Scottish Journey* (1935) through industrial Scotland in the summer of 1934 who saw men who "seemed to me to have nothing to do but think" (1935, p. 143), fails to realise that this very position of unemployment is *not* a departure point for thinking *because it is shameful* and a source of regret and recrimination. As per our analysis of Dauvit in Chapter 2, often an integral ingredient to explaining the disappearance of working-class reality *especially within the consciousness of the working-class person* is the 'thick' reality of locality and intersubjectivity which means the thematisation of 'failure' is fated to be almost never cultivated in a deliberative and free or non-shameful way, because an integral part of living economic failure is having to live with other people having to live one's failure, which often means the exertion of sustained pressure to read one's failure exclusively from the dominant point of view i.e. as a shameful reality to be ended as soon as possible, and certainly not a reality to be explored and used as a point of departure for a project of self-appropriation.

Such is the level of harsh cultural commentary upon poverty that even to attend to it as 'data' is, in a sense, to already be beginning to be free of its grip and to attend to this reality requires one's intellectual life escape from being a cipher for conventionality and conventional responses such as shame. The difficulty for achieving a life of introspection and representation, then, is due to the nature of the reality being inquired into: being the decentred and 'trigger-requiring' reality it is means it is a source of self or 'set of data' that can be disappeared or hidden or euphemised or finessed by talk, or prayed about or forgotten in drink, or released from when happy or endured in silence or enacted in violence or mental ill-health. Only by becoming a worker-inquirer is the worker able to transcend this condition by instantiating, in addition to his deep integration to this reality, a certain alienation or distance from this reality, or a *speculative or even contemplative relation to his immersion in the real*, a reflective relation to his condition of being unable to afford the luxury of practicing introspection.

Taking the first steps on the journey of self-appropriation, then, must be difficult because what it requires is somehow or other developing an open-eyed, deliberate or 'invulnerable' relationship to one's vulnerability, a strong relationship to one's weakness or an articulate relationship to one's being lost for words. Such is the difficulty in pulling this relationship to self off that the worker's internalisation of his already in situ *dasein* and *mitsein* or being-for-others will spontaneously raise the objection: how vulnerable can such vulnerability really be, or how weak can such weakness be, or how silent can such silence in fact be if the same vulnerable, weak and silent worker is able to face up to and recognise them in an open-eyed and deliberate fashion i.e. be invulnerable, strong and articulate in the face of such truths about itself, and deploy these weaknesses and 'wounding' experiences as resources to fuel a reflexive project of self-appropriation.

The defining tension within a project of self-appropriation in a manual labourer is bringing two very different worlds and two very different aspects of the self into a symbiotic relationship and, eventually, conscious alignment with each other. On the one hand the self to be appropriated is the situated labouring or working-class self that will care nothing for intellectual inquiry. On the other hand, the self to be appropriated is "the rational, intelligent, experiencing man" (Lonergan 1990, p. 193). From the existential standpoint of a particular individual, then, he must embark upon the intellectual pursuit of himself and in doing so break with a firmly established 'immediate' relationship to himself, and it is at this point that a further determination comes into view: if it is unlikely a campaign of understanding will be waged unless there is some expectation of the resultant benefits, from where other than theory or 'pure reason' (certainly not from experience) could such an expectation emerge? Also, if the only source of motivation is a purely theoretical source, the fact is that for the consciousness yet to be constituted by theory, any theoretical motivation is no motivation at all. This is the Gordian knot to be untied or the Rubicon to be crossed as this shift from worker to worker-inquirer that leads to the path of cognitional agency is the *conditione sine qua non* of the entire process.

As a result of stepping onto the road less travelled the worker becomes a worker-inquirer, and so far we have argued for the physical and psychological affects of work, including a certain sense of the worker being justified or dignified by his labour; a justification, however, that is a merely serial integration whose reality is tied to the serial reproduction of particular bodily conditions and physical praxis and that is not a permanent possession but something which has to be enacted or brought into existence again and again by fresh effort if it is to remain real. This raises the question: at what other level can the integration of self effected by work exist? To answer this question the worker-inquirer must not only ascend to the level of inquiry but must rise to the level of *conceptualisation* in order to give a more adequate account of himself and the being brought into existence by his doing.

## 6.4 Conceptualisation (or Why Reality Isn't Enough)

French philosopher Simone Weil's *Factory Journal* (1987) gives an account of her struggle to come to terms with her experience of manual labour and an indication of the difficulties involved in the worker-inquirer coming to an adequate self-concept. Reading Weil's account of her eight-and-a-half months working in a factory in 1934-35, it is illuminating to see how she resisted conceiving the new becoming that was happening within herself as a result of her life as a worker, and how she was unable to rise to any kind of conceptualisation of her new 'secondary nature.' The opportunity to conceive the new *dasein* that was occurring within her was resisted insofar as Weil preferred to indulge in a 'flight from contextual being' rather than theorise her industrialised incarnation, with the result that she never set herself the task of thinking what was coming to pass within her. As her editors (in Weil 1987, p. 153) wrote of her time as a factory hand:

> Perhaps even more important than the intellectual conclusions she drew from her factory experience were its psychological effects on her. When she attempted to describe it in letters to friends, she found it inexpressible; she became almost inarticulate and could only sum it up in such generalities as 'it's inhuman.'

Central to Weil's difficulties in thinking her 'worked self' was having to cope with her physical exhaustion and what she felt was the impossibility of intellectual labour as a result. Instead of converting to the importance of embodiment and the importance of *the body* as a means of the self coming-to-know its being-in-the-world via labour, for example, this existential truth which Weil was coming to know in her body was something she was unable to use as a standpoint for her theoretical work. While she had the social and cultural capital to accomplish the task of translating a 'secondary nature' into its adequate conceptualisation or representation but in fact failed to do so, it seems the key factor in explaining her failure to accomplish this was her failure to posit as a goal for herself the task of translating her particular 'existence' into its adequate conceptualisation, and in trying to understand Weil's failure on this point it seems her philosophical training more or less blinded her to the need to discard her categories of 'pure reason,' and emerge from her immersion in factory life with new mental categories to think her new *dasein*. Insofar as Weil failed to align her 'being' with her 'consciousness,' it was as a result of her philosophical training and long immersion in universalism that meant she was ill-equipped to see "it is not possible to strip away our 'second nature' in order to lay bare… human being, because without those contents we would not recognise this subject at all" (Parker 2011, p. 12).

Similarly, when trying to understand how those of little symbolic capital and no training in universalism also fail in this respect, Chapter 2 concerned a consciousness chronically reduced to 'the present' and an existentialism that ordinarily does not reach representational, far less theoretical, self-consciousness. There I also argued that a purely linguistic construction or depiction of contextual reality was of little use when articulating working-class ontology, just as the domination of the public sphere by representations of time as 'progress' is unable to change the reality or the real relation to time effected by manual work or living certain housing conditions. However, in any project of self-appropriation, a reliance upon conceptual and linguistic processes is unavoidable because, to the extent the worker-inquirer's relation to language fails to escape an 'inherited' and then learned and freely practiced determinism, the worker-inquirer will be unable to rise to a project of self-appropriation.

This difficulty is, of course, exacerbated the less material and symbolic resources one has, because a sociality and personality forever tied to the compulsions of the cash-nexus requires of itself first and foremost that it survives such a situation, so that *what is least of all necessary* is a conceptual effort at understanding itself, far less wider society. Indeed such a self whose only dues are money is often the most convinced of all that such is all there is to understand about the self and society; that when the basic obedience of employment is achieved, the self can even imagine itself as indifferent to society, as living intimately within the confines of such financial pressures it is more or less inevitable that such thinking, often becomes the extent of thinking insofar as it is the extent of experiencing the demands of one's society and the conditions for being the self that one is. Insofar as one's basic condition is a vulnerable condition then its *raison d' être* is to simply reproduce its social relations in order to maintain itself (and without any thought to change them according to what is imagined to be right or just), and in the existential 'success' of merely coping and managing, this subjectivity is more or less fated to be content. Men and women who are objectively at risk of moving into poverty at some point in their lives are heavily invested in reproducing social structures, as by doing so they successfully keep a possible poverty precisely at the level of potentiality thanks to the immediate existential security of paid employment, and this is why any acquaintance with a working-class population always involves acquaintance with economism.

In addition to intellectual and financial difficulties, the daily social practice of manual work ordinarily involves an immersion into the practicalities of life, which become a matter of habit and a matter of taste, preference and satisfaction and a source of identity for oneself and one's being-for-others despite its rigors. Those living the body as their fate and living its sui generic self-affirmation, then, routinely feel no need to sally forth upon a Lonerganian project of self-appropriation and jeopardise the solid pre-conceptual realities and knowledges they enjoy thanks to their embodiment of pre-conceptual truths. Because there is a non-conceptual or kinaesthetic knowledge that justifies the worker, there is a freedom from the need for representation that is the freedom of existence 'outside the text' or a freedom from signs, so that attempting to reproduce this bodily justification via rational investigation seems unlikely, and certainly unsatisfactory, so that instinctively they distrust reason to reproduce their embodied 'truths.' More concretely, an 'anti-learning' disposition is often present and can always be justified thanks to pointing towards the class of people who do invest in the realm of meaning and pointing to the objective need to keep making money every week. The issue remains the relation of tension between the existential and intellectual level; the developed cultural prejudices that are enjoyed and so brought to bear against a project of self-appropriation.

While the phrase 'self-appropriation' or 're-thinking human being' seem inoffensive enough, what they involve if they are to be successful is the worker-inquirer being able to bear the weight of his long immersion into 'naturalism' pressing down upon his first efforts of will, which are fated to be resisted *de profundis* so that the idea of having to think about one's being in an open-eyed and deliberate fashion must ordinarily be pre-consciously rejected a thousand times before it succeeds in being sufficiently present to be recognised as a task in itself. The subject then must ordinarily undergo a crisis event in order to emerge from his natural possession of himself. What one reluctantly faces because one has to is precisely that which one does not want to be a source of self, or any more present in one's life than is absolutely necessary, so that there is an existential basis for a campaign against self-appropriation upon one's 'thrown' self in favour of some other self that is free of coerced 'becomings' and unwanted empirical events. (Were I to criticise manual labourers for failing to instantiate a reflexive project upon the basis of the 'signature *dasein*' that they are I would be hypocritical, as I failed to do precisely this as regards my fieldwork housing conditions).

What seems clear from our discussion of Dauvit in Chapter 2 is that some kind of impetus is required to climb out of and transcend immanence, as both employment and unemployment 'disappear' the data that is needed to fuel the project of self-appropriation, insofar as both positions more or less coerce the self into acting and believing that its business is nothing other than the existential and the material. This of course is not to be understood as something that is learned as a proposition, but rather as a de facto unstated truth for the consciousness whose data regarding its existence is that of being continually moored to its material conditions, and which routinely does not have the intersubjective or network resources to raise further questions and escape its imprisonment within habitus. Such is the existential weight or hegemony of an embodied existentialism's judgment as to what is real and worthwhile that it routinely judges there is nothing further to be concerned about, and certainly not a Hegelian or Lonerganian project of self-appropriation, so that the hegemony of 'scarcity thinking' reigns even in conditions of affluence because of an existentialism that freely extends its immersion into material conditions and their determination of human being all the way to an antepredicative 'metaphysics' that is deeply limiting and defining.

In the worker-inquirer's journey to grasp himself intellectually he must find his way to align himself with Marx's *The German Ideology* (1846) where he criticised Feuerbach for beginning with Man in the abstract, and not Man as the subject of a concrete political economy. Likewise, he must ally with Althusser who saw that: "One thing is certain: one cannot begin with man, because that would be to begin with a bourgeois idea of 'man'...'Man' is a myth" (1984, cited in Tubbs 1997, p. 16). The worker-inquirer then must discard his first idea of himself that is conveniently 'at hand' insofar as what is certain is that the kind of being doing brings about has not been the subject of much progress, because those 'thinking being' have traditionally instantiated a leisurely non-working relation to doing, so that this has largely remained a non-question because the traditional producers of knowledge were not bringing their being into being by labouring.

The worker-inquirer, then, does not yet know the reality nor the process of his liberation as he has no experience of it nor a theoretical representation or model of it in his mind. Indeed, insofar as the schemes of perception of the worker-inquirer are conventional he will have difficulty appearing before himself. Parenthetically, we may say that only at a later stage at the completion of cognitional structure will the worker-inquirer put the question to Althusser as to whether Althusser himself conceived a real concrete self and worked out the phenomenology of its liberation, or whether Althusser himself refused particularity and ethnography and in their stead was "forced to posit a subjectless discourse" (Tubbs 1997, p. 16), which brings us back to the starting point of Marx criticising Feuerbach, and calling for a break with a purely imaginary universal Man because no 'secondary nature' or set of social conditions are universal.

It is because the conceptual order is a *sui generic* realm that a set of concrete material and social conditions that are dominant and present, and that never pass out of existential awareness into unconscious structure and which dominate everyday speech and everyday consciousness, can still fail to be the subject or content of an open-eyed and self-conscious reflexive project of self-appropriation. Because the work of translating 'being' into 'consciousness' is difficult at the best of times, something so real and 'infallible' in its reach and transformation of subjectivity and consciousness, can also remain perennially under-developed insofar as its existence remains *tied to seriality*. Also, this very condition of underdevelopment is often the result of an over-development of *dasein* in a particular direction, so that a determinate structuration of self and its continual occupation of intentionality paradoxically works to prevent that same intentionality from engaging with the world of meaning as a possible new medium for the expression or development of this same condition. This condition, then, may indeed create a reflexive project, but a project conducted *against* the realm of meaning, and this is the difference between the reflexive development of the 'worked self' via freedom and choice that follows the paths of least resistance, and something which is quite different: the open-eyed deliberate psychological self-analysis and conceptualisation involved in the project of self-appropriation.

In order to perform an act of intellectual understanding our sights have been set upon conceiving the worked-self as our aim is for the worker-inquirer to achieve self-appropriation, and the self to be appropriated is not only the worked-self but "the rational, intelligent, experiencing man" (Lonergan 1990, p. 193). We have seen that this project must ordinarily fail even to begin because the worked-self is only one aspect of *dasein*, and ordinarily is not the identity that is particularly loved and surrounded by doting attention when the worker is at his leisure. Self-appropriation depends upon the worker translating his *dasein* into his consciousness, but it also recognises that the labourer is not the *dasein* brought into being by doing (Castoriadis 1997) in the same way as a stone is and always is its 'being a stone,' because the worked-self is no thing-like substantive something either 'out there' or 'in there' continually present to the worker, far less the casual observer. The non-substantialist nature of working-class identity then is caught sight of or is revealed in events or moments of strength/vulnerability, or justification or being 'at issue' that are captured by paying attention to the data of oneself, and then thematizing this data and interrogating it for its intelligibility and sorting the data of oneself into patterns, and sifting it as a possible window onto one's historicity, or a key to explaining behaviours, practices and intentionality. To 'fix' himself, the subject must find some way of grasping his non-substance-like self in a substantial manner i.e. in such a way that its being present to awareness escapes its slavery to a merely serial existence and to empirical-come-physical conditions and 'triggering' events. This kind of presence can only be intellectual presence, and so the self must be grasped intellectually, so that a little more of his incarnation becomes habitually present in awareness.

In this simultaneous further immersion into the real and liberation from the real, the real is present in a fuller and richer manner as part of a reflexive project outwith its concrete 'live' triggerings, and for this to happen the worker-inquirer must firstly grasp the data of himself his psyche makes available, and then grasp whether or not they are a pattern and of significance, and then grasp the objective triggering mechanisms or social occasions that make these patterned feelings live within him. If he is to comply with his own cognitional structure, the worker-inquirer's pursuit of self-knowledge must be a pursuit of adequate conceptualisation which rejects recourse to "a cloud of warm incense, a kind of thinking in terms of music, that does not get the length of notions" (Hegel 1967, p. 257). If the labourer is mindful of Hegel's advice that after praxis comes theory, we can say that subsequent to the practice of the body, the mind must attempt to conceive this bodily *dasein* in the spirit of Dilthey as he searches for "the categories of life" and seeks to render *Erlebnis* or "lived experience" (in Makkreel and Rodi 2002, pp. 248-50) by locating the concept that renders the life and the lived experience specific to the manual labourer. If it is clear the conceptualisation of the lived life of labour is destined to play a crucial role, the question to which we now turn is whether it is possible to lay bare this 'second nature' and to grasp it and *conceptually* know it?

## 6.5 The Reduction: (i) *Reductio ad Sensum* & (ii) *Reductio ad Humanum*

The chief defect of all hitherto existing materialism (that of Feuerbach included) is that the thing, reality, sensuousness, is conceived only in the form of the object or of contemplation, but not as sensuous human activity, practice, not subjectively.

Karl Marx *Theses on Feuerbach* (1845)
(in McLellan 1977, p.156)

When Bourdieu (1977, p. 1) wrote that: "It is not sufficient for anthropology to break with native experience and the native representation of that experience," his intention was to justify adopting an objective structuralist approach such as that taken by Lévi-Strauss, for whom anthropology was not about a Malinowskian attempt to understand 'the native's point of view' because natives themselves do not understand the real meaning or function of their practices, myths and beliefs. For Lévi-Strauss (1963), such meaning is only available to structuralist analysis. However, Bourdieu (1977, p. 2) argued that the ethnographer or interpretive sociologist must not only break with the native point of view but, "make a second break and question the presuppositions inherent in the position of an outside observer, who, in his preoccupation with interpreting practices, is inclined to introduce into the object the principles of his relation to the object."

For Bourdieu, then, the unsuspecting analyst is more or less fated to imagine his relation to the object of study is the same as the relation the natives under study have to the object or social practice in question, and the analyst must be aware that this is a fatal error because, if we accept that integral to understanding the lived experience of being a manual labourer is the fact that it is taken up and developed by freedom, this condemns the person who knows nothing of this *dasein* or its many forms to observation and the speculations of 'pure reason.' If this conception of an embodied *dasein* that is enacted by social action means its bearer may be empowered by this invisibility and this inability to be spectated or known, it also divests the observer of the ability to know this *dasein*.

To avoid the snare of 'pure reason' then and establish the project of self-appropriation within the worker it is necessary to do so upon an adequate conceptualisation of that (physical and psychological) structuration brought into being by doing manual labour, and this meant manual labour had to be integral to fieldwork if I was to answer the question as to what constitutes an adequate conceptualisation of the worked self. The search for an adequate conceptualisation of the worked self also faces the difficulty of abstracting from its innumerable instantiations not only in innumerable workers but its innumerable instantiations in one worker over the course of a lifetime, and to tackle this problem I take a chronological approach to the question by focussing upon the subjectivity of the worker beginning his life of manual labour, and in Chapter 2 I introduced the notion of 'being reduced' or the notion of a 'reduction' effected by working insofar as, just as when applying heat to a foodstuff in cooking it is said to be reduced, so the activity of working at its most basic is a physical expending of energy which has biological and physiological consequences that can be analogously described as *reducing* the worker.

In Chapter 2 the term 'reduction' was employed to draw upon the cluster of meanings surrounding the transformation of natural products into human cultural products such as the food served at table in the family home, and was also used in light of its suggesting a change or transformation that is ingested, embodied and occurs via a process of assimilation to the self, and being suggestive of a condition that comes into being as a result of the burning of energy in working and the somatic quality of the becoming that occurs and which we wish to adequately conceive. The metaphor of reduction is chosen, then, insofar as it suggests the interior bio-chemical processes or physicality of this becoming and usefully suggests a 'second nature' that is natural and a process of becoming that is pre-conscious and non-cognitive. Finally, the notion of reduction usefully suggests the impossibility of a 'spectatorial gaze' being capable of suspecting, far less knowing, this 'secondary nature' or contextual *dasein* that comes into being via working, because the 'reducing' effect of work is a reality for the worker alone and does not exist for the casual passer-by and is something which, before any effort of conceptualisation, is already real and part of the self.

In this conception of work, then, there is the daily enacting of a 'secondary nature' and the daily transformation of the natural body into a social and cultural body, and the integration of the worker's social existence and his physical nature as well as his psyche insofar as the ontological consequences of this social action upon the body is not a superficial 'clothing' to be discarded at will because the reality of that which is enacted by doing is not an item of clothing or a veneer overlaying a universal and natural body. The worked-self then is a psycho-physical reduction effected by the expenditure of energy in labouring and, building upon the term reduction, I introduce its Latinate form *reductio* to accord this 'ontology via labour' a conceptualisation of its own and introduce the Latin preposition *ad* meaning 'towards,' to signify the dynamic or mobile nature of this secondary nature; to express the processual and temporal nature of this *dasein* that is brought about by doing (Castoriadis 1997, p. 168), as well as to indicate its intentional existence and dynamic tendency to 'in-form' psychic life.

The conjunction *reductio ad*, then, is used with the intention of conceptualising the non-objective decentred nature of the being of manual labour, and to give priority to the agency of 'the world' in the *dasein* and behaviour and cognitional processes of this decentred social actor. The conjunction *reductio ad* then is used to conceive and indicate not only the historicity of embodiment but its dynamic orientation towards the future as a result of its being taken up by intentional existence into the structure of the person; an embodied and dynamic habitus free of any suggestion of a mechanical programming of behaviour at the point of production that obliterates the exercise of freedom and the play of circumstance.

Integral to the worker-inquirer's socialised *dasein* is a general sensual tendency and, thanks to his working with others, the worker-inquirer will recognise in a pre-theoretical fashion that this condition is not something that is private or unique to himself but is a shared interpersonal reality and a shared basis for behaviour and identity. To account for this further specification of the worked self as something not confined to life as physical existence, further specifications of the condition of 'being reduced' are required, and to this end I introduce the phrase *reductio ad sensum* to conceptualise the fact that not only is there a more or less coerced reduction to physicality but freedom, choice and preference or *amor fati* take up this necessity and develop it, so that the exercise of choice and taste vitalises or 'in-spirits' the *reductio* into becoming a second nature, that makes itself at home in its 'second skin' as it is not only confined to but *celebrates physicality*. The *reductio ad sensum* tendency or modality then is based upon the daily production of a 'simplified' existence as a result of the prioritisation of embodiment as a result of performing a social practice which prioritises the body, and refers to a social practice transformed into a way of life, a grounded orientation towards living, and I use this term to convey the formally dynamic inner conversion to the sensual that occurs within the worker and signifies a determinate comportmental structure which is evidence of a decisive acceptation of a particular measure of the real and source of self: the working body.

The phrase *reductio ad sensum* above all is used to synthesise the living reality of manual labour performed daily by social actors who also exercise choice, so that the reality intended by the term is not a passive registration of the priority of the social world over the self or a surrender to that world, but the reality of the world being taken up into the life of the subject and becoming a quasi-autonomous principle of operation. I propose the view that in manual labour a chemical-physiological template or *gestalt* is established that acts as the *conditione sine qua non* for a bio-physical 'politics of identity' which means that in his relationship to food, eating and sexuality, for example, as well as linguistic and intentional forms of self-expression, the worker generates 'mimetic satisfaction' in these areas of life *as defined by the template or criteria laid down in the worker's bio-chemical-physiological habitus that comes about as a result of chronic labouring*, so that what will be satisfying are those experiences that mimic or reproduce the pattern already laid down. The phrase *reductio ad sensum* then adverts to this more or less coerced and free bio-chemical and psycho-somatic 'politics of identity.'

When Adam Smith in his *Wealth of Nations* (1776) visited a pin-making factory in the village of Pathhead outside Kirkcaldy and described the new post-artisanal division of labour that he saw there, or when during my own fieldwork when working as an agricultural labourer at Kettle Produce or reporting to Pathhead treatment works as a manual operative with East of Scotland Water, there is a basic choice to be made between an 'objective' and a 'subjective' account of the point of production. Insofar as we take the latter approach it must be borne in mind that human experience is not objective (Laing 1982, p. 9), and this applies in a particular way to the experience of manual work and the character of the subjectivity of the worker who does this work which are not available to the observer or casual passer-by or the philosopher contemplating the 'nature' of work as it is a direct result of a particular social organisation of work. One only need think of the artisan and his self-imposed discipline and 'ownership' of the process of making and his 'personal' relationship to time and my own fieldwork experience of the freneticism of conveyor-belt working, or having to complete time sheets every day to account for every minute of every working day, to suspect the difference between the artisan's lived experience of work and that of the industrial manual labourer. My own practice of manual labour meant a very non-objective experience of work, and integral to which is a 'structure of immediacy' that establishes the subjectivity of the worker as a direct result of the pressure of time and completing the work as quickly as possible; of work performed within a temporal horizon captured by the expression 'time is money.'

Whether it is the frenetic pace of work imposed upon the factory worker by machines and conveyor belts or the imposed pace of work of the self-employed squad member on a building site, there is established within the worker a 'structure of immediacy' thanks to a particular organisation of work, but which has been further conditioned by the freedom and choice of the workers themselves i.e. those intrapersonal and interpersonal solidaristic and discursive practices among workers characterised by a sense of urgency and conviction; by what appears to the observer as an obviously libidinal relation to language, self and fellow workers that is free of delicacy, pretence or affectation and is consubstantial with an immersion into spontaneity or immediacy and expressions dominated by being at home in the real, in what is, and a characteristic libidinal relationship the world and lack of distance from the world, and all this in opposition to behaviour that is prudish, strategic or distant or that have a calculating eye on the future.

Given a life where physicality is paramount, the preoccupation with the body over time inevitably results in a source of structuration of *dasein* which cannot be switched off at the end of the working day, and so is fated to be taken up by freedom into intentional life and the psyche, so that it is often in those informal private psychological spaces that are removed from public view and formal regulation that particular structurations can be practiced. Typically, then, it is in the privacy of interiority and intentionality and worker intersubjectivity that the cost of work and the fantasy of being free of its tyranny is expressed in language and developed when and where it is safe to do so. In their intentional behaviours, then, workers will often express that which is repressed at the 'point of production,' so that in their leisure time there is a return of the repressed which explains their 'over-determined' behaviour, such as a raucous sensualism that is a form of 'revenge' upon their frenetic obedience to the will and command of others during the working week. Balance is restored via an interpersonal immersion into the pleasures of the body via food and drink and locality and sociality at the weekend, when among unmarried or single workers we see the full display of libidinal selves and *ad libitum* talk and practices; a linguistic sensualism sourced in the exigencies of paid labour and which becomes their preferred relationship to language and in which is sourced all manner of paralinguistic behaviours.

In this regard, I propose that those behaviours which require self-presence and interpersonal presence such as intimacy, parenting, loving, caring, aggressing, sexuality, gathering as a congregation to practice spirituality, or gathering as part of an audience or supporters of a local team etcetera, are likely to be informed by the *gestalt* laid down in manual labouring; that these practices that require something of the self or 'intimacy' borrow something of their phenomenological reality from manual labour and the social constitution of the psyche. Just as scholastic philosophy argues the material object of perception insofar as it becomes a *res cogitan* exists in a new and qualitatively higher order of existence, so the reality of the physical reduction exists in a higher way in the minds and psyches of labourers and informs all manner of practices.

As a student of male manual work cultures Savage (1999) has remarked upon the objectively imposed and 'de-privatised' self-understandings of manual workers, and I introduce the term *reductio ad humanum* to conceptually fix a further specification of the general 'condition of reduction' that concerns the particular kind of sociation brought into being by manual labouring. Performing paid labour is not the private affair of physical exercise to maintain one's health or the collective effort of team sports, but is a free-market-driven social practice that is integral to the reproduction of society. The term *reductio ad humanum* is introduced to recognise that the worker-inquirer's appropriation of the reality of intersubjectivity is intense and chronic and constitutes a particular kind of interpersonal realm. In performing work, there occurs the construction of a 'we' or 'being with others' (*mitsein*) and a group identity as this kind-of-being is not unique to any individual but something workers share.

As a conceptualisation of this interpersonal realm brought into being by doing among manual workers, the term *ad humanum* is intended to signify the dynamic tendency towards solidaristic behaviours and sentiments that reflects finding in the social practice of work the necessity and rationale for cultivating camaraderie among themselves and in their relations with others inside and outside of the workplace. This *ad humanum* disposition towards others, then, is not a matter of 'fundamental ontology' in the Heideggerian sense of a universal quality, as it is contingent upon a particular context and something exacted from the worker in his informal behaviours and relations to his fellows and only subsequently chosen, so there occurs a 'free' reduction to a 'we' that is firstly more or less coerced and subsequently enjoyed and cultivated. While prescinding from listing particular behaviours and assigning each to one or the other tendency, the term *reductio ad humanum* is introduced to signal a particular quality of relating to self and fellows and to signal an interior condition of having conformed oneself to objective conditions and subsequently having developed a 'second nature' as a result of having freely committed one's self to an ethic and ethos of solidarity. The *reduction ad humanum* then reflects finding in work the founding necessity and rationale for cultivating such behaviours among themselves and in their relations with others, as well as convey the reality of liking and learning this *dasein* so that it becomes a matter of free choice as one's social fate becomes *amor fati*.

In arguing for the reality and practice of this *mitsein* or 'being-with-others,' the term *ad humanum* also adverts to a libidinal intersubjectivity and overt visceral quality in the behaviour of workers at work and outside of work; signals the intersubjective and communal aspect of being and each worker's participation in each other's being, and indicates the experience of being as solidarity and communion with what one's fellow workers are. Among manual workers, then, there is little sense of a solitary pursuit of a unique vocation but an impersonal functionalism which nevertheless does entail over time the cultivation of a 'we;' an enforced production then reproduction of a group identity and a sense of 'membership' that is independent of personal or unique traits as one's fellow workers share in this condition. There is an *ad humanum* relation exacted from the worker in his working (and subsequently non-working) relation to his fellows. If the *possibility* of this fellowship is objectively 'out there,' it is only brought about as an existential condition by being immersed in this relationship, and is only available as a result of the practice of labour and so it is accurately described as an enforced and then learned and then autonomous reduction to a 'we.'

The *ad humanum* term, then, specifies or 'fixes' a quality of relating to self and fellows in similar conditions, and signals the interior condition of having conformed oneself *in one's ownmost dasein* to doing what is required by the job and having freely committed one's self to its exigencies. What has to be committed to is an ethic of solidarity so that the *ad humanum* term is meant to convey that all workers share the same condition effected by working and this has clear solidaristic results. It is a mistake then to imagine the *ad humanum* is the result of the inherent goodness or the universal human nature of the workers as the humane and attractive behaviours it signals have an objective or impersonal foundation and rationale that workers internalise. To complement the reduction to the body, then, there is a 'reduction' to inter-subjectivity and one's neighbour in their ownmost *dasein*, and this 'primitive' pre-theoretical experience of communion that is independent of discursive or linguistic construction is subsequently taken up by language, freedom and deliberation to constitute a kind of 'politics of identity' which will inform all manner of non-workplace activities.

I fundamentally disagree, then, with a writer such as Sartre whose analysis of 'being-with' (*mitsein*) was a direct criticism of Heidegger's analysis of the experience of "we" and whether it can form part of the ontological structure of human *dasein*. I criticise Sartre who held "the experience of the We-subject has no value as a metaphysical revelation" (1966, p. 553) as the more socio-logically sound view is that the grounds for individuation is the intersubjective context, whether it be the family or locality or school or workplace etcetera. My view as to why the "we" experience for Sartre is deemed unable to bear the weight of human being is consubstantial with why the kind of being doing brings about was not something of any real significance for Sartre. In this regard, thinkers who have instantiated a 'non-working' relation to the question of human being have been freed from group memberships and living such memberships as their fate.

Traditional producers of knowledge have not been bringing their thoughts on *dasein* into being after practicing manual labour or obeying the exigencies of group membership, and so in Sartre's well-known analysis of the waiter who is represented as *playing at* being a waiter, this is extended to include workers who are daily required to perform manual labour. A fateful antinomianism that can write: "This obligation is not different from that which is imposed on all tradesmen. Their condition is wholly one of cere-mony" (Sartre 1966, p. 102), involves accepting that a few thou-sand particular acts of labour, for example, have only the slightest of footholds upon *dasein* and are only maintained in being as long as 'the player' plays the game, as according to Sartre's analysis the labourer can choose not to attend to any of his days of labour and have them "collapse in an infinity of particular acts" (Sartre 1966, p. 109), so that Sartre is an exemplary illustration of how embodiment and the reality of intersubjectivity can play no part in a thinker's understanding of human being.

By highlighting within the 'condition of reduction' the two further (Weberian) 'ideal types' of the *reductio ad sensum* and the *reductio ad humanum*, the aim is to capture an existence marked by a privileging of the corporeal and the prioritisation of the body, an *objectively coerced* and then free tendency towards sensation. The terms *reductio ad sensum* and *reductio ad humanum* are based upon the fact that *the condition of reduction becomes free and reflexive* in all its modalities and this has an infinite number of consequences. First and foremost, the reduced *dasein enjoys being itself*, which means it is reflexive and deliberately comports itself towards itself; anticipates itself in its social interaction with others and prefers wherever possible to comport itself towards interaction and the future as the *reductio*. The phrase *reductio ad sensum* refers to the triangulation of the physical, the psychological and the social and the abstract attribute of humanity as 'sociable' and 'sensual' becomes existence in a distinctive orientation of living and experiencing sensuously. This daily integration of 'nature' and 'society' and 'culture' explicitly rejects any divorce or caesura between physiology or nature and nurture and freedom as the action of the various filters of society and culture upon the body are not the superficial matter of "clothing" the body, as this suggests such coding can be removed at will and that there is a constant 'body part' underneath the veneer of society and culture.

While the terms are products of abstraction, they are based upon empirical observation. When conducting fieldwork it is easy enough to spot the kinship or iso-morphism (from the Greek μορφή i.e. *morph*, meaning 'form' or 'shape') between a range of working-class behaviours and note the similarity or iso-morphism that exists between mental and material social conditions as the *reductio* morphs itself into other areas of life and 'informs' other areas of experience. It is also clearly seen how the working class enjoy their *dasein* and how unlikely they are to instantiate any kind of real separation between social structure, reflexivity and knowledge as this would require the 'modernist' mythical ability to dissolve their heavy historicity into thin air and instantiate an impossible immaculate *dasein* à la Sartre. By conceptualising the *reductio* and these two modalities as the habitus specific to the manual labourer, the aim is to develop categories tailored to the life of manual labour as opposed to employing, for example, Bourdieu's generic notion of habitus as a "system of durable dispositions" (1994, p. 190).

I propose the concept of the *reductio* as the habitus of manual labour and propose that it meets Cicourel's (1993) criticisms of Bourdieu's notion of habitus as needing empirical verification and grounding. I also mean to indicate a dialectic exists that is unique to each labourer between the *ad sensum* and *ad humanum* modalities, or between the carapaced behaviours or that complex of toughness Mary Searle-Chatterjee (in Wallman 1979, p. 285) identified among Benares sweepers in India, for example, and the humane *ad humanum* characteristics identified by Scheper-Hughes (1992) in the favellas of Brazil. In this regard, while the *ad humanum* behaviours of solidarity and community are cited by ethnographers such as Scheper-Hughes and Eric Wolf (Schneider and Rapp 1995) as a sign of a more humane society, it has to be borne in mind that these humane behaviours emerge from a position of subordination, so that while it is perhaps inevitable that the humanity contained within *ad humanum* behaviours is interpreted as an integral humanism and vision of a new society, this interpretation only interprets half the data, as these humane behaviours are consubstantial with the *ad sensum* behaviours that emerge from performing a particular social practice. This socially-constructed behaviour often means that when the compulsion of necessity is removed, the compulsion for humane behaviours is likewise removed, so that outwith the necessity of enduring certain conditions the consubstantial solidaristic behaviours and dispositions are more or less fated to disappear over time, and as Willis (1977, p. 185) observed in his ethnography of the English working class: "The couplet accommodation/ resistance is riveted tight."

If we presume we are making some progress in the effort of grasping the practice of labour 'subjectively' and making good the principal defect of all hitherto existing materialisms, it is because the concept of the *reductio* liberates the physical experience of working from its initial conditions of embodied existence, just as the imagination has the power to liberate sensual realities from their physical existence by being able to be 'brought to mind' despite their material or physical absence. To draw upon scholastic terminology, the reduction or *reductio* is the *eidos* or the 'idea' or 'form' (Greek εἶδος) of manual labour. In cognitional terms, the *reductio* is the 'universal' which the intellect abstracts from the individual thing (or labourer in this instance). Insofar as the daily practice of labouring in-forms the psyche, the *reductio* is an ontic a priori comportmental structure or *gestalt* or *imprint* that determines the comportment and intentionality of the worker-inquirer. Finally, this work of 'in-forming' other relationships is the result of the dynamism of 'secondary natures' being taken up by human freedom so that the concrete exercise of freedom must ordinarily be seen as involving the worker-inquirer freely allowing himself to be determined by his circumstances.

If the worker's mode of being is to be captured via language and be represented mentally or verbally it requires conceptualisation, and having been made the matter of reflection, the laboured body's mode of being becomes part of the life of mind as the worker-inquirer's conceptualisation of self gathers its data from its dispersal in real being and real time and real labour, insofar as he transforms these into a *res cogitans*. Attempting to articulate 'working class being' then, means rendering an embodied self mentally and textually, translating a being-in-the-world into its conceptualisation. Insofar as a particular kind of social doing brings about a particular kind of social being, manual labour must be established as a category of being if it is to be thinkable and in this effort, arriving at the idea of a 'reduced' condition is relatively straightforward. However, a more complicated and involved matter is grasping its systematic significance for a range of behaviours and a range of 'forms of consciousness' and how the *reductio* acts as a template for other becomings.

In taking this step the argument is not that the *reductio* is the key to understanding every major relationship or every realm of experience *in any causal or essentialist manner*, as even for manual labourers who are the class fraction for whom this categorisation of being-in-the-world is specifically tailored, and among whom I do argue for the centrality of the *reductio* precisely because other realms of experience are in a relation of dependency or *ontological kinship* to the *reductio*, it is essential to safeguard the contingency and freedom of the empirical data that confirms this argument and safeguard against interpretations of the analysis being presented here as deterministic or mechanistic. I make no 'pure reason' claim or suggestion that a manual labourer's relation to the aesthetic realm, language, gender, nationality, history or the transcendent, for example, are somehow 'fated' to never reach escape velocity from the gravitational pull of the *reductio*, as the question whether the exercise of freedom means the ever-increasing centrality and relevance of the *reductio* as a category of being thanks to its impact upon areas of experience outside of manual labour is something that can never be settled by theory but is an empirical question that can only be settled by empirical research.

The theoretical possibility that the *reductio* may fail to establish itself in a particular labourer for whatever reason must always be freely conceded. My *empirical* argument, then, is that when empirically grasped as a principle of the construction of self across various fronts, the true systematic relevance and cognitional import of the concept of the *reductio* is apprehended by the worker-inquirer for whom the intense effort of work, liberated by the exercise of free choice and taste, means the *reductio is in fact the key* that opens subjectivity to its adequate mental existence in the intellectual life of the worker-inquirer, and therefore must also be the key for the ethnographer insofar as the practice of introspective analysis reveals the *reductio* accounts for and is consubstantial with a libidinal or cathartic investment in a range of other relationships. For this assertion to be evidenced, the worker-inquirer must illustrate to his own satisfaction the homology or consubstantiality of the being brought into being via work with other realms of being, and to make this argument we had to widen our discussion of contextual *dasein* in the previous chapter to recognise how other realms of being such as national identity, for example, are *historically* mediated and contingently configured via the social practice of manual labour.

The heuristic value of arriving at an adequate conceptualisation of the dynamic and multi-faceted structuring effected by labouring then is that it allows us to grasp a decentered reality insofar as "the notion [of the reduction] rises out of the dispersion of sensibility" (Hegel 1967, p. 286). While mindful that "the problematic of representation... as...violence to what it depicts – as if every word is the murder of the thing" (Parker 2011, p. 117), the worker-inquirer thanks to the concept of the *reductio* can press on and appropriate Hegel's (1967, p. 566) assertion that "what is not comprehended through a notion, conceptually determined, *is* not" but without committing himself to the idealist notion that a thing is its representation (Gilfillan 2009). This adequate conceptualisation integrates the discontinuous realms of reality and representation, so that without the concept of the reduction the worker-inquirer would be unable to raise himself above empirical consciousness to intellectual existence. Hence, to achieve intellectual consciousness of his worked self, the worker-inquirer must hit upon the notion of 'the reduction' or some other such concept that does the same integrating work if he is to proceed to the next level of cognitional structure upon the basis of the labouring subject that he is.

Also, the more progress the worker-inquirer makes in this the more he is able to put together the structure of knowing from his own experience. In his practice of introspection, then, the worker has insights into the self and uncovers the patterning of motivation, behaviour and intentional consciousness and the place of the *ad sensum* and *ad humanum* reductions as operative motivations and orientating forces upon the exercise of his freedom and behaviour. However, insofar as the worker-inquirer progresses there is also revealed the mind's natural felicity in following insights and its natural delight in understanding and 'catching on,' so that a point of reflexivity is reached in the process where the worker-inquirer not only catches onto the *reductio*, but catches onto the fact that it is the *reductio* that he repeatedly catches onto. After this point in his inquiry he is able to suspect and anticipate its heuristic value so that he uses it as a hermeneutic to read himself.

Also, in making this progress there is reflection upon reflection that reveals the fact that, not only is the content of empirical consciousness structured, but inquiry itself is structured i.e. insights recur, and at some point there is insight into insight until, finally, the reflexive worker-inquirer becomes aware that his inquiry will not be satisfied with merely following data but requires the integration of all of the data; becomes aware that an act of intellectual synthesis is required to terminate this process. The natural appetite and dynamism of the intellect is what Lonergan characterises as critical reflection heading for a 'grasp of the unconditioned,' the level of judgment that settles the issue and brings the process to an end, and upon completion of this task the worker-inquirer completes the final step of cognitional structure i.e. judgment, and makes the shift from worker-inquirer to worker-inquirer-knower.

## 6.6 The Moment of Being-the-Truth & the Natural Apotheosis of Contextual *Dasein*

If we presume the worker-inquirer has successfully aligned his self-consciousness with his *reductio*-informed behaviour, he has successfully organised his self-understanding along the lines of his history of instantiating a dialectical 'to and fro' relation between 'freedom' and 'unfreedom' i.e. upon the basis of recognising how, when *outwith the actual reduction* in his being-for-himself (and his being-for-others) he is liable to being put 'at issue' in the semiotic 'sea of signs' and discourse, not just by being read by unsympathetic dominant cultural codes but *by the demands of his own rational nature and the demands of cognitional structure*. Upon recognising the presence of a struggle or dialectic between his two histories i.e. the history of justification and the history of being 'at issue,' the worker-inquirer will also have adverted to the fact that his being-for-others and his being-for-himself stands in a particular relation to his condition of being reduced: *that the reductio justifies or frees him in his being-for-others* as it is its own sui generic source of justification outwith the gaze or ken of others.

Also, while his being-for-self and being-for-others is put 'at issue' insofar as he is immersed in the realm of public meaning, having come this far in his journey of self-appropriation he will notice this 'being at issue' or 'being-for-others' is not even primarily the result of symbolic domination in a free-market society but is recognised as being also the result of his rational nature that has been elicited and awakened, and which is restless until it articulates an answer to the questions of his interlocutors. This *intellectual tension* signals he has not yet brought to a successful conclusion the exigencies of cognitional structure which demand he give a reading or account of himself to himself; that he himself in all his contingency puts himself into signs and "into words for the *very* first time" (Heidegger 1962, p. 362), and onto what Lonergan calls the brink of judgment. What is sought above all is a true intellectual judgment of the self he is, because it is cognitional structure and not the class structure and its symbolic codes he is immersed in and which demand the right to pronounce its own judgment. Importantly, from the standpoint of the structure of his own mind, the only relevant criteria for deciding his understanding of himself is being judged in relation to the truth of himself he has laboured to arrive at.

If what is needed is an act of understanding where "the understander and the understood are identical" (Lonergan 1990, p. 238), this judgement can only occur when the data has been marshalled to the point where the intellect can grasp the sufficiency of the data; where subjectivity has been adequately translated into the intellectual order, as only at this point becomes possible the moment of knowing that the *reductio* is true because it reduces the data that is the worker-inquirer's life to its intelligibility. This special act and insight is what is known as a judgment: a 'live' demonstration of the truthfulness of the conceptual apparatus that has been laboriously put in place thanks to understanding one particular act or behaviour via the conceptual apparatus put in place and seeing, for the first time, that in understanding a particular instance of behaviour he thereby understands every other previous behaviour that were instances of the same pattern and dialectic.

*This is the moment when the worker-inquirer passes the structure of himself into his intellectual consciousness for the first time, and the intellect of the worker-inquirer catches or recognises (using the reductio) himself or his dasein in the act of being its being and the adequacy of his conceptual grasp of himself is attained. Insofar as he conceptually catches his dasein in the act of being its being, this act simultaneously recognises and unlocks and understands all of the other data that this act is sufficient to explain i.e. the structure of his life and behaviour. He finally intellectually recognises and sees and knows himself through judgment, so that it is an act of judgment, then, and not desiring or wishing or suspecting, that is the event which puts the worker-inquirer in cognitional possession of himself for the first time; puts the worker-inquirer in possession of the intelligibility of the history and events he has lived through throughout his life, because the moment of judgment is that point in time when the conceptual apparatus laboriously put in place grasps a particular instance of his structured behaviour intellectually i.e. by its idea or eidos (i.e. the reductio), and so by understanding one instance in a long history of such moments of comportment or behaviour is to unlock the intelligibility of an entire history. Judgment, then, releases the intelligibility that until this moment remained tied to its serial existence and confined to the heavy historicity of patterns of affectivity, behaviour and intentionality,* and this moment of apotheosis is the highest natural joy for a rational nature because it releases the self from obscurity and ends the long historicity of doubt sedimented in the lived history of the worker-inquirer's mental life, and which is why the moment of judgment can be described as delivering a lifetime's worth of intelligibility.

Prior to this moment of truth, the worker-inquirer has two sets of data which both concern himself and which he knows are both true, yet pull in two different directions. On the one hand, he knows that he is free or justified as a result of 'being reduced.' However, the worker-inquirer also notices within himself his history of not being free or justified but being 'at issue' in the world of discourse, because in the realm of language he has no account of himself to give himself or others, and so is easily the victim of 'symbolic violence' in his being for interlocutors and is insecure or liable to be 'at issue' in this medium.

In addition to this class structure that positions the worker-inquirer, however, there is another structure, the structure of cognition, that in its own *sui generic* way exercises its own *sui generic* discipline and sovereignty and even 'violence' over the worker-inquirer. The worker's own rational consciousness or his ownmost being-for-his-cognitional-structure reveals his 'cognitional insecurity,' so that the key to overcoming this condition of being liable to 'cognitional violence' is not to have something occur 'out there' within the class structure but to have something occur within himself; a cognitional development or act of cognitional agency within the worker-inquirer that can only happen if he has the adequate self-conceptualisation at hand. Insofar as the real source of his 'symbolic insecurity' is not having a symbolic account of himself, the *reductio* becomes the key to furnishing him with such an account of himself because just as it justifies him while labouring, so it is the key 'sign' that unlocks his self-knowledge or *conceptual justification* and his performing an act of self-understanding, and thanks to the *reductio* he takes possession of the true account of himself and cognitional structure can be completed.

In this exercise of *cognitional agency* there is an obvious similarity between the ethnographic account just given and Lonergan's (1957) account of self-appropriation and Hegel's suggestion (1967, p. 431) that the intellectual life consists in an essence being retrieved from its dispersal in the world; of achieving the 'moment of truth' and the apotheosis where: "Self-consciousness...has attained its true conception of itself...has arrived at a consciousness of its own substance." In Lonergan's account of human understanding, grasping 'the sufficiency of the evidence' is the cause and condition of the act of judgment as a result of the dependency of judgment upon sufficient evidence. In the ethnographically-situated account of judgment just given, I have highlighted the existential requirement of a life both socially-determined and freely chosen in a particular manner since, being 'structured in the truth' of one's being through judgment means *understanding the life actually led* and not some other life the worker-inquirer might have wanted for himself, so that the act of judgment is conditional upon a certain fidelity to a particular situated or class reality, to having been 'condemned' to a life and then having freely determined to choose and having allowed the *reductio* to play the role of 'in-former' of the life actually led.

What needs to be emphasised time and again is that this argument concerning the *reductio* informing subjectivity is an empirical observation and not a theoretical hypothesis, as it is based upon a description of how real lives known by fieldwork are in fact lived, and is not an argument about what another population somewhere else or what another generation might or might not do with their freedom vis-à-vis their social determination. It goes without saying, then, that in a life that has not been constructed and configured in this fashion, the concept of the *reductio* can not play this role in cognitional structure because the concept of the reduction can not explain the data. The act of understanding just described reveals how a life in fact has been lived; that insofar as understanding the life actually led, the *reductio* is the adequate concept that generates this act of understanding. The argument then is that this particular relation to the body and language and the nation and others *is the relation*, and not some other kind of relation; *is the data*, and so in these circumstances only bringing this to the brink of judgment can produce an act of self-understanding. There may be lives that are lived in such a manner that they can be crowned by different kinds of liberating acts of self-understanding that do not take the concrete social praxis of labouring as their starting point *but the lives of manual labours will not be among them.* Finally, *only the act of understanding just described can liberate such a person*, so that all other models of self-understanding will be derivative or additional where they are not illusory.

In giving this account of the integral liberation of integral *dasein* I am not concerned to settle ideological questions such as the causal priority of labour as a structuring agent of *dasein*, but

I am concerned to make the unremarkable argument that the 'condition of reduction' does not invent *ex nihilo* the being of the nation or language or a particular self or a particular *mitsein* but, rather, enters into their social and cultural construction and mundane practice. This is why in Chapter 5 we added to our account of working-class *dasein* the element of nationality and argued nationalism was informed by an integration of id, identity and ideology or nature, nurture and freedom that itself is integrated with the exigencies established within human being by the practice of manual labour. Our argument was not a philosophical position that manual labour is necessarily the source of the libidinal charge of nationalist sentiment on view among locals performing their national identity while gathered to watch a football match, but an ethnographic and empirical observation that in working-class locations and among working-class people this integralism is present throughout the realms of consciousness and experience, and is evidenced in those set-piece occasions where locals gather and come alive to a preferred and privileged sense of themselves. In this phenomenology of physicality, consciousness and cognition, then, I have simply taken seriously realities that are mundane and obvious to any ethnographer of any working-class population, which is that the presence of the dominant structural reality and daily practice of work weighs heavily upon many other relationships and, given that it is difficult for other relationships to reach 'escape velocity' from the gravitational pull of the condition of reduction, we have given an account of intellectual liberation that has harvested the intelligibility that results from such a life.

In giving an account of the natural apotheosis or natural beatitude of contextualised Scottish human being we transcend the analysis of Sartre who was ignorant of this apotheosis but was familiar with the desire for it. For Sartre, Man's decentred or 'dispersed' nature was taken as sufficient reason for the dogmatic assertion of the impossibility of the human subject ever being united with his essence, and when drawing upon Scotus's emphasis upon "the radical indetermination of the will" (Gilson 1980, p. 410) in human beings, Sartre drew the wrong conclusions and, once again, great truths were held captive by great errors. If we take one of the earliest articulations of Man's decentredness such as Mirandola's *On the Dignity of Man* ([1486] 1998, pp. 4-5) we find Scotus's break with Greco-Arabian necessitarianism and the discovery that God has commanded that Man's fate is to be existence-led:

> We have given to thee, Adam, no fixed seat, no form of thy very own, no gift peculiarly thine, that thou mayest feel as thine own, have as thine own, possess as thine own the seat, the form, the gifts which thou thyself shalt desire. A limited nature in other creatures is confined within the laws written down by Us. In conformity with thy free judgment, in whose hands I have placed thee, thou art confined by no bounds; and thou wilt fix limits of nature for thyself. I have placed thee at the centre of the world, that from there thou mayest more conveniently look around and see whatsoever is in the world. Neither heavenly nor earthly, neither mortal nor immortal have We made thee. Thou, like a judge appointed for being honourable, art the moulder and maker of thyself; thou mayest sculpt thyself into whatever shape thou dost prefer. Thou canst grow downward into the lower natures which are brutes. Thou canst again grow upward from the soul's reason into the higher natures which are divine.

What was alien to Scotus and Mirandola was any suggestion that Man is fated to be always separated from himself and, rather than possess himself, is to be continually thrown forward via intentionality to the future and becoming as in Sartre's *Being and Nothingness* (1966). The only solution to this insight into Man's existence-led life being held captive by error is the performance of self-appropriation. In terms of the reconciliation of the Hegelian in-itself and for-itself which both Sartre and Lukacs declare impossible, I have argued the static subsistence of secondary substances (such as the *reductio*) make it possible for intelligence to effect the worker-inquirer becoming equal with himself and achieving the injunction we become coeval with ourselves. The *reductio,* as the contextual existence of the worker, becomes a 'secondary essence' and insofar as it becomes the subject of a project of intellectual appropriation by the worker-inquirer, his essence is grasped and the alleged impossible task of possessing one's essence is achieved.

When Hegel (1967, p. 756) wrote in typical idealist style that "substance...enters existence in the shape of self-consciousness," the sociologist adverts to the concrete ethnographic order where society and history intervene upon human being, and produce many kinds of existences and many forms of life and many 'secondary essences.' Parenthetically, we may say that rejecting a 'metaphysics of substance' in favour of existence paradoxically ends up another species of antinomian thinking for, if today's post-structural deconstruction of ontology and the subject is to be welcomed as the working class, fully existential and decentred and undoubtedly favourable to a post-universalist ontology in which existence has precedence over essence, the fact is this still postpones our arrival at the correct starting point, because existence does not maintain itself immaculate and pure from (becoming) essence because, over time, it becomes essence or a fixed secondary nature, so the determination to start from the 'facts of existence' rather than an essential nature is not an adequate statement of the choices available because there is no such choice ever really available. In the intellectual biography of the worker-inquirer, however, an account of this process of existence becoming essence or habitus can be given. If Hegel is correct that "the object only has truth so far as it has the form of self" (1967, p. 553), then the worker-inquirer comes to the truth of himself once he gets the conceptualisation of himself as worker right i.e. lifts it free of merely endless seriality, and liberates it from its pre-conceptual and primitive day-to-day reality. If the account I have presented here is accurate then we have solved the problematic Hegel and Sartre and Lukacs who in his *History and Class Consciousness* ([1923] 1971, p. 110) described as "the antinomies of bourgeois thought" as he was preoccupied with the crisis of modern European Man and providing a solution to Schiller's (1971, p. 139) articulation of the predicament faced by European culture:

> On the one hand, he [Schiller] recognises that social life has destroyed man as man. On the other hand, he points to the principle whereby *man having been socially destroyed, fragmented and divided between different partial systems is to be made whole again in thought.*

Lukacs' Hegelian brand of Marxism rightfully intuited that only because the proletarian had been transformed in his very *dasein* by the industrial production process was he able to abolish not only his own reification but that of others, and *integral to this was a purely intellectual or cognitional moment that can only occur "in thought."* However, if Lukacs failed to give any account of this cognitional agency, I have given an answer by demonstrating that only when the worker-inquirer has constituted the *reductio* throughout his consciousness is the cognitional act of liberation immanent. If others may wish to pretend for ideological reasons another natural beatitude is possible, I have given an account of a performative verification of my position that also has metaphysical reasons for being confident that no contradictory account will be forthcoming, such as the position that the human intellect is ordained to intelligible being famously expressed by Scotus's phrase: *falsum non est scibile* (cited in Wolter 1987, p. 20). Hence, while there can be dogmatic and wilful assertions of positions contrary to the one developed here, or dogmatic assertions as to its impossibility as in Lukacs and Sartre, there will be no performative account grounding such positions.

This is why a fully-contextualised account of cognitional structure is no small matter, because it safeguards all that cognition achieves and without a cognitional theory one cannot account for a transforming event where a particular data set of behaviours is crowned by a particular act of understanding; where a 'data set' becomes a source of liberation insofar as self-appropriation transforms a nested series of behaviours into a nested series of objects of thought, and judgment transforms these latter into a nested experience of liberation and apotheosis. With Lonergan (1972, p. 292), then, my position is that: "Genuine objectivity is the fruit of authentic subjectivity," so that "the individual and the subjective is a valid position from which to know the general and apparently 'objective'" (Hauke 2000, p. 85). The worker-inquirer, through fidelity to the data and fidelity to the historicity of his refusal to attempt self-appropriation upon any other basis, transforms this existential decision into a fundamental option to thinking his concrete reality that results in knowledge of himself thanks to reproducing at an intellectual level what it has taken him the course of a lifetime to construct at an existential and behavioural level. By this event, the enquirer is liberated in his intellectual and rational consciousness and is freed in his being-for-himself and his being-for-others insofar as the realm of meaning is implicated in these relations.

At the heart of this attempt to think human being in an integral manner and in a way that is free of modernism and materialism is an event, a happening or performative verification. At the moment of completing cognitional structure the worker-inquirer translates his being-in-the-world into his rational self-consciousness and establishes his cognitional sovereignty, thanks to having reduced himself to a 'pure act' and reducing the self to its intelligibility and translating a 'secondary essence' into the content of an act of understanding thanks to making intellectually present to rational consciousness that which has taken a lifetime to assemble. In this achievement, grasping the isomorphism that exists between the order of cognition and the order of fully contextualised human being is the key moment as, at a mere behavioural level, the worker-as-inquirer merely repeats or re-iterates himself behaviourally, and must remain sceptical about claims of a once-and-for-all 'moment of truth.'

Prior to grasping the unconditioned, the worker-inquirer cannot make a judgment as to the true significance of the *reductio* which may be the truth of his being but may not be the truth of himself, as there may well be a further conceptualisation that is required that will allow him to grasp the sufficiency of the evidence about himself and that he has failed to suspect so far. The act of judgment presupposes an adequate conceptual grasp of the self but this conceptual grasp must be distinguished from the act of judgment. Our conceiving manual labour as a category of being involves an act of abstraction from particularity to universality, and insofar as one conceptualisation fits a thousand dispersed acts of labouring, the concept of the reduction establishes the worker-enquirer's intellectual self-awareness. Once the reduction's empirical presence throughout consciousness, experience and behaviour is firmly identified, this allows inquiry to proceed to the next stage in the process of self-appropriation, and raise the question of *the final cognitional significance* of this concept i.e. the question of its truth. Successfully gathering the dispersion of the self via a conceptual grasp of the truth of the self is not yet the act of intellectual synthesis that grasps the connections between the data that must take place in order for the truth that enquiry demands to come into being. As stated, what is required is a 'live insight' into the behaviour and consciousness of the self that reduces all previous and future behaviours and patterns of consciousness to their intelligibility.

From Aristotle we learn that living substances are composed of their matter and their animating form (or *eidos*/idea), and while the real always remains singular so that a science of the singular is impossible, the fact is knowledge of the many (i.e. science) is possible because each human intellect grasps the one form shared by each member of a particular species. It is because many particular intellects grasp the same universal form that is only present and real in the many singular instances that science or objective knowledge of concrete reality in general is possible. For my purpose, then, it is because the *reductio* is the form or eidos of the worked body that sharing in this condition is the basis not only for manual workers' self-recognition and self-knowledge but the objective basis for knowing how they experience and constitute their intersubjectivity. Each particular worker shares the same 'universal' reduction as his own 'private' possession or 'idiosyncratic form,' as it is both a personal possession and shared by others who are doing the same tasks with the same nature and the same shared medium of the human body. As already stated several times, this condition is both individual and personal and a source of solidarity and group identity a basis for social interaction. This explains why the worked self is more or less sovereign in its signification of self, meaning and world; is not simply sovereign in the objective sense that in the cash economy it is the relation to money that is second to none in importance but is sovereign over intentional, psychological and interpersonal life i.e. is an intensely subjective sovereignty vis-à-vis the subject's intentional life and affective horizon, to the extent that any other different reality must negotiate with it in order to become phenomenologically real and present to the self.

If for Aristotle the truth is a product of the mind and we have a natural felicity for understanding, we must not forget that if we are able to master reality intellectually it is because we have firstly been mastered by reality. The truth can neither be received 'second-hand' from someone else or received by a delegate on our behalf or imposed upon us from outside. In the journey towards the wholly interior event of the advent of our truth, our initial steps were occupied with attending to a certain freedom or sense of justification brought about by manual labour. Thanks to work, a freedom and integration of self in relation to place, time, self and others occurs. Next, the notion of a physical structuration or 'reduction' was extended throughout empirical consciousness by adverting to more data on the strength of its consubstantiality with other behaviours, and this consubstantiality was the clue that alerts the worker-inquirer to the fact that not only is there a certain way of relating to a diverse range of realities (self, others, language and nation etcetera), but that it is a preferred way of relating and a preferred sense of identity and sociality or individuation and sociation that is enjoyed and freely selected, and which can also become part of a politics of national identity. We identified this preferred style and characteristic behaviours as consubstantial with the signature of the reduction and concluded the *reductio* is an intense 'libidinal' hermeneutic that the worker-as-inquirer adverts to as having been freely reproduced throughout the polymorphism of his being to the exclusion of other constructions and developments of individuation and sociation.

The worker-inquirer's relations to the use of symbols, language, self and sexuality then are not simply imposed by objective social forces, but are actively taken up in preference to very different kinds of individuations and sociations that are taken up by those immersed and socialised in other class conditions. Next, labour is also the source of a stigma and symbolic violence and a dominated or unfree being-for-others, and this reality has a history in any working-class individual and its reality is responsible for a dialectic of shame and defiance, so that intellectual consciousness constructs and maps a dialectic of freedom/alienation that is played out in consciousness, behaviour and biography. However, the miserablist temptation to imagine endless symbolic violence is to be resisted as, ultimately, it is in this realm of meaning and the sui generic realm of mind that the full development of the *reductio* as a source of self and intellectual agency is reached and, due to an intimate reproduction of self across many relationships, we can say this 'integral being' is the ground of what can be described as an integral rational consciousness insofar as the act of understanding grasps an entire life and reduces a lifetime to its intelligibility so that, if the life of mind torments and calls the worker-inquirer to lose himself in abstraction, it also 'saves' the worker-inquirer so that "knowledge itself [must] be accorded agency" (Parker 2011, p. 91).

In our account of the natural apotheosis of fully contextual Scottish human being, knowledge does indeed exert agency as the structuration effected by the truth is a privileged event and moment when the worker-inquirer becomes the worker-inquirer-knower; is the moment when the agency and structuring effect of truth upon *dasein* occurs, and thanks to the shift from worker-inquirer to worker-inquirer-knower many of the issues of 'pure reason' such as whether complete rational self-knowledge is possible is settled. If Bettoni (1961, p. 73) is correct to assert that "an a priori study of man's nature is impossible. The only way we can know it is by studying its acts," then in light of the fact that an account can be given of a perfect act of self-understanding, it is reasonable to conclude it is proper to Man's nature and that which it brings within range is likewise reasonable and proper to our human nature, and in Chapter 8 I will add one final perfection or one further 'primary colour' to my representation of fully contextualised Scottish human being as a result of the psychological experience of freedom discussed in the next chapter.

# 7

# Self-Actualisation
# & the Psyche

To make ourselves at home in our alienated being.

Marx, cited by Jameson in Lyotard 1984, p. xix

## 7.1 The Secret History of My Shame

If Scheff and Retzinger (2000) are correct to assert that shame is "the master emotion of everyday life," then it seems to follow that every adult should not only have a long history of instances of 'being ashamed,' but should have a greater history of instances of behaving in such a way to avoid adding to his or her history of 'being ashamed.' Insofar as an adult practices introspection, then, he or she should have sufficient data available about himself to be able to recognise that shame may be described as a pattern or thread running through their lives.

However, this assertion of Scheff and Retzinger poses a problem not only for the private practice of introspection but for any kind of 'publication' of what such introspection discovers insofar as, just as with our previous remark about the psychological improbability of unemployed miners grasping their unemployment as an opportunity to explore the *dasein* that comes about as a result of being unemployed, precisely because it is shameful and a source of self that is not nurtured or welcomed but normally only given the most minimal kind of recognition, so this same repression of that which is shameful implies that every adult must not only have a history of shame but a history of repressing this shame i.e. a 'secret' history of shame. How the ethnographer might evidence such contentions, of course, is clearly problematic as the inoffensive-sounding task of uncovering the depth of society within oneself in the project of self-appropriation must include recognising the data of one's history of shame i.e. data that will not be freely attended to, because introspection will meet strong resistance because of fears and insecurities surrounding shame.

To describe the prospects of the worker embarking upon a sustained analysis of how he is caught up in schemes of interpretation that involve feelings of shame and feelings of guilt about shame, then, Zizek's judgment of the practice of psychoanalysis as being "necessary only where it is not possible, and possible only where it is no longer necessary" (in Parker 2011, p. 194) seems to hit the target. The task, then, is to talk of my own 'secret history of shame' as this is the only history I have access to.

I begin by recalling an incident when heading to work in August 2012 on the 6.37 a.m. A few minutes out of Cardenden at the next stop, a man in his early-thirties boarded the train and sat across from me in a carriage which we happened to have to ourselves. After we bought our tickets we got chatting and he informed me that he lived in Bowhill and was an unpaid volunteer scaffie (roadsweeper) based in Dunfermline with Fife Council. I told him that I had not long ago moved to the Dundonald area of the village to get a bigger house as my previous two-bedroom Council house was too small for a family of five. At this, he reciprocated by telling me that he was divorced, and that his former wife who came from Cardenden had custody of their child and despite being from Ballingry (some five miles away) he would like to have his work route closer to Cardenden, but really would not want to have his work route actually in Cardenden because, "a' the bairns wid be gien me cheek an take the pish oot e me." As per the discussion in Chapter 5 of a female informant who was shamed by the remarks of a schoolboy as I sat in her home watching television, so from these few words of a scaffie and his diffident 'knowing' manner of making this remark, I immediately understood his meaning to be that if he worked in Cardenden or the neighbourhood where he was known because he had lived there until his recent split from his wife, he would be liable to be put 'at issue,' and would find this quite 'uncomfortable' because the local children would recognise him.

After he had confided this to me I told him that some years previously when working in Edinburgh for the temping agency Margaret Hodge Staff Consultants at the pension fund company Scottish Widows, I was not earning enough money to live in Edinburgh and so was living with my parents and travelling back and forward between Cardenden and Edinburgh, and how at one point as I had made my way to the train station every morning I passed a group of locals waiting at the 'double block' bus stop on Cardenden Road to be picked up for their day's hired labour of picking potatoes. I recalled how, as it was winter, I wore an old knee-length overcoat of my father's, and as I passed this group shouts of "Ya mink! Ya f***in mink!" were aimed at me, after I was sufficiently beyond the group so that the individual shouting the insults could not be picked out as I had my back to them.

From the day that I realised what was being shouted and that it was being shouted at me, I told my travelling companion that I then realised that this had happened several times before as I remembered having heard shouting on previous occasions as I had passed the group of day-labourers, but had paid no attention. I then recalled that as the days had passed and the shouted insults had continued, I grew more and more tense each day as I approached the group wondering who my tormentor was, and as I was now making a point of intently looking at the group as I passed, I presumed everyone in the group was wondering how I would react and what, if anything, I might do. Having initially decided to ignore the shouts, the next day as I made my way to the station I suddenly deviated from my usual route and walked directly up to the group, and stood face-to-face with the dozen or so individuals, male and female, predominantly young but also with older adults. I asked who was doing the shouting. As I stood there I recognised some older men with whom I made a point of maintaining eye-to-eye contact, perhaps to provoke them into 'breaking rank' and breaking the silence they were all maintaining and address the problem between us. I waited to see if anyone would say anything, but the only thing that was forthcoming was one or two giggles and muffled comments. I walked away not having managed to identify the individual.

Soon after I recalled this incident the train pulled into Dunfermline station, and my informant left the train for his day's work. As I reflected that this was the first time I could remember ever having told someone about this episode, I remembered another occasion of *having my objectivity handed to me*, and the same feeling of 'burning shame' that accompanied it. The incident was from the same period of time when I was working in Edinburgh and concerned a girl called Julia with whom I was 'in love,' and after some months of working with her as part of a team in an office and cultivating her acquaintance, there came a point where I asked Julia in a half-serious and half-joking manner if she would go out with me, as I wanted to have a relationship with her. In the short ensuing conversation we had as we sat in a busy office, Julia had looked me in the eye and with a broad and beautiful smile had pointedly and seriously asked me: "What have you got to offer a girl that would make her marry you?" And in that moment I saw with perfect clarity, thanks to Julia handing me my objectivity, that I was not in love with her but had been merely enjoying being infatuated with her. In two or three seconds, I realised that all along my private fantasies of a life with Julia were mere daydreams that had been 'cathartic' insofar as they gave me psychic release from my subordination thanks to this fantasy being a cipher for the make-believe of living a successful life, as opposed to my reality of being one of the 'working poor' written about by sociologists; and that from the outset and throughout such daydreams were fated to dissolve at the first contact with reality.

The three instances of social interaction described above involve social actors recalling experiences of shame or behaviours motivated by avoiding the possibility of being shamed, and what they have in common is the truism that being placed in the bottom of a hierarchy (low-status job, too poor to buy clothes of high status, too poor to 'afford' a young beautiful woman of some status) teaches those who are thus classified their position in society, and that moments of realising what one's objective position in society is is not a game or 'data' that is material for a project of self-appropriation, as its meaning for *dasein* is of not being of value, and being left to endure the consequences of this objectivity. More generally, it is extremely difficult to raise the question of low status and how a person feels and lives their low status within a hierarchy, a difficulty that becomes more difficult the longer they remain positioned towards the bottom, because this 'historicity' is something of a direct line to a person's capacity for self-worth and a direct line to the history of their failure to have been truly able to esteem themselves.

If we look at the first incident mentioned with the volunteer road sweeper, what was not actually committed to words but could remain implicit, thanks to a shared horizon of meaning that was taken for granted as a result of my living locally and my working-class manner of speaking, was that local children were not liable to pick on or tease my informant because they would recognise him but because of the social meaning or the low status attached to his job, and therefore to him.[132] Our shared horizon of meaning meant we both knew his fear was that, at least on occasion, the mere sight of him picking up litter would trigger a prejudice, so that in a literal sense it *went without saying* that as a result of his visible low status he was likely to be *the victim of children's resentment at those of low status*; that they would act as a cipher for the reality of society and its classificatory system and make him feel ashamed of himself for having to do this kind of work. Also implicitly understood between us was that unlike the anonymous scaffie in the city whom no-one knows or pays attention to, the scaffie in a small provincial locality is known because he or his wife and child lives there.

---

[132] Not only occupations, of course, but localities too are ranked according to status, as evidenced when Muir (1935, p. 107), freshly arrived from the Orkney Isles into lowland industrial Scotland wrote: "The main problem which puzzled me at that time was how all these people could live in such places without feeling ashamed."

In eliciting the resentments of others, then, the scaffie is confronted by the scapegoat mechanism as analysed by Girard (1989) insofar as the lone scaffie cleaning the streets becomes a target for judgments, and draws out of young people their resentments and has heaped upon himself spoken or unspoken insults. When this behaviour occurs, the condition of symbolic domination that normally goes unseen and unheard and unrecognised is caught sight of, and a window is opened onto children's internalization of the cultural system that is aligned with the occupational and class structure. Also, of course, the symbolic domination learned as a child comes back to haunt or tease the adult if we assume this man as a child was as likely to have hurled abuse at a scaffie as the children whom, as a man, he is put 'at issue' by, so that we might say the symbolic domination he suffered as a child is something he colludes in inflicting upon himself as a man.

Likewise, in the second incident concerning my coat, this 'material sign' was a visible provocation that triggered a particular behaviour if I am correct in presuming the daily insults were drawn by my hand-me-down overcoat, and what becomes transparent is that the working class in general have strong resentments and its deprived class fraction can be aggressive and vicious among themselves and to others, and the reason for their aggression is their shame at their deprivation and poverty: if the poor despise the other person they see to be poor, this can only mean they despise and feel shame at the selves they are should social interaction hand them the objective reality of their poverty. If objectively I could truthfully say that in 1993 when I was earning £3.95 an hour from a temping agency, which meant a full-time weekly wage of £138.25, I was not likely to spend money on an expensive overcoat to protect myself from the weather and the culture of resentment that visible signs of 'poverty' provoked in others, the heart of symbolic domination is revealed in the fact that, if my first reaction was incredulity and the wish to shout back at my tormentors: "Why are you shouting that? You are poor as well!," the proof of my own symbolic domination was that I did not shout this because *I did not want to name or commit to words that which went without saying, and thereby reveal what was on my mind and what was on all of our minds: being ashamed of ourselves as a result of our poverty* i.e. it is not poverty, then, but *shame* at poverty that silences and wounds or 'imprisons.'

Similarly, then, in relation to the third incident with myself and Julia, in the two seconds it took her to ask me her question, Julia handed me my objectivity, and revealed to me my symbolic domination not because of what she said but because she silenced me because I was unable to offer any 'resistance' or credible answer *in my own estimation* to her question. In this brief social interaction a woman handed me my semantic poverty, my inability to esteem myself, and only incidentally handed me the true or objective or sociological interpretation of my weeks of fantasising about having a life with her. Julia's unexpected question to me made me realise my 'social worth,' but not because of any kind of insight she had about me but because her question made me come out of my fantasy and face the fact that in my own estimation I had nothing to offer a woman, and that society's voice in me was stronger than my own voice, so that I was lost for words.

By putting my subjective thoughts and feelings for her into another context, and thereby allowing me to glimpse my objectivity thanks to a pretty girl who didn't know me being fated to see me via my objectivity and not my subjectivity, in this social and de-privatised and dis-enchanted context, everything I had rehearsed for our first real encounter suddenly became foolishness *in my own eyes*. My internalisation of the dominant symbolic system explains how a girl who didn't know me could put me 'at issue,' and this power over me came not from Julia but from my immersion into a classificatory system that was suddenly activated from its latent state, so that my objectivity trumped my subjectivity as it suddenly became my existential predicament.

Far more explanatory of my encounter with Julia than not having any 'capital' was not having the freedom (from this classificatory system) to even convince myself that the fact that I had nothing was not important. *Accepting* I couldn't have value for her, rather than dismissing or resisting my 'social' or 'objective' truth as of no or little importance as I tried to win this girl, is the evidence of my symbolic domination i.e. I myself was complicit in my own domination because not only did I not have material things to offer a girl – no shame there – but *I was revealed to myself* as not having the heart to articulate a non-material source of value that I might have had for a very pretty office girl. It was not Julia but *myself that had put myself* 'in my place,' and thanks to her question I realised to my shame and embarrassment that indeed I had nothing of value to offer her and was out of my depth and Julia was out of my league.

In attending to these social interactions, 'shame' is the key to bringing into view the fact that in shame there is 'sociological density' because in each person's secret history of shame the symbolic order is made real. However, talk of a symbolic order is an example of reification insofar as it is people who oppress themselves. Every man who plays the game of *cherchez la femme* is fated to play the social game of distinction and desire to have social status, so that among those of low prestige or status, it seems the issue of having 'psychological space' or 'psychological time' that is publicly sanctioned for them to esteem and value what they are is problematic, so that their 'being working class' will come under pressure to be reduced to the bare sociological minimum and their contextualised *dasein will not be enjoyed, celebrated or cultivated.*

Insofar as such an individual is sensitive to the symbolic order, he faces the paradox that his *dasein* is unreal and unrecognised by himself because for this individual it is unrealistic to imagine he can be anything of public or symbolic value in *his own eyes* by being this being in public. This is because if shame is firstly something that is objectively imposed upon members of the lower orders of class-based societies, it is fated to take on a life of its own within psychological life, but not as shame *per se* but as having morphed into a kind of permanent vigilance against the 'risk of shame' that fuels a more or less permanent resentment among those of low status,[133] so that shame structures behaviour

---

[133] According to Bourdieu (1992, p. 209) "being constantly reminded of your otherness stimulates a sort of permanent sociological vigilance."

565

and a 'scheme of perception' to the extent that, for example, the sight of someone in a shabby overcoat spontaneously triggers the desire to shout: 'Ya mink!' It seems clear that in this particular instance, if this day-labourer were ever himself to wear a shabby item of clothing, and as a hired potato picker he clearly has, he has shown his hand to everyone within earshot that he himself has a history of expressing this same insult at himself, and has revealed himself as someone who has had to actively repress making this judgment about himself, and is revealed as someone whom we can safely say habitually suspects others are either making this judgment about himself or are repressing this judgment about him.

This kind of 'perpetual observance' or standing guard over the possibility of shame and the repressions involved becomes transformed within some individuals into what might be called *a standing ressentiment* which, as always, will have an initial and ongoing objective basis but will have taken on a life of its own, so that in any contextual analysis of the life of the psyche in class-based societies, a sensitivity to repression is needed as it is promiscuous within individuals' relationship to self and intersubjective interaction, and use of language and discourse in particular. In this regard, language is the cipher of choice of real or imagined resentments and hatreds that evidences the condition of being symbolically dominated, and those who are the victims of symbolic violence stand guard against any real or imagined aggressor and are 'armed and ready' to reproduce the very hierarchy or dominant understandings of status by invoking it against themselves – whether their clothes, country or their 'provincial' use of language, such as when they opine, "The Fife accent is horrible."

Those who lack symbolic resources reproduce the dominant reading of their language and they fail to suspect they have become 'mouthpieces' for their own domination, or exercise symbolic violence over themselves and are their own oppressors. In this regard, I recall the daughter of a former miner after reviewing a transcription of the interview I had done with her late father telephoning me to talk about the interview, and having difficulty in bringing herself to say she had concerns about the interview; and when asked what her concerns were, being very reluctant to tell me, and at my suggestion to break an awkward silence that perhaps there was too much swearing in the text and that she wanted me to cut the more 'colourful' language her father used to express himself, she had said this was not the problem. Having then asked if she was concerned about confidentiality, to which she said no, she eventually and 'shamefacedly' said: "Well, it's mair the language."

The problem, then, was that the interview transcript had not been translated into English, and she was embarrassed at reading her father's words in Scots and needed reassurance on this point. Asking her if she wanted me to translate the interview into English she replied, "Ah dinnae ken what Ah want." In the end I assured her by advising the long interview with her father, some seventeen pages of single spaced text, would never be published in its entirety, and that at most one or two short paragraphs might be used at a much later date and in a context with other extracts in Scots from a range of people other than her father, and that not translating Scots into 'proper English' was standard practice among academics.

This anecdote evidences that language is drawn into the hierarchical social structure, and that language is a potential source of embarrassment and shame if used 'in public' or outside of one's village or with strangers from another social class, as it risks bringing shame upon the speaker and his or her people, and not simply on a particular occasion but in any similar 'out of place' context a person's manner of speaking is liable to put them to shame. In this regard Bourdieu (in Jenkins 1992, p. 154) writes:

Linguistic relations are always relations of power and, consequently, cannot be elucidated within the compass of linguistic analysis alone. Even the simplest linguistic exchange brings into play a complex and ramifying web of historical power relations between the speaker...and an audience.

The relations that exist between language and power are also configured by history, and so as not to fall into the "occasionalist fallacy" (Bourdieu and Wacquant 1992, p. 144n) where we explain a social practice such as 'being ashamed of one's language' as an idiosyncratic folly, the process of the delegitimation and 'inferiorisation' of the Scots language has been ongoing for centuries. In the *Old Statistical Account of Scotland* of 1790 (cited in Houston 1924, p. 412) we find the minister at Auchterderran reporting:

> Question 39. Is your accent particularly offensive to the ear of strangers, or are they pleased with it or easily reconciled to it?
> Answer: They complain of its being drawling, and that it impresses them with a belief that the person speaking is sour and ill-tempered.

The consequences for language as a result of political union with England in 1707 included a more or less coerced cultural and linguistic union with England with the result that, while the Scottish middle classes have long become comfortable using English, the working-class Scots vernacular routinely becomes a source of awkwardness, social embarrassment and shame when used outwith the domestic or local context, so that a contextual analysis of language as a social practice evidences the relations between political and culture power, as well as the alliance between political and cultural empowerment/disempowerment. If Chapter 5 argued for an emergent class, nation and culture alignment, this regaining of integral sovereignty thanks to political and constitutional progress also implies the ending of the symbolic domination that results in a cultural inferiority that passes into good provincial common sense. I recall in this regard an East of Scotland Water operative opining, "The Fife accent is horrible" and the same opinion emerging while talking with two locals about a television adaptation of one of Ian Rankin's novels. Having asked whether they thought the programme was unrealistic because the language used was English, their reply was that it had to be in English because the Fife accent was "horrible." Likewise, when watching the television adaptation debut of Rankin's crime novels my wife had complained, "Why are they talking like that? Rebus is from Cardenden but nobody in Cardenden talks like that!"

This comment highlighted for me that only a foreigner whose structures of perception have not become assimilated to domination is able to ask such a question without being suspected of being disingenuous or acting in bad faith as, just like the English schoolboy shaming a Scottish pensioner, so the language question reveals the extent of the Scots' acceptance of the situation where the different classes and their different cultures are not allowed to exist in Scottish television programming, and class and cultural realities have been cleansed from Scottish television programming for so long that only foreigners can sincerely find this cultural subordination very strange. Another mundane instance of how the Scots language has no status or prestige among its speakers came when chatting with a group of mums waiting for their children to come out of school and, when the subject of conversation turned to the school nativity play which that particular year (2010) had been performed by the children in Scots, one mother-of-four was emphatic in her opinion that to tell this sacred narrative in Scots was: "So vulgar! Embarrassing." On this stigmatisation of the Scots language the renowned writer James Kelman (1992, p. 112) has observed:

> Language is the culture—if you lose your language you've lost your culture, so if you've lost the way your family talk, the way your friends talk, then you've lost your culture, and you're divorced from it. That's what happens with all these stupid f***ing books by bad average writers because they've lost their culture, they've given it away. Not only that, what they're saying is it's inferior, because they make anybody who comes from that culture speak in a hybrid language, whereas they speak standard English. And their language is the superior one. So what they are doing, in effect, is castrating their parents, and their whole culture.

Similarly, the writer MacColla (1933, cited in Macdonald 2009, p. 88) had long ago come to the same conclusion of Kelman on the centrality of the language issue in Scotland:

> Language is the very crux of the whole matter. It is idle and windy nonsense to deny the fact, and indeed it is everywhere implied in the invariable and undisguised haste which the conqueror shows the conquered. And in the (sometimes desperate) attempts made by the conquered to retain the native tongue. There you have a tacit admission of the importance of language to peoples – having it they can never be destroyed, and if conquered they will rise again; losing it, they disappear.

In the opinion of Kelman and MacColla and many other 'producers of culture,' so long has been my informants' immersion into their specifically *cultural form of subordination*, that they do not read their evaluations of their regional voices as evidence of cultural domination but as simply recognising the way things are. More generally, it also seems a safe bet that if their language is unable to be valued as a source of status then their provincial Fife regional identity, much as the Scots vernacular they speak, will similarly be unable to act as a source or means of cultural or political conscientisation, so that the mobilisation of this sub-national identity to restore its cultural and historical heritage after a long history of neglect will remain an unimagined project, so that imagining the project of a national Scottish modernity, for example, will not be mediated via this provincial identity. It is unsurprising, then, that none of the presenters on the radio station Kingdom FM, which consciously defines itself as Fife's only dedicated regional radio station, speak in Scots, far less in a working-class accent, so that there is no programming recognition whatsoever of the Scots language spoken by its audience of listeners. Given the institutionalisation of such 'cultural shame,' the SNP Scottish government has begun to encourage Scots within schools, a policy which is praiseworthy but suffers from the familiar middle-class prejudice expressed by Geertz (1993, p. 243) when he characterised many languages as fated to disappear due to being "psychologically immediate but socially isolating."[134]

An alleged 'social suicide' as a result of only being able to speak a provincial dialect when in modern urban centres, of course, is not a great concern in the localities and workplaces of *East of Scotland Water* workers where speaking Scots is simultaneously a marker of authenticity, belonging and intimacy when 'at home' in the provinces, but is also outwith this couthie setting potentially stigmatising. In Adam Smith's 'society of strangers' or the 'bourgeois society' of formal market relations, hierarchies and bureaucratic officialdom, the power of context means a medium of expression that is enjoyed and mediates intimacy becomes potentially shameful and embarrassing, so that it is because "the unequal distribution of linguistic capital…is an aspect of the class system, as mediated by formal education" (Bourdieu, in Jenkins 1992, p. 154) that Scotland's anglicised middle classes, who have managed Scottish education for generations, have driven the Scots language out of many generations of Scottish children, as they understand that it is thanks to gaining control of language that allows classes (and nations) to neglect the languages of rival classes (and nations), and thereby exercise symbolic or cultural hegemony within the very 'hinterland' or the ownmost *dasein* of the dominated. The privileges of power then mean the ability to either save a language or condemn it to marginality and cultural invisibility, and it is the exercise of political power that enables the dominant to 'capture culture' and the public realm and impose their language as the *lingua franca* of the nation and state.

If we keep in mind the views of MacColla and Kelman expressed earlier and add Mead's observation that "a person

---

[134] The Spanish and Basque writer Miguel de Unamuno (1864-1936) confidently argued in a speech in 1901 that it was scientifically demonstrable that the Basque language was unsuited to modernity, while Irish and Scots Gaelic speakers were similarly once openly viewed by Enlightenment intellectuals and the likes of John Stuart Mill (1806-1873) and Thomas Carlyle (1795-1881) as unfit for modernity, despite Gaelic being one of the linguistic mediums through which David I modernised Scotland.

learns a new language and, as we say, gets a new soul...He becomes in that sense a new individual" (1934, p. 283), this implies that the ability to take away or make a people unlearn its native tongue is also the ability to take their 'soul' from them, insofar as language as a social practice seems able to bear the full weight of a person's social consecration or their social dis-grace, insofar as the command of the right kind of language stands in a direct relationship to the person being able to instantiate the 'right' kind of trajectory through social space over the course of his or her life-course. When Rankin (2001) attributes the following words to a (Scottish) writer, "My language – I didn't lose that so much as wipe it off my shoe," it seems plausible to consider the proposition that the person who rejects their language also rejects their means of authentic individuation, because this act of rejection signals they are ashamed to embrace and enjoy their language as their ownmost means of freedom and thought, so that this act reproduces their domination and secures the next generation's cultural subordination insofar as a 'shameful' relationship to their language is passed on to the next generation.

Something else that will follow is that this 'language shame' means such a people will be unfree to develop an interest in their 'shameful' class culture or even their national culture, as much of Scotland's literature was written in Scots at a time when this shame was unknown and when Scottish people had a free relationship to their language. In terms of how the symbolic, intellectual and cultural levels are lived and experienced by the working class, then, we can say that thanks to the hegemony of unionist *cultural modernists*, the realms of experience of language and culture are not rich mediums of imagined community and individuation and sociation among the dominated, and so this 'cultural void' is more or less fated to be interpolated by power, resulting in an individualised/privatised and de-nationalised consumerist relationship to culture where the offerings of global profit-organisations are consumed.

If a truly modern and truly Scottish culture is to develop after independence, then, a range of tasks must emerge to provide ballast and resistance against modernism and globalism, and it is at the level of long-delayed cultural tasks where the 'tasks of freedom' must flourish if a Scottish modernity is to flourish precisely because of its long history of being so heavily policed and populated by a modernist imaginary. This cultural realm has to be re-made in the image of each class and, for the working class, can only happen if it stands upon a new relation to the realm of language if a free Scottish modernity is to happen, with the working class in particular needing to develop their own relationship to the realm of meaning and representation because this is the realm where their symbolic domination is most unsuspected and pernicious, as historically the realm of culture has been surrounded by the ideology of *ars gratia artis*.

For the vast majority, of course, such a development will not occur as a personal achievement precisely because of this relationship to their own language and routinely occupying low-status positions, which means many individuals' self-assuredness disappears if their expertise in practicality is left behind and an occasion arises where they must take their chances in the realm of meaning. I know of men, for example, who are intimidated by having to complete bureaucratic forms, so that such men have yet to enter language and the imaginary *upon their own terms*, and so are fated to never know their way around this reality or medium, as if caught in a perennial fear of 'castration' via language, or fear of losing their integral sense of self and so remain fixed in an infantile 'wholeness' that refuses to suffer the 'loss of self' by entering the realm of language and abstraction.

A *dasein* characterised by integral subordination where the cultural, economic, political and social fields are all in alignment so as to ensure the acceptance of the status quo, means that linguistic subordination is a 'blood relative' of the conviction found on doorsteps of Scotland's economic deficiencies, and is isomorphic with an acceptance of constitutional subordination and what one might describe as *an integral inferiority*. Because "the psychological self does not reside in a tranquil universe of meanings but in a set of conflicts and battles" (Porter 1997, p. 240), the worker who does not objectify himself or register the objectifying gaze of others is unlikely to reach self-knowledge because self-appropriation is about attending to the data of oneself and re-presenting one's life and paying attention to the dialectic or the 'to and fro' of occurrences of symbolic violence and occurrences of 'symbolic consecration' and re-presenting these realities to consciousness. Such is the bread and butter of the worker-enquirer's journey towards self-appropriation.

What the worker-inquirer learns through sifting the data of his experience is that how he feels about himself is a radically decentred piece of 'social ontology' that is 'bought and sold,' or is at the mercy of his social interaction. The worker-inquirer comes to see that he is not in charge of how he is perceived by others, nor is he in charge of how he perceives and feels about himself, as this too is more or less at the mercy of social determination. At this point the worker-inquirer either submits to *amor fati* or looks to muster the resources he has to transcend his fate. In all of this, however, the intellectual life is a unique and special place where the ability to both accept the reality and force of 'social determinism,' but also transcend this determination occurs because, thanks to his intellectual life, the worker-inquirer's social determination is no longer blind, no longer occurs behind his back or beyond his consciousness, so that in his behaviours the worker-inquirer can withdraw his consent and can choose not to be a cipher for his social relations and can choose to take his first steps in autonomy.

In practical life of course the simultaneous acceptance/rejection of society's power is accomplished every day in people's lives, so that if a dialectical relationship of 'transcendence-within-internalisation' of social determinism within people's inner psychological life is rather normal, what is special about the project of self-appropriation is that, the further the worker-inquirer commits to self-appropriation, the more the thrill of the intellectual chase becomes a causal force in his life, so that shame behaviours facilitate discovering with Samuel Beckett that failure is always more interesting (to the inquirer). This counter-reading of self and counter-reading of shame and failure are the fruits of the worker-inquirer's intellectual life, which takes on more psychological reality the more the worker-inquirer is able to "call into question how [he has] been brought into being" (Parker 2011, pp. 140-1), so that the worker-inquirer becomes psychologically strong enough and free enough to contemplate his social determination, and accept the truth that "the individual, before it can determine itself, is determined by the relations in which it is enmeshed" (Adorno, cited in Jacoby 1997, p. 34) and see in his own life the truth of Hayek's (2011, p. 163) remark that, "Man has not developed in freedom" as truths to be accepted as part of the chase of self-appropriation.

A paradox of the intellectual life, then, is that while the practice of introspection and contemplating how radically he is caught and immersed in his social determination, and seems fated to never be free of it, this coming to explicit awareness of the fact of his social determination *frees him to pose the question of his freedom*; frees him to ask himself whether his social determination might some day *not exhaust the self he is*; whether one day his behaviours and thoughts and emotions might include more than what his social position determines they shall be. The point, then, is that *even if only as a matter of 'pure reason' or 'pure desire,' by simply asking these questions the intellectual life begins to deconstruct his conditioned consciousness, already begins his secession from his conditioning* and stops dead in its tracks his long history of having freely and unsuspectingly collaborated in his social determination. At this point, instead of absolutely identifying with the self one is, one can look upon the self as a mask, see oneself as taking on social roles instead of being "Scottish through and through," and sees the sense in the notion of being a 'social actor' engaging in 'strategies,' and this is a significant victory, as one can imaginatively secede from being a cipher for the social structures one occupies insofar as the worker-inquirer can for the first time choose to accept or reject his social determination or his 'roles,' as he opens onto the drama of his freedom.

The freedom to turn to the data of oneself is difficult to achieve when the data in question is not only of no apparent value but is psychologically 'painful' to attend to, because our attention is caught in a social determinism which, to escape from, requires a paradoxical *shameless relation to one's shame* i.e. requires practicing a break with one's normal relation to oneself and practicing a break with one's being-for-others in one's intellectual life and behaviour. Practicing this 'shameless thinking' by being prepared to overcome one's 'decency' and not look away from oneself and others who are ashamed of themselves is of course a delicate affair, and not to be confused with advocating the absurd idea that shame is intrinsically a bad thing. As the following testimony recounting the price paid by miners who returned to work before the 1984-1985 strike ended shows, shame is a powerful weapon in the maintenance of social order:

> When ye look at them, ye ken exactly what they're thinkin. As much as tae say well, eh, are we gaun tae get them noo or dae we wait. An' ye see their wee minds workin.' Ah mean we wernae harmin' the boy bit ye seen it. An' this wis efter the strike. So Ah mean they kent within theirsel. As one e the boys said 'We'll never forget.' Tae watch [Name] gaun aboot the village noo, tae watch [Name] gaun aboot the village noo, tae see [Name] gaun aboot the village noo. They ken within theirsels, everybody's watchin' them. An' it's a case e 'Dae Ah gane here, dae Ah go there? Och Ah'll jist burrel back an' away back hame.' Their personality his totally changed fir the sake e three weeks' work. Ye'd need tae be totally oot yir heid tae get a convoy oot tae yer work an' a convoy back fae yer work.

It is because "social repression operates more commonly through the threat rather than the commission of violence [and]...is therefore mediated by the psychic domain of meaning" (Goodchild 1996, p. 90) that an analysis of 'shame' is the necessary ballast to tackling the question of working out what *a free relation to the condition of domination* involves. If I criticise the superficiality of the modernist nationalist's vision of the post-independent future as a result of his 'dissolution of history,' there is a similar need to resist the fantasy of a psyche that is free of shame or that has an 'immaculate' psyche vis-à-vis social and cultural conditions. If the power of the social and the reality of domination *per se* cannot be overcome, what can be overcome is a dominated relation to the condition of being dominated, and this is a tremendous achievement of freedom because *a dominated (or ashamed) relationship to the condition of being dominated (or ashamed) is an integral aspect of the condition of being dominated*, so that it follows that integral to overcoming the condition of being dominated is overcoming this dominated relationship to one's domination. Something of this paradox is captured by Durkheim's (2010, p. 727) insight that "the individual submits to society and this submission is the condition of his liberation" i.e. the reality of 'being free' only comes via recognising one's prior unfreedom. Likewise, when Todorov (1999, p. 62) asked, "Did the Spaniards defeat the Indians by means of signs?", it is because the answer is yes that the previous chapter talked of the need for the worker-inquirer to perform a specifically cognitional operation before he could gain his freedom in the realm of signs.

## 7.2 Victory in the Land of Signs & Freedom from Objectivity

Man's subjection to the symbolic gives benefits
aplenty in compensation for this subjection.

Parker 2011, p. 140.

The liberating act of self-understanding or 'cognitional agency' outlined in the previous chapter gave little attention to the notion of healing or 'trauma,' and spoke instead of the worker-inquirer arriving to the adequate intellectualisation of the data of his behaviours and emotions, and identified a dialectic or a lived pattern of security/insecurity that was a constitutive part of the worker-inquirer's psychological history, and catching sight of this intentional and behavioural pattern enabled this history to exist as a *res cogitans* in the life of mind, making it thereby permanently available to awareness and free from its plodding serial or episodic or iterative real empirical existence. Also, thanks to cognitional structure and the act of judgment, freedom itself becomes a *res cogitans* i.e. free of its empirical episodic existence and, finally, by understanding himself, *the world* insofar as it is in him also becomes a *res cogitans*, and the worker-inquirer sets the world free of its episodic seriality. When freedom becomes a matter of thinking because one has resolved a lifetime of ignorance, insecurity and pursuit thanks to an act of self-understanding, what becomes a permanent possession and a permanently available possession is not just the ability to know what the social determinism of his unfreedom looks like when such occasions arise, but the power to anticipate these situations and, when they occur, to comport himself differently. While it is certain that society and social situations and the realm of social-interaction will retain their class-character, the worker-inquirer-knower suffers or endures or contests or changes rather than practices 'symbolic violence' upon himself.

For an adequate translation of contextual *dasein* into explicit self-awareness to occur, the conscious ego has to come to recognise and liberate into the light of consciousness that which heretofore only existed pre-consciously, and in Freud's understanding of therapy where "the work of culture and psychoanalysis is that the domain of the ego be enlarged" (Parker 2011, p. 96), so that the 'therapeutic moment' means having patterned areas available to the ego of the worker-inquirer-knower so that he can read these patterns for himself and from the standpoint of himself, so that his working-class identity can roam freely within his psyche. The goal of self-appropriation, then, is not to get the worker-inquirer out of the comfortable immediacy of his id, but to get the prevalence of this comfortable immediacy into the full awareness of his ego. We can say then that just as in the life configured to the *reductio* via manual labour a template is laid down in this social practice which 'in-forms' other relationships and intentional and conscious life, so in light of the act of self-understanding there is a similarly promiscuous in-forming of all manner of relations with freedom, and that thereby become part of *an integral freedom.* As per Hegel's statement "*Wessen ist was gewesen ist.* Essence is what has been" (in Sartre 1966, p. 72) and its psychologisation in Freud's dictum "Where Id was, Ego shall come to be (*Wo Es War, soll Ich warden*)" (in Castoriadis 1987, p. 102), freedom and power become available to the worker-inquirer-knower, and this freedom and power re-structures the psyche.

Just as 'the nation' is routinely a site of projection and transference or a 'fantasy object' that allows the self to be itself 'all over again' in an externalised object, so the same can be said of the self brought about by labouring insofar as the *reductio* in-forms other relationships and is given new life and new objects to make into its image, so that it fuels a politics of identity that sees and reproduces likenesses of itself *ad libitum*: in the nation, the football game or the desired woman etcetera, because each practice or fantasy allows the symbolic/psychological replication of the reduced self, and because these objects allow him to be himself in a thousand different objects and guises and instances. If we add this analysis of the worker-knower's psyche to Aristotle's argument in *De Anima* that the intellect can receive the 'form' of all things and so becomes intellectually united or 'as one' with all intelligible things, so we can say the aspect of *dasein* that escapes social determination is the intellectual life, and so it becomes a special area of freedom and will surrounded by social determinism.

Until the worker-inquirer reaches this level of cognitional life, he is not securely set upon the road of self-appropriation as he has not yet reached the stage where the formally dynamic nature of the structure of cognition i.e. a natural structure that puts itself together, is his own personal experience and habit. While the reign of 'immediacy' upon finding its conceptualisation is overthrown at least in its reign over the life of the mind and imagination, this overthrow is only available as an intellectual development as it is never overthrown or transcended as a structuration of self, so that the space where freedom operates is the tension between immediatism and 'the understood' that was not there previously.

In *The Imaginary Institution of Society* (1987) Castoriadis makes use of the Lacanian thesis that the unconscious is the discourse of the Other within psychic life, so we may say it is in the worker's psyche that the work of social domination is effected and victory for the worker-inquirer in the 'land of signs' means: "my discourse must take the place of the discourse of the Other, of a foreign discourse that is in me, ruling over me: speaking through myself" (Castoriadis 1987, p. 102). However, for Castoriadis, this autonomy refers "not to an attained state but to an active situation; not to an ideal person who has become a pure Ego once and for all...How little it is a question in all of this of a power grab by consciousness" (1987, p. 104). In light of the previous chapter, however, where I gave an account of the purely natural apotheosis of contextual *dasein*, I argue that the *reductio* as the past made present via the body, insofar as it becomes the subject of a project of intellectual appropriation, the 'impossible' Sartrean task of the In-itself being made For-itself is no longer impossible, and a commitment to cognition involves a fundamental rejection of this prognosis of Castoriadis who in his discussion of the relation between the insights of Freud and Marx refused to conceive autonomy involving the purely natural apotheosis of the worker i.e. precisely that which happens via insight into the *reductio*.

The Lacanian thesis of Castoriadis is that in the unconscious lies the discourse of parents, society and history etcetera, while my experience is that to the extent it is brought to the light of consciousness via insight, Ego takes the place of Id and the subject is free not of his reality but free to consciously be and freely contest or reject his 'programmed' self should he so chose. Importantly, the person is now free to be the Tradition as in him the Tradition is now a free autonomous project in a member of a new generation. Castoriadis's a priori defeatism on this point is presumably directly related to his failure to give an account of situated *dasein's* natural perfection or 'being in act,' so that Castoriadis failed to escape the prison of 'pure reason' and did not succeeded in the practical or performative task of exercising cognitional agency. What is required is the performance of self-appropriation before speculating upon the nature of autonomy and what autonomy is from a psychological viewpoint. I argue psychological liberation *must be enjoyed and must satisfy the psyche*, and must involve a 'power-grab' by consciousness so that when Castoriadis denies the possibility of the event of *dasein* becoming 'fully in act,' this is precisely what is possible in the land of signs (but without suggesting a human intellect can be 'in act' in relation to everything about the person's biography, far less can be 'in act' regarding the entire universe of intelligible being).

Long before the concept of the *reductio* and the judgment and knowledge and liberation that it makes possible becomes an existential event in the worker-inquirer-knower, the reduced body and psyche are already sources of freedom. The labourer is justified via the knowledge that he has worked hard, and that knowledge is in his bones and body, and is a source of freedom *inter alia* because a life lived 'outside the text' is a form of protection from the symbolic as the self 'outside the text' is not at the mercy of mind, and so the embodied self acts as a guide when the mind has no idea what to do, so that the worker's body is the intellect's first and last ally in the dynamic search for happiness and truth. The *sui generic* justifications of the body and psyche being reduced is an experience of decentering, of selfhood free of concern for the opinion of any other – including the self enthralled to abstraction and the public realm of meaning.

Because it is the body or our incarnate self that decides which realities are really true and which truths are merely abstract or objective, the body is the most trusted of mediums of the real, and is a more trusted indicator of what we are than the thoughts that run through our head. The body, then, is a *sui generic* source of the reality of the dialectic of 'inferiority/superiority' or justification/alienation, and all along has been witness to the worker's history and his many episodes of freedom/unfreedom and has all along taught him he can not be unfree or autonomous without his body registering his being unfree or autonomous, because the body is what tells him if 'freedom' is not real before he begins to use this condition as a departure point for a project of self-appropriation.

Along with being justified or being 'at issue,' the condition of 'not knowing' is a psychological state that registers in the psyche because the desire to know, precisely because it is a desire and a matter of *eros*, means the person who does not know or does not yet understand is frustrated, because his desire is not satisfied and he has to live with this cognitional and psychological tension. This tension or frustration of 'not knowing' has its reality through time, has its own *historicity* or weight that builds over time and registers in the person's psycho-somatic awareness. In the land of signs, then, every player needs their own theory of the contextual self to be 'at home,' because every other player in the land of signs has a 'theory' of the contextual self that they more or less seek to impose on others. This is why the insight of the last chapter is important as it means the worker-inquire-knower catches up with himself intellectually, and the freedom of becoming coeval with one's history and 'authoring' oneself is sourced in using the *reductio* as the form or idea of the condition and the history of the condition of being symbolically dominated, and grasping this condition as the condition of knowing himself and his history – a kind of cognitional independence day.

Also, this insight has the power to free the worker-inquirer's being-for-others because, if the insight described in the previous chapter is the *conditione sine qua non* for the worker-inquirer understanding himself, then it is also the *conditione sine qua non* for others knowing him i.e. others, in order to know him, must similarly understand what he has understood. Insofar as this is something interlocutors in the land of signs are unable to do, they are delegitimised and divested of the power to interpolate or know the worker's *dasein* and its purely natural apotheosis, and so the worker-inquirer-knower knows he is free of the other players in the symbolic order because what it is that makes him free is that which they can never suspect, far less come to know and use to wield symbolic power over the worker-inquirer-knower. Insofar as objective structures of perception "are only objective inasmuch as they are perceived as such by actors and significant others" (Jenkins 1982, p. 272), in this act of understanding a new player in the scramble for pronouncing upon the proper classification of social reality emerges and the struggle over 'objectivity' and 'reality' is renewed, thanks to the addition of a new player in whom the 'bourgeois edifice' collapses, and this power is a real power grab by consciousness by any standards.

## 7.3 Integral *Dasein*: the Realm of Meaning

At the moment of completing the structure of cognition, then, a revolution occurs within the worker-inquirer-knower as the intellectual order becomes a space where he enjoys a non-dominated or free relation to the realm of meaning. Thanks to his act of self-understanding, the worker-inquirer-knower's relationship to the internalised realm of meaning and the objective symbolic order is re-founded and brings into being a deliberative and open-eyed freedom in relation to its being-for-itself and its being-for-others and its many relations to the objective public realm. This reality which merits the word 'revolution' is the change where that which was a source of risk, regret or disadvantage and shame to the extent that even recognising it, far less thinking upon its basis was resisted, becomes one's anchorage, identity and ballast not only in the realm of meaning but, as the final chapter describes, the advent of the supernatural realm and the appropriation of the Christian tradition, as the long-held desire to understand and the long-term investment in the hope for a successful conclusion is brought to fulfilment.

In her sociological study of emotion, Lutz (1988, p. 3) rejects the idea "that emotion is in essence a psychobiological structure and an aspect of the individual...[while] the role of culture in the experience of emotion is seen as secondary, even minimal." Lutz's understanding of the relationship between affectivity and social structuration helps explain the tremendous catharsis effected by intellectual insight into the self; that the measure of psychological liberation is the measure of the intellectualisation of the amount of 'violent' or wilful or incompetent or humiliating readings that are sedimented in *dasein* and internalised as shame or anxiety, and that are uncovered by introspection and then brought to the cusp of judgment and finally 'relieved' of their intelligibility. The depth of healing of the psyche is the result of the fact that, insofar as any particular behaviour or situation of 'justification' versus being 'at risk' is a structural replica of many prior and future occasions, to free one particular occasion, is to free every other occasion and the range of this freedom is extended retrospectively to the past and prospectively to the future. While liberation is the liberation of relationships and the sublation of relationships configured by the *reductio ad sensum* and *reductio ad humanum* modalities, it is also a conquest in the realm of meaning that owes nothing to the dominant's discourse or wisdom.

The reality of a specifically psychological liberation that accompanies the specifically cognitional act discussed in Chapter 6, then, presupposes the affective life of members of class-divided societies is constituted as much by symbolic as material realities; that the class structure exists not only 'on paper' but in bodies (Wilkinson 2000), and is deeply structuring of psychological life and the constitution of emotions so that class is deeply felt and phenomenologically lived (Charlesworth et al. 2004). The psyche, then, intensely participates in the structuring effect of 'not knowing' or not yet being in possession of the truth, as well as intensely participates in and is structured by being in possession of the truth of itself. If the worker-inquirer lives the "alienation of the subject under the rule of the signifier" (Parker 2011, p. 151), then the worker-inquirer-*knower* knows the end of all 'contemplative' psychologies and the repatriation of sovereignty.

That there is a specifically psychological liberation is unsurprising given the recognition of what Bourdieu terms the homology between social and mental structures and, more generally, the 'clinical' value of this sociologically-informed therapy has long been recognised by sociologists and social psychologists. When asked whether his choice of sociology over philosophy or psychoanalysis was because sociology was a more powerful tool in the project of self-appropriation, Bourdieu replied that "given what I was socially...sociology was the best thing for me to do...I believe that I succeeded in my work: I effected a sort of self-therapy" (Bourdieu and Wacquant 1992, p. 211). And when sociology "gets down to the nitty gritty of real life... it is an instrument that people can apply to themselves for quasi-clinical purposes" (Bourdieu and Wacquant 1992, p. 198). The reason a sociologically-informed act of self-appropriation has 'clinical results' is because, prior to the act of judgment, we might say that the subjective demands of intellectual integrity form a kind of unholy alliance with the objective symbolic domination exercised by more dominant classes insofar as the being-for-others of the cognitional subject lacking self-knowledge more or less collaborates with and makes himself more vulnerable to symbolic readings of himself that are not grounded upon the data of fully contextualised and socialised *dasein*. The act of self-understanding, then, not only fulfils cognitional structure but conquers the 'objective' realm insofar as it has entered subjectivity in the form of socially dominant readings of working-class *dasein*.

Because the worker-inquirer-knower instantiates a history of being a particular self, a particularly constructed historicity is integral to his secondary nature, and a deeply illuminating and freeing judgment of this historicity is possible, and a liberation of the historicity of the psyche and behaviour is also possible. This means the worker-inquirer-knower is free to use formerly despised cultural materials (language, history, provinciality etcetera) as his departure point and criteria for the realm of culture generally and his free participation in these realms of creativity *as himself*. From the position of his development, then, a 'politics of culture' and a programme of cultural renewal upon this new basis is possible, and has as an historical ally in this endeavour a previous era of cultural production in Scotland where a holistic conception of Scottish *dasein* and use of the Scots language was free of any sense of inferiority. Also, in terms of reading and critiquing contemporary Scottish culture upon the basis of this development, the worker-inquirer-knower is able to recognise those 'producers of culture' who are not painting Scottish *dasein* with a full palette of colour and are still producing 'scarcity era' representations, as well as being able to recognise those 'producers of culture' operating from a more holistic understanding of *dasein*.

Upon the basis of a contextual performance of individuation, then, the internalisation of cultural inferiority is no longer simply lived or behaviourally repeated in an iterative sense but exposed to explicit self-awareness, where it can be explicitly rejected as a result of being placed at the disposal of a freedom that is in control and possession of itself. In this act of what might be termed 'cultural agency,' culture in a purely virtual or imaginary sense is liberated from its class-based and geo-politically-based subordinations in which it is actually immersed, and insofar as a specific *cultural subjugation* is understood, there is a liberation of awareness of what is at stake in the cultural realm, and a liberating recognition of what has for so long been repressed and has gone unrecognised at the cultural level, and not only in relation to the past but in relation to the future, the freedom that comes from self-understanding is conditioned by its cultural context and there emerges the 'tasks of freedom' to re-make the Scottish cultural realm from within the horizon of this freshly-acquired freedom that is immediately put at the disposal of intentionality, and which immediately enjoys a new and vital orientation and relation to culture and the 'realm of meaning' as it catches up with the analysis of Beveridge and Turnbull (1989) who identified the eclipsing and repressing of Scottish culture.

Thanks to achieving self-appropriation, then, a series of tasks are unlocked because this achievement is not the personal or private possession of an individual or the private catharsis of an individual, because the *gaudiam de veritate* is also a means for the further development of the *ad humanum* solidarity outwith the 'mirror of production' at the higher level of rational consciousness and cultural effort insofar as the worker-inquirer-knower's self-knowledge is also a sharing in the as yet unrealised liberation of his neighbour and his compatriots. Because similars are similarly understood, to understand one structuration is to virtually understand all structurations and one act of judgment enjoys the empowerment that follows from objective understanding. Through insight, the labourer-inquirer-knower uses the *reductio* to leverage a symbolic revolution not only within himself in a vital fashion but *in others in a virtual fashion* because he shares his condition with others, so that his self-understanding is also the self-understanding of others and a source of intersubjective communion in the truth and the basis for a new form of individuation and sociation.

The joy of being structured in the truth then is the joy of exercising a free relationship to one's self, others, temporality and the realm of meaning for the first time. The happiness of being structured in the truth is ending the symbolic domination internalised and exercised over oneself through one's being-for-others thanks to a dispersed and occasional freedom being raised to a qualitatively higher level of reality; an intellectual freedom liberated from its material and psychological conditions. Only an act of understanding brings this freedom into being because only by being the content of an act of understanding can the occasional or serial freedom of the worker experienced in his bodily and mental justification be freed from the original conditions of the worker-knower being physically, in actual fact, reduced, and become permanently available as an item of knowledge. Thanks to his act of understanding, a physical condition becomes a *res cogitans* and the sense of justification as a result of labouring is spiritualised so that the worker-inquirer-knower does not need to be actually or empirically psychologically 'in danger' or 'at issue' in the symbolic order. In the realm of meaning, *intellectual* freedom is a freedom that is always available to oneself and is a permanent source of anchorage, truth and identity and never a source of regret or disadvantage. While the moment of joy passes, then, there is a permanent imprimatur of empowerment or a 'condition of freedom' available by simply entering the realm of meaning thanks to this 'revolutionary act' which Lacan had in mind as it turns analysand into analyst.

## 7.4 Integral *Dasein*: A Free Relation to Domination

First, alienation is 'real' in its status as the necessary underlying condition for becoming a subject...The real... appears only transitorily at moments of traumatic revelation; it is resistant to symbolisation...Second, alienation is 'real' as gap in the symbolic."

Lacan, cited in Parker 2011, pp. 87-88

If we take the example of an old rich man who is long-accustomed to his status thanks to his long history of being successful, and then suppose that he attempts to achieve a particular goal but happens to fail, the man will acknowledge his defeat and perhaps analyse the reasons for his failure and come to a decision as to whether or not to try again. Acknowledging his attempt and acknowledging his failure will be more or less straightforward, and will cost him little or nothing to do so as one defeat will not ordinarily require him to question himself, far less coerce him into a crisis of self-confidence. Similarly, his being-for-others will not be jeopardised or put 'at risk' by knowing and communicating his set-back, because any intersubjective judgment that he was a failure would be viewed as a wilful and even perverse over-reaction.

The rich man, then, will have a healthy and open-eyed relation to his failure and will not be mastered or defined by it. However, if we take the example of a poor man for whom poverty is a long-established fact, the same historicity which inured the rich man from over-reacting to an instance of failure, in the case of the poor man will more or less coerce him into having a defeated relationship to his condition of being defeated, and it is more or less fated or inevitable that his failure will result in him constituting a particular kind of relation to himself, and that the poor man, as part of his very self, will have an ashamed relation to himself or be unable to look at his defeat clearly in an open-eyed and deliberate manner.

If a deep unwillingness and resistance to recognising sub-ordination and shame is a defining characteristic of the subordi-nate, then thanks to the emergence of what may be termed a free integralism and a dynamic and developmental relation to the self and the realm of meaning having been brought about, a free field of perception contains as integral to itself the free recognition of subordination where it exists within oneself and others. The freedom that results within the worker-inquirer-knower thanks to achieving self-understanding is a wholly interior cognitional event and does not change objective social and cultural conditions at all, so that the worker-inquirer-knower continues in a social and cultural and national context that is immersed in unequal relations of power and symbolic violence. However, as previously stated, the natural environment of human beings is the realm of meaning and in an important sense, to know our domination is to escape it, not as a brute fact of social position but as a symbolic or mental condition.

Something else that is freed is the ability to recognise the will-to-domination as it exists within oneself and in others so that, for all of an earlier emphasis upon the *ad sensum* and *ad humanum* dispositions and behaviours being developed by freedom and chosen in preference to other possible dispositions and behaviours, the worker-inquirer-knower can recognise the 'libidinal charge' accompanying much of working-class behaviour and discourse emerges from a subordinate location within the social hierarchy that was never a matter of choice; a subordination which is often consubstantial with an anti-intellectualism which a free integralism has no hesitation in recognising for the alienated and resentful relationship to intellectual consciousness that it is. Along with the self-understanding of the previous chapter, then, comes an equally radical self-acceptance and freedom to recognise the reality of self-hatred, language-hatred and nation-hatred and the 'nested' or multiple inability to esteem or accept one's *dasein* in all of its density, and this allows into view the full weight of the existential problem of structures of perception which have been trained to only see their comparative inferiority due to their immersion in a geo-political class-based universe of meaning, made all the more powerful by the absence of intellectual self-development.

Freedom to recognise one's own *ressentiment* and one's contempt for subordination and failure in others, brings into relief the fact that the key to psychological individuation is an understanding strong enough to reverse these dominant structures of perception; that only a structure of perception structured according to the standards of one's own cognitional structure is able to break the subject free of internalised social and cultural logics and representations, and decisively intervene into sociological determinisms and ongoing structures of self-perception operating in mass mediated class-based culture. Sartre's helpful insight that: "The slave in chains is free to break them...[but]...it is necessary fundamentally to choose himself on the ground of *slavery*" (1966, p. 703) is only possible when the worker-inquirer understands that because his 'secondary nature' is his means to self-understanding and his means to raise himself up to his natural beatitude, his 'slavery' has tremendous worth, as it is his only means to achieving his natural perfection and achieving the

Hegelian 'negation of the negation' and redeeming the judgment that "all subjected labour is cursed" (Adorno 1974, p. 217).

In embarking upon the project of self-appropriation the worker-inquirer had to obey the exigencies of his rational consciousness, which obliged him to give an account of himself that involved more than an appeal to intuition, poetry or spirituality i.e. a personal intellectual practice. On the presumption that this 'pursuit of self' had to do with knowing something, the procedure we decided most likely to meet with success was the pursuit of self-knowledge upon the basis of being a worker, and to that end we established a set of distinctive empirical data specific to the manual labourer, beginning with the reality brought about by his particular kind of doing as a sui generic bodily justification independent of consciousness. The next task was to show how a reality we had established operated 'outside of the text' not only had significance for consciousness, but exerted an informative 'gravitational pull' upon the whole of intentionality, affectivity and behaviour. In our account we noted the data of justification and established the link between the physical and the psychological, and in the process of self-appropriation an integral aspect of intellectual consciousness became an explicit awareness of the dialectical confrontation with the hierarchical realm of meaning that is intimately connected to the hierarchically ordered material resources of society.

This link between the physical and the psychological necessitated the expansion of the ontology brought into being by work into the symbolic order, where a dialectic of freedom/alienation within consciousness and behaviour was identified. We found that there were many consequences for consciousness and behaviour revealed by a contextual analysis of freedom, as each social class selects itself and develops a class-specific set of characteristics in contradistinction to other class-inflected relations to language and self i.e. freedom is used by each class to privilege its own standpoint and devalue others, while the social institutions and material and symbolic resources at their disposal as they pursue their politics of meaning are, by definition, unequal. Finally, insofar as this dialectic was taken up into the cognitional order, our argument has been that *upon its becoming an intellectual problematic, adequately conceiving physical structuration became a key to the construction and interpretation of other relationships and the content of empirical consciousness until, finally, via an act of judgment, this leveraged a revolution within the worker-inquirer,* and revolutionised the worker-inquirer-knower's relationship to himself and his being-for-others and the realm of meaning. The significance of the concept of the *reductio*, released by the work of reflection from being confined to being merely a conceptualisation of physical structuration, played the pivotal role in constituting the rational self-consciousness of the worker-inquirer-knower, because it re-founds his relationship to the realm of meaning *according to cognitional structure* and in active opposition to the control of meaning exercised by more dominant classes.

This empowerment allows a reading of 'the present as history' as well as a reading of previous attempts to diagnose the signs of the times, such as the revolutionary crisis throughout Europe during the 1920s and 1930s when, for many political activists and engaged observers of the period, the objective social conditions seemed ripe for revolutionary transformation, only to see the failure of revolutionary movements. As understood by the Frankfurt School, this failure was evidence that a purely objective Marxism was insufficient insofar as it was the 'subjective response' of workers to their objective social conditions that had been missing, and was to blame for the failure to bring about revolutionary change. In this light a critical social theory capable of *die anthropologischte wende* or 'turn to subjectivity' was required, and it is here that a paradox is brought into view.

Just as Marxism failed to integrate working-class *dasein* into its vision, so the discipline of psychology has been engaged in a similar search for a liberation psychology that has resoundingly failed, and the root cause of the failure to articulate a liberating or empowering theory of the psyche is that any completion of the 'turn to the subject' discovers that the psyche, precisely because it is immersed in and constituted by the medium of bourgeois capitalist society, is thereby 'contaminated' and unable to act as a source from which to transcend or challenge these same social conditions, with the result that any empirically given psyche cannot act as a starting point for this new psychology. For Jacoby (1997), for example, this search for a new psychology by psychologists such as Fromm, Maslow and Rogers failed, so that it remains a matter of urgency to work out a relationship between psychology and social theory. In this regard, Adler was the first psychologist to write on Marx and psychoanalysis and argued that an "affective state" underlies class consciousness, but in the opinion of Jacoby, this began the move away from the insights of Freudian psychoanalysis towards the sociological consciousness, and this latter is the main culprit in the story of why a post-Freudian psychology has been unable to articulate an *ego psychology* able to liberate the 'bourgeois individual.'

Starting from the basic idea of the psyche as profoundly informed by social or intersubjective conditions, the process of attaining true self-knowledge requires an understanding of social experience as the individual is located in and often dominated by a number of social contexts. Furthermore, if the primary social context to which every adult looks in order to know himself, and to which other adults look to locate him and the social status he has, is the context of the occupational hierarchy, it seems that any theory of psychological development and maturity that was not a social psychology and did not include a contextual account of the psyche in which social conditions are more or less fundamental to attaining maturity, or did not articulate the psychological 'secondary nature' via which maturity was achieved, can not be 'fit for purpose' as it will be a product of 'pure reason' characterised by ahistoricism and universalism.

The task for psychologists then is to articulate a psychology that transcends the legacy of bourgeois universalism and secedes from the 'scarcity era' psychoanalytic theory of Freud, but without falling into the superficiality of the affluence-fuelled 'ego psychologies' of the likes of R. D. Laing and Cooper. I propose that insofar as I have articulated aspects of psychological experience that owe little to a universalist concept of Man and shares little ground with the clichéd account of 'self-actualisation' such as found in Maslow (1968), my account of psychological liberation is a step in the required direction, as in my account there is nothing of the facile ease with which freedom arrives as found in R. D. Laing and there is nowhere to be found readily available policies to usher in all-round equality such as liberation from the family and marriage, or absurd modernist slogans such as 'smash monogamy' or 'free love' or constructivist fantasies such as "nature leaves undefined the object of sexual desire" (Wittman 1970, cited in Johnston and Noakes 2005, p. 59).

Rather than a social ontology characterised by such rationalist and voluntarist fantasies as freedom from marriage and the discipline of economic production and all such superficial individualism, there is instead a free relation to the 'mirror of production' and the freedom that recognises the repression and domination to be resisted, but also the need for repression as found in the institution of the family, Christianity and productive work, for example, and that all psychological theories that attempt to articulate freedom or 'therapy' without mediation via 'secondary natures' are de-contextualised exercises destined to fail, and can only have appeal to those whose social conditioning is such as to inculcate a social ontology infected with the virus of immaculacy.

The epidemic of failed projects aimed at articulating a holistic psychology share the same paradox: on the one hand they fail to articulate their ego psychology upon a particular contextual *dasein* or a real 'secondary nature,' and yet this very flight from the labour of engaging in any real 'secondary nature' is routinely the result of their enthrallment to the 'secondary nature' or social habitus of the middle class. The failure that they all share is that in turning to the subject they *do not turn to their class condition*, but instead turn to this class's signature ideology concerning human *dasein* i.e. that there is an immaculate realm of autonomy and individualism. Hence, while with the advent of affluence and the need for an 'affluent modernity' it is necessary to articulate a fully contextualised account of self-actualisation, it was also more or less inevitable that forms of ego psychology would reach epidemic proportions, and the failure of psychology to give an account of how Man's full nature might emerge in post-affluent Western capitalist societies recapitulates the long standing question of whether a middle-class thinker can produce an account, firstly, of the conditioning of the middle-class psyche and then *upon that basis* give an account of how it is brought to its natural apotheosis.

In attempting this task a great problem has not only been the 'pure reason' fantasy of a universalist psychology and one social class theorising the liberation of every class, but the persistence of contemplative pronunciations against immersion into particularity. A prime example of this is Lukacs, according to whom (in Jacoby 1997, p. 77): "Opportunism mistakes the actual psychological state of consciousness of the proletariat for the class consciousness of the proletariat...[and seeks to] reduce class consciousness...to the level of the psychologically given." Here, then, is the problem: if oppression, liberation and truth are never psychologically given, then they cannot be known or experienced as a vital living achievement, but must remain metaphysical constructs of 'pure reason' unavailable to the worker-inquirer.

While this alleged split between psychological experience and the class consciousness of the proletariat is useful for excusing the 'pure theorist' from having to immerse himself in the life of any concrete working-class population (because if the worker himself is oblivious to the truth of his situation there is no point to ethnographic immersion, and so even 'going native' is no way to know their oppression and liberation), I argue the data gives the evidence of repression and that people are aware there is a social hierarchy of status linked to occupation; that the objective impinges upon comportment and inner psychological life, and this data is in plain sight and open awareness and talked about on morning trains and is enough to make a start on the journey of self-appropriation. This is the basis for rejecting theorists who imagine true class consciousness is foreign to psychological consciousness, so that the notion that true class consciousness has nothing to do with the given empirical consciousness of the working class, or class consciousness lacks all psychic content is a theoretician's fantasy as any theory of class consciousness in which the *sui generic* movements of working-class subjectivity and its cognitional acts are irrelevant to attaining 'class consciousness,' far less its purely natural apotheosis, is fated to be rejected as a form of 'supernaturalism.'

The arrival of general affluence from the nineteen-seventies and nineteen-eighties in Western nation-based societies was often imagined as inaugurating a post-materialist and *post-repression* psyche, free from 'the mirror of production' and the traumas and repressions of family life and Christianity. In the era of affluence, ego psychologists were quick to imagine repression was obsolete as populations were freed to pursue their higher natures. What was envisaged by Carl Rogers or Abram Maslow was in fact a post-industrial and post-affluent fantasy of human beings 'without qualities' or without 'secondary natures.' Such a vision can only emerge from a "totally administered subjectivity" (Marcuse 1972) within consumerist cultures with no anchoring or repressive ballast to imagine the future of the psyche by, and an illustration of *psychological modernism* and the bourgeois fantasy that Man had escaped the 'mirror of production' is found in Carl Rogers for whom the fact of 'social roles' was a violation of our humanity and the real authentic self i.e. the free bourgeois autonomous individual that is supposed to be repressed and locked up within us all is constrained by an artificial social role or mask, and thereby immersed in an alienated mode of human behaviour.

This rank secular form of supernaturalism that has no need for contextualized *dasein* to achieve freedom, is innocent of even the suspicion that 'secondary natures' are the very stuff that is needed to fuel a purely natural freedom – far less the very stuff *to be redeemed*, and that has a vital role to play in brining this redemption about. The problem, then, is how to articulate a humanist psychology *when the very call for such a development is the favoured ideology of one-dimensional society* (Marcuse); how to agree with Jacoby (1997, p. 103) that "the cult of human subjectivity is not the negation of bourgeois society but its substance," and yet transcend that social and intellectual determinism.

My strategy has been to start from the fact that affluence and education allows the working class to cultivate a holistic *dasein* all the way to its natural beatitude, and this holistic *dasein* takes aim at the rather vacuous accounts of developmental psychology developed by the likes of Rogers and Maslow. The flight-from-yet-immersion-in class remains an epidemic in every arts and humanities academic discipline, and if we look at sociology and psychology which in their modernist phases tried hard to be purely secular, and ask if they have succeeded where philosophy and theology failed to historicise and socialise the study of the human psyche and human society, it seems no discipline is able to resist being assimilated to the class structure and truncated 'scarcity thinking' visions of human being.

Just as for Durkheim sociology was necessarily atheist (Richard, in Pickering 1975), so psychoanalysis for Freud was necessarily atheist, and the likes of Parker still call upon psychology to "find another secular path to the revolution in subjectivity that Lacanian psychoanalysis promises" (2011, p. 160). The doxic organisation of the psychological imagination revealed in sentences such as: "Psychoanalysis will only be able to break from capitalism if it explicitly breaks, renews its break, with Christianity and for that matter traverses any appeal to divinity as consolation for the subject" (Parker 2011, p. 154), hardly encourages the hope that psychology will effect the step-change it calls for any time soon. For my part I have given a purely natural path Parker calls on others to deliver, and in the process have transcended the 'scarcity thinking' that is unaware that the period of militant and materialistic thought is over, and to turn to the superannuated cliché that psychoanalysis must necessarily be atheist and reject all supernatural consolation indicates monochromatic 'scarcity thinking,' and the continuing absence in psychology of an adequate model of the purely natural beatitude of the human psyche.

To bring the story of Scottish working-class *dasein's* journey to its conclusion is to bring it to a higher perfection or a beatitude that is 'beyond nature.' In the next Chapter I add the last primary colour to my 'picture' of this *dasein* and turn to the famous *analogia entis* which has not been adverted to until now, but has been fundamental to everything written so far. When describing the 'present as history' as the recovery of an original twelfth-century understanding of 'being modern,' a breakthrough that ultimately failed, I mean to argue that if Christian thinkers had historicised and socialised the *analogia entis* of St. Bonaventure (1221-1274), they would have given every subsequent generation a template of how to imagine a purely natural or social departure point for appropriating the Christian revelation.

The *analogia entis* is the key to an integral psychology and sociology because it more or less demands a purely natural or a purely social departure point for the advent of the supernatural and in this regard, while Hard and Negri pinpoint the twelfth century as the beginning of the modern era and credit Duns Scotus and others with an original 'turn to the subject,' their view that the "discovery of the plane of immanence...[was] founded on an attack on transcendence" (Hardt and Negri 2001, p. 91) and that "the refusal of transcendence is the condition of possibility of thinking this immanent power" (Hard and Negri 2001, p. 92) mistakes an original and historical critique of supernatural*ism* for an attack on the supernatural, and reveals once again modernist thinkers' remarkable ability to snatch error from the jaws of a correct understanding of European modernity.

In grappling with the errors of much mainstream sociology of his time, Yves Simon (1991, p. 129) wrote: "freedom is an intense, excellent and overflowingly powerful mode of causality [and]...it becomes possible to consider coldly the question whether the object of social science comprises...some facts pertaining to the use that human freedom makes of itself." In the next chapter I seek to envisage a social science that takes as its object some of the consequences of human freedom, and argue that one of the uses human freedom makes of itself is *to bring about the advent of the living God* within fully contextualised human *dasein fully in act*, and when making this argument I hope not to be accused of idealism as I have waited until after completing chapters devoted to a range of concrete working, social, housing, political, cultural and psychological conditions before completing our journey by turning to Scottish working-class *dasein's* capacity for the supernatural. The final chapter then argues that just as the 'worked self' is not the whole of Scottish working-class *dasein*, so the purely natural achievements of the worker-inquirer-knower is not the end of his journey. Having completed our account of the person as *imago mundi*, the final task is to give an account of the worker-inquirer-knower as he *co-reveals himself to be imago Dei*, as thanks to accomplishing his self-actualisation or reducing himself to a 'pure act' via a perfect act of self-understanding, the worker-inquirer-knower imitates the living God who is *actus purus* or 'pure act.'

# Part 2
# The Supernatural

# 8

# The Sociological Mediation
# of Christian Redemption

That which is wholly done for us by God, namely deification by
grace, is yet also our highest act and as such properly our own.

John Milbank 2005, p. ix

## 8.1 Integral Sociology & the Proportionate
## *Actus Purus* of 'Secondary Nature'

Initially, a *description* ("positivism") of the religious
phenomena is required: immediately, free of theories, the
phenomena in themselves (cf. the similar demand by Max
Weber for sociology). Religious phenomena are to be
observed naively, as not yet hackneyed.

Heidegger 2004, pp. 14-15

On the 7th of March 1988 I was in bed in St. Mary's Orphanage
on Dum Dum Road in Calcutta (India). It was early on a sunny
Monday morning, and I was lying dreaming. In my dream I heard
a sound and looked up to see what the sound was and saw my
mother standing looking at me. She was standing still, holding out
a telephone towards me in her right hand indicating to me to
come and take the phone. "I think it's Him" she said diffidently.
I went over and put the phone to my ear and said 'Hello?' At this,
I heard a voice say with great enthusiasm: "Paul, the quality!

The quality!" At that moment what I saw changed. Now, looking within myself I saw a vast open expanse set before me. I looked upon this scene as if perched high above, and as I looked down at the scene that stretched out far below me, I saw what I first took for a mass of white slow-moving billowing clouds. I then realised they were in fact enormous clouds of fire and flame, and as they came closer I could see they were fires of deep brilliant orange and red and white and yellow; slow-moving yet coming towards me as if from the centre of some nuclear explosion that had occurred out of sight, deep within me. Then, from within the slowly moving colours that had now expanded to fill the whole of this landscape within me that stretched from horizon to horizon, I realised I was looking upon the face of Jesus who was looking directly at me. As the slow-moving coloured fire rose upwards to crash and break against me, I momentarily became afraid and wondered whether I might burn or come to harm, and wondered what I should do. I decided to stop looking, and I lay down and closed my eyes and readied myself for the impact, wondering what it would feel like. As it reached me I lay completely passive with eyes closed and felt the fire reach me and slowly burn its way through me and expand uniformly and slowly, in every direction outwards to every surface of my body. Realising it was not painful but felt like a deep burning that did me no harm, I relaxed and allowed it to happen. When the uniform pulse of red and orange and yellow fire reached me and slowly burned its way through me, it came to an end. I remained still and kept lying on the bed. After a few moments of marvelling at what had just happened, and with nothing else happening, I opened my eyes to see the bright sunny day outside and got up and got dressed, before heading off for breakfast with the Christian Brothers.

The experience described above happened a week after I achieved an act of self-understanding during the night of 28-29th February 1988, which was the basis for the previous two chapters and is the experiential basis for the argument that, if a methodological 'rule' of interpretive sociology is to follow wherever human *dasein* leads, whether to the structuration effected by living particular housing conditions or the structuration effected by manual labour or the structuration of *dasein* effected by reflexive acts of self-understanding, or experience of the supernatural, then a sociology that is 'fit for reality' cannot be only natural or exclusively naturalistic as it is more or less coerced into including the supernatural as an element of human experience and, as a reasonable extension of that inclusion, a presence or reality in the lives of societies and human history.

An integrally developed *dasein* then requires an integral sociology, a post-secular sociology if the *dasein* under sociological study has mastered self-appropriation and achieved its purely natural beatitude, and received some positive experience of the supernatural. Moreover, however, far more than merely conceding the possibility or actuality of the supernatural, sociology is more or less coerced not only into exploring what sociology can contribute to the alignment of "social science and self-actualisation" (Bhaskar 2012, pp. 117-164) but is more or less coerced into a new self-understanding *insofar as it has a role to play in mediating the living God to socialised human being.*

Because the worker-inquirer's self-actualisation is more than a private psychological affair because it is directly relevant and linked to an entire class condition, it is also directly relevant to the history of social theory and social research that has practiced class analysis, so that the work of self-appropriation is also able to illuminate the failures of 'scarcity sociology' that affluent modernity sociologists must address in the spirit of Archer et al. (2004, p. 168): "More recently, some critical realists...have raised the issue of...spiritual emancipation which has traditionally been the work of religion. This...is a new subject matter for critical realist thought, widely referred to...as a 'spiritual turn,'" while Habermas (2010, p. 18) has called for a post-secular shift to allow advanced post-Enlightenment Western societies to recover their faith in reason:

My motive for addressing the issue of faith and knowledge is to mobilize modern reason against the defeatism lurking within it. Postmetaphysical thinking cannot cope on its own with the defeatism concerning reason which we encounter today both in the postmodern radicalization of the 'dialectic of the Enlightenment' and in the naturalism founded on a naïve faith in science.

While in the spirit of Habermas it is good metaphysical manners to refrain from aggressive and exclusionary sectarianism, by building upon the performative basis of self-appropriation, this post-secularist basis is rooted in the fact that beyond the structuring of the person effected by working or nationality or truth, is the direct supernatural action of the supernatural (or the person of the Holy Spirit in the Christian mind) within the worker-inquirer-knower. Thanks to the worker-inquirer-knower exercising his own 'dictatorship of the proletariat' over himself, the 'analogy of being' (*analogia entis*) becomes an existential truth insofar as his passing the structure of himself into his intellectual consciousness means he 'creates' himself or gives birth to himself as a *res cogitans*, and in this achievement there is an analogy with the procession of the Second Person of the Blessed Trinity i.e. the worker-inquirer-knower by accomplishing his own proportionate *actus purus* makes it possible for him to recognise God as *actus purus*, and that he is an image of this God and also makes God see a very weak likeness of Himself in fully-contextualised 1979 generation Scottish working-class *dasein* fully 'in act,' and is pleased by this and takes pleasure in this and brings this achievement of his creature to a perfection 'beyond nature,' by communicating Himself in the gift of supernatural grace. Hence, in contrast to Corrie's despair in *The Image O' God* (1927):

> Crawlin aboot like a snail in the mud,
> covered wi clammy blae,
> Me, made after the image o' God –
> Jings! But it's laughable, tae.

the worker-inquirer-knower is empowered to write another kind of poetry (Rilke 2009, p. 23):

> What will you do, God, when I die?
> When I, your pitcher, broken, lie?

When I, your drink, go stale or dry?
I am your garb, the trade you ply,
you lose your meaning, losing me.
Homeless without me, you will be
robbed of your welcome, warm and sweet.
I am your sandals: your tired feet
will wander bare for want of me.

If this sociological account of grace is something of a novelty, the sanctification by which the human person participates in the redemption of Christ has been seen since the first days of the Church as creating a new ontological reality within the person, and over the course of two thousand years of speculation there has accumulated a daunting literature devoted to the nature of this transformation and the reality of grace and the presence of the Holy Spirit within human being. In making a contribution to this long durée tradition, the interpretive sociologist is able to understand that the "transformation that a human being undergoes when he is incorporated into Christ" (Kerr 2002, p. 145) is made possible by the operationalisation of fully contextual and fully contingent 'secondary nature' while remaining a supernatural gift beyond nature, and an integral sociology begins to deliver upon the task first sighted in the twelfth-century Latin West which called for "the refraction of the gospel's truths throughout a determinate social structure" (Chenu 1997, p. 38). In their efforts to understand the action of grace or the Holy Spirit within the person, medieval theologians developed the notion of a supernatural *habitus* to describe the structuration brought about by sanctifying grace.

According to Chenu's (1997) *Nature, Man and Society in the Twelfth Century*, in reaching the view that each human being had a purely natural beatitude or a purely natural perfection that is proportionate to or corresponds with human nature, as well as having a supernatural beatitude or perfection that is disproportionate to or beyond human nature, the great leap forward was the discovery of the categories of 'Nature' and 'History' and their import for the historicisation and socialisation of the Christian understanding of salvation, understood as a specifically supernatural structuring of the person, and the term 'super-natural' referring to that which, by definition, is above and beyond 'nature' and the natural powers of the human being. In this regard, the 'discovery' of *nature* and *history* in the work of Alan of Lille (1128-1202) and Alexander Neckham (1157-1217) formed part of a wider mental revolution and renewal of Christendom which called for new theologies and spiritualities to replace a pre-modern monasticism that had privileged sanctification via practicing withdrawal from the world.

These new social and intellectual developments were the context for Scotus's turning to particularity (Llywelyn 2010, pp. 185-223) and contingency and inaugurating a paradigm shift (Picksttock 2003, p. 11) that explicitly conceived Christian salvation in a temporal and processual manner. By the thirteenth century the term *habitus* was used to denote a fixed and permanent reality or a 'second nature' as opposed to a mere 'disposition,' and according to Lonergan (1971, p. 13): "Between Peter Lombard and St Albert the Great there emerged the idea of the supernatural habit," with Lombard affirming against Augustine's anthropological pessimism: "there are many good acts prior to prevenient or operative grace, and that these acts are due either to grace and free choice or even to free choice alone; but by them man merits neither justification nor eternal life" (Lonergan 1971, p, 12).

In Lonergan's view it was Peter, Chancellor of the University of Paris, who made the break from a thoroughgoing pessimism regarding human nature to understand the significance of 'secondary natures' and their causality, thanks to the key distinction between a natural *amor amicitiae erga Deum* (love and friendship for God) and the properly supernatural grace-filled love of God. Thanks to the distinction between *a natural love towards God* and the supernatural life of grace, a purely natural apotheosis was theoretically discovered and defended, along with purely natural knowledges about purely natural realities and knowledge of 'secondary natures.' Insofar as an inherited Augustinian pessimism that insisted every good deed was to be accorded to grace was finally rejected, in its place came the recognition of a natural and dynamic orientation towards God, and in the new mental universe of twelfth and thirteenth-century Europe, nature and 'secondary natures' in the form of the *desiderium naturale* were given their rightful place and human being was accorded a *natural* desire for God to act as an immanent and dynamic anchor for the sacred within humanity itself, while the dogmatic issue that supernatural justification and sanctifying grace were supernatural realities that were God's free initiative alone, and remained beyond the power of nature, was safeguarded.

While the "unique impulse" (Chenu 1997, p. 38) of the twelfth century was an attractive integral humanism overcoming the long winter of Augustinian pessimism concerning human nature, this new appreciation of the human being's purely natural orientation towards and capacity to receive the supernatural was never a unanimous position that commanded consensus, so that if there emerged a turning to the contingent, processual and temporal nature of human beings in their co-operation with the work of their redemption, this did not automatically inaugurate an era of contextual theology.

Kerr (2002) has given an account of the twentieth century's recovery of the dynamic developmentalism at the heart of Aquinas's (1225-1274) account of human beatitude, and how the recovery of this 'version' of Thomism was the achievement of Henri de Lubac (1896-1991), a rediscovery which Milbank (2005) has described as the most important development in twentieth century theology. In de Lubac's version of Thomism, the human being enjoys a *natural* capacity and desire for face-to-face vision of God, and in de Lubac's *integral revolution* – so-called because it rejects the view that each individual has a separate natural beatitude and an additional and separate supernatural beatitude i.e. rejects the "two-storey model of nature and grace" (Kerr 2002, p. 136) in favour of one single or integral order of salvation – it is impossible to separate the natural and supernatural contributions to the unity that is any particular concrete human person, with the important consequence that: "the social and political cannot be separated from the spiritual" (Kerr 2002, p. 148), and "every human being enjoys a de facto relationship to Jesus Christ" (Boff 1987, p. 122).

In constructing my sociological account of Christian redemption or the advent of the supernatural, I reject de Lubac's rejection of the two-storey model of nature and grace, and draw upon the 'discovery' of nature and the emergence of the idea of a 'second nature' or habitus, so that secondary or *socialised* nature can be given its rightful place within what might be termed a sociological 'economy of salvation,' and argue for the theonomic value of 'integral contingency' insofar as the sanctification of the worker-inquirer-knower is prepared for via his contingent 'secondary nature.' Drawing upon Kerr's version of Aquinas, I construct a sociologically-grounded version of Aquinas's analogy between the secondary causation of the creature and the causation of the Creator that Aquinas developed to answer the question of how God causes an individual's salvation.

More concretely, then, just as intelligence liberates the *ad sensum* and *ad humanum* modalities from their original immediacy to the higher level of ideal or cognitional existence, so insofar as supernatural grace builds upon and does not destroy nature, then, insofar as there is the infusion of a supernatural habit, the nested structurations of the *reductio* are simultaneously elevated above themselves and are the condition for the possibility of this elevation i.e. the act of self-appropriation mediates or 'triggers' – but does not cause – the worker-inquirer-knower's supernatural elevation. The argument is that if "God moves the will according to its condition" (Lonergan 1971, p. 130), then He moves it according to its apotheosis i.e. mediates the preparation of the worker for his salvation through his grasping his secondary nature as this is the purely natural or purely socialised means by which, thanks to conceptualisation and the act of judgment, the worker reduces himself to 'pure act.'

More generally, then, the argument is that in industrialised societies, without the necessary class and cultural mediation of 'causality,' a person cannot exercise the co-operation or 'secondary causality' he must exercise if he is to order himself towards his supernatural end. Because God's salvific will is constant and universal, the event of the gratuitous gift of sanctifying grace requires a 'triggering' event on the part of the worker-inquirer-knower who is to receive the gift of grace; as if God's advent is dependent upon a prior event occurring within the person. The heart of the matter turns upon the 'cause' of grace, and for Aquinas "a cause that acts in time, acts at a given time neither sooner nor later. We have to discover why it does not act sooner and what makes it act when it does" (Lonergan 1971, p. 70).

According to philosophical and theological tradition, the predicament faced by human beings is that they are created natures which, unlike angels, are not created in full possession of their faculties and powers and so, because "Nature gives us nothing in act" (Lonergan 1990, p. 161), human beings must achieve their perfection via "a greater actuation of the agent" (Lonergan 1971, p. 71), so that the concrete solution to this human dilemma will consist of locating the mechanism whereby the worker-inquirer-knower operationalises his situated or secondary nature via conceptualisation, language and the structure of cognition. If we accept Kerr's argument (2002, p. 173) that "it is by one's own activity that one is drawn into God" and that the activity that is privileged in bringing this about is achieving self-knowledge as this "gives the created agent a special participation of the pure act of being" (Kerr 2002, p. 163), our sociological account of grace may be stated thus: the concept of the *reductio*, insofar as it is a milestone along the road of language and conceptualisation that the worker-enquirer must travel in his journey towards an adequate account of himself, is also the triggering causal mechanism for the exercise of cognitional agency which reduces the worker-inquirer to 'pure act,' and thereby prepares him for the moment of grace.

The *reductio* categorisation of the situated self is our ethno-graphic account of how the universal *desiderium naturale* is opera-tionalised and culminates in 'triggering' the constitution of Scottish working-class '79 generation *dasein* as *imago Dei*. If this account is valid, then we have a sociologically-grounded solution not only to a theological problematic first sighted in the twelfth and thirteenth centuries, but to a problematic which preoccupied late nineteenth and twentieth century attempts at articulating an inte-gral sociology: evidencing the supernatural purely upon the con-temporary and modern basis of 'integral contingency,' and thereby providing an alternative to the 'modernisation is secularisation' paradigm that has been dominant in sociological theory.

Textual evidence in broad support of this position is provided by Aquinas when he describes preparation for justification "in terms of an Aristotelian promotion" (Lonergan 1971, p. 100) or act of self-understanding which, as well as being its own *sui generic* reality, is also preparatory for grace due to inhering within a created nature that is dynamically oriented to a higher order. Within this ordered order, the purely natural achievements of intellect and freedom and will, act as the conditions for the entitatively distinctive supernatural structuration – the advent of the fire of the Holy Spirit within the soul of the worker-inquirer-knower. The beatitude of the worker-inquirer-knower, then, considered as *imago Dei* must also be an analogous matter of achieving a profound act of knowing and profound act of love. If we follow Aquinas' Trinitarian theology whereby God's happiness or bliss consists in His self-understanding and self-loving, so that a person is *imago Dei* insofar as he or she produces acts of loving and understanding, and where Aquinas describes God as existence 'fully in act' or *actus purus*, the worker-inquirer-knower likewise can refer to his own experience of being 'fully in act' thanks to his operationalising of his situated being, so that a purely sociological means of preparing for the reality of divine love within *dasein* is to firstly establish the reality of purely natural human love within the worker-inquirer-knower, as it is by generating an act of human love that the worker-inquirer-knower co-operates with his sanctification, so that the advent of grace can be described as gratuitous but never purely adventitious.

The joyful experiences of understanding or the *gaudiam de veritate* and the joy or bliss of 'love of self' (as well as acts of knowing and loving others sharing this *dasein*), however, must not be mistaken for experiences of the supernatural, as performing a radical act of self–understanding and a radical love of self are acts within our natural powers. At the same time, however, from the experience of this intellectual operation it is legitimate to draw an analogy between the worker-inquirer-knower 'saying himself' as he passes the intelligible structure of himself into his intellectual self-awareness for the first time, and the procession of the Word in Trinitarian theory. Similarly, it is legitimate to draw an analogy between the procession of the Holy Spirit within the Blessed Trinity and the worker-inquirer-knower's bursting forth into an act of love as a direct result of the joy of self-understanding. These analogies refer to purely natural operations of *dasein* 'fully in act.' However, while we reject any suggestion that it is possible to 'naturalise' or 'socialise' the supernatural, these purely natural and social actions are indeed preparatory for a gift or an operationalisation of human nature beyond nature's powers, so that a great paradox is that the gift of the Holy Spirit that is beyond nature, reason and merit, is at the mercy of our co-operation and, thanks to the necessity of this co-operation, our salvation may be described as a reality which in a real sense is something we co-operate in bringing about.

This view of 'pure nature' is not the view that human beings are able to 'bootstrap' their way to God as no human being is able to lift himself to the supernatural. Rather, the task of human being is one of working out its twofold destiny; both its natural development and its supernatural salvation are connected and are both processual matters whereby, unless the situated self brings not simply the pre-industrial category of 'nature' found in patristic and early medieval theology but the ever-increasing complexity of our integral contingency or 'secondary nature' to its purely natural apotheosis, they do not prepare themselves for the advent of the supernatural moment of grace. As Milbank (2005, p. ix) has it: "That which is wholly done for us by God, namely deification by grace, is yet also our highest act and as such properly our own."

## 8.2 Integral Contingency as Post-Metaphysical Foundation for Experience of the Supernatural

As Christians we must simply accept the fact that there will be ever more man-made reality which is neither 'numinous' nature nor is profane in the bad sense.

Karl Rahner 1970, p. 78

In the writings of sociologist Max Weber who emphasised the other-worldliness of Christianity and identified a more or less antagonistic relationship between the Christian and the World as integral to Christianity, there is no awareness of the great reform movements in the eleventh and twelfth-centuries which wished to fundamentally re-think this relationship. In contrast, contemporary historians (Hollister 1969; Stiefel 1985; Constable 1996; Bisson 2009) identify in twelfth-century Europe a radically new concern to articulate the relations between the sacred and profane, and to find new ways of living and conceiving the relationship between nature and grace as a result of a twelfth-century intellectual revolution (Stiefel 1985) or renaissance (Hollister 1969) or reformation (Constable 1996), which saw efforts at ecclesial and social reform and an evangelical awakening that wished to put the Gospel into practice in post-monastic and secular forms of Christian life.

In the new post-agrarian urban settings that were a feature of twelfth-century Europe, the spread of urban living occurred as a result of an eleventh century agricultural revolution and technological progress which meant larger food surpluses so that greater urban populations could be supported. Rapid urbanisation of more and more of the population in turn led to commercial expansion throughout Europe in the twelfth century, and in its wake a new post-feudal occupational landscape emerged across Christian Europe, along with a concern to integrate this new social order with the traditional concern for salvation.

This movement for the reform of Christian life drew upon a pervasive awareness of living in a New Age, and Europe at this time gave birth to new Christian communities such as mendicant orders like the Franciscans and Dominicans that were committed to non-monastic or secular lifestyles dedicated to serving the laity in urban centres. This 'new evangelisation' also saw the spread of large numbers of lay apostolic groups such as the Humiliati, the Poor Lombards and the Cathars who were also caught up in what historical hindsight can see as the advent of the modern era. While eleventh-century efforts at reform were often aimed at the renewal of monasticism, what emerged in the twelfth century was efforts at social and ecclesial reform outwith inherited feudal and monastic paradigms, thanks to a new understanding that salvation was not to be found in retreating from the world but in "the sacred embrace of the secular condition" (Trinkaus and Oberman 1974, p. 24), and with this came a preoccupation with integrating that which had previously been kept apart i.e. worldly activity and concern for salvation. Among the new religious orders and lay associations were the *fraticelli* who were a lay branch of the Franciscan order who "took an active role in siding with the poor against their lords, sometimes fomenting open revolution and the seizure of lands" (Viladesau 2006, p. 146). For the lay urban poor who wished to have the theological and soteriological significance of poverty stated by the Church, the Franciscan reform provided the 'sacred canopy' that they needed, or "a moral response [to]... what the fate of the socio-economic forces had decreed" (Trinkaus and Oberman 1974, p.7).

The shift to the embrace of the natural and human beyond an Augustinian pessimism was also evident in artistic expression where the 'supernaturalist' formalism of Byzantine iconography was displaced by the naturalism of Giotto (1267-1337), in whose depictions of the Christian mysteries for his Franciscan patrons we have a modern commitment to realism and the rejection of non-naturalistic depictions of the sacred, and in their efforts at keeping abreast of these developments and leaving behind previously solid and enduring social formations, the nominalist school of thought which spread throughout Europe at this time signalled a move away from what Gilson (1980, p. 410) has described as pre-Christian *necessitarianism* toward a new emphasis upon *contingency* which, when applied to theology, placed "emphasis on the absolute freedom of God, rather than on intelligible necessity" (Viladesau 2006, p. 147).

For the likes of a Franciscan such as Duns Scotus, then, the incarnation and crucifixion of Jesus of Nazareth were *freely chosen* means of salvation and not part of a preordained or eternal plan, and thanks to highlighting the freedom of God "to create another world, to choose other means of salvation, and to establish another order" (Trinkaus & Oberman 1974, p. 12) *nominalism trumpeted the importance of contingency* not only as regards the manner whereby God saved Man, but the way Man made his way through life and made his way to God.

If scholars (Cross 1999; Ingham 2003; Llywelyn 2010) do not explicitly state that Scotus places the full weight of the achievement of the redemption brought about by Jesus of Nazareth upon the shoulders of his human nature, it is clear that this is the direction of travel of Scotus's thought, and contemporary Scotus scholarship (Cross 1999, p. 115) argues that in Jesus "the human nature united to the Word is not informed by the Word" according to the mind of Scotus. This claim is revolutionary and utterly fundamental to understanding the tectonic shift within the European Christian mind that is occurring at this point in time. In this regard, in his efforts at articulating a theology of nationality, Llywelyn (2010) has turned to Scotus and the early modern Christian tradition as in Rupert of Deutz (c. 1075-1129) and Alexander of Hales (c.1185-1245) that understood the motive for the Incarnation not as reparation for human sinfulness but as something intended by God before the Creation, and my own articulation of the theonomic or soteriological value of nationality has emerged from a sociological account of *dasein* and a sociological account of contextualized human nature reaching its natural apotheosis.

Insofar as nominalists stood against "the implication that our world is a mere reflection and shadow of higher levels of being" (Trinkaus & Oberman 1974, p. 13), it also broke free of necessitarianism or fatalism in terms of how the Christian was to view the established social and political order i.e. as something that was not part of a preordained plan but a secondary or contingent construct. According to the Scotist doctrine of freedom, then, Christian redemption is not the unfolding of a necessary *a priori* plan but the exercise of freedom in relation to a particular historical context, and the exercise of freedom vis-à-vis the play of events in which the individual who would imitate and come-to-know the God of Jesus of Nazareth is called upon to exercise his freedom in achieving his salvation; each person like the historical Jesus of Nazareth must freely win his or her salvation, and imitate Jesus not by following a pre-conceived and already established route to salvation but by constructing his or her route to salvation upon the basis of his or her unique immersion into their contingent socio-historical-cultural conditions.

This shift from pagan necessitarianism and the return to the Judeo-Christian God of history, was the retrieval of the earlier patristic "emphasis on covenantal and not-necessary relationship between God and his world" (Trinkaus & Oberman 1974, p. 15), and meant a focus upon contingency and particularity cleared the way for a turn to Nature and History, while the significance of the nominalist school for politics was to sound the death-knell for the legitimation of the exercise of arbitrary rule by an individual lord or king (Bisson 2009) and the first articulation of social contract theory in Scotus (Wolter 2001). This, then, was the beginning of the end of the monopolisation of political theology by elites and status quo doctrines regarding the social order, and the 'explosive' pluralisation of rival political ontologies among the different social strata and even within religious orders.[135] In this regard, a piece of social theory that stretched back to St. Paul's letter to the Romans 13: 1-3 was fundamentally weakened: "You must all obey the governing authorities. Since all government comes from God, the civil authorities were appointed by God, and so anyone who resists authority is rebelling against God's decision, and such an act is bound to be punished" (Jerusalem Bible 1968). Once this taboo was lifted from the political consciousness of believers, they were more or less free to conclude any social order which contradicted the Gospel had to be changed.

As a theory of knowledge, the consequences of nominalism had similar far-reaching consequences, such as the end of a naïve realism and the end of uncritical estimations of Man's natural knowledge of God as nominalism claimed no demonstrative knowledge of God was possible, and thereby ruled out any easy victory of 'pure reason' while safeguarding against scepticism

---

[135] In 1323 pope John XXII ruled against the proposition of a group of Franciscans known as the Spiritual Franciscans that the *usus pauper* or the restricted ownership of material goods should be obligatory for all followers of St. Francis (1181-1226).

insofar as it accorded *a new soteriological significance to reason* or man's cognitional life in light of its conviction that, just as God had committed Himself to a freely chosen and established order of salvation, so He had likewise committed the full responsibility or the full weight of knowledge of intelligible being to the natural power of the human intellect. In the nominalist theory of signification, then, "words are the connecting link between the mind and reality and between the world and God" (Trinkaus & Oberman 1974, p. 80), and when Boehner (1990, p. li) writes that nominalism was the original *via moderna* and that, "One historical fact, however, seems to be quite securely established: it was the physics of the via moderna which gave birth to modern physics," we can see in the following passage from Ockham (cited in Boehner 1990, p. 11) something of the trust in reason that Habermas feels has been lost thanks to the freely created cognitional order having been freely ordained to the order of being:

> Properly speaking, the science of nature is not about corruptible and generable things nor about natural substances nor about movable things...Properly speaking, the science of nature is about mental contents which are common to such things, and which stand precisely for such things.

The insight of nominalism, then, was that just as the human mind was made to bear the full weight of knowledge of intelligible being, so the full weight of freedom and working out one's natural and supernatural destiny was to be borne by situated *dasein* as nominalism embraced the centrality and the efficacy of 'post-ontological' verbal covenants or relationships between God and man, relationships that were no less dependable for being contingent and voluntary in origin. Just as for nominalist natural theology the order that prevails in the physical universe is in no sense necessary, so for nominalist social theory, the order that prevails in the social and economic sphere is in no sense necessary. Nominalists, then, took seriously the contingency they saw in nature, in human cognition, in social organisation and at the supernatural level in the manner by which Jesus had redeemed humanity.

Within this perspective, contingency is not simply a brute fact but is providential, and its theonomic value is revealed in the practice of operationalising one's relationship to one's natural and supernatural destiny, which are *not* a matter of following a necessary and universal ontology but of exercising practical and 'cognitional agency' which are dependent upon contingent contextual *dasein* using words, signs and concepts in its intellectual and intentional life, so that ultimately, contingency is providentially designed to bear the weight of the person's redemption, so that Man can work out his salvation upon the basis of "laws voluntarily and contingently established by God" (Trinkaus and Oberman 1974, p. 80). The discovery of the *contingency* of signification where signifiers or mere names (*nomenes,* from which we derive nominalism), whose only form of existence is cognitional (as opposed to also existing as eternal Platonic Ideas or models or templates of things in some non-earthly realm), is the point in time when the Christian mind began the *historicisation* of reason and the end of the reign of metaphysics or 'pure reason' over theology, insofar as the realities or processes of knowing and 'being saved' were entrusted to 'secondary natures' and 'secondary causality.'

In Catholic Scotland the patient study of mental acts or 'cognitional agency' has a long history and in the view of Broadie (2008, p. 2), Scottish intellectual life remained within the benign shadow of the Subtle Doctor until the disastrous wrong-turning of the Protestant Reformation of 1560. "Scotus was the great philosopher of freedom of the Middle Ages" and his influence upon John of Ireland (c.1440-1495) is clear from Ireland's close following of Scotus's doctrine of free will and his adopting the classical conciliarist position in *The Mirror of Wisdom* (1490) and *Commentary on the Sentences of Peter Lombard* (c.1480), which located authority within the Church in the communal nature of the believing community, rather than exclusively in the Pope or the Church hierarchy (see McDonald 1991). Conciliarism, then, was a doctrine that, when politicized, became a 'democratic' argument that located sovereignty within the community or the people rather than Crown or Parliament. As Broadie (2009, p. 5) has put it: "[Scotus's] political philosophy almost certainly had an impact on two of the great documents of early Scotland, the *Declaration of the Clergy* (1310) and the *Declaration of Arbroath* (1320)."

James Liddell's *On Concepts and Signs* (1495) carried on the nominalist tradition's patient study of mental acts, while Lokert's (c.1485-1547) *Writing on the Subject of Notions* (1514) maintained this epistemological turn and its focus upon the cognitional subject as integral to Scottish intellectual life. Indeed, such is the theonomic conception of human reason that in the opinion of Broadie (1990, p. 19), "Ireland has regard for the fact that we do tend...to see our acts as causally determining God to respond." Likewise, in the work of William Manderston (c.1485-1552) when dealing with the question whether the motivations to morality and belief are purely natural or not, he argues: "a person's free will can produce an act which is morally entirely good without God's special help (cited in Broadie 1990, p. 71), and Broadie concludes his discussion of the goodness of human nature and whether there is a purely natural ability to know and love and be moral with the observation that: "Manderston thus places the full weight of responsibility upon our free will" (1990, p. 71). Other significant Scottish nominalists included Lawrence of Lindores (1372-1437) who as inquisitor-general in Scotland not only burned heretics but, in his capacity as rector of St. Andrews University and a devout nominalist, banned the teaching of naive realism.

The relevance of these writers for the project of articulating working-class integral liberation, then, lies in their recognition of *the causality of knowledge* and the need to exercise 'cognitional agency' in achieving a purely natural apotheosis. At this point we may say in the rejection of naïve realism there is a 'coming of age' in Scottish and European intellectual life which consists of inaugurating or recognising a 'perennial' tension that henceforth lies at the heart of the modern Christian consciousness as a direct result of having to reconcile the conviction that the supernatural is at work in socially stratified and unequal societies, and from the twelfth and thirteenth-centuries, theology is more or less coerced into becoming fully contextual insofar as the task of *becoming Christian* is the task of triangulating the autonomous orders of human cognition and the Gospel and human society. Henceforth, integrating or aligning the three levels of cognitional structure, socialised *dasein* and the supernatural is the 'ideal type' synthesis that will keep Christianity alive in the hearts of modern men and women. Also, however, if recognising the need for this triangulation is the achievement of the twelfth and thirteenth-century, it also allows us to see that any subsequent failure to maintain the tension of this new vision will be a regressive opting for one of two equally erroneous and false choices:

1) a regressive supernaturalism that does not recognise and embrace the theonomic value of (i) the purely natural and social life of the person and (ii) a regressive clericalism in the life of the community called the Church.

2) a regressive empiricism/materialism that concludes the empirical realm of nature or 'secondary natures' is the proper object and full extent of human inquiry, knowledge and reality.

I propose that these two 'ideal type' errors can be used to read subsequent eras that were faced with maintaining the threefold tension of 'being human,' 'being modern' and 'being Christian,' or the tension of being *imago mundi* and the transcendent call to be *imago Dei*. In this regard, the advent of experiments in new forms of Christian living in community in the world which sought to combine a life of faith and the attempt to build a new social order during the twelfth-century reform of Christianity was similarly keenly felt during the emergence of industrial civilization throughout Europe in the early nineteenth-century, and triggered the search in industrialising societies for what might be termed an integral or a 'socialised Christianity' in light of Rahner's (1967, cited in Losinger 2000, p. xxix) recognition that: "Today dogmatic theology must be anthropology and such an 'anthropological turn' is necessary." In *The Great Transformation* ([1944] 2001) which charted the advent of free-market society and the production-based society that we inhabit today, Polanyi (2001, p. 176) identified an early example of this triangulation or integralism in Robert Owen's village of New Lanark which was organised upon co-operative principles.

> Owenism was a religion of industry the bearer of which was the working class...it was the beginning of the modern trade union movement. Cooperative societies were founded... determined to devote the profits of the venture to the furtherance of... the establishment of Villages of Cooperation.

In Owen's *A New View of Society* (1816) Polanyi identified the resolve to resist falling into the error of both a regressive otherworldly supernaturalism and a regressive materialism, as Owen fought to retain the 'whole man' in industrialising society and resist the *modernist* anthropology which wishes to 'privatise' and separate 'spheres of social life' (religion, politics, art, economic activity etcetera) and which sociologists would incorrectly come to identify as integral to or a signature characteristic of modernisation itself. Throughout Europe at this time, similar attempts at the integration of Christianity and the new industrial order were seen such as Saint-Simon's *New Christianity* ([1825] 1964) which sought to articulate a vision where new social conditions might stimulate a pan-European response in the form of a European-wide Christian integralism,[136] something which Polanyi viewed as part of European societies protecting themselves

---

[136] Saint-Simon (1760-1825) was influential in the history of sociology for coining important terms such as 'industrialization' and 'positive science,' as well as his role as mentor to August Comte (1798-1857), the founding-father of 'social physics' who was to coin the term 'sociology' in 1839. As an erstwhile French Catholic attempting to align modern social conditions and Christianity, Isidore Augusto Marie François Xavier Comte ended up articulating his hugely influential theory of the three stages of society (see Gane 2006).

from the excesses of the free-market order insofar as the latter involved the 'total mobilisation' of resources, not for subsistence but the never-ending 'godless' pursuit of profit and new markets. Seen in this light, then, much as nationalism is no longer viewed as an irrational throwback to an earlier and simpler social formation but as a reality generated by the very modern conditions of new social formations, so the attempts to articulate a New Christianity were new movements attempting the recuperation of an earlier integralism and an earlier organisation, and not backward or forlorn attempts at returning to the past but fully integral to modernity itself.

## 8.3 The Failure of Supernaturalism as a Paradigm for Sociology

In line with these early attempts at integralism or aligning the old with the new, nineteenth and twentieth-century Europe and North America saw attempts to establish a Christian sociology in order to contest a purely academic and largely secularised sociology. In 1893 the American Institute of Christian Sociology was founded and in 1894 the Oberlin Institute of Christian Sociology was established,[137] while in the following year William J. Kerby introduced the study of sociology to the Catholic University of America. The widepread desire to relate faith to the study of society led to the establishing of *The American Catholic Sociological Society* (ACSS) in 1938, an initiative largely based upon the widely-shared premise that a purely naturalistic social theory could only be an inadequate basis for a discipline concerned with understanding human societies, and the fact that many scholars

---

[137] Such was the widespread acceptance of a Christian standpoint for doing sociology at this time that in volume 1 of the *American Journal of Sociology* (1895, p. 15) we read the following editorial: "To many readers the most important question about the conduct of the *Journal* will be with reference to its attitude to 'Christian sociology.' The answer is, in a word, toward Christian sociology sincerely deferential, towards alleged 'Christian sociologists' severely suspicious."

viewed sociology as threatened by what they saw as the dogmatic secularism of founding figures such as Emile Durkheim[138] whose influence had prevented sociology from dealing adequately with spiritual or religious realities in the life of society. Durkheim's sociology was taken to task for its dogmatic atheism which, in the opinion of his former collaborator Gaston Richard (1923, cited in Pickering 1975, pp. 228-276), had infected sociology with a naturalistic metaphysics so that mainstream sociology has misconstrued the relationship between modernity and religion.

The basis for a Christian sociology, then, was the conviction that the attempt to understand real human beings and their communities and cultures across time "cannot be reconciled with the naturalistic thesis...put forward by so-called scientific sociology" (Sturzo 1947, p. 14). The search for a sociology that recognised the reality of the sacred and the secular was felt to be the only kind of sociology that could be capable of studying human beings and society and history realistically, or as they in fact are insofar as real human beings do not divide themselves or their lives into binary oppositions such as 'material life' and 'religious life.' What was required then was a break with the merely "empirical attitude to social questions and relate social analysis to the true nature of humanity" (Lyon 1983, p. 231), so that in the view of the ACSS, a new sociology was needed to combat positivist sociology which had abandoned every attempt at synthesising or integrating faith (or moral values) and social reality, while in Europe the same concern in the nineteen-thirties saw the development of *sociologie religieuse* or 'religious sociology' associated with the work of Gabriel Le Bras and Jacques Leclerq. This European initiative was a sociology inspired by pastoral concerns, and involved empirical research and collecting demographic data on the changing patterns of church attendance and the different organisational structures of rural and urban parishes, and culminated in the founding of *La Conference*

---

[138] The received view that Durkheim foisted a materialist metaphysics onto sociology has been recently contested by Riley's (2010) *Godless Intellectuals? The Intellectual Pursuit of the Sacred Reinvented.*

*Internationale de Sociologie Religieuse* (CISR) in 1948 at the Catholic University of Louvain, with the aim of pursuing a sociology to serve the needs of the Church. [139]

Despite these developments, however, and the fact that many social scientists held religious beliefs, a supernatural or Christian standpoint for 'doing sociology' failed to establish itself as a legitimate standpoint in the way positivism or, more recently, gender has established itself as a legitimate standpoint for doing sociology. With the benefit of hindsight, it is clear that simply recognising the triple tension of 'being human,' 'being modern' and 'being Christian' and identifying the need to respond by articulating a form of integralism, does not effect the necessary alignment between the human and the social and the supernatural. Insofar as the heart of the matter was enacting or performing this new triangulation through original data and research and conceptual innovations upon the basis of contingent realities such as class-based 'secondary natures' or *industrialised dasein*, the advocates of a non-naturalistic sociology were too caught up in arguing for the *sui generic* reality of the religious sphere of human experience in opposition to the widespread reductionist sociology of religion, and failed to realise that a genuinely Christian sociology had to establish itself upon a sui generic *social* basis, and as long as it was simply an extension or application of theology it would fail to establish itself as a legitimate sociological standpoint. The widely-shared desire for a post-positivist sociology was not in question, but to establish such a new sociology, something much more than this negative unity was required. In the opinion of Lyon (1983, p. 229):

> The Christian sociologists generally followed the mainstream route, without elaborating the implications of their particular

---

[139] Leclercq believed that religion could not be studied by non-religious people without great risk of erroneous interpretations and that "religious sociology could be pursued only by religious minds, and in particular, that the sociological study of the Catholic Church should be done by Catholics knowing theology" (Dobbelaere 1989, p. 381).

metaphysical commitments, some of which could, ironically, have contributed in the long run to a genuinely distinctive sociological outlook.

The longer the project of a religious sociology remained trapped in a form of theologically-inspired intuition, those who were unhappy with a merely dogmatic assertion of the existence or possibility of a Catholic sociology eventually began to suspect that the very idea was misconceived, and the longer this failure to articulate such a new sociology went on, pre-Conciliar Catholics such as Evans-Pritchard (1965, p. 121), for example, not untypically resorted to a professional agnosticism on the question of the possible alignment of the professional anthropologist and the 'private' believer:

> As far as the study of religion as a factor in social life is concerned, it may make little difference whether the anthropologist is a theist or an atheist, since in either case he can only take into account what he can observe. But if either attempts to go further than this, each must pursue a different path. The non-believer seeks for some theory–biological, psychological, or sociological – which will explain the illusion... On this point I find myself in agreement with Schmidt in his confutation of Renan: 'If religion is essentially of the inner life, it follows that it can be truly grasped only from within.'

The failure of a Christian sociology came down to the fact that those in favour of such a project failed to demonstrate 'proof of concept.' Hence, one of the pioneering advocates of a supernatural sociology, Luigi Sturzo (1878-1955), could make the following observation (1947, p. 14):

> I know of no sociologist who as such admits that there can be a free supernatural initiative...I do not say there are no Christian sociologists who believe by faith in the divine revelation; what I do say is that even their sociology remains on the purely natural plane – as if a natural society really existed free from any influence of the supernatural.

From the perspective of the 'integral sociology' that will be outlined in the final section, these first attempts to establish a Christian sociology should be viewed in much the same way in which Strauss (1983, p. 6) viewed Schleiermacher's lectures on the life of Jesus: "The truth is I found myself repelled by almost every aspect of these lectures...Schleiermacher proceeded from a construction of the person of Christ out of the Christian consciousness; this could only impress me as an uncritical presupposition." This harsh judgment is deserved insofar as the responsibility for the failure of a Christian sociology lies with the failure to overcome what I term *supernaturalism*, which I would define as any attempt to found a sociology upon a metaphysical basis. An example of supernaturalism is the following entry for 'sociology' in *The Catholic Encyclopaedia* of 1913 (p. 117):

> Modern non-Catholic sociology hopes to arrive at a metaphysics through the systematic observation and interpretation of present and past social facts and processes. In the Christian-Catholic view of life, however, the social sciences are guided by a sanctioned metaphysics and philosophy. This philosophy is derived not from induction but from Revelation.

The above quote highlights the defining characteristic and defining failure of the supernaturalist approach, which was the inability to realise a Christian sociology *like any kind of sociology* must be founded upon the basis of 'secondary natures' i.e. upon empirical data and research and genuine first-hand discovery. While individual clerics were exceptional in maintaining a commitment to belief and conducting original empirical research (and in the case of Greeley (1989) have the scars to prove it), the fact is responsibility for the failure to establish a Christian sociology lies with those who saw the need to reject 'supernaturalism' but *failed to provide a model of how the supernatural is at work in the industrial era.* The reason behind the failure to establish a Christian sociology was because their entire point of view came "out of the Christian consciousness" (Strauss 1983, p. 6) and was not sourced upon empirical research i.e. the entire basis of their wished-for sociological standpoint was itself removed from any kind of empirical demonstration, and this meant the non-believer had no 'point of entry' to recognise such a project as sociology. The only way a Christian sociology could credibly establish itself as an idea or project was to establish the reality or reasonableness of the supernatural *upon the basis of purely natural empirical research*, and because of its failure to do precisely this Lyon (1983, p. 237) could conclude:

> As with English Christian Sociology...its American counter-part failed to make a systematic investigation of the connections between 'what ought to be' and 'what is'... Christian sociology...did not survive as a distinct entity.

Because of the failure to synthesise or bring into alignment 'what is' i.e. modern life, with 'what ought to be' i.e. the advent of the supernatural to contextual *dasein*, the alignment of modernity and Christianity upon an empirical basis did not happen, and meant the idea of a Christian sociology lost credibility not only among its otherwise progressive supporters but saw some drawing the conclusion that the project of aligning these three realities and producing a Catholic sociology was analogous to constructing a Catholic geometry.[140] In light of this failure, even someone open to the possibility that a purely naturalistic sociology may ultimately be inadequate as a paradigm for sociology can identify Luigi Sturzo as someone who failed to give any account of how the supernatural is at work via 'secondary

---

[140] "Although he [Francis Friedal] and others in this group thought that Catholic sociologists should do sociology in the interests of a theologically inspired social reform, he did not think that the Catholic sociologist qua sociologist inquired into the dynamics of the social world in a manner distinct from other sociologists. As Paul Mundy observed, this point of view considered sociology "an autonomous social science, inherently distinct, analytically 'pure'" (1958: 307) so that there could no more be a Catholic sociology than there could be a Catholic geometry or a Catholic biology" (Kivisto 1989, p. 357).

natures' in industrial society, and thereby failed to overcome supernaturalism, so that even in Sturzo one can conclude that a genuinely sociological inquiry was never underway. As Sturzo (1947, p. 22) himself admitted: "I may be reproached with having left my integralism incomplete, since in my books I have dwelt little...on ethnographical studies."

In this regard John Milbank's *Theology and Social Theory: Beyond Secular Reason* (1990, p. 397) argues that theology must articulate "a full-blown social theory that is grounded in the Christian worldview." For Milbank (2006, p. 9), "Once, there was no 'secular'...[and no] 'purely human'...Instead there was the single community of Christendom," and it was nominalists such as Ockham, following Scotus, who invented and first imagined the space of 'the secular' and the space of 'the political' and 'the social.' This position seems unaware that previous efforts at a Christian sociology ended in failure because of this *a priori* ambition to assimilate sociology to theology, and as someone sympathetic to the call to move beyond 'secular reason,' I fail to find any ethnographic investigation in Milbank that evidences his contention that the supernatural is at work in contemporary society, and so Milbank remains an example of supernaturalism to the extent that his theological vision is not constituted via a pre-theological immersion into any particular ethnographic context.

Unless such a project is established purely upon the basis of 'secondary natures,' it can not command a hearing from those who do not already share a Christian standpoint, and for theology to articulate a full-blown social theory it must begin from the bottom and work its way up, an approach that is the very opposite of that of supernaturalism which is to already have all the answers up its theological sleeve. Whereas social analysis conducted upon a purely natural basis need not justify such an approach as the reality and existence of nature or society is empirically given, when proponents of a Christian sociology begin from the assumption of a reality 'beyond nature' and 'beyond society,' they are more or less faced from the outset with the problem of justifying this belief. As a standpoint for doing sociology, as opposed to a mere private belief of an individual researcher, the supernatural has to be evidenced by some social or empirical means in order to be credible. The project of a Christian sociology was largely stillborn, then, because the problem of evidencing the supernatural upon the basis of *modern contingency* never arose insofar as *it was assumed the fact of the Church and its obvious impact upon society, culture and history constituted empirical evidence of the supernatural at work.*

If the devout supernaturalists, however, can be excused for failing to complete a project they never attempted, those who cannot be excused are those who rightly refused this convenient 'at hand' evidence of the supernatural but who failed to 're-found' the supernatural outwith the visible Church and upon the purely natural or purely social basis of integral contingency. If the supernaturalists applied already established principles from theology to the social order without suspecting that a real effort at coming-to-know that new social order was a precondition for coming-to-know the new categories of being and religious experience that would inculturate the Gospel into terms that modern men and women could understand, the non-supernaturalists likewise failed to articulate a purely natural and purely social post-metaphysical foundation for the supernatural, and so the real failure lay with those who recognised that specifically modern features of culture and society were stumbling blocks to faith and sources of alienation from belief in the supernatural; with those who recognised that the cultural and social realm were realities in their own right which merited their own *sui generic* study as a precondition for discerning whether or not they could mediate higher orders of human experience.

Even would-be post-supernaturalists who saw the reconciliation of the social and supernatural required much more than the Church as evidence of the supernatural *assumed precisely that which needed to be established*: the existence of the supernatural at work in contemporary society. What the advocates of a Christian sociology failed to realise needed to be put to the test was the very possibility of the advent of the supernatural to modernised *dasein*, and so they had unwittingly stumbled upon the fight of their lives; for unless they could bring these two orders into alignment, they would in their own way become *agents of secularisation in their own eyes*. Alternately, if the would-be 'Christian sociologists' had accomplished this then their standpoint would have become immanent to contextual *dasein* and being modern and the 'proof of concept' of a Christian sociology would have been secured, and some of the pain that was to explode into plain view among post-Conciliar generations could have been avoided.

With the benefit of historical hindsight, this failure to establish a Christian sociology was consubstantial or iso-morphic with other failures of Christianity, such as the failure of nineteenth-century Neoscholastic theology to offer a credible *modern* narrative of the supernatural, the failure of nineteenth and twentieth century theologians to 'flesh out' or incarnate God in the modern industrial era, and so in their own way they repeated the much earlier nominalist failure insofar as it had 'discovered' integral contingency, but had ultimately failed to articulate a contextual theology or a post-supernaturalist account of the advent of the supernatural in conditions of modernity; a failure which according to Long (2010) is ongoing in the current post-conciliar context.

The fundamental failure remains the failure to establish the *analogia entis*, or a relationship between the supernatural and the post-agrarian industrial era empirical reality that can overturn or at least offer some kind of resistance to the common sense view of the likes of Corrie when describing his fictionalised Cardenden in *Black Earth* (1939, p.1): "Neither the stars nor the moon seemed interested in the little township beneath them. And why should they? What was down there to interest eternal things?" The failure to compliment the traditional question of natural theology by developing a purely social and modern basis for theology meant attempts at a Christian sociology suffered a perennial identity crisis until calls for a Christian sociology disappeared from the membership of the ACSS by the nineteen-fifties (Varacalli, in Kivisto 1989, p. 358) and, most tellingly of all, the very institutions established to resist the secularisation of social theory themselves succumbed to the forces of naturalism or 'secularisation,' so that in 1970 The American Catholic Sociological Society (ACSS) became The Association for the Sociology of Religion (ASR), while its journal *The American Catholic Sociological Review* secularised itself and became *Sociological Analysis*.

The back-story to this self-secularisation was the older clerical members of the European CISR and the American ACSS tended to favour a theologically-inspired sociology, while a younger generation of lay members of the CISR and ACSS criticised *sociologie religieuse* as theoretically under-developed but, crucially, abandoned the creative tension of locating the supernatural within the realm of secondary natures in their research and methodological debates, so that both the memberships of the ACSS and CISR more or less split between those who advocated the existence of a Catholic sociology and those who "sought to maintain an autonomous sphere for sociological discourse separate from social philosophy and Catholic theology" (Kivisto 1989, p. 356). In continental Europe, Leclercq, like Ralph Gallagher in America, lived to see the secularisation of the organization he had founded at the hands of a new generation of members who were neither clerics nor theologians. By the 1970s the CISR like its American counterpart had become just another academic society concerned with promoting the sociology of religion.

While a younger generation recognised large swathes of populations immersed in modern industrial social and cultural conditions were alienated from the supernatural, insofar as they failed to articulate a relationship between these new conditions and the supernatural, the project of a Christian sociology was unable to challenge mainstream sociology's truism that modernisation entailed secularisation. If no sociologist did more than Max Weber to articulate the sociological thesis of Western secularisation, we look in vain for the Christian sociologist who credibly articulated the counter-narrative of 'modernisation is sacralisation' and resist Weber's thesis that modern processes of rationalisation and differentiation of life-spheres led to secularisation. No Christian sociology demonstrated that the same sociological processes could be embraced as a new starting point for articulating how the supernatural was possible and in fact operative in a new way in conditions of modernity, and how modern processes and new social conditions were ultimately the very conditions, and not simply stumbling blocks, that made experience of the supernatural possible for contemporary men and women socialised and immersed in these modern social conditions.

There is no small irony in the fact that just as an open invitation was extended to the kind of vision for sociology which had been pioneered by the founders of the ACSS and the CISR i.e. a post-positivistic sociology, "there was no one interested in responding to the call" (Fitzpatrick 1978, cited in Kivisto 1989, p. 360). After the pluralisation of standpoints for sociology that emerged from the nineteen-eighties, and in response to Gouldner's call for a Catholic sociology from the perspective of the option for the poor, the theologian turned sociologist Gregory Baum concluded: "I do not think it would be a useful strategy" (cited in Izuzquiera 2006, p. 403-4n). Intriguingly, the fact that the call for a different kind of sociology became mainstream from the nineteen-eighties was itself the result of another history of failure of another kind of sociology, this time the failure of purely naturalistic sociology to emulate the hard sciences and as the next section will detail, the criticisms levelled at attempts at a Christian sociology bore a striking resemblance to purely secular or materialist forms of 'doing sociology' that had a commitment to human liberation.

## 8.4 The Failure of Secularism as a Paradigm for Sociology

If Christian thinkers largely failed to successfully engage with the new industrial era as an opportunity for the re-foundation of their understanding of God's presence to history, and his 'adventability' to industrial *dasein* and *mitsein*, it seemed only a matter of time before purely naturalistic thinkers succeeded where they had failed thanks to being free of any theological baggage, and which meant they could wholeheartedly embraced the new bourgeois free-market era as the new basis upon which to achieve Man's liberation from inequality and poverty, and begin the rational organisation of economy and society. Such theorists of the new post-*gemeinschaft* order had no hesitation in sloughing off any remnants of 'organicism' from their social theory as their materialist recognition and emphasis upon class struggle became installed as a central feature of their social theory and political activism. From the outset, then, a purely natural social theory sought to achieve a materialist conception of Man's integral liberation not only upon non-idealist philosophical sources such as Hegel but upon no appeal to transcendence. As Giddens (1986, p. 4) put it from his modernist/secularist point of view: "In the French Revolution...for the first time in history there took place the overall dissolution of a social order by a movement guided by purely secular ideals – universal liberty and equality."

However, the great strength of mind shown by the likes of Feuerbach (1804-1872) and Marx (1818-1883) in their pursuit of a post-metaphysical foundation for a radically liberating and critical social theory and destruction of all manner of 'supernaturalism' was accompanied by a fatal weakness. When Feuerbach (1957), for example, declared theology to be simply an alienated form of anthropology, and claimed to have discovered the alienated anthropology hidden within theology, he appeared to solve a great riddle for those already wearied of the long failure of philosophers and theologians to articulate the purely natural apotheosis of the fully contextualised human being. Feuerbach's claim answered or 'spoke to' some of the long durée failures of European modernity, and his readers imagined the great achievement of demythologisation had dissolved the 'superstitious' tension of the transcendent and the immanent, and found a kind of liberation in this naturalisation of the European mind and Feuerbach's 'simplification' of the burden of 'being European' and 'being modern' and 'being Christian.' With Feuerbach, the dominant self-understanding of the modern era becomes that of instantiating a caesura with the past (Ardener 1985), and the significance of the issue that had tormented European minds was lost sight of insofar as it was claimed that the solution to what had been troubling the European mind for centuries could be peremptorily summarised as the 'materialist' triumph over 'idealism.'

While Feuerbach gave a plausible explanation for the existence of religion for the dogmatic non-believer by explaining it away, for many non-believers and believers Feuerbach resolved nothing. Perhaps the real achievement of Feuerbach was to 'clear the decks' to allow the question of Man's purely natural beatitude to take centre stage – although the issue of the natural beatitude of Man remained whole and entire, and far from showing history a clean pair of heels, Feuerbach had simply succeeded in resurrecting the twelfth-century problematic of a purely natural human beatitude and failed, just like his twelfth and thirteenth century forebears, to give any account of it, and so the great merit of Feuerbach was precisely his retrieval of this long durée problematic. However, as I will argue, in this regard Feuerbach was to prove to be a template for the failure of Marxism and twentieth century critical social theory's attempts to find an immanent anchor for a purely natural account of integral human liberation.

Despite their mutual antagonism, the tie that bound Christianity and Marxism together was the task of imagining a non-alienated human *dasein* and society, and Feuerbach's *Essence of Christianity* ([1841] 1957) may serve as the watershed text because it is here that the tension of the integral revolution, the link between the twelfth-century and the nineteenth-century industrial era, is taken up again only to fail, because of the failure to articulate the purely natural beatitude of a particular class-based *dasein*. Marx and everyone else, of course, quickly spotted the fact that Feuerbach had given a de-contextualised or universalist treatment of the problem, and was fully confident that a fully contextualised account of human liberation would be forthcoming. However, the fact is that rather than solving a long-standing problem, Marx himself imitated Feuerbach's weakness for liquidating long durée problematics with the stroke of his 'materialist' pen, such as when he wrote that "liberation is an historical and not a mental act" (Marx, cited in Arthur 1970, p. 61).

There is something tragic and comedic in noting Marx's celebrated ending of idealist philosophy occurred wholly within the realm of 'pure reason,' and the same can be said of Marx's theory of working-class liberation, which is drawn entirely from the philosophical reflections of members of society whose ideas Marx was otherwise keen to expose as ideology. As a member of that social elite himself, Marx's ideas on the sociology of knowledge should have meant his own ideas should have remained ideological weapons that could neither know nor liberate working-class *dasein* or *mitsein*. How Marx escaped the social determinations he was quick to identify in the 'idealistic' thought of others, and how he neither needed a contextualised phenomenology of working-class *dasein* nor a theory of working-class liberation from the 'inside' yet could still claim to theorise their freedom *in a non-idealist fashion*, reveals the extent of the reliance upon 'pure reason' by the advocates of what was called 'materialism.'

With the benefit of historical hindsight it is clear to us today that Marx produced a version of Hegel in which the Hegelian subject's dialectical journey to self-knowledge and liberation was replaced by a non-empirically and non-historically verified *theory* of history and *theory* of society. While it is clear that Marx envisaged the need for the de-mystification of consciousness, and despite his purely idealistic disavowal of idealism, Marx did indeed presuppose a purely intellectual or mental liberation, he himself nowhere gave an account of it. The articulation of this particular aspect of human liberation was only taken up by others such as György Lukács (1885–1971) and Karl Korsch (1886-1961) who saw the absence of a 'materialist' phenomenology of mind or account of revolutionary consciousness as a fatal weakness in Marx and one which they sought to correct. In this regard Lukács's *History and Class Consciousness* ([1923] 1971) remains the landmark effort insofar as it attempted a revision of Marxism, and attempted to succeed where the idealist Hegel and the 'materialist' Feuerbach and Marx had failed, by effecting a reconciliation between Hegel's view (in Hodgson 1984, p. 113) that: "Human beings are truly human through consciousness – by virtue of the fact that they think and by virtue of the fact that they are spirit," and the material condition of alienation where a person's real social existence is in conflict with his human essence.

While for Hegel it was Christianity which recognised the "cleavage of the subject, of the ego, from the infinite" (cited in

Hodgson 1984, p. 105), this theological overcoming of alienation became naturalised in Feuerbach and Lukacs as a historical and political imperative of the proletariat to reconcile its existential self with its objective social conditions and achieve the Hegelian 'identical subject-object.' Lukacs, then, recognised (1971, p. 68): "The unique function of consciousness in the class struggle of the proletariat has consistently been overlooked by the vulgar Marxists who have substituted a petty 'Realpolitik' for the great battle of principle," and in his *History and Class Consciousness* (1971) he set himself the task of describing a dialectical process whereby "the proletariat is the identical subject-object of the history of society became truly concrete" (1971, p. 206). However, already in this text, Lukacs (1971, pp. 205-6) had advised his reader:

> The individual stages of this process cannot be sketched in here. They alone would be able to show how proletarian class consciousness evolves dialectically (i.e. how the proletariat becomes a class). Only then would it be possible to throw light on the intimate dialectical process of interaction between the socio-historical situation and the class consciousness of the proletariat.

From the outset, then, it was recognised that some kind of description of this process was desperately needed. However, when writing a new preface to his classic text published in 1967, Lukacs (1971, p. xxiii) not only failed to give what he promised in 1923, but rejected the project of the proletarian coming into intellectual possession of himself as a *res cogitans* as a utopian fantasy:

> But is the identical subject-object here anything more in truth than a purely metaphysical construct? Can a genuinely identical subject-object be created by self-knowledge, however adequate?...We need only formulate the question precisely to see that it must be answered in the negative.

Lukacs's abandoning of the task of giving an account of what the European mind had cut itself in half for all the better to achieve, goes a long way to explaining the failure of radical social theory and the current post-Enlightenment malaise, as it represents another chapter in the long durée failure to find something which the European mind has been searching for since the twelfth-century i.e. an account of the purely natural apotheosis of Man or the 'identical subject-object' via an act of self-understanding. If today such reflexive acts and cognitional agency are deemed imaginary constructs of 'pure reason,' the failure of the Lukacsian project is a crucial factor in explaining the defeatism that Habermas (2010) has alluded to.

Similarly, for Held (1981) and Bronner (1994), the nineteen-twenties and thirties were decisive insofar as the failure of the working classes to challenge the rise of fascism and the capitalist social order meant that, by the nineteen-forties, the Frankfurt School had already displayed a symptomatic malaise regarding the ambition of articulating the purely natural apotheosis of contextual human *dasein* and had become hostile to the idea of the standpoint of the working class being the 'subject of history,' as well as hostile to the related Hegelian and Lukacsian notion of an actual or potential unity between subject and object. In their acclaimed *Dialectic of Enlightenment* ([1944] 1973) Adorno and Horkheimer's view that the proletariat was *not* the revolutionary subject of history was consubstantial with the end of any real belief in the ability of reason to illuminate social and political practice in a revolutionary way. As the defeated Adorno (1974, p. 28) put it: "In the end, glorification of splendid underdogs is nothing other than glorification of the splendid system that makes them so. The justified guilt-feelings of those exempt from physical work ought not become an excuse for the 'idiocy of rural life.'"

This demotion of the proletariat from their starring role thanks to their failure to fulfill their assigned role within the Marxist imagination, more or less signaled the end of the (left-wing) Enlightenment project which, bereft of any anchorage in the working class, led more or less directly to a reliance upon the weapons of 'pure reason' which in turn resulted in a certain despair at reason. If there was a healthy recognition that 'pure reason' was simply incapable of directing political practice or of knowing or liberating different contexts and different contingencies, there was no immersion in particularity, and Horkheimer refused to identify the freedom of the individual with any objective political ideology or social arrangement, either Soviet socialism or Western capitalism, to the point where any kind of social anchor for the project of triangulating humanity and modernity and Christianity was lost. Adorno's 'negative dialectics' theoretically sanctioned this flight from particularity and contingency by affirming the non-identity between the person and his or her social conditions, and referred to the "ontology of false conditions" in the name of an endangered subjectivity. For Adorno, any position which claimed to articulate a relationship of 'identity' between reason and reality was by definition ideology, and such was the contradiction held to obtain between the socialised self and authentic human being that Adorno (in Held 1981, p. 72) spoke of a 'totally administered' subjectivity:

> Adaptation of men to social relationships...has left its mark on them such that...even breaking free mentally...has come to seem a fable and a distant one. Men have come to be - triumph of integration! - identified in their innermost behaviour patterns with their fate in modern society.

Perhaps the theorist associated with the Frankfurt school who came closest to recognising that 'pure reason' had to be overcome by an ethnographic turn was Herbert Marcuse (1898-1979), as already in 1928 he had drawn the conclusion that a phenomenology of *dasein* in the style of Heidegger's *Being and Time* ([1926] 1962) was inadequate because it bypassed material conditions, and that it was fruitless to ask questions concerning concrete human existence in terms of 'existence itself' in the manner of Heidegger, because the division of society into classes meant there were a number of different human existences because there were different social existences. Describing Heidegger's position as one where: "Daily existence...can recall its own actual being; it can take over "being itself (*Siende*) in its dejectedness" (Marcuse 1969, p. 15),

Marcuse was optimistic that: "The labour of the proletarian prevents any self-fulfilment; his work negates his entire existence. This utmost negativity, however, takes a positive turn" (Marcuse, cited in Held 1980, p. 239), although, as per Lukacs, he similarly failed to give an empirical analysis of how 'utmost negativity' could take a positive turn.

This problematic of proletarian autonomy or freedom similarly preoccupied Cornelius Castoriadis (1922-1997) who had also identified the absence of any real analysis of *dasein* within Marxism as a major theoretical weakness. In *The Imaginary Institution of Society* (1987, p. 57) Castoriadis recognised, in contrast to vanguard positions which valorised the role of the Party or an intelligentsia, that "the emancipation of the workers will be the work of the workers themselves:"

> We cannot directly present a theory, even our own, as 'representing the point of view of the proletariat', for the history of the past century has shown that, far from offering the solution to all the problems, the point of view of the proletariat is itself a problem, for which only the proletariat (let us say, to avoid quibbling, labouring humanity) will be able to invent, or will fail to invent, a solution (1987, p. 36).

In the opinion of Castoriadis, an adequate account of the specifically symbolic aspect of domination was necessary if the possibility of the purely natural apotheosis, whereby an uncoerced ego becomes identical with itself, was to be realised. Also, the problem of giving an answer to Lukacs's question (1971, p. 46) "what, then, is the meaning of class consciousness?" for Castoriadis was yet to be answered because "the relation between the revolutionaries and the masses, remains whole and entire" (1987, p. 61). In the aftermath of the fall of the Berlin Wall in 1989 and the global triumph of the neoliberal New World Order, such practico-theoretical problems for many seem more or less obsolete. However, the attempt to articulate the notion of the free or autonomous worker is not simply the last remnants of the old

Hegelian cud, as what lies beneath this project is the twelfth-century turning to immanence as Hegel's phenomenology was from start to finish a more or less obvious attempt to naturalise the Christian's duty to work out his or her salvation.

The modernist phase of social theory started out confidently believing a liberation from religion had happened as a result of the advent of modernity, and to this was added the belief that this liberation was a precondition for the emergence of a fully autonomous social theory.[141] However, when Marx asserted in *Towards A Critique of Hegel's Philosophy of Right* (1844) that "the criticism of religion is the presupposition of all criticism" (cited in McLellan 1977, pp. 63-74), he was paying a debt to Strauss's *Life of Jesus* (1835) as it was Strauss's epochal criticism of supernaturalism both in theology and historical scholarship that informed every subsequent (alleged) materialist critique of idealist philosophical thinking about the nature of society. It was Strauss who had broken the taboo of critiquing religion, and it was thanks to him that demythologisation became the order of the day for a generation of thinkers free to criticise 'everything that exists,' so that Marxism may be described as a school of Straussian demythologisation insofar as Marx's ambition was to do for social theory what Strauss had achieved for theology and the history of religion.

It was from Christian theologians, then, that 'left Hegelians' such as Feuerbach and Marx learned how to 'do sociology' and demythologise the state and religion and bourgeois society, because it was Strauss the demythologising theologian who provided Feuerbach with a model of how to dispense with 'supernaturalism' as a result of nineteenth-century theologians'

---

[141] Probably the most well-known example of the secularisation thesis in social theory and the myth of modern societies being post-Christian, and sociology as the study of modern societies being more or less coerced into being non-religious, is Comte's 'law of the three stages' according to which human history has passed through three stages: (1) the theological stage (until 1300), (2) the metaphysical stage (from c.1300 to 1800) and (3) the positive stage (from 1800) characterised by belief in science (Gane 2006).

search for the historical Jesus of Nazareth as opposed to the Christ of faith. We might make the case then that Marx was not Straussian enough insofar as Marx remained happy to chew the old Hegelian cud, and retained much of the idealist Hegelian edifice which Strauss had already exposed as unhistorical. In his *Defence of My Life of Jesus Against the Hegelians* Strauss (1983, p. 8) observed: "Hegel was personally no friend of historical critique. It annoyed him, as it annoyed Goethe, [to] see the heroic figures of antiquity, to which their higher feeling clung lovingly, gnawed at by critical doubt. If, occasionally, these figures were puffs of mist which they took to be pieces of rock, they did not want to know." In conclusion, then, we may say that despite the great prospects for human freedom opened up by Marxism, this great promise had become largely exhausted by the nineteen-seventies in Western Europe, with Marxism itself criticised as having become an obsolete set of ideas. In the opinion of Piccone and Delfini (1970, p. 38), for example: "Marcuse is the only philosopher who has addressed himself to today's problems as they are…and not as they should be according to some preconstituted ideological scheme."

## 8.5 An Integral Sociology

The similarity between the failure to develop a Christian or supernatural sociology and the failure to develop a purely secular account of integral liberation is striking. What is also interesting is that both projects failed because both failed to articulate a performative account of the purely natural apotheosis of fully contextualised *dasein*. Firstly 'religious' and then 'secular' thinkers attempted to come to terms with the new industrial order emerging around them, and both attempts failed to break with 'pure reason' or 'faith positions' and establish themselves purely upon 'secondary natures.' With the benefit of hindsight it is clear that critical theory in its allegedly 'materialist' guise in fact failed to transcend the (Christian) idealism of Hegel, and reproduced the failure of those Christians who wished to break with supernaturalism, and both projects based their critiques of social conditions upon a merely theological or philosophical rebellion of pure reason that could not find in concrete ethnographic reality the means to leverage the transformation needed.

In light of this shared failure the way is clear for embracing a fuller conception of modernity and the conscious rejection of a false modernist understanding of *dasein*; an understanding of modernity and *dasein* that allies with the artistic modernity of Baudelaire who wished painting to depict the contemporary and the everyday, and that allies with the modernity of Benjamin who wished to recapture "the glow of the profane" (cited in Bronner 1994, p. 6), as these artists draw upon the original inspiration of Giotto to paint modernity and *dasein* with a full palette of colour. Similarly, the way is clear to be modern with Foucault for whom being modern is to cultivate a critical relationship to one's contingency via instantiating a dialectical relationship of accepting oneself while simultaneously 'breaking with' the self, in order to elaborate a critical encounter with one's historicity and fashion one's authenticity and sanctification.

Given this recent history of intellectual failure from the nineteenth and twentieth centuries, one can better appreciate the difficulties faced by twelfth-century theologians trying to break free from philosophy and theology *with only the tools of philosophy and theology to do so*. Inaugurating an anthropological turn against a dominant supernaturalism was clearly a task that ordinarily had to fail, and both the attempt and particular failures are blood relatives of nineteenth and twentieth-century theorists in both the Christian and the Marxist tradition attempting to instantiate an anthropological turn against the dominant idealist philosophers to secure a profane or secular anchor for liberation.

The failure of secular sociology to deliver an account of integral liberation has a direct counterpart in Christian sociology's failure to evidence the supernatural at work in capitalist society, so that the original breakthrough and subsequent failure of the twelfth-century has been recapitulated in secular form and in religious form. While it is now recognised that theology and metaphysics heavily influenced secular theorists in their search for a critique of the industrial capitalist social order, we can see in the rise and fall of Marxism the same rise and fall pattern within the Christian tradition, where a founding 'revelation' simultaneously highlighted the nature of a particular reality and more or less effectively ended the need to dialogue with and learn from empirical reality, so that Marxism like the Church discovered the hard way that a 'truth,' whether religious or secular, when inherited second-hand rather than re-established afresh upon the basis of integral contingency, becomes a set of *a priori* truths that leads to disdain for calls for its experiential verification. If purely naturalistic sociology when faced with the issues of ethnographic verification resorted to the idealism of Hegel which it retained up its 'naturalistic' sleeve, we might characterise the failed project of a Christian sociology as the approach which when faced with the problem of explaining the modern 'adventability' of the living God, always had the answer up its 'theological' sleeve.

Having argued that the error modernism is disastrous for thinking Scottish *dasein* and the nation, we can also say now is the time for a reconciliation or a higher synthesis of these erstwhile rivals that recognises the only solution is to pursue an open-eyed and deliberate tension between fully contextualised *dasein* and the deep ballast (nation, religion, class etcetera) it needs to reach its perfections. Now is the time to recognise that an epistemology incompatible with the *analogia entis* is also likely to have disastrous effects upon the resolve to think human being with a full palette of colour, because the *analogia entis* is in league with the need to break with modernist anthropology and a modernist view of history, because it delivers us from intellectual lives where nothing *final* can be achieved by our understanding our contingent and 'fleeting' secondary natures, and delivers us from national histories where, again, nothing of eternal significance is at play.

Our exercise of secondary causality such as the act of self-understanding that we have described and whose content is contingent, not only safeguards our natural apotheosis but our existential opening to the supernatural and "the novelty and gratuity of Jesus Christ" (Healy 2008, p. 535). If contingency 'captures' eternity, then we are obliged to refuse to entertain a way of being modern or a way of being Scottish or a way of being Christian that is independent of fully contextualised *dasein*.

Similarly, to be rejected is a way of imagining 'being historical' where the destination and the meaning and direction of history is already known, so that contextual *dasein* is again irrelevant to coming-to-consciousness of this destination and journeying to this destination. Also, all such claims to such knowledge which require contextual *dasein* to exercise blind faith are to be rejected as they require each class to instantiate a forgetfulness of its being. If, by definition, the modernist imagination cannot unite the person or a nation with its past then a modernist sociology cannot furnish 'depth interpretations' of thick events such as 1 July 1999 or what is likely to come after 18 September 2014, nor give an account of Scotland today where a twelfth-century long durée patrimony has not only survived but is driving current events and which on any modernist reckoning was never meant to happen.

As the politician quoted at the beginning of Chapter 4 reminds us, twenty-first century nations and peoples are not supposed to go back to the twelfth century to retrieve institutions in order to resolve the problem of how to 'be modern,' and even the modernist nationalist likes to object that this resurrection of 'medievalism' is in fact just the epiphenomenal 'period costume' worn by modern social forces, and certainly not their *conditione sine qua non*. However, theorists of nationalism have more or less established the 'perennial' need for period costume because *it is integral to modernised dasein and mitsein*, and the empirical proof is that four centuries of 'all that is solid melts into air' modernism have not been sufficient to liquidate the need for period costumes because the condition of 'being modern' requires the ballast of the past (or period costume) to constitute the tension of 'being modern.'

Something the Scots know after 1 July 1999 and will know again after 18 September 2014 is that what is glossed as the epiphenomenal need for 'period costume' is in fact the perennial need for a holistic self-understanding that can stand against the "ontology of false conditions" (Adorno, cited in Bronner 1994, p. 181), and because fundamental elements of contextual *dasein* cannot be wished away or dissolved in the acid bath of modernity, the whole of past history and the whole of history to come will continue to be a 'fancy dress' affair as modern nations and modern peoples will not wake up one day and cut themselves in half.

The merit of a fully integral sociology, then, is that the account it is able to generate of Man's purely natural apotheosis is more convincing than any account drawn by the modernist mythology, and from those who choose to paint modern *dasein* with very little colour at their disposal. Another merit is that the account it is able to provide of 'becoming Christian' is far more convincing than any supernaturalist theology lacking any ethnographic content or grounding. If the likes of Carlyle and Nietzsche were right to proclaim the drama of modernity had been the death of God, an integral sociology is able to resurrect the drama of human being and being Christian on the basis of modern secondary natures, and succeed in articulating a phenomenology of Christian redemption.

If "The 'modern[ist] man' – that is to say, the post-Renaissance man - is ready for burial" (Yorck, cited in Heidegger 1962, p. 452) it is because affluence and education have 'democratised' the rejection of impoverished imaginings of *dasein* and so, if even the modernists today in Scotland's anti-independence political parties accept they have been negligent in the 'fancy dress' department, when these erstwhile un-maskers and demythologisers turn upon themselves the structure of perception they train upon others, they are more or less fated to don 'fancy dress' if they are to acknowledge the need for a holistic or integral symbolic structure to match and mirror and model our integral or holistic *dasein* and *mitsein*. Once this step is taken, all forms of bourgeois modernism from Marxism to liberalism become part of the problem to be solved as their faulty view of human *dasein* and their materialism and idealism means *they are profoundly unreal*, and so find themselves in need of new masks and new myths if they are to be suitably dressed for twenty-first century Scotland.

Also, whether social science is to be similarly suitably attired or only fit for the dustbin of intellectual history is a pressing question, as Douglas and Ney's (1998) search for an adequate view of man other than *homo economicus* among Western social scientists reveals the latter's complicity insofar as sociology did not so much release the study of Man from the 'mystifications' of theology and philosophy but re-make the study of Man in the image of a 'scarcity metaphysics.' Insofar as the 'demystifying' and 'demythologising' Hume, Feuerbach, Comte, Marx and Freud wished to erect a new modern 'science of man' and steal back Man's 'essence' from the pedlars of supernaturalism (theologians) and 'pure reason' (philosophers), the effort was to be applauded because in its own clumsy way it was a rebalancing and return to the twelfth-century Franciscan opening to the defeat of super-naturalism and the turning to nature, society and the world. However, insofar as it fell into the same errors of the Renaissance and declined into secularism and modernism, the nineteenth century succeeded only too well and repeated the failure of the twelfth century to secure its breakthrough in the European mind insofar as they dissolved all of philosophy and theology into 'fancy-dress' clothing, which they set about removing in order to reveal Man as they imagined he really is and always had been. However, for as long as the majority of populations remained within the 'dictatorship of scarcity' era, this modernist error only affected a fraction of the population.

Today, however, the struggle to resist modernism in favour of integralism embraces all who are literate and is becoming the general condition. We may also say that for as long as sociological studies were conducted in conditions of scarcity, there was more or less a rationale for 'reading off' behaviour or action from social position, because social conditions meant the practice of a reflexive 'freedom' hardly arose for the vast majority of the population. There was then a crude sense to arguing 'being poor' or 'uneducated' explained why poor and uneducated people were religious, for example, or religion was functional to social cohesion. If this could pass as an explanation of social phenomenon such as religion, a secularist metaphysics or disenchanted view of *dasein* and European history did not necessarily cause too much damage, or obstruct sociological explanation and so sociology was not coerced into examining its modernist assumptions. However, with the loosening of the grip of scarcity upon the practice of freedom from the nineteen-eighties onwards, this 'scarcity sociology' is more or less obsolete, and these explanations explain less and less as sociology is forced to recognise, defend and then shed its modernist assumptions.

If for most of its history sociology turned its attention to a fraction of Man's being and pre-occupied itself with the 'scarcity questions' of social order and conformity (Bauman 1976), this era has come to an end insofar as the relation between 'social structure' and 'superstructure' is now free to be particularised and individuated for each particular social group. More than ever as a result of affluence and deep literacy, then, to continue to confine *dasein/mitsein* and its sociological study into a 'scarcity metaphysics' is regressive, insofar as it disfigures the purely social or immanent realm because such an approach harries and presses the natural and social and cultural to deprive itself of its historicity, religiosity, nationality and locality etcetera.

To persist in such *modernist interpretivism* is to make sociology not the study of the social as it is really experienced and lived and thought about by real men and women, but to align sociology with a mythical account of Man made in the image of the post-Christian nineteenth-century bourgeoisie, and lock the social sciences into a nineteenth-century class myth about human *dasein*. By depriving itself of the means to imagine how men and women live their lives and experience their social and cultural conditions, sociology condemns itself to a myth about Man and not Man himself. I say this despite the deluge of declarations by 'postmodernists' that modernity is at an end as these declarations in fact reproduce the error of modernism *all over again* insofar as the historic opportunity to recapitulate and reappropriate History (and Christianity) is once again avoided in favour of declaring purely imaginary caesuras once again under cover of a turning to the new.

A sociology that recognises the objective social pressures for the privatisation of the realm of meaning and behaviour, so that more and more of conventional beliefs and practices become the free choice of the free individual and so become more or less fated to decline, must not itself fall victim to such pressures and declare issues of fundamental anthropology and ontology a 'private' matter for the individual practitioner of sociology. A discipline which buckles under this pressure which it is obliged to study becomes infected with the modernist germ and proclaims, just as with forebears such as Feuerbach and Marx, that by recognising the 'signs of the times' the discipline thereby comes into alignment with history and society. Another reading, however, of the present moment informed by the ballast of the long durée sees these pressures as the latest terms of engagement of a tension or dialectic that is as old as modernity itself, and one which we really should be learning to recognise by now, so that when faced with the new 'new' we should by now be bringing more balance to our interpretations and more ballast to readings of the 'present as history,' instead of the clichés of capitulation to conditions that are false (Adorno) or, on the other hand, imagining we must begin from scratch and take the latest development as the new standard by which to measure ourselves.

Much as at the outset of the industrialisation of European society in the nineteenth century, so at the outset of the present post-industrialisation of European society, there are those readying themselves to assert once again that 'all that is solid melts into air,' and readying themselves to declare yet another radical break with the past, this time with the modern era. And once again the modernist imagination is as much wrong as it is right. Because it is far easier to proclaim the end of a number of difficult tasks than reconstitute them upon the basis of new conditions, today's post-structuralist rhetoric of 'endings' and the lionising of tropes such as fragmentation, dispersal, decentering and difference, stems not from a bourgeois relation to 'the real' but from a bourgeois relation to a bourgeois myth about history and Man and the present.

What complicates the prospect of reaching any consensus upon the correct understanding of the present as history is the existence of different social classes that are not going away, and the fact that occupying a subordinate or dominant position within a hierarchy does not simply mean that each position is related to a shared reality such as 'history' or 'society' or 'reason' or 'the present' albeit differently, as the very range and nature of objects are different for each different class and are not shared across classes because the relations are different, and so what constitutes 'objectivity' and what there is to be objective about is different.

The emergent turn to and recognition of particularism in social theory signals a crisis for the intellectuals of that social class which has most 'symbolic capital' to lose from the end of universalism, and an opportunity for that class which has most to gain from the end of universalism. On this reading much of the malaise of contemporary social theory stems from the middle class attempting to come to terms with its cultural decline. In its modernist and 'optimistic' phase which corresponds to its historic rise to hegemony, and in its current 'postmodern' pessimistic or post-'heroic' bourgeois phase, the same class relation to the totality remains. Modernism then was the ideology of the confident and emergent bourgeoisie and *was a cipher for this particular class's domination of the modern imaginary and their domination of how the present and the future were imagined.* The post-modern rhetoric of endings, then, signals an imagination becoming aware that it is bereft of historical ballast or 'fancy dress,' and this is the sociological truth that underlies intellectuals' discussions concerning the end of rationalism and universalism, and reveals the recent ideology of postmodernism as the cipher of an erstwhile domination and power to signify the present coming to an end.

If this analysis is not entirely off the mark then the profound knitting together of selves and circumstances that, once seen and appreciated in one group must be conceded as occurring in all groups, means that each class's habitus is equally 'fatal;' that bourgeois *dasein* even in theory *is not* more readily holistic or more dynamic and open to departing from the past and from mere empirical reality, because *in practice* this very freedom means a greater level of freely committing to merely reproducing their socially privileged position at the expense of operationalising any cultural or political leadership of the nation, or developing the historicity of *dasein* and thereby putting social reproduction at risk. In the case of Scotland this fatal grip of habitus or 'secondary nature' has resulted in perhaps the most depoliticised and miserably modernist middle-class Europe has ever seen; a middle class that did not even partially 'correct' Scottish history by leading the modest change of 1 July 1999.

To explain this strange failure of nerve, I argue it is because their social condition is to enjoy the 'privilege' of not having to be more or less coerced into doing something about historical and national *dasein*, that all talk of the historicity and nationality of *dasein* was more or less embarrassing for this class that fulfils none of the leadership roles other national bourgeoisies perform. If a Heideggerian reading of authentic *dasein* emphasises the fundamental exigence whereby "authentic Dasein must 'choose itself'" (Wolin 1990, p. 75), then this is a class that is afraid to mobilise its historicity and nationality and presides over an education system that is deeply ambivalent, if not resentful, towards going beyond the liberal peace, to say nothing about the under-development of all things purely Scottish, or the question of transcendence among them. If this has been a class that has been incapable of inaugurating a Scottish modernity, then from the point of view of the 'end of history' thesis of Fukuyama (1989), his thesis has been true among the Scottish middle classes for centuries.

In contrast to Prime Minister Blair asserting in 1999 when addressing his Party's annual conference: "The class war is over. But the struggle for true equality has only just begun," it has to be asserted that the 'mirror of production' remains intact in the era of affluence, and this diagnosis of the 'present as history' is a perfect example of bourgeois thinking fated to misrecognise the fact that Scottish history is being made by a class which is supposed to be 'finished' thanks to the class war having been won by the middle classes some time in the nineteen-nineties. Socio-economically and cultural-territorially-grounded epistemologies and subjectivities remain intact and still go unrecognised and untheorised in the dominant discourses as a result of three inter-related positions that stem from a class habitus that more or less coerces its bearers into imagining the working class in their image, and that the working class:

1) instantiate the same (bourgeois) relation to the real.

2) have been 'dissolved' by affluence and post-industrialisation.

3) are equally caught up in their individuation reaching escape velocity from a given and determining material base.

If the 1979 working-class generation(s) are arriving to the realm of cultural production they are also fated to give their reading on 'being modern' based upon the fact that they are still confined to their socially and historically and spatially-determined *dasein*; do not ordinarily have the relation to the totality to imagine they have reached 'escape velocity' from the conditions that condition them, so that a still-defining truth is not the escape from being determined by social structure *but the free determination of what this determination means or amounts to*. If no working class escapes the 'mirror of production,' it increasingly does not take up the pre-packaged 'scarcity era' self-image the dominant symbolic order has prepared for it, nor the superannuated accommodations to domination prepared for them by the working-class 1945 generation, and so is increasingly free to work out the extent of their 'being modern' and their natural apotheosis on their own terms.

Furthermore, having articulated a purely natural beatitude, I have deliberately not left the question of transcendence open or simply trusted the 'purely natural' to arrive at the supernatural through the free exercise of its powers, as I do not share in any kind of soft liberal humanist confidence that the purely natural may be left to its own devices on this point. Even achieving a purely natural beatitude requires the exercise of a long 'repression' that leans upon the disciplinary power of (Christian) transcendence. While the appropriation of a holistic view of *dasein* and 'being modern' must be done upon the basis of its own merits, the question of transcendence and Christianity can not be simply left to the free development of *dasein* or the cut and thrust of 'affluent modernity,' because I do not believe that the felt absence of transcendence is inevitable or somehow fated to be widespread, so that 'structures of repression' (in the psychoanalytic sense) such as the family and Christianity within affluent modernity *are simultaneously not needed and more needed than ever* to avoid 'affluent modernity' becoming characterised by nihilism. Liberalism and secularism exert so little disciplinary power over *dasein* and *mitsein* to be capable of modeling even the transcendence necessary to achieve the purely natural beatitude outlined earlier, so that unless there is a free return to structures of repression, there can only be lives more or less immersed in a permanent nihilistic 'crisis of the West,' while those who remain European and Christian will remain defined by and alive to its perennial tasks and tensions.

For the modernist it seems compelling that there is a fragmentation of self, community and de-Christianisation, and to resist this representation of the 'present as history' must be a Canute-like gesture in full flight from the facts. However, insofar as there are populations that retain intact in their biographies the material of a Christian identity and its practices thanks to none of their once-peasant-and-now-proletarian ancestors having had a modernist relation to modernity, the present as history can also be understood as an affluence-fuelled reflexive liberation not *from* tradition but *an affluence-fuelled liberation of Tradition from its long confinement within the 'dictatorship of scarcity' era* insofar as the reflexive 1979 generations radicalise that (Christian) tradition, and instantiate a radical break from the modernist motif of 'modernisation as secularisation.'

While I do not contest the empirical evidence of the de-Protestantisation of Scotland and a similar process among Catholics, the definition of being modern cannot be equated with particular capitulations to modern pressures or social determinations. More concretely, then, if we follow Harvie (2004) and identify a modernisation period from 1950-1971 which saw the start of the decline in Protestantism and political unionism because from this point onwards unionism was modernised and, free of all social embeddedness, had to become the free choice of the free individual to survive, we can say there was an older generation whose behaviour and practices were de-Christianised even while their 'consciousness' or self-understanding was perhaps little de-Christianised, but in the next generation both consciousness and behaviour became aligned, and this resulted in integral de-Christianisation (which if often incorrectly equated with 'secularisation').

While many Scots have become post-Christian to judge by their consciousness and behaviour, to be modern and to be post-Christian or secular are not the same, and so to describe a younger generation that has become fully post-Christian as 'fully modern' implies the believer is somehow not modern or not as modern as the non-believer. Instead of this false interpretation we should understand 'being modern' simply as being subject to a set of objective pressures, and be careful not to identify 'being modern' with a particular set of subjective 'capitulations' or accommodations to an objective set of pressures - while at the same time recognising that it is a safe bet that there will be a 'collective' set of capitulations insofar as many will accommodate themselves to a dominant form of social conditioning that will involve *not* maintaining the full tensions of 'being modern.' This allows us to say that while there may be a majoritarian modernity, there is not one form of 'being modern' but several, and which may be ranked (from a purely secular modernity to a full Scottish modernity to a Catholic modernity etcetera) in order of possessing the fullness of modernity. The predicament of 'being modern' then is universal while the form of the response is particular.[142]

If we complicate things further by adding the radical indeterminacy of the human will and human reason (Scotus) to the indeterminacy of modernity, an appreciation of the ballast that Christianity brings to the 'tasks of freedom' of the 1979 generations is able to emerge. While all can subscribe to the pursuit of a natural apotheosis, the opening to the supernatural and the turn to Christianity ensures a purely natural humanism does not exhaust the new imagining of a free modernity, and I would paraphrase the argument of Mauss (1979, p. 84) that until Christianity "the notion of the person still lacked a firm metaphysical foundation. This foundation it owes to Christianity," and argue that as a result of Man's indeterminacy and the indeterminacy of freedom and affluent-era modernity, the repression or discipline necessary to believe and strive for *even a purely natural beatitude or apotheosis* would otherwise be lost sight of, so that the repressive

---

[142] That modernity has many forms is something that is recognised in sociological theory and is reflected in the European theory of 'modernisation as secularisation' thesis (Weber, Durkheim), and the American theory of 'modernisation as sacralisation' thesis (Parsons 1964; Greeley 1971).

or disciplinary ethos of Christianity is needed because even purely natural perfections must firstly be matters of authority and shared belief before they become matters of purely natural individual achievement.

In this regard, Bourdieu's entire oeuvre and analysis of the social condition suffers from being trapped into an account of *dasein* stripped of all dynamism towards the full range of intelligible being, and his failure to give an account of the purely natural beatitude the sociological imagination is fundamental to achieving is evidence that alerts us to the dangers of over-confidence in pure nature. Bourdieu's failure to give a reading of habitus as it dynamically moves towards its natural and supernatural perfections means that, ultimately, even the incomparable Bourdieu must be termed a pre-integral 'scarcity sociologist' insofar as he does not follow the golden rule of sociological methodology which is to follow *dasein* wherever *dasein* goes, and to think *dasein* in all its colours, and develop a metaphysics if need be that allows the inclusion of *dasein's* reflexive acts and what they lead to. In a similar manner, while Charlesworth (1999) is an exemplary ethnographer and sophisticated analyst, his phenomenological description of working-class *dasein* does not articulate the purely natural apotheosis of English working-class *dasein* and his *Phenomenology of Working Class Experience* (1999) fails to give an account of cognitional agency or intellectual and psychological liberation, far less anything concerning its capacities for the supernatural.

To practice sociology with a full palette of colours is to paint a picture of contextualised *dasein* in free possession of itself, and it is upon this basis that is decided the extent of what is real. To get to this end-point I began by introducing the term *reductio* as a descriptive phenomenological category that occurs when labouring and doing fieldwork among manual labourers. The *reductio* was described as a 'phenomenological datum' by the theorist and while *the concept* relates to he who does conceptual work, the concept does not appear to the worker who is not also an inquirer, so that the reduction is not a phenomenological category of the worker's experience insofar as he does not do the intellectual work of conceiving his patterned experience as generated by his life of manual labour. To commit to conceptual work is to move from being a worker to being a worker-inquirer and set out upon the road of giving a phenomenology of this journey. The fact is one could write endless descriptions of what appears to working-class consciousness or what appears to the student of working-class experience and, while necessary, the point of introspection and phenomenological description is not to remain purely descriptive but to mount to an adequate conceptualisation of working class being in order to arrive at an act of understanding, because the structure of the human mind dictates so because it is a formally dynamic structure. Such is what Lonergan terms following the unrestricted desire for understanding and what scholastics term allowing oneself to be led by the finality of the intellect i.e. living a life dominated by the structure of knowing which puts itself together according to its own natural exigencies.

If this is part of practicing an integral sociology, there is some truth to the argument that to paint *dasein* with a full palette of colour during the 'dictatorship of scarcity' era was fated to appear sociologically naïve and hardly evidence-based. If the accusation of a 'scarcity anthropology' levelled at Western social science by Douglas and Ney (1998) was met with the reply that most modern human beings most of the time did not paint themselves with a full palette of colours and 'fancy dress costumes' and 'sacred canopies' were deemed epiphenomenal to material realities, today, social science will fail to represent post-affluent societies adequately unless it acquires a metaphysics and an epistemology that does more than 'tolerate' human being in all its colours. A social science hoping to explain us to ourselves must articulate a holistic sociology if the 'sociological imagination' is to be relevant and realistic in the era of affluent modernity, because a feature of affluence-era societies is that the 'realm of meaning' becomes volatilised and increasingly differentiated, as each social class and tradition negotiates its survival and reproduction. Among the symbolically dominated, for example, the once-solid reality of Britain was largely based upon the *fides implicita* of the culturally and economically weak, and parents of the '45 generation who have this *fides implicita* relation to the realm of meaning have educated and modernised 1979 generation children who do not reproduce this dominated relation to the symbolic realm, nor their parents' *fides implicita*.

In terms of 'being modern,' then, many who have lived and died within a modern society have not been modern in the manner of an existential predicament as a result of being post-conventional. Many social groups have until recently been modern by proxy whereby an authority figure or institution – church, government, family, parents, husband etcetera – has been delegated the task of negotiating with modernity on their behalf, so that such social groups – women, the working class, the laity etcetera – have only recently had to deal with the predicament of being modern as their personal existential predicament. In terms of a younger working-class generation, I argue that the cocktail of events such as the cultural changes of the nineteen-sixties, affluence, deindustrialization and literacy have more or less coerced this generation into a conscientisation or awakening to the predicament of being modern.

However, even when a whole array of sociological forces are in alignment with each other, because of the radical ontological difference between reality (*res*) and consciousness (*res cogitans*), it is normal for there to be a sharp discontinuity between an individual's objective social reality and his or her consciousness of that reality. This means that the 'historical consciousness' (Gadamer 1979) that is deemed characteristic of post-Enlightenment modern cultures will only point in a clear direction among a fraction of a population. The exercise of freedom and reflexivity is condemned to involve 'the crisis of the West' which may be described philosophically as the condition of being mired in *the radical indeterminacy of reason* or, more sociologically, the situation of members of post-Enlightenment cultures having no rational basis for their beliefs and values, and being more or less fated to search for personal verification of the truths and values they believe in. The values, traditions and beliefs that are inherited as part of membership of groups or institutions to be continued, then, must be personally appropriated in light of rational examination and reflexive freedom. Whereas previous generations enjoyed a *fides implicita* so that many made their way through life through a process of *fides implicita* as their beliefs and values were *socially sanctioned and as real as the reality of society itself* and did not need a personal act of self-appropriation, members of a younger generation are more or less fated to run a rationalist gauntlet before their beliefs and values are intersubjectively or socially verified. In this regard, sociological wisdom teaches us that those beliefs and practices which require the free commitment of the free individual for their survival are destined for long-term decline, so that every kind of belief and every value has to be either in conformity with social power or grounded in personal experience or suffer the fate of long-term decline. Faced with such social pressures, the available cultural resources of a people through which a living connection with the past could be made and which could act as the medium through which a population might find ballast to counteract social determinations and the indeterminacy of freedom and reason becomes all-important.

Faced with this challenge, my predicament has been to take a working-class population that has comparatively little cultural capital and, beginning from manual labourer's *dasein*, argue that insofar as it is reduced to its intelligibility via an act of self-understanding it is capable of an act of self-conscientisation sufficient to destroy one long durée edifice and resurrect another; that insofar as '79 generation producers of culture successfully meet the challenge of producing a 'generational literature' of modern significance, and establish this connection to an older modernity, they break with their symbolic and cultural poverty and simultaneously inaugurate a presumptuous 'betrayal of self' that at the same time makes the tasks of their ownmost selves available to them for the first time. My method of procedure was to stake everything upon the conviction that because the worker is convinced of the reality of his situated self, this is the ground upon which his project of self-appropriation as worker-inquirer is most likely to succeed.

In giving this account we succeeded where both supernaturalist theology and naturalistic social theory have failed, as we articulated the "interrelation of thought and existence *that has ceased to be contemplative*, by the *concrete* demonstration of the identical subject-object" (Lukacs 1971, p. 215) and by providing the missing ethnographic content, and the missing performative event, we have also provided the first ethnographically grounded account of how the worker-inquirer-knower is a dynamic image of the Blessed Trinity and how, in the first place: "it is by one's own activity that one is drawn into God" (Kerr 2002, p. 173) and secondly, how *extra mundum nulla salus* (Schillebeckz 1990, p. 12) and, thirdly, how "that which is wholly done for us by God, is yet also our own highest act and properly our own" (Milbank 2005, p. ix) and in the fourth place how "a greater actuation of the agent...gives the created agent a special participation in the pure act of being" (Kerr 2002, p. 173 & p. 163) and fifthly, how the worker-inquirer-knower is "consciously a conditioned being" (Gadamer, cited in Rabinow and Sullivan 1987, p. 103) and, sixthly, how "eternity appears, not as such, but diffracted through the most perishable" (Adorno, cited in Held 1980, p. 212-3) and, seventhly, how actual being can take over "being itself (*Siende*) in its dejectedness" (Heidegger, cited in Marcuse 1969, p. 15) and in the eighth place, how "the proletariat is the identical subject-object of the history of society" (Lukacs 1971, p. 206) and, ninthly, how "utmost negativity, however, takes a positive turn" (Marcuse, cited in Held 1981, p. 239) and, tenthly, how "the emancipation of the worker is the work of the worker himself" (Castoriadis 1987, p. 57) and, finally, constructed a purely natural or sociological "straight gate through which the Messiah might enter" (Benjamin 1992, p. 255).

# Epilogue

At journey's end and looking over the road travelled, it is clear that in coming to understand my data the ground upon which I stood shifted on more than one occasion. As stated in the introduction, my intention for a long time was simply to write a study of working-class nationalism at the time of its historic triumph in 1999, but as I came to understand the significance of nationalism went far beyond achieving political independence, I understood that the focus of my study had to enlarge to include a study of 'being modern,' and what *a working-class project of modernity* might look like.

If catching sight of this new question meant a change in perspective was required, a shift that was resisted for much longer came as a result of it becoming clear that I could not carry on the fiction of not acknowledging, as integral to my methodology, the fact that I was caught up in the drama I was attempting to give an account of, and so I felt more or less compelled to go 'all the way' in my reflexivity, and so my focus became enlarged again to include an element of auto-ethnography and experiences that I had previously never imagined I would need to include and disclose. This 'coming clean' with my reader seemed my only option, as it meant I could avoid artificially ending my journey and pointing vaguely to a future direction of travel that I would leave for another day, and so I decided to include the section on Special Ontology. This final enlargement of focus also meant a change in the title was necessary, and so what was originally meant to be a straightforward study of Scottish nationalism became a phenomenology of Christian redemption and an argument for a new integral sociology capable of recognising the free imagining of integral human being.

If these were some of the motivations for changes in the range and scope of the text, a more practical consideration that led to including the final three chapters came from my students and their not unreasonable expectation that I should model how the study of society can be of some public service and engage with the 'signs of the times,' and how sociology integrates with and illuminates personal life. Just as I was taught that part of the purpose of studying sociology and anthropology is to become coeval with the times, so I feel a responsibility to model such a sociology and ethnography and so I tell my students to judge a sociology by whether or not it *recognises* them, and whether it can take the full weight of their lives. It is obvious to me that sociology must be integral to answering the question of the proportionate or natural beatitude of people who spend their lives as members of societies, so that sociology is indispensable because it enables the gathering of the necessary data that makes possible the act of self-appropriation that 'squeezes' historicised and socialised *dasein* of its intelligibility. However, this conviction had to be learned, and it is because I have learned *as an ethnographer and sociologist to* place the entire weight not only of our purely natural beatitude but Christian redemption upon the shoulders of the particular 'secondary nature' that is Scottish working-class *dasein* that, like a mathematician, I am able to 'show the working' behind my claim that an integral sociology can stand upon the shoulders of Scotus insofar as "the guiding idea of Duns Scotus [was] to safeguard contingency (*servare contingentiam*)" (Boehner 1990, p. xxi).

A necessary element of 'safeguarding contingency' is to reject *modernism* as a coercive force that would turn us into tourists vis-à-vis our ownmost *dasein* insofar as we are coerced into imagining nothing of lasting value will accrue to us by thinking our contingent and 'fleeting' selves, and this is why how we imagine what it is to 'be modern' is central to how we imagine ourselves and our future, and why a proper respect before 'contingency' is so important. I have argued, then, that as a result of being infected by the modernist imagination, many intellectuals have been in flight from the very times they imagine they reduce themselves to and define themselves by; have been in flight from the new tasks demanded by the new times and have failed the 'new being' brought into being by the industrialisation of society and humanity because of a false and superficial metaphysics that lacks historicity and transcendence. The modernists are enthralled to the mistake of imagining they can better serve the representation of the *novum* by abandoning the task of achieving their own integral holism, and so they abandon the task of re-making Tradition anew through the medium of the new and thereby fail to fulfil the original 'signature dialectic' of being modern.

I also, of course, recognise that critics of modernity often make the fatal mistake of imagining they can better preserve historicity, transcendence and tradition by resisting the challenge of the new and, as I have adverted to, I am not insensitive to the modernist temptation because when studying the social class that is arguably most reduced to their socio-economic 'secondary nature,' the working-class mind can not fail to see much that is indispensable in the modernist spirit if 'being and time' or 'history and reason' are ever to come into alignment within consciousness. If affluence and literacy make the synthesis between the Old and the New possible to more and more people as never before, what has to be resisted as never before is the democratisation of the *modernist imagination*, which imagines all kinds of fictitious caesuras in human being and human history. This resistance to modernism then must be brought into focus and made an explicit part of our consciousness of the 'present as history.'

To safeguard contingency is to safeguard a drama that has an unknown end and a journey that must put the inquirer at risk. The individual who would put sociology to the test must also undertake the long task of 'translating' his or her life into their intellectual self-consciousness, as this is a precondition of being able to put their lives onto the scales of a sociology and judge whether or not the latter is 'fit for purpose.' While students readily recognise they belong to a particular territory, generation, class or religious tradition and that this fundamentally impacts upon their lives, something more personal and exacting is necessary for a deeper appropriation of the sociological imagination i.e. a prolonged effort of practicing reflexivity and gathering the data and its patterns in their lives, and passing all of this through the sociological lens and their native cognitional structure. Having translated something of my own *dasein* into my own intellectual self-consciousness, I have shown the indispensable nature of sociological reasoning in achieving my own self-appropriation and that the 'sociological imagination' is capable of its original promise of succeeding where the instruments of 'pure reason' are fated to fail.

Another aim of this book was to model the process of self-appropriation *to a working-class audience*, and in this regard everything I have written here was first developed while I instantiated what Bourdieu refers to as a *split habitus*; a dual worker-come-intellectual *habitus* as a result of living in the relative poverty of someone who had only ever performed minimum wage level jobs until the age of forty. My hope is that my descriptions and my outlining of the conceptual 'building blocks' of working-class *dasein* may be a stimulus for working-class readers to do the work of reproducing and identifying these elements within their own experience in their own journeys of self-appropriation, so that my hope is to be of some use to the reader achieving self-appropriation by arming him or her with a template of how to achieve an integral self-understanding.

The restoration of the Scots pairlament is only part of a much larger and exciting task of achieving a kind of thinking characterised by systematically reopening the long durée of Scottish history, and the question of a Scottish modernity and the task of re-thinking human being. Thinking through these questions is an integral part of the 'tasks of freedom' of the '79 generation(s) among whom the long haul of overthrowing modernism in favour of the retrieval of an original discovery of the modern era is at hand. Re-founding our imagination and politics and culture upon our ownmost ontology and reversing four centuries of attempting to live without the synthesis of culture, history and *dasein* are within the performative grasp of the '79 generations, and I would hope that by achieving independence some time after 18 September 2014, the modernist organisation of and imagining of Scotland will come to an end among us, and a deeper rejection of modernism will be at hand, and this will determine whether we are successful or not in achieving an intergenerational project of reflexivity after independence that can think working and middle-class *dasein* and the 'present as history' to its foundations and to its limits.

In achieving this re-foundation my view is that a cognitionally-based empowerment of human being upon its ownmost *dasein* ensures the post-1979 generations are able to re-imagine Scotland's culture and to think locality, class, nation, governance and the question of transcendence outwith the paradigms of modernism, supernaturalism and secularism. This development also challenges conventional sociology as to whether it is able to recognise this development using prefabricated categories developed to think previous eras, and it seems to me that to think *dasein* and *mitsein* to the extent of their capacities, as opposed to their merely current empirical state, requires a new kind of sociology insofar as it requires the sociologist resolving to equip himself or herself not only with the usual suspects of class, status, generation, gender and nationality, but with the "attempt to contemplate all things as they would present themselves from the standpoint of redemption" (Adorno 1974, p. 247).

To retrieve the tension of being modern beyond the 'scarcity imagination' that has dominated us until now and be modern according to the original Catholic conception of modernity in Europe, not by dissolving or liquidating half of the tensions it brings but by respecting the tensions between the natural, social, economic and material realms, and the transcendent or supernatural aspects of desire and human experience, is to practice an 'affluent modernity' that is modern without the *scarcity metaphysics* that demand Man must live by bread alone, and that imagines that to turn to the present we must invent epistemologies and ontologies that disrespect and disqualify and misrecognise much that is integral to late-modern human being.

In order to not repeat previous errors, however, talk of affluence and a release from scarcity must avoid becoming another flight from reality in the very effort at capturing the emergent and con-temporary, so that integral to rejecting the modernist imagination is accepting, for example, that we are not heading for the classless society any time soon, as this recognition frees the imagination to resist facile imaginings of a future independent Scotland and recognise that class is not being dissolved but is rather being purified of post-war accommodations and compromises, and class among the '79 generation is being liberated from the insecurities of 'scarcity modernity.' Similarly, if we are heading for a humanity that sees the issue of transcendence being similarly released from previous answers such as the *supernaturalism* that was served up by 'scarcity Christianity,' this helps us dismiss its illegitimate off-spring that is *secularism*, and allows into view the fact that if Scotland is about to arrive for the second time to a sovereign and free modernity, it is also arriving late to the need to avoid dangerous forms of integralism. While *dasein* and *mitsein* must struggle to be free of all forms of subordination, an empowered Scottish *dasein* must consciously dis-align itself from any kind of regression to pre-Christian forms of integralism, so that if the turning to the full historicity and territoriality of *dasein* and *mitsein* in opposition to liberalism and bourgeois modernism and Marxist materialism is necessary, the 'repressions' of Christianity are also needed if an empowered Scottish *dasein* and *mitsein* are to steer clear of neo-pagan versions of integralism (de Benoist 2004; Sunic 2011; Krebs 2012) after independence.

The objective sociological forces that are aligned with the reopening of the question of transcendence reveals all the more starkly the need to reconcile the reality of class with a sociology of the living God as a result of particular questions being more or less fated to become relevant and pressing such as: what image will be revealed to a younger working-class generation as it looks into the 'mirror of production' having exercised reflexivity and cognitional agency beyond the confines of the 'dictatorship of scarcity'? What image will a post-materialist and post-scarcity and post-secular and post-supernaturalist look in the 'mirror of production' reveal? These questions remain for every working-class generation as they remain 'fixed' to the mundane exigencies of reproducing what might be termed *affluent subsistence*, but are also disposed to not reproduce symbolic accommodations to their domination but to break from centuries-old geo-political relations by the deployment of a long durée symbolic patrimony, or any number of more superficial beliefs should they choose. If 'Thatcher' broke every rule in the carefully constructed and carefully managed house of cards that was the United Kingdom, she paid the price by aiding and abetting a retaliatory integralism, because by destroying all-British industries and all-British trade unions the London-based neo-liberal economic project of globalisation destroyed the bases for the symbolic reproduction of Britain among the Scottish working class, and unwittingly opened the gates to the Scots politicising upon the twelfth-century basis of a 'two-storey' or integral sovereignty. But for this development the United Kingdom may well have lasted another three hundred years as a result of a largely inert and certainly de-politicized historicity and nationality, but *due to the advent of a purely Scottish context* an entire symbolic and institutional realm has been more or less overthrown, so that today *Scottish society* and *Scottish politics* exist as imaginary and institutional entities in their own right and have very little of the fake existence of 'Scottish civic life' endured throughout the years of political union with England.

As the classless society is not at hand, this brings into sharp relief the question of what the middle-class contribution to the new Scottish imaginary will be in light of the fact that its domination of the public realm and all public institutions after independence will have been reproduced across not two but three constitutional eras. What seems clear is the level of *cultural leadership* exercised by the middle classes in Scotland is at an historic all-time low, and insofar as they may justly be described as having led the retreat from an integral or Scottish modernity and sovereignty, their fate within the Scottish imaginary seems sealed for the foreseeable future because, unlike the working-class generations which were more or less coerced into taking action and a more or less open reckoning with their traditional political and cultural allegiances, the Scottish middle classes have not been objectively coerced into undergoing this process and so have largely failed to re-imagine themselves.

If earlier I described the Scottish Labour Party as having failed to do much more than simultaneously oppose nationalism and yet dance to its tune, the middle-class Conservative Party in Scotland has contributed even less to Scottish political life, and this curious position of a middle class is no doubt directly related to the fact that during the 1979-1997 period this class experienced a 'democratic surplus' thanks to political union with England, while the working class suffered a 'democratic deficit' because of political union with England. Insofar as the middle-class does not claim any credit for the creation of the Scottish parliament, so the long-awaited advent of a Scottish modernity will perhaps uniquely among European nations be characterised by the absence of the middle class which seems to have slipped into invisibility within the Scottish imagination to such an extent that Marx's dictum about the workers having no country seems to have been directed at the wrong class as far as Scotland is concerned. This class's deep misalignment with the present moment is also no doubt the result of their 'scarcity thinking' in an age of affluence, and insofar as "the class consciousness of the bourgeoisie is geared to economic consciousness" (Lukacs 1971, p. 64), this has blinded them to historicity and nationality, and led directly to their invisibility within Scottish culture.

If the return of Scotland is no longer scorned as a hapless return to 'medieval particularism' by the affluent metropolitan middle classes, it is because this re-nationalization of politics and political power has been aligned with or integrated with their social reproduction, so that even the traditionally anti-nationalist Left-Liberal middle classes more or less genuflect to culture and history, and some kind of holistic *dasein* after the firework display of 1 July 1999. Likewise, formerly 'vanguard modernists' among the working class in the shape of socialist party activists now support independence, and concede more than one colour is necessary to paint a realistic portrayal of working-class *dasein*, and that not only must the project of a Scottish modernity be disentangled from political union with England but the project of 'being modern' is essentially compromised by union with England.

These developments signal a much-needed and long-awaited change in the symbolic order has occurred in light of the fact that, while Scotland's GDP per capita ranking against OECD countries puts Scotland as the eighth richest nation in the world (Scottish Government 2013), such bare facts of material affluence have not been enough to make the Scottish middle and working-classes break with 'scarcity thinking,' and that what has been decisive for the victory of nationalism has been the decline of one structure of meaning and the emergence of another which, while helped by affluence, requires more. This 'more' has been a *formative experience of conflict and contestation* across the generations, and for the '79 generation Thatcherism and the deindustrialization of the nineteen-eighties and the triumph of neoliberalism are the key experiences that meant the ideologies of unionism, internationalism and socialism have evaporated in the heat of battle, with the 1979 working-class generation having been taught the lesson that achieving sovereignty was not just about taking political control via independence but taking control of culture and the imagination. The nation, then, has been re-imagined and there has been a successful re-imagining of the *telos* of politics much as the '45 working-class generation successfully nationalised the State via the creation of the Welfare State so that the political realm became congruent with the nation, and a younger generation has re-created politics along Scottish lines and in achieving this shift at a political and symbolic level, *sovereignty at the level of the symbolic* is understood as crucial in their pursuit of integral sovereignty.

However, if the advent of the Scots parliament was simultaneously the result of an exercise of freedom that was more or less coerced by events, the fifteen years that have passed since 1999 has created a political context and a political dialectic whose centre of gravity is Scotland and which owes little to extrinsic events for its nature and development. Thanks to the retrieval of the original twelfth century advent of the modern era, the question is whether Scotland can not only embark on its own modernity but can proceed to complete the unfinished project of modernity (Habermas 1981, in Entreves and Benhabib 1996, pp. 38-55) by an alignment of the project of modernity with the fundamentals of the earlier Catholic invention of modernity (Habermas 2010, pp. 15-23). To depict this retrieval of this historical ballast in order to orient a movement to face the present and future, Nairn (1997) has used the Janus-faced metaphor, while McCrone has used the metaphor of a younger generation having to deploy its deepest anchors in response to Thatcher when describing the nineteen-eighties and nineteen-nineties in Scotland, so that this generation's nationalism is the response of *their very ownmost being* insofar as the 1979-1997 period forced 'the question of being' onto their generational self-consciousness.

Articulating an adequate response to (English) neoliberalism meant not only articulating a response to this first iteration of Thatcher but to every subsequent 'Thatcher' that was to come along, so that when in May 2010 the next iteration duly arrived to Downing Street, it is an indication of the sea-change in meaning that has occurred that every 'new Thatcher' becomes a living reminder of Scots' deeply inadequate way of 'being modern' and 'being Scottish,' so that increasingly the only rational response is to reject all conceptions of 'being Scottish' and 'being working class' that are complicit in reproducing the existence of the zombie category of the United Kingdom, and every acolyte 'systems of meaning' that is embarrassed or ambivalent at exercising sovereignty and the mobilisation of integralism as they are complicit in perpetuating political and cultural subordination.

Affluence brought an end to the period of reducing class interests to purely economic matters and has coerced working-class populations out of their crass materialism and into imagining the post-industrial and post-materialist tasks of constructing new visions of *dasein* and *mitsein* and identifying their cultural interests and a post-industrial narrative. This transcending of 'materialism' is no private choice or idiosyncrasy but a sociological exigence that has become something of a death sentence for those left-wing socialist political parties which are more or less fated to shift to the middle-ground and struggle to retain their traditional working-class voters, insofar as both fail to imagine the multichromatic post-materialist 'tasks of freedom' that are upon them. If populations are a people as well as a members of social classes it is because they are structured as much by geography and history as by social structure, so that it is an impossible task to separate these two aspects of one integral reality as the 'social structure' itself has its historicity because it is steeped in time and place and nation.

The agency of territory, history and social structure, then, act to effect an 'internment into the present' among populations and suggests the unlikelihood of any class playing the role of the subject of history, and instead the likelihood of classes and nations *inter-ciphering* or acting as the mouthpieces for each other and the embedded positions they occupy. Hence, framing the question of agency in the tired manner of 'structuralism versus humanism' is unhelpful as constraining structural conditions simultaneously predispose classes to act in a historically significant and freeing manner, and because we live in nation-based societies, the social structure has its being within history and within the nation so that the 1979-1997 period saw not only issues of class being raised thanks to the triumph of neoliberalism but the geo-political relationship of union with England emerged simultaneously as integral to how to respond to class identity being put 'at risk' at this time. It is because this social structure continually puts their integral being 'at issue' that integral to *their historicity and nationality and locality* is a long history of conflict and 'risk management,' so that the working class reproduce within themselves and their communities a sharp concern for safeguarding the historicity and nationality and locality of *dasein* and *mitsein*.

For every nationalist, 18 September 2014 will be a straightforward matter of Scotland beginning to catch up with normal national development and implementing a tried and tested formula that other nations have used to resolve the predicament of how to settle the practical political question of how-to-be-in-the-world. However, I propose that both 1 July 1999 and 18 September 2014 can also be a unique rejection of a false view of human being and a false view of modernity insofar as a *working-class nationalism* rejects a false view of 'being modern' in a moment of self-affirmation, having itself been subjected to a very full project of *modernist* modernisation, so that the Scottish working class are perhaps the first to be coerced into rejecting a non-holistic practice and understanding of modernity. This is a new development because if no-one today takes offence at 'fancy dress costume' or holistic conceptions of *dasein*, what many still find very offensive and what is still very divisive is the working class opting for an integral *practice of itself* that mobilises and politicises upon the basis of this self-understanding. Until very recently the Scottish working class were just as reductionist as their middle-class 'managers' in leaving divisive non-materialistic matters well alone in order to keep to the 'liberal peace,' and we may say until 1967 this class left half of its *dasein* out of its politics lest any 'inflated' holistic issues of identity jeopardise their immediate economic interests, so that if the temptation to 'economism' or 'scarcity thinking' among the working class is fated to remain so long as the mirror of production (Baudrillard) remains, so it is likely that their mobilising and politicising nationality may be relatively straightforward with the real prize after independence being the emergence of a self-understanding free from non-integralist forms such as liberalism and materialism.

The 'thick events' of 1 July 1999 and 18 September 2014 require 'thick explanations,' and insofar as they are the result of a history of preceding political events and the effects of affluence and a symbolic revolution that uncoupled the '79 generation from the symbolic order of their parents' generation, these dates in Scotland's history represent something that no previous generation has achieved: an electorally significant new integration of nation and state or the re-socialisation of the nation along class lines. After 1979-1997 (and again after 2010) only the inheritors (Bourdieu) and politically 'over-represented' middle-class Conservatives fail to draw the nationalist conclusion, so that after this time a new class-nation-culture alignment was more or less fated to make its way onto the stage, but not as the mouthpiece for the superannuated clichés of modernism. If many of the '45 working-class generation do not participate in this alignment it is as a result of belonging to traditions that are defined by the disavowal of imagining *dasein* in a holistic manner and their appropriation of union, Empire and a secularised Protestantism which they use to imagine themselves.

This working-class generation, then, are defined by their internalisation of categories that collude with their subjugation so that the members of the local history group revealed a lifelong alienation from the deep narrative of Scotland and their lifelong work of 'forgetting' that is a homage to a job well done by such a symbolic order. There is, however, a transvaluation of symbolic systems underway insofar as the meaning of social positionality, nationality and locality between the generations has changed from being an 'eternal' imprisonment in subordination to being the departure point for an empowering project insofar as a basic 'social ontology,' that in one generation was complicit in consigning people into the invisibility of shame, has become the ballast or pearl of great price that purchases the tasks of freedom and secures the resumption of an unfinished project of integralism in the next generation; a positionality that in one generation meant being condemned to an eternal treadmill of catching-up, but in the next generation is the freedom from all such imposed relations to history and the present-day order thanks to breaking from a cultural subordination.

If at any time there is no surer sign of being dominated and having surrendered to power than having appropriated the signification of history developed by the dominant, so there is no greater sign of appropriating the 'tasks of freedom' than the conscious rejection of the signification work of elites. If there is a healthy rejection of the old unionist cud among the working class, it seems the Scottish middle classes are still largely trapped in a 'dominated' or unfree relation to their domination of Scottish society, insofar as they fail to break with their domination or their traditional exercise of power. These tensions can only heighten in the run up to September 2014 as both classes come under pressure from the weight of the historic moment to break with the modernist signification of history, and to the extent they manage this, their contribution to the 'present as history' will be more than simply working out the terms of their surrender to the clichés of modernism. If "an ethically constituted nation lives in direct unity with its own substance, and...on its organized distribution into the spheres of the various classes, each with its particular way of acting which co-operates to form the whole" (Hegel 1967, p. 710), then we can say that just as the individual intellectually recapitulates the life led by an act of self-understanding, so a nation's history can be recapitulated, and can be made to come into alignment with itself *ad fontes* once again in the event of a 'yes' vote in September 2014, so that the tear in the nation's substance and story can be finally healed.

If the opportunity for a nation to become identical with itself once again is rare, in the case of the individual person it is true to say that he or she ordinarily is free at any time to embark upon the project of self-appropriation, notwithstanding it is a task that requires years of effort. My account of the fundamental 'secondary ontology' of working-class *dasein*, then, was preparatory to the act of self-appropriation and agreement with Aristotle's teaching of the unique value of truth and that a man can only possess himself by knowing himself. In this regard Christian theologians teach that men, unlike angels, are not born in full possession of their powers and so require childhood and youth to come into full possession of their powers. Similarly, no man can know himself immediately but must make a long effort to do so, as a man does not possess his existence like the stone in his hand which is always identical with itself and always is what it is and suffers no diremption within itself. Unlike a stone, however, a man only comes fully into possession of himself intellectually and when this happens there is then *and only then* the apotheosis of *dasein* and thought being integrated and the predicament whereby "human reality as for-itself is a lack and that what it lacks is a certain coincidence with itself" (Sartre 1966, p. 147) is resolved. Conceptual self-knowledge then is a perfection of an antepredicative or merely embodied way of being working class and is the only basis upon which to recommend the intellectual life (Sertillanges 1947) to the working class as a means of liberation.

In taking from Hegel the dialectic of *being and nothingness* Sartre recognised this dialectic "historicises itself in the time of Duns Scotus" (Sartre 1966, p. 669), so that at this point in European history the insistence upon the radical indeterminacy of *dasein* opened the way to the dissolution of a universal Man by the action of time and place and history, and with the benefit of hindsight we can see that this was just the opening salvo in the shift to immanence and humanity by this son of St. Francis, as it was simultaneously a turning to the world, time, history and social structure. Happily, self-appropriation transcends the dispersal and deconstruction of the subject insofar as the dispersal of self can be 'totalised' into its adequate concept so that lives can be intellectually recapitulated. Such is the privilege of intellection and it is how we answered the dogmatism of Sartre (1966, p. 268) when he adverts to the "perpetually indicated but impossible fusion of essence and existence." More generally, insofar as "Scotus stood at the centre of a paradigm shift in the late Twelfth century" (Pickstock 2003, p. 11), he and others effected a turning to the soteriological value of the social realm and it is at this point that can be seen the origin of the social sciences thanks to Scotus and his contemporaries and near-contemporaries being men who "never lost sight of...the burden of our freedom" (Broadie 1990, p. 51). The Scottish Enlightenment, then, was regressive when seen in this younger and earlier light, and is exemplified in the example of Hume who was a devout unionist whose much-lauded 'science of Man' had no use for the exercise of sovereignty upon the basis of his ownmost *dasein*, other than its dissolution via union with England thanks to his view that this was the only road to the modernisation of Scotland and to accomplishing the shift from *gemeinschaft* to *gesellschaft*.

Today's modernist nationalists of course will not repeat the mistakes of eighteenth-century 'scarcity unionists' as they understand that if modernity is to be real it must bend to Scottish *dasein*, and be refracted through this medium if it is to occur at all. Fully-contextualised Scottish *dasein*, then, is the condition for the possibility of modernity in Scotland rather than the sacrificial victim to be offered up that modernity may come. Like every nationalist, I too am a nationalist because it is in my modernising interests but my imagining of modernity "takes modernity back to its Scotist roots" (Pickstock 2003, p. 14) and in the interests of identifying the social carrier of this vision I have outlined the fundamental ontology of a particular situated or contextualised *dasein* and its natural condition and its natural and supernatural beatitude, by building upon a real ethnographic foundation as opposed to entrusting such a project to a particular economic theory or a particular view of worker exploitation or a particular view of history or a particular religious tradition.

In the specific case of Scotland today, to be coeval with the times is to be concerned with the emergence of a full or whole ontology in which *political independence* is only a part, and in which a break with *modernist* nationalism is necessary as there can be no question of independence being the remedy for all the ills of Scotland but rather one of the *conditiones sine qua non* of the larger project of modernity which simultaneously includes the drama of social subordination and the drama of human knowing and the drama of secondary natures being released from out-dated conceptions and subjugations and, for some of us at least, the advent of the supernatural as integral elements of this drama. In arguing modernism has to be consciously rejected the aim is to avoid an epidemic of 'successful lazy nationalism' that in proportion to becoming popular rushes into making all of the mistakes of modernism. In this regard modernism is consubstantial with the imaginations of left-wing liberal authors who as part of their class condition seem fated to imagine the immanent end of all sorts of repressive and determining realities rather than the democratisation and nationalisation of a long durée tension and project.

This misrecognition became an epidemic in post-structuralism and post-modernism and is exemplified in many pre-1989 Marxist and liberal intellectuals who proclaimed with invincible confidence that nationalism was a spent force, and argued for an internationalist organisation of geo-political space until the fall of the Berlin Wall in November 1989 and the subsequent collapse of the USSR. The post-modern flight from History reveals its kinship with modernism's original attempt to re-signify or re-imagine the real history of Europe whereby it became a 'pre-history' spent in preparation for the arrival of Man no longer mystified in his consciousness with regard to himself, and this has been the signature fantasy of the middle-class intellectual as this 'beginning from scratch' fantasy continually dilutes the meaning of European history and is the cipher for this class's myth about itself because, at all times, *thanks to its social condition*, this class views participation in real historic Traditions as obsolete because *this myth is how this class imagines it achieves its true historical consciousness*, so that anything that threatens its modernist self-understanding or its 'leadership of history' is automatically seen as a threat to its hegemony, and any fidelity to any belief or tradition that jeopardises this is more or less fated to be rejected.

To take the obvious examples, then, as soon as the disciplines, repressions and rigors of family, community and church were conceived to be purely human constructs with no *analogia entis*, the motivation to maintain these tensions and institutions in conditions of modernity was weakened, and instead of maintaining a tension there was the surrender to new social conditions, with the result that thinkers more or less coerced themselves into a spectatorial gaze upon history and society and their own *dasein* as they liquidated the work of synthesising Tradition and the New, and thereby deconstructed the tasks of freedom without knowing it. This is why the imagined liquidation of Tradition was the precondition for their emergence to domination of European commercial society because participating in and esteeming the historical Christian tradition was fated to become beneath its self-estimation because at some point retaining belief involved jeopardising their new hegemony. If the middle class is just as much in need of transcending its ownmost modernist relation to history just as the working class too must break with their 'unfree' relation to their condition of domination, this is unlikely because the middle class's 'signature predicament' arises from its social condition which is to never be coerced into facing what the lower classes *because of their social conditions* are more or less coerced into facing i.e. the existential need to break from its accommodations to the *status quo*, so as to rise to a practice and imagining of power or sovereignty or agency and be forced to change society in the process.

Because of the very early liquidation of its institutions and its holistic conception of *dasein* as a result of its failings and poverty and a powerful and insecure Protestant English monarch on its border, Scotland is arriving late to what every other country already knows i.e. that to be modern it is a *condicione sine qua non* to *not* reject the ballast of the past. If the 'dictatorship of scarcity' prevented the '45 generation from making their geo-political relations in their ownmost image, and if their scarcity way of 'being modern' followed established British lines, a new working-class generation's affluent and reflexive way of 'being modern' and *new way of being working class* sees them reaching beyond eighteenth-century compromises with English power to the original twelfth-century template in order to re-imagine itself.

As an ethnographer of the working class, my modernity and my nationalism are sociologically grounded in an emergent '79 working-class generation thanks to the advent of affluence and the extension of higher education. In this reading, the wider significance of Scottish nationalism is that it is an attempt to address the crisis of the European imagination via the appropriation of this original European vision of modernity; an attempt to recapture a vision that synthesises transcendence and history and which retains the *analogia entis* and, by rejecting supernaturalism, disenchanted nature and human society as it discovered the purely natural and social or public realm, and recognised and maintained the tension between immanence and transcendence and the soteriological value of 'secondary natures.' This vision of every social formation and every secular station in life and every standpoint (class, nationality, generation, gender etcetera) occupied by the Christian-in-the-world being 'charged' with a theonomic dialectic was lost sight of firstly by the Renaissance and then the Protestant reformation, and thereafter by the secular modernism of the nineteenth century era of commerce. The worker-inquirer-knower-Christian, then, must recover all of this if the twenty-first century is to simultaneously retrieve and inaugurate another era of Scottish modernity.

1 July 1999 and 18 September 2014 are the empirical events that evidence historicity and nationality remain integral to modern *dasein* because these are the days when the Scots go back three hundred years of pseudo-modernity to retrieve a twelfth century institution (Brown and Tanner 2004) to salvage the adequate

medium to express their nationality, historicity and social condition by and resume their adequate *being-in-the-world*. It is clear then that some aspects of *dasein* can not be opted out of or privatised despite three hundred years of trying, and the failed modernist experiment of the United Kingdom and non-holistic self-understandings are coming to an end insofar as the Scots decide this is no longer imaginable. As a result of the fifteen years that have passed since 1 July 1999 the presence of England within the Scottish imagination has declined precipitously, and yet at the election of May 2010 to the British parliament in London when the Scots elected 50 (out of a possible 51) members of parliament who were not Conservatives only to have a Conservative government imposed upon them, it remains clear that Scotland remains within the '1979-1997 syndrome.'

As a result of the unprecedented level of 'brokenness' of Britain, the following year the Scots concluded that the Scottish National Party best reflected and represented them, and judged the SNP as the most competent defenders and promoters of their historicity and nationality or their 'palette of many colours.' The electoral success of the SNP then is based upon the fact that more and more Scots have a particular conception of themselves that means being governed by politicians who lack this same particular imagining of Scotland feels like an intolerable absence of themselves from their own public sphere. 'The people' wish to be represented by politicians who share the same imagining of Scotland that they have, and if this is how the Scots wish to connect with their political representatives it is because they want their holistically conceived and enacted-via-practice *dasein* and *mitsein* to be the medium of their imagination and culture and politics and intellectual and cultural and spiritual lives, and when Lesley Riddoch stated that Scottish independence is a cause to which "people are bringing their entire selves" she was adverting to this desire for an integral politics.

Because of this integralism and the desire to practice it, the current post-devolution period is palpably an interregnum period where until independence is achieved we must wander between two worlds, one dead and the other about to be born, and in this interregnum it is difficult not to write Heideggerian-like sentences such as Scotland "has a calling to renew the question of Being" (Fried 2000, p. 41), or that the Scots on 18 September 2014 fundamentally must choose themselves, and choose to pursue the society they want to make at this historic turning of the tide. In 2007 and 2011 the Scottish electorate judged the SNP as the party that was conscious of what was at stake, while 'scarcity thinking' unionists continued to beat their monochromatic drum of 'scarcity thinking' and lead the call for a return to 'bread and butter' issues. Increasingly, the truth for unionist politicians is they have nothing interesting to say to the electorate to reverse their electoral fortunes and reanimate their parties because unionist politicians peddle a *dasein deficit* insofar as they do not allow themselves or the electorate to imagine a holistic or integral conception and practice of *dasein* and *mitsein* that would allow politicians and people to burn with the desire to put an end to the many suppressions of holism that literacy and affluence now make it possible to finally recognise and bring to an end.

A parliament that intervenes into the imagination as much as the economy is what is wanted; a parliament that has an adequate conception of *dasein* and that understands its electorate identify with being a proletariat as well as being a people and has no need for the 'scarcity imagination' that says they must choose between independence and the good society. The 2014 Independence Referendum, then, is the day the Scots have given themselves to put many errors right once and for all, so that if Scotland votes 'yes' on 18 September 2014 it will be because its people have stopped imagining the future with only half of themselves and have had enough of trying to exist in the modern era upon the basis of renouncing their ownmost selves and their ownmost tasks.

We await their decision.

# References

Adams, G. 1996. *Before The Dawn: An Autobiography*. London: Heinemann.

Adorno, T. 1974. *Minima Moralia: Reflections from a Damaged Life*. London: Verso.

Adorno, T. and Horkheimer, M. 1973. *Dialectic of Enlightenment*. London: Allen Lane.

Altorki, S. 1986. *Women in Saudi Arabia: Ideology and Behaviour Among the Elite*. New York: Columbia University Press.

Anderson, B. 1983. *Imagined Communities: Reflections on the Origin and Spread of Nationalism*. London: Verso.

Anderson, B. 1991. (2nd ed.) *Imagined Communities: Reflections on the Origin and Spread of Nationalism*. London: Verso.

Anderson, B. 1998. *Spectre of Comparisons: Nationalism, Southeast Asia and the World*. London: Verso.

Anson, P. F. 1970. *Underground Catholicism in Scotland*. Standard Press.

Antonio, R. J. 1981. 'Immanent Critique as the Core of Critical Theory.' *British Journal of Sociology*. 32(3): 330-345]

Archer, M., Collier, A. & Porpora, D. 2004. *Transcendence: Critical Realism and God*. London: Routledge.

Ardener E. 1985. 'The Decline of Modernism in Anthropology' in Overing, J. (ed.) *Reason and Morality*. London: Tavistock, pp.47-70.

Ash, M. 1980. *The Strange Death of Scottish History*. Edinburgh: The Ramsay Head Press.

Bambery, C. (ed.) 1999. *Scotland, Class and Nation*. London: Bookmarks Publications Ltd.

Barnes, J. (ed.) 1984. *The Complete Works of Aristotle*. Vol. 2. Princeton, NJ: Princeton University Press.

Barth, K. 1994. 'Enduring and emerging issues in the analysis of ethnicity,' in Vermeulen, H. & Govers, C. (eds.) *The Anthropology of Ethnicity: Beyond Ethnic Groups and Boundaries*. Amsterdam: Het Spinhuis, pp.11-32.

Baudrillard, J. 1975. *The Mirror of Production.* Translated by Mark Poster. St. Louis: Telos Press.

Bauman, Z. 1976. *Towards a Critical Sociology: an Essay on Commonsense and Emanicpation.* London: Routledge & Kegan Paul.

Bauman, Z. 1999. *Culture as Praxis.* London: Sage Publications.

Bauman, Z. 2000. *Liquid Modernity.* Cambridge: Polity Press.

Bauman, Z. 2001. *The Individualised Society.* Cambridge: Poility.

Beck, U. 1992. *Risk Society: Towards a New Modernity.* London: Sage.

Beck, U., Giddens, A. and Lash, S. 1994. *Reflexive Modernization: Politics, Tradition and Aesthetics in the Modern Social Order.* Stanford University Press.

Bell, D., Caplan, P. & Karim, W. 1993. *Gendered Fields: Women, Men and Ethnography.* London: Routledge.

Benjamin, W. 1992. *Illuminations.* London: Fontana Press.

Bennie, L., Brand. J. & Mitchell, J. 1997. *How Scotland Votes: Scottish Parties and Elections.* Manchester: Manchester University Press.

de Benoist, A. 2004. *On Being a Pagan.* Atlanta, GA: Ultra.

Van den Berg, A. 1988. *The Immanent Utopia: from Marxism on the State to the state of Marxism.* Princeton University Press.

Berger, J. 1979. *Pig Earth.* London: Writers & Readers Publishing Cooperative.

Berger, P. 1967. *The Sacred Canopy: Elements of a Sociological Theory of Religion.* New York: Anchor Books.

Berger, P. & Luckmann, T. 1987. *The Social Construction of Reality: a Treatise in the Sociology of Knowledge.* London: Pelican Books.

Berman, M. 1983. *All That is Solid Melts into Air: The Experience of Modernity.* London: Verso.

Bernstein, B. 1971. *Class, Codes and Control: Applied Studies towards a Sociology of Language.* London: Routledge & Kegan Paul.

Bettoni, E. 1961. *Duns Scotus: the Basic Principles of his Philosophy.* Translated by Bernardine Bonansea. Washington: Catholic University of America.

Beveridge, C. and Turnbull, R. 1989. *The Eclipse of Scottish Culture: Inferiorism and the Intellectuals.* Edinburgh: Polygon.

Beveridge, C. & Turnbull, R. 1997. *Scotland After Enlightenment: Image and Tradition in Modern Scottish Culture.* Edinburgh: Polygon.

Bhabha, H. K. (ed.) 1990. *Nation and Narration*. London: Routledge.

Bhaskar, R. 2012. *Reflections on MetaReality: Transcendence, emancipation and everyday life*. London: Routledge.

Biedelman, T. O. 1989. 'Agonistic Exchange: Homeric Reciprocity and the Heritage of Simmel and Mauss,' *Cultural Anthropology* 4: 227-59.

Billingham, P. 2007. *At the Sharp End: uncovering the Work of Five Contemporary Dramatists*. London: Methuen.

Bisson, T. 2009. *The Crisis of the 12th Century: Power, Lordship and the Origins of European Government*. Princeton University Press.

Blacking, J. (ed.) 1977. *Anthropology of the Body*. New York: Academic Press.

Blair, T. 1999. Speech to Labour Party Conference. Bournemouth, England. Tuesday September 28th.

Blauner, B. 1964. *Alienation and Freedom: the Factory Worker and His Industry*. University of Chicago Press.

Blondel, M. 1984. *Action (1893): Essay on a Critique of Life and a Science of Practice*. Translated by Oliva Blanchette. Notre Dame, ID: University of Notre Dame Press.

Boehner, P. (ed.) 1990. *Ockham, Philosophical Writings: A Selection*. Indianapolis: Hackett Publishing Company.

Boff, C. 1987. *Theology and Praxis: Epistemological Foundations*. Maryknoll, NY: Orbis Books.

Borg, G. 1998. *Borg's Perceived Exertion and Pain Scales*. Human Kinetics.

Bourdieu, P. 1977. *Outline of a Theory of Practice*. Cambridge: Cambridge University Press.

Bourdieu, P. 1979. *Algeria 1960*. Cambridge: Cambridge University Press.

Bourdieu, P. 1984. *Distinction: A Social Critique of the Judgement of Taste*. London: Routledge.

Bourdieu, P. 1990. *The Logic of Practice*. Stanford University Press.

Bourdieu, P. 1991. *Language and Symbolic Power*. Cambridge: Polity Press.

Bourdieu, P. 1994. *In Other Words*. Cambridge: Polity.

Bourdieu, P. 1998. *Practical Reason: On the Theory of Action*. Cambridge: Polity Press.

Bourdieu, P. 2001. *Masculine Domination*. Cambridge: Polity Press.

Bourdieu, P. and Passeron, J. C. 1977. *Reproduction in Education, Society and Culture*. London: Sage Publications.

Bourdieu, P., Passeron, J. C. & Saint Martin, M. 1994. *Academic Discourse: Linguistic Misunderstanding and Professorial Power*. Translated by Richard Teese. Cambridge: Polity.

Bourdieu, P. & Wacquant, L. J. D. 1992. *An Invitation to Reflexive Sociology*. Cambridge: Polity Press.

Boyle, R. & Lynch, P. (eds.) 1998. *Out of the Ghetto? The Catholic Community in Modern Scotland*. Edinburgh: John Donaldson.

*Braveheart*. 1995. Directed by Mel Gibson. 20th Century Fox. Icon Productions [DVD].

Braverman, H. 1974. *Labour and Monopoly Capitalism: the Degradation of Work in the Twentieth Century*. Monthly Review Press.

Brierley, P. 2011. *UK Church Statistics, 2005-2015*. Tonbridge: ADBC Publishers.

Brierley, W. 1935. *Means Test Man*. London: Methuen.

Broadie, A. 1990. *The Tradition of Scottish Philosophy*. Edinburgh: Polygon.

Broadie, A. 2008. 'Scottish Philosophers in France: the Earlier Years.' *The Journal of Irish and Scottish Studies*. 2(1): 1-12.

Broadie, A. 2009. *A History of Scottish Philosophy*. Edinburgh University Press.

Bronner, S. E. 1994. *Of Critical Theory and Its Theorists*. Oxford: Wiley-Blackwell.

Broun, D. 1999. *The Irish Identity of the Kingdom of the Scots in the Twelfth and Thirteenth Centuries*. Boydell Press.

Broun, D., Finlay, R. J. & Lynch, M. (eds.) 1998. *Image and Identity: The Making and Re-making of Scotland Through the Ages*. Edinburgh: John Donald Publishers Ltd.

Brown, A., McCrone, D. & Paterson, L. 1996. *Politics and Society in Scotland*. London: Macmillan Press Ltd.

Brown, C. G. (2nd ed.) 2001. *The Death of Christian Britain: Understanding Secularisation 1800-2000*. London: Routledge.

Brown, G. and Alexander, D. 1999. *New Scotland New Britain*. London: The Smith Institute.

Brown, K. M. and Tanner, R. J. (eds.) 2004. *The History of the Scottish Parliament. Volume 1. Parliament and Politics in Scotland, 1235-1560*. Edinburgh University Press.

Brubaker, R. 1996. *Nationalism Reframed: Nationhood and the National Question in the New Europe*. Cambridge: Cambridge University Press.

Van den Bruck, A. M. 2012. *Germany's Third Empire*. London: Arktos Media Ltd.

Buchan, D. (ed.) 1994. *Folk Tradition and Folk Medicine in Scotland: The Writings of David Rorie*. Edinburgh: Canongate Academic.

Burawoy, M. 1979. *Manufacturing Consent: Changes in the Labour Process Under Monopoly Capitalism*. University of Chicago Press.

Burawoy, M. 1985. *The Politics of Production: Factory Regimes under Capitalism and Socialism*. London: Verso Books.

Burawoy, M., Burton, A., Ferguson, A. A. and Fox, K. J. 1991. *Ethnography Unbound: Power and Resistance in the Modern Metropolis*. Berkeley: University of California Press.

Burawoy, M. (ed.) 2000. *Gobal Ethnography: Forces, Connections and Imaginations in a Postmodern World*. Berkeley: University of California Press.

Calhoun, C., LiPuma, E. and Postone, M. 1993. *Bourdieu: Critical Perspectives*. Chicago: University of Chicago Press.

Campbell, A. 2011. *Fife From Above*. Deveron Publications.

Castoriadis, C. 1987. *The Imaginary Institution of Society*. Translated by Kathleen Blamey. Cambridge: Polity Press.

Castoriadis, C. 1997. *World in Fragments: Writing on Politics, Society, Psychoanalysis and the Imagination*. Stanford University Press.

Catholic Directory, 2000. Archdiocese of St. Andrews and Edinburgh. Glasgow: Burns Publications Ltd.

*The Catholic Encyclopedia*. 1913. Vol. 14. London: Caxton Publishing.

Caws, P. 1997. *Structuralism: A Philosophy for the Human Sciences*. New Jersey: Humanities Press.

Chapman, M. 1978. *The Gaelic Vision in Scottish Culture*. London: Croom Helm.

Charlesworth, S. 1999. *A Phenomenology of Working Class Experience*. Cambridge: University of Cambridge Press.

Charlesworth, S., Gilfillan, P. and Wilkinson, R. 2004. 'Living Inferiority,' *British Medical Bulletin*; Oxford University Press; Vol. 69: 49-60.

Chatterjee, P. 1993. *The Nation and Its Fragments: Colonial and Postcolonial Histories*. Princeton, NJ: Princeton University Press.

Chatterjee, P. 1996. 'Whose Imagined Community?' pp. 214-225, in Balakrishnan (ed.) *Mapping The Nation*. London: Verso.

Chenu, M. D. 1997. *Nature, Man and Society in the Twelfth Century*. Toronto: University of Toronto Press.

Cicourel, A. V. 1993. 'Aspects of Structural and Processual Theories of Knowledge,' pp. 89-115, in Calhoun, C., LiPuma, E. and Postone, M. *Bourdieu: Critical Perspectives*. Chicago: University of Chicago Press.

Clancy, T. O. 1997. 'Columba, Adomnan and the Cult of the Saints in Scotland,' *Innes Review*; 48(1): 1-26.

Clifford, J. & Marcus, G. E. (eds.) 1986. *Writing Culture: The Poetics & Politics of Ethnography*. University of California Press.

Cohen, A. P. 1978. 'Ethnographic Method in the Real Community,' *Sociologia Ruralis*, 18(1): 1-22.

Cohen, A. P. (ed.) 1982. *Belonging: Identity and Social Organisation in British Rural Cultures*. Manchester: Manchester University Press.

Cohen, A. P. 1985. *The Symbolic Construction of Community*. London: Routledge.

Cohen, A. P. 1987. *Whalsay: Symbol, Segment and Boundary in a Shetland Island Community*. Manchester: Manchester University Press.

Cohen, A. P. 1996. 'Personal Nationalism: A Scottish View of Some Rites, Rights, and Wrongs,' *American Ethnologist*, 23(4): 802-815.

Cohen, A. P. 1997. 'Nationalism and Social Identity: who owns the interests of Scotland?' *Scottish Affairs*, 18: 95-107.

Cohen, R. 1978. 'Ethnicity: problem and focus in anthropology,' *Annual Review Anthropology*, 7:379-403.

Comaroff, J. 1985. *Body of Power, Spirit of Resistance*. University of Chicago Press.

Connerton, P. 1989. *How Societies Remember*. Cambridge: Cambridge University Press.

Constable, G. 1996. *The Reformation of the Twelfth Century*. Cambridge University Press.

Constable, N. 1997. *Maid to Order in Hong Kong: Stories of Filipina Workers*. Ithaca and London: Cornell University Press.

Corrie, J. 1939. *Black Earth*. Routledge: London.

Corrie, J. 1985. *Plays, Poems and Theatre Writings*. Edited by Linda Mackenney. Edinburgh: 7:84 Publications.

Craig, C. 1996. *Out of History: Narrative Paradigms in Scottish & British Culture*. Edinburgh: Polygon.

Craig, C. 1999. *The Modern Scottish Novel: Narrative and the National Imagination*. Edinburgh University Press.

*Crash*. 2004. Directed by Paul Haggis. New York: Lions Gate Films [DVD].

Critchley, S. 2007. *Infinitely Demanding: Ethics of Commitment, Politics of Resistance*. London: Verso.

Cross, R. 1999. *Duns Scotus*. New York: Oxford University Press.

Csordas, T. (ed.) 1994. *Embodiment and Experience: the Existential Ground of Culture and Self*. Cambridge: Cambridge University Press.

Davidson, N. 2000. *The Origins of Scottish Nationhood*. London: Pluto Press.

Davies, W. 1992. 'The Myth of the Celtic Church,' pp. 12-21, in N. Edwards and A. Lane (eds.) *The Early Church in Wales and the West*. Oxford: Oxbow Monograph 16.

Derrida, J. 1976. *Of Grammatology*. Baltimore: The John Hopkins University Press.

Deutsch, K. 1969. *Nationalism and is Alternatives*. New York: MIT.

Devine, T. 1999. *The Scottish Nation 1700-2000*. London: Penguin Books.

Devine, T. (ed) 2000. *Scotland's Shame? Bigotry and Sectarianism in Modern Scotland*. Edinburgh: Mainstream Publishing

Dobbelaere, K. 1989. 'CISR, An Alternative Approach to Sociology of Religion in Europe: ACSS and CISR Compared,' *Sociological Analysis*. 50(4): 377-387.

Dolan, C. 999. 'Taxi for White!' *Product*. December 1999/January 2000 issue. p. 49. Edinburgh: Red Herring Arts and Media.

Douglas, M. & Ney, S. 1998. *Missing Persons: A Critique of the Social Sciences*. University of California Press.

Durkan, J. 1994. 'Scottish Reformers: the Less than Golden Legend.' *Innes Review*, vol. 45:1-28.

Durkheim. E. 2010. *Sociology and Philosophy*. Abingdon, Oxon.: Routledge.

Edwards, R. A. 1979. *Contested Terrain: the Transformation of the Workplace in the Twentieth Century*. New York: Basic Books.

Eley, G. & Suny, R. G. (eds.) 1996. *Becoming National: A Reader*. Oxford: Oxford University Press.

Ellingson, L. 2006. 'Embodied Knowledge: Writing Researchers' Bodies into Qualitative Health Research.' *Qualitative Health Research*, 16: 298-310.

Engelke, M. 2002. 'The problem of belief: Evans Pritchard and Victor Turner on "the inner life." ' *Anthropology Today*. 18(6): 3-8.

d' Entrèves, M. P. and Benhabib, S. (eds.) 1996. *Habermas and the Unfinished Project of Modernity*. Cambridge: Polity Press.

Evans-Pritchard, E. E. 1965. *Theories of Primitive Religion*. Oxford: Clarendon.

Faubion, J. D. (ed.) 1995. *Rethinking the Subject: an Anthology of Contemporary European Social Thought*. Boulder: Westview Press.

Farnsworth-Alvear, A. 2000. *Dulcinea in the Factory: Myths, Morals, Men and Women in Colombis's Industrial Experiment, 1905-1960*. Duke University Press.

Feingold, L. 2010. *The Natural Desire to See God According to St. Thomas and His Interpreters*. Ave Maria, Florida: Sapientia Press.

Ferguson, A. 1966. *An Essay on the History of Civil Society 1767*. Introduction by Duncan Forbes. Edinburgh University Press.

Feuerbach, L. 1957. *The Essence of Christianity*. Translated by George Eliot. New York: Harper and Row Publishers.

Fife Free Press. 2001. 'Villagers Seek Action to Halt Hooligans.' October 12.

Finlay, R. J. 1994. *Independent and Free: Scottish Politics and the Origins of the Scottish National Party 1918-1945*. Edinburgh: John Donald Publishers Ltd.

Foley, D. 1989. 'Does the Working Class have a Culture in the Anthropological Sense? *Cultural Anthropology*, 4(2): 137-162.

Fried, G. 2000. *Heidegger's Polemos: from Being to Politics*. New Haven: Yale University Press.

Fukuyama, F. 1989. 'The End of History?' *The National Interest*, Summer.

Gadamer, H. G. 1979. *Truth and Method*. London: Sheed and Ward.

Game, A. and Metcalfe. A. 1996. *Passionate Sociology*. London: Sage.

Galbraith, K. 1969. (2nd ed.) *The Affluent Society*. London: Penguin Books.

Gallagher, T. (ed.) 1991. *Nationalism in the Nineties*. Edinburgh: Polygon.

Gallagher, T. 2013. *Divided Scotland: Ethnic Friction and Christian Crisis*. Argyll Publishing.

Gane, M. 2006. *Auguste Comte*. London: Routledge.

Geertz, C. 1988. *Works and Lives: The Anthropologist as Author*. Cambridge: Polity Press.

Geertz, C. 1993. *The Interpretation of Cultures*. London: Fontana Press.

Gellner, E. 1964. *Thought and Change*. London: Weidenfeld and Nicolson.

Gellner, E. 1983. *Nations and Nationalism*. Oxford: Blackwell.

Gellner, E. 1994. *Encounters With Nationalism*. Oxford: Blackwell.

Gellner, E. 1997. *Nationalism*. London: Weidenfeld & Nicolson.

Gellner, E. 1996a. 'The Coming of Nationalism and its Interpretation: the myths of nation and class,' in Balakrishnan, G. (ed.) *Mapping The Nation*. London: Verso.

Gellner, E. 1996b. 'Do Nations have Navels?'*Nations and Nationalism*, 2(3): 366-370.

GERS 2012. *Government Expenditure and Revenue Scotland 2010-2011*. Edinburgh: Scottish Government.

Giddens, A. 1973. *The Class Structure of the Advanced Societies*. London: Hutchison.

Giddens, 1981. *A Contemporary Critique of Historical Materialism. Vol. 1. Power, property and the state*. Berkeley and Los Angeles: University of California Press.

Giddens, A. 1986. *Sociology: a Brief but Criticial Introduction*. London: Macmillan.

Giddens, A. 1990. *The Consequences of Modernity*. Cambridge: Polity Press.

Giddens, A. 1991. *Modernity and Self-Identity: Self and Society in the Late Modern Age*. Cambridge: Polity Press.

Gilfillan, P. 2009. 'Fundamental Ontology versus Esse est percipi: Theorizing (Working Class) Being and Liberation;' *Space and Culture*. 12(2): 250-262.

Gilfillan, P. 2011. 'Scottish Nationalism and a New Generation's Answer to the Question of Being-in-the-World.' *Concept*. Vol. 1 No. 1. January Issue.

Gilfillan, P. (forthcoming). 'Social Class and Christianity: Imagining Sovereignty and Scottish Independence;' in Titus Hjelm (ed.) *Is God Back? Reconsidering the New Visibility of Religion*. London: Bloomsbury Academic.

Gilfillan, P., Phipps, A. and Aitken, E. 2013. 'A Research Report on the Reception of the 2005 Religious Observance Guidelines in Scotland.' *British Journal of Religious Education*. 35(1): 98-109.

Gilsenan, M. 1996. *Lords of the Lebanese Marches: Violence and Narrative in an Arab Society*. London: I. B. Tauris Publishers.

Gilson, E. 1980. *History of Christian Philosophy in the Middle Ages*. London: Sheed & Ward.

Gimpel, J. 1977. *The Medieval Machine: the Industrial Revolution in the Middle Ages*. London: Victor Gollancz Ltd.

Girard, R. 1989. *The Scapegoat*. Baltimore: The John Hopkins University Press.

Glen, D. and Hubbard, T. 2008. *Fringe of Gold: the Fife Anthology*. Edinburgh: Birlinn Ltd.

Glenrothes Gazette, 1999. 'Apathy Kills Gala in North Glenrothes,' 27 May.

Gloryhammer. 2013. *Tales from the Kingdom of Fife*. [MP3] Eisenerz, Styria, Austria: Napalm Records.

Goldie, M. 1991. 'The Scottish Catholic Enlightenment,' *Journal of British Studies*, 30: 20-62.

Goodchild, P. 1996. *Deleuze & Guattari: An Introduction to the Politics of Desire*. London: Sage.

Gordon, D. M., Edwards, R. and Reich, M. 1982. *Segmented Work, Divided Workers: The historical transformation of labor in the United States*. Cambridge University Press.

Gorz, A. 1997. *Farewell to the Working Class: An Essay on Post-Industrial Socialism*. Translated by Michael Sonenscher. London: Pluto Press.

Gouldner, A. W. 1971. *The Coming Crisis of Western Sociology*. London: Heinemann Educational Books Ltd.

Gray, A. 1981. *Lanark: A Life in Four Books*. Edinburgh: Canongate Press.

Greeley, A. 1971. *The Jesus Myth*. New York: Doubleday.

Greeley, A. 1989. 'Sociology and the Catholic Church: Four Decades of Bitter Memories,' *Sociological Analysis*. 50(4): 393-397.

Greenfeld, L. 1992. *Nationalism: Five Roads to Modernity*. Cambridge, Mass.: Harvard University Press.

Habermas, J., Brieskorn, N., Reder, M., Ricken, F. and Schmidt, J. 2010. *An Awareness of What is Missing: Faith and Reason in a Post-Secular Age*. Cambridge: Polity Press.

Hall, D. 1968. *A Choice of Whitman's Verse*. London: Faber and Faber.

Handler, R. 1984. 'On Socio-Cultural Discontinuity: Nationalism and Cultural Objectification in Quebec,' *Current Anthropology*, 25(1): 55-71.

Handler, R. 1985. 'On Dialogue and Destructive Analysis: Problems in Narrating Nationalism and Ethnicity,' *Journal Of Anthropological Research*, 4:171-182.

Haraway, D. J. 1991. *Simians, Cyborgs, and Women: the Reinvention of Nature*. London: Routledge.

Harding, S. 1995. 'Social Class differences in mortality of men: recent evidence from the OPCS Longitudinal Study,' *Population Trends*, No. 80: 31-8.

Hardt, M. and Negri, A. 2000. *Empire*. Harvard University Press.

Harris, C. R. S. 1927. *John Duns Scotus*. Volume 2. Oxford: Clarendon Press.

Harvie. C. 1993. 'The folk and the gwerin: the myth and reality of popular culture in 19th century Scotland and Wales.' *Proceedings of the British Academy*, 80: 19-48. Oxford University Press.

Harvie, C. 1998. (3rd ed.) *Scotland and Nationalism: Scottish Society and Politics 1707 to the Present*. London: Routledge.

Hauke, C. 2000. *Jung and the Postmodern: the Interpretation of Realities*. London: Routledge.

Hayek, F. A. 1944. *The Road To Serfdom*. London: Routledge.

Hayek, F. A. 1976. *Law, Legislation and Liberty. Volume 2. The Mirage of Social Justice*. The University of Chicago Press.

Hayek, F. A. 1985. *New Studies in Philosophy, Politrics, Economics and the History of Ideas*. London: Routledge.

Hayek, F. A. 2011. *Law, Legislation and Liberty. Volume 3, The Political Order of a Free People*. University of Chicago Press.

Healy, N. J. 2008. 'Henri de Lubac on Nature and Grace: a Note on Some Recent Contributions to the Debate,' *Communio: International Catholic Review*. Winter, 35: 535-564.

Hearn, J. 1998. 'The Social Contract: Re-framing Scottish Nationalism.' *Scottish Affairs*, 23:14-26.

Hearn, J. 2000. *Claiming Scotland: National Identity and Liberal Culture*. Edinburgh: Edinburgh University Press.

Hechter, M. 1975. *Internal Colonialism: The Celtic Fringe in British National Development 1536-1966*. London: Routledge and Kegan Paul.

Hechter, M. 1976. 'Ethnicity and Industrialisation: on the cultural division of labour,' *Ethnicity*, 3(3):214-224.

Hegel, G. W. F. 1967. *The Phenomenology of Mind*. Translated by J. B. Baillie. London and New York: Harper & Row.

Hegel, G. W. F. 1984. *Lectures on the Philosophgy of Religion. Vol. 1. Introduction and The Concept of Religion*. Edited by Peter C. Hodgson. Berkeley: University of California Press.

Hegel, G. W. F. 1991. *Elements of the Philosophy of Right*. Edited by Allen W. Wood. Cambridge University Press.

Heidegger, M. 1962. *Being and Time*. Translated by John Macquarrie and Edward Robinson. Oxford: Blackwell.

Heidegger, M. 1982. *The Basic Problems of Phenomenology*. Translated by Albert Hofstadter. Bloomington: Indiana University Press.

Heidegger, M. 1998. *Pathmarks*. Edited by William McNeill. Cambridge University Press.

Heidegger, M. 2004. *The Phenomenology of Religious Life*. Translated by Matthias Fritsch and Jennifer Anna Gosetti-Ferencei. Indianapolis: Indiana University Press.

Held, D. 1981. *Introduction to Critical Theory: Horkheimer to Habermas*. University of California Press.

Held, D. 1988. 'Farewell to the Nation State,' *Marxism Today*, December, pp. 12-17.

Hellman, J. 1991. 'The Ant-Democratic Impulse in Catholicism,' *Journal of Church and State*, Vol. 33(3): 453-471.

Herzfeld, M. 1997. *Cultural Intimacy: Social Poetics in the Nation-State*. London: Routledge.

Hoberman, J. M. 1984. *Sport and Political Ideology*. London: Heinemann.

Hobsbawm, E. 1997. *On History*. London: Weidenfeld and Nicolson.

Hobsbawm, E. & Ranger, T. (eds.) 1983. *The Invention of Tradition*. Cambridge University Press.

Hodgson, P. C. (ed.) 1984. *G. W. F. Hegel. Lectures on the Philosophy of Religion. Vol. 1. Introduction and The Concept of Religion*. Berkeley: University of California Press.

Hoggart, R. 1957. *The Uses of Literacy: Aspects of Working Class Life*. London: Chatto & Windus.

Hollister, C. W. 1969. *The Twelfth Century Renaissance*. London: Wiley.

Houston, A. M. 1924. *Auchterderran, Fife: A Parish History*. Paisley: Alexander Gardner Ltd.

Howell, D. 1986. *A Lost Left: Three Studies in Socialism and Nationalism*. University of Chicago Press.

Hroch, M. 1993. 'From National Movement to the Fully-Formed Nation,' *New Left Review*, 1/198: 3-20.

Hudson, B. 1994. 'Kings and the Church in Early Scotland,' *Scottish Historical Review*, vol. 73(196):145-170.

Husserl, E. 1964. *The Phenomenology of Internal Time-Consciousness*. Indiana University Press.

Husserl, E. 1975. *Logical Investigations*. Translated by P. J. Bossert. The Hague: Martinus Nijhoff.

Hutchison, L. (ed.) 1986. *Corrie and Cardenden*. Edinburgh: The Workers Educational Association.

Hutchinson, J. & Smith, A. D. (eds.) 1996. *Ethnicity*. Oxford University Press.

Ingham, M. B. 2003. *Scotus for Dunces: an Introduction to the Sublime Doctor*. New York: Francuscan Institute Publications.

Ingold, T. (ed.) 1990. *The Concept of Society is Theoretically Obsolete*. Group for Debates in Anthropological Theory, Department of Social Anthropology, University of Manchester. London: Publishing Solutions.

Izuzquiera, D. 2006. 'Can A Gift Be Wrapped?' *The Heythrop Journal*. 47(3): 387-404.

Jackson, A. (ed.) 1987. *Anthropology at Home*. ASA Monographs 25. London: Routledge.

Jackson, M. 1989. *Paths Toward a Clearing: Radical Empiricism and Ethnographic Inquiry*. Indiana University Press.

Jacoby, R. 1997. *Social Amnesia: A Critique of Contemporary Psychology*. Transaction Publishers.

Jameson, F. 1982. *The Political Unconscious: Narrative as a Socially Symbolic Act*. Cornell University Press.

Jameson, F. 1984. 'The Politics of Theory: Ideological Positions in the Postmodern Debate.' *New German Critique*. 33: 53-65.

Jedrej, C, and Nutall, M. 1996. *White Settlers: the Impact of Rural Repopulation in Scotland*. Harwood Academic Publishers.

Jenkins, R. 1992. *Pierre Bourdieu*. London: Routledge.

*The Jerusalem Bible*. 1968. Translatd by Alexander Jones. London: Darton, Longman & Todd.

Johnston, T. 1920. *The History of the Working Classes in Scotland*. Glasgow: Forward Publishing.

Johnston, H. and Noakes, J. A. (eds.) 2005. *Frames of Protest: Social Movements and the Framing Perspective*. Rowman and Littlefield Publishers.

Joyce, J. 2010. *Ulysses*. Wordsworth Editions Ltd.

Kapferer, B. 1988. *Legends of People, Myths of State*. Washington DC: Smithsonian Institution Press.

Kapferer, B. 2001. 'Anthropology. The Paradox of the Secular.' *Social Anthropology*. 9(3):341-344.

Kehoe, S. K. 2013. *Creating a Scottish Church: Catholicism, Gender and Ethnicity in Nineteenth Century Scotland*. Manchester University Press.

Kelman, J. 1992. *Some Recent Attacks: Essays Cultural and Political*. Stirling: AK Press.

Kennedy, C. 2000. *The Future of Politics*. London: Harper Collins.

Kerr, F. 2002. *After Aquinas: Versions of Thomism*. Oxford: Blackwell.

Kidd, C. 1993. *Subverting Scotland's Past: Scottish Whig Historians and the Creation of an Anglo-Scottish Identity 1689 - c.1830*. Cambridge University Press.

Kilminster, R. 1998. *The Sociological Revolution: from the Enlightenment to the Global Age*. London: Routledge.

Kivisto, P. 1989. 'The Brief Career of Catholic Sociology,' *Sociological Analysis*, 50(4): 351-361.

Kravitz, P. (ed.) 1997. *The Picador Book of Contemporary Scottish Fiction*. Surrey: Ted Smart.

Krebs, P. 2012. *Fighting for the Essence: Western Ethnosuicide or European Renaissance?* Arktos Media Ltd.

Kropotkin, P. A. 1906. *The Conquest of Bread*. New York and London: G. P. Putnam's Sons.

Kuper, A. 1988. *The Invention of Primitive Society: Transformations of an Illusion*. London and New York: Routledge.

Laing, R. D. 1982. *The Voice of Experience*. New York: Pantheon Books.

Lakov, G. and Johnston, M. 1999. *Philosophy in the Flesh: the Embodied Mind and its Challenge to Western Thought*. New York: Basic Books.

Lash, S. and Urry, J. 1987. *The End of Organised Capitalism*. Cambridge: Polity Press.

Latour, B. 1993. *We Have Never Been Modern*. Cambridge: Harvard University Press.

Lévi-Strauss, C. 1963. *Structural Anthropology*. Translated by Claire Jacobson and Brooke Schoepf. London: Penguin Books.

Lévi-Strauss, C. 1972. *The Savage Mind*. London: Weidenfeld and Nicolson.

Liddell, H. 1999. Horsburgh, Frances. 'Salmond defends SNP's funding plans as Liddell goes on attack.' *The Herald*, 19 February, p. 6.

Llywelyn, D. 2010. *Toward a Catholic Theology of Nationality*. Lexington Books.

Local History Group. 1989. *Auchterderran of Yesteryear*. Vols. 1-5. Edinburgh: The Workers Educational Association, South East Scotland District.

Lonergan, B. 1957. *Insight: A Study of Human Understanding*. London: Darton, Longman & Todd.

Lonergan, B. 1967. *Verbum: Word and Idea in Aquinas*. Edited by David B. Burrell. Notre Dame, IN: University of Notre Dame Press.

Lonergan, B. 1971. *Grace and Freedom: Operative Grace in the Thought of St. Thomas Aquinas*. London: Darton, Longman and Todd.

Lonergan, B. 1972. *Method in Theology*. London: Herder & Herder.

Lonergan, B. 1990. *Understanding and Being*. E. A. Morelli and M. D. Morelli (eds). Collected Works of Bernard Lonergan. Vol. 5. Toronto: University of Toronto Press.

Long, S. A. 2010. *Natura Pura: On the Recovery of Nature in the Doctrine of Grace*. New York: Fordham University Press.

Losinger, A. 2000. *The Anthropological Turn: the Human Orientation of the Theology of Karl Rahner*. Translated by Daniel O. Dahlstrom. New York: Fordham University Press.

Lukács, G. 1971. *History and Class Consciousness: Studies in Marxist Dialectics*. Translated by Rodney Livingstone. London: Merlin Press.

Lutz, C. 1988. *Unnatural Emotions: Everyday Sentiments on a Micronesiam Atoll and their Challenge to Western Theory*. University of Chicago Press.

Lynch, M. 1992. *Scotland: A New History*. London: Pimlico.

Lyon, D. 1983. 'The Idea of a Christian Sociology: Some Historical Precedents and Current Concerns,' *Sociological Analysis*. 44(3): 227-242.

Lyotard, J. F. 1984. *The Postmodern Condition: A Report on Knowledge*. Manchester University Press.

Mac Colla, F. 1967. *At the Sign of the Clenched Fist*. Edinburgh: M. Macdonald.

Mac Colla, F. 1975. *Too Long in this Condition*. Thurso: Caithness Books.

MacCormick, N. 1996. 'Liberalism, Nationalism and the Post-Sovereign State,' *Political Studies*, XLIV, pp.553-67.

Macdonald, F. 2010. 'Understanding our Present – anticipating our Future.' *Theology in Scotland*, 17(2): 83-93.

Macdonald, I. 2009. 'The Very Heart of Beyond: Gaelic Nationalism and the Work of Fionn Mac Colla.' *eSharp*, Special Issue: Spinning Scotland: Exploring

Literary and Cultural Perspectives, pp. 82-96. http://www.gla.ac.uk/esharp [Accessed 12 June 2013].

Macdonald, S. 1997. *Reimagining Culture: Histories, Identities and the Gaelic Renaissance*. Oxford: Berg.

MacDougall, I. 1993. *'Hard Work, ye Ken:' Midlothian Women Farmworkers*. East Linton: Tuckwell Press.

MacDougall, I. 1995. *Hoggie's Angels: Tattie Howkers Remember*. East Linton: Tuckwell Press.

Macintyre, S. 1980. *Little Moscows: Communism and Working Class Militancy in Inter-War Britain*. London: Croom Helm.

Macleod, D. 2010. 'Reformed Theology in Scotland.' *Theology in Scotland*, 17(2):5-31.

Makkreel, R. A. and Rodi, F. (eds.) 2002. *Wilhelm Dilthey Selected Works, Volume III: The Formation of the Historical Sciences*. Princeton & Oxford: Princeton University Press.

Mannheim, K. 1936. *Ideology and Utopia*. London: Routledge.

Mannheim, K. 1970. 'The Problem of Generations.' *The Psychoanalytic Review*. Vol. 57(3): 378-404.

Marcel, G. 2001. *The Mystery of Being. Volume 1: Reflection and Mystery*. Translated by G. S. Fraser. South Bend: St. Augustine's Press.

Marcus, G. E. & Fischer, M. M. J. 1986. *Anthropology as Cultural Critique: an Experimental Moment in the Human Sciences*. University of Chicago Press.

Marcuse, H. 1969. 'Contributions to a Phenomenology of Historical Materialism.' *Telos*, Fall, pp. 3-34.

Marcuse, H. 1972. *One Dimensional Man*. London: Abacus.

Maritain, J. 1954. *Approaches to God*. New York: Harper and Brothers.

Marx, K. and Engels, F. 1974. *The German Ideology*. Edited and introduced by C. J. Arthur, London: Lawrence and Wishart.

Marx, K. and Engels, F. 1996. *The Communist Manifesto*. London: Pluto Press.

Maslow, A. 1968. *Towards a Psychology of Being*. New York: Van Nostrand.

Mauss, M. 1979. *Sociology and Psychology: Essays*. Translated by Ben Brewster. London: Routledge.

Mauss, M. 1990. *The Gift: The Form and Reason for Exchange in Archaic Societies*. London: Routledge.

McCrone, D. 1992. *Understanding Scotland: the Sociology of a Stateless Nation*. London: Routledge.

McCrone, D. 1998. *The Sociology of Nationalism: Tomorrow's Ancestors.* London: Routledge.

McCrone, D. (2nd ed.) 2001. *Understanding Scotland: The Sociology of a Stateless Nation.* London: Routledge.

McCrone, D., Kendrick, S. & Straw, P. (eds.) 1989. *The Making of Scotland: Nation, Culture and Social Change.* Edinburgh University Press.

McLellan, D. 1977. *Karl Marx: Selected Writings.* Oxford University Press.

McRoberts, D. 1959. 'Material Destruction Caused by the Scottish Reformation.' *The Innes Review*, Vol. 10(1): 126-172.

Mead, G. H. 1934. *Mind, Self and Society.* University of Chicago Press.

Mendieta, E. (ed.) 2005. *The Frankfurt School on Religion.* London: Routledge.

Meneley, A. 1996. *Tournaments of Value: Sociability and Hierarchy in a Yemeni Town.* University of Toronto Press.

Milbank, J. 2005. *The Suspended Middle: Henri de Lubac and the Debate Concerning the Supernatural.* Grand Rapids: Eerdmans.

Milbank, J. 2006. (2nd ed.) *Theology and Social Theory: Beyond Secular Reason.* Oxford: Blackwell.

Mill, J. S. (2nd ed.) 1861. *Considerations on Representative Government.* London: Paker, Son and Bourn.

della Mirandola, G. P. 1998. *On the Dignity of Man.* Translated by Charles Glen Wallace, Paul J. W. Miller and Douglas Carmichael. Indianapolis, IN: Hackett Publishing Company, Inc.

von Mises, L. 2012. *Liberalism.* Translated by Ralph Raico. Important Books.

Morris, C. M. 1987. (2nd ed.) *The Discovery of the Individual 1050-1200.* Toronto: University of Toronto Press.

Morris, W. D. 1949. *The Christian Origins of Social Revolt.* London: George Allen & Unwin Ltd.

Morrison, T. 1999. *Bluest Eye.* London: Vintage.

Muir, E. [1935] 1985. *Scottish Journey.* London: Flamingo-Fontana Books.

Mulholland, N. 2011. 'The Challenge of Cultural Self-Determination,' pp. 198-210, in Gerry Hassan and Rosie Illet (eds) *Radical Scotland: Arguments for Self-Dertermination.* Edinburgh: Luath Press Ltd.

Myers, F. R. 1993. 'Place, Identiy and Exchange in a Totemic System,' *in* Fajans, J. (ed.) *Exchanging Products, Producing Exchange*, Oceania Monograph, 43. Sydney: Oceania Publications.

Nadel-Klein, J. 1997. 'Crossing a Representational Divide: from West to East in Scottish ethnography,' pp. 86-102 in James, A., Hockey, J. & Dawson, A. (eds.) *After Writing Culture: Epistemology & Praxis in Contemporary Anthropology.* London: Routledge.

Nagel, T. 1986. *The View from Nowhere.* Oxford University Press.

Nairn, T. 1977. *The Break-Up of Britain: Crisis and Neonationalism.* London: New Left Books.

Nairn, T. 1981. (2$^{nd}$ ed.) *The Break-Up of Britain: Crisis and Neonationalism.* London: Verso.

Nairn, T. 1994. *The Enchanted Glass: Britain and its Monarchy.* London: Radius.

Nairn, T. 1997. *Faces of Nationalism: Janus Revisited.* London: Verso.

Nairn, T. 2000. *After Britain: New Labour and the Return of Scotland.* London: Granta Books.

Nash, J. 1993. *We Eat the Mines and the Mines Eat Us: Dependency and Exploitation in Bolivian Tin Mines.* Columbia University Press.

Nast, H. & Pile, S. (eds.) 1998. *Places Through the Body.* London: Routledge.

Obeyesekere, G. 1979. 'The vicissitudes of the Sinhala-Buddhist identity through time and change,' in Roberts, M. (ed.) *Collective Identities, Nationalism and Protest in Modern Sri Lanka.* Colombo: Marga.

Obeyesekere, G. 1981. *Medusa's Hair: an Essay on Personal Symbols and Religious Experience.* University of Chicago Press.

O'Callaghan, J. P. 2003. *Thomist Realism and the Linguistic Turn: Toward a More Perfect Form of Existence.* University of Notre Dame Press.

Offe, C. 1985. 'Work: the key sociological category?' pp. 129-150, in Offe, C. *Disorganised Capitalism: Contemporary Transformations of Work and Politics.* Cambridge: Polity Press.

Olwig, K. F. and Hastrup, K. (eds.) 1997. *Siting Culture: the Shifting Anthropological Object.* London: Routledge.

Ortner, S. 1995. 'Resistance and the problem of ethnographic refusal,' *Society for Comparative Study of Society and History*, 37: 173-193.

Ouroussoff, A. 1993. 'Illusions of rationality: false premises of the liberal tradition,' *Man* 28(2):281-298.

Overing, J. (ed.) 1985. *Reason and Morality.* London: Tavistock Publications.

Owen, R. (2$^{nd}$ ed.) 1816. *A New View of Society: or, Essays on the Formation of the Human Character Preparatory to the Development of a Plan for Gradually*

*Ameliorating the Condition of Mankind*. London: Longman, Hurst Rees, Orme and Brown.

Parker, I. 2011. *Lacanian Psychoanalysis: Revolutions in Subjectivity*. London: Routledge.

Parsons, T. 1964. 'Christianity and Modern Industrial Society,' pp. 273-98, in L. Schneider (ed.) *Religion, Culture and Society*. New York: John Wiley.

Paterson, L. 1996. 'Does nationalism matter?' *Scottish Affairs*. 17, Autumn, 112-19.

Paul VI, 1975. *Evangelii Nuntiandi*. Rome: Libreria Editrice Vaticana.

Pefanis, J. 1992. *Heterology and the Postmodern: Bataille, Baudrillard and Lyotard*. Duke University Press.

Perry, E. J. (ed.) 1996. *Putting Class in its Place: Worker Identities in East Asia*. Berkeley: University of California Press.

*The Phantom Menace: Star Wars Episode 1*. 1999. Directed by George Lucas. San Francisco: Lucas Film.

Piccone, P. and Delfini, A. 1970. 'Herbert Marcuse's Heigeggerian Marxism.' *Telos*, 6: 36-46.

Pickering, W. S. F. (ed.) 1975. *Durkheim on Religion*. London: Routledge.

Pickstock, C. 2003. 'Modernity and Scholasticism: a Critique of Recent Invocations of Univocity.' *Antonianum*, 78(1):3-46.

Pina-Cabral, J. de and Pine, F. (eds.) 2008. *On the Margins of Religion*. New York and Oxford: Berghahn Books.

Pirenne, H. 1936. *Economic and Social History of Medieval Europe*. London: Routledge and Kegan Paul.

Platonov, A. 1996. *The Foundation Pit*. Translated by Robert Chandler and Geoffrey Smith. London: The Harvill Press.

Polanyi, K. 2001. (2nd ed.) *The Great Transformation: the Political and Economic Origins of our Time*. Boston: Beacon Press Books.

Porter, R. 1997. *Rewriting the Self: Histories from the Middle Ages to the Present*. London: Roputledge.

Rabinow, P. and Sullivan, W. M. 1987. *Interpretive Social Science: a Second Look*. University of California Press.

Rahner, K. 1970. *Grace in Freedom*. London: Catholic Book Club.

Rankin, I. 1986. *The Flood*. Edinburgh: Polygon.

Rankin, I. 1987. *Knots and Crosses*. London: Orion Books Ltd.

Rankin, I. 1999. *Dead Souls*. London: Orion Books Ltd.

Rankin, I. 1999. *The Sunday Times.* 3 October.

Rankin, I. 2001. *The Falls.* London: Orion.

Rapport, N. 2002. 'The Truth is Alive': Kierkegaard's anthropology of dualism, subjectivity and somatic knowledge,' *Anthropological Theory*, 2:165-183.

Reid, I. 1998. *Class In Britain.* London: Polity Press.

Relph, E. 1989. 'Geographical Experiences and Being-in-the-world: the Phenomenological origins of Geography,' pp. 15-31, in David Seamon and Robert Mugerauer (eds.) *Dwelling, Place and Envoronment: towards a Phenomenology of Person and World.* Columbia University Press.

Richard, G. 1923. 'L' Athéisme dogmatique en sociologie religieuse,' in W. S. F. Pickering 1975. *Durkheim on Religion.* London: Routledge, pp. 228-276.

Rilke, R. M. 2009. *Poems from the Book of Hours.* New York: New Directions.

Rondet, H. 1972. *Original Sin: the Patristic and Theological Background.* Ecclesia Press.

Ross, A. 1958. 'Introduction'. *Innes Review*, Vol. 9: 5-23.

Ross, A. 1959. 'Reformation and Repression.' *Innes Review*, vol. 10: 338-381.

Royce, J. 2001. *The Problem of Christianity.* Washington, DC: The Catholic University of America Press.

Ruby, J. (ed.) 1982. *A Crack in the Mirror: Reflexive Perspectives in Anthropology.* Philadelphia: University of Pennsylvania Press. 'Introduction,' by Barbara Myerhoff and Jay Ruby, pp. 1-35.

Sahlins, M. 1976. *Culture and Practical Reason.* University of Chicago Press.

Sahlins, M. 1995. *How Natives Think About Captain Cook, For Example.* University of Chicago Press.

de Saint-Simon, H. 1964. 'New Christianity' pp. 81-116, in *Social Organisation, the Science of Man and other Writings.* Edited by Felix Markham. New York: Harper and Row.

Sartre, J. P. 1963. *The Problem of Method.* Translated by Hazel E. Barnes. London: Methuen & Co.

Sartre, J. P. 1966. *Being and Nothingness: a Phenomenological Essay on Ontology.* Translated by Hazel E. Barnes. London: Pocket Books.

Savage, M. 1999. 'Sociology, Class and Male Manual Work Cultures,' pp. 23-42, in J. Mcilroy, N. Fishman and A. Campbell (eds.) *British Trade Unions and Industrial Politics: The High Tide of Trade Unionism, 1964–1979.* Aldershot: Ashgate.

Scheff, T. J. and S. M. Retzinger 2000. 'Shame as the Master Emotion of Everyday Life,' *Journal of Mundane Behavior*. Vol. 1(3): 303-324.

Scheper-Hughes, N. & Lock, Margaret 1987. 'The Mindful Body: A Prolegomena to Future Work in Medical Anthropology,' *Medical Anthropology Quarterly* 1(1): 6-41.

Scheper-Hughes, N. 1992. *Death Without Weeping: The Violence of Everyday Life In Brazil*. University of California Press.

Schillebeeckx, E. 1990. *Church: the Human Story of God*. New York: SCM Press.

Schneider, J. and Rapp, R. 1995. *Articulating Hidden Histories: Exploring the Influences of Eric R. Wolf*. Berkeley: University of California Press.

*The Scotland Act*, 1998. Edinburgh: The Stationery Office Ltd.

*Scotland on Sunday*. 1998. 'Unison Branch Demands Union Donate Funds to SNP'. 25 October.

*Scotland on Sunday*. 1998. 'Big Business in Secret Bid to Save Union,' 1 November.

*The Scotsman*. 1998. 'Gloves off a Holyrood Campaign Launched,' 12 November.

*The Scotsman*. 1999. 'Economists Back Independence,' 9 April.

Scottish Government, 2013. *Scotland's International GDP Per Capita Ranking*. Edinburgh. www.scotland.gov.uk/Resource/0039/00390896.pdf [Accessed 7 March 2014]

Scottish Television, 1999. 'Scotland Today' news Bulletin, Broadcast 2 April.

Scott-Moncrieff, G. 1956. *Catholic Edinburgh*. Glasgow: The Catholic Truth Society of Scotland.

SCCC, 1999. *The School Curriculum and the Culture of Scotland*. Dundee: Scottish Consultative Council on the Curriculum.

Searle-Chatterjee, M. 1979. 'The Polluted Identity of Work: a Study of Benares Workers,' pp. 269-286, in Sandra Wallman (ed.) *Social Anthropology of Work*. London: Academic Press.

Seawright, D. & Curtice, J. 1995. 'The Decline of the Scottish Conservative and Unionist Party, 1950-92: Religion, Ideology or Economics?' *Contemporary Record*, vol. 9(2): 319-42.

SES, 2011. *Scottish Election Study*. School of Government & Public Policy, University of Strathclyde. http://www.scottishelectionstudy.org.uk/index.htm [Accessed 15 June 2013]

Segal, D. & Handler, R. 1992. 'How European is Nationalism?' *Social Analysis*, 32: 1-15.

Sertillanges, A. D. 1947. *The Intellectual Life: its Spirit, Conditions, Methods.* Translated by Mary Ryan. Cork: Mercier Press.

Shields, R. 1999. *Lefebvre, Love and Struggle.* London: Routledge.

Siegelbaum, L. & Walkowitz, D. 1995. *Workers of the Donbass Speak: Survival and Identity in the New Ukraine, 1989-1992.* New York: State University of New York Press.

Simon, Y. 1991. *Practical Knowledge.* Edited by Robert J. Mulvaney. New York: Fordham University Press.

Skeggs, B. 1997. *Formations of Class and Gender: Becoming Respectable.* London: Sage Publications.

Smith, A. 1986. *The Ethnic Origins of Nations.* Oxford: Blackwell.

Smith, A. D. 1996. 'Memory and Modernity: reflections on Ernest Gellner's theory of Nationalism,' Annual Public Lecture of Nations and Nationalism. LSE, London.

Stewart, C. 2001. 'Secularism as an Impediment to Anthropological Research.' *Social Anthropology,* 9(3): 325-328.

Stiefel, T. 1985. *The Intellectual Revolution in Twelfth-Century Europe.* London: Croom Held.

Strauss, D. F. 1983. *In Defence of My Life of Jesus Against the Hegelians.* Translated and edited by Marilyn Chapin Massey. North Haven, CT: Archon Books.

Van Steenbergen, B. 1990. 'Potential influence of the holistic paradigm on the social sciences. *Futures,* 22(10): 1071-1083.

Stoller, P. 1989. *The Taste of Ethnographic Things: the Senses in Anthropology.* The University of Pensylvania Press.

Sturzo, L. 1947. *The True Life: Sociology of the Supernatural.* Translated by Barbara Barclay. Geoffrey Bles.

Sunic, T. 2011. *Against Democracy and Equality: The European New Right.* Arktos Media Ltd.

Tanner, J., Davies, S. and O'Grady. B. 1992. 'Immanence Changes Everything: a Critical Comment on the Labour Process and Class Consciousness,' *Sociology,* 26(3): 439-453.

Tambiah, S. 1986. *Sri Lanka: Ethnic Fratricide and the Dismantling of Democracy.* Chicago: University of Chicago Press.

Tamir, Y. 1993. *Liberal Nationalism.* Princeton University Press.

Taylor, S. and Markus, G. 2006. *The Place-Names of Fife.* Volume 1. Donington: Shaun Dyas.

Taussig, M. 1992. *The Nervous System.* London: Routledge.

Thatcher, M. 1993. *The Downing Street Years.* London: Harper Collins.

Thompson, E. P. 1967. 'Time, Work-Discipline and Industrial Capitalism,' *Past and Present*, 38:56-97.

Todorov, T. 1999. *The Conquest of America: the Question of the Other.* University of Oklahoma Press.

Tönnies, F. 2001. *Community and Civil Society.* Edited by Jose Harris. Cambridge University Press.

Trinkaus, C. and Oberman, H. 1974. *The Pursuit of Holiness in Late Medieval and Renaissance Religion.* Amsterdam: E. J. Brill.

Tubbs, N. 1997. *Contradiction of Enlightenment: Hegel and the Broken Middle.* Aldershot: Ashgate.

Turner, B. 1991. *Religion and Social Theory.* London: Sage.

Turner, R. 1980. 'We're A' Jack Tamson's Bairns: Central Lowland Scotland as a Culture Area.' Abridged version in *Proceedings of the Association for Scottish Ethnography*, Vol. 1 1984.

Turner, R. [n.d.] 'Gala Day as an Expression of Community Identity' in Anthony Jackson (ed.) *Way of Life and Identity.* North Sea Oil Panel Occasional Paper No. 4, pp. 63-78.

Turner, V. 1957. *Schism and Continuity in an African Society.* Manchester University Press.

Tyrrell, G. 1909. *Medievalism: a Reply to Cardinal Mercier.* London: Longmans, Green and Co.

Veitch, K.1997. 'The Columban Church in Northern Britain, 644-717: A Reassessment,' *Proceedings of the Society of Antiquaries of Scotland*, 127: 627-647.

Verran, H. 2002. 'Transfering Strategies of Land Management: Indigenous Land Owners and Environmental Scientists,' pp. 155-181 in M. de Laet (ed.), *Research in Science and Technology Studies.* New York: JAI Press.

Viladesau, R. 2006. *The Beauty of the Cross: the Passion of Christ in Theology and the Arts, from the Catacombs to the Eve of the Renaissance.* Oxford University Press.

Voas, D. 2006. 'Religious decline in Scotland: New Evidence on Timing and Spatial Patterns.' *Journal for the Scientific Study of Religion.* 45(1): 107-118.

Volosinov, V. N. 1986. *Marxism and the Philosophy of Language.* Translated by Ladislav Matejka and I. R. Titunik. Harvard University Press.

Walkerdine, V. 1996. 'Working-class women: psychological and social aspects of survival,' in Wilkinson, S. (ed.) *Feminist Social Psychologies: International Perspectives.* Open University Press.

Wallerstein, I. 1979. *The Capitalist World Economy.* Cambridge University Press.

Wallerstein, I. 1980. 'One man's meat: the Scottish great leap forward,' *Review*, 3(4): 631-40.

Wallman, S. (ed.) 1979. *Social Anthropology of Work*. London: Academic Press.

Weber, E. 1976. *Peasants into Frenchmen: Modernization of Rural France 1870-1914*. Stanford University Press.

Weber, M. 1989. *The Protestant Ethic and the Spirit of Capitalism*. London: Unwin Hyman.

Weil, S. 1987. *Formative Writings 1929-1941*. Edited by Dorothy Tuck McFarland and W. Van Ness. London: Routledge & Kegan Paul.

Welsh, I. 1993. *Trainspotting*. London: Secker and Warburg.

Wight, D. 1993. *Workers Not Wasters: Masculine Respectability, Consumption and Unemployment in Central Scotland*. Edinburgh University Press.

Wilkinson, R. 2000. *Mind the Gap: Hierarchies, Health and Human Evolution*. London: Weidenfeld & Nicolson.

Williams, B. F. 1989. 'A Class Act: Anthropology and the Race to Nation Across Ethnic Terrain,' *Annual Review of Anthropology* 18:401-44.

Willis, P. 1977. *Learning to Labour: How Working Class Kids Get Working Class Jobs*. Farnbrough: Saxon House.

Wolin, R. 1990. *The Politics of Being: the Political Thought of Martin Heidegger*. New York and Oxford: Columbia University Press.

Wolter, A. 1987. *Duns Scotus: Philosophical Writings*. Indianapolis: Hacket Publishing Company.

Wolter, A. 2001. *John Duns Scotus: Political and Economic Philosophy*. New York: The Franciscan Institute.

Worsley, P. 1982. *Europe and the People Without History*. University of California Press.

Yack, B. 1996. 'The Myth of the Civic Nation', *Critical Review*, 10(2): 93-211.

Zerubavel, E. 1997. *Social Mindscapes: An Invitation to Cognitive Sociology*. London: Harvard University Press.

Zimmermann, D. 2003. *The Jacobite Movement in Scotland and in Exile, 1746-1759*. New York: Palgrave Macmillan.

Zizek, S. 2000. *The Fragile Absolute: or, why the Christian Legacy is worth Fighting For*. London: Verso.

Zweig, F. 1961. *The Worker in an Affluent Society*. London: Heinemann.

# Index

Lightning Source UK Ltd.
Milton Keynes UK
UKOW05f0205170815

256968UK00002B/101/P